The Migration Conference 2021
Selected Papers

The Migration Conference 2021
Selected Papers

Compiled by
Ibrahim Sirkeci

TRANSNATIONAL PRESS LONDON
2021

Conference Series: 20
The Migration Conference 2021 - Selected Papers
Compiled by Ibrahim Sirkeci

Copyright © 2021 Transnational Press London

First published in 2021 by TRANSNATIONAL PRESS LONDON in the United Kingdom, 13 Stamford Place, Sale, M33 3BT, UK.
www.tplondon.com

Transnational Press London® and the logo and its affiliated brands are registered trademarks.

Requests for permission to reproduce material from this work should be sent to:
admin@tplondon.com

Paperback
ISBN: 978-1-80135-097-6
Digital
ISBN: 978-1-80135-098-3

Cover Design: Nihal Yazgan

Transnational Press London Ltd. is a company registered in England and Wales No. 8771684

CONTENTS

PEOPLE

The Migration Conference Executive Committee

Prof Ibrahim Sirkeci, IBBS, UK (Chair)

Prof Jeffrey H. Cohen, Department of Anthropology, Ohio State University, USA

Prof Philip L Martin, Department of Agricultural Economics, University of California Davis, USA

The Migration Conference Transnational Advisory Committee

Prof Deborah Anker, Harvard University, United States

Prof Gudrun Biffl, Krems, Austria

Prof Lucinda Fonseca, University of Lisbon, Portugal

Prof Elli Heikkila, Migration Institute of Finland, Finland

Prof Mohamed Khachani, AMERM & University of Rabat, Morocco

Prof Beatrice Knerr, Kassell University, Germany and Hefei University, China

Prof Markus Kotzur, Universität Hamburg, Germany

Prof Jonathan Liu, Global Banking School, UK

Prof Apostolos G Papadopoulos, Harokopio University of Athens, Greece

Prof João Peixoto, University of Lisbon, Portugal

Prof Michela C. Pellicani, University of Bari "Aldo Moro", Italy

Prof Giuseppe Sciortino, University of Trento, Italy

The Migration Conference Scientific Committee

Africa

Agnes Igoye, Ministry of Interior Affairs, Uganda

Prof Mohamed Khachani, AMERM & University of Rabat, Morocco

Dr Rania Rafik Khalil, The British University in Egypt, Egypt

Dr Sadhana Manik, University of KwaZulu-Natal, South Africa

Prof Claude Sumata, National Pedagogical University, DR Congo

Dr Ayman Zohry, Egyptian Society for Migration Studies, Egypt

Americas

Dr Bharati Basu, Central Michigan University, USA

Prof Jeffrey H. Cohen, Ohio State University, USA

Dr José Salvador Cueto-Calderón, Universidad Autónoma de Sinaloa, Mexico

Dr Ana Vila Freyer, Universidad Latina de México, Mexico

Dr Pascual Gerardo García-Macías, Universidad Técnica Particular de Loja, Ecuador

Dr Torunn Haaland, Gonzaga University, USA

Prof Liliana Jubilut, Universidade Católica de Santos, Brazil

Prof Philip L Martin, University of California Davis, USA

Dr Eric M. Trinka, James Madison University, USA

Karla Angélica Valenzuela-Moreno, Universidad Iberoamericana, Mexico

Dr Hassan Vatanparast, Saskatchewan University, Canada

Prof Rodolfo García Zamora, Autonomous University of Zacatecas, Mexico

Dr Monette Zard, Columbia University, USA

Asia-Pacific

Prof Ram Bhagat, International Institute for Population Sciences, India

Dr Amira Halperin, University of Nottingham Ningbo, P.R. China

Dr Sadaf Mahmood, Government College University, Pakistan

Dr Shweta Sinha Deshpande, Symbiosis School for Liberal Arts, India

Prof Nicholas Procter, University of South Australia, Australia

Dr Ruchi Singh, Prin.L.N.Welingkar Institute of Management Development & Research, India

Dr AKM Ahsan Ullah, University Brunei Darussalam, Brunei

Dr Zhongwei Xing, University of Technology Brunei, Brunei

Dr Xi Zhao, Hefei University, P.R. China

Eastern Europe

Dr Merita Zulfiu-Alili, South East European University, N. Macedonia

Dr Olga R. Gulina, RUSMPI- Institute on Migration Policy, Russian Federation

Dr Tuncay Bilecen, Kocaeli University, Turkey, UK

Prof Dilek Cindoglu, Kadir Has University, Turkey

Dr Yaprak Civelek, Anadolu University, Turkey

Dr Z. Banu Dalaman, Istanbul Ayvansaray University, Turkey

Dr Sevim Atilla Demir, Sakarya University, Turkey

Prof Vladimir Iontsev, Moscow State University, Russian Federation

Dr İnci Aksu Kargın, Uşak University, Turkey

Prof Sebnem Koser Akcapar, Ankara Social Sciences University, Turkey

Dr Oksana Koshulko, Alfred Nobel University, Ukraine

Dr Murat Lehimler, Urban Development and Social Research Association, Turkey

Dr Armagan Teke Lloyd, Abdullah Gul University, Turkey

Dr Vildan Mahmutoğlu, Galatasaray University, Turkey

Dr Nermin Oruc, Centre for Development Evaluation and Social Science Research (CREDI), Sarajevo, Bosnia and Herzegovina

Dr Gökay Özerim, Yaşar University, Turkey

Prof Irina Savchenko, Linguistics University of Nizhny Novgorod, Russian Federation

Prof Ali Tilbe, Tekirdag Namik Kemal University, Turkey

Dr Fethiye Tilbe, Namik Kemal University, Turkey

Dr Onur Unutulmaz, Ankara Social Sciences University, Turkey

Dr Deniz Eroglu Utku, Trakya University, Turkey

Dr Pınar Yazgan, Sakarya University, Turkey

Dr Sinan Zeyneloglu, Kent University, Turkey

Western Europe

Dr Nirmala Devi Arunasalam, Oxford Brookes University, United Kingdom

Dr Bahar Baser, Coventry University, United Kingdom

Dr Gülseli Baysu, Queen's University Belfast, United Kingdom

Prof Petra Bendel, Friedrich-Alexander University of Erlangen-Nuremberg, Germany

Dr Gul Ince Beqo, University of Bari, Italy

Prof Aron Anselem Cohen, University of Granada, Spain

Dr Martina Cvajner, University of Trento, Italy

Dr Carla de Tona, Independent Researcher, Italy

Dr Sureya Sonmez Efe, University of Lincoln, United Kingdom

Dr Deniz Cosan Eke, University of Vienna, Austria

Dr Alina Esteves, Universidade de Lisboa, Portugal

Dr Sarah E. Hackett, Bath Spa University, United Kingdom

Dr Serena Hussain, Coventry University, United Kingdom

Prof Monica Ibáñez-Angulo, University of Burgos, Spain

Prof Markus Koller, Ruhr University Bochum, Germany

Dr Emre Eren Korkmaz, University of Oxford, United Kingdom

Prof Jonathan Liu, Ming-Ai (London) Institute, United Kingdom

Dr Altay Manço, Institut de Recherche, Formation et Action sur les Migrations, Belgium

Dr A. Erdi Öztürk, London Metropolitan University, United Kingdom

Isabella Piracci, Avvocatura Generale dello Stato, Rome, Italy

Dr Sahizer Samuk-Carignani, University of Pisa, Italy

Prof Giuseppe Sciortino, University of Trento, Italy

Dr Selma Akay Sert, University College London, UK

Dr Caner Tekin, Ruhr-Universität Bochum, Germany

Irene Tuzi, Sapienza University of Rome, Italy

Dr Emilia Lana de Freitas Castro, Berlin, Germany

Dr Ülkü Sezgi Sözen, University of Hamburg, Germany

Near East

Dr Rania M Rafik Khalil, The British University in Egypt, Egypt

Dr Simeon Magliveras, King Fahd University of Petroleum and Minerals, Saudi Arabia

Dr Bradley Saunders, American University of Bahrain, Bahrain

Dr Paulette K. Schuster, Hebrew University Jerusalem, Israel

Dr Omar Al Serhan, Higher Colleges of Technology, United Arab Emirates

Dr Md Mizanur Rahman, Qatar University, Qatar

Dr Liat Yaknich, Beit Berl College, Israel

The Migration Conference Local Organisation Committee

Prof Ibrahim Sirkeci, IBBS, UK (Chair)

Dr Nirmala Devi Arunasalam, IBBS, United Kingdom

Dr A. Erdi Öztürk, London Metropolitan University, United Kingdom

Dr Aytac Yerden, Gedik University, Turkey (IT)

Ege Cakir, Middle East Technical University, Turkey (Admin)

Cagdas Torbacioglu, Transnational Press London, UK (Admin)

Nihal Yazgan, Transnational Press London, UK (Admin)

ABOUT THE MIGRATION CONFERENCE 2021

The 9th Migration Conference, TMC 2021 was held from 6 to 10 July 2021 and hosted on MS Teams as a virtual conference.

The TMC 2021 London was a forum for discussion where experts, young researchers and students, practitioners and policy makers working in the field of migration have joined the debate and exchanged their knowledge and experiences in a friendly and frank environment. The Migration Conference 2021 London was held as a virtual conference due to COVID-19 Pandemic and travel restrictions. The conference was organised in thematic streams of about 60 parallel sessions and six plenary sessions over five days. About 500 participants from over 60 countries have participated.

Similar to the past conferences, The Migration Conference 2021 entertained the following distinguished scholars delivering keynote speeches:

Theresa Alfaro-Velcamp, Sonoma State University, USA

Élise Féron, Tampere University, Finland

Ruth Gomberg-Muñoz, Loyola University Chicago, USA

James F. Hollifield, Southern Methodist University, Dallas, USA

Camilla Orjuela, University of Gothenburg, Sweden

Pia M. Orrenius, Federal Reserve Bank of Dallas, USA

Rodolfo Cruz Piñeiro, El Colegio de la Frontera Norte, Mexico

Hna. Leticia Gutiérrez Valderrama, Scalabrinian Missionary and Diocese of Sigüenza-Guadalajara-Spain.

The conference venue was initially set as Ming Ai Institute in London, UK but due to ongoing COVID-19 related restrictions, the event moved online and was hosted virtually. Hopefully in TMC2022, we will be back to a "normal" face to face event.

We thank our hosts, reviewers, participants, supporting organisations and the team of volunteers who collaboratively made the event a success.

In this volume, we put together a self-selected collection of conference papers submitted after the conference integrating the debates and comments from the audience. There is no particular order for the articles included in this book but it merely registers the contributions presented at the TMC2021.

Ibrahim Sirkeci (Chair) and Chungwen Li (Co-Chair)

The Migration Conference 2021 Chairs

SUPPORTERS OF THE MIGRATION CONFERENCE 2021

- Ming-Ai (London) Institute, United Kingdom (TMC2021 Host)
- International British Business School (IBBS), United Kingdom
- Association Marocaine d'Etudes & de Recherches sur les Migrations (AMERM), Morocco
- Centre for Development Evaluation and Social Science Research (CREDI), Sarajevo, Bosnia and Herzegovina
- Global Migration Research Centre, Social Sciences University of Ankara, Turkey
- Institut de Recherche, Formation et Action sur les Migrations, Belgium
- Migration Institute, Finland
- Migration Policies Research Centre, Istanbul Ayvansaray University, Turkey
- Research Centre in Economic and Organizational Sociology (SOCIUS), Universidade de Lisboa, Portugal
- Ruhr-Universität Bochum, Centre for Mediterranean Studies, Germany
- Sino-German Economic Development and Innovation Research Centre, Hefei University, P.R. China
- The Global Mobility Project, The Ohio State University, USA
- Unidad Académica en Estudios del Desarrollo, Mexico
- Universidad de Burgos, Spain
- Universidad Latina de México, Mexico
- Universidad Tecnica Partocular de Loja, Ecuador
- Universität Hamburg, Germany
- University of California, Davis, Gifford Center for Population Studies, USA
- University of Nottingham, Faculty of Humanities and Social Sciences, China
- Urban Development and Social Research Association, Turkey
- Western Balkans Migration Network (WB-MIGNET), Bosnia and Herzegovina
- Yaşar University Jean Monnet Migration Chair, Turkey
- Association Marocaine d'Etudes & de Recherches sur les Migrations, Morocco
- Remittances Review
- Migration Letters
- Journal of Posthumanism
- International Journal of Religion
- Yeiya
- Göç Dergisi
- Journal of Gypsy Studies
- Border Crossing
- Kurdish Studies
- Transnational Press London, UK

MIGRATION NARRATIVES IN THE FIRST PERSON: LIFE STORIES OF BRAZILIAN IMMIGRANTS IN PORTUGAL

Patricia Posch and Rosa Cabecinhas

Considering the increasing number of Brazilians migrating to Portugal in the last years, we conducted Life Stories interviews with 25 Brazilians who migrated to the North of Portugal from 2015 onwards, analysing their perceptions about their migration experience. The findings were analysed in the light of Cultural Studies and Social Psychology theories, uncovering texts and contexts about the case of Brazilian migration to Portugal.

Brazilians are currently the largest immigrant community in Portugal, representing 27,8% of the total immigrant population in 2020 (SEF, 2021). In the middle of 1980s, what is now known as the first migratory wave of Brazilians to Portugal began, driven by the economic slowdown in Brazil and by the perception of more favourable economic conditions in Portugal for joining the European Economic Community (EEC). Among those who migrated were highly qualified professionals, political exiles, and Portuguese relatives who returned to Portugal.

In the mid-1990s, a new phase of this migratory flow began, known as the second wave. Portugal's entry into the Schengen Area, together with the country's transition to a service-based economy, have attracted many Brazilians. This flow was marked by its feminisation and by the migration of individuals with low qualifications, who would fill vacancies with low qualification requirements in construction, the food industry and tourism. With the global economic crisis in 2008, this flow began to slow down, giving way to new migrations of these now Brazilian immigrants in Portugal or their return to Brazil.

This situation started to change in 2017 when the flow of Brazilians to Portugal grew by 5% compared to the previous year. That growth continued, reaching the 44% mark in 2019 (SEF, 2018; 2020), shaping what researchers have designated as a third migration wave (França & Padilla, 2018) or even a fourth wave (Fernandes, Peixoto & Oltramari, 2021). Following this growth, some questions arise: Why have Brazilians been migrating to Portugal in the last years? What are their migration trajectories? How is their life in Portugal? Questions like these gave rise to the research underpinning this paper.

Although we can find the answers in various spheres, such as in the media or in institutional discourses, we have chosen the Life Stories method to seek these answers from another viewpoint: the perspective of immigrants themselves. This method is significant for Migration Studies because it conceives individuals as a synthesis of contemporary subjectivity. Their perception of their own life is not exempt from the influences of the values and meanings that they inherit through culture. Thus, the narratives and discourses they construct about themselves can be a valuable data for studying broader social phenomena.

With that in mind, the fieldwork consisted of Life Story interviews with Brazilians who migrated to Portugal from 2015 onwards. Hence, the findings of this paper relate to a recent migration flow. There was also a geographical filter given that the research focused on immigrants living in the Northern Region of Portugal due to the remarkable growth of this area as a destination of choice for Brazilians migrating to Portugal in recent years. Between December 2020 and April 2021, we interviewed 25 Brazilian immigrants that matched these criteria.

Looking back on their life in Brazil, interviewees recalled it as fast-paced, having to deal with their professional and personal responsibilities at one time - especially those who lived in large central areas such as Rio de Janeiro and São Paulo. Interviewees also recalled that their lives were structured and stabilized, with few financial struggles. It is interesting to note that some of them even used the term "privileged" when recalling their living conditions in Brazil in times before their migration.

As for the reasons prompting their migration, there is a significant shift: the predominance of economic reasons for second wave immigrants, as found in Góis and Marques (2015), changed to those like safety and the political context of Brazil. The perceived cultural differences also played a great weight in these people's decision to migrate, reflected in the divergence with "the moral values of the Brazilian culture" and the affinity to the so-called "European culture" mentioned by some participants.

The actual decision to migrate is mostly made within the family. However, it was noted that men played an important role in many cases by sparking the first idea of migration or making the final decision about it. Moreover, this situation contrasts with that of second-wave immigrants, for whom, according to Góis and Marques (2015), migration was a decision made suddenly. For those who migrated in the last years, migration is a strategic and planned movement, and this planning sometimes begins two or three years earlier as part of a broader life project.

The primary sources of information used were social networks and online content. Those produced by Brazilians already living in Portugal were the preference, specially YouTube videos and personal blogs. These future immigrants wanted more practical information about the changes that migration would bring to their lives, such as obtaining documents, living conditions and job opportunities in Portugal, information that they claim they were not getting from the media in general. Moreover, although Capoano and Barros (2021) suggest that the urge for more practical and closer-to-reality information increases as the date of migration approaches, the participants in our research seem to have used it throughout the planning period.

Hiring consultancy services was also frequently mentioned in the planning phase. These consultants were often, in fact, Brazilians who already lived in Portugal and who helped, usually for large sums of money, those who were still in Brazil with the bureaucratic procedures of migration both in Brazil and in Portugal. Some also relied on this service for more practical issues, such as renting apartment flat, buying kitchen utensils or even tips on the best supermarket.

When addressing their current life, it was interesting to note the immigrants' awareness that there was a profile of "the Brazilian immigrant" back when multiple social representations emerged, which now underlie discrimination. When our interviewees acknowledged the existence of this stereotype, their explanations revealed they sought distance and distinction between them and the idea of a Brazilian immigrant from other times. As seen in Festinger (1954), changing personal opinion within a social group is a process within the framework of comparisons. It is not an arbitrary process but rather influenced by social relations. On the other hand, when it comes to differentiation between Brazilians and Portuguese, language, especially accent, seems to play an important role, confirming previous studies on this topic (e.g. Brasil & Cabecinhas, 2018). Some interviewees mentioned that they tried to change the way they spoke to fit in more smoothly, while others stressed that the Brazilian variant of Portuguese language is part of a culture they did not want to leave behind.

Regarding work experiences, professional disqualification, a situation observed in several studies on international migration, was also widely reported. This means highly qualified professionals in Brazil who did not have their diplomas and previous experiences recognised in Portugal, or even who accepted job opportunities below their qualification as a way to enter the labour market. They also refer to the "Brazilian employee" stereotype and how this impacts the lives of recent migrants in Portugal, who face prejudice based on the negative experiences employees and co-workers have had with Brazilian immigrants they have worked with before.

The interviewees also mentioned prejudice and discrimination within social relations in general, although amid an ambiguity of conceptions that led to different valuations of discrimination experiences. There was a reference to different "nuances" of discrimination, which made it hard to recognise and assert beyond doubt that such a situation had occurred. According to Corsby (1984), the reluctance to admit a situation of discrimination on an individual level could mean a way of avoiding personal discomfort at having to assume the role of a victim and, consequently, naming the perpetrators for the experienced situation. Moreover, although prejudice can be described as a judgment about an individual or a group as a result of the process of social categorisation (Eagly & Diekman, 2005), discrimination occurs when prejudice acts through their effective exclusion from specific domains of social life. In this sense, some immigrants claimed to have experienced discrimination from the Portuguese, but even when they related, they did not undergo any form of exclusion from society.

Furthermore, participants sometimes justified prejudice against Brazilians stemming from the Portuguese experiences with Brazilian immigrants from previous migration waves with a different social status than newly-arrived Brazilian immigrants (Posch & Cabecinhas, 2020a). By doing so, these immigrants feel that they can establish social relations with the Portuguese and maintain their belonging to the Brazilian community for fear of social sanctions (cf. Tajfel, 1974) on the part of other immigrants. The analysis of these findings in the light of immigrants' acculturation strategies (e.g. Berry, 2001; Sam & Ward, 2021) suggests that misconception or attenuation of discriminatory situations might be a way to mitigate situations that could consolidate the distinction between Brazilians and Portuguese.

As to the relationship with other Brazilian immigrants, an aspect that stood out was the reference to what the immigrants called the "Brazilian ghettos": groups of Brazilian immigrants who intentionally interact mainly with each other and perpetuate their Brazilian cultural practices in Portugal. It is interesting to note that these alleged "ghettos" were mentioned as both a cause and a consequence of Brazilians integration with other social groups in the country. Some interviewees believe that immigrants should adopt Portuguese culture instead of perpetuating Brazilian cultural practices since they perceive this is one of the factors causing integration difficulties with other social groups. Others consider that Brazilian have no other option but to interact with other compatriots in a culturally different social relationship dynamic. Nonetheless, there is also a perception of the Brazilian immigrants with different perceived social status among the broader Brazilian community in Portugal, who now share a common social position: to be an immigrant in Portugal. Such perception was often used to justify the challenges in interacting with other Brazilians, leading to prejudice within the Brazilian community.

As for the future, there were notably different perceptions of time. Some immigrants understand the medium-term to be three months, while it is six months or even a year for others. We infer that these different perceptions stem from migration experience itself, related to the experiences and the pace at which things happen in their lives.

Focusing on medium-term objectives, especially as it is a valuable information in the backdrop of COVID-19, the return to Brazil emerged as a tangible possibility for many of these immigrants (Posch & Cabecinhas, 2020b), although the reasons for it vary. While some plan to return because they miss their family, others have decided to return because they feel that Portugal is not their place and can be "more themselves" in Brazil. Also, it is worth noting that this return was a certainty for some who migrated to study and intend to return to Brazil as soon as they complete their study plan. Getting a job was also within the medium-term horizon of these immigrants. However, it is interesting to note that while for some this was a matter of financial need, for others, getting a job was an option, something that relates more to their mental health and idleness than their income. Entrepreneurs, especially those who migrated in 2020, at the beginning of the COVID-19 pandemic, planned to invest further in their businesses and fulfil a business plan that the pandemic hampered. Also, those who had to work in areas other than their area of education hoped they would soon have an opportunity to work with what they graduated.

These were some of the main findings of the referred ongoing research. The following stages of the research include developing further analyses based on the collected data, comparing to the results with the previous migration waves, and linking them to the social, economic and cultural contexts that led to the current state of the situation. An intersectional analysis (e.g. Crenshaw, 1991; Bastia, 2014) is also considered to understand how other variables and their intersection can help discern the overall results and unveil many others.

Financial Support

The development of this work received the support of Fundação para a Ciência e Tecnologia, I.P., by the means of a doctoral grant with the reference SFRH/BD/137855/208, within the scope of the Human Capital Operational Program (POCH). The proofreading of this paper was supported by national funds, through Fundação para a Ciência e a Tecnologia, I.P., within the scope of the project UIDP/00736/2020.

References

Bastia, T. (2014). Intersectionality, migration and development. *Progress in Development Studies*, 14(3), 237-248. doi:10.1177/1464993414521330

Berry, J. W. (2001). A Psychology of Immigration. *Journal of Social Issues*, 57(3), 615–631. doi:10.1111/0022-4537.00231

Brasil, J.A. & Cabecinhas, R. (2018). Ties that (Un)bind? The Case of Latin Americans in Portugal and Spain. *Revista del CESLA. International Latin American Studies Review*, 22, 115-134.

Capoano, E., & Barros, V. T. de. (2021). Panorama web de la inmigración brasileña a Portugal: periodismo desinteresado y redes sociales en alza. In: González, J. S. & García, J. G. (eds.) *Digital Media. El papel de las redes sociales en el ecosistema educomunicativo en tiempos de Covid-19*. Madrid: McGraw-Hill Interamericana de España, 553-576.

Crenshaw, K. (1991). Mapping the Margins: Intersectionality, Identity Politics, and Violence against Women of Color. *Stanford Law Review*, 43(6), 1241–1299. doi:10.2307/1229039

Crosby, F. (1984). The Denial of Personal Discrimination. *American Behavioral Scientist*, 27(3), 371-386. doi:10.1177/000276484027003008

Eagly, A. H., & Diekman, A. B. (2005). What is the Problem? Prejudice as an Attitude-in-Context. In: Dovidio, J. F., Glick, P. & Rudman, L. A. (eds.) *On the Nature of Prejudice: Fifty Years after Allport*. Oxford: Blackwell Publishing, 19-35.

Festinger, L. (1954). A Theory of Social Comparison Processes. *Human Relations*, 7, 7-117. doi: 10.1177/001872675400700202

França, T., & Padilla, B. (2018). Imigração Brasileira para Portugal: entre o surgimento e a construção mediática de uma nova vaga. *Cadernos de Estudos Sociais*, 33(2), 207–237. doi:10.33148/ces2595-4091v.33n.220181773

Fernandes, D., Peixoto, J., & Oltramari, A. P. (2021). A quarta onda da imigração brasileira em Portugal: uma história breve. *RELAP - Revista Latinoamericana de Población*, 15(29), 34–63. doi:10.31406/relap2021.v15.i2.n29.2

Góis, P., & Marques, J. C. (2015). Percursos e trajetos migratórios dos brasileiros. In: Peixoto, J., Padilla, B., Marques, J. C. & Góis, P. (eds.) *Vagas Atlânticas: Migrações entre Brasil e Portugal no Início do Século XXI*. Lisbon: Mundos Sociais, 39–58.

Posch, P., & Cabecinhas, R. (2020a). Being Present Through Absence: the Semiotic Construction of Recent Brazilian

Migration To Portugal in the Brazilian Media. *Comunicação e Sociedade, 38*, 201–217. doi:10.17231/COMSOC.38(2020). 2592

Posch, P., & Cabecinhas, R. (2020b). Facing a pandemic away from home: COVID-19 and the Brazilian immigrants in Portugal. In: Sirkeci, I. & Cohen, J. H. (eds.) *COVID-19 and Migration: Understanding the Pandemic and Human Mobility*. London: Transnational Press London, 105-117.

Sam, D. L., & Ward, C. (2021). Three generations of psychological acculturation research: Theoretical advancements and methodological challenges. In: Bender, M. & Adams, B. G. (eds.) *Methods and assessment in culture and psychology* (pp. 17–40). Cambridge: Cambridge University Press, 17-40. doi:10.1017/9781108675475.003

SEF. (2019). *Relatório de Imigração, Fronteiras e Asilo 2018*. https://sefstat.sef.pt/Docs/Rifa2018.pdf

SEF. (2020). *Relatório de Imigração, Fronteiras e Asilo 2029*. https://sefstat.sef.pt/Docs/Rifa2019.pdf

SEF. (2021). *Relatório de Imigração, Fronteiras e Asilo 2020*. https://sefstat.sef.pt/Docs/Rifa2020.pdf

Tajfel, H. (1974). Social identity and intergroup behaviour. *Social Science Information, 13*(2), 65-93. doi:10.1177/0539018474013 00204

HIGHLY SKILLED SYRIAN REFUGEES MOVING TO THE WEST: 5 CASE STUDIES

Duaa Al-Namas

Introduction

Syria and Syrians have been going under a non-ending conflict for the last decade, which led to the displacement internally and internationally of more than 13 million individuals, between adults and children, -not to mention those killed-. Some of whom have lost their homes, families, jobs, and all aspects of life including dreams, causing the fleeing of about 6 million Syrians to neighbouring countries, looking for safety and shelter for themselves and their children. That in return had its impact on the host countries, and inhabitants. However, the life of Syrian refugees themselves, their education, their jobs and their future plans, has faced dramatic changes and challenges till they have settled in some countries. Challenges and forces has pushed some of them to make a second move to Europe.

This paper will look into the reasons of out-migration of skilled Syrian refugees who initially went to neighbouring countries after 2011, and later to the West on another journey of hope of finding better opportunities and the betterment of their lives. In order to better understand the reasons from the refugees themselves, I conducted some qualitative interviews, and will explore the push and pull factors in these migration flows and the methods of entry into Europe and Canada. I will also analyse what other policies, other than having high social and human capital, played a role in facilitating these flows.

Skilled Syrian refugees moving to the West

Human capital and social capital each have a significant and positive role on the movement of highly-skilled people nationally and internationally. A skilled person needs to have both in order to manage and complete a journey and reach to his/her aspirations. The same applies to the skilled Syrian refugees, that was clear from some Western countries' governments and their representatives, coming to Turkey, Jordan, and Lebanon in search of the skilled Syrian refugees, especially those with high skills, high education attainment, or those who used to be working in particular professions back in Syria before the conflict had started.

Yet, in the case of skilled Syrian refugees, in addition to human and social capital, other factors interfere in aiding the mobility of these skilled people, such as countries changing their regulations and policies across the world, in a process of allowing the maximum possible number of refugees and asylum seekers to find safety, shelter and maybe settlement. These changes took place as a response to the worst refugee crises took place in our world since the Second World War, and to the mass migration of Syrian refugees. Some countries were faster than others in their response, yet, eventually most countries caught up. Migration policies of nation-states was one of the main factors as favouring those with more human capital whereas restrictions were imposed on others even if they are forced migrants and needed humanitarian assistance and protection.

For this research paper I conducted interviews with five cases, 4 males and 1 female between the ages of 30 and 38; 3 of whom went to Europe and 2 went to Canada from Turkey, Jordan and Lebanon, through regular and irregular routes (see Appendix 1). Each case interviewed was special and unique in itself, each case presented different perspective and views, in an exceptional way in dealing with aspects of skilled people, refugees, movement and adapting to life in different parts of the world.

Challenges in Turkey, Jordan and Lebanon

The reason why many Syrians left to the West was mainly centred around the challenges they faced in Turkey, Jordan, and Lebanon; mainly issues of language, work, education, policies and opportunities in general. Finding opportunities to support a person's own and family financially, physically and psychologically was very difficult for most of the Syrian refugees where ever they sought refuge at the beginning of the Syrian conflict. Hoping to find better future and opportunities was one of the main reasons for many Syrians who went on a second journey to the West, especially the skilled Syrians.

Although **language** was not an issue for those who went to Arab countries, learning the language was the main difficulty the Syrian refugees faced in Turkey, as at the first period, the government did not provide Turkish language courses, nor guided them to ways of learning the language.

As for **work** Finding a decent job for many of the Syrian refugees in all three countries (Jordan, Lebanon and Turkey) was a great challenge, as Syrian refugees felt looked down upon, skilled or not skilled, educated or not educated and finding a decent job was a challenge to all. Though it must be noted, that it was easier for those with human and social capital, like those who had relatives and friends in the countries they moved to at first. In addition, to those who spoke other languages, like English in Jordan and Lebanon, and Kurdish for those who came to Turkey. Yet the work load was really heavy for those who found jobs, and the payment they got was insufficient. All in all, opportunities were very limited, reflecting negatively on many Syrian specifically the educated and skilled ones.

As for **education,** to be able to start or continue education for a Syrian refugee, in any level whether primary, secondary or high school was not permitted for Syrian kids at the beginning (between 2011 and 2015) until policies changed. The same applies for undergraduate university students and higher education students. Again, this had a very negative impact on many Syrian refugees, specifically for the educated and skilled ones.

As for some **policies,** like acceptance into education sector, making equivalence of education certificates (if available), accepting their skills and approving them, work permits, given country's residency and later citizenship, all these policies were not available between 2011 and 2015, hence the increased movement to the West by Syrian refugees around 2015/2016, as these policies among others are basic rights of human been in the West. Some of these policies are still absent in Jordan and Lebanon, yet, it became available to some extent in Turkey, and is much more feasible in the West.

Settlement and adaptation in the West

Syrians in their hundreds of thousands took the dangerous routes via sea and land to migrate to Europe with many losing their lives on the way through irregular routes. Western governments were late in taking action to accommodate Syrian refugees through regular routes. Though it was a delayed action, yet some western governments representatives came to countries neighbouring Syria, looking for Syrian refugees and giving them a new chance and hope for a better life in a new country, with all basic rights and opportunities provided as well as being financially supported was much appreciated by many Syrians. In addition to changing policies in many sectors in these Western countries to adapt for the Syrian refugees coming to be new residents, this by itself gave a very positive impact on Syrian refugees moving from Turkey, Jordan and Lebanon to the West.

Yet Syrians still faced many challenges in trying to fit in these communities. As for the **language;**

hence it was a major challenge in some countries, it was positively reflected in the integration process and adaption to the new country. Syrian refugees faced similar difficulties to that in Turkey, yet western governments provided language courses to help with the matter, following their arrival. This helped four of the five cases interviewed with the exception of interviewee 3, who found it difficult to learn Swedish, when compared with other Western languages. This is besides difficulties in validating educational qualifications, similar to a study of Bucken-Knapp et.al. (2018).

As for **income support and Work;** providing regular and sufficient income to Syrian refugees on arrival to the country, in addition to given them the country's residency, and work permit, released a massive part of the pressure of finding an adequate job to support one's own and family basic needs, with their human dignity being preserved. Nevertheless, opportunities were provided to work in some council centres if competences were met, and if not, opportunities to improve their language, skills and education level were also provided to match the required level of expectances in different fields and aspects of labour sector. On the **educational** front, to many of the Syrians interviewed, it was very important to have a sufficient level of education and the country's spoken language. The best way to gain this was through providing educating and language centres for refugees as an immediate action and activity to be taken by refugees, after settling in a suitable accommodation.

In addition to changes in **Policies;** which were applied differently by different countries, in the East and the West. These policies on their own could be counted as push and pull factors, where in the East it is a push factors, but in the West is a pull factors. This was clearly mentioned by one of the interviewees, where he said: *"I can't stay in the Arab countries, I will never be a citizen or get the rights of a citizen, where ever I go in the West I will be granted the legal residency at least, plus money, work and education opportunities"* (Interviewee 4). This was agreed on to be true by all the interviewees, and Western policies changes supported this idea even further, by given the residency to most of the correspondents on arrival, enhancing the integration process by miles instantly.

Conclusion

This paper looked into reasons of out-migration of skilled Syrian refugees to Europe and Canada, after trying to settle in some neighbouring countries in the Middle East, such as Jordan, Lebanon and Turkey, and concentrated on cases went out from Turkey to Europe. From the interviews, it can be seen that human and social capitals can play a role to some extent in the integration process for some of the Syrian refugees, those who managed to get to Europe. This is besides having luck on their side as one of the interviewees described his experience. From my point of view, I think flexibility played the major part in the process of integration, flexibility in the acceptance of moving in the first time, and again in the second time, flexibility in learning new skills, new languages, and acceptance of new cultures, and flexibility in adapting to new life all together.

Language is a huge obstacle for many migrants, and refugees, though it was the main reason why some Syrian refugees choose to move to Jordan and Lebanon and not Turkey. However the geographical position of these people in Syria at the beginning of the conflict played a role on deciding to which neighbouring country they moved. Nevertheless, Turkish Language amongst other obstacles in Turkey was the main reason for many highly-skilled Syrian refugees as well as other skilled migrants to move out of Turkey to Western countries at the nearest possible chance.

On the educational aspect, as it was not possible for the Syrian refugees between 2011 and 2015 to join the education sector. Syrian refugees opened there own primary, secondary and even high schools, within Turkish cities, using mainly the Arabic language, Syrian teachers, and supported by the Turkish government and the UN for wages, which was very low (about 500TL at 2012, went up to 1200TL by 2014). This actually had led to late integration within the Turkish society, and to some extent a rejection of the Syrian refugees by some sections of the Turkish society later on. However, this was not the case in Jordan, or Lebanon, since the language didn't differ, Syrians didn't face the same challenge to be included within the public education sector for kids, yet, they faced a different form of challenge on this aspect, as the numbers were too high to be managed by the education sector in Jordan and Lebanon, with very limited resources and high population density, with an established history of hosting many other refugees from different nationalities.

As for policies changing; it is argued in this study that these policies were taken much later than expected, had these policies been put in place couple of years earlier, it would've resulted in better and quicker integration of Syrian refugees, especially the skilled ones, and might have had a different impact on their decision to move to Europe. In addition to having different impacts on the host society and on Syrian refugees themselves. Yet neighbouring countries, particularly Turkey, still bore the biggest number of refugees and continues to support their integration as still the bulk of the refugees still reside in neighbouring countries with the hope of returning home.

[[Word count 2100]]

Appendices

Appendix 1: Table of interviewees, Syrian refugees moved to the West

Interviewees	Interviewee1	Interviewee2	Interviewee3	Interviewee4	Interviewee5
Age	30	33	36	37	31
Gender	Male	Male	Male	Male	Female
Place and city of origin	Aleppo / Syria	Qamishli / Syria	Damascus/Syria	Syria	Dara'a / Syria
Country living in at the present time	Germany	Canada	Sweden	Germany	Canada
Marital status	Single	Married	Single	Married	Single/Engaged
Number of Children	N/A	1	N/A	N/A	N/A
Academic qualifications/Education	Finished second year- philosophy	Electrical Engineering-Damascus University	Civil Engineering-Damascus University	Graduate of Medical Doctor - Damascus University	University graduate in child education from Syria
Occupation in Syria	Not worked in Syria	Worked in a petrol company	Civil Engineer	Surgeon specialist – Digestive system	Primary school teacher
Occupation at the present time	Working with mentally disabled students in a public center	Working as a sales man in a furniture company	Working as administrative in a consultation office	Working as a surgeon in a public hospital	Continuing education
Wages (Low/ Good/ Very good)	Very good	Very good	Good	Very good	Good
Method of Travelling	Irregular	Regular	Irregular	Regular	Regular
Main Difficulties	Language,Waiting for things to happen (Time)	Language, Waiting for things to happen (Time)	Language, Waiting for things to happen (Time)	Language, Waiting for things to happen (Time)	Language, Waiting for things to happen (Time)
Would come back to Turkey or Syria	Yes, for visits only	Maybe, when my daughter grows up	Never	Never	I would love to, if things go back to Normality

22

Bibliography

Ager, Alastair and Strang, Alison. (2008). *Understanding Integration: A Conceptual Framework* Journal of Refugee Studies Vol. 21, No. 2 Published by Oxford University Press.

Akcapar, Şebnem Koşer, (2005-2006). Turkish Highly Skilled Migration to the United States New Findings and Policy Recommendations. Istanbul/ Turkey. KOÇ University.

Akcapar, Şebnem Koşer, (2010). Re-Thinking Migrants' Networks and Social Capital: A Case Study of Iranians in Turkey. *International migration.* Vol. 48 (2). Blackwell Publishing Ltd

Akcapar, Şebnem Koşer, and Şimşek, Dogus. (2018). *The Politics of Syrian Refugees in Turkey*: A Question of Inclusion and Exclusion through Citizenship. Social Inclusion. 6(1), pp. 176–187

Başol, Dünya. (2018). *Syrian Refugees on the Way to Europe.* Ankara Policy Center (APM).

Bélanger, Danièle & Saracoglu, Cenk (2018). *The governance of Syrian refugees in Turkey*: The state-capital nexus and its discontents, *Mediterranean Politics.*

Betts, Alexander and Collier, Paul (2017). *Refuge, Rethinking Refugee Policy in a Changing World.* Oxford University Press.

Blackburn, Christine Crudo, and Jr. Lenze, Paul E. (2019). Syrian Forced Migration and Public Health in the European Union. Lexington Books. London.

Bucken-Knapp, Gregg, Fakih, Zainab, Spehar, Andrea. (2018) *Talking about Integration*: The Voices of Syrian Refugees Taking Part in Introduction Programmes for Integration into Swedish Society.

Elveren, A. Y. (2018). *Brain Drain and Gender Inequality in Turkey*, Springer Nature, https://doi.org/10.1007/978-3-319-90860-1_3

Içduygu, Ahmet and Toktas, Sule (2002). How Do Smuggling and Trafficking Operate via Irregular Border Crossings in the Middle East? Evidence from Fieldwork in Turkey

Içduygu, Ahmet. (2011). *Europe, Turkey, and International Migration: An Uneasy Negotiation.* Koç University Visiting Fellow, Robert Schuman Centre for Advanced Studies, European University Institute (EUI),

Knappert, Lena, Kornaub, Angela, Figengüla, Meltem. (2018). *Refugees' exclusion at work and the intersection with gender: Insights from the Turkish-Syrian border.* Journal of Vocational Behavior, 105, pp.62-82.

Memisoglu, Fulya & Ilgit, Asli. (2017). "Syrian refugees in Turkey: multifaceted challenges, diverse players and ambiguous policies". Mediterranean Politics

Nielsen, Selin Yıldız. (2016) .*Perceptions Between Syrian Refugees and Their Host Community*, Turkish Policy Quarterly. Volume 15 Number 3.

Yılmaz, Gaye. Doğa Karatepe, İsmail. And Tören, Tolga. (2019). *Integration through Exploitation: Syrians in Turkey.* Labor and Globalization. Volume 17. Edited by Scherrer Christoph. Rainer Hampp Verlag, Augsburg, München.

TÜRKİYE-YUNANİSTAN SINIRINDA YAŞANAN KİTLESEL GÖÇ HAREKETİNİN VE GELEN GÖÇMENLERİN EDİRNE YEREL BASININDA TEMSİLİYETİ*

Jale Avyüzen Zobar

Özet

Bu çalışma, Türkiye'nin açık kapı politikasını uygulamaya geçirmesinin ardından Yunanistan sınırına gelen kitlesel göç akınında göçmenlerin yaşadığı problemlere odaklanmaktadır. Çalışmada, Türkiye-Yunanistan sınırında neler olduğuna dair yaşananların ve göçmenlerin karşılaştığı problemlerin Edirne yerel basınında nasıl yer aldığı ortaya konulacaktır. Birinci yılı dolan kitlesel göç hareketinde kentte bulunan vasıflı yerel gazetelerin haberlerinde göçmenlerin temsiline ve yaşanan hak ihlallerinin nasıl ele alındığına ışık tutulacaktır. Çalışmanın amacı, göç konusunda medyanın rolünü anlamak ve göçmenlerin insan hakları açısından yaşadıkları sorunların medyada nasıl temsil edildiğini göstermektir. 2020 yılında yaklaşık bir ay süren kitlesel göç akını sırasında Edirne'ye gelen göçmenlerin deneyimlerini, pratiklerini ve hak kayıplarını içermesi açısından bu çalışma, sınırlı bir alanda üretilen haberlerin içeriğine odaklanacaktır.

Giriş

Göç, üzerinde ortak bir tanımlamaya gidilebilen bir kavram değildir. Farklı bağlamları ve bakış açıları nedeniyle sürekli tartışılan ve üzerinde ortak bir tanım bulunmayan göç, aslında sosyal tarihi de anlamlandırmanın bir yoludur. Belki de bir kliş olarak belirtebileceğimiz 'göç, insanlık tarihi kadar eskidir' söylemi, insanın ve toplumların yolcuğunu daha derinlikli bir şekilde yorumlamamız gerektiğine işaret etmektedir. Nitekim Afrika'dan dünyaya yayılan insanoğlu, yerleşik yaşama geçmeden önce avcı-toplayıcı olarak çevreyle ilk ilişkisini kurmuştur. Bu ilişki de bir tür göçü barındırmaktadır. Şöyle ki, kaynakların kıtlaştığı, hastalıkların baş gösterdiği zaman dilimlerinde avcı-toplayıcı kabileler bölge değiştirerek hem yeni yaşam alanlarını keşfetmiştir hem de kaynaklara ulaşmak açısından bir takım sorunları göç ederek aşmıştır. Bu nedenle göç, insanlığın sosyal tarihini yazmıştır. Buradan bakıldığında göç, bir zaman dilimine sığamayacağı için süreçselliği de önem kazanmaktadır. Özellikle günümüz dünyasında gerek kitle iletişim araçlarının varlığı gerek küreselleşme gerekse de politik ve kültürel bir takım süreçlerle bezenen göç, süreç bağlamında hareketliliğin bir noktada durmayacağını gösteren bir olgudur.

Gerek tarihsel gerekse de kültürel yapı bakımından oldukça zengin bir mutfak sunan göç olgusu, bünyesinde çok çeşitli parametreleri barındırmaktadır. Göç, en kaba tanımıyla bir hareketlilik halidir. Bu hareketliliğe sebep olan etkenler ve bu hareketliliğin eyleme döküldüğü andan itibaren karşılaşılan bir takım noktalar, kimi zaman travmatik, politik, güvenlik ve daha birçok açıdan "tartışmalı" görüntüler sunarken, kimi zaman da insan hakları açısından özellikle ulus devletlerin karar alma süreçlerinde ne derece katı olabileceklerini gösteren olaylar kamuoyuna yansımaktadır. Bu nedenle tek bir koşul ile açıklanamayan, tıpkı kendisi gibi dinamik sebepleri olan göç ile toplumsal hareketlilik arasında önemli

---

* İstanbul Üniversitesi Sosyal Bilimler Enstitüsü Antropoloji ABD Doktora Öğrencisi.

bir bağlantı vardır. Grupların sahip olduğu eşitsizlikler zemininde düşünüldüğünde ortak bir amaç ile kitlesel göçün büyük bir parçasını oluşturan mülteciler, yine toplumsal hareketlilik bağlamında önemli özneler olarak karşımıza çıkmaktadır. Özellikle günümüzde toplumsal hareketlerin kendisi; farklı eylemleri, fikirleri, örgütlenme biçimleri ile farklı toplumsal kesimlerin kamusal ve politik alanda seslerini ve taleplerini duyurmalarında ve katılımın daha geniş kesimlere yayılmasında önemli işlevleri yerine getirmektedir (Şanlı, 2005, s. 12). Bu nedenle, göçün ve göçmenlik hallerinin bu durumun önemli bir parçasını oluşturduğunu söylememiz mümkündür. Bu çalışmada, medya organlarının toplumsal hareketliliğin bir kısmını oluşturan göçmenlerin temsiline ve uğradıkları insan hakları kaybına karşı nasıl tavır aldıklarına bakılacaktır. Medyada yaratılan temsillerin bu çalışmadaki yeri önemlidir çünkü temsil, anlam ve dilin kültürle ilişkisini sağlamaktadır. En nihayetinde kullanılan dilin yarattığı anlamlar temsillerin birer yansımasıdır (Hall, 2017, s. 23). Oluşturulan bu yeni temsiller ise fikirleri kategorize ettiği gibi üzerinde örtük bir perde bulunan eşitsizlikleri de derinlikli hale getirmektedir (Varol, 2016, s. 44).

Kamusal alanda göç hareketliliğine etki eden önemli siyasi gelişmeler her daim var olmuştur. Söz konusu gelişmeler, insan hareketliliğini arttırdığı gibi bunun sonucunda da bir takım olaylar yaşanmaktadır. Türkiye'nin 2011 yılından bu yana Suriyeli mültecilere[1] yönelik uyguladığı *açık kapı politikası* bunun bir örneğini oluşturmaktadır. Yaşanan kitlesel göçle birlikte "misafir" olarak kabul edilen insanların ülkede kalıcı hale gelmesi sonucunda toplumsal uyum sorununun da görülmesiyle Türkiye, politikalarını gözden geçirmiştir. Tüm bunlarla birlikte 27 Şubat 2020 günü İdlib'de 33 Türk askerinin hayatını kaybetmesi sonucunda Türkiye-Yunanistan sınırında göç hareketliliği meydana gelmiştir (Anadolu Ajansı, 2020). Aynı günün ilerleyen saatlerinde Reuters haber ajansı, Türkiye'nin Suriyeli mültecilerin Avrupa'ya geçişini engellememe kararı aldığı haberini sunmuştur (Independent, 2020). Yaşanan gelişmelerin ardından AK Parti Sözcüsü Ömer Çelik, Türkiye'nin mültecileri tutabilecek gücünün kalmadığını açıklamıştır (Anadolu Ajansı, 2020). Basına yansıyan haberlerin ardından Türkiye-Yunanistan sınırında olağanüstü bir göç hareketliliği yaşanmıştır. Bu çalışma, Türkiye'nin 27 Şubat-27 Mart 2020 döneminde yaşanan gelişmelerin ardından uygulamaya soktuğu *açık kapı politikası* üzerine Edirne'ye gelen göçmenlerin yaşadıklarını ve bunların kentteki yerel gazetelerde nasıl ele alındığını inceleyecektir.

Kent merkezinde günlük yayın yapan 8 yerel gazetenin haberleri üzerinden yaşanan göç hareketliliğini ele alacak olan bu çalışmanın amacı, göçmenlerin yaşadığı hak ihlallerinin haberlere nasıl konu olduğu ve gazetelerdeki temsillerin nasıl oluşturulduğunu ortaya koymaktır. Medya çalışmalarında temsil, toplumsal eşitsizlikleri ortaya koyduğu gibi kimi zaman da söz konusu eşitsizlikleri derinleştirmektedir. Bu bağlamda, Van Dijk'in eleştirel söylem analizi yöntemi üzerinden çalışma yapılacaktır. Dijk'in de ifade ettiği gibi, eleştirel söylem analizi sunduğu geniş perspektif ile haberin üretim sürecine hakim olan dil ve onun kullanımı, toplumsal alanda sosyal gruplar arasında yaşanan eşitsizliklerin çağrışımlarını ortaya koymaktadır (Dijk, 2001, s. 352-354). Çalışmada, haberlerin ele alınışında ayrımcı unsurlar barındırıp barındırmadığı da göz önünde bulundurulacaktır. Ayrıca kente gelen kişilerle yapılan röportajların da paylaşılması, göç hareketliliğinde meydana gelen sorunları anlamlandırmak açısından önemli bir rol oynayacaktır.

Çalışmanın verilerine geçmeden önce Edirne'deki mülteci hareketliliğine ilişkin bir takım bilgilerin aktarılması yaşanılanların anlaşılır olmasını kolaylaştıracaktır. 2011 yılından bu yana Türkiye'de önemi giderek artan göç olgusuyla birlikte Göç İdaresi Genel Müdürlüğü'nün verilerine göre Mart 2020

---

[1] Türkiye'nin 1951 tarihli Mültecilerin Hukuki Statüsüne Dair Sözleşmesi'ne taraf olmasıyla birlikte coğrafi kısıtlama getirmesi sonucunda Avrupa sınırları dışından gelen kişiler, mülteci statüsünde kabul edilmemektedir. Ancak buradaki kullanım, Suriyelilerin varlığının sosyolojik açıdan kullanımıyla ilgilidir.

itibariyle ülkede 3 milyon 587 bin 266 Suriyeli geçici koruma altında yaşamaktadır (TBMM, 2020, s. 6). Suriyeli nüfusun yanı sıra Irak, Afganistan, Somali, İran gibi ülkelerden gelen ve uluslararası koruma talebi olan 300 bin sığınmacı mevcuttur. 28 Şubat 2020 tarihinde Türk askerine yönelik düzenlenen saldırının ardından Türkiye'nin açık kapı politikasına başvurmasıyla birlikte Edirne'deki sınır kapılarına çok sayıda mülteci ulaşmıştır. Türkiye'nin söz konusu çıkışı ve sınırların gevşetildiğine dair yapılan açıklamaların üzerine Yunanistan kendi sınırlarını kapatmıştır. Türkiye ile Yunanistan sınırını oluşturan Pazarkule Sınır Kapısı'nda bulunan ve tampon bölge olarak ifade edilen alanda 1 ay bekleyişleri süren göçmenler, burada sert müdahalelerle karşılaşmıştır. Türkiye ile Avrupa Birliği arasında 18 Mart 2016 tarihinde imzalanan AB Mutabakatı ve Vize Serbestisi Anlaşması'nın uygulanmaması üzerine ve yaşanan sıcak gelişmelerin ardından sınır bölgesinde günlerce zor koşullarda mücadele veren mülteciler, aradıkları uluslararası korumayı bulamamıştır. Gelen grupta görece az sayıda Suriyeli mültecinin yanı sıra İran, Afganistan, Pakistan, Fas ve Kuzey Afrika uyruklu mülteciler yer almıştır. TBMM İnsan Haklarını İnceleme Komisyonu Göç ve Uyum Alt Komisyonu'nun hazırladığı raporda belirtildiği üzere, Türkiye'nin konjonktürü gereği mültecilerin "kendi tercihlerine göre yaşamalarına izin verildiği ve buna destek olduğu açıklamaları" iç kamuoyunun tansiyonunu düşürmek için atılan bir adımdır. İdlib'te Türk askerinin uğradığı saldırı sonrasında alınan bu karar, söz konusu görüşü bir anlamda doğrularken, Avrupa Birliği ve Birleşmiş Milletlerin gözü önünde uygulanan insanlık dışı muameleler, mültecilerin politika alanının adeta "malzemesi" olduğunu da ortaya koymuştur. Bu süreçte İçişleri Bakanı Süleyman Soylu, günlük olarak sınırı geçebilen mültecilerin rakamlarını paylaşarak, kamuoyunda dikkatleri çekmiştir. Bakan Soylu, alanın boşaltılmasından iki gün önce 150 bin 600 mültecinin sınırı geçtiğini ve 4 bin 600 mültecinin ise bekleyişinin devam ettiğini duyurdu (Sputnik, 2020). Edirne İl Sağlık Müdürlüğü ve Edirne Valiliği'nin verilerine göre söz konusu dönemde 4 mülteci kullanılan gerçek mermilerin vücutlarına isabet etmesi sonucunda hayatını kaybedenler, yüzlerce mülteci ise yaralandı. Tüm bu olaylara rağmen Türkiye'nin mültecileri sınırdan uzaklaştırmak yerine günlerce bekleyişlerini desteklemeleri ve güvenlik güçlerinin mültecilere yönelik kolaylaştırıcı tavrı öte yandan Yunanistan güvenlik biriminin insanlık dışı muameleleri, yaşanılanların siyasetin gölgesinde gerçekleştiği konusunda dikkat çekmektedir. TBMM İnsan Haklarını İnceleme Komisyonu Göç ve Uyum Alt Komisyonu, mültecilerin Türkiye'de yaşamaktan dolayı mutlu olduklarını ancak bazılarının Avrupa'da ailelerinin olduğunu ve bu sebeple sınırı geçmek istediklerini rapor etmesi de söz konusu dönemdeki hareketliliğin belirli bir amaç doğrultusunda yapıldığını ifade etmemiz mümkündür. Hukuken karşılığı olmayan ancak siyasette çok sık tekrarlanan bir söylem olarak mültecilerin misafir edildiğine dair kullanımlar ve sosyal politika açısından uygun bir yaşam hakkı bulamayan mültecilerin Avrupa'ya gitme isteği bir hayalden ve istekten öte bu bağlamda bir zorunluluk doğurmuştur. Söz konusu kitle arasında büyük bir kısmı oluşturan Afgan mülteciler de olduğu gibi Türkiye'den ya da üçüncü bir ülkeden uluslararası koruma hakkı bulamayan göçmenler, bir anlamda sınırın açılması için beklemek zorunda kalmıştır. Bununla birlikte yaşanılan göç hareketliliğinde Yunanistan'ın mültecilere karşı uyguladığı sert müdahale ve tavır uluslararası hukuku açık bir şekilde ihlal etmiştir. Türkiye'nin de taraf olduğu 1951 Cenevre Sözleşmesi'ni çiğneyen Yunanistan, en ağır şekliyle sınır hattında mültecilere sert yüzünü göstermiştir.

Çalışmanın Amacı

Medya organları tarafından üretilen haberler ve paylaşımlar, hakim sosyo-kültürel ve ekonomi-politik yapı göz önünde bulundurularak kamusal alana yayılmaktadır. Söz konusu haberler, bir takım dilsel ve göstergesel kodlar zemininde üretildiğinde ya da bu noktalar, toplumsal yapıda var olan bir takım kalıplar ve söylemlerle bezendiğinde ortaya teknik araçlar ile dolayımlanmış bir düşünce çıkmaktadır. "Üretilen" bu fikirler, toplumsal alanda zaten var olan eşitsizlikleri derinleştirdiği gibi yeni toplumsal kalıplar üretmekte ve sınırları da yeniden tanımlamaktadır (Shoemaker & Reese, 2002, s. 127). Daha açık bir ifadeyle dünyadan haber veren medya içerikleri, yaşadığımızı zannettiğimiz dünyanın bir parçası değildir aksine haberdar olabildiğimiz dünyanın bir parçasıdır. Bu sebeple gerek bilinçli bir şekilde gerekse de bilinçsizce olsun medya araçlarının kamuoyuna sunduğu etiketlemeleri, ayrıştırıcı söylem taşıyan içerikleri toplumsal alanda yargı üretmekle birlikte belirli tutumları da tetiklemektedir (Akçalı, 2006, s. 13). Oluşturulan bu kalıp yargılar, belirli sınıflamalara tabi olup kullanılan dil de bir tehdit unsuruna dönmektedir. Burada ortaya çıkan stereotipler, söz konusu grubun temsiliyetini sunmaktadır. Temsiliyete baktığımızda ise toplumsal alanın sosyal haritasını sunması adına medya araçları ve söylemleri dikkatli bir şekilde ele alınmalıdır. Temsiliyetin ve söylemlerin medya araçlarıyla dolaşıma sokulduğu andan itibaren bir takım düşünceler meşru kılınmakta, modern ağ toplumlarında toplumsal yapıdaki hareketlilikleri de belirlemektedir (Dijk, 2000, s. 36). Meşru kılınan bu fikirler ise yeni ırkçılık, ötekileştirme, cinsiyetçi, türcü ve daha çok çeşitli yapıda olmaktadır. Medya içerikleri üzerinden yapılan söylemsel pratikler, van Dijk'ın işaret ettiği gibi modern toplumun büyük bir parçasını oluşturan enformasyon araçlarının yeni bir ırkçılık geliştirmekte ve bunlar da metin, görüntü, konuşma gibi şeyler üzerinden aktarılmaktadır. Belirli tutum ve ideolojilerle örülmüş, iktidar ilişkileri bağlamında özellikli hedefi olan içeriklere karşın alıcılar da haberlerden istenen ve beklenen bir etki yakalamaktadır. Tüm bunlardan hareketle van Dijk'ın yeni ırkçılık olarak adlandırdığı medya araçlarının ve söylemlerinin temelinde mülteciler gibi devletlerin ve toplumsal alanın "kabulü dışında kalan" mültecileri ve onların karşılaştıkları problemleri ele alış şekli bu çalışmanın temelini oluşturmaktadır. Çalışmanın sınırlandırılması amacı ile 2020 yılında Edirne ilinde meydana gelen göç hareketliliği sırasında kentte aktif bir şekilde hizmet veren yerel medya haberlerine bakılarak, söz konusu dönemdeki hak ihlalleri, söylemler ve bunların gazete sayfalarına nasıl taşındığı ele alınacaktır.

Çalışmanın Yöntemi

Kentteki günlük yayın yapan yerel gazetelerde üretilen haberler, çalışmanın odak noktasıdır. Aşağıdaki tabloda, kentte yayın hayatı devam eden gazeteler yer almaktadır.

Tablo 1. kentte yayın hayatı devam eden gazeteler

ÇALIŞMA GRUBUNDAKİ GAZETELER

Gazete	Künye
Yenigün Gazetesi	Yenigün Gazetesi Yenigün Ofset Gazetecilik & Matbaacılık *"Gündemi Bizle Yakalayın"*
Hudut Gazetesi	Yeni Hudut Gazetecilik ve Matbaacılık San. Ve Tic. Ltd. Şti. *"Güvenilir Haberciliğin Adresi"*
Gündem Gazetesi	Yeni Gündem Radyo Medya ve İletişim A.Ş. *"Günlük Siyasi Bağımsız Gazete"*
Sonhaber Gazetesi	Sonhaber Gazetecilik & Matbaacılık Ltd. Şti. *"Güvenilir Habercilik"*
Vatandaş Gazetesi	*"Gücü Özgürlüğünde"*
Edirne Haber Gazetesi	Baz Basın Yayın Ve Medya A.Ş. *"Haberin Doğru Adresi"*
Edirne Gazetesi	Edirne Gazetecilik & Televizyonculuk & Matbaacılık *"Gündemi belirler, Edirne'nin En İyi Gazetesi"*
Edirne'nin Sesi Gazetesi	Erçetin Medya İnş. ve Tic. Aş.

Çalışmada ortaya konulan bulgular, Teun van Dijk tarafından geliştirilen eleştirel söylem analizi çerçevesinde ele alınmıştır. Eleştirel söylem analizinin medya içeriklerine ve metinlerine uygulama konusunda önemli çalışmaları bulunan van Dijk, söz konusu analizin, "toplumsal ve siyasi içerikli konuşmalar ve metinlerin öne sürdüğü ve yeniden ürettiği; eşitsiz, egemen ve istismar eden sosyal tahakküm yollarını araştıran söylem araştırmalarının bir türü" olduğunu belirtmektedir (Dijk, 1993, s. 251-252). Bu yöntem bize toplumsal alanda meydana gelen olayları söylemsel açıdan daha geniş bir perspektif ile görmemize yardımcı olmaktadır. Eleştirel söylem analizi, sosyal ve kültürel yapılar, ilişkiler ve uygulamalar bağlamında metinlerin sürdürülen politikaya ve iktidar anlayışına ne şekilde hizmet verdiğini de göstermektedir. Örtük ilişkilerin üzerindeki perdeyi kaldırarak daha derin anlamları açığa çıkarması bakımında bu yöntem aynı zamanda araştırmacıların da görüşlerini çekinmeden ifade etmenin bir yolunu sunmaktadır.

1980'lerden itibaren Avrupa ülkelerinde yaşayan mülteci, göçmen ve azınlıkların medyadaki temsillerini sorunsallaştıran Teun van Dijk, söz konusu grupların basında yasadışılık, suç, saldırganlık ve şiddet gibi olaylarla ilişkilendirildiğini ve bunların sonucunda çeşitli stereotiplerin oluşturulduğunu dile getirmiştir (Gölcü & Dağcı, 2017, s. 21). Bu temsil ve olumsuz tasvirlere baktığımızda ise, olumsuzluk üzerine inşa edilmiş olan "öteki-sunumu" sistematik olarak olumsuz "özsunumla" yani kendisini ırkçı olmayan, hoşgörülü yurttaş olarak sunmaktadır (Dijk, 2005, s. 338). Kentte yayın hayatına devam eden 8 gazetenin 2020 yılı Mart ayı boyunca yaptığı yayınlar çerçevesinde 74 haber, çalışmanın odak noktasına uygun olarak seçilerek, analiz edilmeye uygun görülmüştür. Seçilen haberler ise, Dijk'ın eleştirel söylem analizi noktasında önerdiği çalışma başlıkları kapsamında değerlendirilmiştir (Dijk, 1993, s. 264). Bu başlıklar şu şekildedir:

- Yargılama (Gerçeklerden Kaynaklanarak Olumsuz Değerlendirmeler Yapma)
- Retorik görünüm (Olumlu Davranışların Gizlenmesi-Olumsuz Davranışların Ön Plana Çıkarılması)
- Lexical Stil (Negatifliği ya da Pozitifliği İma Eden Kelime Tercihleri)
- Hikayeleştirme (Yaşanılan Olumsuzlukları Kişisel Deneyimlere İndirgeme)
- Olumsuz Davranışların Yapısal Vurgusu (Başlıkta, Spotta, Ara Başlıkta, Girişte)
- Güvenilir Kaynaklardan Alıntı Yapma

Yargılama

Bu başlıkta analiz edilen haberlerde, kente gelen mültecilerin sebep oldukları gerçek durumlar üzerinden üretilen ayrıştırıcı ve yargılayıcı söylemlere bakılacaktır.

"Avrupa Hayali Sınır Kapılarına Dayandırdı" (Edirne'nin Sesi, 02.03.2020) başlıklı haberde Avrupa'ya gitmek için kente gelen mültecilerin gelişi haberleştirilmiştir. Haberde gelen mültecilerin içinde bulundukları durum ve hukuki varlıkları göz ardı edilerek bir hayal uğruna kitlesel göçün yaşandığı ifade edilmiştir. Haberin içerisinde kullanılan *"Edirne mülteci yuvasına döndü"* alt başlığı ise, gelen mültecileri ile kentliler arasında bir çizgi çekerek, öteki bağlamına oturtulmuştur.

"Karaağaç Çiftçisi Tepkili: Tarlamızı Ekemiyoruz" (Gündem, 12.03.2020) başlıklı haberde mültecilerin sınır hattına giderken semtteki tarlaları kullandıklarını ve büyük bir kitle oldukları için hareketlilikten dolayı çiftçilerin tarlalarını ekemedikleri haberleştirilmiştir. Haberde mültecilerin kente akın ettiği ve bundan dolayı çiftçilerin zor duruma düştüğü ifadesi kullanılarak, haber söyleminde yargılayıcı bir anlatım kullanılmıştır.

"Balıkçı kan ağlıyor" (Hudut, 10.03.2020) başlıklı haberde sınır hattına gelen mülteciler nedeniyle Pazarkule ve Kastanies Sınır Kapılarının kapalı olduğu ve bunun sonucunda Yunan turistlerin Edirne'ye gelemedikleri, balık pazarı esnafının işlerinde durgunluk yaşadığı haberleştirilmiştir. Mültecilerin hedef gösterilmesine bir örnek olan bu tarz haberler söz konusu dönemde çeşitli esnaf gruplarıyla görüşülerek tekrarlanmıştır. "Bu Suriyeliler çıktığından beri Bulgar Yunan vatandaş gelmiyor" ifadesinin haberde kullanılması ise ayrıştırıcı bir dil kullanımına örnektir. "Suriyeli mülteci" şeklindeki ayrımcı dil ifadesi yabancı düşmanlığına zemin hazırlamaktadır.

"Coronavirüs ve Mülteciler Ulus Pazarını Vurdu" (Edirne, 29.02.2020) başlıklı haberde mülteci grubu nedeniyle kente yabancı turistin gelmediği, her hafta kurulan Ulus Pazarı'na bu durumun yansıdığı ve ekonomik durgunluk yaşandığı haberleştirilmiştir. Bu bağlamdaki haberde de mülteciler, olay çıkaran, sorun teşkil eden gruplar olarak gösterilmiş ve ötekileştirici bir dil kullanılmıştır.

"İnatçı Mülteci 13'üncü kez Yunanistan'a Gitmeyi Deniyor" (Edirne, 10.03.2020) başlıklı haberde bir mültecinin Türkiye'den daha önce birçok kez ayrılmaya çalıştığı haberleştirilmiştir. Haberde mültecinin Pakistanlı olduğunun belirtilmesi ve inatçı sıfatı ile güçlendirdiği haberdeki anlam, kişinin neden bu kadar göç etmeye çalıştığını anlamlandırmaktan uzak kalarak, yargılayıcı fikri meşru hale getirmektedir.

Retorik Görünüm

Bu grupta analiz edilen haberlerde dilin retorik açıdan kullanımı ve hangi bağlamlarda anlamların yeniden üretildiğine bakılmıştır.

"***Umut Otogarı***" (Vatandaş, 09.03.2020) başlıklı haberde Edirne'ye gelen mültecilerin büyük bir kısmının otogarda kendilerine yaşam alanı kurdukları haberleştirilmiştir. Mültecilerin içinde bulunduğu zorlu şartlardan öte ortaya çıkan tablonun sosyal hayatı olumsuz etkilediği haber metninde ön plana çıkarılmıştır. Metinde kullanılan mültecilerin "Edirne'ye akın ettiği" ifadesi de sık sık tekrarlanan bir söylem olmuştur.

"***Türk Hemşireden Yunan Sınır Güvenliğine İnsanlık Dersi***" (Edirne Haber, 04.03.2020) başlıklı haberde Pazarkule Sınır Kapısı'nda Yunanistan sınır güvenliğinin attığı gaz bombalarından etkilenen çocuklarla ilgilenen sağlık personeli haberleştirilmiştir. Biber gazlı müdahaleden etkilenen çocuklara hemşirenin çikolata vermesi, insanlık dersi olarak tanımlanırken, Türk olduğu vurgusu da mültecilerin yaşadığı hak ihlalinden ziyade bir milli kimliği öne çıkarmaya çalışmaktadır. Mültecilerin hak ihlallerinin gerçekçi bir anlatı ile haberleştirilmesi yerine örtük anlamlarla sunulması, yaşanılanların ikincilleştirilmesine sebep olmaktadır.

"***Suriyeli Göçmenin Cumhurbaşkanı Sevgisi***" (Edirne Haber, 05.03.2020) başlıklı haberde Gaziantep'ten Edirne'ye gelerek Avrupa'ya gitmeye çalışan bir mültecinin oğluna cumhurbaşkanının adını vermesi haberleştirilmiştir. Sınır hattında seslerini duyurmaya çalışan mültecilerin hak ihlallerinden ziyade daha soft haberlerin yapılması yaşanılan olumsuzlukları geri plana düşürmektedir. Benzer bir şekilde haberdeki mültecinin uyruğunun da belirtilmesi haber söyleminde sıklıkla tekrarlanmıştır.

"***Yunan Irkçılar Mülteci Avına Çıktı***" (Yenigün, 05.03.2020) başlıklı haberde Kastanies sınırındaki Yunan güvenlik güçlerine "destek" olmak için gelen avcılar haberleştirilmiştir. Haber metninde "ülkelerinde göçmenleri istemeyen ırkçı Yunan halkı" ifadesi ayrımcı ve ötekileştirici bir söylem inşası üzerine kuruludur. Mültecilerin yaşadığı zulmü anlatmak için bir başka grubu hedef alan bu söylemler, eleştirel bir çözümlemeden oldukça uzaktır.

Lexical Stil

Bu grupta analiz edilen haberlerde mültecilerin tanımlanmasında kullanılan negatiflik barındıran ve mültecilerle ilişkilendirilen bir yaklaşımın varlığı gözlemlenmiştir.

"***Yunan'a Akın Var***" (Edirne, 03.03.2020), "***Göçmenler Sınıra Dayandı***" (Edirne 29.02.2020), "***Göçmenler Edirne'ye Akın Etti***" (Edirne Haber, 29.02.2020), "AB Yolunda Sınır Tanımadı" (Gündem, 29.02.2020) başlıklı haberde kullanılan "***göçmenler Edirne'ye adeta akın etti***" ifadesi, "***Edirne'ye Mülteci Akını***" (Hudut, 29.02.2020), "***Sınıra Akın Başladı***" (Sonhaber, 29.02.2020) başlıklı haberlerin hepsi, Türkiye'nin göçmenleri durdurmama kararı almasının ardından yaşanılan hareketliliği ifade etmek için yazılmıştır. Sınıra dayanma, akın etme, dalga, düzensiz göçmenlerin 'yakalanması' kelimelerinin tercih edilmesi, haberlerin belirli bir doğrultuda şekillenmesine neden olmuştur. Bu kelimelerin tercih edilmesi negatiflik barındıran bir ifade olduğu gibi kamuoyunda bir tehdit olarak algılanmayı tetiklemektedir. Benzer bir şekilde "korkulan oldu" şeklindeki bir anlatının da haber metinlerinde sıklıkla tekrar etmesi yıkıcı bir anlama işaret etmektedir. "Korku" kelimesinin sıklıkla tekrar edilmesi de benzer bir kullanımının örneğidir.

"***Köpeğinin pasaportu var onun yok!***" (Gündem, 11.03.2020) başlıklı haberde, İspanya'ya gitmek için sınırda bekleyen bir mültecinin hikayesi haberleştirilmiştir. 7 yıl önce kendisine Avrupa'dan gelen bir arkadaşı tarafından "hediye edilen" köpeğinin pasaportu olduğunu ancak mültecinin pasaportunun olmadığı kıyaslanarak, türcü bir dil kullanılmıştır.

"**Akın durdu, bekleyiş sürüyor**" (Gündem, 11.03.2020) başlıklı haberde, yine göç hareketliliğinin akına benzetilmesi ve bu kelimenin haber metninde çok sık kullanılması, yerel halk üzerinde bir algı oluşturmaktadır. Haber metninde Edirne Belediye Başkanının görüşlerine yer verilerek, halkın sakin kalması ve sabırlı olması için çağrıya yer verilmesi de bu algıyı görünür kılmıştır.

Hikayeleştirme

Bu gruptaki haber analizlerinde yaşanılan sorunların bireysel anlatılarla dolayımlanmasını ele almaktadır.

"**Mülteci Akını ile Sınav**" (Edirne, 03.03.2020) başlıklı köşe yazısında yaşanan kitlesel göç hareketi ele alınmıştır. Söz konusu deneyimle ilgili "Böyle kalıcı ve de arkası da kesilmeyecek bir durumda Edirne büyük sıkıntılar yaşayacak, bir şekilde 'Mülteci Akını ile Sınav' vermek zorunda kalacaktır. Güvenlik-Huzur boyutunun yanı sıra, beslenme, temizlik ve sağlık konusu beklenmedik kitlesel sorun ve rahatsızlıklara neden olacaktır" kente gelen kişilerin potansiyel açıdan "rahatsızlık vereceği" düşüncesi ile yoğrulmuştur. Gazeteler aracılığıyla kamuoyuna ulaşan bu düşünceler, toplumsal kalıpları tekrarlamaya, meşru kılmaya, ayrımcılığın sürekli kılınmasına neden olmaktadır.

"**Mültecilerin Sırtından Geçinenlere Engel Olunmalı**" (Vatandaş, 03.03.2020) başlıklı köşe yazısında gelen mültecilere karşı kötü niyetli olan yerel halkın tavrı eleştirilmiştir. Ancak bununla birlikte "*Aç sefil her şeyini kaybetme korkusu yaşayan insanlardan çekinmek gerekir. Kimlikleri dahi olup olmadığından şüphe duyulan bu insanlarla Edirneliler arasında tatsız bir olay olduğunda önce Türkiye'de bu olayı kendi çıkarına yorumlayan malum basının daha sonra da ülkemizi karalamak kötü göstermek isteyen yabancı basının malzemesi oluruz*" ifadeleri tıpkı bir önceki örnekte olduğu gibi peşin hükümlere besleyen bir üsluptadır.

"**Yoğun hijyenik kirlilik hastalıklara davetiye çıkarıyor. Sığınmacılar Karaağaç'tan derhal çekilmelidir**" (Vatandaş, 16.03.2020) başlıklı köşe yazısında, kente geldikten bir süre sonra mültecilerin bir takım sorunlara sebep oldukları belirtilerek, suçlayıcı bir dil kullanılmıştır. Metinde geçen "*Sayın Cumhurbaşkanımız, ani bir kararla; "Bu kadar sığınmacıyı biz bakamayız. Onlara yurt dışına çıkışı serbest bıraktık." Diyerek on binlerce sığınmacıyı Edirne'nin üzerine saldı. Olan bizim Karaağaç semtimize oldu. Karaağaç Halkı bu hijyenik kirlilikten korkarak mahalle bakkallarından dahi alışveriş yapmaya korkuyorlar. Sığınmacıların traş olduğu berberlere gitmekten korkuyorlar. Ve hatta berberler dahi onları görünce dükkanlarını kapatıyorlar. Bu korku ve tedirginlik Karaağaç Halkının hakkı mı?*" ifadeleri, söz konusu düşüncenin meşru kılınmasında oldukça etkili gibi gözükmektedir.

Olumsuz Davranışların Yapısal Vurgusu

"**Çiftçi perişan!**" (Vatandaş, 09.03.2020) başlıklı haberde mültecilerin açlıktan tarlalardaki mahsulleri yedikleri haberleştirilmiştir. "Göçmenlerin Pazarkule Sınır Kapısı ve çevresindeki sınır hattına ulaşmak için Karaağaç'ta bulunan tarlaları kullanması, bölgede üretim yapan çiftçilerin büyük zararlar yaşamasına neden oldu. Tarlalardaki mahsullerin kullanılamaz hale geldiğini, su boruları ile elektrik panolarının patladığını ve yaklaşık 50 bin lira zarar ettiğini söyleyen Üretici Mustafa Öztürk, yetkililerden yardım beklediğini ifade etti" ifadeleri yerli üreticinin sorununu anlatırken öte yandan genelleştirici bir dil kullanarak, tüm mültecilerin ortak bir davranış sergilediği belirtilmiştir. Ayrıca mültecilerin yaşamsal ihtiyaçlarının yetmediği belirtilmeyerek, sebep olunan diğer olumsuzluklar sıralanmıştır.

"**Tarım alanları zarar gördü**" (Yenigün, 02.03.2020) başlıklı haberde Pazarkule Sınır Kapısı'nda bulunan göçmenlerin tarlalara zarar verdiği haberleştirilmiştir. Haberde "*Yunanistan'ın asker ve polis takviyesinde bulunması, gaz bombası kullanması ve plastik mermi atışında bulunmasının ardından uzun bir bekleyişe geçen ve koşuşturan büyük mülteci grubu bu sırada çevreye de zarar verdi*" ifadeleri mültecilerin yaşadığı ihlali dile getirmekten çok uzaktır. Genelleştirici bir dil kullanımı ve asıl olumsuzlukların ifade edilmeyişi, söylemsel analiz açısından önemlidir.

"*Edirne ekonomisi durdu*", "*Esnafımız sabretsin*" (Hudut, 03.03.2020) başlıklı haberlerde yaşanılan mülteci hareketliliği nedeniyle kent ekonomisinin zarar gördüğü haberleştirilmiştir. Haber metninde kullanılan *"Seyahat, turizm bunların hepsi ikinci planda. Söylemek istemiyorum ama savaş var."* ifadeleri, kamuoyunda panik oluşturabilecek, tedirginlikleri hat safhaya çıkarabilecek kullanımlardır. Burada mültecilere yönelik pratiklerin arka planda tutulması ve olumsuz davranışların yapısal vurgusu, olumsuzluk kurgusu üzerinden inşa edilmiştir.

"*2 milyon göçmen gidecek*" (Edirne, 04.03.2020) başlıklı haberde Kamu Baş Denetçisi Şeref Malkoç'un alana gelerek yaptığı ziyaretlerdeki açıklaması haberleştirilmiştir. Haberde kullanılan *"yakında 2 milyon göçmen bu duvarlara, tel örgülere rağmen Avrupa'nın içlerine gidecektir."* ifadeleri, insan haklarına sığmayan müdahalelere rağmen mültecilerin her koşulda Avrupa'ya gönderilecek olması yapısal açıdan tehlikeli bir dil kullanımına örnektir.

Güvenilir kaynaklardan alıntı yapma

"*Meclis Doyran'a geldi*" (Gündem, 05.03.2020) başlıklı haberin alt başlığında kullanılan *"Yardımcı olsak 200 bin kişi geçiririz"* söylemi, TBMM İnsan Hakları Komisyonu'nun incelemelerine dayandırılmıştır. Bu haberde, Türk güvenlik güçlerinin mültecilerin sınır geçişlerine yardım ettiği yönünde yabancı basında yer alan haberlere karşı bir söylem kullanılmıştır.

"*Yunan Yaralıyor, Türkiye Koruyor*" (Edirne, 09.03.2020) başlıklı haberde ve **"*Yunanistan Ayırdı, Türkiye Kavuşturdu*"** (Edirne, 06.03.2020) başlıklı haber, **"*İşte Gidiyor Özel Harekat*"** (Edirne, 06.03.2020) başlıklı haberlerde emniyet kaynakları birincil bilgi kaynağı olarak gösterilmiştir. Kaynak kullanımının tek yönlü olması medya içeriğinin de hakim ideolojik anlayışa hizmet etme noktasında iç kamuoyunun tansiyonunu düşürmeye yarayan bir kullanıma örnektir.

"*Sınır Savaş Alanı Gibi*", "*PÖH Nefes Aldırmıyor*" (Edirne, 13.03.2020) başlıklı haberlerde askeri bir terminoloji dili kullanılarak haber aktarımı tek yönlü bir alana çevrilmiştir.

Sonuç

Bu çalışmada, ülkelerin politika alanlarında oldukça önemli bir etki uyandıran göç olgusu ve medya araçları üzerinden üretilen içeriklerin kullanım dili arasındaki ilişki ele alınmıştır. Sınırların giderek keskinleştiği ve göçün güvenlikli hale getirildiğini bir zaman diliminde medya içeriklerinin bu olguyu ele alışı giderek önem kazanmaktadır. Hakim bir anlayışa hizmet veren medya dili ile insan hakları ihlalini ortaya koyan ve pratikleri analiz ederek, sebep-sonuç ilişkisi koyan medya dili arasındaki bağlantı, yaşananları toplumsal alanda anlamlandırmaya yaramaktadır. Medyanın ayrıştırıcı ve ötekileştirici bir dil kullanması zaten çeşitli paradokslar barındıran göçmenlik hallerini ve göçün temsilini zorlaştırdığı gibi bir çatışma yaratmaya da neden olabilmektedir. Bu nedenle eleştirel söylem analizi, medya çalışanlarının ve içerik üreticilerinin her daim takip etmesi gereken önemli bir iştir. Çalışma kapsamında, 28 Şubat 2020 tarihinde hükümetin açıklamalarıyla başlayan göç hareketliliğinin Edirne'de yansımaları incelenmiştir. 1 aylık süreçte kentte sınırların açılması için bekleyişlerini sürdüren mültecilerin karşılaştıkları sorunların yerel gazetelerde nasıl işlendiği ele alınmıştır. İnsan hakları ihlallerine önemli bir derecede yer veren kent gazeteleri bir yandan bilinçli ya da bilinçsiz bir şekilde kullandıkları dil ile göç durumunu daha da zorlu bir hale getirmiştir. Mültecilerin bir sorunun kaynağıymış gibi ele alınışları göçün ve bu alanda üretilen politikaların esas analizlerinin önünü tıkamaktadır. Açık kapı politikasının yalnızca mültecileri bulunduran ülkelerin uygulaması gereken yöntem değildir. Yerinden edilerek, gelecek tahayyülü bulunmayan insanların kendilerini güvende hissetmeleri açısından yük paylaşımının yapılması insani bir sorumlulukken, devletlerin uyum politikaları, milli kimlik ve daha çeşitli parametrelerce uyuşmaması nedeniyle kapıların daha da sıkı kapatıldığına şahit olmaktayız. Göçün engellenmesi adına geri itme, sığınmacı botlarının patlatılması ve tampon bölgede sıkıştırmak gibi insanlık dışı uygulamaların engellenmesi adına bu alan daha derinlikli bir bakışı gerektirmektedir. Fakat bunun karşısında Edirne yerel gazetelerinde olduğu gibi haber metinlerinin üretim sürecinde mültecilere eşit hak ve alanların sağlanmaması yüzeysel bir bakışı ve sonucunda da derin problemleri tetiklemektedir. Özellikle haber kaynaklarının ağırlıklı olarak emniyet ve yetkili birimlerin oluşturması asıl öznelerin göz ardı edilmesine neden olmaktadır. Olumsuz tanımlama ve uyrukların özellikle belirtilmesi ayrımcı bir dil kullanımına işaret ederken, bu sorunların çözümü adına öncelikle haber metinlerinin üretim süreçlerinde söz konusu kalıpların kullanımı terk edilmelidir. Böylelikle temsillerin kalıp yargılara dönüşmesinin önüne geçilebilir.

Kaynakça

Akçalı, Selda (2006). Gündelik Hayat ve Medya: Tüketim Kültürü Perspektifinden Okumalar, Ankara: Ebabil Yayıncılık.

Gölcü, A, Dağlı, A. (2017). "Haber Söyleminde 'Öteki'yi Aramak: Suriyeli Mülteciler Örneği", Akdeniz Üniversitesi İletişim Fakültesi Dergisi , (28)

Hall, S. (2017). "Temsil İşi", Temsil Kültürel Temsiller ve Anlamlandırma Uygulamaları, (Editör: Hall, S.), Çev. İdil Dündar, İstanbul: Pinhan Yayıncılık.

Sanlı, Leyla (2005). Politik Kültür ve Toplumsal Hareketler, İstanbul: Alan Yayıncılık.

Shoemaker, P & Reese, S. (2002). "İdeolojinin Medya İçeriği Üzerindeki Etkisi", Medya Kültür Siyaset, Süleyman İrvan(Der.), Ankara: Ark Yayınları.

Türkiye Büyük Millet Meclisi, (2020). İnsan Haklarını İnceleme Komisyonu Göç ve Uyum Alt Komisyonu Türkiye-Yunanistan Sınır Bölgesindeki Sığınmacı Geçişlerinin Yerinde İncelenmesine İlişkin Rapor.

Van Dijk, T. (2001). "Critical Discourse Analysis", Deborah Tannen, Deborah Schiffrin & Heidi Hamilton (Eds.), Handbook of Discourse Analysis, Oxford: Blackwell.

Van Dijk T. (2005). "Söylemin Yapıları ve İktidarın Yapıları", Medya İktidar İdeoloji. Mehmet Küçük (der. & çev.), Ankara: Bilim ve Sanat Yayınları.

Van Dijk, T. (2003). "Söylem ve İdeoloji: Çok Alanlı Bir Yaklaşım," Söylem ve İdeoloji, Barış Çoban ve Zeynep Özarslan (Ed.), İstanbul: Su Yayınları.

Van Dijk, T. (2000). "New(s) Racism", Simon Cottle (Ed.), Ethnic Minorities and The Media, London: Open University Press

Van Dijk, T. (1993). "Principles of Critical Discourse Analysis", Discourse & Society, Volume 4 (2).

Van Dijk T. (2005). "Söylemin Yapıları ve İktidarın Yapıları", Medya İktidar İdeoloji. Mehmet Küçük (der. & çev.), Ankara: Bilim ve Sanat Yayınları.

Varol, F. S. (2016). Temsil, İdeoloji, Kimlik, İstanbul: Varlık Yayınları.

Web Kaynakları

https://www.aa.com.tr/tr/politika/ak-parti-sozcusu-celik-artik-multecileri-tutabilecek-durumda-degiliz/1747670 (Erişim Tarihi: 12.04.2021).

https://www.aa.com.tr/tr/turkiye/hatay-valisi-dogan-idlibde-hava-saldirisinda-33-mehmetcigimiz-sehit-oldu/1747454 (Erişim Tarihi: 12.04.2021).

https://www.indyturk.com/node/138766/haber/reuters-haberini-%C3%BCst-d%C3%BCzey-t%C3%BCrk-yetkiliye-dayand%C4%B1rd%C4%B1-t%C3%BCrkiye-suriyeli-m%C3%BClltecilerin (Erişim Tarihi: 12.04.2021).

https://tr.sputniknews.com/turkiye/202003261041689936-soyludan-sokaga-cikma-yasagi-sorusuna-yanit-gerekirse-tedbirleri-yukseltebiliriz/ (Erişim Tarihi: 15.05.202

IDENTITIES PUT TO THE TEST OF MIGRATION: THE CASE OF RUSSIAN HOMOSEXUALS AND BISEXUALS IN FRANCE AND IN CANADA

Katia Hartmann

The context of this research

The project to realize this research has become me for reasons that are both political and personal. On the *political* level, it must be remembered that in 2013, following the adoption of the law against the "propaganda of homosexuality" in St. Petersburg, amendments have been made to the federal law on the "Protection of children against information that influence their health and development". The law against the "propaganda of non-traditional relations among minors", adopted than, banishes any encouragement of relations between same-sex people. Following these legislative changes and the increase of discrimination and violence, more and more LGBT people have arisen the question: **can they stay living in Russia or should they leave**? On the *personal* level, in 2012, I became a volunteer of the association called Alliance of heterosexuals and LGBT for equality. By participating in public actions, I lived all the danger of "legalized" homophobia: physical aggression, moral harassment, lack of legal protection. In other words, all that people who claim equality and tolerance in totalitarian Russia.

Problematic

At the beginning, I focused on the issue of "private life", more particularly, on the strategies used by LGBT to protect themselves after the adoption of the liberticide laws by the Putin government. With the adoption of the law against "propaganda", LGBT were considered a threat to demography and for morality and even for the sovereignty of Russia. The right of LGBT people has been presented as a threat to national identity. New emissary goats serve the state to achieve its political and ideological purpose. At the beginning of my work, I distinguished three types of protection of "privacy": to hide or live in the closet, to make a coming-out and militate to defend the constitutional rights of citizens, or to emigrate. In my field research, I wanted to understand why LGBT people migrate. What is their migration "career"? What strategies they deploy to settle abroad and to register in other ways to see homosexuality and bisexuality.

I realized during my work, that classic sociology of migration should be supplemented by another sociology, that of identities – they are numerous in this research: homosexual or bisexual, opponent, activist, migrant. It was important to study this issue of identities if I wanted to understand the difficulties of life in the country and the process of acculturation in France and in Canada.

The question of identity: difference between women and men

First, there is the time of acceptance of homosexual and bisexual identity. Coming-out is a fundamental step of the "career" of my respondents. It takes into practice the form of a process that begins with the awareness for the most part, women and men face the same difficulties in this coming-out process. But it seems to me that the break with family is particularly painful for women.

Then it is militant identity. From coming-out and when a sense of pride is associated with their sexual orientation, some people decide to combat discrimination and homophobia in Russia. They thus give themselves a new identity – the militant identity. For many interviewees, the 2011-2012 election in Russia were the trigger, the turning point in their lives. Respondents – women and men – then participated in spectacular public actions. Some of men residing in St. Petersburg then disengaged from LGBT movement, no longer seeing the utility of the actions or being the victim of burnout. A good part of these militant men still decided to stay in their country of origin, while most of the militant women I have met, chose to emigrate.

And, finally, I will speak about the migration and recomposing of identities of homosexual and bisexual women and men. It happens a turning point where people say, "This time is too much", This time it is no longer possible". But what is "too much" and "not possible"? Life in Russia, discrimination, stigma, humiliations, aggressions? YES, and there are the reason why LGBT people migrate.

There is always the choice – migrate or not.

For MEN it is especially the question of security that prevails and the absence of the image of a Russian straight man – as Putin, the question of freedom of expression. Regarding WOMEN, I also see the weight of positive reasons that push them to migrate:

1. There is a more positive turning point – conjugal and family motivations. Women fall in love and migrate to give a fulltime to their couple.

2. Some couple with children migrates not to lose them because of the bill that has proposed to remove to homosexual parents the custody of their children.

3. Other women migrate to be able to base a medically assisted reproductive family and libe normally in a country where LGBT rights are protected.

How is the process of acculturation going to the recomposing of identities?

Upon arrival in a new country, cultural shock gives wings to migrants. At first, they see everything in pink color, they can be themselves without any discrimination. But this phase of Honey Moon passes and the problems of migrants arrive: administrative procedures, stereotypes on Russia and especially on the Russian women who are "looking for a man", and, of course, the depression.

Passing this phase of euphoria and a crisis phase, my respondents understand that there is no return to Russia. So, they only must adapt a new society and to recompose their identities. The process of multistage acculturation that women and men are crossing differently.

1. When confronting the Russian community in the host country, men come up against stereotypes about male Russian men. As for women, they come up against stereotypes about Russian women: heterosexual, looking for a husband to stay abroad. Everything shows that the Russian community propagates the same values as Russian society: traditional family values and the subordination to men.

2. Consequently, the process of assimilation into the host society involves the loss of Russian identity, with attempts to obtain French or Canadian identity. To do this, my respondents look to the LGBT community rather than the Russian community. Assimilation involves complete rejection of one's culture of origin and 100 per cent adaptation to the host society, which is the case at the start of a migratory "career".

3. However, once settled abroad, some of my respondents go back to their origins. Many participants felt a mixture of two cultures and talked about the importance that their original culture plays in their cultural identity today – they want to preserve Russian cultural

heritage, have Russian decorative objects, books, food.

The question of recomposing identities is linked to the question of returning to Russia. This concerns only women because men are afraid to return to Russia and be aggressed again. "You can love Russia only from afar", says one of the lesbians, who currently lives in France. And when I say "come back" it is never final, it can be for one or max two weeks. Why do women come back to Russia after a long process of acculturation which is sometimes painful when they already formed a new identity – Western identity – opposite of Russian. The causes of this return can be the desire to reconcile with the parents, nostalgia, or sometimes the return to Russian activism to share their French or Canadian experience.

But !!!!

When they return, their new western identity is not accepted either by relatives or by activists with whom they share the same cause a few years earlier. They thus come ti the radical decision – never to return to Russia !!!

So, I was able to show you briefly that in addition to physical migration, there is another that we can call "migration identity". The migratory process brings about profound changes in identity. From the recognition of their homosexual and bisexual identity, the people concerned change their identity and find themselves part of the LGBT community. Research has shown how the suffering endured in Russia led some homosexual and bisexual people to migrate, these people acquired yet another identity – migrant. Once there, it is another form of discrimination that often affects them – racism – and which still forces them to redefine their way of situating themselves in society. Most of the people concerned deny their Russian origin and try to become French or Canadian. However, the temporary return to Russian, attempted by lesbian and bisexual women, leads them to suffer a new form of discrimination – their compatriots attribute to them another deviant identity – the western identity.

LIFE STORIES OF THREE SYRIAN MIGRANT WOMEN IN TURKEY: RIGHTS AND GENDER EQUALITY EXPERIENCES

Hulya Sahin-Erbektas

Abstract

This paper includes the life stories of three women who migrated to Turkey from Syria through forced migration. Thoughts of Syrian women, who participated in the research, related to gender roles and gender equality; and their gains in new rights and new freedom fields provided by civil rights after coming to Turkey are discussed based on the participants' standpoints. This research uses one of the qualitative data collection techniques "life story". Life stories of these women consist of their life in Syria, migration process and their life in Turkey. This paper contains answers to these questions: "What is the life story method", "What are the contributions of life story method to the feminist standpoint approach, and to the participants who share their story".

Keywords: forced migration, women rights, gender equality, life story.

Introduction

This study focuses on the Syrian women who migrated to Turkey from Syria through forced migration. It presents a comparison of how women have experienced human rights in gender inequality and gender roles. In this study, there are three objectives. The first of these is to convey thoughts and experiences of the participant Syrian women on gender equality and women's rights in Syria prior to migration; the second is to investigate whether these women have experienced any change in their thoughts on gender equality and women's rights in their new life after the migration to Turkey and to present what aspects these changes were based on if there is any change; the final objective is to reveal what the future expectations of these forced migrant women are.

Method

In this study "Feminist-Standpoint Theory" has been used. There are a lot of different perspectives or ways of being a feminist, because to make sense of the social reality or describing real-life cannot be possible from one single viewpoint. Based on Haraway[1] (2004), there is no typical or essential women's life form from which feminisms start their thought. Additionally, there is no single feminist research method. For this reason, the Feminist Standpoint Theory helps us present different experiences of femininity from different perspectives. Based on these, Standpoint epistemology is used in this study. In this research frame, the information and experiences of Syrian women who live in Turkey with regards to gender roles that are prior to migration and post-migration were accepted as a piece of the social reality. In the research, the subject of knowledge is Syrian women. The participants' way of knowing differs from both men and other women. This difference can be explained by the theory of intersectionality. Finally, through Feminist Standpoint theory, the women living a life that was marginalized, transform into a subject who can speak (Harding, 2004: Somay, 2017). At this point, the

---

[1] "There is no typical women's life from which feminisms start their thought…"

way of gathering evidence which is the life story has much importance.

The life story is one of the methods of qualitative data collection that has been used by the inquiry fields such as psychology, sociology, and anthropology. Atkinson, who is one of the pioneers of the life story, states that "life story provides ageless elements and motifs that tie us with our roots, through the entire life course" (Atkinson, 2001). Life story interviews ensure a lot of benefits for both researchers and participants. For this research, to make ordinary people the subject of history, to include multiple points of view in the production process of the information, to give power to the narrator, to ensure flexibility for both researcher and narrator have great importance through the life story method.

Demographic Information of Participants

Table 1. Demographic Information of Participants

Pseudonyms	Age	Education	Place of Residence in Syria	Marital Status	Occupation in Syria	Occupation in Turkey
Samira	28	Undergraduate academic degree	İdlib	Single	Music Teacher	Interpreting at schools
Fatma	52	University drop out	Halep	Her husband has passed away	Tutoring Teacher	Interpreting at projects
Ayşe	32	Undergraduate academic degree	Halep	Married	Recently graduated	Interpreting at schools

This research was conducted with three Syrian immigrant women who have different criteria. Since the life story method requires very long processes and multi-stages, it was decided to interview three women who have features that are essential for the study. These features are the participants have different ages, marital statuses, and occupations. The other important features are knowing how to speak Turkish and to have a university education. One of the women's criteria that was determined, being able to speak Turkish, is important in terms of the stories being able to be transmitted first-hand without the need for a translator. The other criterion is that the women have a university education because of the desire to reach the thoughts and experiences of educated women on gender equality and women's rights.

Findings

The findings were discussed in three parts as pre-migration, migration process, and post migration.

The Women's Life in Syria

The women's life in Syria represents the pre-migration stage. I will discuss just some of the topics in this section in the following slides. This section includes three findings from their life in Syria. These are "Patriarchal System", "Women's Educational Rights", and "Attending the Work-life and Domestic Unpaid Labor".

Patriarchal System

The first of these is Patriarchal System. Patriarchal thought and Islamic religion are the most important elements that give direction to Syrian society. Patriarchal codes have expanded on each layer of their society. The women were raised by their mothers with the idea that says: "A woman goes from her father to the husband; she goes from her husband to tomb". Women who have grown up with such a mentality have developed some ways of bargaining by using patriarchal thought and religion in order to exist, such as accepting marriage in order to continue their education life, having sons, and being silent and obedient.

Women's Educational Rights

Similarly, attending the educational life in Syria, in practice, since there are no laws protecting women's rights, women do not benefit from the rights of making education mandatory or restrictions applying to early age marriages.

Attending the Work-Life and Domestic Unpaid Labor

Syrian women have the right to work in the public sphere. However, according to the participants' statements, Syrian women think about work in the public sphere as a difficulty and an obstacle to their primary responsibility such as doing household chores, making themselves attractive, or being a good wife.

The Process of The Migration

The participants migrated as a family with a man representing the family. They have not taken the decision to migrate themselves. In this research, for two of them the person who is the decision maker is their father. The other participant (Fatma), because her husband has passed away, stated that she would never take a migration decision if it were for herself, made the decision herself on behalf of their family. Being a female migrant alone in a society with such a strong patriarchal network is very difficult in terms of both making decision and being able to migrate. Moreover, the costs of being a "manless immigrant" are high.

Women migrating alone may face many dangers on the way. Smugglers at the border might confiscate their belongings and demand more money. Women who are alone in the migration process also risk a journey under the threat of harassment and rape.

Post Migration

Participants are aware of the rights and practices in Turkey that can improve their lives after coming to Turkey. In particular, they are very satisfied with the practices such as women's benefiting from their education rights, the obligation of civil marriage, the legal prohibition of polygamy, and the absence of restrictions on women's participation in working life. However, at the same time, the participants indicated that they could not accept the examples they saw in Turkey, showing hesitancy in expressing a positive opinion on the individual decision-making freedom of women in Turkey.

Conclusion

About Their Life in Syria

Although the participants think that they have a lot of rights in Syria, it was not possible to find the exact equivalent in juridical resources. Moreover, the restrictive nature of the social structure does not allow them to exercise their rights even if they have rights in some areas. Women have difficulty distinguishing between religious practices, legal practices, and traditions, and they have difficulty specifying what rights they have in Syria. When they cannot use their legal rights with the effect of social control mechanisms, they don't fight for these rights, and they show behaviors adapted to the system.

What Have Changed in the Lives of Syrian Women in Turkey?

In this study, changes include the marriage decision and starting a new family according to the participants. When two of the participants migrated to Turkey, they hadn't yet been married. One of them (Ayşe) was married during the research period. The other participant (Samira), when we started the interview, she was saying that she wanted to marry a Turkish man. Nearly all Syrian migrant women had told her that she should marry a Turkish man because they are better than Syrian men. According to participant women's opinions (points of view) perspectives, Syrian families (Syrian men as the head of the families) have been affected by Turkish families after the migration. Hence, before the marriage, their fathers allowed them to meet with a man who intends to marry. Moreover, they mentioned that they gained the right to select their husband. Besides, one of the participants (Ayşe) mentioned that she feels better because she is married to a Turkish man. She defined the Turkish men as kind people, who gives their wives the right of saying something or making a decision. She feels more valuable herself in their marriage. The other change in the participants' life is being involved in working life. Although the Syrian women can work in Syria, they couldn't have any relationship with people as a citizen or colleague. They succeeded to leave their neighborhood that they thought they could never leave. They are happier to have left the oppressive environment.

Future Expectations

Participating women in the study did not mention a plan for themselves in their expectations for the future, and they made requests related to their families. Being together with my children, giving birth to my child, raising him; they used expressions such as getting married, having children after marriage, being happy with my husband and children. It was stated that they are very pleased to live in Turkey. It is concluded that they are not willing to go to a country other than Turkey in the future. However, one of the participants stated that she would like to live in Malaysia if she had the chance to choose to live in a different country. The participant wants to live in Malaysia, which she was said is a developed country in terms of Islamic aspects, while giving women rights such as education and work, and that she wants the rights implemented in accordance with Islamic rules.

References

Atkinson, R. (2001). *The Life Story Interview.* In Gubrium, J. F., ve Holstein, J. A. Handbook of interview research (pp. 120-140): SAGE Publications, Inc. doi:10.4135/9781412973588

Haraway, D. J. (2004). *The Haraway Reader.* New York: Routledge.

Harding, R. (2004). Social Enterprise: The New Economic Engine? *https://doi.org/10.1111/j.0955-6419.2004.00338.x*

Somay, B. (2017). *Çokbilmiş Özne.* İstanbul: Metis Yayınları.

RECOGNITION AND EXERCISE OF THE SOCIAL RIGHT TO EDUCATION. CHALLENGES AND OPPORTUNITIES IN A MULTICULTURAL INCLUSION PERSPECTIVE

Elena Girasella

Abstract

The slight increase in the number of refugees who had access to university education in 2019 is far from the UNHCR's target of the inclusion of 15% of the refugee population in tertiary education by 2030 (UNHCR, 2019) and it is reasonable to assume that the SARS-CoV-2 coronavirus pandemic will explain its negative effects even in this topic. This work is intended to contribute to the affirmation of the right to education as a social right. The contribution is based on the assumption that the enhancement of the knowledge and skills of migrants, refugees and asylum seekers represents one of the main levers of inclusion and development. Investing in education and facilitating access to the highest levels of education not only guarantees full personal development but it also generates indisputable added value to the entire community. The assessment of a positive impact that goes beyond the private sphere is justified by the quantity and quality of the migration flows in this century. Notwithstanding these simple remarks, the choice to undertake an educational path is still residual. It is, in fact, one of the most difficult paths to deal with, starting from the problem of demonstrating the level of previous studies by the documents. Regardless of age, precondition, motivation and expectations, the reception system implemented by the host countries causes the loss of the background of knowledge and skills which, on the contrary, should be recognised and further supported. The chosen point of view looks at the migration phenomenon as a matter of high political value, it can be ascribed to the capacity of institutions to guarantee sustainability and inclusion, through processes that, first of all, enhance human resources brought by the migration phenomenon and, moreover, that include in the social system people of different cultures and languages. The level of inclusion of immigrants is certainly related especially to the politics and legislative acts that the legal system adopts to overcome cultural, ideological and religious differences. In this framework, it must be considered that the concept of integration does not correspond to that of homologation and that the government intervention will be all the more effective the more it will be able to ensure coexistence and compatibility between different cultures, through its different institutional structures, within the constitutional principle of pluralism and that of equality, and, at the same time, guaranteeing to the immigrants an adequate level of rights, especially the social ones. Looking at the Italian university system we will try to give an account of its most recent evolution in the indicated direction. To do this, we will consider the legal framework and we will examine how it leads to the necessity to expand the sphere of social rights to be recognised to the individuals, besides any status linked to citizenship. Lastly, by illustrating the main experiences emerging from the Italian context, we will examine the way the contribution of universities in favour of the inclusion of migrants, refugees and asylum seekers is expected to become increasingly important.

The exercise of the 'social' right to education in favour of migrants

Focusing on the right to education in favour of migrants, refugees and asylum seekers, it is necessary to firstly frame their relevance in terms of the effective exercise of the right to education, understood as a social right, well beyond the narrow core of educational services aimed at meeting the minimum requirements for access to education.

It's known that, on the general level of borders control (in the European migration policy and further), the instances of securitization prevail but, looking at the individual dimension of the phenomenon, we have to work on a common ground law that protect people over any sovereign policy[1]. So, we define the legal recognition of rights as belonging to the person and not to legal entities, and as such recipients of different levels of protection according to the various types of subjective status. In order to understand how different levels of protection have evolved, let's briefly examine the European legal culture. Starting from the last decade of the 20th century, the European legal culture has extended legal (human) rights to non-EU citizens. The international debate on the issue has flourished mainly due to the need to understand the changes related to globalization in parallel with the consequent new migratory flows, both outside Europe but also within Europe, following the collapse of the former Soviet regimes. As Sabino Cassese so aptly observed, "*with so many residents from other countries, states become places that host not only local citizens, but also residents, to whom many of the rights that are guaranteed to citizens must be recognized (practically all, except those of political nature (...) The result is a separation between rights and belonging to the original community, the nation; a devaluation of citizenship; the need to look at the rights of the foreigner through a different prism from that of citizenship, leading them not to national law, but to human rights recognized at the supra-state level*[2]".

To date, no common migration policy has been developed, or rather a community one with specific reference to the sphere of influence of the European Union political institutions. It is true that migration is at the center of the international political agenda as a phenomenon of massive and structural significance, certainly not contingent on emergency phases. It is also true that, despite huge EU interventions (obviously more financial than political), their management remains today a matter left to the more or less sovereign choices of individual states[3]. Moving from the collective to the individual dimension, the issue opens up to different interpretations. On the general level of border control and the governance of flows, the instances of security and legality seem to prevail. Therefore, from the perspective of individual rights, the numbers lose their meaning, and the primary interest of the person emerges. Starting from this primary interest, the ability to guide responsible solutions also includes the community. Within the European legal framework, Italy has created a constitutional charter unanimously considered to be at the forefront in terms of the recognition of rights, conferring them not only to citizens but to humans as such (Article 2). This intrinsic openness has led constitutional jurisprudence to copiously intervene by extending the rights and duties attributable to non-citizen foreigners. The various aspects of the Italian legal structure in include certain polities that are in favour of refugees as well as foreign minors[4]. We refer to the right of education already universally recognized on the basis of the Universal Declaration of Human Rights of 1948 which, in Art. 26 states: "Everyone has the right to education. Education must be free at least as regards elementary and fundamental classes. Elementary education must be compulsory. Technical and

---

[1] Benhabib Seyla, Another Cosmopolitanism, Oxford University Press, Oxford 2006; Étienne Balibar, We, the People of Europe: Reflections on Transnational Citizenship (Princeton & Oxford: Princeton University Press, 2004.

2 Cassese Sabino, Stato in Trasformazione, Estratto in Rivista Trimestrale di Diritto Pubblico Anno LXVI Fasc. 2 – 2016. Milano, Giuffrè Editore, 2016.

[3] Till the last main important Pact on migration and Asylum, see on the topic: IOM, Views on the Roadmap for the EU's New Pact on Migration and Asylum, August 2020, https://eea.iom.int/publications/iom-views-roadmap-eu-new-pact-migration-and-asylum.

4 For a further analysis, A. Germanà, E. Girasella, G. Moschella, Higher education as a lever to promote inclusion: the role of "frontier universities", in H. Gülerce, E. Girasella, M. Skoufi (edited by), Migration, social entrepreneurship and social inclusion, Editoriale Scientifica, Napoli, 2021, pp. 23 – 37.

vocational education must be made available to all, and higher education must be equally accessible to all on the basis of merit ". Specific reference to refugees came with the Geneva Convention of 1951 (and subsequent Additional Protocol of New York of 1967) which stated in Article 22: "1. The Contracting States will grant refugees, as regards primary education, the same treatment accorded to citizens; 2. The contracting states shall accord refugees the most favorable treatment possible and, in any case, no less favorable than that accorded in the same circumstances to foreigners in general". The scope is significant, for our purposes it is sufficient to recall what is stated in Section VII - Recognition of the qualifications of refugees, displaced persons and persons assimilated to refugees: "Each Party shall take all possible and reasonable measures within its own educational system, in compliance with constitutional, legal and administrative provisions, to develop appropriate procedures that make it possible to evaluate in a fair and effective way whether refugees, displaced persons and persons assimilated to refugees meet the conditions required for access to higher education, of complementary higher education programs or the exercise of a professional activity, and this even if the qualifications obtained in a Party cannot be proved by documents certifying them ". Five years after its promulgation, Italy ratified the Convention thus overcoming the traditional concept of equivalence in favour of the so-called "finalized" recognitions that universities manage in the academic field by virtue of their autonomy: "The competence for the recognition of cycles and of the periods of study carried out abroad and of foreign qualifications, for the purpose of accessing higher education, continuing university studies and obtaining Italian university degrees, is attributed to universities and university education institutions, who exercise it within their autonomy and in compliance with their respective legal systems, without prejudice to bilateral agreements on the subject ".

2. Beyond the recognition of the right to study: the exercise of the right to study by migrants

Migrants face a number of structural barriers and problems in gaining access to the educational and academic system. The recognition of diplomas, certifications and skills acquired abroad remains complicated. Schools, teachers and the education system in general are not well equipped to manage multi-ethnic pupils and classes, and struggle to deal with issues related to multiculturalism. Foreigners have very few options when it comes to accessing very high qualifications, specialized training courses or scholarships. In general, most young migrants or second-generation students find it difficult to access high schools that prepare their studies for a university course; on the contrary, they are often "confined" to technical and professional institutes. In this context, the integration potential of the educational education system for the young migrant population therefore remains limited.

This is what emerges in summary in one of the most recent analyses carried out by Italian Caritas[5] which also took into consideration the barriers to education and specialized training of migrants[6]. Statistics provided by the United Nations High Commissioner for Refugees (UNHCR) also give an unflattering picture[7]. According to the latest global report and the focus on "Strengthening the education of refugees in times of crisis" we see that, with reference to minors, only 63% of refugee children attend primary school (globally the percentage is of 91%) and that the adolescents enrolled in

---

[5] See the CARITAS 2019 Report, available in English, https://www.caritas.eu/wordpress/wp-content/uploads/2019/05/CommonHomeItalyEN.pdf and, only in Italian, the 2020 CARITAS report, https://www.caritas.it/caritasitaliana/allegati/9090/RICM_2020_Finale.pdf.

[6] From others point of view relating to the same conclusions, see: Colombo M., Scardigno A.F. (2019), La sfida dell'integrazione culturale per i rifugiati, i richiedenti asilo e i minori stranieri non accompagnati in La formazione dei rifugiati e dei minori stranieri non accompagnati. Una realtà necessaria, Quaderni CIRMiB Inside Migration 2-2019, VP-Vita e Pensiero, Milano, pp. 11-15.

[7] UNHCR, Doubling our impact third country higher education pathways for refugees, 2019 https://www.unhcr.org/5e5e4c614.pdf.

secondary school are 24% (84% globally). Of the 7.1 million minor refugees, substantially more than half do not go to school. With particular regard to refugee access to higher education at university, the percentage stands at 3%, a figure which, however, should not be disheartening if read looking at its constant growth compared to previous surveys. It is the international organization itself that reminds us of the ambitious goal of collaborating in order to guarantee, by 2030, university access to at least 15% of refugee students worldwide. What we have seen theoretically to be peaceful, in terms of recognition of the right to education and study, therefore does not seem to find concrete confirmation if we look at their effective exercise. My thesis is that, on this level, the cultural and practical preconditions must be created to favour their exercise.

3. The commitment of universities to enhance the knowledge and skills of migrants, refugees and asylum seekers

In general, the Italian university system allows enrolment to anyone who has completed at least twelve years of schooling. It is not necessary, for our purposes, to enter into the merits of the different regulations, even though they can be found in non-EU education systems, it will suffice here to emphasize the importance of being able to recognize and therefore enhance the training courses already carried out by migrants, before arriving in Italy. Out of any easy rhetoric, it is in fact obvious to imagine how many migrants of age have previous schooling of some kind, capable of being evaluated. The issue of recognition of qualifications is therefore the first step to be taken. In Italy, the Information Center on Mobility and Academic Equivalences (CIMEA) operates on a practical level in this sense. CIMEA was designated in 1984 by the then Ministry of Education as the official Italian center belonging to the NARIC network - National Academic Recognition Information Centers of the European Union and to the ENIC network - European National Information Centers of the Council of Europe and of the UNESCO. Following the ratification law of the aforementioned Lisbon Convention, CIMEA is thus identified by the same Dicastery, now MUR - Ministry of University and Research, as a national information center on the procedures for the recognition of qualifications in force in Italy, in the Italian higher education system and qualifications evaluated on the national level. CIMEA provides applicants with its own technical-administrative opinion regarding the requests for recognition of qualifications, this is a free service if the applicants have already been recognized as refugees. Universities can thus rely on the information deriving from the so-called "Certificate of comparability" issued by CIMEA following an investigation that is based on all the documentary evidence that the applicant is able to provide and, if insufficient, on the verification of the declarations made to support the lack of documentation. CIMEA has also recently introduced the innovative blockchain technology, through which the "diplome" service, a portfolio for each holder of qualifications can be developed, where potential students can upload their qualifications, even non-academic qualifications, to be verified of the authenticity of the study qualification of the young migrant who also becomes the owner of their own declarations, thus reducing in some way the risk of false or inauthentic productions of titles. In addition to this important assessment tool, CIMEA has finally promoted the dissemination of the Qualifications Passport for Refugees, an assessment procedure that academics can use in the event of absence or poor documentation of the qualifications of young refugees. Recently, the UNHCR wanted to promote a system initiative to network the Italian universities most committed to the front in question by launching the "Manifesto of inclusive universities" to which fifth-one universities adhere to date[8]. All this network works to guarantee some necessary preconditions, after the enrolment, in order to make successfully the academic path of such

---

[8] See the website of the UNHCR Italy initiative, https://www.unhcr.org/it/le-universita-aderenti-al-manifesto-delluniversita-inclusiva/. For a deep analysis about the public engagement commitment of universities, see Davies Sarah R., Research staff and public engagement: a UK study. Springer, 2013.

fragile target of students and this means, above all, enhancing the commitment designing flexible rules, because every case is a single case.

Balibar Étienne, We, the People of Europe: Reflections on Transnational Citizenship (Princeton & Oxford: Princeton University Press, 2004.

Benhabib Seyla, Another Cosmopolitanism, Oxford University Press, Oxford 2006.

CARITAS, Report 2019, Europe 2020: Where are we now and What way forward? 5 years after committing to poverty reduction & employment growth; Report 2020, XXIX Rapporto Immigrazione, https://www.caritas.it/caritasitaliana/allegati/9090/RICM_2020_Finale.pdf.

Cassese Sabino, Stato in Trasformazione, Estratto in Rivista Trimestrale di Diritto Pubblico Anno LXVI Fasc. 2 – 2016. Milano, Giuffrè Editore (2016).

Colombo M., Scardigno A.F. (2019), La sfida dell'integrazione culturale per i rifugiati, i richiedenti asilo e i minori stranieri non accompagnati in La formazione dei rifugiati e dei minori stranieri non accompagnati. Una realtà necessaria, Quaderni CIRMiB Inside Migration 2-2019, VP-Vita e Pensiero, Milano, pp. 11-15.

Davies Sarah R., Research staff and public engagement: a UK study. Springer, 2013.

Germanà Antonino, Girasella Elena, Moschella Giovanni, Higher education as a lever to promote inclusion: the role of "frontier universities", in H. Gülerce, E. Girasella, M. Skoufi (edited by), Migration, social entrepreneurship and social inclusion, Editoriale Scientifica, Napoli, 2021, pp. 23 – 37.

IOM, Views on the Roadmap for the EU's New Pact on Migration and Asylum, August 2020, https://eea.iom.int/publications/iom-views-roadmap-eu-new-pact-migration-and-asylum.

UNHCR, Doubling our impact third country higher education pathways for refugees, 2019 https://www.unhcr.org/5e5e4c614.pdf.

LA PROTECTION JURIDIQUE INTERNATIONALE DES MIGRANTS (PJIM)

Ali El Mhamdi

Introduction

Le migrant désigne une personne qui quitte son pays d'origine pour s'installer de manière temporaire ou permanente dans un pays dont elle n'a pas la nationalité.

L'accomplissement de tout projet migratoire s'accompagne souvent de défis multiples aux premier rang desquels la violations des droits humains. La précarité des personnes qui en sont les victimes a rendu nécessaire une protection juridique internationale(PJIM).

L'ONU s'y est attelée en adoptant progressivement un dispositif organisationnel universel protecteur dont la mise en place a été favorisée par l'évolution de la doctrine juridique qui reconnait à partir de 1945 l'individu come sujet de droit international en lui accordant des droits subjectifs fondamentaux connus sous le concept des droits humains. Ce sont des droits inaliénables auxquels peuvent légitimement prétendre de tous les êtres humains, sans distinction de race, de sexe, de nationalité, d'origine ethnique, de langue, de religion ou de toute autre situation. Tous les États sont tenus de les respecter, les protéger et les garantir. La PJIM obéit à une double exigence difficile à conci

La PJIM obéit à une double exigence difficile à concilier : la souveraineté des Etats et la garantie du respect des droits humains fondamentaux sachant que les impératifs de la première limitent forcément la portée de la seconde .C'est ce dont on peut se persuader dans les développements qui suivent articulés en trois parties : le cadre juridique, la mise en œuvre et ses limites

I: Le cadre juridique de la PJIM

A: Repères historiques

La PJIM procède de l'idée des droits de l'homme, née de la philosophie de lumières qui s'est imposée progressivement aux XVII et XVIII siècle dans le droit constitutionnel national à travers les étapes suivantes

- ✓ Petition of Rights de 1628, Habeas Corpus de 1679 en Angleterre.

- ✓ Bill of Rights de la Virginie de 1776.

- ✓ Déclaration des Droits de l'Homme et du Citoyen de 1789 en France.

- ✓ Promotion du standard minimum international à partir des années 1920 aux termes duquel tout être humain est doté de droits fondamentaux lui garantissant le respect de sa dignité.

- ✓ L'adoption de la charte de l'ONU en 1945 marque la naissance de l'individu comme sujet de droit international avec trois conséquences majeures à savoir :

L'adoption de la charte de l'ONU en 1945 marque la naissance de l'individu comme sujet de droit international avec trois conséquences majeures à savoir :

* l'Etat ne pouvait plus traiter ses ressortissants à son gré sans intervention de la société internationale .L'exercice de la souveraineté de l'Etat sur son territoire est désormais limité par l'obligation du respect des droits humains

* Fin de l'impunité garantie par la justice pénale internationale pour les criminels abstraction faite de leurs statuts, qui violent le droits humain.

* Mise en place du statut de Rome de 1998 créant la CPI.

B: L'encadrement juridique universel

1- Les sources universelles.

✓ Déclaration universelle des droits de l'homme.

✓ Pacte international relatif aux droits civils et politiques.

✓ Pacte international relatif aux droits économiques, sociaux et culturels.

✓ Convention sur l'élimination de toutes les formes de discrimination raciale.

✓ Convention sur les droits des enfants.

✓ Convention sur la discrimination à l'égard des femmes.

✓ Convention de 1951 relative au statut des réfugiés.

✓ Convention de l'ONU sur la protection des droits de travailleurs migrants et les membres de la famille de 1990.

2- Les sources régionales

✓ Convention européenne des droits de l'homme et des libertés fondamentales adoptée par le Conseil de l'Europe

✓ Convention américaine des droits de l'homme et le système interaméricain adoptée le 22 novembre 1969.

✓ Charte africaine des droits de l'homme et des peuples.

3-Droit pénal international en rapport avec la migrations:

Les deux « Protocoles de Palerme » se rapportant à la Convention de

l'ONU contre la criminalité transnationale organisée, adoptés en 2000.

4-Le droit international du travail

✓ Conventions, recommandations et normes élaborées par l'OIT.

✓ Convention n° 97 sur le travailleurs migrants de 1949 modifiéeset complété à plusieurs reprises.

✓ Déclaration de l'OIT relative aux principes et droits fondamentaux au travail de 1988. Déclaration de l'OIT relative à une justice sociale pour une mondialisation équitable de 2008.

5-Le droit des réfugiés

La protection des réfugiés et des personnes déportées est assurée essentiellement par la convention de Genève de 1951 relative au statut des réfugiés telle qu'ella a été complétée par le protocole du 4 Octobre 1967.

2: Les protections spécifiques

♦ Le droit à la nationalité

L'article 15 de la Déclaration universelle des droits de l'homme dispose que.

Tout individu a droit à une nationalité. Nul ne peut être arbitrairement privé de sa nationalité, ni du droit de changer de nationalité. »

Plusieurs textes de droit international consacrent le droit Tout enfant à un nom à l'enregistrement de sa naissance et d'acquérir dès sa naissance la nationalité de l'Etat sur le territoire duquel il est né.

♦ La question de l'apatridie

L'apatride est une personne dépourvue de nationalité, qui ne bénéficie de la protection d'aucun État. Plusieurs textes internationaux tentent de supprimer les cas d'apatridie et Le HCR a pour fonction statutaire de fournir une protection internationale aux apatrides.

♦ La protection des femmes

Les femmes sont victimes de violence dans la plupart pays du monde en raison de leur sexe. Le droit international a prévu des textes généraux et spécifiques pour en assurer la protection.

- ✓ Les textes généraux relatifs à la protection des femmes.
- ✓ Charte de l'ONU.
- ✓ Déclaration universelle des droits de l'homme.
- ✓ Pacte relatif aux droits civils et politiques.
- ✓ Pacte relatif aux droits économiques sociaux et culturel

Les textes spécifiques relatifs à la protection des femmes:

- ✓ Convention sur l'élimination des discrimination à l'égard des femmes.
- ✓ Déclaration et le programme d'action de Vienne en 1993
- ✓ Déclaration de Pékin et Pékin plus 5 en 1995 et 2000,
- ✓ Statut d la CPI qui prévoit entre autre le « crime lié au genre »

D- La protection des enfants

L'intérêt de la protection de l'enfant est apparu dans États occidentaux à partir du XIXe siècle, dans le contexte des grandes lois sociales. La protection s'est faite en plusieurs étapes à savoir : Les dispositions imitant le travail des enfants ; L'instruction publique obligatoire ; La Déclaration de Genève de 1924 et la Convention Internationale des droits de l'enfant1989 (CIDE) L'article 3 §1 de la CIDE énonce pour la première fois la locution « intérêt supérieur de l'enfant »,

II: Les modalités de mise œuvre

A: Les institutions dédiés à la PJIM

1: Le Haut commissariat aux droits de l'homme (HCDH)

- ✓ Le HCDH est une agences spécialisée de l'ONU. Ses missions essentielles sont :
- ✓ Coordonner les activités des droits de l'homme des organes de l'ONU
- ✓ Intégrer les droits de l'homme dans les activités onusiennes
- ✓ Promouvoir, contrôler et de renseigner sur le respect des droits de l'homme et du droit international humanitaire dans le monde,

2: Le conseil des droits de l'homme

Le Conseil est un organe subsidiaire de l'Assemblée générale de l'ONU Il siége et à Genève. Il prend en 2006 la suite de la commission des droits de l'homme, créée en 1946 pour élaborer les textes de protection des les droits de l'homme qui constituent l' un des trois piliers de l'ONU avec la paix et la sécurité ainsi que le développement.

3: La Commission de la condition de la femme

La commission est un organe intergouvernemental créée en 1946 pour préparer des rapports et recommandations au Conseil économique et social sur les droits de la femme. Composée de 45 experts élus par les Etats membres du Conseil économique et social, se réunit une fois par an.

La Déclaration et le Programme d'action de Beijing de 1995 constituent une initiative visionnaire jamais établie en faveur de l'autonomisation des femmes

Pour marquer le 25e anniversaire du Programme d'action de Beijing, ONU Femmes lance une nouvelle campagne intitulée « Génération Égalité : Pour les droits des femmes et un futur égalitaire ».

4: ONU- Femmes

C'est l'entité onusienne consacrée à l'égalité des sexes et à l'autonomisation des femmes. Porte-drapeau mondial des femmes et des filles, l'organisation a été créée pour accélérer les progrès dans la réponse apportée à leurs besoins spécifiques partout dans le monde.

B. Les mécanismes de suivi et de contrôle

1-L'action des mécanisme conventionnels

- ✓ Comité des droits de l'homme.
- ✓ Comité contre la torture.
- ✓ Comité des droits économiques et sociaux.
- ✓ Comité des droits de l'enfant.
- ✓ Comité contre la discrimination raciale.

Les comités exercent trois types d'activités

- ✓ Examen des rapports périodiques.

- ✓ Examen des communications.

- ✓ Production de directives ou d'observations générales.

2. La justice internationale

La CIJ est compétente pour traiter de « tout point de droit international », La CPI Créée en 2002, et avant son entrée en vigueur les tribunaux pénaux ad hoc.

C: La condition juridique des migrants en situation régulière

Les règles de droit qui encadrent aux plans national et international la protection des migrants sont réductibles à sept catégories:

- ✓ Droit interne du pays d'origine.

- ✓ Droit interne du pays d'accueil.

- ✓ Accords bilatéraux en matière de protection mutuels des investissements.

- ✓ Accords bilatéraux pour éviter la double imposition.

- ✓ Accords bilatéraux en matière d'emploi, de sécurité sociale.

- ✓ A accords de coopération judiciaire.

- ✓ Conventions internationales relatives aux droits humains.

1: Les droits fondamentaux dans les pays de résidence

- ✓ Egalité de traitement entre les migrants et les nationaux dans les conditions de travail notamment sur les plans de recrutement, salaire, accidents de travail et droits syndicaux.

- ✓ Octroi aux migrants et aux membres de leurs familles résidant du régime de sécurité sociale

2: La protection diplomatique et consulaire

La protection diplomatique est une procédure par laquelle un Etat intervient au bénéfice d'un de ses ressortissants en vue de la réparation d'un préjudice causé un par des mesures contraires au droit international.

La protection consulaire permet à un Etat de défendre les droits et intérêts de ses ressortissants. L'État d'origine agit pour le compte de ses ressortissants. Il les aide à défendre leurs droits dans le respect de l'ordre juridique de l'État de résidence.

3- Les migrants en situation irrégulière et la question de la réadmission

Le droit international coutumier impose à tout pays de réadmettre ses ressortissants en situation irrégulière . Les mesures d'éloignement doivent respecter les conditions suivantes:

- ✓ Identification des personnes à réadmettre.

- ✓ Respect des droits des migrants et des voies de recours.

- ✓ Décision de justice définitive et exécutoire.

✓ Rapatriement par vol régulier et notification à l'avance aux autorités. du pays d'origine des dates de retour des intéressés.

III: Les limites de la PJIM

A: Les prérogatives de l'Etat liées à la souveraineté

Tous les Etats disposent du droit souverain de contrôler leurs frontières, de définir librement les modalités de gestion des flux migratoires et des conditions d'entré, de sortie et de séjour des étrangers

B: les impératifs de l'ordre public et de la sécurité nationale

Les migrants sont tenus de se conformer à la législation et aux impératifs de l'ordre public de l' État d'accueil.

C: Les Lacunes du droit d'asile

✓ L'octroi du statut de réfugié procède d'une décision discrétionnaire.

✓ L'obligation de non-refoulement, faite aux Etats n'implique pas l'octroi d'un permis de résidence aux demandeurs de droit d'asile

✓ La Convention ne prévoit pas de procédure uniformisée pour l'octroi du statut de réfugié,

Conclusion

La déclaration universelle des droits de l'Homme a brisé le lien entre citoyenneté et nationalité en interdisant formellement aux États de discriminer les personnes en fonction de leur nationalité.

L'ampleur du phénomène migratoire, les impératifs de la souveraineté, alliés aux contraintes de l'ordre public national, ont fait émerger dans les Etats d'accueil l'idée la prévalence du concept de la nationalité sur celui de la citoyenneté.

Aussi longtemps que les critères d'admission et d'expulsion des étrangers relèvent de la souveraineté exclusive des États, le rêve d'une communauté internationale garante de la protection effective des droits humains des migrants demeure inachevé. Il se heurte à la difficile - et parfois tragique - réalité que vivent aujourd'hui les migrants à travers le monde.

VISUAL REPRESENTATIONS OF THE REFUGEE EXPERIENCE FROM THOSE EXPERIENCING IT. A CASE STUDY OF REFUGEES FROM SYRIA INTO GREECE

Anastasia Chalkia, Joanna Tsiganou, and Martha Lembesi

Introduction

The usual tools we, the sociologists, use in our study of the social experience are based on transcribing textualised information to meaningful knowledge. However, within the mounting vein of visual sociology new means have been added,[1] which when used solely or additionally, might help us to comprehend more fully narratives of life experiences.[2] Our paper focuses on the travelling and host experiences into Greece of refugees from Syria. It is based on a qualitative research conducted in 2019-2020 with Syrian refugees incomers to Greece. It is in the scope of our paper to address the framing of the refugee experience not only in terms of the discourse resulting out from the face-to-face interviews with our research population but mainly in terms of the visual representations of the refugee experience as exhibited in their own photographs.

Thus, our conclusions are based on two distinct types of mediation. The mediation of an interpreter and the mediation of a visual instrument. Being haunted by Ferrell's question on why "we never, never talk about photography",[3] and despite the "deep mistrust" of images[4] in disciplines like sociology, where the uses of visual material have long been marginalized, we have decided to include photographs generously offered to us by our respondents picturing their social worlds. The intention was to capture those aspects of the refugee lived and living experiences that words could not. The original impetus behind the inclusion of these images was to illustrate stories and not solely as a means of documenting social processes. So we have used photographs as both illustration and evidence. As we all know visual representations have always had an evidentiary role. Thus we use the visual fragments as a complementary theoretically and methodologically informed understanding, as one that seeks not simply to supplement but also to expand our conceptual tools to a direction attuned to the fraught relations between words and images. After all, Georg Simmel has long ago claimed that of our five senses, the 'eye has a uniquely sociological function'.[5]

Framing the respondents meanings on their travelling experience, their reception and integration into Greece, certain broad analytical and interpretative categories were formulated based on respondents' narrations.

---

[1] Indicatively, Harper, D. (2012). *Visual sociology*. London: Routledge.

[2] Brown M. & Carrabine E., eds. (2017). *Routledge International Handbook of Visual Criminology*. London: Routledge.

[3] Ferrel J. (*2017*). "We never, never talked about photography? Documentary photography, visual criminology, and method", in Michelle Brown & Eamonn Carrabine, eds, 2017, Routledge International Handbook of Visual Criminology. London: Routledge, pg. *40-52*.

[4] As in Holliday, R. (2000). "We've been framed: Visualising methodology". *Sociological Review*, 48(4): 503–521.

[5] Simmel, G. (1908/1921). "Sociology of the senses: Visual interaction". In Park, R.E. & Burgess, E.W. (Eds.) *Introduction to the science of sociology*. Chicago, IL: University of Chicago Press. pp. 356–361.

The decision to depart

The widespread violence of war in Syria and the activities of ISIS lie underneath decisions for migration. The main driving force is to put as much distance as possible (in terms of time and space) from "what" is happening in our respondents' homeland. Narratives are describing a "doom's day" scenery with experiences of disasters, deaths and a constant as well as a permanent threat to life. Visual representations of Syrian refugees' "exodus" from Syria energize further social imagery adding more material fruitful to comprehend their decision to depart.

"You can see the destruction of my home, of shops and of the neighborhood"

"Since I quit university studies I had to work for my living as a taxi driver and a bomb hit my car"

Our respondents as no longer "owners of soil" have chosen to refer to images of destruction in order to illustrate more vividly their shattered lives and the conditions of immense social deprivation of basic goods as shelter, food, electricity and water supply, but also access to means to get a decent living and education. All consequences of war. All driving forces for departure. Life plans have been abandoned in front of the terror of living under war. The decision to depart is also owed to an irrevocable overturn of life plans and the chattering of life prospects. Yet, the "exodus" for our respondents is dictated by the agony and anxiety to protect their children, to keep them safe and secure, by all means available, their life chances and prospects of life. Thus certain attempts are made to ameliorate trauma through the comforting embrace of the Greek hospitality. Certain attempts are also made not only to advance their educational credentials as a means of mobility within the host social formations but also as a more accessible and promising way to their children social integration to host societies.

"The first time the kids near the see!..."

Keeping kids safe, happy and secure"

Developing a "sense of belonging" through entertainment practices dominant in the host country.

Family reunion and family union

In some cases, relocation occurs within Syria, in other cases abroad, in order 'to reunite the family' in times or conditions of uncertainty, a family with strong ties and social bonds within the Syrian sociocultural milieu. So, family's reunion is projected as a place of salvation and strength to overcome difficulties in juxtaposition to fragmentation, impotency and loss. It is a source of empowerment and warmth. It also represents continuity and hope. Additionally the relevant visual representations involve not only family in reunion but also family in union.

"I hold on to the memory when I met my children after four years apart! I met one of my sons a month after I had arrived on an island in Greece. My other son came here to Athens. We took photos and videos to look at".

Although Greece represents a country for "transit", a country for a temporal and intermediate stop to the minds of our respondents, they are faced with a mechanism of a prolonged and rather permanent state of reception. Being at such a 'limbo' state intensifies our respondents' anxiety and complicates the process of their integration both in our country as well as in the countries of their final destination. Despite the fact the Greece in the imaginary of our respondents represents a familiar (due to the climate conditions) and easily accessible place (due to the geographical proximity to their country of origin) it also represents a place of convenience for entering Europe. However, our respondents lived experiences indicate their entrance to a dystopia of unfulfilled expectations. Their narrations are indicative of marginality intensified by exclusion from work, difficulty in communication due to language barriers, isolation from social life and endosmosis with the natives due to prejudice and discrimination maximized with each new wave of refugee incomers. To these our respondents cope mainly by building ethnic enclaves.

A celebration day with a respondents' male cousins in a central park of Athens.

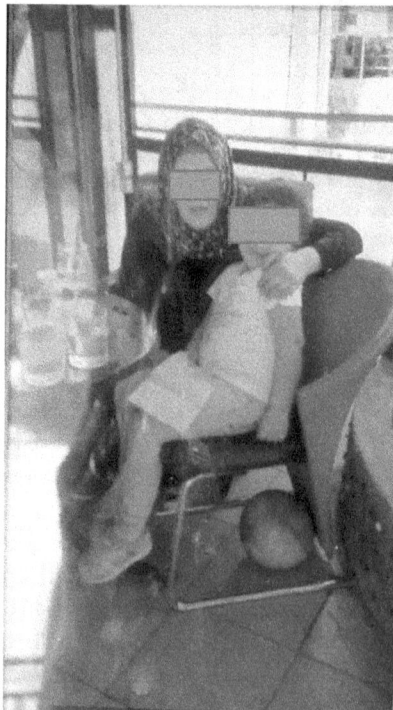

Happy moments shared by grandma and grandchield as life goes on …

A journey of no return and no returns

The migratory experience of Syrian refugees is a journey of 'no return'. A collective trauma is identified based on the pain of an irrevocable uprooting and a strong sense of nostalgia for people and places that were lost forever, also for those who are 'left behind'. This is more reflected in the faces and speech of the women respondents. Men in their social imaginary continue to be the breadwinners who must 'stand up to the circumstances'. On the other hand women feel free to expressing their pain, being conceptualized through their traditional domestic and reproductive roles within the family domain. Thus the refugee experience has no returns for the deeply rooted perceptions of gender relations under the long established patriarchal structure prevalent in the country of origin. The refugee experience has no returns also in terms of reception to the country of immediate destination (namely Greece). Visual representations elaborate on this further by recruiting the male "body" to indicate not only strength but also as the unique remaining asset. With all material assets lost, the male body serves not only as a unique remaining resource for exploitation but also as a reminder of national, social, cultural and religious identity. At the same time the "body" becomes the sole bearer of hope.

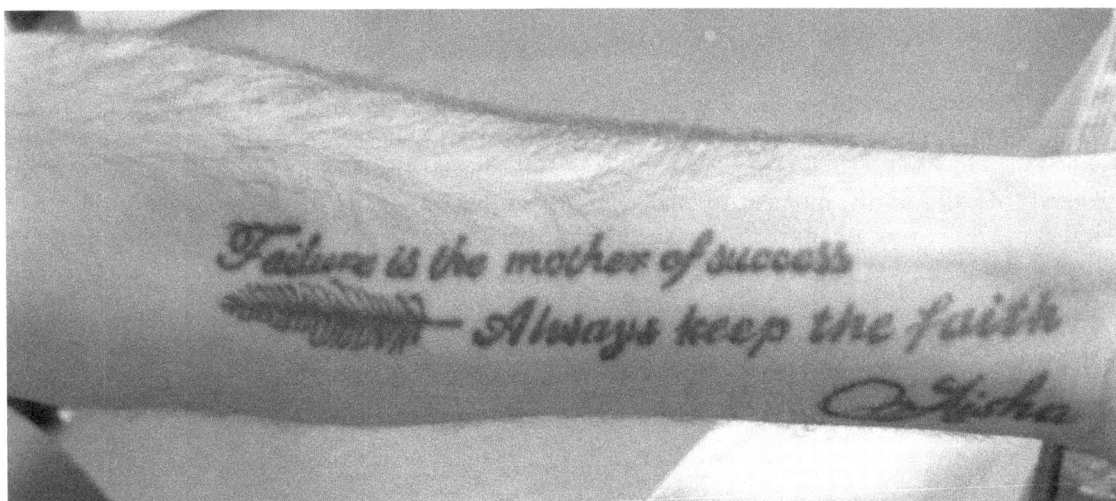

"Failure is the mother of success. Always keep the faith"

However, the refugee experience helps to unearth not only the enforcement of the patriarchal patterns of domination or religious oppression but also their questioning and dispute. Visual representations elaborate on this further by recruiting the female "body" not only as a carrier of trauma and suffering but also as a carrier of women's' emancipation and claims to self – determination according to the morals, mores and norms of conduct met at the host country. The presentation of self in Goffman's terms[6] becomes important the same way as it has been important to the natives as well as in the rest of the world.

---

[6] Goffman E., (1959). *The Presentation of Self in Everyday Life*, Anchor Publications, USA.

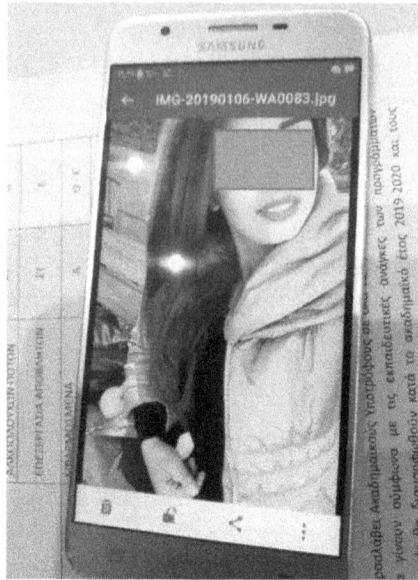

"This is the perfect day of my life. The first day here in Athens. .. I took off my burka. I came in the morning with it and in the evening I had abandoned it. In my country I had to wear a burka and the color should be black. Can you imagine a woman not being able to take off the burka in front of her brother! I decided at that moment to take it off and at that moment I decided to walk in the street without it... I felt very ashamed ... But when I came back home, I was already being feeling better".

"When I first got money, I went to a hairdresser and did my hair. I changed the color. I took off the burka but I am not allowed to go out with a short sleeve... In time... who knows... But I feel like I can't put on shorts...In Syria I wore all black even gloves (Burga). I thought I was invisible! As a prisoner I walked with my prison".

Conclusions

Our paper is a study on methods rather than substance. Our aim was to show the contribution of visual representations to the broadening of our understandings of the Syrian refugee experience. In fact, visual representations helped us to comprehend more fully the cultural determinants of Syrian refugees living experience and built upon their verbal narrations. Thus we were enabled to conclude that inferences on cultural diversification between "us" and "them" might not hold the strong face validity attributed to them. We became more knowledgeable of the various routes of refugees "escaping" in order to cope with the refugee trauma. Either by resorting to retreat, to fatalism, to resignation or by holding on their own country's religious beliefs and social norms or by resorting to emancipatory and empowerment mechanisms in order to adapt and/or to belong to their host socio-cultural environments. All these traits are common and shared in other cases of dealing with collective tragedies and are not met at the migratory collective experience alone.

İSLAM KÜLTÜR TARİHİNDE GÖÇÜN ETKİSİ: İLK DÖNEM KUR'AN YORUM ÇALIŞMALARI BAĞLAMINDA BİR İNCELEME

Ömer Dinç*

Giriş

İslam dininin ilk dönemlerden itibaren geniş coğrafyalara yayılmasının temel etkenleri arasında göç unsurunun bulunduğunu söylememiz gerekir. Hz. Peygamber'in Mekke'den Medine'ye, ilk Müslümanların Habeşistan'a gerçekleştirdikleri yolcukları dikkate aldığımızda, İslam'ın daha etkili ve hızlı bir şekilde yayılmasına göçün tesir ettiğini tarihsel bir gerçeklik olarak ifade edilebiliriz. Bunun yanında Hz. Peygamber dönemi sonrasında, Müslümanların çeşitli şehir ve bölgelere göç etmek suretiyle, genelde İslam dinini insanlara tebliğ etmeleri, özelde ise dinî kültürün oluşması bakımından Kur'an'ı açıklama ve izah faaliyetlerini icra ettikleri görülür. Bu faaliyetlerin İslam'ın Arap yarımadası dışındaki pek çok coğrafyada kabul edilmesine olanak sağladığı gibi, aynı zamanda Müslümanların kültürel yapılanmalarının giderek yaygınlık kazanmasına önayak olduğunu söyleyebiliriz. Özellikle Kur'an'ın yorumlanması sürecinde önde gelen pek çok sahabînin, değişik yerlere gitmek suretiyle kendi çizgileri ekseninde birer tefsir ekolü oluşturduklarını görmekteyiz. Ayrıca bu bölgelerdeki Müslümanların, Kur'an'ın açıklanması ve yorumlanmasına ilişkin kendilerine gelen sahabîlerden aldıkları bilgileri, başka coğrafyalara gitmek suretiyle aktardıkları ve bu durumun Kur'an'ın açıklanması faaliyetleri bağlamında bir gelenek haline geldiğini belirtmeliyiz.

Bu çalışmada, Hz. Peygamber sonrası dönemde pek çok sahabînin Kur'an'ı diğer bölgelerdeki insanlara öğretme ve açıklamak için hangi bölgelere göç ettikleri hususu üzerinde durulacaktır. Bu hususu iki aşama ve iki isim üzerinden incelemeyi planlamaktayız. Bu çerçevede tefsir faaliyetlerinin başlangıç evresindeki isimlerden İbn Mesud'u, tefsirin ilmî bir disiplin olduğu evrede ön plana çıkan Yahya b. Sellâm'ı örnek olarak ele alacağız. Bunun akabinde söz konusu bölgelerde gerçekleştirdikleri çalışmaların, İslam'ın gelişmesi ve ilerlemesi bağlamında nasıl bir etkide bulunduğu meselesi incelenecektir. Ayrıca Arap yarımadası dışındaki coğrafyalara göç eden bu sahabîlerin, kendi kurdukları okullarda yetiştirdiği pek çok şahsın, sonraki dönemlerde başka bölgelere giderek öğrendiklerini diğer insanlara ulaştırmaları ve bu durumun etkileri meselesi de ele alınacaktır.

Tefsir Faaliyetinin Sahabe Dönemi ve İbn Mesud

Mekke'den Irak bölgesine giden önemli sahabîlerden Abdullah b. Mesud'un, hem o bölgenin Müslümanlaşma sürecini yönetmesi hem de Hz. Peygamber'den öğrendiği Kur'an'ı insanlara açıklaması ve yorumlaması neticesinde bir okul tesis etmesi, göç faktörünün İslam'ın entelektüel yönünün gelişimine katkıda bulunması açısından değerlendirmek mümkündür (Kesler, 2005, s. 36).

İslam'ı ilk kabul edenler arasında bulunan İbn Mesud, müslüman olduğu zaman 15-16 yaşlarındaydı. Annesine nisbetle İbn Ümmi Abd diye de anılan İbn Mesud'un ailesi hakkında fazla bir bilgiye sahip değiliz (Küçükkalay, 1971, s. 6). Çocukluk ve gençlik fakirlik içerisinde geçen İbn Mesud'un asıl hayatı İslam'la birlikte başlamıştır (Cerrahoğlu, 1996, s. 84). Müslüman olduktan sona daima Hz. Peygamber'in

* Hitit Üniversitesi İlahiyat Fakültesi, Tefsir Anabilim Dalı, omer_dinc25@hotmail.com

yanında bulunan ve ona destek olan İbn Mesud,(Çalışkan, 2020, s. 41) Kur'an'ı Mekke'de aşikâr okuyan ilk sahabî olması açısından dikkat çekmektedir. Ayrıca cennetle müjdelenmiş on sahabiden birisi olarak zikredilmektedir. Habeşistan'a hicret eden ilk müslümanlar arasında yer alan İbn Mesud, aynı zamanda Medine'ye de ilk göç edenler arasında bulunmaktaydı (İbn Sa'd, 2001, s. 2:295; Zehebî, 2000, s. 63).

İbn Mesud'un aslında göç hikayesinin genelde dinin özelde ise Kur'an'ın öğretilmesiyle bağlantılı olduğu hicretin ilk yıllarında ortaya çıkmaktadır. Zira İbn Mesud, Kur'an ve tefsirle meşguliyetini Müslüman olduğu dönemden itibaren başlatmış, hem onun öğrenilmesi hem de öğretilmesi konusunda ciddi bir seviyeye ulaşmıştır. Öyle ki Hz. Peygamber'in övgüsüne mazhar olacak şekilde Kur'an'ı en iyi okuyanlar arasında olup vahiy katipliği yapmış önemli sahabilerden sayılmaktadır. Mekke ve Medine döneminde Kur'an eğitiminde vazife alan İbn Mesud, bu görevini ömrünün sonuna kadar devam ettirmiştir. Hz. Peygamber'in vefatından sonra dahi bu vazifeyi devam ettiren İbn Mesud, son göç yeri olan ve kendisinden sonra tefsir ekolünün oluşumuna öncülük ettiği Kufe'de dini meselelerin çözümünde müracaat edilen isim olmuştur (Dâvûdî, 2008, s. 220; Küçükkalay, 1971, s. 24). Bu görevlendirilmesi onun resmî bir statüde olmasının da ötesinde bunu dinî bir sorumluluk gereği olarak yerine getirmiş ve Kufe bölgesinin İslam'I her yönüyle öğrendiği yegane kaynak olmuştur.

Ömrünün son kısmını göç ettiği bölge olan Kufe'de geçiren İbn Mesud, yaşadığı zaman diliminde birçok alanda, özellikle tefsir, fıkıh, hadis ve kıraat sahasında pek çok öğrenci yetiştirmiştir. Yetiştirdiği bu öğrenciler onun izini takip ederek genelde İslamî ilimlerde özellikle tefsirde "Kufe Ekolü" denilen bir tefsir okulunun inşasına zemin hazırlamıştır (Kesler, 2005, s. 34).

İbn Mesud'un Kufe'de özellikle Kur'an'ın anlaşılması ve yorumlanması bağlamında tefsir tarihinin önemli bir dönüm noktasında olduğunu ifade etmeliyiz. Bu durumun en somut delili ise kendisinin Kur'an'ın tefsiri konusunda ulaştığı noktadır. Ondan nakledilen bir rivayete göre İbn Mesud, Allah'ın kitabının nerede, ne zaman, hangi şartlar altında nâzil olduğunu bildiğini, kendisinden bu hususta daha bilgili olan varsa ona her şekilde ulaşabileceğini beyan etmiştir (et-Taberî, 2001, s. 1:75) Onun Kufe bölgesinin dinî anlayışını şekillendirmesi ve kendisinden sonra geleceklere kaynaklık etmesi dikkat çekmektedir. Bunun en önemli sebeplerinden birisi, Kufe bölgesinde yeni Müslüman olanların dini anlama ve yorumlama çabalarının sorgulayıcı ve aklı esas alan bir yaklaşımı benimsemelerinden ileri gelmektedir (Çalışkan, 2020, s. 42; Küçükkalay, 1971, ss. 62-64). İşte İbn Mesud da kendi yurdunu bırakarak dini insanlara öğretme ve ulaştırma maksadıyla geldiği Kufe bölgesinin bu anlayışını dikkate almıştır. Çünkü İbn Mesud, nassları zahiri üzerine anlamayı değil, hikmet ve maksat anlayışı üzerinden değerlendirmeyi esas almıştır (Gengil, 2021).

İbn Mes'ud'un hem dinî metinleri anlama yaklaşımı hem de Kufe toplumunun yapısını dikkate alması, ilerleyen aşamada İslam düşünce tarihinin en önemli temsilcileri arasında olan Hanefi mezhebinin kaynağını teşkil etmiştir (Ebu Zehra, 1999, ss. 37-39). Nitekim Hanefî mezhebi, İbn Mesudun öğrencileri olan, Mesruk b. el-Ecda, Alkame b. Kays gibi isimlerden aktarılan birikim ve dinî anlayış neticesinde gelişim göstermiş, asıl kimliğini Ebû Hanife ile kazanmıştır (Gengil, 2021). Dinin anlaşılması, Kur'an'ın yorumlanması hususu İbn Mesud'un Kufe'de temellerini attığı bir anlayışı üzerinden yüzyıllar boyu sürmüştür.Hatta İbn Mesud'un bu etkisi, tefsir geleneğinin Hanefî mezhebi damarını en açık bir şekilde temsil eden Mâtürîdî'de belirgin olarak görülmektedir. Ona göre sahabeden bir görüş tercih edilecekse öncelik İbn Mesud'a aittir demiştir (el-Mâturîdî, 2005, s. 15:236).

Tefsirin İlmî Disiplin Evresi ve Yahyâ b. Sellâm

Kendi yurdundan göç etmiş ve Kur'an'ın anlaşılması ve açıklanması faaliyetini başka coğrafyalara taşıyan en önemli müfessirlerden birisi de Yahyâ b. Sellâm'dır. Tefsir çalışmalarının ilmî bir disiplin haline geldiği evrenin temsilcisi olan Yahyâ b. Sellâm, göç ettiği bölgelerde tefsir tarihinin akışını ve durumunu değiştirmiş önemli isimlerden sayılmaktadır. Kufe'de doğmuş ancak küçük yaşlardan itibaren ailesiyle birlikte bulunduğu şehirden göç etmeye mecbur kalmıştır. İlk göçü Basra'ya olan Yahya b. Sellâm tefsir, hadis ve dil ilimleri tedrisini çok güçlü bir şekilde tamamladı (Dâvûdî, 2008, s. 305). Yaşadığı dönemde bir ilim adamının çeşitli coğrafyalara yaptığı seyahatler, onun ilmî gelişimi için kritik öneme sahipti. Yahyâ b. Sellâm'da bu düreçte birçok merkeze seyahatlerde bulunduğu gibi doğup büyüdüğü coğrafyaya geri dönmemiştir. Zira Kur'an'a dair topladığı tefsir malumatını çeşitli şehirlerde insanlara aktarmış ve gittiği her yerde alannda saygın birisi olarak karşılanmıştır. Hayatının yaklaşık son yirmi yılını geçireceği ve kendi memleketinden ayrılarak göç ettiği Kuzey Afrika'ya doğru yola çıkmıştır (Cerrahoğlu, 1970, ss. 7-19). Mısır'da kaldığı geçici sürede pek çok ilim halkasına katılmış, Abdullah b. Vehb'in de aralarında bulunduğu sayısız ilim adamı onun tefsir, hadis ve diğer alanlarındaki bilgisinden istifade etmiştir. Ardından 182/798 senesinde şu anki Tunus bölgesinde bulunan Kayrevan'a yerleşti ve ömrünün geri kalan yirmi yıllık kısmını burada tamamladı (Nüveyhiz, t.y., s. 730). Ardından 182/798 senesinde şu anki Tunus bölgesinde bulunan Kayrevan'a yerleşti ve ömrünün geri kalan yirmi yıllık kısmını burada geçirdi. Kayrevan'da kurduğu ilim meclislerinde yazdığı tefsir eserini insanlara aktarıp Kur'an'ın açıklanması ve yorumlanması çalışmalarına aralıksız olarak devam etmiştir (Uzun, 2011, ss. 189-190). Yahya b. Sellâm, çeşitli coğrafyalarda elde ettiği genelde dinî özelde ise tefsir birikimini Kuzey Afrika bölgesine taşıyan ve burada tefsir sahasında önde gelen ilk müfessir olmuştur.

Yahya b. Sellâm'ın vefatından sonra tefsirini, oğlu Muhammed, Kayrevan camiinde uzun yıllar okutmuş, üzerine bazı ilaveler yapmıştır Torunu ve daha başkaları onun tefsirini hem Kayrevan çevresine hem de Endülüs'e yaymışlardır. Kuzey Afrika ve Endülüs Tefsir Geleneğinin kaynağı Yahya b. Sellâm'dır.Örneğin Kuzey Afrika tefsir geleneğinin önemli temsilcilerinden Hud b. Muhkem el-Hevvârî (ö. 280/893) Yahya b. Sellam'ın tefsirini ihtisar eden bir tefsir çalışmasını kaleme almıştır.Aynı şekilde Endülüslü müfessir İbn Ebî Zemenîn de Yahya b. Sellâm'ın hacimli tefsirini ihtisar etmiş ve bu da Endülüs tefsir çalışmalarını beslemiştir (Çalışkan, 2020, ss. 138-139).

Sonuç

İslam dinin kültürel birikiminin oluşumunda kendi yurtlarını bırakıp dinî ve ilmî gayelerle göç eden şahısların payı büyüktür. Bunun somut örnekleri de tefsirin başlangıç ve gelişim aşamalarında görmekteyiz. Tefsirin ilk evresi olan sahabe döneminin öncü şahsiyetlerden İbn Mesud'un Kufe'ye göç etmesi hem İslam düşünce tarihini hem de tefsir tarihini etkilemiştir. İbn Mesud dinî anlayışını gittiği coğrafyanın dinamikleriyle harmanlayarak özgün bir boyut kazandırmıştır. Bu hususun en açık yansıması Hanefi mezhebinin teşekkülü ile bu zihniyeti devam ettiren müfessirlerin olmasıdır. İbn Mesud yalnızca bir bölgeyi değil aynı zamandaa başka diğer coğrafyaları aşan bir düşünce dünyasının kurucu figürü olmuştur. Tefsirin gelişim ve disipline olduğu bir evrede ise Yahya b. Sellâm'ın etkisinin dikkat çekici olduğu görülmektedir. Doğduğu Kufe bölgesinden küçükken göç eden Yahya b. Sellâm Basra, Kahire gibi pek çok şehre göç etmiş ve en sonunda Kayrevan şehrine gelmiştir. Tefsir dersleri ve kaleme aldığı tefsir çalışması Kuzey Afrika ve Endülüs tefsir geleneğinin en temel kaynağı olmuştur. Yahya b. Sellâm göç ettiği yerlerdeki dinî ve kültürel birikimi söz konusu bölgelere taşıyarak kültürel değişim ve dönüşüme katkı sağlamıştır. Bu çerçevede İslam'ın kültürel mirasının yayılması, belirli etki ve değişimlerin olmasının, tarihî süreçteki öncü şahısların göç etmesiyle ortaya çıktığını söylemek gerekir.

Kaynaklar

Cerrahoğlu, İ. (1970). *Yahya b. Sellam ve Tefsirdeki Metodu*. Ankara:Ankara Üniversitesi İlahiyat Fakültesi Yayınları.

Cerrahoğlu, İ. (1996). *Tefsir Tarihi*. Ankara: Fecr Yayınları.

Çalışkan, İ. (2020). *Tefsir Tarihi*. Ankara: Bilay Yayınları.

Dâvûdî, Ş. (2008). Tabakâtu'l-Müfessirîn.

Ebu Zehra, M. (1999). *Ebu Hanife* (O. Keskioğlu, Çev.) Ankara: DİB Yayınları.

el-Mâturîdî, E. M. M. b. M. b. M. (2005). *Te'vîlâtu'l-Kur'ân* (C. 1-17). İstanbul: Dâru'l-Mîzân.

et-Taberî, M. b. C. (2001). *Câmiu'l-beyân an te'vîli âyi'l-Kur'ân* (C. 1-26). Kahire: Dâru Hicr.

Gengil, V. (2021). *Mâtürîdî'de Tefsirin İmkânı*. İstanbul: İz Yayıncılık.

İbn Sa'd. (2001). *et-Tabakâtu'l-Kübrâ*. Kahire: Mektebetü Hanci.

Kesler, M. F. (2005). *Irak Tefsir Ekolü*. Ankara: Akçağ Yayıları.

Küçükkalay, H. (1971). *Abdullah İbn Mesud ve Tefsir İlmindeki Yeri*. Konya: Denizkuşları Matbaası.

Nüveyhiz, A. (t.y.). *Mu'cemu'l-Müfessirîn*. y.y.

Uzun, N. (2011). *Hicri II. Asırda Siyaset-Tefsir İlişkisi*. İstanbul: Pınar Yayınları.

Zehebî, M. H. (2000). *et-Tefsîr ve'l-Müfessirûn* (C. 1-3). Kahire: Mektebetü Vehbe.

THE COVID-19 PANDEMIC AND SYRIAN WOMEN REFUGEES IN A GENDER PERSPECTIVE[1]

Senem Gürkan[2] and Erkan Perşembe[3]

Introduction

The last days of 2019 brought some dramatic changes in all facet of our lives. The world faced with coronavirus disease (COVID-19), which was declared as "pandemic" on March 11, 2020 by The World Health Organization and on the same date, the first case was seen in Turkey (SB, 2020; WHO, 2020).

The pandemic had unprecedented impacts all over the world and undoubtedly affected each and every individual, bringing new practices and changes in social life, called "new normal" (Akca and Tepe-Küçükoğlu, 2020). These impacts can be seen both during the downturn and the subsequent recovery period, constituting the major aspect of the sociology of COVID-19.

Upon the Effects of COVID-19 Pandemic

The effects of the pandemic have been more intense in some groups, although it has been felt less in some groups, but it continues to exist widely in all segments of society. The literature on pandemic has shown that people in vulnerable / disadvantaged groups with special conditions such as poverty, old age, disability, gender-based discrimination, refugees are affected more negatively and / or exposed to discrimination compared to other segments of the society (EU, 2020; Ünalp-Çeper, 2020; Hopman and Allegranzi, 2020; Kıran, 2020).

Regarding gender and pandemic, the same related literature has demonstrated that immigrants (refugees and/or asylum seekers) have faced with new problems that arise during the pandemic process, as well as their current problems before the pandemic process (EU, 2020; Ünalp-Çeper, 2020; Shrivastava and Shrivastava, 2020; Raju and Ayeb-Karlsson, 2020).

These are the problems such as not being able to access adequate information due to language restrictions, registration problems of the unregistered refugees, losing their jobs, inadequate health, nutrition and accommodation conditions during the filiation process and inability to access to the hospitals or healthcare services. As this is the case all over the world, these people, who have been terminated from their jobs or working as seasonal agricultural workers, have encountered obstacles due to accommodation and transportation problems. Other problems are that many do not have health insurance, and are afraid of being deported if they consult to formal services (Mardin, et al. 2020). In addition, since these individuals could not be directly included in the population, their use of services was indirect (Kılıç, 2020).

The Turkish Ministry of Health, the World Health Organization, the United Nations High Commissioner for Refugees, some municipalities, Non-Governmental Organizations (NGOs) and

---

[1] This study is an expanded version of the abstract presentation which was presented at the Migration Conference 2021 held on 6-10 July 2021 in London (online) by the authors.
[2] Erkan Perşembe, Prof. Dr., Ondokuz Mayıs University, Samsun, Turkey, 0000-0002-1659-3301, erkanper@omu.edu.tr
[3] Senem Gürkan, Ph.D., Samsun, Turkey, 0000-0002-2061-6385, senemgrk@yahoo.com

international organizations have been working on accessing the necessary services to solve the problems these groups face during the pandemic process. Although documents translated into Arabic were published by these institutions and organizations, and hygiene kits such as masks, gloves and disinfectants were sent to the relevant staff, adequate measures could not be taken for the ongoing pandemic process and effects.

Budak and Bostan (2020) made a study to reveal how the Syrian immigrants in Kilis, Turkey, were affected by the pandemic, and revealed that 30% of these immigrants did not have enough information about the pandemic, and that approximately 45% did not have personal protective equipment and / or had a limited amount. Moreover, the anxiety levels were found to be above the average. Women, Turkish citizens and married people are said to be more sensitive to pandemic measures.

In his study investigating how Syrian immigrants in Lebanon were affected by the pandemic process, Trovato (2020) revealed that the pandemic process was not democratic, it affected marginalized groups more, and these effects were especially in the areas of social tension, livelihood, security, evacuation, and physiological and psychological health. Similarly, Raju and Ayeb-Karlsson (2020) determined that immigrants living in camps were more likely to be affected by the virus due to dense population, poor health and thirst, insufficient health resources, lack of livelihood, financial and social security.

Specifically, in Turkey, according to the data from Ministry of Interior Diractorate General of Migration Management (2020), Syrians under temporary protection, 3,6 million of population, on one hand, have been trying to cope with the problems such as integration, poverty, unemployment, hunger, etc.; on the other hand, have faced with some problems stemming from the pandemic period. Mardin, et al. (2020) underlined that gender-based influences, especially those faced by women, came to the fore in Turkey. Gender inequality, which is one of the sources of these problems, has caused these women to be negatively affected both before and during the pandemic period (Marsella and Ring, 2003; Yakushko and Chronister, 2005). As the relevant literature states, the pandemic process has paved the way for the end and / or slowdown of the actions on gender discrimination in recent years. Therefore, the acquisitions are eliminated and the inequal status have deepened and caused new problems (Gausman and Langer, 2020; Ergönen, Biçen and Ersoy, 2020; Altun, 2016; Çelebi Boz and Şengün, 2017; UNFPA, 2020).

Şahin- Erbektaş (2020) revealed that the views of Syrian women, who have adopted patriarchal codes, coincide with their gender roles; and their beliefs about gender equality are not strong. Baklacıoğlu and Kıvılcım (2015) argued that within the patriarchal structure of Syrian society, women are more backward than women in Turkey.

Gender Role Stress

In spite of the fact that the concept of gender is thought to be feminized in society and generally studied over women, the concept also includes men and individuals of other genders. All these expectations for both sexes cause gender role stress in men and women.

Gender roles that exist in social memory and in the culture of societies become permanent by being transferred from generation to generation through socialization process (Demirbilek, 2007). These roles consist of what is expected from individuals depending on their gender. For instance, society expects men to behave towards norms such as success and high status, physiological, psychological and emotional power, and not behaving as feminine (Burn, 1996). So, the women are positioned inside home, private sphere whereas men are positioned to public sphere (West and Zimmerman, 1987).

In other words, there is a form of masculinity and femininity that exists and is expected to be achieved in society (Demren, 2003; Oktan, 2008). Some roles arise only from the gender of the people, and these expectations cause stress in individuals (Koç, Haskan Avcı and Bayar, 2017). It is stated that the pressures related to the male gender role and the stress resulting from these pressures can harm both men and women in terms of their social and individual consequences (Bayar, Haskan Avcı and Koç, 2018).

Thus, it would not be wrong to say that the COVID-19 pandemic made changes in the gender roles of women and men. During the pandemic, while childcare and housework increased for women's unpaid domestic labor, men were also involved in this process, and there was a shift in gender stereotypes at this point (Alon, et al, 2020; Zeybekoğlu-Akbaş and Dursun, 2020). Although both sexes are influenced by the pandemic, it is supported by the data in the literature that women (especially immigrant women) are more likely to be affected (Ergönen, Biçen and Ersoy, 2020; Altun, 2016: 187; Çelebi Boz and Şengün, 2017: 362). UNFPA (2020) drew attention to gender equality and inequality during the pandemic period with the words *"The pandemic affects women and men in different ways"*.

In line with all these data and information, the aim of this study is to reveal the consequences of the COVID-19 pandemic on Syrian women refugees in Samsun in a gender perspective. Within this respect, these research questions were tried to be replied:

1. How has the COVID-19 pandemic had effects on Syrian women refugees from a gender perspective?

2. Has the gender role stress of Syrian women refugees in Samsun showed differences according to their marital status?

3. Has the gender role stress of Syrian women refugees in Samsun showed differences according to their educational background?

Methodology

Methodologically, the research was conducted through the periods and methods of mixed research method, combining both qualitative and quantitative research paradigms.

Research Design

The qualitative dimension of the study was carried out through grounded theory to reveal how the COVID-19 pandemic has had effects on Syrian women refugees from a gender perspective, which means that the embedded -grounded- data in the interviews of the participating women were revealed through themes (Giles, 2002).

The quantitative dimension of the study, on the other hand, was carried out through correlational survey model to find out the changes between two or more variables (Karasar, 2006).

Participants

The participants of the study were 32 Syrian women refugees, between the ages of 18 and 71 (average 39,6), living in İlkadım, Canik and Atakum districts of Samsun province. The participants were chosen via snowball or chain sampling technique providing access to a participant first and then to other participants referred by that participant (Patton, 1987). The descriptive information of the participants is given in Table-1:

Table 1. The descriptive information of the participants

VARIABLE	Groups (N)	%
Age		
	18-22 (n=4)	12,5
	23-27 (n=3)	9,4
	28-32 (n=3)	9,4
	33-37 (n=5)	15,6
	38-42 (n=6)	18,75
	43-47 (n=5)	15,6
	48 and above (n=6)	18,75
Marital Status		
	Married (n=24)	75
	Single (n=8)	25
Number of Children		
	0 (n=2)	6
	1 (n=1)	3
	2 (n=7)	22
	3 and above (n=22)	69
Educational Background		
	Illiterate (n=9)	28
	Literate (n=8)	25
	Primary School (n=6)	19
	Secondary School (n=5)	15,5
	High School (n=4)	12,5
Occupation		
	Housewife (n=21)	66
	Service industry (cleaning) (n=4)	12,5
	Beauty expert (n=2)	6,25
	Translator (n=2)	6,25
	Garment worker (n=1)	3
	Student (n=1)	3
	Teacher (n=1)	3
	TOTAL (n=32)	100

When Table 1 is examined; it can be seen that the 12.5% (n=4) of the participants were between the ages of 18-22, 9.4% were 23-27 and 28-32 (n=3 each), 15.6% (n=5) were 33- 37, 18.75% (n=6) were 38-42, 15.6% (n=5) were 43-47, and 18.75% (n=6) were 48 and over. Looking at the marital status, which is another variable, it can be seen that 75% (24 people) of the participants were married and the remaining 25% (8 people) were single. In addition, 2 people (6%) had no children, 1 person (3%) had only one child, 7 people (22%) had two children, and 22 people (69%) had 3 or more children. In terms of the educational backgrounds of the participants, it can be observed that the 9 (28%) were illiterate, 8 (25%) were literate, 6 (19%) were primary school graduates, 5 (15.5%) were secondary school graduates, and the remaining 4 (12.5%) were found to be high school graduates. In terms of the occupations of the participants, 21 people (66%) were housewives, 4 people (12.5%) were employed in the service industry (cleaning), 2 people (6.25% each) were beauty experts and translators. It was determined that 1 person (3% each) was a garment worker, teacher and a student.

Data Collection and Analysis

The data were collected by the researchers themselves by using in-depth interview technique through online interviews to minimize the risk of the transmission of the virus. A semi-structured interview form and questionnaire form, which was compiled from the former researches (Karataş, 2020; Budak and Bostan, 2020; Trovato, 2020; Raju and Ayeb-Karlsson 2020), were used. The demographic questions were age, marital status, number of children, educational background and occupation of the participants. The open-ended questions that were asked to the participants were as follows:

1. As a refugee, what kind of problems have you faced with during the COVID-19 pandemic?

2. As a woman refugee, what kind of problems have you faced with during the COVID-19 pandemic?

3. How has COVID-19 pandemic influenced your domestic relations and responsibilities?

4. How has COVID-19 pandemic influenced your working life and social life?

5. What changes has COVID-19 pandemic brought to your life?

Three step qualitative data analysis model that was developed by Miles, Huberman and Saldana (2015) was applied to the data gathered as a result of the interviews. These steps are data condensation, data display and conclusion drawing and verification. As seen in Table 2, the data were visualized and the findings were interpreted among themselves.

As to the quantitative data, Feminine Gender Role Stress Scale (FGRSS), developed by Koç, Avcı and Bayar (2017), was conducted to the participants to measure the gender role stresses of the female participants. It is a 5 Likert-type scale including 20 items and no diverse item. The Confirmatory Factor Analysis has shown that there are 4 factors (χ^2/df=3,18, RMSEA=,08, SRMR=,04, GFI=,87, AGFI=,83, CFI=,98 and NNFI=,98). The scale has an internal reliability of (Alpha=,93) Cronbach Alfa.

The analysis of the quantitative data was conducted through SPSS 22.0, IBM (Statistical Package for Social Sciences). Descriptive statistics (mean, standard deviation, median, minimum, maximum, frequency, percentage) were used to evaluate the data. The Kolmogorov-Smirnov test (when the degree of freedom is more than 50) and Shapiro-Wilk test (when the degree of freedom is less than 50) were used to reveal the approximate normality of quantitative data. A P of less than 0,05 was considered significant. Independent Samples t Test was used to find out if the gender role stress of Syrian women refugees in Samsun showed differences according to their marital status. One Way ANOVA was used to find out if the gender role stress of Syrian women refugees in Samsun showed differences according to their educational background.

Procedure

The data was collected between 30.01 and 10.03. 2021 by the researchers themselves. The data collected by recording through online interviews lasting around 40-50 minutes. The data set was created by the researchers in accordance with the rules of Turkish grammatical rules. Participants were informed that participation in the study was voluntary, their answers would be confidential, the data would not be used for purposes other than this research, and they could withdraw from the study at any time they want. There was no participant who refused to participate in the study.

Ethical Issues

Ethics committee approval was obtained from Turkey Ministry of Health on 08.01.2021 and Ondokuz Mayıs University Ethical Committee of Social and Humanities Sciences on 29.01.2021 with the number of 2021/13. In any part of the study, the private information of the participants was not included, and all of the examples given during the study were coded according to the date and order of the interviews such as P1, P2, etc.

Limitations and Assumptions

This study was conducted in İlkadım, Canik and Atakum districts of Samsun province of Turkey with limited participants who had no language problems. Therefore, at the beginning of the study, it was assumed that the participants, that is, the sample has the power to represent the population.

Findings and Discussion

How has the COVID-19 pandemic had effects on Syrian women refugees from a gender perspective?

From the interviews with the participants, it was found out that the gender effects of the COVID-19 pandemic on Syrian female refugees living in Samsun can be divided into 7 themes given in Table 2:

Table 2. The gender effects of the COVID-19 pandemic on Syrian female refugees living in Samsun

	Frequency (n)	Per cent (%)
Increase in economic difficulties	12	37,5
Increase in household responsibilities	5	16
Increase in domestic violence	5	16
Psychosocial effects	4	12,5
Increase in health problems	3	9,4
Decrease in women's participation in social life	2	6
Increase in polygamy	1	2,6
TOTAL	32	100 %

According to Table 2, 37.5% (n=12) of the Syrian women refugees living in Samsun stated that the COVID-19 pandemic caused the increase in their economic problems, and 32% (n=5 each) mentioned the increase in household responsibilities and the increase in domestic violence. 12.5% (n=4) of the women mentioned the psychosocial effects of the pandemic, while 9.4% (n=3) of the women revealed that the pandemic caused an increase in their health problems. 6% (n=2) of the participants revealed that women's participation in social life decreased due to the pandemic, and the remaining 2.6% (n=1) revealed that the pandemic caused polygamy to increase.

The participants mentioned that the most difficult factor they faced during the pandemic was the increase in economic hardships, as supported by the studies in the literature. In the context of the increase in economic difficulties, the existing COVID-19 literature reveals that one of the effects of the pandemic is related to working life in the economic framework. In this period, pandemic has affected people in the lower part of the society more economically (Davidai, 2020) due to working from home or flexible working system and the loss of jobs of most individuals (Zhou and Chen, 2020; ABS, 2020). Ginette (2020) stated that 435 million of women are to live on 1,90USD per day by the further years. The Syrian women refugees, most of whom worked informally before the pandemic, especially in areas such as cleaning and care, faced unemployment and poverty by breaking away from their working life during this period. (Blundeell, 2020; Kumar, Culbertson, Constant, Nataraj, Unlu, et al., 2018; Rahman, Narayan and Shakil, 2020). They have experienced difficulties due to economic difficulties and poverty to meet their basic needs (Karadağ-Caman, Çınar, Çevik, Mardin, Nergiz and Karabey, 2020).

"All of the men in my family are doctors. My family did not allow us, the girls, to get education. Our financial status in Syria was very well, I had a beauty centre in Damascus. We had to come to Samsun, but my elder brothers are still in

74

Syria. First, we found a job, we bought a flat. But with pandemic, they discharged us. We do not pay rent for home; however, we have no money. We do not know whether to be sad for health or for starvation. Everything is really expensive." *(P9, 30, married with 2 children, secondary school, cosmetician).*

"Sometimes I could not buy bread, or sometimes medicine. These bad days are still going on. I miss my country. However, some of you are insensitive. What's my fault if my kids don't have a computer, I can't buy medicine, but I want to work and I can't find a job? Our teacher at school gave us a computer, God bless her! My husband's boss sometimes sent pasta, sometimes milk. Please let these days pass, let's have our fill with ease. What my husband earns is not enough anymore, everything is too expensive." *(P11, 41, married with 3 children, secondary school, housewife).*

As another factor, the participants claimed that the pandemic process triggered an increase in their responsibilities at home. Among the most unpaid chores of women is the responsibility of care as well as housework. The care of children, the elderly, sick and disabled individuals, which are among those informal responsibilities of women in the private sphere, can be considered in this group. In addition to these responsibilities of women during the pandemic process, the care of their children has been added as education has been suspended in educational institutions at all levels (university, schools, kindergartens, courses, etc.) and distant education was started. Moreover, the rate of women losing their jobs during the pandemic process has been higher than that of men. The sum of all these factors has caused the repercussions of the pandemic to make women parallel to their traditional roles in their private spheres (Tokyay, 2020).

"Previously, I would finish my work until the children came from school, then we would meet with friends who had children. We were going to parks. At the weekends, we were going for a picnic at the seaside. I don't have time even to look out of the window anymore. Children always attend distant education classes at home. As I'm afraid of the spread of the virus, when my husband comes from work, I wash everything in my hand, because I don't have a machine. My father doesn't go to the shop anymore, he always wants tea and coffee at home, I'm not done. Now I'm like a sewing machine needle, I only find time to sit while I sleep." (P14, 36, married with 3 children, secondary school, housewife).

"I'm a grandma, a wife, a teacher. I am at home; I have many things to do at home. All my grandchildren are at home, four kids are doing homework every time. I don't know what to do: to cook, to clean, to iron, to help them with their homework?" *(P31, 67, married with 8 children, illiterate, housewife).*

"I am an artist; I had an atelier in Syria. When I came here in Samsun, I became an art teacher. With this virus, we long for money and health. My domestic work has increased; breakfast, dishes, online courses of children, lunch, dishes, courses again, cleaning, washing, etc. I will get mad!" (P11, 37, married with 5 children, high school, teacher).

Just like the participants, many studies in the literature suggest that the situation of especially refugee women has worsened during the pandemic process as they live in unhygienic and unhealthy conditions such as camps or slums. Moreover, there has been an increase in domestic violence during the process of staying at home. These women, who are afraid to report their spouses who resort to violence for reasons such as language barrier, xenophobia and fear of deportation, have stayed away from both judicial and health institutions (Mardin, et al. 2020). Some studies in the literature confirm that the curfews and quarantine practices that were implemented during the pandemic and still being implemented increase the cases of domestic violence, and that the elderly, children and family members of the disabled, especially women, are exposed to violence in various forms (UNFPA, 2020; WHO, 2020; Altun, 2016: 187; Gausman and Langer, 2020). One of these studies demonstrates that the rate of violence against women and children increased 45.9% during quarantine. 23.7% of them faced with psychological violence, 10.3% of them faced with economic violence, while 4.8% of them digital, 1.7% physical violence and 1.4% were subjected to sexual violence (Socio Political Field Research Center, 2020). In addition, it is claimed that the reasons for this violence are the increase in the compulsory time spent at home, the stress caused by unemployment and economic difficulties, the increase in panic and fear, and the decrease in social communication (Ergönen, Biçen and Ersoy, 2020).

"I have been living here in Turkey for seven years, this is my sixth year in Samsun. I graduated from the university in Samsun and I started to work as a translator at my kids' school. Sometimes I heard about violence from families at school. There is a lot of violence against women and children, and I would have witnessed it a lot in my neighbours in Aleppo. They carried this habit here exactly, I heard a lot when translating these works in the courts, they saw us as a very violent nation. I blushed before. But I've heard much worse in quarantine: I have a student, six siblings, grandparents, all living in my upper street together. I saw her at the grocery store a few days ago and she said her father was in jail. He always used violence against his mother and children, and the adults did not like his mother and their voices were not heard. Finally, the neighbours complained and sent him to jail. This is a very sad situation." (P15, 36, married with two children, high school, translator).

In parallel with the existing literature, the participants also stated that one of the problems that emerged in the lives of individuals with the pandemic is psychosocial problems, that women's problems increased and women are affected psychosocially more than men as a result of the differentiation of power balances in the family during the pandemic (Çelebi Boz and Şengün, 2017: 362; Ekiz, Ilıman and Dönmez, 2020:140; Karataş, 2020). People experience fear and panic when they encounter situations that they are not accustomed to, or even that can be considered as radical, such as a pandemic, and their feelings of hope and confidence can be damaged (Beck, 1992). More specifically, it is stated that pandemic periods cause the following psychosocial conditions in humans: stocking food and cleaning materials and shopping for possible diseases and deaths caused by diseases; negative attitude towards communities that are the source of the virus; unreasonable application to health care institutions due to anxiety and risk of contamination; non-compliance with practices such as isolation, social distance and curfew, and the increase of unfounded information pollution and conspiracy theories about the pandemic (Taylor, 2019). In particular, it reveals that disadvantaged groups are more affected by the negative effects of the pandemic, and that they feel more deeply about coping with stress and adapting to the new normal (Taştan, 2020).

"I have come to this age; I have not faced such bad days. The war left us homeless and landless, we settled in your hometown, I was separated from all my friends and relatives. But I wasn't bored as I am today. We can't see people, we can't see air, the birds are too far away. My brothers in the camp in Hatay are in a very difficult situation, they got sick, the virus destroyed the camps, they are worse than dying. I am sick of my lungs; they cannot come to us. May Allah not show us these days again, may flowers bloom all over the world." (P27, 58, single (her husband died), mother of 6 children, illiterate, housewife).

Another problem stated by the participants and the literature is that the pandemic process has negatively affected individuals' living a healthy life (Kluge, Jakab, Bartovic et al, 2020). Women working in the health sector and care services, where women are heavily employed, day workers and short-term workers who do not have social rights such as sick leave and/or paid leave, unemployment benefits, and migrant workers working illegally within the borders of a country, have been from the segments that are more affected by the pandemic process in terms of health (ILO-1st edition, 2020:3-6). In more detail, some of the women refugees working without social security in factories and cleaning services were dismissed, and some of them were more exposed to the risk of contagion because they could not work from home (Blundeell, 2020). These groups have a higher probability of contracting the disease, as well as difficult access to health services (Sunar, 2020).

"We were cleaning apartments in the city. We were not unemployed, but we were very sick. The people living in those apartments did not tell us that they had Coronavirus. My sister and me caught the virus, then we infected our relatives without knowing it. Then I quit the job, I won't go there yet, I'm so sorry." (P7, 26, married with 3 children, literate, service industry -cleaning).

Another effect of the COVID-19 pandemic is the decrease in women's participation in social life due to the emergence of changes in daily life areas (Kıran, 2020). It can be argued that one of the situations that reinforces this issue is that the pandemic has increased women's responsibilities at home (Tokyay, 2020). Participants also talked about this situation with the following words:

"We all live at … Street. When the children were at school, we were going to each other's gardens and houses with friends. Sometimes we went on picnics with husbands when there were children. We are at home now, maybe for ages, we are so bored." (P4, 22, married, mother of 2 children, literate, housewife).

"Before the pandemic, every week, we were going to an aunt's home, cleaned it and had coffee with friends there. Now all of us are at home, no friends, no coffee. I wish the virus was over. While we missed our land before, now we miss our days here last year." (P22, 44, married with 4 children, literate, housewife).

During the pandemic, another factor affecting the situation of women in the context of gender has been the increase in polygamy. It can be argued that increased conflict situations within the family in the event of a pandemic (Ümmet, 2007; Kluwer, 2020) trigger this situation. One of the participants made the following statements regarding her husband's marriage to a second woman during this period:

"With us, men marry many wives. Not like you here, there are many women, up to four. One is registered in the state, but sometimes none of them are registered in the state. My husband was only in love with me. He said that I was his soul, everything. He is a carpenter. They do well here, Turks love furniture, my husband earns lots of money. When he got money, he got a new woman. I knew this would happen one day, because his father has three women, too. I thought he would follow his example. He still loves me, I know. But now he has one another wife other than me, living in a different house!". (P16, 39, married, mother of 3 children, literate, service industry -cleaning-).

2/3. Has the gender role stress of Syrian women refugees in Samsun showed differences according to their marital status and educational background?

To find out if the gender role stress of Syrian women refugees in Samsun showed differences according to their marital status, firstly, the process to find the distribution of the data was applied. As the P of less than 0,05 was considered significant, the data showed normal distribution. So, Independent Samples t Test was used.

Tablo 4. The Comparison of the Gender Role Stress Averages and Marital Status and Educational Status of the Syrian Women Refugees living in Samsun

		WM ± SD	Test Stat.	p
Marital Status	Married (n=24)	77,458 ± 6,255	2,032	0,051*
	Single (n=8)	71,25 ± 10,553	1,574	0,151*
Educational Background	Illiterate (n=9)	72,556 ± 9,901		
	Literate (n=8)	77,25 ± 9,881		
	Primary School (n=6)	76,167 ± 3,764		0,055**
	Secondary School (n=5)	75 ± 5,244		
	High School (n=4)	81,5 ± 2,38	3,080	

*Independent Two Samples t Test, ** One Way (ANOVA)

As seen in Table 4, according to the results of the t Test, the Levene test showed that there was no homogeneity of the variances. The P-value (Sig)<0.05 showed that there are no significant differences between groups. The analysis conducted to reveal whether the gender role stress of Syrian women refugees in Samsun showed differences according to their marital status have demonstrated that the married participants (77,458) experience higher levels of gender role stress than those of the single ones (71,25).

This finding is in line with the literature stating that married women experience more gender role stress than single women; and, gender-based effects of the pandemic on women are more negative (Marsella and Ring, 2003; Yakushko and Chronister, 2005; Gausman and Langer, 2020; Ergönen, Biçen and Ersoy, 2020; Altun, 2016; Çelebi Boz and Şengün, 2017; UNFPA, 2020; Şahin- Erbektaş, 2020; Baklacıoğlu and Kıvılcım, 2015).

Table 4 also shows the test to find out if the gender role stress of Syrian women refugees in Samsun showed differences according to their educational background, firstly, the process to find the distribution of the data was applied. As the *P* of less than 0,05 was considered significant, the data showed normal distribution. So, One Way ANOVA was conducted to the data collected. Each educational status was found to distribute normally and the Levene test showed that there was no homogeneity. So, Robust (Welch) value was checked and no difference was found between the groups in terms of means (p>0,05). In other words, the analysis conducted to reveal whether the gender role stress of Syrian women refugees in Samsun showed differences according to their educational backgrounds have demonstrated that there is no statistically significant difference between the educational backgrounds of these women; all these women, regardless as their educational backgrounds, experience similar levels of gender role stress. It can be interpreted from these findings that this situation supports the literature data suggesting that immigrant women, who are among the disadvantaged groups, are affected by gender inequality at a higher level than normal during the pandemic process (Mardin, et al. 2020; Marsella and Ring, 2003; Yakushko and Chronister, 2005; Gausman and Langer, 2020; Ergönen, Biçen and Ersoy, 2020; Altun, 2016; Çelebi Boz and Şengün, 2017; UNFPA, 2020).

Results and Discussion

The COVID-19 pandemic, which has had impact on the whole world, undoubtedly affected each and every individual. The literature on pandemic has shown that people in vulnerable / disadvantaged groups with special conditions such as poverty, old age, disability, gender-based discrimination, refugee and asylum, are affected more negatively and / or exposed to discrimination compared to other segments of the society. Specifically, in Turkey, Syrians under temporary protection, on one hand, have been trying to cope with the problems such as integration, poverty, unemployment, hunger, etc.; on the other hand, have faced with some problems stemming from the pandemic period. Gender inequality, which is one of the sources of these problems, has caused these women to be negatively affected both before and during the pandemic period and this inequality causes Syrian women refugees experience high levels of gender role stress.

The findings of the study have put forth that the gender effects of the COVID-19 pandemic on Syrian female refugees living in Samsun can be divided into 7 themes. These effects are, respectively, increase in economic difficulties, increase in household responsibilities, increase in domestic violence, psychosocial effects, increase in health problems, decrease in women's participation to social life and increase in polygamy.

The analysis conducted to reveal whether the gender role stress of Syrian women refugees in Samsun showed differences according to their marital status have demonstrated that the married participants experience higher levels of gender role stress than those of the single ones. Moreover, the analysis conducted to reveal whether the gender role stress of Syrian women refugees in Samsun showed differences according to their educational backgrounds have demonstrated that there is no statistically significant difference between the educational backgrounds of these women.

As a result, the COVID-19 pandemic has reinforced the gender-based discrimination faced by Syrian women refugees, one of the disadvantaged groups; together with the social inequalities, oppression and poverty within the framework of traditional gender roles that society has assumed for women and men. Because the grounded information revealed from the discourses of the participants showed that the work of Syrian women in the private sphere has increased more than their routine during the pandemic process, exacerbated their existing problems, and that women have been more confronted with their traditional roles at home due to the economic, social and psychosocial problems brought by the pandemic.

In addition to this, it is thought that the social impact of the pandemic was felt more in women and that these women lost some of the acquisitions they gained until the pandemic in the context of gender equality. Just as the current literature reveals, the pandemic has made economic class distinctions clear, thus affecting the disadvantaged groups and poor more than other segments of society.

According to the World Health Organization, the European Union, the United Nations and the World Health Organization, the gender inequality faced by Syrian women refugees have deepened within this period.

It is thought that the fact that there is no difference between the gender role mean scores of the participants and their educational status and that the married people experience more gender role stress than the single ones can be interpreted in two ways: First, the participants have no awareness of gender or have gender beliefs that are in line with the patriarchal structure. The second and vice versa is that, as the literature supports, the COVID-19 pandemic has made the gender-based effects of Syrian women refugees more deeply and intensely felt.

References

ABS- Australian Bureau of Statistics. (2020, 05 01). Household Impacts of COVID-19 Survey. Australian Bureau of Statistics: https://www.abs.gov.au/ausstats/abs%40.nsf/mediareleasesbyCatalogue/DB259787916733E4CA25855B0003B21C?OpenDocument

Akça, M. And Tepe-Küçükoğlu, M. (2020). COVID-19 ve İş Yaşamına Etkileri: Evden Çalışma. Uluslararası Yönetim Eğitim ve Ekonomik Perspektifler Dergisi, 8(1): 71-81.

Altun, F. (2016). "Afetlerde Psikososyal Hizmetler: Marmara ve Van Depremleri Karşılaştırmalı Analizi". Çekmece İzü Sosyal Bilimler Dergisi. 4 (8-9), 183-197.

Baklacıoğlu, N.Ö. and Kıvılcım, Z. (2015). "Sürgünde Toplumsal Cinsiyet: İstanbul'da Suriyeli Kadın ve LGBTİ Mülteciler. İstanbul: Derin Yayınları.

Bayar, Ö., Haskan Avcı, Ö. and Koç, M. (2018). Üniversite öğrencilerinde erkek toplumsal cinsiyet rolü stresinin yordanması. Çukurova Üniversitesi Sosyal Bilimler Enstitüsü Dergisi , 27 (2) , 70-83 .

Beck, U. (1992). Risk society: Towards a new modernity. London: Sage Publications.

Blundell R, Dias MC and Joyce R. (2020). COVID-19 and inequalities. Fiscal Studies; 41: 291-319.

Burn, S. M. (1996). The social psychology of gender. Mc Grav-Hill.

Çelebi Boz, F. and Şengün, H. (2017). "Afet ve Kalkınma İlişkisinde Kadın". The Journal of Academic Social Science Studiess. 59, 360-371.

Davidai S, Day MV, Goyatocchetto D, et al. COVID-19 provides a rare opportunity to create a stonger, more equitable society. Https://psyarxiv.com/hz4c7

Demirbilek, S. (2007). Cinsiyet ayrımcılığının sosyolojik açıdan incelenmesi. Finans Politik & Ekonomik Yorumlar, 44(511), 12-27.

Demren, Ç. (2003). Erkeklik, ataerkillik ve iktidar ilişkileri. Hacettepe Üniversitesi Kadın Sorunları Araştırma ve Uygulama Merkezi, Erişim tarihi: 05.12.2019. http://www. huksam. hacettepe. edu. tr/erkek. htm.

Mardin, D. Et al. (2020) COVID-19 Sürecinde Türkiye'de Göçmen ve Mültecilerin Durumu, Sağlık ve Toplum Özel Sayı, 112-118.

Ekiz, T., Ilıman, E., and Dönmez, E. (2020). "Bireylerin Sağlık Anksiyetesi Düzeyleri İle COVID-19 Salgını Kontrol Algısının Karşılaştırılması". Uluslararası Sağlık Yönetimi ve Stratejileri Araştırma Dergisi. 6(1), 139-154.

Kıran, E. (2020) Prominent Issues About The Social Impacts of Covid-19, Gaziantep University Journal of Social Sciences 2020 Special Issue 752-766

Ergönen, A. T., Biçen, E. and Ersoy, G. (2020). "COVID-19 Salgınında Ev İçi Şiddet". Adli Tıp Bülteni. 25, 48- 57.

EU (04.05.2020) COVID-19 coronavirus outbreak and the EU's response, European Council, https://www.consilium. europa.eu/en/policies/covid-19-coronavirus-outbreak-and-the-e-u-s-response/

Budak, F. and Bostan, S. (2020) The Effects of Covid-19 Pandemic on Syrian Refugees in Turkey: The Case of Kilis, Social Work in Public Health, 35:7, 579-589, DOI: 10.1080/19371918.2020.1806984

Gausman, J., and Langer, A. (2020). Sex and gender disparities in the COVID-19 pandemic. Journal of Women's Health, 29(4), 465-466.

Hopman J and Allegranzi B (2020) Managing COVID-19 in low- and middle-income countries. JAMA. https://doi.org/10.1001/jama.2020.4169

ILO (2020). " ILO Monitor 1st Edition COVID-19 and the World of Work: Impact and Policy Responses", 18 March 2020, ss.3-6.https://www.ilo.org/wcmsp5/groups/public/---dgreports/---dcomm/documents/briefingnote/wcms_738753.pdf

İçişleri Bakanlığı Göç İdaresi Genel Müdürlüğü (2020). Geçici Koruma Altındakiler, https://en.goc.gov.tr/temporary-protection27, Erişim Tarihi: 26 Nisan 2020

Karasar, N. (2006). Bilimsel Araştırma Yöntemi. Ankara: Nobel Yayın Dağıtım.

Karataş, Z. (2020). COVID-19 Pandemisinin Toplumsal Etkileri, Değişim ve Güçlenme. Türkiye Sosyal Hizmet Araştırmaları Dergisi 4(1), 3-15

Kılıç M. (2020). Pandemidönemiinsan Hakları Siyaseti: Hak ve Özgürlükler Düzeninin Kırılganlaşan Doğası, Adalet Dergisi, 2020/1 64. sayıss.17-55

Kluge HHP, Jakab Z, Bartovic J et al (2020) Comment refugee and migrant health in the COVID-19 response. Lancet 2019:2019–2020. https://doi.org/10.1016/S0140-6736(20)30791-1

Kluwer, C. (2020). Families in time of Corona. (Erişim Tarihi: 11.06.2020). https://nias.knaw.nl/food-for-thought/families-in-times-of-corona/

Koç, M., Avcı-Haskan, Ö. and Bayar, Ö. (2017). Kadın Toplumsal Cinsiyet Rolü Stres Ölçeği'nin (KTCRSÖ) geliştirilmesi: Geçerlik ve güvenirlik çalışması. Mehmet Akif Ersoy Üniversitesi Eğitim Fakültesi Dergisi, 41, 284-297.

Kumar, K. B., et al. (2018). Opportunities for All: Mutually Beneficial Opportunities for Syrians and Host Countries in Middle Eastern Labor Markets. Santa Monica, CA: RAND Corporation.

Trovato, M.G. (2020). Dwelling in emergency. The effect of the COVID 19 pandemic on Syrians displaced in Lebanon. Landscape Design and Ecosystem Management Department, Faculty of Agricultural and Food Sciences/American University of Beirut. Available at URL http://admigov.eu.

Marsella, A. J., and Ring, E. (2003). Human migration and immigration: An overview. In L. L. Adler and U. P. Gielen (Eds.), Migration: Immigration and emigration in international perspective (pp. 3–22). Westport: Praeger. (Google Scholar)

Miles, M.B, Huberman, M. and Saldaña, J. (2015). Qualitative data analysis-a methods sourcebook. (3. Baskı). USA: Sage Publications.

Oktan, A. (2008). Türk sinemasında hegemonik erkeklikten erkeklik krizine: Yazı-tura ve erkeklik bunalımının sınırları. Selçuk İletişim, 5(2): 152-166.

Karadağ, O. et al. (2020). Situational Brief: Report On Forced Migrants And Covid-19 Pandemic Response in Turkey https://csd.columbia.edu/sites/default/files/content/Situational%20Brief%20-%20Migrants%20COVID-19%20Turkey.pdf

Zeybekoğlu-Akbaş, Ö. and Dursun, C. (2020) Avrasya Sosyal ve Ekonomi Araştırmaları Dergisi (ASEAD), ASEAD CİLT 7 SAYI 5 Yıl 2020, S 78-94 .

Patton, M. Q. (1987). How To Use Qualitative Methods in Evaluation. Newbury Park, CA: Sage.

Rahman, Z. Narayan C. D., and Shakil A. (2020). Rapid Survey on Immediate Economic Vulnerabilities Created by COVID-19 and the Coping Mechanisms of Poor and Marginal People. Bangladesh: BRAC Institute of Governance and Development.

Raju, E. and Ayeb-Karlsson, S. (2020). COVID-19: How do you self-isolate in a refugee camp?. International Journal of Public Health (2020) 65:515–517 https://doi.org/10.1007/s00038-020-01381-8

Shrivastava, S. R. and Shrivastava, P. S. (2020). Effective Containment of The COVID-19 Pandemic Among Migrants and Refugee: World Health Organization. TJFMPC, 14(2): 163-165.

Sosyo Politik Saha Araştırma Merkezi, (2020). "COVİD-19 Karantinasından Kadının Etkilenimi İle Kadın ve Çocuğa Yönelik Şiddete İlişkin Türkiye Araştırma Raporu".

Sunar L. (13 Nisan 2020). Salgınla mücadelenin ilk eşiği: Eşitsizlikler. Toplumsal Yapı Https://tyap.net/sgmi

Şahin- Erbektaş, H. (2020). Türkiye'ye Zorunlu Göçle Gelen Suriyeli Kadınların Haklar Ve Toplumsal Cinsiyet Eşitliği Bağlamındaki Deneyimleri. Hacettepe Üniversitesi Sosyal Bilimler Enstitüsü Sosyoloji Anabilim Dalı, YL, Ankara.

T.C. Sağlık Bakanlığı. (2020). COVID-19 (SARS-CoV-2 Enfeksiyonu) Rehberi. https://covid19bilgi.saglik.gov.tr/depo/rehberler/COVID-19_Rehberi.pdf

Taştan, C.(Ed.). (2020). "Kovid-19 Salgını ve Sonrası Psikolojik ve Sosyolojik Değerlendirmeler". Polis Akademisi Yayınları. Yayın no: 90. Ankara.

Taylor, S. (2019). The psychology of pandemics: Preparing for the next global outbreak of infectious disease . Newcastle upon Tyne: Cambridge Scholars Publishing.

Titan A. (2020). The Impact of COVID-19 on Gender Equality, NBER Working Paper No. 26947, April 2020, Cambridge

Tokyay M. (2020). Rapor: Pandemi sürecinde kadınlar daha da yoksullaşıyor. (24 Mayıs 2020) https://tr.euronews.com/2020/05/24/rapor-pandemi-surecinde-kad-nlardaha- da-yoksullas-yor

UNFPA (2020)." Birleşmiş Milletler Nüfus Fonu, (2020). "Toplumsal Cinsiyet Perspektifinden COVID-19 Cinsel Sağlık, Üreme Sağlığının ve Haklarının Korunması ve Toplumsal Cinsiyet Eşitliğinin Teşvik Edilmesi".

UNFPA. (2020, March). Toplumsal Cinsiyet Perspektifinden Covid-19: Cinsel Sağlık, Üreme Sağlığının ve Haklarının Korunması ve Toplumsal Cinsiyet Eşitliğinin Teşvik Edilmesi. UNFPA: https://www.unfpa.org/sites/default/files/resource-pdf/Turkish_-COVID-19_A_Gender_Lens_Guidance_Note.pdf

United Nations. (2020). A UN framework for the immediate socio-economic response to covid-19. Retrieved 5 August 2020 from: https://www.undp.org/content/undp/en/home/coro-navirus/socio-economic-impact-of-covid-19.html

Ümmet, D. (2007). Üniversite öğrencilerinde sosyal kaygının cinsiyet rolleri ve aile ortamı bağlamında incelenmesi (Yayınlanmamış yüksek lisans tezi), Marmara Üniversitesi.

West C. and D.H. Zimmerman. (1987). Doing gender. Gender and Society. 1 (2). 125-151.

WHO (2020). WHO. https://www.who.int/reproductivehealth/en/

WHO (2020). Rolling updates on coronavirus disease (COVID-19). https://www.who.int/ emergencies/diseases/novel-coronavirus-2019/events-as-they-happen

Yakushko, O. and Chronister, K.M. (2005). Immigrant Women and Counseling: The Invisible Others. Journal of Counseling ve Development, 292-298.

Zhou, Y. and Chen, L. (2020). "Twenty-Year Span Of Global Coronavirus Research Trends: A Bibliometric Analysis". International Journal of Environmental Research and Public Healty. 17, 1-12, doi:10.3390/ijerph17093082.

Ünalp-Çepel, Z. (2020) Neoliberalizmin Kovid-19 Testi ve Avrupa Birliği: Dezavantajlı Gruplar Örneği, Ulisa: Uluslararası Çalışmalar Dergisi, 4, 1, 33-50.

Azcona, G. (2020) "From Insight to Action: Gender Equality in the Wake of Covid-19" UN Women. https://www.unwomen.org/ /media/headquarters/attachments/sections/library/publications/2020/ genderequality-in-the-wake-of-covid-19-en.pdf?la=en&vs=5142

GÖÇ AYDINLANMA SAĞLAR MI? KARŞILAŞMA VE YÜZLEŞME PRATİĞİ OLARAK GÖÇ VE KİMLİĞİN DÖNÜŞÜMÜ

Mehmet Evkuran[1]

Özet

Toplumsal sorunların çözümünde dinden yararlanmak mümkün müdür? Eğer mümkünse nasıl? Dinlerin ve inançların merkezi sayılan Ortadoğu, günümüzde dünyanın en kaotik coğrafyası haline gelmiştir. Savaşlar, istikrarsız yapılar, radikalizm sosyal hayatı çoktandır tehdit etmeye başlamıştır. Bu sürecin en önemli sonuçlarında biri kitlesel göçlerdir. Göç İslam dünyasında kültürel ve politik olduğu kadar dinsel etkileşimi de arttırdı. Üst kimlik olarak İslam'a vurgu yaparak sorunları çözmeye çalışmak bir dereceye kadar yararlı olabilir. Ancak bu yaklaşım kültürel farklılaşmalardan kaynaklanan sorunların çözümünde yetersiz kalacak gibi görünüyor. Bu çalışmada kültür ve kimlik sorunlarının çözümünde din-göç eksenindeki sorunlar tartışılmıştır.

Anahtar Kavramlar: Din, kimlik, göç, dinsel özdeşlikler, kültürel farklılaşmalar, uyum.

Does Immigration Provide Enlightenment?

-Immigration as a Practice of Encounter and Confrontation and Transformation of Identity -

Abstract

Is it possible to benefit from religion for solving social problems? If yes, how? The Middle East, considered the center of religions and beliefs, today it has become the most chaotic geography in the World. Wars, unstable structures, radicalism began to threaten social life. One of the most important results of this process is mass migration. Migration has increased cultural and political as well as religious interaction in the Islamic world. Trying to solve problems with an emphasis on Islam as a supreme identity may be beneficial to some issues. But this approach will be insufficient in solving the problems arising from cultural differentiations. In this study, some problems in the axis of religion-immigration in the solution of culture and identity problems are discussed.

Keywords: Religion, identity, immigration, religious identities, cultural differences, harmony.

Din ve Kimlik Edinme Pratikleri: Dünyanın Karşısında/İçinde/Kenarında Olmak...

Anlam ve değer arayışı, gelişmişlik düzeyi ne olursa olsun düşünce ve duygu (akıl ve arzu da denebilir) varlığı olan insanın vazgeçilmez bir sorunudur. Kimlik tanımlamaları değer ve anlam arayışlarına bağlı süreçlerdir. Kimlikler boşlukta oluşmaz; zaman ve mekân bağlamlarında tanımlanır ve gelişir. Bu nedenle zamanın ve mekânın değişmesi/dönüşmesi ile birlikte, kimlik krizlerinin ortaya çıkması sürecin doğal bir sonucudur. Zaman-mekân ve kimlik ilişkilerindeki sorunları ya da imkânları tetikleyen temel

---

[1] Prof. Dr. Mehmet EVKURAN, Hitit Üniversitesi İlahiyat Fakültesi Çorum/TÜRKİYE.

olgulardan birisi göçtür.

Toplumlar sorunlarını çözmeye çalışırken, tarihlerinde yer alan figürlere yönelik özdeşleştirmelere başvururlar. Özdeşlik, yeni olanın sürpriz yanlarını gidermekte ve yaşanan krizi yabancı olmaktan çıkarmaktadır. Yanı sıra sorunları çözmek için gerekli olan zihinsel saflık, odaklanma, motivasyon ve eyleme geçme gibi unsurları sağlamaktadır. Yaşanan sorun ve sıkıntının yeni bir şeyey olmadığı eskiden bu yana karşılaşılan bilindik bir durum olduğunu algısı, toplumsal iletişimi ve dayanışmayı sağladığı gibi toplumsal-tarihsel kimliği de yeni şartlar bağlamında yeniler ve güçlendirir. Ancak kimliğin izlediği bu yöntemin sıkıntıları da bulunmaktadır. Karşılaşılan sorunları özdeşleşme üzerinden sürekli olarak geriye dönük analojilerle karşılaşma eğilimi, yeni ve farklı olanların gözden kaçırılmasına yol açacaktır. Her olayın kendi biricikliği ve tarihsel tikelliği içinde ele alınması gerekir. İnanca ya da ideolojiye süreklilik kazandırma adına geriye dönük analojilerle dolu bir dünya inşa etmek, hayatın canlı akışının dışında kalmak, reel hayatı zorlamak, radikalizme ve ötekileştirmelere yol açmak gibi sorunlar doğuracaktır.

Müslüman coğrafyanın kendi içinde yaşanan ya da Avrupa ve ABD'ye yönelik göçlerin kendilerine özgü koşulları ve sonuçları vardır. Bu göçler, doğurduğu siyasal, ekonomik ve toplumsal problemlerin dışında daha kökende kimlik ve değerlerle ilgili sorunları tetiklemiştir. Özellikle zamana ve mekâna aşırı bağlı kimlikler bu süreçte daha derin savrulmalar yaşamaktadır.

Dinin dünya kurma işlevi çok yönlü ve çok boyutlu bir süreç olarak çalışır. Din, fizik ile metafizik arasında anlambilimsel ve etik bağlar kurar. Öyle ki dindar bir insan karşısındaki ağacı, dağı, ormanı, hayvanı sadece kendinde bir şey olarak görmez. Öte yandan din, bireyi ve toplumu tarihsel akış içine yerleştirir, onları konumlandırır. Genel olarak tarihe ve tikel olaylara bir anlam ve amaç katar. Dindar bireyler, tikel olayları da, onların tarihselliklerini aşan bir anlam dünyasına yerleştirerek anlamaya çalışırlar. 'Çalışırlar' çünkü Tanrı'nın iradesinin ne olduğu ve hükümlerinin nasıl tecelli edeceği insanlar tarafından tam olarak bilinemez.

Dinin tarihe ve olaylara yüklediği anlamın araştırılması çok yönlü ve boyutlu çalışmaları gerektirmektedir. Ön temel ayrım din kavramının daha özelde ise dinsel inanç kavramının çerçevelenmesinde yatmaktadır. Sosyolojik yaklaşım, gerçek ve sahte inanç ayrımına bakmaksızın tarihsel ve toplumsal hayatta gözlemlediği yaşayan inançları dikkate alır ve dinsel inanç araştırmasını bu zeminde gerçekleştirir. Teolojik yaklaşım ise daha farklı biraz da zorlu bir şey yapmaya çalışır. Dinsel inancı sahihlik kavramı üzerinden temellendirmeye ve temel metinlerde (nasslarda) ve ilk tebliğcinin söyleminde anlatıldığı saf, katışıksız şekliyle imanı tespit etmeye yönelir. Bu yönelim zorluklarla ve problemlerle doludur, çünkü sahih ve saf imanı tespit etmek için pek çok iman şeklinin elenmesi zorunluluğu ile karşılaşılır. Bu tarihsel süreçte dinselleşmiş ve iman olarak tanımlanmış pek çok inancın direncinin harekete geçmesine ve din içinde bir iman ve sahih inanç mücadelesinin başlamasına yol açacaktır.

Problem dinin dünya koruma işlevi ile oldukça yakından bağlantılıdır. Din dünyayı nasıl korur? Hangi dünyayı korur? Kimim dünyasını koruma altına alır? soruları, salt teolojik değildir. Sosyolojik ve politik olarak tanımlanmış farklı dünyalara göndermeler yapar. Açıkçası ortada tek bir dünya yoktur. Her toplumda başta yönetim ve zenginlik olmak üzere sınıfsal bir bölümlenme ve eşitsizlikler söz konusudur. Egemen sınıfın kendi statüsünü korumak ve sürekli kılmak üzere değerlerden yardım aldığı ve dine dayandığı tarihsel bir gerçektir. Öte yandan muhalefet eden ya da pasif bir hayatı tercih eden geriye kalanların da kendilerine göre bir din ve değer anlayışı geliştirdiği ya da bunları kendi konumuna göre algıladığı görülmektedir. Bununla birlikte yönetici ve egemen sınıfın dinden yararlanma ve dini düşünceyi yönlendirme konusunda daha avantajlı olduğu açıktır. Farklı dünyalar arasında kalan dinin hangisinin dili ve meşrulaştırıcısı olduğu, dinin toplumsal işlevini anlamak için temel noktalardan birisidir.

İslam vahyi, vahiy geleneği açısından imanın yenilenmesini, düzeltilmesini ve saflaştırılmasını temsil ediyordu. Denebilir ki İslam, gizemciliğe, kutsallaştırmaya ve aracılığa meydan okuyan söylemiyle dünyada yeni bir dinsel-toplumsal kimliğin önünü açmaktaydı. İslam tarihi de son derece açık, akışkan ve hareketli gelişimi ile toplumsal kimlik üretimi konusunda oldukça verimli bir saha inşa etmiştir. İslamî politik-teolojik kimlikler hala canlıdır ve bu tarihsel dinamizmi günümüz post-modern dünyasına taşımıştır.

Dinin tarihin sonraki aşamalarındaki politik-teolojik gücü ve etkisi özdeşleştirmeler üzerinden gerçekleşir. Geçmişteki bir olay, kişi ya da ilişki teolojik söylemin gücü ile modellenir ve tarih üstü bir figür olarak kodlanır. Ebedî bir temsil başlar ve dinin metafizik ve sosyal gücü bu figürde toplanır. Artık bundan sonra dindar birey ve kitlelere bu temsil yön verir.

Özdeşlik kurmanın kadim dünyadaki en etkin araçları mit, efsane, masal, kıssa, hikâye anlatımlarıdır. Bu anlatıların akışı, rol alan iyi ve kötü figürler, bunlar arasında gerçekleşen olaylar ve sonuç birer arketip oluşturma potansiyeline sahiptir. Böylece anlatıya kulak veren ve kendini kaptıran dinleyici/okuyucu anlam ve değer arayışı konusunda çok temel sorularının cevaplarını bulmuş ve evrendeki ve toplumdaki statüsüne, duruşuna ve eylemlerine bir yön ve içerik kazandırmış olur. Dinî metinlerde anlatılan olaylar da inananlara rol model oluşturan güçlü modellerle özdeşlik kurma ve onların temsil ettiği değer ve davranışları hayatına taşıma imkânı sunar.

Modern dünyada ise bu ihtiyaç kültür ve sanat endüstrisi tarafından karşılanmaktadır. Modern medeniyet hikâye ve kıssa üretme konusunda elindeki tüm araçları kullanmaktadır. Edebiyat ve sanatın kitleler üzerindeki gücü iletişim teknolojilerinin devasa gelişimi ile daha artmıştır. Küresel dünyada internet imkânları kullanılarak, bir dünya görüşü doğrultusunda üretilen hikâye/kıssaların tüm dünyaya dağıtılması da mümkün olmuştur. Kısacası özdeşlik kurulacak model ve figür sayısı ve çeşitlenmesinde paradigmaları zorlayan artış yaşanmaktadır. Küresel dünyanın bir vatandaşı olmak düşüncesi en çok Batı dışı toplumlarda rağbet gören parlak ve çekici bir ideolojiye dönüşmüştür. Göçlerin genellikle Batı ülkelerine yönelik olması ve göçmenlerin gelişmiş bir Batı ülkesinde yaşamlarına devam etmek niyetinde olmaları, bu sürecin sonuçlarından birisidir. Ortaçağda Batı'da anlatılan *Binbir Gece Masalları* edebiyatı tersine dönerek Batı güzellemeleri halini almıştır.

Göç ve kimlikler konusunda yukarıda yer alan tartışma ve değerlendirmelerde işaret edilen sorunların İslam dünyası üzerindeki yansımalarını gözlemlemek mümkündür. Daraltarak ele alırsak özdeşleştirmeler ve temsil; misafir (Yıldız, 122), hicret kavramları üzerinden inşa edilmektedir. Bu çalışmada daha çok son iki kavram üzerinde durulacaktır.

Tarihsel Figürler ve Özdeşliklerin İnşası

Ülkemizde göç olgusu üzerine yapılan çalışmalarda zaman zaman kavramsal benzerlikler üzerinden geçmişte ve günümüzde yaşanan göçler arasında özdeşlikler kurulduğu görülmektedir. En sık karşılaşılan benzeştirme ise hicret ile göç kavramları arasında kurulan bağlantılardır. İslam tarihinde yaşanan ve İslam tarihinin başlangıcı sayılan hicret, ilk Müslüman toplumu için keskin ve radikal bir kırılma noktasıdır. İslam peygamberi önce Müslümanlara göç etmeleri için talimat vermiş ve ardından da kendisi Mekke'yi terk ederek Medine'ye hicret etmiştir. Mekke'de gittikçe çekilmez hale gelen ve zorlaşan hayat şartları nedeniyle bazı Müslümanların, peygamberin tavsiye ve yönlendirmesiyle daha güvenli olduğu düşünülen ve Hristiyan bir kral tarafından yönetilen Habeşistan'a sığındıkları bilinmektedir. Hz. Muhammed de bireysel bir girişim olarak akrabalarının bulunduğu Taif'e bazı umut ve beklentilerle gitmiş ancak sert bir şekilde reddedilmiş kovulmuştur.

Medine'ye yönelik hicret, bu kez daha planlıydı ve önceden gereken stratejik hazırlıklar yapılmıştı.

Nitekim bunun olumlu sonuçları olmuş hicret, Müslümanlara yeni bir dünyanın kapıları açılmıştır. Medine'de gittikçe güçlenen İslam, kısa sürede egemenliğini inşa ederek Arap Yarımadasına sığmayan bir dinî-politik harekete dönüşmüştür.

Hicreti karakterize eden en temel özellik, zulümden adalete, baskıdan özgürlüğe kaçıştır. Kendisinden kaçılan mekâna ve insanlara atfedilen olumsuz değerler etik olduğu kadar teolojiktir. Kur'an'da açıkça ifade edildiği gibi zulüm, şirk, haksızlık dolu bir yerde yaşamak insanı Allah'tan uzaklaştırdığında, yapılması gereken şey her şeyi geride bırakıp daha güvenli ve huzurlu bir yere gitmektir. Mekke'nin zorunlu şartları altında Müslümanların zihninde kaçıp gitmek ve başka bir mekânda inancını yaşamak düşüncesi ilk zorlu sürecin ilk günlerinde belirmiş olduğu tahmin edilebilir. Nitekim başta Yunus ve Nuh peygamberler gibi kendi halklarının azgınca ve ölçüsüzce davranışları karşısında umudunu yitiren ve görev yerini terk etmek isteği duyan bazı peygamberlerin kıssası hatırlatarak, Müslümanlara sabretmeleri ve inançlarını korumaları, sabredenlerin sonunda üstün gelecekleri anlatılmıştır. İlerleyen süreçte inen ayetlerde ise göç-hicretin de bir seçenek olduğu, geçmişte yaşamış bazı inanan gurupların ve kavimlerin (Ashab-ı Kehf, İsrailoğulları vs.) hicretleri anlatılarak Müslümanlar zihinsel olarak hicrete hazırlanmıştır.

İslam tarihçileri hicreti sonuçlarına ve kazanımlarına göre değerlendirmişler ve Mekke'nin terk edilmesini yenilgi, baskıya boyun eğme, davadan vazgeçiş olarak değil geçici bir geri çekilme, gelecek zafer için kendini yenilemek, inancını uygun bir mekânda ve mesaja açık insanlarla yükseltme/güçlendirme, oku daha uzağa ve ileriye atmak için yayı germek olarak değerlendirmişlerdir. Nitekim tarihsel olarak da süreç böyle gerçekleşmiştir. On yıl gibi dinler tarihinde çok kısa sayılabilecek bir sürenin ardından Medine'de güçlenen Müslümanlar Mekke'ye dönerek terk ettikleri vatanlarına muzaffer olarak dönmüşlerdir.

Hz. Peygamberin Medine'ye hicret etmesinin ardından toplumsal ilişkileri ve dengeleri düzenlemeye yönelik çok önemli uygulamaları olmuştur. Bunların başında 'Muahât (kardeşlik)' adı verilen uygulama gelmektedir. Buna göre Mekke'den Medine'ye hicret eden her bir Müslüman Medine'nin yerlisi olan başka bir Müslüman ile kardeş olarak eşleştirilmiştir. Bu uygulama bir yandan tüm mal varlıklarını geride bırakan ve mağdur bir pozisyona düşen Mekke'li Müslümanlara bir destek anlamına gelirken diğer yandan da Medineli Müslümanların yükünü de rasyonel biçimde yaymış ve hafifletmiştir. Böylece göçten kaynaklanan toplumsal ve ekonomik sorunlar en aza indirgenmiştir. Bu uygulama, Mekkeli ve Medineli Müslümanları tanımlamak için de bir kavramsallaşmanın oluşmasına neden olmuştur. Mekkeli Müslümanlar 'muhacir (hicret/göç eden)', Medineli Müslümanlar ise 'ensâr (yardımcılar)' olarak anılmıştır. İslam'ın sonraki tarihlerinde benzer göç ve mağduriyet olayları yalandığında peygamberin bu uygulaması sorunları çözmek için bir model olarak alınmış ve uygulanmıştır. Nitekim günümüzde Irak, Suriye, Afganistan ve diğer Müslüman ülkelerden ya da Bulgaristan gibi Müslümanların azınlık olarak yaşayıp da zulüm gördüğü Batılı ülkelerden ülkemize gelip sığınan insanlara karşı 'muhacir-ensâr' modellemesinden ilham alınarak davranılması gerektiği söylemleri yaygınlaşmıştır.

Muhacir-Ensâr kavramsallaştırmasının kullanılması, İslam dünyasında günümüzde yaşanan göç ve mağduriyet sorunlarının çözümünde kitlelerin desteğini almak açısından önemli bir bakış açısı sunsa da bazı açılardan sorunları dışarıda bırakmaktadır. Anadolu'da şu an yaşayan kitleler tarihsel göçler sonucu oluşmuştur. Göç ve doğurduğu zorlukların gündelik dil, atasözleri, deyişler ve halk müziği üzerinde derin izleri bulunmaktadır. Göç-göçmen sever bir kültür içinde yetişip büyüyen birisi göç eden insanların duygularını anlama konusunda zorluk çekmeyecektir. Bu, Anadolu halkının göçmenlere sıcak ve içten yaklaşmasının temel nedenlerinden biridir. Diğer neden ise İslam dininin ilke ve değerleri ile ilgilidir. Yukarıda sözünü ettiğimiz muhacir-ensâr söylemi ve yardımlaşmanın İslamî ve ahlaki bir görev olarak kodlanmış olması sığınmacılara olumlu ve kucaklayıcı yaklaşmayı sağlamaktadır. Toplum kesimlerinin göçmenlere yardım konusundaki özverisi, devletin üzerindeki yükü hafifletmekte ve sorunların çözümünde büyük kolaylıklar sağlamaktadır.

Bununla birlikte özdeşlikler kurma politikalarının yeterli olmadığı bazı konular ve sorunlar da göze çarpmaktadır. İlk olarak göçlerin yaşandığı ülkeler, uzun süredir etnik, mezhebî ya da kabile çatışmalarının ve siyasî baskıların hüküm sürdüğü bölgelerdir. Sözünü ettiğimiz bu problemli coğrafya yüzyıllardır Müslüman halkların yaşadığı ve İslam ülkesi olarak bilinen ülke topraklarıdır. Dolayısıyla dinsel özdeşlik modeline uymayan ilk nokta, göçlerin yönü ve istikameti sorunudur. Burada bir uyuşmazlık vardır. Ülkelerini terk edenlerin büyük çoğunluğunun Müslüman kimliğini taşıdığı doğrudur. Ancak bu göçmenlerin nihaî arzusu ve hedefi Hristiyan, seküler, laik Batılı ülkelere gitmek ve orada hayatlarına devam etmektir. Bu görüntü, İslam dünyası açısından oldukça acı ve incitici bir tablodur. Göçlerin basit ve açık bir kesinlikle inkârdan İslam'a küfürden imana olduğu söylenemez. Belki ironik olacak ancak kendisinden kaçılan şey İslam olmasa da onu temsil etme iddiasını taşıyan dinî yapı ve zihniyetler olan mezheplerdir. Günümüz İslam dünyası, farklı İslam anlayışları/yorumları ve onları temsil eden siyasî yapılar tarafından domine edilmektedir. Buna bağlı olarak ortaya çıkan çatışmaların ve mağduriyetlerin nedenlerinin araştırılmasında dinî duygu ve düşüncelerin olumsuz etkilerinden de söz edilmesi zorunlu olmaktadır. Nitekim Ortadoğu'daki gelişmeleri anlamak için yapılan çalışmalarda mezhep kimlikleri problemleri öne çıkmaya başlamıştır.

Dinsel özdeşleştirmeler konusundaki ikinci sorun kültürler arasındaki farkların yeterince fark edilememesidir. Buna bağlı olarak kültürel farklılıklardan kaynaklanan sorunların yönetilmesi zorunluluğu temel bir konu olarak ortada durmaktadır. Aynı dine inanmak bir üst çatı oluşturmakta ve kriz dönemlerinde gereken empati, bütünleşme ve yardımlaşmayı sağlamaktadır. Ancak insanlar uzun süreli ilişkilerde kalıcı değerler üretmek zorundadırlar. Bu süreçte kişisel ve grupsal yaşam tarzı, değer algısı ve kültürel kodlar yavaş yavaş etkinleşmeye başlar. Suriye, Irak, Afganistan ve İran'dan gelen geçici sığınmacı ve göçmenler ülkemizde farklı şehirlerde ikamet edilmektedirler. Ülkelerindeki güvenlik sorunları ve kaos devam ettiği için artık kendileri ve çocukları için ülkemizde bir hayat kurmaya çalışmaktadırlar. Eğitim, ticaret, sanat vs. alanlardaki ilişkiler zamanla kültürler arasındaki farklardan kaynaklanan uyuşmazlıklara sahne olmaktadır. Toplumsal hayatta göçmenlerin daha fazla görünür olması iletişimin artması, entegrasyonun gelişmesi ve ortak değerlerin paylaşılması açısından önemlidir ve teşvik edilmesi gereken bir süreçtir. Ancak bu süreçte zaman zaman ortaya çıkan sorunların toplumsal gerilimlere ve hatta göçmen karşıtlığını anımsatan çatışmacı düşüncelere yol açtığı görülmektedir. Bu bağlamda kültürel farklılıklarla ilgili sorunların yönetilmesi konusuna daha yakından ilgi gösterilmesi ve çözüm odaklı politikalar üretilmesi gerekmektedir.

İnsanların kendi kültürlerini bir anda terk etmeleri için ortada hiçbir neden yoktur. Üstelik bir kültür yol olduğunda sadece kendisi değil beslendiği ve içerdiği diğer kültürler imkânlar da yok olmaktadır (Maalouf, 15 vd.). Yapılan bilimsel araştırmalar göçe bağlı kimlik sorunlarını ve bunların klinik yansımalarını ortaya koymaktadır. Buna göre insanların, hastalıklar dışında yaşadıkları bozucu etkilere karşı geliştirdikleri en önemli savunma mekanizmalarından biri kimlik alanında görülmektedir. Bu durumlarla karşı karşıya kalan birey milli, etnik ve dini duygulara daha sıkı bağlanmakta, bu yönlerini sosyal yaşantısında daha çok vurgulamaktadır. Göç söz konusu edildiğinde ise etnik kimlik, yurtdışında ulusal kimliğin önüne geçebilmektedir.

Kültür statik bir yapı değildir. Her kültürün kendine özgü karakteristik özelliklerinden söz edilebilir. Göç eden ya da yer değiştiren bireyler, gittikleri yere kültürlerini de beraberlerinde götürmektedirler (Çağırtkan, 2615). Ancak bu onun değişim geçirdiği gerçeğini örtmemektedir. Göçmenler ile ilgili çalışmalarda kültür sorununu ele alan çok sayıda akademik çalışma yapılmaktadır. Bunlardan bir kısmı özcü ve indirgemeci bir yöntem izleyerek göçmenlere değişmez, sabit ve sert bir kültürel kimlik atfetmekte ve yaşanan sorunları kültürel farklılaşma ve kimlikler arası çatışma kuramlarına göre ele almaktadır. Bunun yanında kültürün esnek ve değişken yönünü dikkate alan ve kültürel geçişleri, dönüşümleri ve melezleşme teorileri ekseninde göçmenlerin kültürel sorunlarına yaklaşan akademik çalışmalar da bulunmaktadır. Yapılan çalışmalarda göçmenlerin ülkemizde yaşarken edindiği sosyal ve kültürel alışkanlıklar ve yaşadığı dönüşümler ortaya konulmaktadır.

Bu çalışmalardan birisinde Suriye'den göç ederek Türkiye'ye yerleşen ve şehirlerimizde yaşamaya başlayan göçmen kadınların davranışları konu edilmiştir. İlke olarak göçmenlerin kendi kültürel kimliğini korumak için bir direnç oluşturdukları ve bu çerçevede yaşadıkları yerel-kültürel hayata dikte etmeye çalıştıkları gözlemlenmiştir. Göçmen kadınlarda görülen kültürel etkileşim sürecinin ise dıştan içe bir hareket ile ilk olarak giyim kuşamdaki değişimler şeklinde kendini gösterdiği ileri sürülmüştür. Kültürel çatışma ortamının oluşmasına sebep olan bu durumun göçmen bireyleri asimilasyon ile kültürel uyum arasında bir yere sürüklediği, iki farklı kültür arasında kalmaktan kültürel uyuma doğru bir dönüşüm sürecini başlattığı sonucuna ulaşılmıştır (Yeter, 100). Çalışmada yapılan görüşmelerde, göçmenlerin içinde yaşadıkları sosyo-kültürel yapıya direnmek yerine uyum gösterme eğiliminde oldukları ve bunun bir göstergesi olarak da genelde evli göçmen kadınların yerel kıyafetleri olan "ferace" yerine, muhafazakâr bir şehir olan Kahramanmaraş'ın dini-sosyal kültürünün "türbanını" simgeleyen "uzun manto" sunu giymeye başladıkları belirtilmiştir (Yeter, 99).

Sonuç

Günümüz küresel dünyasında özgün ve saf kimliklerden söz etmek imkânsız hale gelmiştir. Kültürlerin ve kimliklerin karşılaştığı, karşı karşıya ya ada etkileştiği pratiklerin başlıcalarından biri göçtür. Dünyanın belirli bölgelerinde özellikle Ortadoğu'da bitmek bilmeyen savaş ve kaos nedeniyle, bu ülkelerden çok sayıda insan yurtlarını terk etmek zorunda kalmıştır. Göçler büyük çoğunlukla Batı ülkelerine gerçekleşmektedir.

Türkiye Ortadoğu'da yaşanan zorlukların en büyük yükünü çeken ülkedir. Çok sayıda göçmen ve sığınmacıya kapılarını açmış ve barınma imkânı sağlamıştır. Göçmenlerden Türkiye'yi Batı ülkelerine geçiş yapmak üzere geçici bir sığınma yeri olarak görenlerin yanında hayatını sürdürmek üzere kendi vatanı seçenler de vardır. ikincilerin oranının daha yüksek olduğu söylenebilir.

Şehirlere yerleştirilen göçmenler merkez-çevre kavramlarının yeni boyutlar kazanmasına, çevreyi temsil eden yerli kesimlerin kendi sosyal statülerini ve kimliklerini *merkez* olarak inşa etmelerine neden olmaktadır. Çözülmeye ya da esnemeye başlayan yerel değerlerin göçmenler üzerinden yeniden keşfedilmesi, daha doğrusu yeniden inşa edilme düşüncelerinin güçlendiği de görülmektedir.

Göçmenler arasında yapılan pek çok akademik çalışma kültürel uyum ve ortak değerler inşa etme konusunda eğilimlerin güçlendiğini ortaya koymaktadır. Göçmenleri aşağılamak, dışlamak, kültürel öteki olarak kullanarak yeni ve sert bir politik-kültürel söylem inşa etmeye çalışmak büyük sorunlar doğurabilir. Bunun yanında İslam ortak paydasına vurgu yaparak ve ensar-muhâcir figürlerine dayanarak var olan kültürel farklılıkları görmezden gelmek, toplumsal gerilimlere yol açabilir. Kültürel farklıkları yönetmek için politikalara geliştirmek ve kültürel uyum konusundaki imkânları araştırmak göçmenlerin kimlik sorunlarının sağlıklı şekilde çözülmesi için kaçınılmaz görünmektedir.

Kaynaklar

Çağırtkan, Barış, "Göç, Hibrit Kimlik ve Aidiyet: Yeni Toplumlar, Yeni Kimlikler", *İnsan ve Toplum Bilimleri Araştırmaları Dergisi*, c. 5, sayı 8, 2016, ss. 2613- 2623.

Maalouf, Ameen, *Ölümcül Kimlikler*, Çev. Aysel Bora, 34. Baskı, Yapı kredi Yayınları, İstanbul, 2012.

Yeter, Elife, "Suriyeli Göçmen Kadınların Dini-Kültürel Kimlik Oluşturmalarında Yerel Dini Kültürün Etkisi: Kahramanmaraş Örneği", ANTAKİYAT/Hatay *Mustafa Kemal Üniversitesi İlahiyat Fakültesi Dergisi,* Cilt 1, Sayı 1, 99-126.

Yıldız, Sümeyye; Çakırer-Özservet, Yasemin, "Türkiye Göç Politikalarının Entegrasyon ve Yerel Yönetimler Açısından İncelenmesi", *Ortadoğu'daki Çatışmalar Bağlamında Göç Sorunu* içinde, Ed. Paksoy, H. Mustafa; Yıldırımcı, Elif; Sarıçoban Kazım; Özkan, Ö

SALGIN DÖNEMİNDE UZAKTAN EĞİTİM VE YABANCI UYRUKLU ÖĞRENCİLER
-ÇORUM İL MERKEZİ ÖRNEĞİ-

Yakup Çoştu[1]

Giriş

2020 yılı başından itibaren COVID 19 salgını tüm dünyada hızlı bir şekilde yayılım göstermiş ve başta sağlık alanı olmak üzere ekonomik, sosyal ve kültürel hayatın tüm alanlarında önemli değişim ve dönüşümlerin yaşanmasına neden olmuştur. Günümüzde yaşanan salgının etkilediği alanlarından biri de eğitim alanı olmuştur. Millî Eğitim Bakanlığı, Sağlık Bakanlığının tavsiyeleri doğrultusunda, hastalığın yayılım hızının artma ve yavaşlamasına göre örgün eğitimde birtakım uygulamaları yürürlüğe koymuştur. Bu uygulamaların başında ise, uzaktan eğitim modeli yer almaktadır. Bu model, öğrencilerin zaman ve mekân bağlamında birbirlerinden ve öğrenme kaynaklarından uzak olmayı içermektedir. Çeşitli kitle iletişim imkanları üzerinden yürütülen bu eğitim modelinde, eğitimsel kaynaklara ulaşabilme ya da onlardan yararlanma eşitliğinde ciddi sorunların ortaya çıktığı gözlemlenmiştir. Özellikle, dezavantajlı gruplar bu süreçten en çok etkilenenler olmuştur.

Kendi anavatanlarının dışında azınlık olarak bulunan göçmenlerin, ev sahibi topluma uyum sağlama süreçleri sosyal bilimciler tarafından ele alınan önemli araştırma konuları arasında yer almaktadır. Özellikle, genç kuşak göçmenlerin ev sahibi topluma yönelik sosyal ve kültürel uyumunda, okullaşma ve dil öğrenimi önemli rol oynamaktadır. Eğitim, genç göçmenler için yeni sosyal ortamlara ve hayat şartlarına uyum sağlamanın ve göç sürecinin olumsuz etkilerinden uzaklaşmanın önemli bir aracıdır. Ülke genelindeki yabancı uyruklu göçmen nüfusu dikkate alındığında, Türk eğitim sistemi için göçmen öğrenciler konusu, artık göz ardı edilemez bir gerçek haline dönüşmüştür.

Çorum il genelinde, İçişleri Bakanlığı Göç İdaresi Genel Müdürlüğü'nün yayınladığı istatistiklere göre, 30.06.2021 tarihi itibariye, geçici koruma kapsamında 3.270 Suriyeli bulunmaktadır. İkamet izni ile Çorum'da yaşayan göçmen sayısı 2.222 kişidir. Uluslararası koruma kapsamında yer alan ve uluslararası koruma arayan göçmen sayısı ise 12.000 civarındadır (https://www.goc.gov.tr/). Net olmamakla birlikte Çorum il genelinde yabancı göçmen sayısı 17.000 civarında olduğu tahmin edilmektedir. Çorum il genelinde Milli Eğitim Müdürlüğüne bağlı okullarda (ana sınıfı, ilkokul, ortaokul ve lise) okuyan yabancı uyruklu öğrenci sayısı ise, toplam 3.246'dır (Çorum MEB, Nisan 2021).

Türkiye'de COVID 19 salgını sürecinde örüğün eğitimde uygulanan uzaktan eğitim modelinde ortaya çıkan eşitsizliklerden dezavantajlı gruplar içerisinde yer alan göçmen öğrenciler de etkilenmiştir. Bu çalışmanın temel konusunu, Çorum il merkezinde ikamet eden göçmen toplulukların İl Milli Eğitim Müdürlüğüne bağlı ilkokul, ortaokul ve liselere kayıtlı öğrencilerinin salgın (COVID 19) sürecinde uzaktan eğitimden faydalanma durumlarının tespit edilmesi oluşturmaktadır. Bu kapsamında, uzaktan eğitime katılım, derse devam, ders başarı durumu, okul-öğrenmen-veli irtibatı gibi hususlar eğimde fırsat eşitliği kapsamında betimsel olarak araştırılmıştır. Bahsi geçen konu, araştırmanın çalışma

[1] Prof. Dr. Hitit Üniversitesi İlahiyat Fakültesi, Din Sosyolojisi Anabilim Dalı, Çorum. e-posta: yakupcostu@hitit.edu.tr

grubunu oluşturan Çorum İl Merkezinde yabancı uyruklu öğrencilerin bulunduğu ilkokul, ortaokul ve liselerde görev yapan ve sınıflarında yabancı öğrenci bulunan öğretmenler ve okul idareecileriyle yapılan yarı yapılandırılmış mülakat tekniğiyle elde edilen bulgular üzerinden tartışılmıştır.

Uzaktan Eğitim ve Yabancı Uyruklu Öğrenciler

Bilişim, iletişim ve ulaşım imkanlarının hızla geliştiği küresel dünyamızda, insan hareketlilikleri yanında karşılıklı bağımlılık, tarihsel dönemlere oranla, artmıştır. Bu durum, bir taraftan homojenliği yaygınlaştırırken diğer taraftan da farklılıkların ifade edilebilmesine zemin hazırlamıştır. Artan bağımlılık toplumların etkileşimini yoğunlaştırmış ve benzerliğin yayılımını kolaylaştırmıştır. Diğer taraftan da mevcut teknolojik gelişmeler farklılıkların kendilerini ifade edebilme ve tanıtabilme imkanını artırmıştır. Günümüzün dünyası, söz konusu bu birbirine zıt iki farklı sürecin aynı anda olduğu bir mekân haline dönüşmüştür.

Günümüzde yaşanan hızlı sosyal ve kültürel gelişmeler, eğitim alınında da gözlemlenmektedir. Özellikle eğitim teknolojilerinde -eğitim teknikleri, malzemeleri vb.- ilerlemeler farklı ve alternatif eğitim modellerinin ortaya çıkmasını sağlamıştır. Uzaktan eğitim modelinin gelişimine zemin hazırlayan bu gelişmeler, eğitim alanında farklı bir tecrübenin oluşmasını sağlamıştır.

Klasik/örgün eğitim modelinden farklılaşan uzaktan eğitim modelinde, öğreten/öğretmen ile öğrenen/öğrenci fiziki olarak farklı mekanlarda veya birbirinden uzak bir biçimde bulunmaktadır. Öğretim faaliyeti ise, bilişim teknolojisinin imkanları üzerinden planlanmakta ve yürütülmektedir. Buna göre, uzaktan eğitimde üç unsuru yer almaktadır: i) öğreten, ii) öğrenen ve iii) ortam (Tezcan, 2021).

Uzaktan eğitimin bir unsuru olarak "ortam" kullanılan eğitim teknolojilerini ifade etmektedir. Radyo, televizyon, internet bağlantısı olan bilgisayar, tablet ya da telefon, eğitime konu olan hususlarla ilgili oluşturan metin ve görseller (slayt, video, vb.) teknik unsurlar, uzaktan eğitimin önemli bir parçasını oluşturmaktadır. Bu modeldeki amaç, örgün olarak yürütülemeyen eğitim faaliyetinin bilişim ve iletişim teknolojileri vasıtasıyla yürütülebilmesini ve bireylerin kendi kendine öğrenme kabiliyetlerinin geliştirilmesidir.

Uzaktan eğitim modelinin, iş ve işlemlerin yürütülmesinde sağladığı kolaylıklar yanısıra zamanı iyi kullanma, bireyin kendi kendine öğrenme yetisinin geliştirilmesi, kitle eğitimin daha ucuz ve kolay olması gibi pek çok avantajlı yönleri bulunmaktadır. Bunun yanı sıra, sınırlı toplumsallaşma, teknik araçlara ulaşımdaki zorluk, motivasyon eksikliği gibi dezavantajlı yönleri de bulunmaktadır.

Örgün eğitimden farklı olarak birtakım teknik araç ve gereçler üzerinden yürütülen uzaktan eğitim modelinde en önemli husus, söz konusu bu teknolojik ürünlere sahip olma durumudur. Bu da belli bir maddi imkânı zorunlu kılmaktadır.

Eğitim temel amacının bireyin sosyalleşmesine zemin hazırlayarak kişilik ve kimlik kazanımını sağlamaktır. Bu nedenle eğitimden, tüm vatandaşların eşit bir biçimde faydalanması, eğitim imkanlarına eşit ve adaletli bir şekilde ulaşması beklenmektedir. Eğitimde fırsat eşitliği hususu bu konu üzerine odaklanmaktadır. Fakat, dezavantajlı gruplar olarak ifade edilen kesimler, toplumun geri kalan kesimiyle benzer ve eşit imkanlara sahip olamamaktadır. Örneğin, cinsiyet, ırk, din ve dil ayrımı, siyasal etkenler, nüfusun nicel ve nitel özellikleri, coğrafi (kırsal ve kentsel alandaki eğitim imkanları) olumsuzluklar, gelir dağılımındaki eşitsizlikler gibi hususlarda eğitimde fırsat eşitsizliğini besleyen hususlardır.

Dezavantajlı gruplar içerisinde yer alan çoğunluk toplum içerisinde azınlık olarak yaşayan göç unsuru topluluklar da eğitime ulaşma, yaralanma, eğitim teknolojilerine sahip olma gibi hususlarda birtakım eşitsizliklerle karşı karşıya kalabilmektedirler. Bu grupların çoğunlukla ekonomik yetersizlikleri, alt sosyo-kültürel tabakalara aidiyetleri, eğitime ulaşmada ciddi sorunları barındırmaktadır.

Çalışmanın bu kısmında Çorum İl merkezinde yerleşik çoğunluğu Iraklı ve Suriyeli yabancı uyruklu göçmenlerin okul çağındaki çocuklarının, uzaktan eğitimden yararlanma durumlarına değinilecektir.

Tablo 1. Eğitim-Öğretim Yılına Göre Çorum İl Geneli Yabancı Öğrenci Dağılımı

Eğitim Öğretim Yılı	Ana Sınıfı / İlkokul	Ortaokul	Lise	Genel Toplam
2020/2021	1657 %51,04	1288 %39,67	301 %9,27	3246 %100
2019/2020	1803 %53,44	1075 %31,86	350 %10,37	3374 %100
2018/2019	1820 %54,22	1078 %32,11	329 %9,80	3357 %100
2017/2018	1560 %56,09	834 %29,99	284 %10,21	2781 %100
2016/2017	906 %56,63	478 %29,88	161 %10,06	1600 %100

(Çorum Milli Eğitim Müdürlüğü, Nisan 2021)

Tablo 1'de Çorum il i genelinde eğitim-öğretime devam eden yabancı uyruklu öğrencilerin sayıları yer almaktadır. Yabancı öğrencilerin okullaşma oranı yıllara göre değiştiği görülmektedir. Çorum İl genelinde yerleşik yabancı göçmenlerin okul çağındaki kayıtlı çocukların sayısı, toplam göçmen nüfusunun %20'sini aşkındır. 2011 yılından itibaren Çorum'da yerleşik olan göçmen nüfusu yeni doğanlarla her geçen gün daha da artmaktadır. Bu nedenle, genç göçmenlerin yerleşik topluma uyum süreçlerinde okullaşma oranı son derece önem arz etmektedir. Dezavantajlı gruplar içerisinde yer alan bu kesimin, eğitim sistemi içerisine dahil edilmeleri, onlara verilen dil öğretimi başta olmak üzere, sosyal, kültürel eğitsel destekler göçmen çocukların yaşadıkları topluma uyumunu kolaylaştırmaktadır.

Tablo 2. Çorum İl Geneli Cinsiyete Göre Yabancı Öğrenci

Cinsiyet	İlkokul	Ortaokul	Lise	Toplam
Kız	823 %53,41	486 %31,54	178 %11,55	1541 % 00
Erkek	906 %50,31	648 %5,98	177 %9,83	1801 %100
Toplam	1729 %51,74	1134 %33,93	355 %10,62	3342 %100

(Çorum Milli Eğitim Müdürlüğü, Şubat 2019)

Yukarıda tablo 2'de ise, Şubat 2019 tarihi itibariyle Çorum il genelinde eğitim gören yabancı uyruklu öğrencilerin cinsiyete göre dağılımı yer almaktadır. Buna göre, kız öğrencilerin erkek öğrencilere oranla daha fazla eğitim kademelerinde yer aldığı görülmektedir. Ortaokul ve lise kademelerinde erkek öğrencilerin sayısal azlığı, bu öğrencilerin eğitim alma yerine ekonomik aktivite içerisinde bulunmalarından kaynaklandığı düşünülmektedir. Çorum il merkezi genelinde, okul çağında (ortaokul ve lise) olması beklenen genç/ergen yabancı erkek göçmenlerin çeşitli hizmet alanlarında yoğun olarak çalıştığı gözlemlenmektedir.

Tablo 3. Çorum İl Geneli Ana Sınıf ve İlkokula Kayıtlı Yabancı Öğrenci Dağılımı

	Ana Sınıf	1. Sınıf	2. Sınıf	3. Sınıf	4.Sınıf
Çorum İl Merkezi	55 %66,26	299 %87,94	355 %87,43	374 %87,38	364 %91
İlçeler	28 %33,73	41 %12,05	51 %12,56	54 %12,61	36 %9
Toplam	83 %100	340 %100	406 %100	428 %100	400 %100

(Çorum Milli Eğitim Müdürlüğü, Nisan 2021)

Tablo 3'te Çorum il geneli ana sınıfı ve ilkokullarda kayıtlı yabancı uyruklu öğrenci dağılımı yer almaktadır. İlçelerde (İskilip, Bayat, Alaca, Sungurlu, Mecitözü) de yadsınamayacak oranda yabancı öğrencinin kayıtlı olduğu görülmektedir. Diğer eğitim kademeleri verilerine bakıldığında (Tablo 4, 5) ana sınıfı ve ilk okulda kayıtlı yabancı uyruklu öğrenci sayısı yüksektir.

Tablo 4. Çorum İl Geneli Ortaokula Kayıtlı Yabancı Öğrenci Dağılımı

	5. Sınıf	6. Sınıf	7. Sınıf	8. Sınıf
Çorum İl Merkezi	418 %93,09	340 %92,89	261 %94,56	192 %97,46
İlçeler	31 %6,90	26 %7,10	15 %5,43	5 %2,53
Toplam	449 %100	366 %100	276 %100	197 %100

(Çorum Milli Eğitim Müdürlüğü, Nisan 2021)

Tablo 4'te Çorum il geneli ortaokullarda kayıtlı yabancı uyruklu öğrenci dağılımı yer almaktadır. Aşağıdaki Tablo 5'te de Çorum il geneli Liselerde kayıtlı yabancı uyruklu öğrenci dağılımı yer almaktadır. Her iki tabloda da görüldüğü üzere, eğitim kademlerinde sınıflar ilerledikçe öğrenci sayıları azalmaktadır. Sınıfların ilerlemesine paralel bir biçimde genç/ergen öğrencilerin okullaşma oranlarının azaldığı görülmektedir. Bu durum, eğitim alması beklenen öğrencilerin, daha çok kayıt dışı ekonomik aktiviteye yönelmeleriyle açıklanabilir.

Tablo 3, 4 ve 5'de de görüldüğü üzere Çorum il geneli yabancı öğrenci okullaşma oranları eğitim kademleriyle paralel bir biçimde düşmektedir. Yine, örgün eğitim yapılan dönemde, Mayıs 2019 tarihi itibariyle, yabancı uyruklu öğrencilerin okula devam/sürekli devamsızlık dağılımlarında, tüm eğitim kademelerinde söz konusu öğrencilerin yaklaşık yarısının sürekli devamsız olduğu tespit edilmiştir (Çoştu, Yılmaz ve Bulut, 2020). Örgün eğitim sırasında okullaşma oranındaki düşüş, başka bir ifadeyle okula devam /dersleri düzenli takip etmeme durumu, uzaktan eğitime geçilen 2019-2020 bahar dönemi ile 2020-2021 güz ve bahar dönemlerinde daha da fazla yaşanmıştır. İl Milli Eğitim Müdürlüğü yetkilileriyle (Suriyeli Çocukların Türk Eğitim Sistemine Entegrasyonunun Desteklenmesi Projesi (PIKTES) yetkilileri) yaptığımız görüşmede, uzaktan eğitimin modelinin gerçekleştirildiği dönemlerde yerli öğrencilerin bu modele katılım oranı %70 civarında iken, Çorum İl genelinde okullarda kayıtlı toplam yabancı uyruklu öğrencilerin yaklaşık %10'nunun uzaktan eğitimden istifade ettiği belirtilmiştir.

Tablo 5. Çorum İl Geneli Liseye Kayıtlı Yabancı Öğrenci Dağılımı

	9. Sınıf	10. Sınıf	11. Sınıf	12. Sınıf
Çorum İl Merkezi	118 %97,52	102 %99,02	41 %97,61	35 %100
İlçeler	3 %2,47	1 %0,97	1 %2,38	-
Toplam	121 %100	103 %100	42 %100	35 %100

(Çorum Milli Eğitim Müdürlüğü, Nisan 2021)

Yabancı uyruklu öğrencilerin uzaktan eğitime katılım düzeyi, derse devam durumu, ders başarı durumu, okul-öğrenmen-veli irtibatı gibi hususlarla ilgili olarak, ilkokul, ortaokul ve lise kademesinde görev yapan ve sınıfında yabancı öğrenci bulunan sekiz (8) öğretmen ve dört (4) okul idareciyle 15-28 Mayıs 2021 tarihlerinde yapılan görüşmeler -pandemi şartların nedeniyle telefon yoluyla- gerçekleştirilmiştir. Elde edilen bulgular çokluk ve sıklık değişkenine göre aşağıda sınıflandırılmıştır:

Ekonomik yetersizliğe bağlı eğitim teknolojilerine ulaşmadaki eksiklik

Uzaktan eğitim, 'dijital uçurumun' ve 'eşitsizliğin' büyümesine neden olmuştur. Bu durum hem yerli hem de göçmen ailelerin çocuklarının eğitime erişmelerini zorlaştırmıştır. Alt sosyo-ekonomik tabakada yer alan ailelerin çocuklarının televizyon, bilgisayar, tablet, akıllı telefon ve internet bağlantısı gibi modern eğitim teknolojilerine erişimdeki yetersizlikleri, onların uzaktan eğitme katılımını sınırlandırmıştır. Göçmen ailelerin içerisinde bulundukları ekonomik yetersizlikler, uzaktan eğitimin yapıldığı dönemlerde çocuklarının okul derslerine devam etme oranlarının, örgün eğitim dönemine göre, daha düşük olmasına neden olmuştur. Sınıfında kayıtlı yabancı öğrenci bulunan öğretmenlerin ifadelerine göre, her on yabancı uyruklu öğrenciden en fazla 4 ya da 5 tanesi uzaktan eğitime katılmıştır. Sürecin uzamasına paralel bu sayı azalmıştır. Bu duruma daha çok dijital uçurum neden gösterilmiştir.

Ailelerin çocukların eğitimine yönelik ilgisizlikleri

Çalışma grubuyla yapılan görüşmelerdeki bulgulardan çokluk ve sıklık değişkenine göre, ikinci sırada göçmen ailelerin çocuklarının okullaşma konusundaki ilgisizlikleri olarak ifade edilmiştir. Çorum il genelindeki yabancı göçmenlerin çoğunluğunun uluslararası koruma (genellikle Irak kökenli), bir kısmının da geçici koruma (Suriyeli) statüsünde olduğu bilinmektedir. Okul öğretmenleri ve okul idarecilerinin beyanlarına göre, bu göçmen topluluklarının her iki kesiminin, çocuklarının okula devamının ve böylece eğitim almalarının sağlanması hususunda ilgisiz oldukları görülmektedir. Buna çoğunlukla, ailelerin öncelik sıralamalarının etkili olduğu belirtilmiştir. Özellikle daha alt sosyo-ekonomik tabakadan göçmen ailelerin, daha çok geçim ve yaşam mücadelesi, onların çocuklarının eğitimlerinin önüne geçmektedir. Öte yandan, göçmen aile bireylerinin Türkçe dil yetersizlikleri hem okul-aile irtibatında, hem de EBA TV etkinliklerinin yürütülmesinde kısıtlayıcı rol oynamıştır.

Bir evde çeşitli eğitim kademelerine kayıtlı birden fazla öğrencinin olması

Evdeki okul çağındaki öğrenci sayısının fazlalığı, eğitim teknolojilerine ulaşmada kısıtlayıcı bir rol oynamaktadır. Bu da çoğunlukla daha küçük yaştakilerin uzaktan eğitime katılımına imkan verirken, ileri yaştakilerin eğitimden kopmasına ve başka (özellikle ev içi emeğe katkı sağmamak amaçlı) alanlara yönelmelerine neden olmaktadır.

Pandemi sürecindeki ekonomik gelir kaybının, okul çağındaki genç/ergen göçmenleri hane bütçesine katkı sağmamaya yöneltmesi

Çalışma grubumuza (özellikle okul idarecileri) katılanlar tarafından, erkek ergen/gençlerin hane ekonomisine katkı amaçlı çeşitli iş alanlarına, kızlarında ev içi işlere yönelmeleri uzaktan eğitime katılımı olumsuz etkilediği ifade edilmiştir.

Pandemi/karantina koşullarının göç öncesi travmayı hatırlatması, öğrencilerin derse devam/uzaktan eğitime katılım oranlarını etkilemiştir

Katılımcılarca, pandemi koşullarının bazı göçmen aile çocuklarının göç öncesi ve göç sırasında yaşadıkları olumsuz travmaları hatırlatması ya da yeniden canlanmasına neden olduğu, bununda uzaktan eğitime katılımı olumsuz etkilediği belirtilmiştir.

Sonuç

Pandemi (COVİD 19 salgını) dünya genelinde olduğu gibi Türkiye'de de, toplumsal alanın tüm kesimlerinde daha önce tecrübe edilmeyen yeni ve benzersiz durumları ortaya çıkartmıştır. Eğitim alanında ise, insanların daha önce pek gündeminde olmayan ama kendi içerisinde teknolojik imkanlara bağlı olarak hızlı gelişim gösteren uzaktan eğitim modelinin yaygınlaşması söz konusu olmuştur. Bu model bünyesinde, birtakım avantajları ve dezavantajları barındırmaktadır. Özellikle eğitim teknolojilerinin hızla gelişmesi ve modern eğitim materyallerinin çeşitlenmesi uzaktan eğitimim daha fonksiyonel yapılabilmesini sağlamıştır. Fakat, modern uzaktan eğitim teknolojilerine sahip olup olmama durumu ise, eğitimde fırsat eşitliği konusunda yeni bir tartışmayı da gündeme getirmiştir.

Pandemi sürecinde MEB, Türkiye genelinde çoğunlukla uzaktan eğitim modeliyle eğitim faaliyetlerini sürdürmüştür. Bu amaçla, özellikle EBA TV üzerinden ders anlatımları gerçekleştirilmiştir. Ayrıca öğretmenler de farklı uzaktan eğitim araçları üzerinden ders anlatımı, ders aktiviteleri, ders ödevlendirmesi gibi çeşitli eğitsel faaliyetleri yürütmüşlerdir. Uzaktan eğitim sürecinin yürütüldüğü zaman dilimlerinde, bu eğitim modeline dahil olma ve dersleri takip etme tüm öğrenciler için geçerli bir durumdur. Fakat bu süreç, dezavantajlı gruplar için birtakım eşitsizliklerin gün yüzüne çıkmasına neden olmuştur Dezavantajlı gruplar içerisinde yer alan yabancı uyruklu öğrenciler de bu eşitsizlikten son derece etkilenmişlerdir.

Çalışma gurubunuzdan elde edilen bulgular çerçevesinde uzaktan eğitimin yürütüldüğü bu süreçte yabancı uyruklu öğrencilerin;

- Eğitim teknolojilerine ulaşamama/sahip olmama durumu, onların uzaktan eğitime katılımını sınırlandırmıştır.

- Akademik başarısı iyi olan yabancı uyruklu öğrenciler, uzaktan eğitim uzamasına bağlı olarak (bu eğitim modelin verimsiz bulunması, devam mecburiyetinin olmayışı, öğrenciler mağdur olmasın diye ilk dönemde -2019-2020 bahar dönemi- yüksek notların verilmesi gibi) süreç içerisinde eğitimden kopmuşlar ya da ayrılmışlardır.

- Genç/ergen erkek öğrenciler hane bütçesine katkı amaçlı ekonomik aktiviteye yönelmişler, kızlarda ev içi işlerle meşgul olmayı tercih etmişlerdir.

- Türkçe dil öğrenimini yavaşlatmıştır.

- Türk öğrencilerle olan temas zayıflatmış ve sosyalleşme kanalları değişmiştir.

Bu sonuçlar çerçevesinde son olarak şunlar söylenebilir: Eğitime ara verme, eğitimden kopma ya da uzaklaşma, yabancı uyruklu öğrencilerin yaşadıkları topluma uyum sağlamaları açısından bir risk oluşturacaktır. Bu risk ilerleyen zamanlarda, yabancılaşma, akabinde toplumsal dışlanma ve marjinalleşmeyle sonuçlanabilecek toplumsal süreçlere zemin oluşturabilecektir. Olağan dışı dönemlerde de olsa, eğitim çağındaki bireyleri eğitim dairesi içerisinde tutmanın alternatif yollarının aranması önem arz etmektedir. Bu durum eğitimde fırsat eşitliği kapsamında tüm öğrenciler için aynı geçerliktedir. Azınlık olarak yaşayan toplulukların, çoğunluk toplum içerisindeki sürekilikleri, genç nesillerinin eğitim sistemine entegre olabilmeleriyle doğru orantılıdır.

Kaynakça

Tezcan, M. (2021), Eğitim Sosyolojisinde Güncel ve Çeşitli Konular, Ankara: Pegem akademi

Çoştu, Y., Yılmaz, M., Bulut, İ. (2020). "İlköğretim ve Orta Öğretim Yöneticileri ile Öğretmenlerinin Yabancı Uyruklu Öğrencilere Yönelik Tutumları: Çorum İl Merkezi Örneği", *The Migration Conference 2020 Proceedings Migration and Integration*, London: TPLondon, 65-72. https://www.goc.gov.tr/

ANTI-IMMIGRANT NARRATIVES IN TIMES OF REAL CRISIS. AN AUTOMATED CONTENT ANALYSIS OF ITALIAN POLITICAL COMMUNICATION ON SOCIAL MEDIA

Anita Gottlob and Luca Serafini

In this paper, we explore how the narrative on immigration changes when society is threatened by 'real' risks, i.e., during the COVID-19 health crisis. We compared the salience and engagement of posts published on Facebook between December 2019 and November 2020 by politicians and by the Italian news media; post selection used a dictionary related to immigration. Along with prior research on anti-immigration narratives, we also operationalized risk narratives on immigration by constructing a second dictionary for post selection. Our findings suggest that the political discourse and risk narratives on immigration decreased during times of 'tangible crisis' for right-wing populist parties and news media.

Introduction

The strongest discourses against immigration are linked to widely accepted social myths in media and public sentiment portraying immigrants, and irregular migrants, as a threat to nations in general, or as a challenge over resource competition, personal safety, or social values (Chouliaraki & Zaborowski, 2017). Far right and right-wing populist (RWP) parties operates by fuelling this uncertainty by exaggerating possible risks of immigration to host nations, while promising their voters a resolution from this uncertainty, thereby portraying themselves as the sole representatives of ordinary people's interests in opposition with political issues which threaten national identities (e.g., immigration) (Gründl & Aichholzer, 2020; Heinisch, 2019; Heisbourg, 2015).

In this context, social media has been found to be particularly suitable to the communication of populist actors, as it relies on a direct communication to voters without institutional mediation (Ernst et al., 2017; Gerbaudo, 2014). Furthermore, misperceptions on immigration can be further amplified: algorithms of platforms such as Google and Facebook filter content for audiences based on the principle of "personalization" (Pariser, 2011). The selective exposure, enhanced by the filtering mechanisms of the algorithms, and the consequent formation of "echo chambers" (Sunstein, 2017), determine a progressive polarization of the positions within niches that are not communicating with each other.

In this paper, we explore how the representation of migrants and the discussion on the topic of migration can change in political communication and online news media, when the host-society is occupied with managing 'real' risks, such as that of Covid-19. Specifically, we aim to understand whether the communication on migration from far right and populist parties, such as the Lega and Fratelli d'Italia, and the 5 Star movement (Mosca & Tronconi, 2019; Rodujiin, 2019) changes (in terms of salience and risk language) on social media, during times of 'tangible crisis'.

Literature review

In public and political discourse, the topic of migration is often referred to as a crisis (e.g., the 'refugee crisis of 2015') as well as the COVID-19 pandemic of 2021. Crises are defined in scientific literature as 'exceptional events that may interrupt journalistic routines and create opportunities for newly emerging aspects and interpretation of an issue' (Horsti, 2008). The discursive construction of a crisis is highly linked to the concept of risk (Hier & Greenberg, 2002). A vast body of literature shows that the public concern over immigration is often influenced by mediatized accounts of migrants and refugees as a risk to society, regardless of statistical accuracy (De Rosa et al., 2021; Caricati, 2018; Sniderman et al., 2004). In this work, we consider risks associated to migration as a 'constructed' or perceived risk (Slovic, 2004).

In contrast, the risk stemming from the COVID-19 pandemic is mediatized in more concrete terms, as statistics of daily new hospitalizations and deaths are available and visible. Consequentially, for our analysis, we identified two distinct periods in which the number of cases of COVID-19 was particularly high in comparison to other periods in Italy. We labelled these two periods 'waves of tangible crises', to represent two periods in which presumably the risk stemming from COVID-19 was strongly perceived (and real) by the Italian population.

Data and Methods

We performed an automated content analysis based on a dictionary approach, to compare the salience and engagement on posts related to migration by Italian media and politicians on Facebook during the first and second wave of COVID-19 infections in Italy over a period of almost 12 months, from December 1st, 2019, to the 15th of November 2020. Here, we compared our observations between the above-mentioned 'waves of tangible crises', of high infections rates to pre-and post-wave periods (of low infection rates). Our sample included a total of 276.809 posts of four Facebook pages of media outlets, and 71.875 posts on eight Facebook pages of political parties.

In a second step, we operationalized risk-related terms on migration by constructing a 'risk- and threat dictionary' in line with prior research on anti-immigration narratives in the media and on social media (Maltone-Bonnenfant, 2011; Milkowska-Samul, 2018). We also performed a manual content analysis to cross-validate for false negatives, and to see in what context these terms were used. Finally, we measured how engagement levels on the analysed posts by political leaders and mainstream media sites online developed over time.

Results and Discussion

The findings indicate that on average, during the two periods of high COVID-19 infection rates (tangible crisis), posts on migration by far right and populists' politicians decrease by a remarkable amount (first wave: -35% for LEGA, -28% for FDI and -82% for M5S. Second wave: -34% for LEGA, -31% for FDI and -65% for M5S) compared to periods of lower infection rates (see figure 1). A similar trend is visible for engagement levels of online users with the same pages, suggesting that the political discourse on migration as well as the exposure to the topic for Facebook Italian users decreased during those periods. In contrast, center-left parties exhibit much less variation during all phases. Therefore, the narrative of these parties on the issue of migration does not seem to be affected by the COVID crisis. The trend of right and far-right newspapers mirrors that of right-wing politicians, with significant drops (albeit less marked than those of politicians) both in the number of posts and engagement during the first and second wave, and a strong rise between these two phases, when the number of COVID-19 cases in Italy had dropped (see figure 2).

Results also show a decreasing trend in risk-related migration posts and engagement activity relative to all migration-related narratives is visible during both waves for all the analyzed posts, with a subsequent increasing trend after the first lockdown phase. In the manual analysis, we observed that as expected, left-wing politicians cited/paraphrased risk-related terms to criticize anti-immigration claims and opinions of far-right politicians condemning way.

Figure 1.

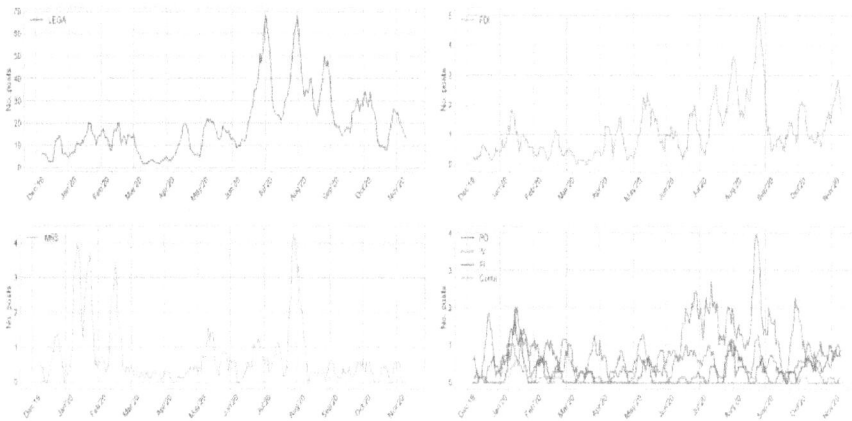

Figure 2.

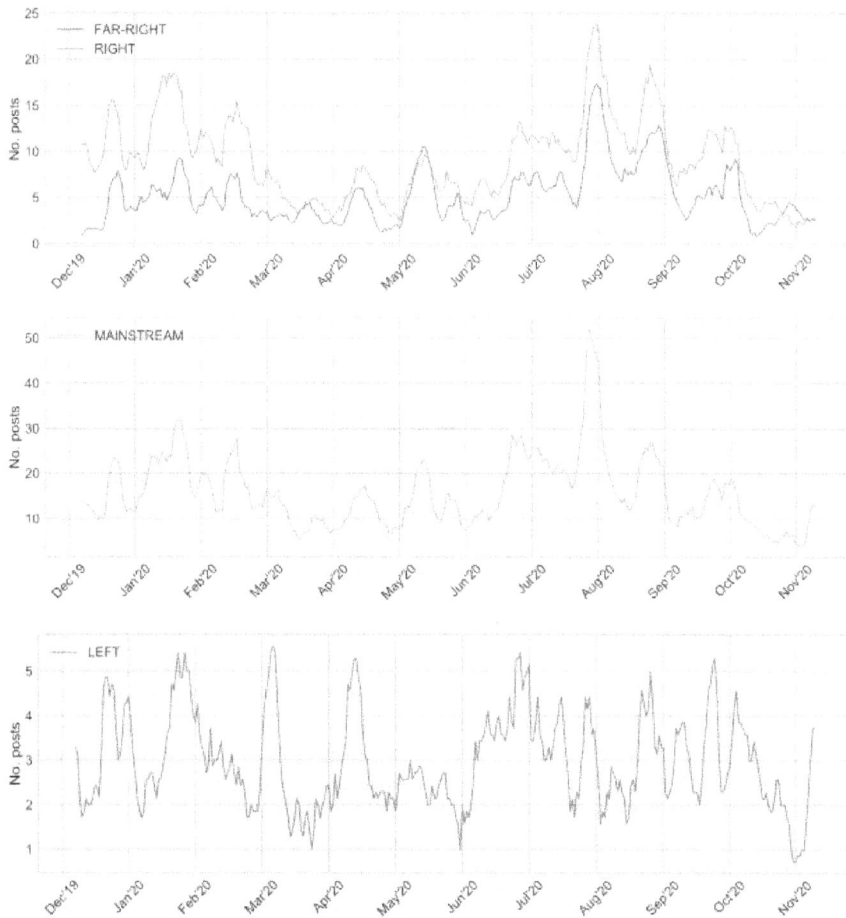

Notably, during the first wave, the Italian government proposed a law for the regularization of 600,000 immigrants, which was then approved in May 2020. Under normal conditions, such a law would have raised a wave of protests from right-wing parties and would have produced a spike in immigration-related posts. Subsequently, towards the end of the first wave up until August 2020, the salience of the migration topic, as well as migration posts including risk and threat terms, increased by a considerable amount in RWP politicians. During this period, in Italy the virus had almost disappeared, with an average of 100-200 daily infections (unlike many other European countries where infections were more numerous). Therefore, we postulate that when the virus was no longer an "internal" threat to the country, the narrative of the virus as an "external threat" brought by immigrants regained strength, similarly to what happened in the period preceding the first wave. For example, in the months between May and August 2020, there were cases of migrants tested positive to COVID-19 who arrived in Italy on NGO ships: right-wing leaders such as Matteo Salvini and Giorgia Meloni posted on these events almost daily and stressed that there was a concrete danger of NGOs and boats with immigrants bringing the virus back to Italy.

Altogether, the findings suggest that, in the short-term, the political discourse on migration as well as the exposure to the topic for Facebook Italian users decreased in times of tangible crisis. Crucially, this happened also at a time when key policies regarding immigration and regularization of migrants were discussed and decided by the Italian government, receiving unexpectedly low reactions.

Conclusion

In conclusion, considering the implications that the infodemic, misinformation and conspiracy theories surrounding COVID-19 on social media has for trust in governing institutions (Boberg et al., 2020), decreased focus on anti-immigration narratives within RWP rhetoric might be replaced by other characteristic features of populist communication (for details on populist communication see Aalberg et al., 2918). For instance, a recent study by Eberl, Huber & Greussing (2020) shows that the COVID-19 pandemic provides fertile ground for populists' opposition to scientific and political elites. An interesting question for further research would thus be to investigate whether in times of tangible crises, anti-immigration narratives in RWP rhetoric observed in our results are replaced by antagonism to scientific and political elites.

References

Aalberg, T., Esser, F., Reinemann, C., Strömbäck, J., & Vreese, C. H. de. (2018). Populist Political Communication in Europe.

Boberg, S., Quandt, T., Schatto-Eckrodt, T., & Frischlich, L. (2020). Pandemic populism: Facebook pages of alternative news media and the corona crisis--A computational content analysis. arXiv preprint arXiv:2004.02566.

Caricati, L. (2018). Perceived threat mediates the relationship between national identification and support for immigrant exclusion: A Cross-National Test of Intergroup Threat Theory. International Journal of Intercultural Relations, 66, 41–51.

Chouliaraki, L., & Zaborowski, R. (2017). Voice and community in the 2015 refugee crisis: A content analysis of news coverage in eight European countries. International Communication Gazette, 79(6-7), 613-635.

De Rosa, A. S., Bocci, E., Bonito, M., & Salvati, M. (2021). Twitter as social media arena for polarised social representations about the (im) migration: The controversial discourse in the Italian and international political frame. Migration Studies.

Ernst, N., Engesser, S., Büchel, F., Blassnig, S., & Esser, F. (2017). Extreme parties and populism: An analysis of Facebook and Twitter across six countries. Information, Communication & Society, 20(9), doi: 10.1080/1369118X.2017.1329333

Eberl, J. M., Huber, R. A., & Greussing, E. (2020). From Populism to the 'Plandemic': Why populists believe in COVID-19 conspiracies.

Gerbaudo, P. (2014). Populism 2.0: Social media activism, the generic internet user and interactive direct democracy. In Social Media, Politics and the State: Protests, Revolutions, Riots, Crime and Policing in the Age of Facebook, Twitter and YouTube (pp. 67-87). Taylor and Francis. DOI: 10.4324/9781315764832

Gründl, J., & Aichholzer, J. (2020). Support for the Populist Radical Right: Between Uncertainty Avoidance and Risky Choice. Political Psychology, 41(4), 641–659.

Heisbourg, F. (2015). The strategic implications of the Syrian refugee crisis. Survival, 57(6), 7-20.

Heinisch, R. K., Massetti, E., & Mazzoleni, O. (2019). The People and the Nation: Populism and Ethno-Territorial Politics in Europe. In Betz, Hans-Georg; Habersack, Fabian (2019). Regional nativism in East Germany: the case of the AfD. In: Heinisch, Reinhard; Massetti, Emanuele; Mazzoleni, Oscar. The people and the nation: populism and ethno-territorial politics in Europe. Abingdon: Taylor & Francis Group, 110-135. (pp. 110–135).

Hier, S. P., & Greenberg, J. L. (2002). Constructing a discursive crisis: Risk, problematization and illegal Chinese in Canada. Ethnic and racial studies, 25(3), 490-513.

Horsti, K. (2008). Europeanisation of public debate: Swedish and Finnish news on African migration to Spain. Javnost-the public, 15(4), 41-53.

Maltone-Bonnenfant, C. (2011). L'immigrazione nei media italiani. Disinformazione, stereotipi e innovazioni. Line@ editoriale, (3), 62-78.

Mosca, L., & Tronconi, F. (2019). Beyond left and right: the eclectic populism of the Five Star Movement. West European Politics, 42(6), 1258-1283.

Pariser E. (2011). The Filter Bubble. New York, Penguin Press.

Slovic, P., Finucane, M. L., Peters, E., & MacGregor, D. G. (2004). Risk as analysis and risk as feelings: Some thoughts about affect, reason, risk, and rationality. Risk Analysis: An International Journal, 24(2), 311-322.

Sniderman, P. M., Hagendoorn, L., & Prior, M. (2004). Predisposing factors and situational triggers: Exclusionary reactions to immigrant minorities. American political science review, 98(1), 35-49.

Sunstein, C. (2017). #Republic. Divided Democracy in the Age of Social Media. Princeton, Princeton University Press

FROM HERE TO THE BORDER, I'M MEXICAN, AND FROM THE BORDER OVER THERE I'M AMERICAN: A LOOK INSIDE RETURN MIGRATION AND ITS COMPLEXITIES

Irasema Mora-Pablo and M. Martha Lengeling

Introduction

Mexico and the United States have a long history of two bordering countries living together and separately. Within Mexico, Guanajuato is the third state which has the most returnees coming back to Mexico (INEGI, 2010). This movement of people between the two countries has its pros and cons. In the University of Guanajuato, a large public university, we have seen this influx of return migration in our student population of BA in English language teaching (ELT). These young people are multicultural, and they have come back to Mexico with a substantial range of knowledge, practices, as well as linguistic and cultural experiences. Yet their return is not always easy for them, and they find a place within our BA as a way to fit themselves within Mexico. They are often seen as an outsider in their own native country and may even experience negativity when coming back.

In this article we explore this phenomenon of our BA students' challenges they have encountered when coming back, the constructed discourses that mark their presence, and what the consequences they have regarding their identity development in Mexico. These students have returned from different parts of the United States due to illegal status in the US, family issues, or their migratory status. Their English is a linguistic capital which helps them to enter our BA in ELT, yet their use of Spanish is often seen as deficit by Mexicans.

From the analysis of the data, we found that these returnees go through a complex identity development which changes depending on where they are, and how their identity is influenced by their past, present, and possible future (Norton, 2013). When they come back to Mexico, they experience challenges of inserting themselves within society and specifically in our BA. They often feel doubt regarding who they are and their use of languages: English and Spanish. Their identity is influenced by what they experienced in the United States and their experiences as Mexicans. The phrase *ni de aquí ni allá* (neither from here nor from there) is often used to isolate these transnationals and describe how they have identity issues in both countries. One may see that their identity is a mixture of a variety of languages, educational experiences, and cultural practices which cause problems of how they are viewed as complex individuals who are often rejected in both countries.

Mexico and the US: A complex history of migration

Mexico and the US have a long and complex history of migration which has evolved over time (FitzGerald 2016). Lately, between 2009 and 2016, 2.2 million Mexicans were deported and an additional 1.4 million returned voluntarily (Fundación Bancomer BBVA, 2018). Hazán (2014) points out that between 2005 and 2014, nearly 2.4 million people who had spent most of their lives in the US returned to Mexico for a variety of reasons. Most of these were US born children or Mexican young adults who were taken by their families at an early age, had received education in the US and had visited Mexico on a few occasions or none. We identify this population as transnationals since they have links with both countries and have developed identification with either one or both cultures (Mora Vázquez *et al.,* 2018).

As multicultural subjects (Kleyn, 2017), these young people returning to Mexico, with a vast repertoire of knowledge, practices, and cultural experiences, are unaware of the anger to which they will be subjected. Returnees, in some situations, do not exist (Hamann & Zuñiga, 2011; Tacelosky, 2018). Schools and educators continue to minimize the social phenomenon and, when returnees are recognized, they are generally seen as foreigners and often mistreated. Where does this abuse originate? When returning to Mexico, school is not easy for transnationals. According to Despagne and Jacobo-Suárez (2019), "adaptation in the Mexican education system represents a convoluted, challenging, and oftentimes painful process, as once they are in Mexico, they are caught between two worlds posing cultural, linguistic and identity conflicts" (p. 2).

Methodology

The methodology of this research is qualitative and narrative inquiry with retrospective perspective. The data was collected using autobiographies, biograms, and semi-structured interviews of 32 participants who were studying a BA in ELT in central Mexico. These participants faced various reasons to return to Mexico such as deportation, family reasons, migratory status, to name a few. The data analysis was carried out using paradigmatic cognition. For the purposes of this paper, we will focus on two participants, Edgar and Gemma, who belong to the same family. The research questions we aimed to answer were:

> RQ1: What are the challenges they have experienced when returning to Mexico?
>
> RQ2: What are the implications for the returnees' identity formation processes when being in Mexico?

Data Results and Discussion

At the time of the study, participants were working as English language teachers. This was not their first choice, but because they spoke the language, they were offered a job as English teachers. The themes we will discuss are: 1) facing challenges while being in the US, 2) troubles with identity; 3) coming back to Mexico and 4) living in two worlds.

As for the challenges of living in the U.S. and adapting to the ways of life in a new country, Edgar narrates how he felt on the spot because his accent gave him away in front of his friends:

> They [my friends] told me like "Dude, you don't look Mexican. You don't look Latino but where are you from?… You have an accent and where's that accent from?" and I didn't like that. I didn't like that they acknowledged more my accent than what I was saying. So, I started practicing and practicing a little more and grabbing those accents.

He worked very hard to acquire an American accent, but soon he realized that this was not the main problem for him.

> I learned a lot in very little time, but I was bullied by all my peers; it was sort of a funny thing though, because the peers I thought would aid me were the ones that would give me the hardest time…Latinos.

He felt discouraged but still, he pursued his studies in high school and tried to improve his language skills as much as he could. At a given moment, he questioned how other counterparts felt more American than Mexicans, but he was always aware of his legal situation in the US, and the following is what he says:

I never considered myself being American because I think, I always knew I wasn't American, since I was born in Leon, Guanajuato. I am Mexican. My likes are Americanized.

His sister, on the other hand, experienced bullying when coming back to Mexico. She started her middle school in Mexico, and she had adaptation problems because her academic linguistic skills in Spanish were not at the level she was expected by her teachers. She mentions:

I didn't know how to write. I knew how to speak it [Spanish], and I would understand it. But when you put me to read, I would read and the teachers would call it "*mocho*" [mutilated], and their method was to put me next to another girl, so I would copy her notes, and that's how my whole third year of middle school here in Mexico was: me sitting in each class with a specific girl in my class. And I would just copy her notes, and that was their method.

She asked her parents to send her back to the US, but they refused, as she was a young girl, and they were afraid she would make bad decisions while in the US away from the family. For Gemma, her experience as a returnee made her realize that she was living in two worlds and that now, as she was studying a BA in English language teaching, she had come to terms with this dual identity:

When I'm here [Mexico], it depends on the situation. I'm kind of very undecided about who I am. I have a very Mexican side: "Oh, I'm Mexican!" And I'm as proud as I am of my American side. Just like when someone says something bad about the United States, I get defensive, but when they say something bad about Mexico, I also get defensive. So, I am very indecisive about who I am. So, I always say that from here to the border I am Mexican, from the border to there, I am American.

For both Gemma and Edgar, their identity formation process is based upon their lived experiences in two countries: the US and Mexico. They have experienced discriminatory acts and were questioned by their Mexican peers about their linguistic proficiency in Spanish. At times they did not feel they could fit into a specific national identity completely; however, they also created a hybrid identity of being bilingual and return migrants. The results here imply deficiencies in terms of equality in the Mexican educational system and it highlights linguistic bullying in both Mexico and the US. It seems as if they were punished for being bilinguals. They continually negotiate their identities and emotions and show flexibility as individuals. Through time the participants seemed to resolve some issues of identity, constant movement, and insecurity. One way of solving their identity conflicts was to become English language teachers. Gemma found a place where she felt she belonged and was appreciated. Edgar has come to terms with his life in Mexico but also acknowledges his American side as well.

Conclusion

Identity is not singular and is made up of many facets. Identity transformation is complex and continual, redefining all aspects of self, as well as taking into consideration discrimination in the school system (by teachers and peers), and problems with the languages of English and Spanish. The participants constantly negotiated their identity in a different language depending on where they were situated, and what made it more difficult was the discrimination which is associated with the two languages and cultures. A more inclusive discourse is necessary, where return migrants can be accepted as citizens of two worlds, or more, and not defined as half citizens where something is missing.

References

Despagne, C., & Jacobo Suárez, M. (2019). The adaptation path of transnational students in Mexico: Linguistic and identity challenges in Mexican schools. *Latino Studies,* 17(4), 428-447. https://doi.org/10.1057/s41276-019-00207-w

FitzGerald, D. (2016). 150 Years of Transborder Politics: Mexico and Mexicans Abroad. In N. L. Green, & R. Waldinger (Eds.), A century of transnationalism. Immigrants and their homeland connections (pp. 106–131). University of Illinois Press.

Fundación BBVA Bancomer. (2015). Situación Migración México. Primer Semestre 2015. BBVA Research Mexico.

Hamann, E. T. & Zúñiga, V. (2011). Schooling and the everyday ruptures transnational children encounter in the United States in Mexico. In C. Coe, R. Reynolds, D. Boehm, J. M. Hess & H. Rae-Espinoza (Eds.) *Everyday ruptures: Children and migration in global perspective* (pp.141-160). Vanderbilt University Press.

Hazán, M. (2014). Understanding return migration to Mexico: Towards a comprehensive policy for the reintegration of returning migrants (San Antonio: MATT Working Paper), 22.

Instituto Nacional de Estadística y Geografía (INEGI) (2010). *XII Censo de población y vivienda.* INEGI.

Kleyn, T. (2017). Centering transborder students: Perspectives on identity, languaging and schooling between the U.S. and Mexico. *Multicultural Perspectives, 19*(2), 76-84. doi:10.1080/15210960.2017.1302336

Mora Vázquez, A., Trejo Guzmán, N. P. & Mora-Pablo, I. (2018). 'I was lucky to be a bilingual kid, and that makes me who I am': the role of transnationalism in identity issues". *International Journal of Bilingual Education and Bilingualism*, 24(5), 693-707. https://doi.org/10.1080/13670050.2018.1510893

Norton, B. (2013). Identity and language learning extending the conversation (2nd ed.). Multilingual Matters.

Tacelosky, K. (2018). Teaching English to English speakers: The role of English teachers in the school experience of transnational students in Mexico. *MEXTESOL Journal, 42*(3), 1-13.

INTEGRATION CHALLENGES OF PAKISTANI DIASPORA INTO WEST EUROPEAN SOCIETIES; A GENDER SENSITIVE ANALYSIS WITH A FOCUS ON GERMANY

Sadaf Mahmood, Beatrice Knerr, and Izhar Ahmad Khan

Abstract

In the 21st century, the integration of immigrants has become a major challenge for the European Union Countries as a large share of the immigrants preferred to stay there. Thus, poor integration is challenging for both, the immigrants and the host society. The researcher intended to rigorously study the integration challenges of Pakistani immigrants residing in Germany. For that purpose, a survey was conducted with 264 Pakistanis, 50% of them were females, above 18 years of age, and living in Germany for more than three months on a legal status was inclusion criteria. Human capital remained an important factor for integration.

Key words: Social Integration, Pakistani diaspora, Germany

Introduction

Integration of immigrants has become a major challenge for different countries. An enormous number of immigrants made their path to stay in their host country because of higher income and better quality of life. Understanding the social integration of migrants into host societies, especially into high-income countries, is one of the major areas of 21st-century migration research (Palo et al., 2006, Loch, 2014; Maliepaard & Schacht, 2018). Social integration for immigrants means developing a sense of belonging to the host society, i.e., accepting the cultural norms, acting as per norms, building social capital, and participating in social life and cultural activities. For natives, it is defined as considering and accepting the migrants as members of the society (Laurentsyeva & Venturini, 2017).

With the reference to the Pakistani immigrants in Germany, in 2019, 75,495 Pakistanis officially resided in Germany; 11,870 of them holding a permanent residence permit, 4,875 being students, and 16,090 holding a residence status as family members. Including those without their personal migration history (i.e., born in Germany, like second-generation migrants and persons with one parent being Pakistani) the number of residents with a 'Pakistani migration background', reached 124,000, 35.5% of them without their personal migration experience (BAMF, 2020). Around 30,000 of the migrants reached Germany after 2015 (Haider, 2018).

Objectives

Keeping in view the above situation, we examine the integration challenges of Pakistani immigrants with a focus on Germany, one of the major host countries for Pakistanis. We applied a gender-sensitive approach to compare the situation of male and female respondents. In the light of the empirical research findings, study-based recommendations for shaping appropriate policies are offered.

Justification

Over time, the number of Pakistani immigrants tends to increase in Germany. Concerns related to the social integration of Pakistani migrants across Europe are the subject of public discussions. Most of these Pakistanis are males, but the share of females is growing as well. Poor integration causes problems for both, the immigrants and the host societies. For that purpose, a sound data and information basis are required. There is a dire need for studies to dig out this phenomenon of integration challenges for all. So, social integration and especially based on gender need to be studied. This research article intends to contribute to that by considering the integration challenges of the Pakistani Diaspora in the European Union, with a special focus on Pakistani immigrants who are residing in Germany especially females. The findings of the study are useful for shaping policy measures and are highly relevant beyond the focus of the countries considered here.

Review of Literature

Erdal (2013) & Ager & Strang, (2008) stated that social integration is the willingness of the state to integrate migrants by offering those benefits and migrants adaptation of the local culture and their interaction with the locals. The key markers of integration are employment, housing, education, and health. Several studies found that education, duration of stay in the host society, and interaction with other nationalities helped in integration (Dalgard and Thapa, 2007; Haque, 2012; Mahmood, 2017; Wessendorf & Phillimore, 2018). Migrant communities are trying to socially assimilate with locals or from the local's perspective and local population accepting them as members of society. This is a debate of social inclusion and exclusion which is also relevant to understand social integration (Bass, 2018; IOM, 2021).

From the perspective of the Pakistani immigrants in West Europe, Erdal (2013) interviewed thirty Pakistanis that how they feel about dual loyalties and integration in Norwegian society. Dual national loyalty was not a hurdle in their way of integration for both genders. In terms of gender and social integration, one of the key factors is marriage. Olwig (2011) investigated that the Pakistani diaspora marries mostly with other Pakistanis and in Denmark local views it as forced marriages arranged by parents. Amjad (2017) found that integration among women is mainly in the domain of employment, education, and marriage.

Mohiuddin, (2017) stated that religion was one of the significant markers of the identity of people of Pakistani origin and Liebert *et al.,* (2020) found integration depends on equal employment opportunities and social inclusion. We built our theoretical and conceptual framework on David Lockwood's (1964) theory of social system to refer to the concept of Pakistani immigrants' integration in Germany.

Data & Methods

We collected our empirical data by using face-to-face interviews with a structured questionnaire with 264 Pakistani individuals, 50% of them were females selected through the snowball sampling technique. The descriptive and inferential statistics were applied with the help of the Statistical Package for Social Sciences (SPSS).

Results & Discussion

Personal characteristics

The results show that 66% of females and 77.3% of males were holding Pakistani citizenship while the remaining was holding German citizenship. The majority of the male in the data were students (78%) while the majority of the females (44.8%) were housewives or dependents to their family members. The f/m value of 0.3 shows the low share of women in the students' category. The majority of our respondents were 25 years to 35 years old. Most of the women were married, and more females than males were living, as indicated by the f/m-a value of 2.0. The f/m-value for higher secondary education was 2.7, while for Graduation and Masters from Pakistan it was 0.6 and 0.7 respectively which shows that males were more educated than females.

Social integration

Marking the indicators on a five-point Likert scale, the majority of the respondents strongly agreed that a lack of German language competencies is a barrier towards their social adjustment in Germany; with an f/m value of 1.1, this was almost equal among males and females. Just 0.8% of the females and 2.3% of male respondents strongly disagreed with this statement. More than 70% of both genders strongly agreed that they could easily perform their religious practices in Germany, with an f/m value of 1.1, while the f/m value of those who agreed that the hijab worn by the ladies was acceptable in Germany was 1.5. The majority of the female respondents felt lonely in Germany, with an f/m value of 1.3 for 'strongly agree', and 1.5 for 'agree'. 35% of the respondents expressed that they felt discrimination in Germany for being Pakistani. Being Pakistani, 1.4 value of f/m describes those respondents who strongly agreed that they found German nationals friendly towards them.

Referring to the frequency of meeting with German friends, other international friends, and those from the Pakistani community, the responses were almost the same for those who met often and those who rarely interacted with German and other international friends (Table 1). The f/m values were 0.3 and 0.6 for those who met very often and often German friends, and 1.7 and 3.9 for those who rarely and rarely did so. Similarly, f/m 0.3 and 0.6 values applied for those who frequently met with their other international friends, even though the f/m was 2.9 for respondents who rarely met with other nationals. The frequency of meeting Pakistanis was higher. In a nutshell, male respondents were more social than females according to these indicators.

Table 1. Frequency of social meetings with different communities (Total=264, Female=132, Male=132)

Indicators	Levels*	Female	Male	F/M
Germans friends	1	5.3	17.4	0.3
	2	19.7	35.6	0.6
	3	26.5	24.2	1.1
	4	31.1	18.2	1.7
	5	17.4	4.5	3.9
Other nationals	1	6.1	18.2	0.3
	2	28.8	49.2	0.6
	3	25	22	1.1
	4	31.1	10.6	2.9
	5	9.1	0.0	9.1:0
Pakistani nationals	1	47.7	62.1	0.8
	2	34.8	25.8	1.3
	3	9.8	9.1	1.1
	4	6.8	3.0	2.3
	5	0.8	0.0	0.8:0

*1-Very often, 2-Often, 3-Sometimes, 4-Rare, 5-Never
Source: Author's survey

Conclusion & Recommendations

It is concluded that there are several stakeholders of integration including migrants, their families, the government of host and sending societies as well as the local community at the destination area. The language (German and English both) and the interaction with the local community and other nationals play a significant role in the integration of the Pakistani immigrants in Germany. These accounts are useful for shaping policy measures and are highly relevant beyond the focus of the countries considered here (Mahmood, 2017). The government should focus on the education, skill development, language learning (English and German), and labor force participation of females. The government of Pakistan should offer affordable language courses before their departure. In the future, the problems of Pakistani children especially the second and third generations should be studied. A gender comparison should be applied to the educational attainments of second and third generations.

References

Ager, A., & Strang, A. (2008). Understanding integration: a conceptual framework. *Journal of Refugee Studies*, 167-190. doi:10.1093/jrs/fen016

Amjad, R. (2017). Introduction:An age of migration. In R. Amjad, *The Pakistani diaspora Corridors of oppurtunity and uncertainty* (pp. 1-21). Lahore : Lahore School of Economics.

Bass, L. E. (2018). Social inclusion in a context of global migration. *Societies Without Borders, 2*(2), 1-4. Retrieved from https://scholarlycommons.law.case.edu/swb/vol12/iss2/2

Bundesamt für Migration und Flüchtlinge (BAMF) (2020). Migrationsbericht 2019. Bundesamt für Migration und Flüchtlinge - Infothek - *Migrationsbericht* 2019: 1,6 Mio. Zugewanderte

Dalgard, O. S., & Thapa, S. B. (2007). Immigration, social integration and mental health in Norway, with focus on gender differences. Clinical Practice and Epidemiology in Mental Health, 3(1), 24-34.

Erdal, M. B. (2013). Migrant Transnationalism and Multi-Layered Integration: Norwegian-Pakistani Migrants' Own Reflections. *Journal of ethnic and migration studies*, 983-999. doi:10.1080/1369183X.2013.765665

Haider, S. (2018, 06 05). Why are Pakistanis so successful at finding jobs in Germany? Retrieved from Deutsche Welle: https://www.dw.com/en/why-are-pakistanis-so-successful-at-finding-jobs-in-germany/a-44083455

Haque, K. (2012). Iranian, Afghan, and Pakistani Migrants in Germany: Muslim Populations beyond Turks and Arabs. Chloe: Beihefte zum Daphnis, 46(1), 193-206.

IOM. (2021, 07 04). *Regional Office for the European Economic Area, the European Union and NATO*. Retrieved from IOM: https://eea.iom.int/migrant-inclusion-and-social-cohesion

Liebert, S., Siddiqui, M. H., & Goerzig, C. (2020). Integration of Muslim Immigrants in Europe and North America: A Transatlantic Comparison. *Journal of Muslim Minority Affairs*, 196-216.

Laurentsyeva, N., & Venturini, A. (2017). The Social Integration of Immigrants and the Role of Policy-A Literature Review. Intereconomics, 285-292. doi:DOI: 10.1007/s10272-017-0691-6

Lockwood, D. (1964). Social integration and system integration, in: Zollschan, K. and Hirsch, Walter (eds.), Explorations in Social Change. Routledge and Kegan: London, 244-251

Mahmood, S. (2017). Human capital, occupational status, and social integration of Pakistani immigrants in Germany: Gender Perspectives (Vol. 20). Kassel University press GmbH.

Maliepaard, M., & Schacht, D. D. (2018). The relation between religiosity and Muslims social integration: a two-wave study of recent immigrants in three European countries. *Ethnic and racial studies*, 860-881. doi:https://doi.org/10.1080/01419870.2017.1397280

Mohiuddin, A. (2017). Muslims in Europe: Citizenship, Multiculturalism and Integration. *Journal of Muslim Minority Affairs*, 393-412. doi:https://doi.org/10.1080/13602004.2017.1405512

Olwig, K. F. (2011). 'Integration': Migrants and Refugees between Scandinavian Welfare Societies and Family Relations. *Journal of ethnic and migration studies*, 179-196. doi:10.1080/1369183X.2010.521327

Palo, D. d., Faini, R., & Venturini, A. (2006). The social assimilation of immigrants. *IZA papers (discussion paper series)*, 2-34.

Wessendorf, S., & Phillimore, J. (2018). New Migrants' Social Integration, Embedding and Emplacement in Super diverse Contexts. Sociology, 123-138. doi:https://doi.org/10.1177%2F0038038518771843

EXPERIENCES OF SOCIAL AND PSYCHOLOGICAL ADAPTATION AND IDENTITY FORMATION OF SECOND-GENERATION IMMIGRANT TURKISH STUDENTS IN NORTH CYPRUS: PRELIMINARY RESULTS

Ayşenur Talat Zrilli and Şerif Türkkal Yenigüç

Abstract

This study focuses on the processes of social and psychological adaptation and identity formation of university students in North Cyprus who have a migrant background, namely those who have at least one Turkish parent who migrated from Turkey and settled in North Cyprus after 1975. It aims at identifying this population's acculturation strategies (Berry, 1997) and identity styles (Berzonsky, 2004) as well as exploring the relationship between the two by drawing on semi-structured in-depth interviews.

Introduction

This study focuses on the processes of social and psychological adaptation and identity formation of university students in North Cyprus (NC) who have a migrant background, namely those who have at least one Turkish parent who migrated from Turkey and settled in NC after 1975. It aims at identifying this population's acculturation strategies (Berry, 1997) and identity styles (Berzonsky, 2004) and exploring the relationship between the two by drawing on semi-structured in-depth interviews.

The group under scrutiny is oftentimes referred to as *second generation immigrants*, because, although they may not have gone through the movement themselves, it is assumed that many of their socio-psychological experiences, especially those that relate to their ethno-cultural/national identity, is affected by the immigration of their parent(s); and although their experiences cannot be equated with that of their parents', they are unique in their own right. In the case of NC, to our knowledge, these experiences have not yet been extensively studied.

Historical and Contextual Background

1975 is the year that marks the division of the island of Cyprus with a military operation of Turkey which ended the interethnic war between Turkish and Greek Cypriots with a ceasefire. This initiated a process of displacement of the Greek Cypriot (GC) population to the southern part and the Turkish Cypriot (TC) population to the northern part of the island, creating two ethnically homogeneous sections. In the northern part TCs proclaimed a separate state, initially the Turkish Federated State of Cyprus and in 1983 the Turkish Republic of Northern Cyprus. Following these developments, the TC state signed an agreement with Turkey to bring and settle an agricultural labour force in NC (Kurtuluş & Purkis, 2014; Talat Zrilli, 2019). Since that year further waves of immigration from Turkey to NC continue in form of labour migrations, student migrations and more recently, migrations of skilled and highly skilled labour. Today a numerically large section of the population in NC has a migration background from Turkey.

Within the initial migratory movement incoming groups were incited to settle through enticements such as allocation of houses, agricultural land, workshops and citizenship. Yet, although these may have created circumstances that eased the initial adaptation of these immigrants, there was no extensive integration policy as the nationalist elite both in NC and in Turkey assumed that immigrants would automatically assimilate. They were assuming this since they had a primordialist conception of ethnic and national identity, believing that populations in Turkey and in NC were identical due to their common 'roots', 'blood' and 'kinship'. It can even be argued that immigrants from the Turkish mainland were brought to the island as part of a nationalistic project so as to constitute an important part of the TC nation-state that was being built during the era (Talat Zrilli, 2019). However, contrary to the assumptions of automatic assimilation of the incoming groups by the nationalistic elite, studies focusing on TCs' encounters with Turkish immigrants show that there exists cultural differentiation between them (Navaro-Yashin, 2005). Similarly, studies on immigrants' experiences report their hardships of adaptation as well as prejudice and discrimination they face in the labour market, in the political arena and in everyday life (Bryant & Hatay, 2000; Kurtuluş & Purkis, 2014).

Theories and Concepts

The present study holds a constructivist approach to 'identity' implying that individuals have an active role in the process of constructing their own realities. It also aims to take into regard theories and models which were developed by the disciplines of psychology and sociology, thus forming an interdisciplinary perspective. In this regard Berzonsky's (2004) 'identity styles', Berry's (1997) 'acculturation strategies' and constructivist sociological theories about ethnic identity (Cornell & Hartmann, 2007) constitute this study's theoretical-conceptual background.

According to Berzonsky (2004), people employ problem-solving strategies to construct their *identity styles*. Berzonsky proposes that this process may be influenced by social and cultural interactions and observational as well as direct learning experiences. Three different identity styles are identified: 'informational style', 'normative style' and 'diffuse avoidant style'. Yet in the context of migration, identity becomes an even more complex matter as immigrants experience *acculturation* (Redfield, Linton & Herskovits, 1936). In this context, immigrant groups need to make certain decisions regarding their own cultural heritage and the culture of the majority society. According to Berry (1997), immigrant groups can choose to follow the *assimilation strategy* when they abandon their own cultural identity; *separation strategy* if they avoid interaction with majority society and keep own cultural heritage; *integration strategy* when they maintain own cultural identity to some degree and participate in the majority society and culture; and finally *marginalisation* when they are unable or unwilling to maintain own culture while also being excluded from the majority culture. Berry argues that the openness of the majority society to include immigrants plays a key role as it will enable or put barriers to mutual contact and accommodation between groups. This study aims to understand acculturation strategies of the immigrants as described by Berry's (1997) model and their identity styles as described by Berzonsky (2004). Moreover, it aims to discover the relationship between the acculturation strategies and identity styles if these exist.

Methods and Data

Focus group and individual semi-structured in-depth interviews with at least 30 university students with migrant backgrounds are planned to be carried out. A guiding questionnaire is utilised which focuses on the following main themes: Presentation of (ethnic) identity; acculturation strategies and identity styles involved in identity construction; identification and relations with the place of origin in Turkey and with the TC society.

Participants are being recruited via various channels using social media platforms, by direct approach and by suggestions from other participants. Participants are asked to fill out an initial questionnaire through which information is gathered on their and their parents' demographic characteristics, their relations and identification with Turkey and Cyprus, and their expressions of own ethnic identity. In-depth interviews conducted afterwards are later transcribed verbatim and analysed by paying attention to themes that are deduced from Berry's (1997) and Berzonsky's (2004) models and from topics that arise in the interviews.

Preliminary Results

At this point in the study, six participants have completed the demographic forms and two have participated in-depth interviews. In the following a juxtaposition of the two participants of in-depth interviews will be presented. They are given the pseudo names Ali and Ayşe. Whereas both of Ali's parents immigrated from Turkey; in Ayşe's case only the mother had a migration background. Ali and his family were living a rural area. His father was reported as working in non-skilled and semi-skilled job in private sector and mother was reported as a stay-at-home parent. Ayşe and her parents were living in an urban area. Her mother was reported to be a civil servant and her father was reported to be working in the private sector.

Both Ali and Ayşe claimed to associate more with Cyprus than with Turkey saying that their social environment played the key role in their sentiments. They both underlined that it was their social networks rather than their 'ancestral roots' which mattered in this regard. Both participants claimed to endorse the TC culture, which, in their opinion, was characterised by a lifestyle, mentality, and world view quite different from Turkish culture. They claimed that TC culture offered greater freedom to individuals in their everyday lives and in expressing their opinions compared with Turkish culture. Ayşe underlined feeling 'safer' in Cyprus as a young woman than she does in Turkey, which she claimed played a huge role in her feelings towards both countries. Both informants reported that they had clashes with their parents from time to time because they demanded to live by TC cultural standards and be awarded greater individual freedom.

Even though both informants were committed to TC and Cypriot identities, their perceptions of what defined 'Cypriotness' was different. In explaining his identity related feelings and perceptions Ali resorted to nationalistic symbols and discourses. For instance, he expressed his pride for participating in a TC national sports team. Ayşe on the other hand, expressed that she associated with the TC political left which is committed to finding a peaceful solution to Cyprus problem. Ayşe's perception of 'Cypriotness' explicitly included the GC side too. She reported seeking contact with GCs by participating in bi-communal activities. She also expressed discontent with Turkey's interventionist policies in Cyprus.

Participants also described identity related challenges: Ali expressed feeling stressed when TC and mainland Turks define him differently, as a 'Turk' and as a 'Cypriot' respectively. Ayşe, on the other hand, expressed that she felt 'incomplete' about her Cypriot identity. She claimed to be conscious about not being 'completely Cypriot' because of her mother's migration background. She stated that she sometimes felt insecure about her ethnic identity.

In the light of Berry's acculturation model, both participants seem to be following an assimilationist strategy of acculturation, claiming that they identify themselves more with Turkish Cypriotness in terms of lifestyle, mentality, and world view. They underlined their differentiation from mainland Turks in those respects. However, there were some differences between the participants explanations: Whereas

Ali declared that problems with relatives living in Turkey played a role in his distancing from Turkey; Ayşe based her alienation from her Turkish background on ideological reasons. Although she had close relations with her relatives in Turkey, she claimed to be very dissatisfied with the current political and social atmosphere there.

It can be argued that the two participants were using different strategies to overcome their identity related challenges. Ali seems to be following the foreclosure identity style in Berzonsky's (2004) model as he mainly relied on his sentiments about the TC national sports team and his father's identity descriptions when constructing his identity. He did not report resorting to any other sources to explore his identity. Ayse, on the other hand seems to be following the informational style as she is actively exploring her identity and seeking information by applying to various sources such as other native TCs and GCs.

Final Remarks

So far, our research supports our initial claim about identity being a construct which is continuously shaped and reshaped by individuals in everyday life. Our data indicates that there is heterogeneity among second generation immigrants in the way they construct their ethno-national identities. Social networks within which the person participates seem to play a critical role in the process of acculturation and accompanying construction of ethnic identity. Nevertheless, parents' migration background may be creating challenges for second-generation immigrants as these find themselves in situations of conflict and stress about their identity; and engage in various strategies to claim and validate them.

References

Berry, J. W. (1997). Immigration, acculturation and adaptation. Applied Psychology: An International Review, 46, 5–68.

Berzonsky, M. D. (2004). Identity processing style, self-construction, and personal epidemic assumptions: A social-cognitive perspective. European Journal of Developmental Psychology, 1, 303-315.

Cornell, S. & Hartmann, D. (2007). Ethnicity and race: Making identities in a changing world (2nd ed.). Thousand Oaks.

Bryant, R., & Hatay, M. (2020). Sovereignty suspended: Building the so-called state. University of Pennsylvania Press.

Kurtuluş, H., & Purkis, S. (2014). Kuzey Kıbrıs'ta Türkiyeli göçmenler. Türkiye İş Bankası Kültür Yayınları.

Redfield, R., Linton, R., & Herskovits, M. (1936). Memorandum on the study of acculturation. American Anthropologist, 38, 149–152.

Talat Zrilli, A. (2019) Ethno-nationalism, state building and migration: The first wave of migration from Turkey to North Cyprus. Southeast European and Black Sea Studies, 19(3), 493-510.

"BRAIN DRAIN" MIGRATION AS A CONSEQUENCE OF CORRUPTION IN THE REPUBLIC OF KOSOVA

Adrianit Ibrahimi and Besa Arifi

Abstract

Over 344.660 people have left Kosovo only during 2008-2018. The average education level of them was higher than of the resident population, resulting in a significant brain drain from Kosovo during the past decade. On the other hand, the struggle against corruption still continues. Therefore, corruption is among the main push factors for brain drain migration from Kosovo.

Germany remains the most preferred final destination for Kosovo migrants meanwhile the most damaged sectors from brain drain are the health sector, the IT sector, the construction sector, the social workers, and the craftsman.

Keywords: Corruption; Brain drain; Kosovo

Introduction

The number of residents in Kosovo is 1,782,115 based on the last estimation in 2019 (Kosovo Agency of Statistics, 2020, p. 12). Referring to this estimation of the Kosovo population, the paper aims to map the flow of brain drain from Kosovo during the last years. In order to a have a bigger picture of the situation, the focus was on the following migration statistics: **a)** the number of *visa applications*, **b)** the number of *asylum applications*, **c)** the number of people found to be *illegally abroad*, and **d)** the number of *temporary residence permits*. Indeed, the analyses of these categories of statistics may have resulted with the shaping of the main trends of brain drain from Kosovo during the last years. Nevertheless, the follow-up research about the push and pull factors for such trends has enlightened that **pervasiveness of corruption in Kosovo in last decade has created fertile ground for brain drain migration.**

While corruption is pushing forward the youth of Kosovo to leave their country for a better life, the most damaged sectors from brain drain are the health sector, the IT sector, the construction sector, hoteliers and tourism (Balkans Policy Research Group, 2020, p. 21). On the other hand, the main beneficiary of this brain gain from Kosovo is Germany.

Brain-Drain from the Republic of Kosovo

People are always on the move from one place to another because they are pushed or pulled from different reasons and circumstances. How far they move and how long they stay depends on the new push and pull factors that may be available for the new place of residence. From this point of view, migration is like a never-ending circle but with different intensities in different times and places. However, migration is not always the "win-win solution". When skilled and professional people move away from one country, this is called brain drain (European Commission, 2021). In the meantime, for the destination country of those people, this is called brain gain (European Commission, 2021). For instance, the Republic of Kosovo is experiencing significant migration trends within brain drain crisis.

During 2012-2015, Kosovo had to deal also with irregular migration crisis when over 135.000 citizens of Kosovo had filed asylum applications to the EU countries (Halili Xhevdet, 2017, pp. 90, 91). Among these asylum seekers from Kosovo, more than 75% belong to the 0-34 age group which represents the majority of the population and the working power in the Republic of Kosovo. Worth noting is that those citizens from Kosovo who migrated had higher levels of education on average than the resident population, resulting in a significant brain drain from Kosovo during the past decade (World Bank Group, 2018, p. 21).

Based on a research from European Policy Institute of Kosovo, during 2008-2018 a total of 344,660 people left Kosovo searching for a better life in the EU. Among them, 141,330 were found to be illegally present in the EU while the other 203,330 Kosovo citizens have filed asylum applications in the EU. Consequently, only within a decade (2008-2018) approximately 1/5 or 19.5% of the Kosovo population "made a run for a great escape" (European Policy Institute of Kosovo, 2019, p. 2).

The dismay of political and economic circumstances can be considered as the main causes for this decline of population but among a lot of other decisive push and pull factors. For instance, 43% of the youth perceive that corruption and nepotism is among the biggest challenges for living in Kosovo. Moreover, almost 58% of the youth would likely or definitely consider migrating in the near future (European Policy Institute of Kosovo, 2019, p. 10).

From 2014 until 2019, an average of 87,059 citizens from Kosovo have filed visa applications for the Schengen Zone every year (Schengen Visa Info, 2014-2020). This means that approximately 4.9% of the population in Kosovo has annually filed applications for visas to the Schengen Zone. This may be not directly linked with migration purposes but confirms that 4.9% of the people in Kosovo constantly seek to travel to the EU. Of course, lack of visa liberalization for Kosovo does hinder those people to move freely as its their basic human right but still denied unfairly only for Kosovo in Western Balkan.

Tab. 1. Number of visa applications from Kosovo to the Schengen Zone

Year	2014	2015	2016	2017	2018	2019	2020
#No.	74,286	80,175	77,800	90,478	90,840	108,774	26,036
%Perc.	4.2	4.5	4.4	5.1	5.1	6.1	1.5

Source: (Schengen Visa Info, 2014-2020)

Worth noting is that the number of visa applications has grown almost every year since 2014 and until the zenith in 2019 when 108,774 Kosovo citizens or 6.1% of the population have filed visa applications for the Schengen Zone (Schengen Visa Info, 2014-2020).

Fig. 1. Trend of visa applications from Kosovo to the Schengen Zone

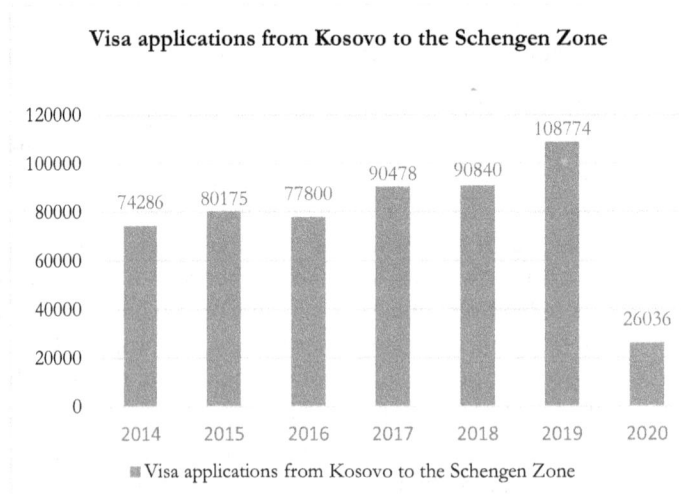

Visa applications from Kosovo to the Schengen Zone

Source: (Schengen Visa Info, 2014-2020)

At the end of 2018 approximately 854,198 citizens of Kosovo were living abroad, the majority of them in Germany and Switzerland (Balkans Policy Research Group, 2020, p. 13). From 2011 until 2018, the number of temporary residence permits for citizens of Kosovo has grown every year. Most of those permits are for working and for family reunion (Balkans Policy Research Group, 2020, p. 19). The Balkans Policy Research Group in 2020 has concluded that corruption, nepotism, youth unemployment, poor health and education system are the main push factors for migration from Kosovo (Balkans Policy Research Group, 2020, pp. 14, 19).

Fig. 2. Number of residence permits for citizens of Kosovo in the EU

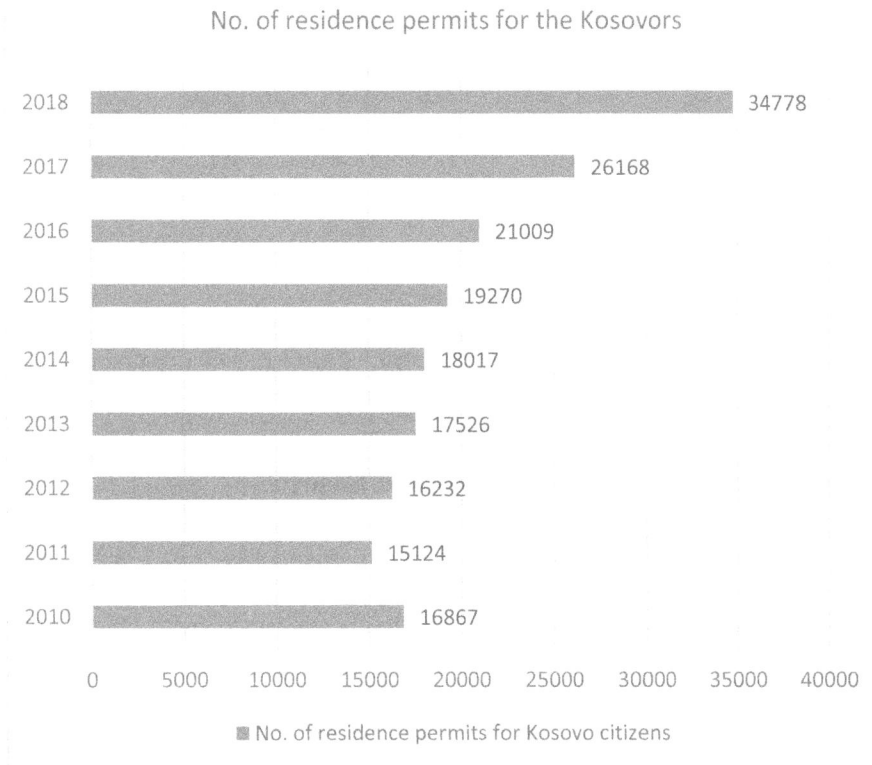

No. of residence permits for the Kosovors

Year	No. of residence permits for Kosovo citizens
2018	34778
2017	26168
2016	21009
2015	19270
2014	18017
2013	17526
2012	16232
2011	15124
2010	16867

No. of residence permits for Kosovo citizens

Source: (Balkans Policy Research Group, 2020, p. 19)

From 2010 to 2018 approximately 184,991 citizens of Kosovo have gained temporary residence permits in the EU countries. The most affected sectors from migration in Kosovo are the IT sector, construction, hoteliers and tourism (Balkans Policy Research Group, 2020, p. 21). However, the health sector in Kosovo is definitely the most damaged from brain drain (Ahmetxhekaj, Shkumbin, 2019).

Germany remains the main preferred destination for migrants from Kosovo. It is estimated that in 2017 over 433,000 citizens from Kosovo were living in Germany and more than 66% of them are in working relations (GAP Institute, 2020, pp. 23-24). Only during 2016-2018, over 67,272 citizens or 3.78% of the population in Kosovo have applied for a job in Germany (GAP Institute, 2020, p. 15). From those 67,272 job applications in Germany filed only within three years, the Federal Agency for Employment in Germany has pre-approved 64,517 applications or 96% of them (GAP Institute, 2020, p. 23).

Fig. 3. Pre-approved job applications of Kosovars from Germany

Pre-approved job applications of the Kosovo citizens from the German Federal Agency of Employment

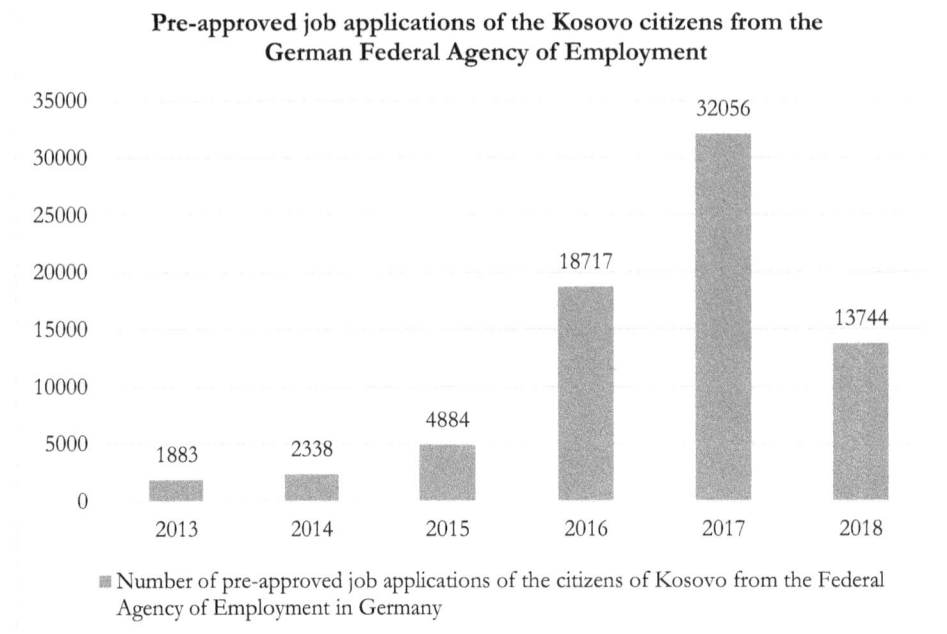

■ Number of pre-approved job applications of the citizens of Kosovo from the Federal Agency of Employment in Germany

Source: (GAP Institute, 2020, p. 23)

Relations between corruption and brain drain in Kosovo

Kosovo is still struggling in the fight against corruption. Based on the Corruption Perceptions Index (CPI) for 2020, Kosovo has scored only 36/100 points and ranked no. 104/180 (Transparency International, 2020). Meanwhile, the Gallup Research Migration Center has published its survey on the Potential Net Migration Index (PNMI) where Kosovo has been assessed with -48% net loss of youth population and -43% brain drain because of migration during 2015-2017. Kosovo has been assessed with -42% PNMI which is the highest negative score indicating net population loss in the region (Gallup Research Migration Center, 2018). It is conclusive that Kosovo is ranked very low from both indexes CPI and PNMI. From this point of view brain drain migration and the fight against corruption in Kosovo are closely linked to each other.

Kosovo has a relatively high birth rate and the youngest population in the region with 25% of the population under 15 years (Eurostat, 2019). Having such a young population indicates also the potential for migration of the youth. However, having a young population is not a push factor itself for brain drain. Just try to imagine the youth in Kosovo when they graduate from university but cannot find jobs because of corruption affairs. Meanwhile just a two hours' flight away is Germany where young doctors, nurses and IT's are very welcomed. Therefore, we cannot blame the youth for running after a better welfare. Instead, we shall recognize and overcome the brain drain crisis from Kosovo. At this point, the struggle with corruption in Kosovo is a main concern! Referring to the Report on Kosovo for 2020, corruption is certainly the consequence of the political influence in the judicial system and not only (European Commission, 2020, pp. 5, 43). Therefore, corruption is among the main push factors why the professional youth is leaving Kosovo.

Conclusions

Kosovo is facing with brain drain crisis. Approximately 1/5 of the population has left Kosovo only during 2008-2018. These migrants are mainly young people representing the majority of the population and the working power in Kosovo. Moreover, the average education level of them is higher than of the resident population. The main preferred destination is Germany while the most damaged sectors in Kosovo from brain drain are the health sector, IT, construction, the social workers and the craftsman.

The dismay of political and economic circumstances can be considered as the main causes for this decline of population but among a lot of other decisive push and pull factors. Nevertheless, the youth perceive that corruption is among the biggest challenges for living in Kosovo. Consequently, they would likely or definitely consider migrating in the near future. From this point of view, corruption is on top of the list with push factors for brain drain in Kosovo, followed from youth unemployment, lack of visa liberalization, poor health and education system.

References

Ahmetxhekaj, Shkumbin. (2019). *BalkanInsight - BIRN*. Retrieved June 27, 2021, from BalkanInsight - BIRN: https://balkaninsight.com/2019/12/04/brain-drain-will-the-last-doctor-in-kosovo-turn-out-the-lights/

Balkans Policy Research Group. (2020). *Kosovo: Trendet e migrimit kërkojnë një qasje të re të politikave*. Pristina: Balkans Policy Research Group. Retrieved June 14, 2021, from https://balkansgroup.org/wp-content/uploads/2020/10/Kosovo_Trendet-e-Migrimit-kerkojne-nje-qasje-te-re-strategjike-.pdf

European Commission. (2020). *Kosovo 2020 Report*. Brussels: European Commission. Retrieved February 03, 2021, from https://ec.europa.eu/neighbourhood-enlargement/sites/near/files/kosovo_report_2020.pdf

European Commission. (2021, June 11). *European Commission - Migration and Home Affairs*, Brain Drain - Definition. (E. Commission, Producer, & European Commission) Retrieved June 11, 2021, from European Commission - Migration and Home Affairs: https://ec.europa.eu/home-affairs/what-we-do/networks/european_migration_network/glossary_search/brain-drain_en

European Policy Institute of Kosovo. (2019). *The great escape*. Pristina: European Policy Institute of Kosovo. Retrieved June 13, 2021, from https://cdn.website-editor.net/8a3b242c12494d76b2b60ea75852e5f4/files/uploaded/THE%2520GREAT%2520ESCAPE.pdf

Eurostat. (2019). *Eurostat - European Statistics*. (European Commission) Retrieved June 23, 2021, from European Commission: https://ec.europa.eu/eurostat/news/themes-in-the-spotlight/western-balkans-2019

Gallup Research Migration Center. (2018). *www.news.gallup.com*, Potential Net Migration Index. Retrieved June 30, 2021, from www.news.gallup.com: https://news.gallup.com/migration/interactive.aspx

GAP Institute. (2020). *Emigrimi i fuqisë punëtore të Kosovës në Gjermani - Vlerësim i shkurtër i kthimeve pozitive dhe negative*. Pristina: GAP Institute & The Expert Council of German Foundations on Integration and Migration - Research Unit. Retrieved June 16, 2021, from https://www.institutigap.org/documents/82484_emigrimi_gjermani_.pdf

Halili Xhevdet, I. A. (2017). Causes for the Irregular Migration Crises: Case of Kosovo. *Strategos, 1*(2), 79-98. Retrieved June 12, 2021, from https://www.researchgate.net/publication/321757677_Causes_for_the_Irregular_Migration_Crises_Case_of_Kosovo

Kosovo Agency of Statistics. (2020). *Population Estimation, 2019*. Pristina: Kosovo Agency of Statistics. Retrieved June 20, 2021, from https://ask.rks-gov.net/en/kosovo-agency-of-statistics/add-news/population-estimation-2019

Schengen Visa Info. (2014-2020). *schengenvisainfo.com*. Retrieved June 19, 2021, from Schengen Visa Info - Statistics - Specific Schengen Visa Statistics: https://statistics.schengenvisainfo.com/

Transparency International. (2020). *Corruption Perception Index 2020*. Transparency International - the global coalition against corruption. Retrieved February 03, 2021, from https://www.transparency.org/en/cpi/2020/index/ksv

World Bank Group. (2018). *Western Balkans Labor Market 2018*. Washington: World Bank Group. Retrieved June 28, 2021, from http://documents1.worldbank.org/curated/en/565231521435487923/pdf/124354-Western-Balkans-Labor-market-trends-2018-final.pdf

"THE YOUNG AND THE RESTLESS": SECOND GENERATION CHINESE MIGRANTS IN THESSALONIKI

Georgia Sarikoudi

Introduction

This presentation is a part of my postdoctoral research that is still in progress and regard the study of the "Second Generation of Immigrants from Albania and China living in Thessaloniki" and is funded by the State Scholarship Foundation (IKY). The aim of the research is to study the dynamics of the formation of the second generation, the interaction and conflicts with compatriots and their wider social environment, their relations with their place of origin, their degree of integration into Greek society and their plans for the future. Today though, I will focus only on Chinese families and the way young immigrants form their identity in a transnational world.

The ethnographic material that supports this paper was collected from August 2020 until June 2021 in Thessaloniki and was based on qualitative research method: mainly open informal discussions and semi-structured interviews along with participant observation. However, the pandemic changed my plan and I had to redefine my methodology. Many of our conversations took place online and only recently I was able to visit people's home and be a part of their daily life.

I conducted twelve semi-structured interviews with second generation people (7 of Chinese origin and 5 of Albanian origin) and 2 interviews with first generation immigrants (one woman from Albania and one from China, parents of two informants) but the range of people I met and talked to regularly consisted of thirty people (aged eighteen to fifty-seven). I need to clarify that when I refer to 2nd generation[1] I include children who were born in Greece by at least one immigrant parent and children who came to Greece before the age of 12 in order to examine whether children who came as immigrants have shaped a different perception of the Greece, their identity and their future plans than the ones developed by those who were born in the host country.

Immigration in Greek literature

In Greece, the first studies on the issue of immigration appeared in the 1960s and focused on the immigrants from Greece to foreign countries. The interest in the phenomenon of migration reappeared in the late 1980s as a result of the massive migration flows from the Balkan and Eastern European countries. This phenomenon raised the issue of diversity and the challenges immigrants posed to Greek society. The anthropological studies that began to be produced from 2000 onwards dealt with immigration, not as a problem, but gave voice to the subjects themselves and shed light on some aspects of the issue that other common scientists had not dealt with. Such issues are gender migration, household migration and second generation.

Of the studies conducted on immigrant communities, most concern the case of Albanian community

---

[1] There is a great discussion in the social sciences literature on who belongs to the second generation and who to the one-and-half (1.5) generation. However, I do not intend to analyze the issue further here, as it is beyond the scope of today's announcement. For a better understanding of the discussion on second generation immigrants see Michail 2014.

(Pratsinakis, 2005; Lamprianidis-Hatziprokopiou 2008; Kokkali, 2011; Michail, 2014; Michail and Christou, 2016 and 2018; Vathi, 2019) and only few the Chinese (Tonchef 2007, Rosen 2011 and 2018; Theodoraki 2013, Matziropoulou 2013). The literature regarding the Chinese immigration to Greece is mostly concerned with the entrepreneurship of immigrants in big urban centers (Athens and Thessaloniki) and the emergence of multicultural spaces in the urban landscape. However, there is no information on the settlement of their households, their coexistence with the local population and / or other nationalities or the experiences of the second generation as well as a comparative perspective of the migrant communities.

Chinese immigrants in Thessaloniki

The first Chinese immigrants came to Thessaloniki at 1995 and they were 20-30 middle aged men that arrived by illegal paths. Until 2000, there were no more that 300 people and by 2004 there were around 1500 people and about 80 Chinese shops. By 2005, there has been a successive of Chinese immigrants from China due to a law that was passed that year regulating entry, residence and social inclusion in the country of third-country nationals. Thanks to these programs, many immigrants brought their families to Greece and decided that their settlement in Thessaloniki would be permanent. Today, the number of Chinese immigrants in the city of Thessaloniki stands at about 5,000 of the registered foreigners of the city, according to the census of 2011. Most Chinese live and work on the west side of the city, near the train station. There they have created an entire neighborhood, the Greek Chinese city, which is perceived by the red lights and colorful walls. In recent years, however, many Chinese have settled on the east side of the city, especially those who do not trade or open shops in other neighborhoods far from the center. However, due to the previous lack of Chinese school in the city, many parents chose to leave their young children behind in China in order to go to school there, to learn the language well, before coming to Greece. While as many children as were born here or did not leave for China attend Greek schools, public or private. In recent years the Chinese community has set up a Chinese school for kids who want to learn their native language.

Second generation Chinese

Young people of Chinese descent have a complex attitude towards their nationality. The way Chinese immigrants were portrayed by the Greek media played a key role in shaping their ethnic identity. The identification of Chinese with mafia and underwold was identified in the conscience of most Greeks. This stereotypical representation of foreigners in the hegemonic discourse intensified the stigmatization and marginalization of this community that was considered inferior. So, the children, when they began to realize their different national identity, they experienced it through the negatively charged identity. Huan Li, a 20 years old man, remembers that he didn't want to go to school because his classmates were making fun of his origin. *"It didn't matter how good I was speaking the language, I had this weird name and slanted eyes, that differentiate me from my classmates. That was enough for them to make my days at school like hell"*. Because of these stigmatizing experiences, many of these youngsters have developed a strong sense of alienation from their ethnic identity, sometimes hiding their origin and rejecting anything to do with China.

As national identity was losing its significance, other forms of identity and belonging emerged. For many of the Chinese youngsters Thessaloniki or even the neighborhood where they grew up is the place of reference, for their belonging. These places are the locus of their daily interaction. In these places they find the space to express their personal interests and form their multiple identities. The multiple identities they adopt are evident in their narrations. Young immigrants tend to describe themselves through non-ethnic identity features, while the urban identity they project shows the importance of the city in their identification processes.

The poor emotional contact of parents with their children also contributed to this distancing from national identity. The fact that most of the migrant parents work many hours to make ends meet diminishes the time they spent with their children. Therefore, this situation decreased the prospects for parents and children to communicate and connect and also confined parents' ability to attend their children's experiences, happiness or disappointments. The little time the family spent together gradually led to an alienation and the children felt that there is no interaction among them and the gap between them grow. *"I feel that I basically grew up alone. My parents were all day in the shop and when we were all together in the house, there was no qualitative time and talk. I feel more attached to my friends"*. Lao Chan doesn't claim that his parents are indifferent towards him, he acknowledges that they are trying hard to provide him with any material and economic support they can, but he expects more in an emotional level. According to him, his parents are the typical stereotypic image of the taciturn and suave Chinese. Thus, Lao Chan fells closer to his peers. He gets affected and embrace a youth culture far away from his ethnic customs and habits. This dissonant acculturation challenges parent–child relationships and family hierarchies. Peer-to-peer networks emerge as a very important and dynamic group in the construction of the identity of second-generation immigrants. The long absence of the parents from home and the lack of supervision favored the children to spend time with their friends in the neighborhoods or through online games. The streets and the computer become the places where young people express their personality and form relationships and identities (Soysal, 2001).

Conclusion

There are many factors that influence and shape the identity of Chinese youth in Thessaloniki. Youngsters get more influenced from peers and school than family, especially during adolescence. They get emotionally detached from their parents who don't spend enough time with their children and feel powerless and afraid of losing the control of their family. Especially in the case of Chinese, the racism and stigmatization that the second generation experienced made them develop a strong sense of alienation from its nationality and identify itself not on the basis of their ethnic identity, but on other, alternative identities. Youth interests and emotional ties between peers are the most important elements of their identity. The trend towards experimentation, consumption and doubt of everything are considered important indicators of youth identity that do not associate with any particular nationality.

Literature

Kokkali, I. (2011) Absence of a 'community' and spatial invisibility: migrants from Albania in Greece and the case of Thessaloniki. In F. Eckardt and J. Eade (Eds). T*he Ethnically diverse city*, Berlin: Berliner- Wissenschaafts-Verlag, pp. 85-114.

Matziropoulou, Th. (2011) Chinese immigration in Thessaloniki. In D. Syrri (ed). *Living with Immigration*. Athens: Ianos-Navarino Network.

Michail D. (2014) Albanian Immigration in Greece. Studies and Issues. Anthropological and Interdisciplinary Approaches. Athens: Stamouli. [in Greek]

Michail, D. and Christou, A. (2016) Diasporic youth identities of uncertainty and hope: second-generation Albanian experiences of transnational mobility in an era of economic crisis in Greece, *Journal of Youth Studies* 19 (7): 957-972.

Michail, D. and Christou, A. (2018) Youth mobilities, crisis, and agency in Greece: second generation lives in liminal spaces and austere times. *Transnational Social Review: A Social Work Journal* 8 (3): 245-257.

Pratsinakis, M. (2005) Aspirations and Strategies of Albanian Immigrants in Thessaloniki. *Journal of Southern Europe and the Balkans* 7 (2): 195- 212.

Pratsinakis, M., Hatziprokopiou P., Grammatikas, D. and Labrianidis, L. (2017) Crisis and the resurgence of emigration from Greece: trends, representations, and the multiplicity of migrants trajectories. In: B. Glorius and J. Dominguez-Mujica (Eds). *Migration and crisis: Understanding migration dynamics from Mediterranean Europe*. Bielefeld: J. Transcript Verlag, pp: 75-102. Availiable at DOI: 10.14361/9783839434789-004 (accessed 13 Mai 2021).

Soysal L. (2001) Diversity of experience, experience of diversity: Turkish migrant youth culture in Berlin. *Cultural Dynamics* 13(1): 5–28.

Theodoraki, S (2013) *The Chinese neighborhood of Athens in transition. Investigations and Prospects.* Master thesis at the Department of Architecture at National Metsovio Polytechnic.

Tonchef, P. (ed) (2007) Asian Immigrants in Greece. Origin, Present and Prospects. Department of Asian Studies [in Greek]

Vathi, Z. (2019) Identifications of Albanian-origin teenagers in Thessaloniki and the role of ethnicity: A multi-scalar perspective *Global Studies of Childhood* 9 (1): 29-41

MEASUREMENT OF ETHNIC DIVERSITY AND ITS EFFECT WITH THE RECENT IN-MIGRATION RATE

Tiara Maureen

Introduction

Ethnic diversity has its appeal to study. Ethnic Fractionalization Index (EFI) and Ethnic Polarization Index (EPOI) are the measurement of ethnic diversity that have been used in research (Taylor & Hudson, 1972; Montalvo & Reynal-Querol, 2005; Reynal-Querol, 2002; Arifin et al., 2015). EFI indicates a degree of fractionalization or ethnic heterogeneity. The EPOI indicates a degree of ethnic polarization probability of conflict that may appear from the presence of large ethnic groups.

Indonesia is known as its ethnic diversity. In Population Census 2010, Statistics Indonesia classifies 1,343 ethnicities into 31 major ethnic groups, but there has been no further research on the measurements of ethnic diversity in Indonesia using those ethnic classification. Ananta et al. (2015) measured ethnic diversity in Indonesia using the ethnic classification in Ananta et al. (2014) with a new method called New Classification (NC). Wasino (2011) said that ethnic diversity in Indonesia is caused by migration. Riau and Riau Islands are one of the provinces that have in ethnic composition changing from the increasing in-migration flows to the region (Gayatri, 2010; Ananta, 2016). According to the 2010 Population Census (SP2010) results, According to the results of SP2010, Riau Islands has the highest rate of recent in-migration in Indonesia at 15.88% and the Riau Province at 6%. Recent in-migration reflects the displacement state of five years ago and can be more reflect the current state of migration.

Researches on the internal migration behavior of various ethnic groups according to migrant characteristics such as region of residence, age, gender is useful to see how ethnic groups are dispersed as a result of internal migration, which can then be compared between regions (Raymer, Smith, & Giulietti , 2011). Other researches used a quantitative approach to see internal migration of ethnic groups and their impact on migrant populations and characteristics (Stillwell & Hussain 2008; Finney & Simpson 2008; and Stillwell & Phillips, 2006).

Based on previous reviews, the objectives of this study are; describe the composition of the population recent in-migration patterns of ethnic groups in Riau and Riau Islands Provinces in 2010, measure ethnic diversity using EFI and EPOI and see how recent in-migration rate affects EFI and EPOI with simple regression analysis.

Literature Review

Reynal-Querol (2002) and Montalvo & Reynal-Querol (2005) measured EFI and EPOI values between countries. The EFI value can indicate the level of ethnic heterogeneity and EPOI indicates the level of ethnic polarization which can indicate the probability of conflict. EPOI can predict the probability of ethnic conflict better than EFI. The likelihood of conflict is greater when an area contains two or more ethnic groups of nearly the same size. Ananta et al. (2016) described ethnic diversity in Papua and West Papua with EFI, EPOI and showed how in-migration rate affects ethnic diversity in Papua and West

Papua with simple regression analysis. The results showed that in-migration rate had a positive effect on the EFI value, but didn't affect the EPOI value. Research with a quantitative approach to ethnic internal migration and its impact on the population and characteristics of migrants. Stillwell & Duke-Williams (2005) found that the ethnic composition of in-migration in the UK is similar to the ethnic composition of the whole population.

Methodology

The object of this research is 19 districts/cities in Riau and Riau Islands Province in 2010. We use secondary microdata SP2010 which covers 10% of the Riau and Riau Islands population in 2010. Descriptive analysis is used to see the ethnic composition and its in-migration patterns by age, sex, and area of residenceSimple regression analysis is used to see the effect of recent in-migration on EFI and EPOI. The formula of EFI and EPOI refers to Montalvo & Reynal-Querol (2005) with the following equation:

$$EFI_i = 1 - HHI = 1 - \sum_{j=1}^{m} s_{ij}^2 \tag{1}$$

$$EPOI_i = 1 - \sum_{j=1}^{m} \left(\frac{0.5 - s_{ij}}{0.5}\right)^2 s_{ij} \tag{2}$$

s_{ij}: proportion of j-ethnic group (j:1 ... m) in region-i (i:1 ... n)

Findings

In 2010, The Malays is the ethnic group with the largest population in Riau and Riau Islands Province. The other three largest ethnic groups are the Javanese, Batak and Minangkabau ethnic groups. The composition of migrants by ethnic group in Riau and Riau Islands is similar to the composition of the whole population by ethnic group. The largest percentage of migrants is from Javanese Group. However, ethnic groups of recent in-migrants in Riau Islands is more diverse than Riau. It indicates that the high in-migration rate has contributed to the ethnic diversity of the population.

The migration pattern of ethnic groups is also seen from the characteristics of migrants such as gender, age, and area of residence. In both provinces, the percentage of male migrant in most ethnic group is bigger than female. But, Sumatran and Betawi in Riau and Batak group in Riau Islands have more female migrants. Then, most of the ethnic groups in the two provinces also have the same migration pattern in terms of age. The migration rate is quite high at the age of 5-15 years in each ethnic group and increased at the age of 16-22 years until it reaches the peak at the age of 23-54 years. According to the area of residence, in Riau, most ethnic groups migrated to urban areas. Meanwhile in the Riau Islands, all ethnic groups mostly migrated to urban areas. Besides that, differences in migration patterns are found in minority ethnic groups.

Table 1. EFI, EPOI, and the largest percentage of ethnic groups in Riau Province and Riau Islands, 2010

Kabupaten/Kota	EFI	EPOI	Etnis Terbesar
Provinsi Riau	0,81	0,55	Jawa (29,13%)
Kuantan Singingi	0,57	0,78	Melayu Riau (59,99%)
Indragiri Hulu	0,69	0,76	Melayu Riau (42,43%)
Indragiri Hilir	0,80	0,59	Banjar (31,73%)
Pelalawan	0,80	0,58	Jawa (31,35%)
Siak	0,79	0,58	Jawa (36,42%)
Kampar	0,72	0,70	Melayu Riau (42,95%)
Rokan Hulu	0,77	0,63	Jawa (38,08%)

Bengkalis	0,78	0,63	Jawa (32,04%)
Rokan Hilir	0,72	0,70	Jawa (44,38%)
Kepulauan Meranti	0,64	0,77	Melayu Riau (53,22%)
Kota Pekanbaru	0,79	0,58	Minangkabau (37,99%)
Kota Dumai	0,82	0,54	Jawa (30,54%)
Provinsi Kepulauan Riau	**0,85**	**0,46**	**Jawa (24,76%)**
Karimun	0,79	0,59	Melayu (36,78%)
Bintan	0,79	0,58	Jawa (32,84%)
Natuna	0,66	0,82	Melayu (44,55%)
Lingga	0,38	0,56	Melayu (78,19%)
Kepulauan Anambas	0,50	0,72	Melayu (67,90%)
Kota Batam	0,87	0,43	Jawa (28,03%)
Kota Tanjung Pinang	0,82	0,55	Jawa (27,99%)

Source: 2010 Population Census, Statistics Indonesia

Based on Table 1, the value of EFI in Riau and Riau Islands are 0.81 and 0.85. Those province have high ethnic heterogeneity. But, Riau Islands is more heterogeneous ethnic than Riau. The most homogeneous region is Lingga Regency and the most heterogeneous region is Batam City. Interestingly, the ethnicity with the largest percentage in Batam is not ethnic Malay, but Javanese as migrants ethnic. It indicates that high migration flow can cause the increasing ethnic heterogeneity.

The EPOI values of Riau and Riau Islands are 0.55 and 0.46. Riau is more ethnically polarized than the Riau Archipelago. Natuna Regency has the largest EPOI and Batam City has the smallest EPOI. 5 out of 12 districts/cities have an EPOI value of more than 0.7. It need to be considered because the level of ethnic polarization identifies the presence of two or more ethnic groups with the same size and has a greater chance of ethnic conflict.

Figure 1. Quadrants of EFI and EPOI

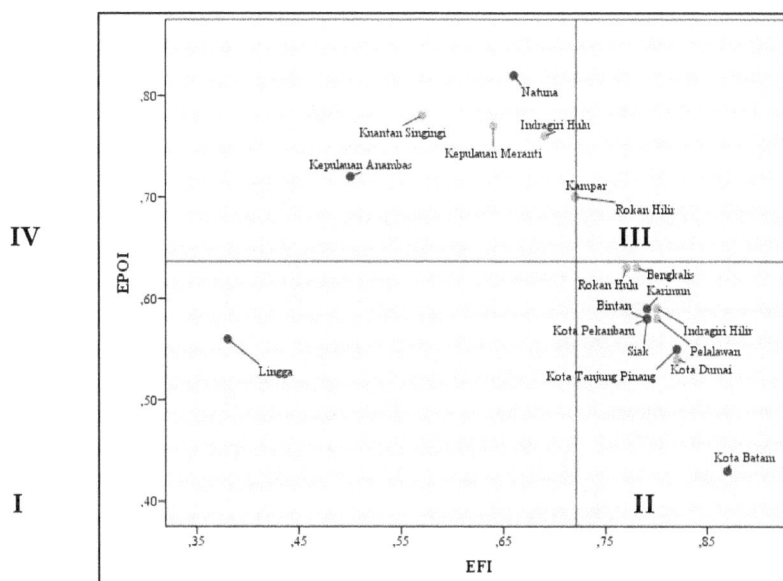

Based on the EFI and EPOI quadrants (Figure 1), at a low EFI, ethnic fractionalization and ethnic polarization is linearly positive. However, at the medium EFI, the correlation is zero. Meanwhile, for a high EFI, the relationship with polarization is negative. The level of polarization decreases at high fractionalization. Quadrant II shows areas with high EFI and low EPOI. These are heterogeneous but not ethnically polarized, so they may have less probability of conflict. But, five out of seven region in Quadrant IV have a medium-high EFI with a high EPOI. Those need special attention because the probability of conflict may be higher than others.

However, as said by Esteban et al. (2012), EFI and EPOI only show the level of ethnic diversity and the potential for conflict. The reality of conflict still depends on other aspects, including the culture of each ethnic group and the prevailing system in society. EFI and EPOI are not the main determinants of internal conflict, but they can be important indices that can help make better policies.

How In-Migration Rate Affects EFI and EPOI

Based on the results of simple regression analysis, at the 95% confidence level, the recent in-migration rate has positive effect on the EFI. These results are in line with the results of Ananta et al (2016) that in-migration rate has positive effect on ethnic heterogeneity. Then, the rate of recent in-migration has a negative effect on the EPOI. This result is different from the research of Ananta et al. (2016) that in-migration rate in Tanah Papua areas doesn't affect the EPOI. The high in-migration rate made Riau and Riau Islands more heterogeneous. Meanwhile, ethnic heterogeneity in Tanah Papua is mainly due to the very varied indigenous Papuan ethnicities. The high polarization in several areas in Papua is also due to the very diverse indigenous ethnicities that trigger greater conflicts between ethnic Papuans. Meanwhile, Riau and Riau Islands have a high ethnic polarization in some areas due to the presence of migrants. Therefore, in comparing the ethnic polarization between regions, it is necessary to pay attention to the composition and culture between ethnicities and conditions in the region. Several regions may have the same level of polarization, but produce different intensity of conflict.

Conclusion

We conclude that the population of Riau and the Riau Archipelago consists of various ethnicities. Those have have a high level of ethnic heterogeneity and a medium level of ethnic polarization. The composition of migrants by ethnic group in Riau and Riau Islands is similar to the composition of the whole population by ethnic groups. Recent migration in ethnic groups tends to be carried out by male migrants, age group 23-54 years old, and residing in urban areas. Differences in migration patterns are found in minority ethnic groups.

References

BPS. (2011a). Migrasi Internal Penduduk Indonesia: Hasil Sensus Penduduk 2010. Jakarta: Badan Pusat Statistik.

BPS. (2011b). Kewarganegaraan, suku bangsa, agama, dan bahasa sehari-hari penduduk Indonesia: Hasil sensus penduduk 2010. Jakarta: BPS.

Ananta, A. (2016). Changing ethnic composition and potential violent conflict in Riau Archipelago, Indonesia: an early warning signal. Population Review, 45(1).

Ananta, A., Arifin, E., Hasbullah, M., Handayani, N., & Pramono, A. (2014). A New Classification of Indonesia's Ethnic Groups (Based on the 2010 Population Census). Institute of Southeast Asian Studies Working Paper Series.

Arifin, E., Ananta, A., Utami, D., Handayani, N., & Pramono, A. (2015). Quantifying Indonesia's Ethnic Diversity:Statistics at National, Provincial, and District Levels. Asian Population Studies, 11(3), 233-256.

Finney, N., & Simpson, L. (2008). Internal Migration and Ethnic Groups: Evidence for Britain from the 2001 Census. Population, Space and Place, 14(2), 63 - 83.

Gayatri, I. (2010). Nationalism, democratization and primordial sentiment in Indonesia: problems of ethnicity versus Indonesianness. Journal of Indonesian Sciences in Humanity 3, 189–203.

Montalvo, J., & Reynal-Querol, M. (2005). Ethnic Polarization, Potential Conflict and Civil Wars. American Economic Review 95(3), 796-816.

Raymer, J., Smith, P., & Giulietti, C. (2011). Combining Census and Registration Data to Analyse Ethnic Migration Patterns in England from 1991 to 2007. Population, Space and Place, 17(1), 73 - 88.

Reynal-Querol, M. (2002). Ethnicity, Political Systems and Civil War. Journal of Conflict Resolution, 46, 29-54.

Wasino. (2011). Multikulturalisme dalam Perspektif Sejarah Sosial. Semarang: Kementerian Kebudayaan dan Pariwisata.

Stillwell, J., & Hussain, S. (2008). Ethnic Group Migration within Britain during 2000-01: A District Level Analysis.

Stillwell, J., & Phillips, D. (2006). Diversity and Change: Understanding the Ethnic Geographies of Leeds. Journal of Ethnic and Migration Studies, 32(7), 1-21.

Taylor, C., & Hudson, M. (1972). The World Handbook of Political and Social Indicators. Ann Arbor, MI: ICSPR.

EXTRATERRESTRIAL MIGRATION AND THE TRANSPORTATION MODEL FOR A SPACE COLONIZATION AND MANUFACTURING SYSTEM: ANALYZING THE RISKS OF ARTIFICIAL ORBITAL DEBRIS ACCUMULATION

Stefani Stojchevska

Abstract

This research examines artificial orbital debris accumulation as a threat to extraterrestrial migration within Earth-orbit subsystems consisted in Wagner's "Transportation Model for a Space Colonization and Manufacturing System". The collision hazard to the ESS and SSPSs is analyzed by two factors: [1] orbital region and [2] nature of operations, where a constructive correlation is exhibited between official space environment statistics data analysis and collision hazard probability-related calculations. Kessler Syndrome predictions are additionally analyzed regarding the near-Earth components of Wagner's model, with the ESS in particular consideration.

Introduction

The "Transportation Model for a Space Colonization and Manufacturing System" designed by Lynn A. Wagner describes a computer model written in Q-GERT simulation language. Being stationed within the Earth-Moon system, the Space Colonization and Manufacturing System (SCMS) consists of six major subsystems whose names correspond to the physical location that they occupy: [1] Low Earth Orbit, [2] Geostationary Earth Orbit, [3] Low Lunar Orbit, [4] Unstable Lagrangian Point Two, [5] Stable Lagrangian Point Four, and [6] Stable Lagrangian Point Five. (Wagner, 1982, p.17) While Wagner's model exhibits promising predispositions for constructing extraterrestrial habitats, given that it was conceptualized in 1982, artificial orbital debris accumulation is drastically increasing within the near-Earth region ever since the launch of Sputnik I in 1957, simultaneously questioning whether artificial orbital debris poses a serious threat to extraterrestrial migration. The SCMS requires for an Earth Space Station (ESS) to reside in Low Earth Orbit (LEO), while a Satellite Solar Power Station (SSPS), considered as the major product of the SCMS, will be constructed in Geostationary Orbit (GEO), initially utilizing two Earth orbits. (Wagner, 1982, p.28) The hazard to space operations from debris is a function of the nature of those operations and the orbital region in which they take place. The orbital region is important because the debris flux encountered by a spacecraft varies greatly with orbital latitude and, to a lesser extent, orbital inclination. The nature of the operations is a factor because the same piece of debris that could cause serious damage to one type of spacecraft might do little harm to a spacecraft with a different configuration or orbital altitude. (Committee on Space Debris, Commission on Engineering and Technical Systems, Division on Engineering and Physical Sciences, & National Research Council, 1995, p.79) Both factors shall be analyzed in continuation;

Orbital Region

In the SCMS there will be two Earth orbits utilized. The first will be a LEO which will be the orbit of an ESS. The orbit selected will be a near-circular orbit with an altitude/inclination of 426 km/28.5 deg, while the second orbit will be a GEO which will be the orbit where SSPSs will be placed. This is a near-circular orbit with an altitude/inclination of 35,740 km/0.0 deg, and has a period of 23 hours 56 minutes (the time for one revolution of the Earth) which causes the SSPS to appear to remain "fixed" over one location on the Earth's equator. (Wagner, 1982, p.21)

Figure 1. Spatial density distributions, for objects 10 cm and larger, for three different years

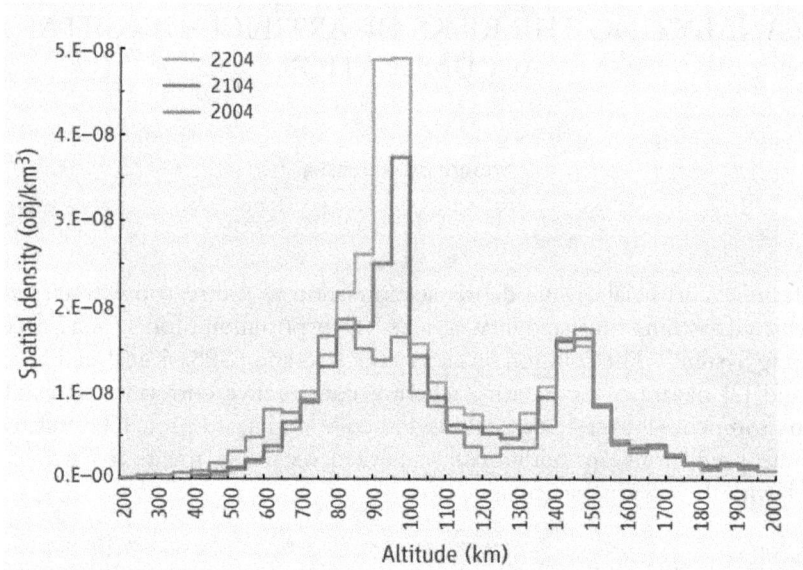

Note. Adapted from "Risks in Space from Orbital Debris" by J.-C. Liou and N.L. Johnson, 2006, SCIENCE, 311, p.341.

Stationing the ESS in LEO creates the risk of collision with other orbiting objects, including artificial orbital debris. In order to calculate the collision hazard for an object in orbit, such as the ESS, the rate of occurrence parameter would be the product of that object's cross-sectional area (AC), average spatial density of all other objects (SPD), average relative velocity (VR) between the object under consideration and all other objects, and the time (T), which is the length of time the object is exposed to the given population density, SPD. (Kaman Sciences Corporation, Engineering Sciences Division, 1992) Equation (1) estimates the probability of a collision between a given object and another object in a given volume:

$PC = 1 - exp\,(-\,AC{*}SPD{*}VR{*}T)$ (1)

where:

PC = probability of collision for the duration of time, T

AC = Cross-sectional area, km2

SPD = Spatial density, objects/km3

VR = Relative velocity, km/s, and

T = Time at risk, seconds

Wagner does not explicitly mention such values for the ESS, hence, remaining parameters may be approximately adopted from the International Space Station (ISS) due to presumed similarity and generally displayed in the form of an example problem: The ESS as an orbiting object of cross-sectional area 700 m2 (this value may vary depending on the ESS configuration) and a mass of 430,500 kg in a

132

426 km near-circular orbit;

SPD: For a near-circular orbit at 426 km, as shown in figure 2, the spatial density can be found by considering an inner radius (lower altitude boundary) of 400 km altitude and an outer radius (upper altitude boundary) of 450 km altitude, i.e. formulating a 400-450 km altitude "shell". Figure 1 plots spatial density values out to 2000 km altitude, where the peak density in LEO evolves throughout the years of 2004, 2104 and 2204 in a continuous manner. While the current peak density still remains at an altitude of around 800 km, collisions will continue to occur in the LEO environment over the next 200 years, primarily driven by the high collision activities in the region between 900- and 1000-km altitudes, and will force the debris population to increase. (Liou & Johnson, 2006, p.340) Since spatial density represents the number of objects that reside in a given volume of space (per cubic kilometer), calculations would depend on up-to-date satellite catalogues data within the above-specified altitude shell, as the ESS lies within the low sub-region.

Figure 2. The ESS within a LEO Altitude "Shell" (400-450 km)

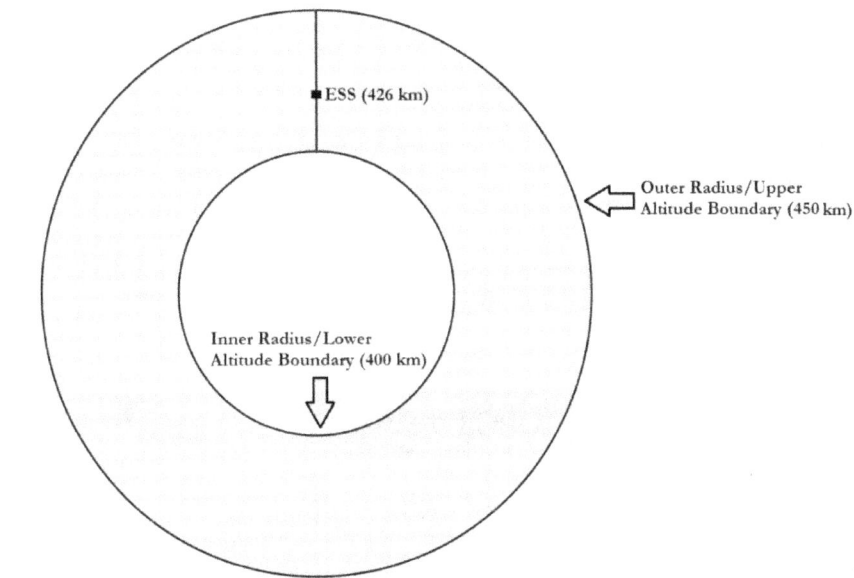

T: Regarding the time at risk, since the ESS is stationed within an orbit which is subject to decay by atmospheric drag, one must consider the lifetime of the ESS when calculating debris collision risk. To calculate the lifetime of the ESS, the ballistic coefficient is needed. The ballistic coefficient is found by:

$$BC = \frac{C_d \cdot A}{m}$$

(2)

where:

BC = Ballistic coefficient, m2/kg

Cd = Drag coefficient, 2.0 to 2.2

A = Cross-sectional area, m2, and

m = Mass, kg

VR: Considering the ESS placement in LEO, the average relative velocity is assumed to be about 10km/s;

AC: Depending on its configuration, like the ISS (700 m2 and 2300 m2), the average cross-sectional area of the ESS may vary. For accuracy, the average collision cross-sectional area between the ESS and all other objects with which it could collide should be used in equation (1) instead of the physical cross-sectional area. The average collision **cross-sectional** area is found by:

$$XC = \frac{1}{n} \Sigma ([AC]^{0.5} + [AC_i]^{0.5})^2$$

(3)

where:

XC = Average collision cross-section

AC = Cross-sectional area of the object

AC_i = Cross-sectional area of object_i in population, and

n = number of objects

Equation (3), however, can be simplified by assuming that all objects in the population are small compared to the object under consideration (ESS). Thus, the collision cross-section can be substituted by the cross-sectional area of the object for a reasonable first order approximation. (Kaman Sciences Corporation, Engineering Sciences Division, 1992) This refers to the assumption of considering space debris approximately up to 10 cm in the population, as well as the possibility for the ESS cross-sectional area value to vary, depending on the ESS configuration.

Table 1. Components of the Probability of Collision (PC) for the ESS in LEO

Variable	Definition	Unit of Measure	Approximate Value	Estimated Function
SPD	Spatial Density	objects/km3	N/A	Formulating an altitude "shell" by considering the lower and upper altitude boundary
T	Time at Risk	sec	N/A	Function of the length of time the ESS poses a risk to space debris and the ESS lifetime
VR	Relative Collision Velocity	km/s	10	√2 the orbital velocity of LEO
AC	Cross-sectional area	km/2	0,0007	Projected area of the ESS along the trajectory

Values displayed in Table 1 reflect the input parameters of (1), while the "Estimated Function" column describes the particular approach dependent on one or more factors. It is proposed to estimate the spatial density by formulating an altitude shell (400-450 km). Regarding the time at risk, the ESS lifetime is required, where the BC = 0,003 m2/kg, given the following values: $Cd = 2.07$; $A = 700$ m2; $m = 430, 500$ kg; More study is required in order to achieve precise calculations in near future.

NOTE: The ESS is, technically, located in Very Low Earth Orbit (VLEO) - below approximately 450 km in altitude. It would not continuously remain at 426 km altitude – as the orbit decays, its altitude will decrease. Since the current peak density in LEO is at an altitude of around 800 km and would continuously evolve in the region between 900- and 1000-km altitudes over the next 200 years, ESS altitude decrease would not contribute to significant debris collision-related threats, although reducing spacecraft drag in VLEO might be necessary;

Figure 3. Flux distribution against local azimuth based on Earth-fixed coordinate system

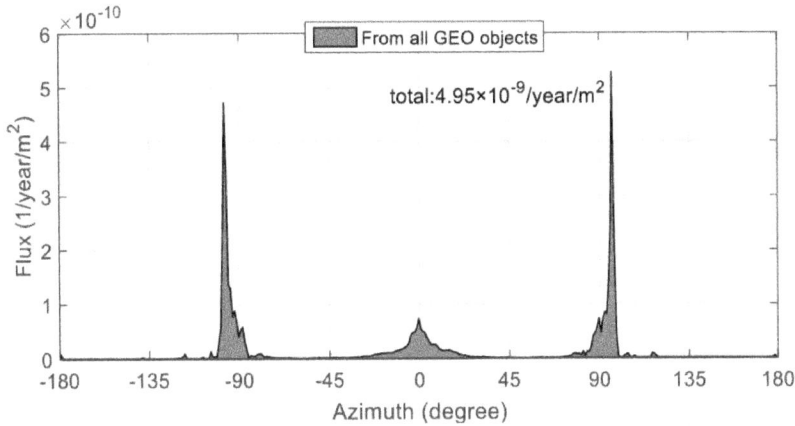

Note. Adapted from "GEO space debris environment determination in the earth fixed coordinate system" by W. Dongfang, P. Baojun and X. Wei-ke, 2016, *Acta Astronautica*, 118, p.219.

Placing SSPSs in GEO, on the other hand, is associated with significantly lower spatial density. Collision hazard calculations in GEO may also be estimated by (1), being based on the kinetic theory of gases, which assumes that objects are randomly distributed and can all pose a collision risk to each other. (Chrystal et al, 2011, p.17) Consequently, the four parameters of the PC equation correspond to the flux distribution for 0.0 deg that appears to be below 1, as figure 3 displays. One should consider GEO's altitude/inclination of 35,740 km/0.0 deg, indicating that the plane of the SSPSs' orbit is equated to Earth's equatorial plane, as well as that SSPSs are stationed within an orbit which is not subject to decay by atmospheric drag;

Figure 4. An adapted "Risk Cell" as a Subset of the GEO Arc at the SSPS's altitude/inclination

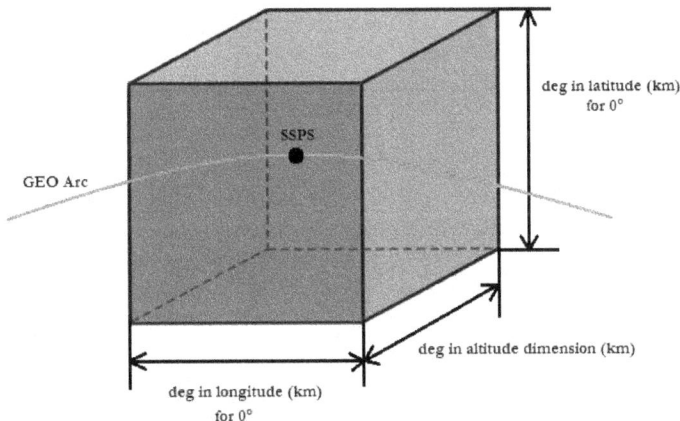

According to Chrystal et al (2011), the creation of a "risk cell" is presented, primarily aimed at estimating the spatial density, and from which the remaining parameters are dependent on. Given that the SPD analysis, in particular, is specifically modified to eliminate station-kept satellites and account for the longitudinal bunching of trapped objects, adapting the "risk cell" concept toward estimating debris collision risk regarding SSPSs might prove to be significantly beneficial. Figure 4 displays an identically designed "risk cell" which addresses collision hazards in GEO where SSPSs will be placed, given the altitude/inclination of 35,740 km/0.0 deg, respectively. Proposed dimensions would correspond to Earth's equator values in relation to 0 deg, such as the longitude (111.320 km) and latitude (110.574 km), as well as depth regarding altitude dimension. Understandably, more research is required regarding the adaptation of such concept.

Table 2. Components of the Probability of Collision (PC) for SSPSs in GEO

Variable	Definition	Unit of Measure	Approximate Value	Estimated Function
SPD	Spatial Density	objects/km3	N/A	Function of dividing the total number of space debris in each risk cell by the volume of the risk cell
T	Time at Risk	sec	31 557 600	The length of time the SSPS poses a risk to space debris within the "risk" cell for annual collision probability
VR	Relative Collision Velocity	km/s	0.5	Function of the orbital velocity of the SSPS and space debris (as colliding objects) and the angle at which the SSPS and space debris strike
AC	Cross-sectional area	km/2	0,0001	Measure of how the SSPS and space debris (as two impacting objects) will interact during the collision, depending on both the impacted SSPS and piece of space debris hitting it

Approximated values displayed in Table 2 reflect the input parameters of (1), while the "Estimated Function" column describes particular approaches influenced by Chrystal's "risk cell", where the most crucial step is to define a distinctive risk cell as a subset of the GEO arc at the SSPS's altitude/inclination. With the SSPS acknowledged as a spacecraft at risk, the longitudinally-dependent probability of collision value may be calculated. Particularly regarding the spatial density, the total number of space debris in each risk cell is found by determining the amount of time space debris resides in each cell consider the dimensions of longitude, altitude and latitude/inclination;

Nature of Operations

The main activities of the SCMS are to build space colonies, to build Satellite Solar Power Stations, and to process lunar and asteroidal ore. The major component of the transportation system is the Inter-Orbital Shuttle (IOS) which moves most goods between the points in the SCMS and is unloaded, serviced and loaded at each of the facilities. (Wagner, 1982, p.ix) Within the near-Earth region, the ESS will receive the Heavy Launch Vehicle (HLV) from the Earth and transfer the HLV's cargo to an IOS for transport to other parts of the SCMS. (Wagner, 1982, p.27) On the other hand, the SSPS will be construed in GEO to supply the Earth with inexpensive electrical power from sunlight. The SSPSs are built in parts and then transported in IOSs to GEO to be constructed. (Wagner, 1982, p.28) This indicates that the SSPS and particularly the ESS are the main spacecrafts crucial for the SCMS, hence, necessary to be protected from collision hazards.

Figure 5. Wagner's LEO and GEO Subsystems

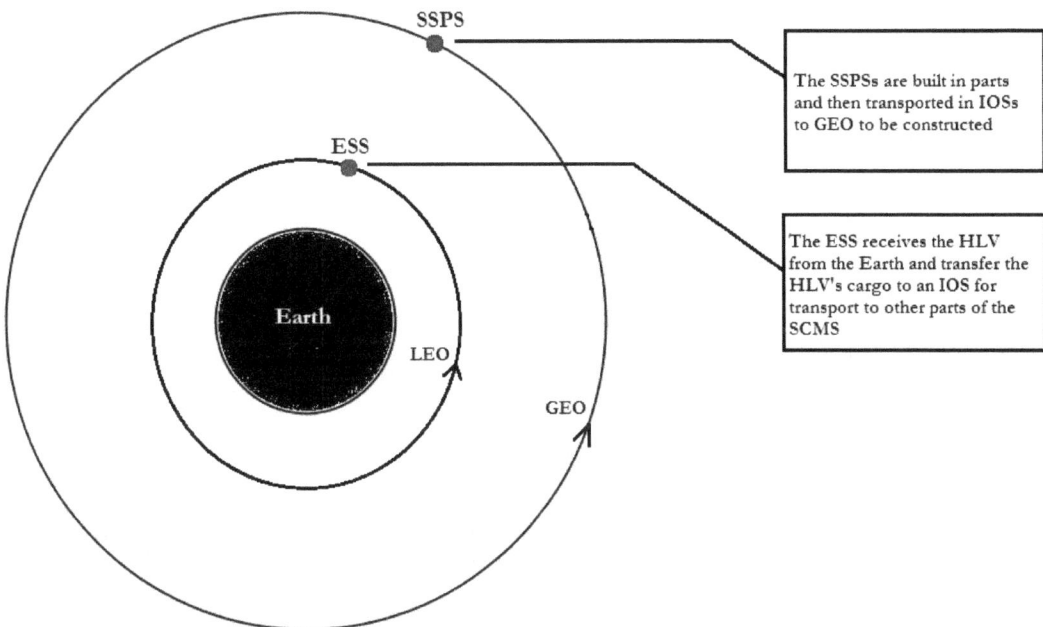

The "Nature of Operations" factor addresses both the configuration and orbital altitudes of the spacecraft. While the configurations of the ESS and SSPS can only be approximated, their orbital altitudes are explicitly defined and being 35,314 km apart. Consequently, collision velocities vary with orbital altitude and inclination. In LEO, collision velocities vary from almost 0 km/s to greater than 15 km/s. On the other hand, orbital velocities are directly related to altitude – objects in lower-altitude orbits move faster than objects in higher orbits. Orbital velocity for circular LEO orbits varies from almost 8 km/s (skimming the top of the atmosphere) to about 7 km/s (at 2,000 km). In GEO, orbital velocity is about 3 km/s. (Committee on Space Debris et al, 1995, p.89) This indicates that the ESS has significantly higher chances of being struck by space debris, disabling the task of transferring the HLV's cargo to an IOS for transport to other parts of the SCMS, thus disrupting the entire process. Correspondingly, this section manifests particular ESS considerations;

Figure 6. Normalized collision velocity distribution as a function of the debris velocity for a spacecraft with orbit inclinations of 28.5 •, 63 •, and 90 •

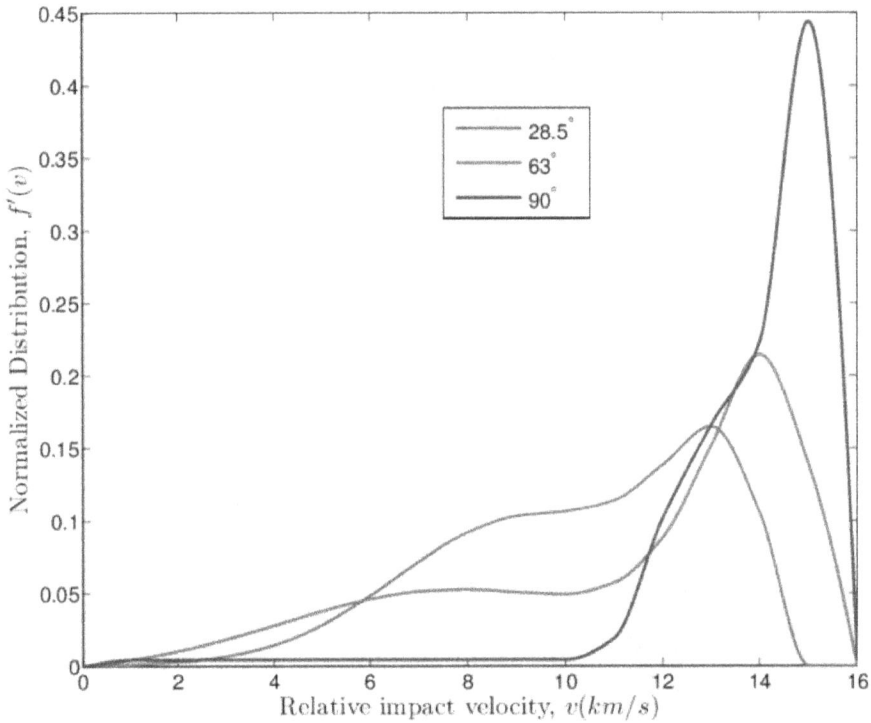

Note. Adapted from "Bare-tape scaling laws for de-orbit missions in a space debris environment," by S.B. Khan, 2014, Departamento de F´ısica Aplicada a la Ingenier´ıa Aeronautica.

Figure 6 displays numerically normalized velocity distribution function with catalogued objects at various inclinations as a function of a LEO object's velocity. (Khan, 2014, p.16) Given that the ESS is stationed at an inclination of 28.5 deg, the relative impact velocity of approximately 13 km/s reaches its peak at a normalized distribution of approximately 0.15 of value (notated by the green line). Regarding the collision velocity, we identify the ESS and a piece of debris (presumably 10 cm and larger) as two orbital objects with velocity vectors v1 and v2. Furthermore, it is important to consider the angle at which the piece of debris would possibly strike the spacecraft. Near the collision point these can be represented as straight lines making an angle θ between them. For a head-on collision θ = 180º (π radians), and θ is zero for a 'tail' collision. The collision velocity vector $\mathbf{v_c}$ is found by subtracting vector $\mathbf{v_2}$ from vector $\mathbf{v_1}$. This is accomplished geometrically by reversing the direction of $\mathbf{v_2}$ and laying it next to $\mathbf{v_1}$. The resultant velocity $\mathbf{v_c}$ is drawn from the tail of the first vector to the head of the second. To calculate the magnitude of the collision velocity v_c we use the cosine rule on triangle ABC:

$$v_c{}^2 = v_1{}^2 + v_2{}^2 - 2\ v_1\ v_2\ \cos(\ \theta\ )\ (4)$$

If we consider two circular orbits at the same altitude (but with different inclinations) then:

$v_1 = v_2 = v_o$ (the orbital velocity)

138

and we can then write the collision velocity as:

$$v_c = \sqrt{2}\, v_o\, (\, 1 - \cos(\theta)\,)^{\frac{1}{2}}$$ (5)

Moreover, if we assume circular orbits, then the orbital velocity varies only as function of the height of the orbit. This can be calculated directly using Kepler's law, or derived from Newton's second law of motion and gravitational force law. Also, for a head-on collision the maximum collision velocity is twice the orbital velocity. (Australian Space Academy, n.d.) Hence, considering the ESS, the approximate value for 400 km is 7.84 v_o (km/s), while the maximum collision velocity is 15.68 km/s.

To protect their spacecraft against the debris hazard, designers can calculate typical collision velocities and impact angles and then, if necessary, modify their spacecraft design to protect the areas most likely to be struck by debris. (Committee on Space Debris et al, 1995, p.88) This analysis, however, only presumes the ESS's technical realization. Since Wagner's model is written in Q-GERT, such simulation language allows a graphical presentation of the system to be modified to experiment with different transportation strategies. The subsystems are distinguished from each other not by position but by the flight times between them. It will, therefore, be possible to "move" the site of a subsystem to match what the production engineers and celestial-mechanics experts finally settle on. (Wagner, 1982, p.18)

Kessler Syndrome

In addition to collision hazard probability estimates, it is generally presumed that continued creation of space debris will lead to the Kessler syndrome, when the density of objects in LEO is high enough that collisions between objects and debris create a cascade effect, each crash generating debris that then increases the likelihood of further collisions. At this point, certain orbits around Earth will become entirely inhospitable. (ESA, 2020) Implying that time is limited in relation to solving the artificial orbital debris accumulation issue we simultaneously question whether the ESS would be endangered by the Kessler Syndrome in the long run?

The impact rate on the ESS, dI/dt, can be approximated according to the spatial density of objects in LEO, by using the equation:

$$\frac{dI}{dt} = S\bar{V}_s A_c$$ (6)

where Vs is an average relative velocity, Ac is the cross-sectional area of the ESS, and I is the total number of impacts with the ESS at time t. (Kessler & Cour-Palais, 1978, p.2638) Considering previous estimates within this research, the average relative velocity and cross-sectional area values are determined. The collision rate between all objects, dC/dt, is given by:

$$\frac{dC}{dt} = \frac{1}{2}\int S^2 \bar{V}_s \bar{A}_{cc}\, dU$$ (7)

where C is the number of collisions between objects, Acc is an average collision cross-sectional area of the objects, and dU is an element of volume. (Kessler & Cour-Palais, 1978, p.2638) Regarding the initial predictions, since the actual growth rate has been only slightly lower than the lowest assumed rate in 1978, it is instructive to compare the 1978 predictions with the actual collision rate. To-date, there have been four known accidental hypervelocity collisions between catalogued objects, as shown in Table 3.

Table 3. Random Collisions between Catalogued Objects

Date	Objects involved	Altitude	Number of fragments
23 Dec 1991	Cosmos 1934 Debris from Cosmos 926	980 km	2
24 July 1996	Cerise spacecraft 1986 Ariane explosion fragment	685 km	1
17 Jan 2005	Thor-Burner 2A rocket 2000 Chinese explosion fragment	885 km	4
10 Feb 2009	Iridium 33 Cosmos 2251	790 km	>1500

Note. Adapted from "The Kessler Syndrome: Implications to Future Space Operations" by D.J. Kessler, N.L. Johnson, J.-C. Liou and M. Matney, 2010, 33rd Annual AAS Guidance and Control Conference, p.4.

Figure 7 compares the rate of these collisions with the 1978 predictions. All except the 1996 (Cerise) collision likely contributed to the current hazard to spacecraft from the small debris; only the 2009 (Iridium) collision was catastrophic and contributes to future collision cascading. The observed collision rate would be in close agreement with the 320 object/year growth rate if the adopted collision cross-section were increased by about 50%. (Kessler et al., 2010, p.5) Simultaneously, specific LEO regions under notable risk are identified. Although the ESS would still be exposed to debris-related collision hazards, its altitude is not equated to the LEO peak density. Besides integrating above-mentioned equations, national forces would consult a catalogue of identified pieces of debris and monitor the ESS orbit in order to detect a piece of debris and determine whether it has potential to threaten the ESS.

Figure 7. Number of Collisions Predicted in 1978 between Catalogued Objects Compared to the Observed Collision Rate

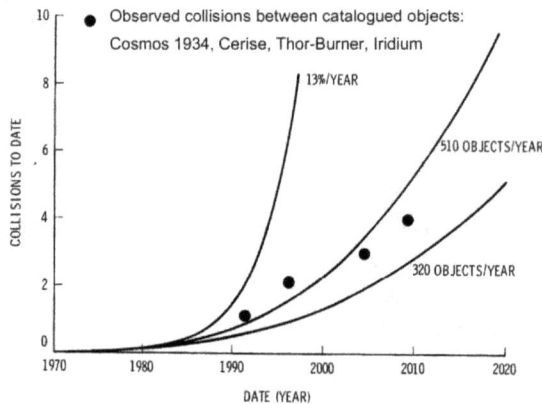

Note. Adapted from "The Kessler Syndrome: Implications to Future Space Operations" by D.J. Kessler, N.L. Johnson, J.-C. Liou and M. Matney, 2010, 33rd Annual AAS Guidance and Control Conference, p.5.

On average over the last two decades, 12 accidental 'fragmentations' have occurred in space every year – and this trend is unfortunately increasing. Fragmentation events describe moments in which debris is created due to collisions, explosions, electrical problems and even just the detachment of objects due to the harsh conditions in space. (ESA, 2020) Moreover, the stability of the orbital debris environment depends not only on the rate fragments are generated, but also on the rate fragments decay from orbit. Without atmospheric decay, it would require only two objects maintained in orbits that cross each other to represent an unstable environment. The rate of orbital decay can be predicted within 10% to 20% accuracy, if the area-to-mass ratio is known and if the initial orbit is known. (Kessler et al., 2010, p.5) Consequently, their end-of-life operations methods vary, as the ESS orbit is prone to atmospheric decay, while the SSPS orbit is not.

Figure 8. Number Fragmentation Events

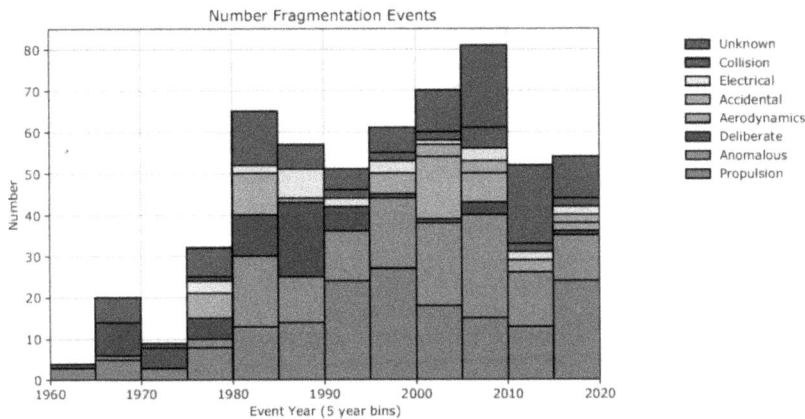

Note. Adapted by "The current state of space debris" by ESA, 2020.
(https://www.esa.int/Safety_Security/Space_Debris/The_current_state_of_space_debris)

All things considered, spacecrafts, such as the ESS and SSPSs, are subject to orbital debris impact damage, which has the potential to degrade performance, shorten the mission, or result in catastrophic loss of the vehicle or crew. Hence, their ultimate protection from orbital debris would become an absolute necessity. In fact, a specific comparison can be made regarding the ISS, which is the most heavily protected spacecraft with shields or barriers installed on the U.S. modules to protect it from damage by orbital debris as large as 1 cm. To avoid debris larger than 10 cm, NASA has had the ISS conduct approximately 27 collision avoidance maneuvers since 1999, the most recent of which was in September 2020 when a piece of debris was expected to pass within 1 mile of the Station. (National Aeronautics and Space Administration OIG, 2021, p.7) Identical collision avoidance maneuvers may also be applied to the ESS and SSPSs, in correspondence to the environment evolution of the debris population.

Conclusions

Although this research analyzes the extraterrestrial migration concept in an indirect manner, obtained results show that hazards to the ESS and SSPSs, as well as astronauts engaged in associated activities within those spacecrafts, are quite plausible regarding artificial orbital debris accumulation. More precisely, debris collision-related threats are not severely endangering regarding current LEO and GEO space environments. Given the predictions of continuous debris population growth, however, the risks are prone to significantly increase in the future. While effective space debris mitigation undertakings are encouraged, Q-GERT simulation language allows divergent transportation strategies assessments. Moreover, the potential realization of Wagner's model cannot be understood in isolation, as philosophical, psychological, anthropological, ethical and legal constructs must be correspondingly scrutinized. The near-Earth subsystems of Wagner's model, nevertheless, manifest realistic predispositions for long-term human migration to space in near future, simultaneously enabling a breakthrough within the new epoch of the Anthropocosmos.

References

Australian Space Academy. (n.d.) *Collision Velocity in Low Earth Orbit*. https://www.spaceacademy.net.au/watch/debris/collvel.htm

Chrystal, P., McKnight, D., & Meredith, P. (2011). *Space Debris: On collision course for insurers?* Zurich: Swiss Reinsurance Company.

Committee on Space Debris, Commission on Engineering and Technical Systems, Division on Engineering and Physical Sciences, & National Research Council. (1995). *Orbital Debris: A Technical Assessment*. Washington: National Academies Press.

Dongfang, W., & Wei-ke, X. (2016). GEO space debris environment determination in the earth fixed coordinate system. *Acta Astronautica*, 118, pp. 218-223.

ESA. (2020, October). *The current state of space debris*. European Space Agency. https://www.esa.int/Safety_Security/Space_Debris/The_current_state_of_space_debris

ESA Space Debris Office. (2021). *ESA's Annual Space Environment Report*. Darmstadt: European Space Agency.

Kaman Sciences Corporation, Engineering Sciences Division. (1992). *On-Orbit Collision Hazard Analysis in low-Earth orbit using the Poisson Probability Distribution (Version 1.0.)* Alexandria, Va.: Kaman Sciences Corporation, Engineering Sciences Division.

Kessler, D.J. & Cour-Palais, B.G. (1978). Collision Frequency of Artificial Satellites: The Creation of a Debris Belt. *Journal of Geophysical Research*, 83, p.2638.

Kessler, D.J., Johnson, N.L., Liou, J.-C., & Matney, M. (2010). The Kessler Syndrome: Implications to Future Space Operations. 33rd Annual AAS Guidance and Control Conference, 1-15.

Khan, S.B. (2014). Bare-tape scaling laws for de-orbit missions in a space debris environment. (Doctoral Thesis). Madrid: Departamento de Física Aplicada a la Ingeniería Aeronautica.

Liou, J.-C. & Johnson, N.L. (2006). Risks in Space from Orbital Debris. *SCIENCE*, `311, p.341.

National Aeronautics and Space Administration OIG. (2021, January 27). *NASA's Efforts to Mitigate the Risks Posed by Orbital Debris*. Report No. IG-21-011. National Aeronautics and Space Administration OIG. https://oig.nasa.gov/docs/IG-21-011.pdf

Wagner, L.A. (1982). A Transportation Model for a Space Colonization and Manufacturing System: A Q-GERT Simulation. (Master's Thesis). Dayton, Ohio: Faculty of the School of Engineering of the Air Force Institute of Technology.

APOROFOBIA Y NACIONALISMO:
EL RECHAZO HACIA EL INMIGRANTE (POBRE)

Laura Natalia Rodríguez Ariano[1]

Gran parte de las migraciones del siglo XXI son forzosas y no van en busca de un sueño, suerte y fortuna, buscan de un trabajo, huyen de sus países de origen debido a los problemas políticos, sociales y económicos.

Algunas externalidades negativas hacia las migraciones a nivel mundial e impulsan los movimientos nacionalistas actuales, son discriminación, violencia e intolerancia que, al mismo tiempo desatan las diferentes fobias hacia el que es considerado diferente, *el otro*, el que no pertenece al lugar, ya sea por tener características físicas, ideológicas y costumbres distintas.

El objetivo principal de este trabajo es analizar cómo influye la aporofobia en los crecientes nacionalismos del siglo XXI y las consecuencias en el ser humano como un ente de reciprocidad, dentro de las diferentes relaciones de poder. De esta manera, se analiza el rechazo a la población inmigrante por parte de las sociedades anfitrionas, en específico a los inmigrantes irregulares.

Para evitar equívocos, la definición que se empleará de nacionalismo será la de John Keane[2], donde marca la diferencia entre nacionalismo (como algo despectivo) a diferencia del patriotismo (parte positiva del amor a la patria).

El nacionalismo carece del respeto que pertenece a la identidad nacional. No tiene temor y penuria del presente ni del pasado, supone que la *culpa* es de los extranjeros y de los <<enemigos de la nación>>. De acuerdo con Keane, el nacionalismo, se encuentra lleno de petulancias discriminatorias y se tratan de introducir el pensamiento en la sociedad anfitriona. Por consiguiente, el nacionalismo es la lucha por la identidad nacional, fundamentalista que tiende a la codicia por el poder y la gloria del Estado-nación.

Aporofobia

Actualmente vivimos en un mundo, donde el ser humano ha denotado más distinciones entre el <<*nosotros y el ellos*>> haciendo una fuerte alusión hacia la otredad, lo que le es distinto, lo que no es parte de su entorno. El rechazo frente a esta otredad resulta un factor inamovible para las personas, donde muchos dejan a flor de piel sus *espíritus animales* y el poder adquisitivo juega un papel fundamental al diferenciar y menospreciar a otro ser humano por su capacidad adquisitiva. Se trata de un problema de pobreza, característica común entre la población, **aporofobia.**

Se presenta en discursos políticos y plataformas electorales, siendo uno de los principales desafíos de la democracia del siglo XXI. Se trata de un problema de pobreza y sirve para entender en gran parte los conflictos políticos y sociales en la actualidad. La aporofobia[3], aunado a la intolerancia por raza,

---

[1] Doctoranda en Ciencias Sociales, en el área de relaciones de poder y cultura política en la Universidad Autónoma Metropolitana, unidad Xochimilco, Ciudad de México. Maestra en relaciones internacionales y licenciada en economía ambas por la UAM-X.
[2] En vida y muerte de la democracia, 2018.
[3] Sin justificar ningún tipo de rechazo, esta provoca odio a la población de bajos recursos.

etnia, preferencia sexual, religión o extranjería propicia una animadversión aún más grande a la inmigración, en específico a la inmigración irregular.

Esta supuesta nueva manera de diferenciar y violentar a los seres humanos, propicia un rechazo exacerbado hacia los inmigrantes y es originada (no en su totalidad, pero si potenciada) por las elites gobernantes y las más altas esferas políticas a nivel mundial. Donde, la demagogia y la mentira son elementos predominantes para atacar al inmigrante de bajos recursos que llega con una expectativa de mejorar su nivel de vida.

Cabe destacar que los inmigrantes, en específico los indocumentados, tienen las tasas más altas de desempleo, precariedad y las peores condiciones laborales que el resto de los trabajadores o una persona que tiene regularidad en su estatus migratorio. Consecuencia de lo anterior son personas más vulnerables a caer en pobreza.

El *problema*[4] de la alteridad

Conforme pasa el tiempo el ser humano ha denotado más distinciones entre el <<*nosotros y el ellos*>> El rechazo hacia la otredad resulta un factor inamovible, donde muchos dejan a flor de piel sus espíritus animales y el poder adquisitivo juega un papel fundamental al diferenciar y menospreciar a otro ser humano.

La inmigración irregular, es vista como *el otro*, el diferente, es perseguida y violentada de manera cruenta y salvaje. La idea que permea en el <<imaginario colectivo>> sobre otredad es la de considerarla como un intruso, no se toma en cuenta los beneficios que aportan los inmigrantes y solo se maximizan las dificultades que, de acuerdo al discurso anti-inmigratorio neo-nacionalista, van a causar al lugar de destino. Esta concepción peyorativa del <<*otro*>> se reproduce a través de la transmisión cultural basada en la conservación del poder y es promovida por la identidad colectiva predominante.

En la aporofobia, la otredad se encuentra condicionada por los estigmas y estereotipos que se le han impuesto a los irregulares pobres, comienza en un nivel conceptual, se extiende por las expectativas que la población receptora tiene y culmina con los actos discriminatorios que llevan a cabo.

Consecuente, los discursos y delitos de odio son las herramientas principales por los que existe una estigmatización en la que se deshumaniza a las personas, en este caso a los inmigrantes pobres, los áporos[5] y se les convierte en el blanco de diferentes tipos discriminación.

Todos somos homo reciprocan

Los mecanismos de reciprocidad son muy sencillos y el ser humano los realiza de manera consciente e inconsciente. En otras palabras, la persona que propicia un beneficio y aporta será parte del grupo <<nosotros>> y la persona que no aporta y provoca algún malestar será parte de <<los otros>>.

La reciprocidad, es el núcleo de nuestras sociedades basadas en el contrato, es decir, el dar y recibir. Vivimos en sociedades contractuales.

La interrogante de las sociedades contractuales que termina siendo un inconveniente es ¿Qué pasa con aquellos que no pueden dar nada a cambio? Porqué si la clave de la sociedad es el intercambio, aquellos que no tienen nada que ofrecer quedan rezagados y esos son los pobres, los áporos. Los que no tienen posibilidades para entrar al intercambio porque no pueden devolver algo que, de acuerdo a la sociedad

---

[4] Las cursivas son mías
[5] Los áporos son los disminuidos psíquicos, los enfermos mentales, los inmigrantes, los refugiados y los que en cada ámbito de la vida social no tienen los recursos para entrar al ciclo del intercambio.

anfitriona, le parezca conveniente o interesante para entrar en esta dinámica.

¿Por qué odiamos a los pobres?

Una variable importante y que nos ayuda a introducir una mirada de manera general a este tipo de conflictos sociales, es la globalización. En la coyuntura actual regida por el neoliberalismo, las sociedades globales se desarrollan en torno al capital, como promotoras del consumismo y la búsqueda de un beneficio económico. Por esta razón, se genera un sentimiento de rechazo hacia las personas que, por su situación de pobreza, no pueden ingresar a una sociedad basada en el intercambio.

La consolidación del sistema capitalista a nivel mundial vulnera los derechos fundamentales de las personas y propicia la distribución inequitativa de la riqueza, tiene como consecuencia el empobrecimiento, en mayoría de las personas que habitan los países denominados Sur.

La lógica capitalista consiste en despreciar a los pobres y admirar a los ricos, sin tomar en cuenta que pobreza es el fracaso de una sociedad. La incógnita es ¿Se rechaza por ser pobres o porqué son extranjeros? La respuesta es simple, se rechaza al pobre en general, puede ser connacional, extranjero, mujer, hombre incluso un familiar. A los grupos neo-nacionalistas no les interesa cultivar ni erradicar la pobreza, solo les interesa que los áporos no lleguen en sus países.

¿Mecanismo de defensa biológico?

Se tiene la creencia, que la aporofobia y la xenofobia tiene unas bases cerebrales; se dice que este rechazo es natural en el ser humano y es un mecanismo de defensa biológico que ocurre en el córtex del lóbulo prefrontal.

Autores como Eagelman y Evers afirman sobre la necesidad de sobrevivencia en el ser humano. Es decir, lo que nos interesa es sobrevivir y de la mejor forma posible, por lo tanto, intentamos rodearnos de personas que nos resultan agradables, similares y que nos aportan algo. Es por esta razón que nos sentimos más identificados con aquellos con los que compartimos una lengua, cultura, costumbres incluso religión. Este instinto de supervivencia, es un mecanismo de disociación que nos permite rechazar o apartar todo aquello que nos molesta o perturba.

Es importante mencionar que, el mecanismo de defensa es respecto al miedo que nos propicia lo diferente y lo desconocido, lo cual no justifica en absoluto ningún delito en contra de ningún ser vivo, disfrazado de fobia.

Lo que disgustan son los inmigrantes pobres

Normalmente se habla de xenofobia, de prevención y rechazo al extranjero. Esto no solo se trata de una situación de extranjería, ya que existen extranjeros que se reciben con mucho entusiasmo, sin embargo, los pobres son los que incomodan y cuando vienen de fuera más. Es decir, lo que disgusta es la pobreza, y eso si viene acompañado de xenofobia y racismo incrementa la intolerancia y discriminación entre los seres humanos.

Cuando se habla de pobreza, no solo se trata de pobreza económica, sino del individuo que no tiene nada que intercambiar en cuanto a favores, en cada ámbito de la vida social, esta persona que no tiene algo interesante por aportar[6], en consecuencia, es excluido y relegado.

Partidos de ultraderecha

Los extranjeros pobres son los que incomodan a los nuevos partidos de ultraderecha que caracterizan

---

[6] De acuerdo al discurso anti-inmigratorio

un nuevo orden mundial, principalmente en los países receptores de inmigrantes, donde la aporofobia es una particularidad que predomina en el resurgimiento de los nacionalismos en occidente.

Desde los últimos años los partidos <<nacionalistas de occidente modernos>> presentan actitudes discriminatorias que cobran fuerza, en este caso la aporofobia es una problemática global y no es característico de un solo país.

Es evidente el punto de inflexión mediante el cual se generan percepciones, puntos de vista sesgados y discriminatorios hacia las personas por su origen o procedencia, aunado por su capacidad de reciprocidad. Marca una diferencia grande entre países emisores y países receptores. Al mismo tiempo se conciben dos tipos de recepciones: <<*las que importan*>> y <<*las que no interesan*[7]>>, una raíz de esta distinción es la aporofobia, factor que caracteriza la entrada e inserción en una sociedad.

Conclusión

Con el paso del tiempo, la cultura de occidente ha adquirido nuevas connotaciones donde la apariencia importa más que la esencia, donde al hombre o mujer se le considera exitoso por sus posesiones materiales y no por su persona o conocimiento. Esta es una de las principales razones por las que el ser humano tiende a realizar juicios de valor negativos hacia personas con pocos recursos.

Los diferentes tipos de intolerancia disfrazadas de fobias propician una nueva forma de realizar política; los gobernantes de varios países utilizan mecanismos de exclusión como parte de sus campañas y discursos políticos para conseguir un resultado favorable dentro del voto popular. En donde, no tienen mucho por ofrecer y buscan *a quien echarle la culpa*[8] de los problemas coyunturales en los que se encuentra su país, prometiendo acabar con los causantes de su inestabilidad social, económica y política.

En la mentalidad capitalista predomina el rechazo a los inmigrantes tiene un componente aporófobo.

No se puede entender al racismo y xenofobia como elementos aislados que surgen en las relaciones humanas. Atrás de esto, existe una estructura que legitima y reproduce los idearios de pertenencia y exclusión, ejecutando políticas discriminatorias y validando conductas inaceptables. Como sociedad tenemos la obligación el poder de reconocer y erradicar los comportamientos, discriminatorios que tenemos internalizados.

No se puede hablar de democracia ni de derechos humanos si se continúan realizando prácticas discriminatorias. Todas las personas tienen un valor y tienen algo positivo por ofrecer. Merecen que sus derechos humanos sean respetados y garantizados.

La aporofobia es un problema importante y refleja la situación mundial, nos invita a analizar sobre quien está siendo relegado y porqué motivos. Finalmente, la pobreza es una condición que todos debemos enfrentar, no por una situación económica o de reciprocidad, sino por razones más importantes como humanidad.

Bibliografía

Chul Han, B. (2018). *La expulsión de lo distinto*. Herder España.

Cortina, A. (2013). *¿Para qué sirve realmente la ética?* Ediciones Paidós, España.

Cortina, A. (2017). *Aporofobia, el rechazo al pobre*. Paidós, España.

Descartes, R. (1972). *Las pasiones del alma*. Península, España.

Eagleman, D., & Ramis, D. A. (2013). *Incógnito: Las vidas secretas del cerebro (Argumentos nº 449)* (1.ª ed.). Editorial Anagrama, España.

---

[7] Como lo menciona, Huntington.

[8] Las cursivas son mías.

Evers, K. (2010). Neuroética. Cuando la Materia se despierta. Katz, España.

Flores, J. (2003). *Totalitarismo. Revolución y negación del pasado.* Universidad Autónoma Metropolitana, México.

Fukuyama, F. (2019). *Identidad.* Ediciones Culturales Paidós, España.

Keane, J. (2018). Vida y muerte de la democracia/ Life and death of democracy. Fondo de Cultura Económica, México.

Todorov, T. (2017). *El miedo a los bárbaros.* Galaxia Gutenberg, España.

PERSPECTIVES OF MIGRATIONS FROM CENTRAL AMERICA AND MEXICO TO THE UNITED STATES UNDER THE NEW BIDEN GOVERNMENT

Rodolfo García Zamora and Selene Gaspar Olvera

Abstract

After four years of his anti-immigrant policy, which continued the deportations from previous governments, President Trump militarized the border, expanded the wall's construction, dismantled the asylum and refugee policies, and subordinated Mexico and Central America to his regional immigration and security policies, which significantly reduced migratory flows from these countries and accentuated the double crisis of both Covid-19 and the economic collapse in the region. The arrival of the new government creates the possibility of reestablishing collaboration mechanisms between countries in the management of migratory flows with a human rights approach to restore access to asylum and refuge, reverse the separation of families, stop the construction of the wall and participate in a proposal for economic development in Central America with a US $ 4 billion investment that affects the structural causes of migration.

Introduction

At the end of Peña Nieto's government, in December 2018, there was a complicated scenario for human mobility in the country, which comprised six migratory dimensions: as a country of origin, transit, return, internal displacement, and growing asylum and refuge for migrants. The latter, despite the multiple proposals from migrant organizations and civil society to create public policies regarding development, migration, and human rights, some of which became part of the Special Migration Program published on April 30th, 2014 in the Official Gazette of the Federation, without being binding, and with a 50 million pesos budget. Even now, the current migration policy of national security and binational assistance for Mexicans in the United States has proven to be insufficient, and the country's regulations and institutional capability are increasingly overcome and questioned by the new modalities of human mobility (García Zamora, R. 2019b).

From a 40-years-old perspective, the incoherence of the Mexican government stands out because, despite the great importance and contribution of migrants to the operation of the country and the presence of six dimensions of human mobility throughout the nation, has yet not been able to build the appropriate public policies or the regulatory framework to address migration adequately. Human mobility remains absent in the budgets and the national agenda (García Zamora, 2019 to), even though there are over 38.5 million inhabitants of Mexican origin in the United States, 11.5 million permanent inhabitants in that country since 2020 with 5.9 million undocumented people, and 640 thousand "dreamers" who, as a whole, have transferred 40 billion dollars in family remittances during that year with a growing increase in the flows of transmigrants through the southern border.

In his presidential campaign, and at the beginning of his government in 2018, López Obrador promised to build a new national project and to create public policies to influence the causes of international migration. However, after two years of government, there has been neither a comprehensive strategy for economic, social, and institutional transformation nor any development or migration policies with a human rights approach as the central part of the national agenda. On the contrary, there is still a pervasive immigration policy focused on national security towards transmigrants, corporatism, and welfare towards Mexicans in the United States. Faced with Trump's anti-immigrant and anti-Mexican government, the current government continues to subordinate to the migration policy and regional security of the United States, as the previous administration; especially in what refers to the migratory caravans of Central America during 2018 and 2019 when, faced with the threat of charging duties to Mexican exports in that country, during June the Mexican Foreign Minister formally signed and agreed to subordinate to the US government policies.

During the 2000 - 2015 period, there were many proposals from migrant organizations and the transnational civil society to design public policies on migration and were included partially in the Special Migration Program (2014). However, the Fourth Transformation government not only disregarded them and forgot to update and enforce its Program but also excluded human mobility. Paradoxically human mobility, as a migratory, human, and governance crisis, is visible at the northern and southern borders and in the migration corridors from Chiapas to Tamaulipas and Baja California, and it is developing growing tensions and dysfunctionalities between the federal government, the state, and the municipal governments, but especially with the United States. The response was dispatching the National Guard, turned de facto into Mexico's "migratory patrol" to reduce the entry of migrants from Central America, to regulate those in transit through the country, and to control and prevent the irregular entry into the United States of 70 thousand migrants "returned" due to the new agreements with Mexico.

After two years of the current government, the cracks in economic development and migration have become clear within the Fourth Transformation exactly when human mobility, in its different dimensions, requires a State policy with adequate plans, programs, projects, and budgets. Not only is the incoherence between the migratory reality and the absence of adequate public policies for the Mexican migrant community evident, despite its historical contributions of remittances to the country in 2019 and 2020 with 36.4 thousand and 40.6 billion dollars, but also the budgetary exclusion of the most important programs for migrants in the Federation's Expenditure Programs 2020 and 2021, risking a historical fracture with the current government and with the entire Mexican State.

Currently, at the beginning of 2021, with Joe Biden at the head of the United States government, there is a promise to change the immigration policy in his country by sending an immigration reform to the Congress, which includes: respect for human rights, suspension of the construction of the wall, restoration of the rights of asylum and refuge, alternatives to regularize 10.5 million undocumented migrants and the definitive solution to, at least, the 640 thousand "dreamers" with DACA (80% of them were born in Mexico without counting those who are not in the program) and the commitment to invest in Central America for its economic development, the issue is whether the Mexican State will have the political will to carry out institutional changes that allow the inclusion of migration as a central part of the national agenda, public policies and budgets with a new normative and institutional architecture.

This paper will analyze the evolution of international migration from Central America and Mexico from 2015 to 2020, its impact, challenges, and the possibilities for advancing in creating new collaboration mechanisms with the Biden government for the management of a regulated, safe, and orderly migration to the United States taking a human rights perspective and a regional development strategy that affects the structural causes of international migration.

International migration from Central America and Mexico 2015-2020

The consequences of the 2007 - 2009 economic crisis in the United States led the region's management from a neoliberal dream to a neoliberal nightmare. There was a dramatic reduction in migration, a drop in remittances, and an increase in anti-immigrant policies against their economies, prey to the neoliberal cage of trade agreements with the United States and its control and security strategy. These effects were differential between Mexico and Central America (Guatemala, Honduras, and El Salvador) due to the enormous differences in their economic and institutional structures and the processes of economic, social, political, and environmental violence that generated a different migrant typology during the past four decades. While Mexico is about economic migrants who often have strong social networks, migrants from Central America forcefully relocate due to extreme poverty, the growing violence of criminal organizations, and natural disasters. This situation was evident in increased migrant flows from Central America since the end of the 1990s and in its most tragic expression: the massacre in San Fernando, Tamaulipas during 2010, when the murder of 73 mostly Central American migrants happened. The latter was one of the triggers to recognize that insecurity and violence were growing in Mexico on both borders and the different migratory routes that link migratory movements from Guatemala to the Rio Grande from the United States (García Zamora and Gaspar Olvera, 2020b, p. 56).

There has been a much more complicated situation in Central America because of a delay in its rural economic structure resulting not only from its trade agreement with the United States but also from its enormous dependence on remittances, which represent over 15% GDP in countries such as Honduras and El Salvador; the permanent political instability and generalized violence, which has increased forced migrations in recent years, as evidenced by the famous "caravans" of late 2018 and the first months of 2019.

The synchronicity of the economic crisis in Mexico and the region, with the migratory and border problems, led Gustavo Mohar (Excelsior, April 14, 2019) to consider that Mexico is experiencing an unprecedented crossroads in the history of its migration policy at the border and in what refers to security. According to Mohar, the explanations is in three facts: it is the first time that the president of the United States refers to the migration from Mexico using rhetoric and lies in favor of his re-election strategy; secondly, the massiveness and, thirdly, the diversity of migration from Central America, mostly forced by violence and by the stance of the new Mexican government to assume the defense of migrants' human rights as the axis of its migration policy and looking to facilitate transit through national territory with a humanitarian visa.

According to Alejandro Canales (2019), there is a complex migration scenario in Mesoamerica, particularly for the area of the northern countries of Central America (El Salvador, Guatemala, and Honduras) because of the number of people who migrate south-north trying to arrive in America; the complexity of this process links to both: the various factors that drive migration, and the policies and regulations enforced in the countries of origin, transit, and destination. In these countries, migration triggers by structural social, and economic factors, poverty, social inequality, low-level development, and economic growth, a productive matrix with low-level productivity and specialized in primary-exporting goods, maquila and services, added to conditions of violence and public insecurity, political instability, and organized crime networks. The above creates low expectations for a better future for children and descendants in the places of origin and, in this context, emigration, which in other regions could be a natural process, is one of the few options that the population has to try to get out of their oppressing conditions.

Canales (2019) highlights the risk and vulnerable situations during the migratory flow from Central America to the United States. They begin with departure, followed by the transit through Mexico, and continued until the stay of migrants in the destination country because of the irregular nature of their migratory status and the growing participation of girls, boys, and women. Vulnerability and risks manifest in particular ways for cross-border migrations in both the south and north of Mexico and between Central American countries due to violence and criminal organizations, who are involved now as the new "regulators" of migratory flows. Among the multiple causes and consequences of migration, the risks and vulnerabilities of the migrant population stand out as the chronic weakness of the nation-states to design and implement policies and programs that contribute to addressing the problems that affect and violate the fundamental rights of the migrant population.

Regarding the above, he points out that, for example, in the case of Mexico, it is easier to resort to a migration control policy based on a strategy of mass apprehensions and deportations (more than 150 thousand annually in the last decade) rather than assuming migrants' vulnerable situation and develop policies and programs to address it; simple and basic policies such as granting temporary visas to the population in transit would contribute to a substantial reduction of risks and attacks perpetrated by organized crime and the Mexican authorities themselves.

For Alejandro Canales and Martha Rojas (ECLAC 2017), the migration scenario in the Mexico-Central America region is complex, particularly in the area comprised by Mexico and the countries of the so-called Northern Triangle (El Salvador, Guatemala, and Honduras), and given the magnitude of people migrating in the south-north direction. The complexity of this process links to both: the various factors that drive migration, and the policies and regulations enforced in the countries of origin, transit, and destination. However, in any context, the human rights of migrants constitute a central aspect on which the measures implemented throughout the migration process should focus. This task is the main challenge for public policies because they should be comprehensive and holistic and consider the structural causes and factors associated with migration. The human rights approach should exist to effectively safeguard migrants, not to justify detention or dissuasion.

The challenge of the States, according to the cited researchers, would be to undertake greater efforts and strengthen their institutions, to cooperate at different scales (local, national, and international), and to concur with different sectors looking to encourage the so-called governance of migration; to act beyond rhetoric, or meetings, and to function as an effective mechanism which objective would be the respect and protection of the rights of migrants; of course, such actions would require various monitoring mechanisms.

Manuel Orozco and Mariellen Malloy (2017) considered three defining dynamics of Latin American immigrants' trends in the United States: the challenges they face, immigration policies, and future trends. Regarding the challenges, they point out the importance of migrants in the United States despite their undocumented situation and vulnerability; the importance of remittances in Central America and Mexico, the trend of a more qualified and increasingly female migratory flow, the United States' perspective of migration as a matter of national security and a reduced offer of proposals for the integration of migrants in that country or policies that integrate migration with development policies in the countries of origin. Orozco and Malloy proposed four ways to improve migration policies: decoupling migration from national security policies, reform the US immigration policy in stages, and integrate the economic development process into immigration policies looking to facilitate legal migration and the successful integration of undocumented immigrants residing in the United States.

The statistics presented in Graph 1 and Table 1 illustrate that El Salvador, Guatemala, Honduras, Nicaragua, and Mexico are net population expellers, five of the seven Central American countries.

Belize, Costa Rica, and Panama show positive balances. The seven Central American countries have the United States as their principal destination. This characteristic of Central American migration, mainly undocumented immigrants, makes Mexico a transit place for migrants from those countries. Traditionally the United States has been the main destination country for Mexicans, which has favored life in that country for almost 12 million Mexicans and 13.7 million Americans whose parents were born in Mexico. The proximity of Mexico with the United States; the long tradition of Mexicans migrating to that country, and the anti-immigrant policies of the past 15 years mean that the largest number of international immigrants in the country comes precisely from the United States (according to the United Nations, 71.9% of immigrants in Mexico were born in that country).

Graph 1. International emigrants and immigrants from Central American countries, 2019

Emigrants / Immigrants

Mexico: Emmigrants:

Immigrants

Gráfica 1. Emigrantes e inmigrantes internacionales de paises centroamericanos, 2019

■ Emigrantes ■ Inmigrantes

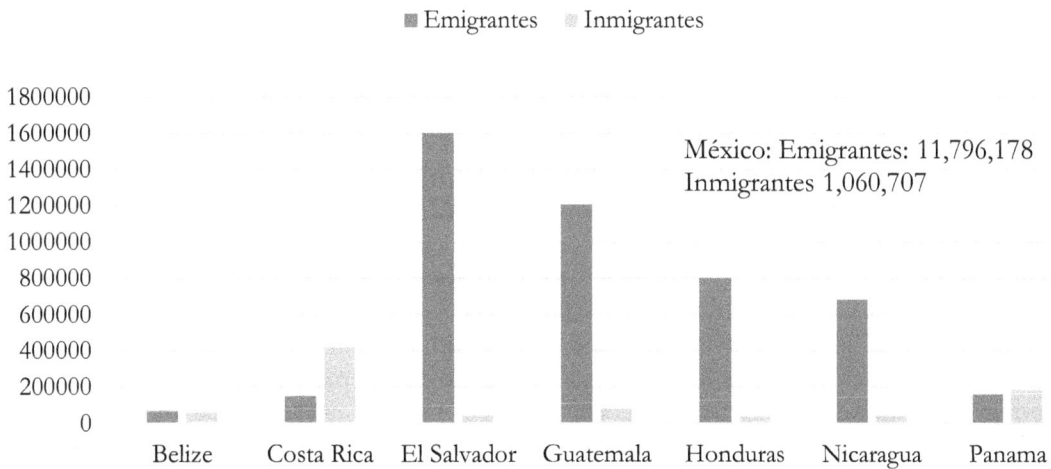

México: Emigrantes: 11,796,178
Inmigrantes 1,060,707

Fuente. Naciones Unidas, 2019. Matriz de origen y Destino.

Source: United Nations, 2019. Origin and destination matrix.

Table 1. Central American migrants: top three countries of residence, 2019

Destinations	Belize	Destinations	Costa Rica
United States	58,472	United States	99,285
Canada	2,123	Nicaragua	11,283
Mexico	2,029	Panama	8,260
Destinations	El Salvador	Destinations	Guatemala
United States	1,429,155	United States	1,070,743
Canada	51,207	Mexico	44,178
Guatemala	19704	Belize	25876
Destinations	Honduras	Destinations	Mexico
United States	655,995	United States	11,489,684
Spain	57,764	Canada	85,825
Mexico	15,300	Spain	53,158
Destinations	Nicaragua	Destinations	Panama
United States	302,845	United States	125,329
Costa Rica	296,541	Costa Rica	11,592
Spain	25,969	Spain	4,399

Source. Own elaboration with data from the United Nations. Origin - Destination matrix, 2019.

Prospects and challenges of migration policies in Central America and Mexico before the Biden government

In July 2018, Andrés López Obrador won the presidential elections with the massive support of 30 million voters and promised to build a New Non-neoliberal Nation Model that would privilege, as axes of the Fourth Transformation in Mexico, national sovereignty, employment, and wellness. His national Development Plan (2019-2024) promises a GDP growth of 6% and the disappearance of migration out of necessity by 2024. However, Covid-19 broke out in Mexico towards the end of February 2020, and the country had been immersed in a long process of low economic growth for over twenty years with decreases during 2019; a double pandemic occurred: the structural crises of health and economy. The impact of Covid-19 deepened them, and there was an expected decrease of -7% of GDP and over 800 thousand unemployed people by May 2020. This adverse situation was even more complicated by the impact of the double pandemic in The United States, with an estimated decrease of -5% of GDP and the loss of over 36 million jobs for the second week of the same month. The consequences imply a large number of unemployed Mexican migrants and the risk of an increase in migration to return to the country, facing the greatest health, economic, and employment crisis in the last 80 years.

Before the arrival of Covid-19 in Mexico, and during 14 months, López Obrador's government enforced the same austerity and macroeconomic stabilization policy at all costs and with a social welfare policy of income transfer to the young and the elderly. Despite his anti-neoliberal rhetoric, in the face of a double pandemic, austerity persists along with the repeated rejection of a progressive tax reform and the temporary contracting of debt before countries like China, the European Union, the United States, and others radically increase their public investment, their fiscal stimuli, and their debt in order to reactivate their economies. Thus, the Mexican government deepened austerity and inclined to trust the trade agreement with the United States and Canada (T-MEC), on July 1st, 2020, as the main instrument to reactivate the national economy, along with the questioned megaprojects in the South of the country and the new airport in the capital (Garcia Zamora and Gaspar Olvera, 2020a).

At the beginning of January 2021, when the deepening of the structural crisis in Honduras, the violence, the impact of Covid-19, and two hurricanes caused the departure of two new caravans to the United States passing through Guatemala and Mexico, these countries governments' were greatly alarmed by the pressure of the change in the presidency of that country which announced a progressive turn in migration policy, though it might be affected by the recurrence of new caravans; this situation generated the intervention of the Guatemalan police and army to stop and force the return of the migrants to Honduras, their country of origin. In Mexico's case, there was a reinforcement of surveillance at the southern border with the National Guard and announced that only those with a visa and a medical study of not contagion by Covid-19 could enter the country. In fact, the two caravans were stopped but not the undocumented migration in transit through Mexico, motivated by the announcement of a more flexible immigration policy proposal in the United States. The national press reported constant arrests, orchestrated by traffickers, of multiple groups of Central American migrants in the south of the country and, the most serious, another massacre: 19 migrants in Camargo Tamaulipas on January 22nd, 2021, mostly Guatemalans.

In the context above, the governments of Mexico, Guatemala, Honduras, and El Salvador raised the need to establish regional alliances and to strengthen their work and their strategic information exchange with the United States to address the migration crisis in the region. The representatives of the first countries agreed to collaborate in the comprehensive management of migration processes, considering irregular migration, security, and the fight against migrant smuggling and trafficking. They ratified their interest in advancing in orderly, regular, and safe migration management, especially in the current stage of Covid-19 and with special attention to small migrants. They recognized that the current migration dynamics constitute a regional challenge that no country can solve alone. Faced with "rumors" that immigration policies will change soon, a representative of the United States embassy in Mexico declared that the immigration policies implemented in recent years by his country continue in force, including restrictions on border crossings, expulsions due to Covid-19, and the migrant protection protocols (La Jornada, January 12nd, 2021).

During the second week of January 2021, the spokespersons of the Mexican government presented the development plan in the south of the country and Central America to the representatives of the Biden team; they initially agreed to address "the root causes of migration" (La Jornada, January 15th, 2021). Faced with the recurrence of the structural causes of forced migration in Central America, aggravated by the hurricanes at the end of 2020, a concerted international humanitarian action is necessary to meet, even if it is circumstantial, the essential needs of migrants in their own country. The latter requires the participation of both: the governments involved (United States, Mexico, Guatemala, and Honduras) and that of international organizations. The root causes of the phenomenon of migration must be removed and resolved in the medium and the long term, namely the lack of economic conditions and the insecurity caused by violence. The next US president, taking his electoral promises into account, is expected to carry out the immigration reform and seriously consider the project of the Mexican president, Andrés Manuel López Obrador, who is looking to promote the creation of jobs, security, and stability (La Jornada, January 19th, 2021) in the nations of origin of the migratory flows.

When the Economic Commission for Latin America (ECLAC) presented its regional economic development proposal for southern Mexico and northern Central America in May 2019, requested by the Mexican government as a substantive alternative to the causes of international migration, we noted its theoretical correctness. It comprised a holistic perspective taking integral, equitable, and sustainable human development into consideration and as the way to eradicate the structural causes of migration. However, it is necessary to integrate the Puebla Panama Plan's antecedents, its advances, and limitations, in addition to considering the enormous problems for its application. The above implies structural economic and social inequalities between the different countries; huge institutional differences; absence of Central American States with the capacity to build and promote development strategies in each seeking to generate synergies in a joint effort; the value of the impact of the neoliberal policies of forced austerity in all of the region's countries, the resulting and increasing debt, and the absence of public policies for regional and sectoral development (as well as the absence, and dismantling, of a developing State in Central America and Mexico) which, under the current conditions, make unfeasible a proposal like the one above. The absence of a comprehensive strategy to confront insecurity and violence in the area, together with inequality, trigger forced mass migration, that is, another limitation for the ECLAC proposal; in conjunction with the United States imperial actions in the region, seeking territorial, economic, commercial, energy, and military control, and opposed to massive investment looking to promote comprehensive economic development and the reversion of poverty and violence (García Zamora and Gaspar Olvera, 2020a, 110).

After several weeks since the triumph of Joe Biden as president-elect of the United States, Andrés López Obrador sent the official letter to congratulate him. Based on this, Jorge Durand (La Jornada, December 20, 2020) highlights Obrador's favorable stance towards migrants from Mexico and the world since it will allow the continuation of the plan to promote the development and well-being of the communities of southeastern Mexico and the countries of Central America. However, for Durand, Biden's agenda is more complex due to the political context of his country and the issues that comprise it: the construction of the wall, the definitive legal solution for the "dreamers" and beneficiaries of the "TPS" program (Temporary Protection for Central Americans and the Caribbean), the suspension of the MPP (Stay in Mexico Program with 70 thousand migrants returned to Mexico), responding to thousands of refugee applicants, the delay of a million cases in the immigration courts, the separation of thousands of migrant children from their parents, the profitable business of private detention centers, and the promise of a comprehensive immigration reform that will legalize the situation of 10.5 million migrants with irregular residence (Budiman Abby, PEW RESEARCH CENTER, 2020) who, despite their immersion in a context in which there was an increase in border patrol arrests since the end of 2020, still announced new migrant caravans from Central America.

Jorge Durand considers that thinking about development plans for Central America is illusory considering the above context and the health and economic crisis. Development is and has been elusive for low-income countries with few resources and many problems. But, beyond the temporary assistance plans and programs, the root lies in the neoliberal model. AMLO is a lonely Quixote who lashes out (verbally) against a model and an ideology entrenched to the core of society and is even willing to risk increasing the minimum wage in times of crisis. Even so, Biden and the leaders of the Central American countries will hardly question the economic model.

On the part of Mexico, Jorge Durand (La Jornada, January 3rd, 2021) highlights the great institutional weakness that is the migration issue, its absence from the national agenda, and the lack of a State policy on development, migration, and human rights that responds to the importance of mobility not only in economic, social, and cultural reproduction but in many other dimensions. He considers that the immigration issue is the worst crisis faced by AMLO in his first two years in office because it put the country in suspense, had to turn back the openness policy, and yielded to Trump's pressure and blackmail. Despite this, according to him, it is not given due importance to the issue and the problem by mutilating the functions of the Ministry of the Interior, by delegating migration functions to the Ministry of Foreign Relations, or by leaving a small Migration Policy Unit, which does not define or propose any policy because of the marginality of its situation, equipment, and resources; a National Institute of Migration as the ram of the migratory policy of national security with a police approach. The official narrative of converting the Consulates in the United States into advocates for Mexicans in that country remains rhetorical in the face of their precariousness, the reduction of budget, the labor problems of their staff, and a growing and unsatisfied demand for services.

Faced with the possibility of a proposal for an immigration reform by Biden, Durand argues that Mexico has to create one of its own considering new mechanisms for collaborating with the United States and Central America. Policies cannot go back to the old stage of "non-immigration policy" from the 80s and 90s of the previous century. The economic, demographic, social, political, and cultural importance of the Mexican community in the United States and the transmigrants flows in Mexico demand the recovery of a shared effort and responsibility of the region's countries. In the case of Mexico there are several factors of great importance that require it, such as the 5 million undocumented people, 250 thousand temporary workers of the field and services (H2A and H2B) that need temporary visas with full respect for labor and human rights, the Stay in Mexico program imposed by Trump that caused the deportation of 70 thousand Central Americans to the country, the problem of Central American development that is the structural cause of the growing migratory flows, unmanageable with rhetorics as a magic solution and lacking serious policy proposals, the problem of growing migration in transit through Mexico due to delay and violence, migrant smuggling, the inadequacy of the immigration containment policy and the regulatory framework, impunity and persistent corruption encouraging new massacres, and the incoherence towards Mexican migrants who send historic amounts of remittances to the country but continue to lack full respect of their rights and are excluded from official programs and budgets (La Jornada, January 3rd, 2021).

Faced with the challenges and opportunities presented by the arrival of Biden to the United States government for having a favorable attitude towards migrants, the caravans coming from Honduras and arrived in Guatemala at the beginning of 2021 face the indifference of their corrupt and irresponsible government, the military containment of the second country, the threat from the Mexican government of only allowing the entrance to those with visa and a negative Covid medical study, the reinforcement of the presence of the National Guard on the border and the announcement by the United States that there will be no flexibility for the entry of new migrants. In the facts, Jorge Durand (La Jornada, January 17th, 2021) confirmed the persistence of the structural causes of migration: poverty, corruption, natural disasters, violence, and state irresponsibility, the collaboration of the other countries on containment strategies and regional security, and the lack of a comprehensive development plan for Honduras, Guatemala, and El Salvador that involves, in the first place, their states, with plans, programs, projects, and budgets supported by the United States, Mexico, and international organizations.

At the end of January 2021, when it became known that President Biden had already sent an immigration reform proposal to Congress, which must follow all the procedures for debate and eventual approval, Jorge Durand (La Jornada, 2021, January 31st) called attention to some aspects of the new context for its debate. The radical change, in recent decades, of former undocumented migrant "workers" who have become undocumented migrant "residents", 80% of them with over 15 years of residence in the United States, a fact that can be favorable to 4 million Mexican migrants for their regularization, along with the additional police, legal, and fiscal requirements (in particular, the use of false security); the fall in the flow of Mexican migration, the main contribution of irregular and cheap migration since the Great Recession of the United States in 2007-2010, and the increase in Central American migration; the repeated confirmation of the impossibility of deportation of 10.5 million undocumented people (despite the fact that from 2008 to 2018 it was estimated at 4 million people deported and returned to Mexico); the reduction of the North American population of working age due to aging and the pressure of the pandemic, as well as the urgency for economic reactivation, generate the need for more migrant workforce. In what refers to Mexico and Central America, Durand points to the fact that the last migrant caravans have been detained by the Mexican National Guard and by the Guatemalan police and army, a strategy that will probably continue due to the negative impact that the arrival of new migrant contingents to the northern border requesting refuge would have on the debate on the immigration reform, which will not prevent the continuation of clandestine migration, as has happened during the pandemic stage, and the persistent polarization of the United States, which already has 70 million voters in favor of Trump and who, after his second exoneration in February, threatening to continue supporting him in his anti-immigrant initiatives; as in the case of Texas and the prosecution strategy.

Migration policies challenges in Mexico under the Biden government, the Covid-19, and the economic crisis

On the migration policies issue and the possibility of collaboration with the countries of the region, after the arrival of Biden to the United States government, Daniel Villafuerte and Carmen García (2020) mention that there is great uncertainty due to the asymmetry of power among the participants, and it is what may largely explain the subordination of the current Mexican government to the migration and security policy of the United States since the Washington agreements in June 2019. The trade-off between "cooperating" with the United States government or not doing so carries economic and political consequences for the country, as evidenced by President Trump's threats to impose tariffs on Mexican exports otherwise.

They argue that the human mobility scenario is considerably complex for Mexico because it is trying to meet the interests and pressures of the United States. The Mexican government has stated that the solution for irregular migration lies in solving the structural problems in Honduras, Guatemala, and El Salvador, for which, during 2019, presented a regional development proposal prepared by the ECLAC. This proposal is currently stoped because of both the disinterest of the United States and the Central American countries, as well as the lack of a budget, estimated at 35 billion dollars; a complicated goal to achieve under the current Covid-19 pandemic and an objective that has transformed into a new wall on the southern border due to persistent migratory flows, with or without caravans. For the authors, the exodus will deepen in the coming years during the Fourth Transformation, not only because of its consequences in terms of poverty, unemployment, and violence but also because of the absence of measures from the regions' governments to face the serious economic crisis and vulnerabilities in the face of the emergencies caused by environmental phenomena, which also have seriously affected a large number of the population.

Villafuerte and García (2020) argue that Mexico is alone now, and the countries of the North of Central America have no interest in making deep reforms to avoid forced migration. Their economies are highly dependent on remittances: in 2019, Guatemala received $10.508 million, El Salvador $5.65 billion, and Honduras $5.523 million (Graph 2). Remittances are the top source of foreign exchange for the three countries. However, the human cost of money is very high and not only because of the number of disappeared and dead. The scenario is uncertain, and Trump has lost the presidency, but the nightmare is not over. Trumpism is present in both Houses, but especially in a deeply divided society in terms of the proportion of votes for the Republican and in divided families, "Trump is like the catalyst for an earthquake that has just divided two continents' ideas. Once the Earth divides like this, there is no going back" (La Jornada, November 7th, 2020).

Graph 2. Main remittances recipient countries in Central America, Mexico, and the Caribbean, millions of dollars, where remittances exceed USD 3.000 million (2016-2019)

Gráfica 2. Países principales receptores de remesas en Centroamérica, México y el Caribe, en millones de USD, donde las remesas sobrepasan los USD 3.000 millones (2016-2019)

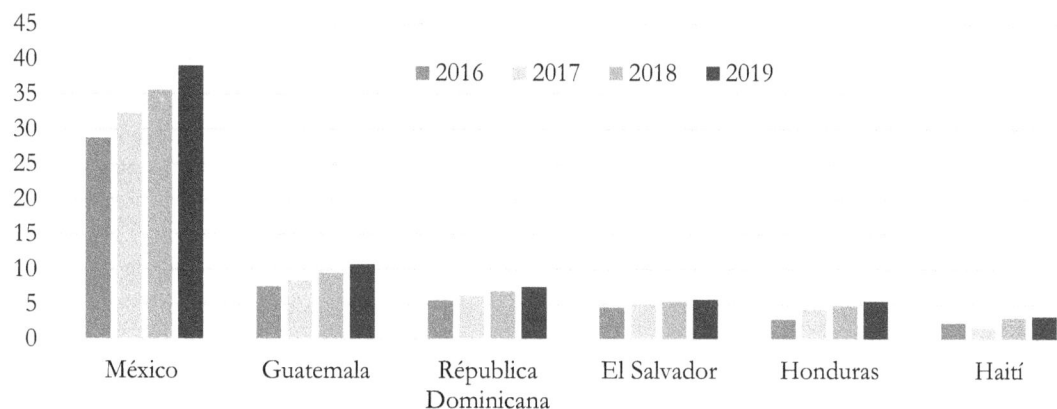

Fuente: Elaborado con datos del ONU, OIM. Banco Mundial.

For his part, Rafel Fernández de Castro (El Financiero, January 22nd, 2021) argues that the government of Andrés Manuel López Obrador must establish its own policy, one that promotes orderly, safe, and legal migration to avoid a crisis in the northern border that causes the "derail" of the immigration reform, proposed by Joe Biden. From his perspective, "We have to have our immigration policy and understand that Mexico is now a place of arrival, that is why in 2019 there was a historical maximum of 70 thousand asylum applications. We have to have a regional perspective and include Central America. That seems of great importance to me in order to understand ourselves with Biden".

When Democrats presented their immigration reform proposal on February 18th, 2021, Joe Biden perceived it as an act of redress towards a migrant community that has waited too long to emerge from the shadows and as a new attempt to regain the lost trust of the Latino electorate, a segment with growing political and electoral influence. "Immigration is an irrefutable source of our strength and is essential to who we are as a nation. The past four years of misguided policies have exacerbated the already bankrupt immigration system and highlighted the critical need for reform. The legislation I sent to Congress will bring much-needed changes to an immigration system in which reform is long overdue and will responsibly manage the border with smart investments, address the root causes of irregular migration from Central America, modernize our legal immigration pathways, and will create a hard-earned path to citizenship for many, including dreamers, agricultural workers, and TPS holders" (La Jornada, February 19th, 2021).

Conclusions

The triumph of Biden in the presidential elections of the United States and his proposal for a comprehensive immigration reform to Congress, which has already generated a negative reaction from the broad conservative sector of that country, means a new context of opportunity for collaboration between the governments of Central America and Mexico in the management of migratory flows from a perspective of integral development and human rights. The new situation implies the recognition that, as suggested by David Brooks (La Jornada, January 25th, 2021), the Democratic victory and the immigration reform proposal are the results of the struggle and progress of broad social groups against the fascist Trump government, a process in which Latino organizations played and still play a major role. Now, with Biden's immigration proposal, a new stage of political struggle opens, in Congress and the country, for which a broad transnational alliance is required not only of Mexican and Central American migrant organizations but also of social groups in order to promote a profound change in economic and social public policies that affect the structural causes of international migration. In this effort to support the new immigration reform proposal, which may have an important impact on the future of the region, the role of the Central American governments in building the institutional framework comprising comprehensive and sustainable human development, the involvement of the United States and Mexico with economic, technical, and administrative support is essential. During 2020-2021, with the Covid-19 pandemic and the economic, energy, and security crisis, there is a fight for the future of Mexico that lies between the recovery of the control of public policies, currency, territory, and the functions of the developing State, and the reinforcement of neoliberalism that, for 38 years, has intensified the causes of international migration and growing dependence on remittances.

Provided the above context, and in the face of the deep national crisis in what refers to economy, Covid, and migration, as well as the growing tensions with the United States after the announcement of the ambitious goals of the National Development Plan 2029-2024, the fundamental questions are: Will the Mexican government be able to break the "neoliberal cage" of public debt, forced austerity, massive layoffs, and increased indebtedness? Is the government looking to regain control of the national economic policy, currency, and credit, to promote (through comprehensive tax reform) solid public investment as a lever for a comprehensive strategy for regional and sectoral economic development to achieve the set goals? Which, let us not forget, would comprise not only a 6% increase in GDP by 2024 but also an increase in employment and welfare to provide the right not to emigrate due to necessity or violence.

The ECLAC proposal is a good diagnosis of investment opportunities, economic growth, and regional integration. However, it does not recognize the deep structural and institutional problems of the four countries (particularly the absence of an institutional framework for development in the Central American states and the dispute in Mexico to reestablish or eliminate it); it also omits the enormous power of the United States in the region and, so far, the lack of interest in its development as well as the dictatorship of the austerity policies of the International Monetary Fund and the World Bank with its consequences: growing debt, forced economic adjustment programs, greater recession, unemployment, greater social and political crisis, increasing violence, and forced mass migrations.

If the Mexican government does not take advantage of the majority presence, in both Congress and the Senate, of its party and allies and does not promote a new national development strategy along with a State policy on Migration with a focus on integral development and human rights, the neoliberal cage, imposed for 38 years, will be strengthened as the model of death with all its destructive consequences for the national economy, social cohesion, and sovereignty; it will deepen violence and the subordination to the Northern Empire together with Central America (García Zamora and Gaspar Olvera, 2020, b).

Bibliography

Brook David (La Jornada, January 25th, 2021) "Nosotros". Available at: https://www.jornada.com.mx/2021/01/25/opinion/023o1mun [19022021].

Budiman Abby (PEW RESEARCH CENTER, 2020). *Key findings about U.S. immigrants.* Available at: https://www.pewresearch.org/fact-tank/2020/08/20/key-findings-about-u-s-immigrants/

Canales Cerón Alejandro. I and Martha Luz Rojas Wiesner (CEPAL, 2018). *Panorama de la migración internacional de México y Centroamérica.* CEPAL. Document prepared in the framework of the Latin American and Caribbean Regional Meeting of Experts on International Migration in preparation for the Global Compact for Safe, Orderly and Regular Migration . https://repositorio.cepal.org/bitstream/handle/11362/43697/1/S1800554_es.pdf [19022021].

Canales Cerón, Alejandro. I, Juan Alberto Fuentes Knight and Carmen Rosa de León Escribano (2019). *Desarrollo y migración. Desafíos y oportunidades en los países del norte de Centroamérica.* CEPAL-FAO. Available at: https://repositorio.cepal.org/bitstream/handle/11362/44649/1/S1000454_es.pdf [19022019].

Durand Jorge (La Jornada, December 20th, 2020) "AMLO, Biden y la migración". Available at: https://www.jornada.com.mx/2020/12/20/opinion/016a1pol [19022021].

Durand Jorge (La Jornada, January 3rd, 2021) "Los pendientes de AMLO" Available at: https://www.jornada.com.mx/2021/01/03/opinion/013a1pol [19022021].

Durand Jorge (La Jornada, January 17th, 2021) "La caravana hondureña". Available at: https://www.jornada.com.mx/2021/01/17/opinion/014a1pol [19022021].

Durand Jorge (La Jornada, January 31st, 2021) "Residentes migrantes indocumentados". Available at: https://www.jornada.com.mx/2021/01/31/opinion/013a2pol?partner=rss [19022021].

Fernández de Castro Rafael (El Financiero, January 22nd, 2021) "Reforma migratoria de Biden puede descarrilarse si la 4T no atiende crisis en frontera sur". Available at: https://www.elfinanciero.com.mx/nacional/crisis-en-la-frontera-descarrilara-reforma-migratoria-de-biden-especialistas [19022021].

García Zamora Rodolfo (2019) México. La Nación desafiada. Análisis y propuesta ante la migración y la falta de desarrollo en México. Miguel Ángel Porrúa-UAZ.

García Zamora Rodolfo y Selene Gaspar Olvera (2020 a) *Migración y Desarrollo Económico. Grietas en la Cuarta Transformación en México 2018-2024.* Transnational Press London. ISBN: 978-1-912997-47-3. 221 pp.

García Zamora Rodolfo y Selene Gaspar Olvera (2020,b). "México. Crisis económica y crisis migratoria al inicio del nuevo gobierno" in Alicia Girón y Eugenia Correa (Coordinators) *México. Hacia la incertidumbre.* IIES-DGAPA-UNAM.

La Jornada (November 7th, 2020). Biden, más cerca de la Casa Blanca; afina agenda de gobierno. Available at: https://www.jornada.com.mx/2020/11/07/ [19022021].

La Jornada (January 12th, 2021)"Gobiernos de Centroamérica urgen a crear alianza contra crisis migratoria: SRE". Available at: https://www.jornada.com.mx/notas/2021/01/12/politica/gobiernos-de-centroamerica-urgen-a-crear-alianza-contra-la-crisis-migratoria-sre/ [19022021].

La Jornada (January 19th, 2021) "Migración: por una solución de raíz". Available at: https://www.jornada.com.mx/notas/2021/01/19/opinion/migracion-por-una-solucion-de-raiz/ [19022021].

Mohar Gustavo (2019) "La encrucijada migratoria", Excélsior, México, April 14th. Available at: https://www.excelsior.com.mx/opinion/gustavo-mohar/encrucijada-migratoria-i/1307594 [19022021].

Orozco Manuel y Mariellen Malloy (2017). "Tendencias y asuntos políticos que repercuten en México --y los países centroamericanos" in Isabel Álvarez Echandi (Compilator) *Mirando al Norte. Algunas tendencias de la Migración Latinoamericana,* DFLACSO, Ford Foundation.

Villafuerte Solís, Daniel y María del Carmen García Aguilar (2020). "Fin de la era de Trump y las promesas de Biden: ¿nuevos aires en la política migratoria de la Cuarta Transformación? Migración y Desarrollo, UAZ, volume 18, number 35, second semester 2020. Available at: https://estudiosdeldesarrollo.mx/migracionydesarrollo/wp-content/uploads/2021/01/35-5.pdf [19022021].

MASCULINITIES AT THE CROSSROAD: WAR, MIGRATION AND URBAN POVERTY IN THE CASE OF SYRIAN MEN IN ANKARA

Saeid Mozafari[1] and Halime Ünal Reşitoğlu[2]

Abstract

This study by focusing on the Syrian refugee men living in Ankara's lower-class neighborhoods aims to draw an image of the impacts of the crucial conditions such as the war, the forced migration and the poverty on their masculinities. In this context, this study intends to answer the following questions: What are the forms of masculinities in crises and how are they perceived by Syrian men? How new masculinities are mediated through the conditions of forced migration and urban poverty in the case of Syrian refugee men in some neighborhoods in Ankara? This fieldwork uses qualitative research methods such as in-depth interviews with Syrian refugee men in Ankara.

Key Words: Masculinities, Crisis, Forced Migration, Urban Poverty, Syrian War

Introduction

Since the commence of the Syrian Civil War on March 15, 2011, a massive wave of forced migration towards neighboring countries has begun. Due to Turkey's social, geographical and political characteristics, as well as the close historical and cultural relations between the two countries, Turkey has become the country that hosts the most Syrian immigrants among the other countries such as Lebanon, Jordan and Egypt. Correspondingly, according to the statistics of the Turkish Migration Administration in May 2021, 3,670,717[3] Syrians under Temporary Protection Status live in different provinces of Turkey. Moreover, the number of registered Syrians living in Ankara was declared as 101,103. Hence, Syrian refugees who are the object of the different researches have almost never been the object of researches within the framework of masculinity as a problematic. However, living in poverty conditions due to factors such as deadly civil war, hazardous forced migration and being refugee has a significant impact on gender relations. To put it differently, living conditions such as war, forced migration and poverty can bring about serious damages to the reconstructing mechanisms of masculinity and can lead to fractures in masculinities.

As a result, this study which is based on fieldwork has focused on the changes and transformations in the masculinities of married Syrian men living in the poor districts of Ankara, combined with the factors of war, forced migration and urban poverty. In other words, this study questions the nature and form of the fractures experienced by poor married Syrian refugee men as fathers or husbands under the conditions of socio-economic pressures. In this regard, the fieldwork was conducted through in-depth interviews with 17 married Syrian men, aged between 25 and 60, living in mostly Syrian-populated neighborhoods such as Önder and Ulubey in Ankara. The interviews were also mostly conducted in their homes, and observations were made through systematic noting.

---

[1] MA. Candidate in Sociology at Ankara Yildirim Beyazit University, Turkey.
[2] Prof. Halime Ünal Reşitoğlu, Department Of Sociology, Ankara Yildirim Beyazit University, Turkey.
[3] Directorate General of Migration Management, statistics of May 2021, accessed 09.06.2021.

The Effects of Civil War and Forced Migration On Syrian Men's Masculinities

One of the most obvious data showing the devastating effects of war, forced migration and poverty on masculinity mechanisms is that Syrian men before the civil war could fulfill their gender roles as breadwinners and protectors of their families. They also emphasized that they had experienced a 'privileged' masculinity in terms of being a 'Syrian man' who could afford his family needs. On the one hand, the effect of brutality and vulnerability created by the war, and the feeling of desperateness, sense of loss and fear caused by a process of risky forced migration, and on the other hand, the exclusion, unemployment, informal work and living conditions of refugees made Syrian men's masculinities "easier" before the war. Therefore, it all paved the way for the formation of more fragile and difficult masculinities in Turkey.

As a result, according to our data, Syrian men living in Ankara fall short of fulfilling their traditional gender roles as the 'Syrian male' which was a more powerful position before displacement. Therefore, on the one hand, they experience a feeling like "*I cannot protect my family*" that is due to the brutality of the war, on the other hand, they are exposed to unemployment and low wages in informal jobs as refugees who have lost everything. Hence, they cannot fulfill the needs of their families as male breadwinner. Therefore, the insistence of the participants on the convenience of being a man before and even during the war in Syria implies the existence of fractures in their masculinities as a consequence of their conditions.

Refugees as Urban Poor: Fractures in The Reproduction of Syrian Men's Masculinities

Refugees with the status of temporary protection in Turkey can obtain a work permit if they have a passport, although the process is quite difficult. However, it is known that the major part of Syrians who came to Turkey as a result of the civil war do not have passports. Therefore, this situation drives Syrians to informal jobs where precarious working relations are dominant. There are three main characteristics most frequently seen in the data related with informal working conditions: Firstly, Syrian refugees are swindled by their employers without being paid. Secondly, they are often unemployed due to the lack of permanent jobs. Thirdly, they are subject to the lowest pays despite laborious working conditions. Under these conditions, it is observed that especially in Ankara where work conditions are burdensome, Syrian refugee men generally experience a permanent unemployment due to the barriers such as language, nationality and ethnicity, as a result, they are doomed to spend more times at home with their families. For instance, a 57-year-old interviewee stated that when collecting wastes, he would walk 15 km a day but he was generally unemployed. Tearily and sorrowfully he said that he had to stay at home due to the effects of the Pandemic, even though he and especially his wife did not enjoy the situation:

Two Different Representations of "Wounded Masculinity" Emerged On The Basis of Generation And The Level of Conservativeness

Drawing on our research findings, the urban poor Syrian men living in Ankara have faced an inability and fractures in their masculinities as a result of arduous processes such as war, forced migration and poverty. However, the formation of these fractures varies depending on the factor of generation and also the level of conservatism that represent some of our interviewees. Hence, this differentiation has revealed two main representations of masculinity.

Religion and Generation: Reproduction of Power Relations at Home

Living under the conditions of refugee life in Turkey, Syrian men's masculinities take specific forms. In this sense, among others, we can speak of a wounded masculinity as seen among Syrian men over 35-years-of-old who have also strong religious implications and belongings. Accordingly, it was frequently observed during the interviews that there were many religious symbols and indicators in both the answers to the questions and the design of the house. Furthermore, the traditional gender relations based on patriarchy and also mediated by religion have been internalized by the members of Syrian refugee families. It shows that this process of internalization helps the Syrian men who are in a crisis in their masculinities in filling the gap caused by harsh conditions such as unemployment, social exclusion, rough working conditions and discrimination. To illustrate, for instance, a 43-year-of-old interviewee who answered some questions with verses from the Qur'an stated that when his family could not meet their needs due to hard economic conditions such as hunger his heart as a man ached with pity for his family. However, he asserted that not only this situation did not affect the relations within his family but also he was still mostly the decision-maker at home.

Another feature of this representation of masculinity is that some of our interviewees denied the existence of a crisis and fractures in their masculinities. For example, a 51-year-old unemployed interviewee tried to hide his situation and not to accept it by answering the questions related to masculinity. While turning serious, he said that *"I am always the head of the house, I say the last word"* (G10). However, the same interviewee in another context related to the questions asked about gender roles and responsibilities stated that he had a hard time under the conditions of displacement, so, he lost control of his family and as a result, his masculinity was fractured. In this framework, on the one hand, Syrian men over 35-years-of-old who pretended that there are no fractures in their masculinities at the same time clearly expressed their failures and inabilities with regard to gender responsibilities.

The third feature of the representation is the reproduction of gender-based discriminatory perspectives against women. Accordingly, some of interviewees' answers to the questions related to women were in alignment with the patriarchal gender values in both Syria and Turkey. For instance, some Syrian men over 35-years-of-old used the following sentences: *"women must stay at home and not work outside"*, *"women's role is to do the housework and take care of the children"*, *"in our tradition, women can work outside and go shopping only if they are widowed, otherwise Syrian men won't let them do so"*.

"Alternative Masculinity"

A significant common feature of the second group of men in our schema is that they are under 35-years-of-old, but they are not conservative in the context of traditional gender relations and experience changes in their masculinities in Turkey. Young Syrian men who claimed they could meet the needs of their families more easily in Syria, clearly stated that in Turkey they feel like themselves as failed men despite what they do at their best. The recognition of this fracture in masculinity has paved the way for a range of transformations in gender relations within families. Firstly, they saw their family ties were strengthening while a sense of unity appeared after their forced migration. Regarding the second point of change, it is seen that the young generation of Syrian men settled in Turkey had to include their wives into decision-making mechanisms at home while sharing their feelings in different situations with them. In other words, new generations of Syrian men have more egalitarian and sharing attitude towards women. During the interviews of the interviewees in this group, there are frequently heard sentences such as *"women are half of the society, I repeat it, they are the half"*; *"women can work outside, I see no problem in this"*, *"women have rights like men"*.

Conclusion

To sum up, the data gathered in this study show that a deadly and miserable war, a risky process of forced migration, and a state of poverty as a refugee have staggering effects on the forms of masculinity. Syrian men who reproduced successfully their masculine authority by fulfilling the requirements of prewar gender roles are faced with fractures in their masculinities as a result of the consequences of this process. However, the reaction of Syrian men to this loss of authority differs depending on generation and the level of conservatism. In this regard, while old Syrian refugee men who have internalized their patriarchal roles based on religion preserve their power as men, young Syrian men have encountered with an alternative form of masculinity which is somehow more egalitarian. Therefore, in the context of our research we can speak of transformations in gender relations as experienced by Syrian refugee men in Ankara.

References

Connell, R. W. (2005). *Masculinities*. University Of California Press, Berkeley, Los Angeles.

Directorate General of Migration Management, statistics of May 2021, accessed 09.06.2021. (https://www.goc.gov.tr/gecici-koruma5638).

Moblo, B. (2008). Failed Men: The Postwar Crisis of Masculinity in France 1918-1930.

Sancar, S. (2016). *Erkeklik İmkansız İktidar*. İstanbul: Metis.

Saraçoğlu, C, Belanger, D. (2015). Mekân, Yer Ve Şehir: Türkiye'de Suriyeli Karşıtlığının Kentteki Görünümleri. *Eğitim, Bilim ve Toplum*, 46-73.

GENDER DIFFERENCES IN POST-CRISIS EMIGRATIONS FROM SPAIN[1]

Sandra Lopez-Pereiro

Abstract

The Great Recession and its further consequences activated new emigration flows from Spain which did not stop with the signs of recovery. The general situation of job insecurity and unemployment seems to be one of the main triggers of this flow, and it does not affect men and women in the same way. Knowing that the point of departure is not the same, this research aims to explore the gender differences in trajectories, motivations, and discourses of the Spanish migrants who left the country after de crisis and onwards. The results show that gender still matters, also in destination, and that it is necessary to focus future research in precarity, care-giving and maternity.

Key words: Spanish emigration, gender differences, Intra-European Migration, precarity, reasons for migrating.

Introduction and justification

The map of migrations in Spain has changed dramatically during the last decades. The country started the new century becoming a major destination of migration for the first time in its history. However, this trend was challenged by the 2008 crisis and its further consequences, which caused a decrease in the number of arrivals and the activation of new emigrant flows (López de Lera, 2020). More than a decade after 2008, before the COVID situation, macroeconomic indicators showed signs of recovery, but the labour market was still damaged and characterised by high levels of insecurity. Consequently, emigration flows showed a decrease, although they were far from stopping completely (Alba & Fernández Asperilla, 2020).

When dealing with a migration phenomenon that seems strongly connected to working conditions and precarity, gender can play an important role which deserves attention. Well-known gender differences in expectations, work conditions and caring responsibilities (Borderías et al., 2011) are important elements which influence migratory motivations, trajectories, and discourses. This research aims to explore those differences as well as guiding future research on the topic by analysing post-crisis native migrants from Spain.

Literature review

Recent emigration from Spain is a very diverse phenomenon (Domingo i Valls et al., 2014) which can be framed within "liquid migration" (Engbersen, 2012) in some aspects, but whose main trigger was the impact of the consequences of the 2008 crisis (Romero-Valiente, 2018). Thus, although it relates to post-materialistic motivations, it is undeniably connected to job insecurity, precarity and life-conditions.

The Spanish labour market, which has historically been affected by structural problems, was extremely

---

[1] This research is embedded within a thesis dissertation in progress and the NUEMIG project, funded by the Spanish Ministry of Economic Affairs.

damaged by the Great Recession. The output is still visible nowadays in unemployment and under-employment rates, job insecurity and generalised precarity. Even though the first steps of the 2008 situation affected more to men, austerity and further job deterioration have had a higher impact for women (Karamessini & Rubery, 2013).

In the Spanish context, both unemployment and job conditions present a darker landscape for women (Millán-Vazquez De La Torre et al., 2015). More specifically, female unemployment in the country is generally around a 4% higher than male's (INE, several years). Referring to conditions, Labour National Survey shows that there is more than a 11% of women who would desire to work more hours than they do —against around a 7% of men— and that temporality is 5% higher for women (íbid.). In addition, the division of housework in Spain remains highly gendered (Canzio, 2021), making women the ones who bear the burden of responsibilities when it comes to caregiving

This happens in a landscape where, on average, women are better educated than men. Interestingly, there are more highly skilled men than women who migrate (González-Enríquez & Triandafyllidou, 2016).

The point of departure is gendered, so it seems reasonable that the migration processes are gendered too. However, literature has not extensively explored yet the role played by gender in recent migration of Spanish natives. In general, there is a gap regarding gender analysis of highly educated migrations (Kofman, 2014) which is maybe extended to intra-European migrations.

Nevertheless, even in the apparently most privileged migration, women still suffer from 'doble disadvantage' (González-Enríquez & Triandafyllidou, 2016) and mobility continues to be connected to social protection and gender (Bermudez & Oso, 2020).

Objective

The aim of this research is to identify the gender differences in trajectories, motivations, and discourses of recent Spanish migrants.

Data and methods

The research is based on the fieldwork of the NUEMIG project, funded by the Spanish Ministry of Economic Affairs and developed during the summer of 2018 in the 3 major destinations of emigration from Spain: United Kingdom, France, and Germany. Almost 50 semi-structured interviews of post-crisis migrants were analysed, 23 women and 26 men. The interviews were developed according to the objective of analysing the recent emigration processes from Spain, without any specific gender approach.

The analysis process was developed under the guidelines of Udo Kucartz's (2014) thematic analysis using the MAXQDA software.

Results and discussion

Gender differences have been detected in different levels. Results have been summarized in three thematic axes.

Motivations to leave

Job conditions and unemployment are the most mentioned motivations to leave, but men and women live them differently. The references to the salary and work recognition are quite more common among men.

168

> Well... economically we make a very good living, I can do whatever I want, I can travel, right now as I am self-employed you can afford to... go on holiday whenever you want. And also for training, here in France they pay you... there is a... they give you money for training every year, at the end of the day here training is also tax deductible, you get tax deductions, there are many, many advantages at the same level... both economically and in many aspects.

> (Interviewee 60)

On the other hand, women tend to refer explicitly to the economic crisis as an expulsion trigger much more often.

There is a motivation that appears in several men respondents: making money with the aim of returning to the origin country and creating their own enterprise. Becoming their own boss is perceived as a good way of escaping from bad labour conditions. This goal is almost absent of the women agenda and when it appears is just one of many possible future ways. In contrast, some of them mention the pursuit of personal independence as one of the reasons to migrate. This aim does not appear in men's interviews.

The other common source of reasons to migrate are personal relationships. It is frequent to leave to follow a partner who has found a better job abroad. There has been detected a frequent strategy of moving out to the place where the partner who experiences more difficulties to have a quality job, which is usually a woman. Perhaps because of this, more men have declared to have migrated for love.

Labour and live trajectories

The paths of men and women are not radically opposite, but there are important differences.

One of the main differences detected in the interview is that for woman it exists a "door" into the labour market and into learning the language of the destination place: the *au pair* work. It is a very common first step in the migratory trajectory of women which is not available for men. The experience is usually connected to exploitation and precarity, so it does not necessarily translate into an advantage.

It has also been detected that men arrive to a job which fulfils their expectations in a higher degree. More women consider themselves to be in a transition point instead of having already arrived at a consolidation point.

Another field of differences is the construction of a network of contacts in the destination. In the case of men, collective sports haven been reported as a way to get to know new people and making friends. This is not common among woman, who tend to use more social networks and activism as socialization tools.

Along the trajectories of women, it is visible that they put more efforts in tracing solid labour paths. That is reflected in a higher concern about their language and education level, the search of backup mechanisms and the acceptance of unpleasant jobs to gain experience:

> I made the decision that, as it was my job, in my first job I had to have at least 2 years of experience to be able to do another job because otherwise it's like.... I could have left earlier because I put up with a lot, but I thought it was better for my future. So I did that. I stayed for 2 years and when I had 2 years, I said "goodbye, dude".

> (Interviewee 41)

Discourses on maternity and family

Regarding discourses, it is remarkable that men praise more the conditions of the country of destination. In contrast, women tend to be more critical with the origin and not so benevolent with the opportunities that the destination offers.

More specifically, this analytic divergence increases when maternity comes out. Men see more clearly the advantages of having a child within the frame of opportunities that the destination country offers, and they minimize the consequences of being far from family. They even see it as an investment for the future;

> If we're going to have a child, it would be great if they learnt German so that they could get an education, you know, so that... I don't know, so that they could grow up here, because I don't know if you've noticed, but here there are some incredible playgrounds. Besides, there are conditions for fatherhood and motherhood that we still don't have in Spain and... and of course, that would be... that would be a kind of investment in the future.

(Interviewee 9)

On the contrary, women often detect the disadvantages of having a child far from the family. Even if they admit the advantages of the destination, the lack of a strong network of contacts is perceived as an important drawback.

Similarly, women are more sensitive with the gaps of gender equality on the destination, whilst men are usually blind to them. Here are the words of a woman emigrated in Germany who, despite have perceived an improvement in her work conditions as a woman, detects the hidden sexism about maternity:

> I mean, the funny thing about this issue of maternity leave, the fact that you get paid maternity leave and all this, actually hides the fact that Germany is very sexist. They want mothers to stay at home for three years with the baby.

(Interviewee 43)

Referring to family in origin, the discourses also show some differences. In general, interviewees answer with a dual narrative when they are asked about their parents. On the one hand, they declare that their parents are happy and proud. On the other hand, they talk about the suffering that their absence is producing to their beloved ones in origin. Women usually pay more attention to the bad side, being more aware of the disadvantages that their parents are experiencing because of their decision of migrating.

Conclusions

The main conclusion is that gender analysis cannot be ignored in this kind of migrations, even if they could be comparatively 'privileged', because they exist and they play a role which should not be bypassed by research and by public policies.

Women's motivations are more connected to labour conditions in origin. Even when the process improves their situation, it remains comparatively worse than their male compatriots. Maybe because of the added difficulties, women tend to develop more cautious trajectories and to keep more backup mechanism in case they fail. Their discourses are more critical.

It is essential to develop more research focused on maternity, care-giving responsibilities, and precarity to map how these topic affect to migration experiences.

Reference list

Alba, S., & Fernández Asperilla, A. (2020). *Emigrar después de la crisis. Crecimiento económico y nueva migración española* (Fundación 1º de Mayo (ed.)). Los libros de La Catarata. https://doi.org/8413520339

Bermudez, A., & Oso, L. (2020). Recent trends in intra-EU mobilities: the articulation between migration, social protection, gender and citizenship systems. In *Ethnic and Racial Studies* (pp. 2513–2530). Routledge. https://doi.org/10.1080/01419870.2020.1770828

Borderías, C., Torns, T., & Bengoa, C. C. (2011). *El trabajo de cuidados: Historia, teoría y políticas.* Los Libros de La Catarata. https://books.google.es/books?id=OgtlDwAAQBAJ

Canzio, L. I. (2021). Division of housework within couples in Spain: Consequences of educational differences and women's gender-egalitarian beliefs. *Papers, 106*(1), 59–94. https://doi.org/10.5565/rev/papers.2750

Domingo i Valls, A., Sabater Coll, A., & Ortega Rivera, E. (2014). ¿Migración neohispánica? El impacto de la crisis económica en la emigración española. *EMPIRIA. Revista de Metodología de Ciencias Sociales*, 39–66.

Engbersen, G. (2012). Migration transitions in an era of liquid migration Reflections on Fassmann and Reeger. In M. Okólsi (Ed.), *European Immigrations: Trends, Structures and Policy Implications* (pp. 91–106). Amsterdam University Press.

González-Enríquez, C., & Triandafyllidou, A. (2016). *Female High-Skilled Emigration from Southern Europe and Ireland after the Crisis* (A. Triandafyllidou & I. Isaakyan (eds.); pp. 44–68). Palgrave Macmillan UK. https://books.google.es/books?id=Rmf-CgAAQBAJ

Instituto Nacional de Estadística. (several years). *Encuesta de Población Activa*. Retrieved June 25, 2021, from https://www.ine.es/dynt3/inebase/es/index.htm?padre=982&capsel=986

Karamessini, M., & Rubery, J. (2013). Economic crisis and austerity: challenges to gender equality. In M. Karamessini & J. Rubery (Eds.), *Women and Austerity: The Economic Crisis and the Future for Gender Equality* (pp. 314–351). Taylor & Francis.

Kofman, E. (2014). Towards a gendered evaluation of (highly) skilled immigration policies in Europe. *International Migration, 52*(3), 116–128. https://doi.org/10.1111/imig.12121

Kuckartz, U. (2014). *Qualitative Text Analysis: A Guide to Methods, Practice and Using Software.* SAGE Publications. https://books.google.es/books?id=9B2VAgAAQBAJ

López de Lera, D. (2020). Continuities in intra-European mobilities: what's novel in the new Spanish emigration? *Ethnic and Racial Studies, 43*(14), 2531–2550. https://doi.org/10.1080/01419870.2020.1738517

Millán-Vazquez De La Torre, M. G., Santos-Pita, M. del P., & Pérez-Naranjo, L. M. (2015). Análisis del mercado laboral femenino en España: evolución y factores socioeconómicos determinantes del empleo. *Papeles de Población; Vol. 21 Núm. 84 (2015): Papeles de Población.* https://rppoblacion.uaemex.mx/article/view/8320

Romero-Valiente, J. M. (2018). Causes of the current Spanish emigration: "external mobility" and the impact of the economic crisis. *Boletin de La Asociacion de Geografos Espanoles, 2018*(76), 303–328. https://doi.org/10.21138/bage.2524

REPRESENTATIONS OF THE HOLY LAND: THE IMPRESSIONS OF FILIPINOS AND INDONESIANS OF LIVING AND WORKING IN SAUDI ARABIA

Simeon S Magliveras and Sumanto Al Qurtuby

Introduction

Focusing on both professional and "unskilled" Filipino and Indonesian expatriate laborers in Saudi Arabia, this paper examines how these two transnational communities envisage their lives in the Kingdom. Saudi Arabia's Filipinos and Indonesians are remarkable because (1) the groups are the largest Southeast Asian transnationals population in the Kingdom and (2) Filipinos are primarily Christian while Indonesians are generally Muslim. This paper explores the different imaginations and impressions about Saudi Arabia. Moreover, Indonesia and the Philippines share similar geographies, parallel colonial pasts, and contemporarily, use immigration as a development strategy. Saudi Arabia is a magnet for Filipinos and Indonesians because it affords them relatively high salaries, economic prosperity, political stability, and for Muslims, access to Makkah and Madinah. This paper studies (1) underlying motives of Filipinos and Indonesians in the Kingdom, and (2) their perceptions about their Saudi experience.

Migration to Arabia: A Brief History

Filipino migration in contemporary times began after the 1899 Philippine-American war (Espiritu 1995; Okamura 2013; del Rosario 2005). After their defeat, the United States replaced the Spanish four hundred years of colonialism with their own. As a result, in 1906 the first Filipinos migrated to the United States continuing for most of the 20th Century continuing even after the Philippines gained independence from the United States in 1946 (ibid) thus, beginning their saga as a transnational people.

The Filipino government established bilateral relations with Saudi Arabia in 1973 (Philippines Embassy 2014). Shortly thereafter, the first Filipinos went to the Kingdom of Saudi Arabia as Engineers to assist in the development of Saudi Arabia with the backing of the United States. In those early days, overseas works used the mantra, "Katas ng Saudi", the fruits of Saudi, as a phrase meaning, build a better future for home from working abroad (Pedregossa 2019). Since then, almost a million Filipino men and women now are legally employed in Saudi. The majority of Filipinos hold support positions as they are relatively well educated and speak English. In contrast with many transnational labor strategies the Philippines deploys almost equal numbers of men and women to Saudi (Johnson 2011).

Moreover, the diversity of types of positions held for Overseas Filipino Workers (OFW's) in Saudi Arabia is bested only by the United States. As a result, Filipinos hold significant positions in Saudi Arabia but have limited authority. Not allowing Filipinos much social capital, they are treated less than westerners with equal qualifications. Moreover, Filipinos are paid less (Margold 1995). Regardless of these known inequities, Filipinos see Saudi Arabia as a very desirable destination[1] for work to support

[1] Filipinos see all the gulf states as very desirable destinations. However, they have learnt that Saudi is a place where more money can be saved because there are fewer distractions.

their families back in the Philippines (Magliveras 2019a ;2019b).

The Filipino portion for the study was conducted with Filipinos presently working in, or had previously working in Saudi Arabia. Over fifteen laborers and professional, men and women from the ages of 24-75 were interviewed. The professional participants were secretarial support staff, dental assistants and nurses. However, several had more authoritative positions as construction sites engineers, or dentists. All of the participants were either Catholics or non-denominational Christians[2].

In contrast with the Philippines, Indonesian have greater temporal connection with the Arabian Peninsula. Although there are no exact numbers or official statistics of Indonesians in Saudi Arabia, according to Sa'adullah Affandy[3], a labor attaché of the Indonesian Embassy in Riyadh, more than a million of Indonesians currently live in the Kingdom. Many Indonesians living in Saudi Arabia today are the product of an established lengthy contact between people of the Arabian Peninsula and the Malay–Indonesian archipelago because of pilgrimage[4]. In fact, Indonesians have journeyed to Makkah, or more generally, to the Hijaz, long before the existence of the modern Kingdom of Saudi Arabia[5]. Not surprisingly, there is a district called *Kampung Jawah*,[6] named after a "Javanese Village", in Makkah which signifies the endurance of Malay-Indonesians in Arabia[7]. The *Kampung Jawah* later became one of the Islamic learning centers for both generational residents and new Malay-Indonesians arriving in Makkah[8].

After performing Hajj in past centuries, the majority of pilgrims returned to Indonesia. Those who stayed in Makkah did so for several reasons. First, is because they needed money. They took jobs to purchase provisions to return to the Malay-Indonesian archipelago or to pay their debts. Many pilgrims ran out of money and supplies because the journey to Makkah was so arduous and expensive. Some worked on dates plantations or in small shops, while others assisted pilgrims. Others even became a slaves so they could not pay their debts. In recent decades, a great number of pilgrims deliberately chose to stay in Makkah after finishing their pilgrimage rituals because they wanted to work, live, and die in Arabia. They settled in places such as Jeddah[9] because Jeddah offered such jobs as shopkeepers and bus drivers, etc.

The second reason Indonesians in the past chose to live in Makkah was to study or learn the Islamic sciences while simultaneously performing rituals at the Haram Mosque in Makkah and the Nabawi

---

[2] For this study, being Christian is salient. If the participants were not Christians, the results and conclusion about the Filipino transnationals might be significantly different. As a result, the voices of the Filipinos in this study represents a segment of the majority Christian population of OFW's and does not represent OFW's of other faiths/non-faiths. There is a large Muslim Filipino community in the Philippines and thus, there are Muslim Filipinos in the Kingdom of Saudi Arabia (KSA) too.

[3] Interview with Sa'adullah Affandy, December 31, 2020.

[4] The million Indonesians mentioned in the text does not include those who travel annually to the Muslim's sacred places of Makkah and Madinah. During the Covid-19 pandemic, holy sites were at times either closed or very restrictive to visitors outside the Kingdom.

[5] The modern Kingdom of Saudi Arabia was established in 1932

[6] The word "Jawah" does not really mean "Java Island". It refers to the Malay-Indonesian archipelago, and the term "al-Jawi" at the time referred to people from this area, including the Pattani of Southern Thailand. However, "Kampung Jawah" in Makkah is mostly inhabited by people from Indonesia's various ethnic groups such Javanese, Sumatrans, Madurese, Makasarese, Sundanese, Betawians, and many others.

[7] The *Kampung Jawah* is located in the district of Shamiah or Shi'ib Ali,

[8] In past centuries, Indonesians journey to the Hijaz was mainly guided by performing one of Islam's main five pillars, the Hajj (Hurgronje 1970; Azra 1992; Diederich 2005). Despite facing many difficulties such as treacherous seas, disease, limited food resources, and an odyssey taking many months at a time, the number of Indonesian Hajj pilgrims in the past centuries were extensive. Between 1850 and 1860, 1600 Hajj pilgrims, and about 2600–4600 in the 1870s, and 1880s. About 15 percent of all pilgrims to Makkah were from the Indonesian archipelago. Steamship technology and the opening of Suez Canal in 1869 made Makkah more accessible resulting in an increase of Indonesians pilgrims. However accurate numbers of Indonesians travelling to Makkah are difficult to calculate. Estimates of 8000-10000 Malayan peoples ventured for pilgrimage. Many eventually settled in Makkah, creating small Indonesian enclaves shaping the *Kampung Jawah*.

[9] Jeddah is a bustling city near Makkah

Mosque in Madinah[10]. Unlike any other places of worship, Muslims believe that worshiping and conducting religious activities in these mosques, that God guaranteed the practitioner entrance into paradise after death because hundreds of thousands of rewards would be granted to the practitioner. A desire for both Islamic learning and performing rituals compelled many Indonesian Muslims to stay longer in the Haramain[11]. While some settled permanently in Makkah, many remained months or even years before returning home. Before WWII, this type of religious and intellectual contact between Indonesia and Arabia is apparent. Moreover, resulting from this contact a great number of Indonesian Islamic scholar/teachers in the Haramain established Islamic schools in Makkah. Their legacy is still witnessed today (Al Qurtuby 2019).

In addition to Hajj/Umrah pilgrims after WWII, Indonesian immigration was marked by the presence of at least three groups. The first group are those seeking "unskilled" menial labor and skilled professional employment who worked in the oil industries, construction companies, hotels, and hospitals[12]. The second group of Indonesians are those studying in *rubat* or universities[13]. The third group of Indonesians are students studying the 'secular' sciences and engineering[14].

Of course, the underlying motives of Indonesian immigrants in the Kingdom vary enormously. Indonesians do pursue employment as professionals or menial laborers for themselves but they also do it to help by sending families remittance. Furthermore, immigrants go to Saudi Arabia to acquire Islamic knowledge, to study secular sciences, to perform religious rituals, to visit the holy shrines, and/or to seek a "quick pass" to Heaven. Filipino labors have a dissimilar set of motives to go to Saudi Arabia.

Saudi as a Stepping Stone and Experiencing the World

For younger educated professional Filipinos in this study, Saudi Arabia provided two main reasons for coming to Saudi Arabia. First, travelling and working is envisaged as an adventure. They romanticized the idea of traveling abroad and seeing the world beyond the Philippines. The second reason young Filipinos decided to go Saudi Arabia is because it was a relatively easy destination to travel to, and it is believed to be an easy way to fast-track their careers.

By going to Saudi Arabia, Filipino participants receive work experience and are paid a good wage. They believe that on returning to the Philippines with the experience and a specialization, they leapfrog difficult advancement processes. Another common belief was that Saudi could be a stepping stone to careers in the West, where they would have better working conditions and better pay. The stepping stone strategy which may have been an initial reason for coming to Saudi Arabia had mixed results. Several participants returned to the Philippines after many years finding that their careers did not advance while those who stayed in the Philippines did. Advancement, likely depends on the type of careers rather than actual experience[15]. Moreover, those in this study hoping to go west did not succeed. Every professional either moved back to the Philippines or stayed in the Middles East[16]. That said,

---

[10] The Haram Mosque in Makkah and the Nabawi Mosque in Madinah are two most sacred places in Islam.
[11] Makkah and Madinah
[12] It is essential to note that the post-WWII "labor force" is made up of both Muslims and non-Muslims. Non-Muslims are usually Christians –Catholics/Protestants
[13] Islamic sciences in multiple Islamic learning centers: *rubats* are informal Islamic boarding schools such as *rubat* Sayyid Alawi in Makkah. An example of a university is the Islamic University of Madinah.
[14] Students in Saudi secular science universities are mostly at Master and PhD level students in Saudi universities.
[15] Accountants and site engineers in this study did not seem to advance their careers if they chose to work in the same type of position back in the Philippines. However, nurses and dental assistants who actually had more advance degrees than they were hired for in Saudi did advance.
[16] After completing their contracts in KSA several took jobs elsewhere in the GCC. While others who hope to go to more developed

being an OFW is a 'rite of passage' to adulthood. The adventure of seeing new places, being on one's own or advancing one's career is part of the package. It is a rite of passage to be independent economically and to a breadwinner for the family who are in great financial need.

Family

Family is the most important factor to becoming an OFW. The family[17] are directly dependent on the income OFW's bring from overseas (Parrenas 2005)[18]. As a result, able bodied adults are willing to 'sacrifice' the comfort of living at home to work abroad as OFW's. When asked why they came to Saudi Arabia, the majority of the participants referred to family directly. Several participants wanted to leave but when discussing their next move, they referred to themselves as the breadwinners of the family and found risking leaving problematic. The younger participants who talked of career advancement, in later discussions about their frustrations about living in Saudi, often referred to troubles about sending enough money home to support their family[19]. In addition, participants all express joy of sending big boxes of gifts for Christmas, Easter, and birthdays[20]. Family is always central where and how they choose to live or how they get their basic needs.

Concept of Sacrifice

OFW's face many difficult challenges[21]. They look for ways to extend their salaries by doing extra work or saving their housing allowance by living in crowded conditions for their family back home. Sacrifice and love[22] are always indicated when participants discuss the trails of becoming an OFW in KSA. A metaphor of an OFW's existence is "love and sacrifice". It is not a coincidence that love and sacrifice core to Christianity. To express love, one must sacrifice. Thus, OFW's sacrifice themselves for the betterment of their loved ones. They live for the benefit for their children, parents and extended family.

Indonesians Perceptions of Saudi Arabia

Indonesian transnationals perceptions of Saudi Arabia vary immensely depending on their degrees of religiosity, professions, education, or experiences. Some have shared grievances because of unpleasant experiences with their employers, while others have expressed joy and happiness because of the good/pleasant experiences with their bosses. Those who had hostile experiences tend to have negative attitudes towards Saudi Arabia while those who enjoyed their experiences see the Kingdom positively.

A great deal of Indonesian Muslims living in the Kingdom[23] also consider Saudi Arabia a "second home". They have a persistent relationship with Saudi. Devout Muslims generally see Saudi Arabia as a good place to live being able to visit Makkah and Madinah for Umrah[24] whenever they desire. Moreover, they also view the Kingdom as a fine place to live because of the absence of 'haram' food and drink[25]. Many even hope to die in Makkah or Madinah because these "sacred places" guarantee

---

counties stayed because they were happy with the living and working conditions.

[17] The family usually means the extended family: parents, grandparents, aunts and uncles, and their progeny

[18] Parrenas (2005) suggests that even when both parents have well-paying jobs, salaries are not enough to support a family.

[19] Some employers were not timely in paying their employs which cause stress on individuals whose families depended on them.

[20] The Balikbayan boxes are an important practice which has been explained as not merely a gift box but as a way of taking control of raising children in their absence, as supplementing families with food items or an expression of identity (Blanc 1996, Alburo 2005, Patzer 2018)

[21] Challenges can range from purely economic ones, such as serious basic needs of family members. But it can also be about dealing with bureaucratic systems in the Kingdom, or about employee abuses, all of which is beyond the scope of this papers.

[22] Much has been written about Christian understandings of sacrifice and love (Kerns 2008, Daly 2009, Mablin & Mangus 2014). Pedregosa (2019) suggests that Christian values and understanding of OFW' s sacrifice is encapsulated in the understanding of the community hero, the bayan. OFW's are envisaged in present day Philippines as heroes sacrificing their lives to support their families and their communities.

[23] Indonesian Muslims living in the Kingdom are refered to as "*mukimin*"

[24] Umrah is a pilgrimage to Mekkah and/or Madinah

[25] Pork or alcohol are typical examples of haram, or forbidden, food and drinks.

them a place in heaven.

However, non-practicing Muslim professionals or menial laborers do not see Saudi Arabia a place for religious practice. They compare working in Indonesia to Saudi Arabia. They consider the Kingdom a good place to make money, to send remittance home, to help build houses in their county, or to save money for their personal futures. Unlike the devout Muslims, their goal is not to live and die in the Kingdom. For the professional, rather, there are other benefits to working for important companies[26]. Employees receive free annual tickets home, free housings, and support for their children's education, etc. Professional employees tend to see the Kingdom positively.

Filipino Perceptions of Saudi Arabia

Filipino perceptions of Saudi Arabia also vary greatly. However, in contrast with Indonesians, Christian Filipinos see their experience in the Kingdom directly related to work and to their employers' attitudes towards them. If they have adequate living conditions, salaries, and support, then they feel very good about their sojourn. They are willing to sacrifice their everyday living conditions, but if employers[27] do not pay them in a timely manner, and they cannot send support home then their experience is intolerable[28].

Conclusion

This paper suggests that Filipinos appear to come to Saudi Arabia for purely secular imperatives, resembling the reasons non-practicing Indonesians Muslims coming to the Kingdom. However, one could argue that there is a deeper set of moral grounds rooted in Christian cosmology of love and sacrifice. Indonesians are driven by similar secular economics and consequentially different religious/moral imperatives. But, because of Indonesian long-standing relationship with the Arabian Peninsula they are better prepared for what awaits them. In conclusion, the motivations of the two communities diverge, they share the same impression towards Saudi Arabia as a site for a better livelihood.

References

Alburo, Jade. "Boxed in or out? Balikbayan boxes as metaphors for Filipino American (Dis) location." *Ethnologies* 27.2 (2005): 137-157.

Al Qurtuby, Sumanto. Saudi Arabia and Indonesian Networks: Migration, Education and Islam.London, UK: IB Tauris & Bloomsbury (2019)

Azra, Azyumardi. The Transmission of Islamic Reformism to Indonesia: Networks of Middle

Eastern and Malay-Indonesian Ulama in the Seventeenth and Eighteenth Centuries. Ph.D

Dissertation, Columbia University (1992)

Blanc, Cristina Szanton. "Balikbayan: a Filipino extension of the national imaginary and of state boundaries." *Philippine Sociological Review* 44.1/4 (1996): 178-193.

Daly, Robert J. Sacrifice unveiled: The true meaning of Christian sacrifice. Bloomsbury Publishing, 2009.

Diederich, Mathias. "Indonesians in Saudi Arabia: Religious and Economic Connection."in

Madawi Al-Rasheed (ed.), *Transnational Connection and the Arab Gulf*, pp. 128-146. London,

Routledge (2005)

Espiritu, Yen. *Filipino American Lives*. Temple University Press, 2010.

Gorospe, Vitaliano R. "Christian renewal of Filipino values." *Philippine Studies* 14.2 (1966): 191-227.

Hurgronje, C. Snouck.. Mekka in the Later Part of the 19th Century: Daily Life, Customs and Learning. The Moslims of the

[26] Important multi-national companies would be like ARAMCO, or Sabic

[27] There appears to be little knowledge about good or bad companies such as the knowledge Indonesians have acquired over time.

[28] An example of such unbearable situations is when one of the participants was a site engineer. The non-Filipino engineers were put up hotels in a town and transported to the site every day. He was given a container to live in for ten months with a port-o-potty on site in the desert. He went to Qatar to work after his contracted had ended.

East Indian Archipelago (transl. Johan Monahan). Leiden: Brill.(1970)

Kearns, Cleo McNelly. *The Virgin Mary, Monotheism, and Sacrifice*. Cambridge University Press, 2008.

Magliveras, Simeon S. "Halo-Halo, Nostalgia and Navigating Life for Overseas Filipino Workers (OFW's) in the Kingdom of Saudi Arabia" in *Exclusion and Inclusion in International Migration: Power, Resistance and Identity* ed. Dr A. Teke-Lloyd. Transnational Press, London (2019)

Magliveras, Simeon S. "Filipino Guest Workers, Gender Segregation, and the Changing Social/Labour-Scape in the Kingdom of Saudi Arabia." *Migration Letters* 16.4 (2019): 503-512.

Margold, Jane A. "Narratives of Masculinity and Transnational Migration: Filipino Workers in the Middle East." *Bewitching Women, Pious Men: Gender and Body Politics In Southeast Asia* (1995): 274-98.

Mayblin, Maya, and Magnus Course. "The Other Side of Sacrifice: Introduction." *Ethnos* 79.3 (2014): 307-319.

Johnson, Mark. "Freelancing in the Kingdom: Filipino Migrant Domestic Workers Crafting Agency in Saudi Arabia." *Asian and Pacific Migration Journal* 20.3-4 (2011): 459-478.

Okamura, Jonathan Y. Imagining the Filipino American Diaspora: Transnational Relations, Identities, and Communities. Routledge, 2013.

Parreñas, Rhacel Salazar. Children of Global Migration: Transnational Families and Gendered Woes. Stanford University Press, 2005.

Patzer, Helena. "Unpacking the Balikbayan Box. Long-Distance Care Through Feeding and Food Consumption in The Philippines." *Studia Socjologiczne* 231.4 (2018): 131-148.

Pedregosa, Lawrence. "A Popular-Theological Anthropology of Bayani: Liminal Unity of Overseas Filipino Workers in their Expression of Love as Sacrifice." *MST Review* 21.2 (2020): 21-55.

Philippines Embassy https://riyadhpe.dfa.gov.ph/about-us/historical-background (2014) last retrieved 6/16/2021

Rosario, Teresita C. Del. "Bridal Diaspora: Migration and Marriage Among Filipino Women." *Indian Journal of Gender Studies* 12.2-3 (2005): 253-273.

Silvey, Rachel. "Filipino Diaspora: Emergent Geographies of Labor and Love." (2013): 98-112.

NEW PATTERNS OF MIGRATION IN MEDITERRANEAN: NORTH-SOUTH

Boutaina Ismaili Idrissi

Abstract

The foreign migration to Morocco, mainly Spanish and French, has deep historical roots. Fueled by economic, social and cultural reasons since the mid-20th century, this phenomenon gained momentum recently in the aftermath of the 2008-2009 economic crisis.

The paper tries to shed light on this new form of migration, its dynamics and features and to what extent it is due to structural or cyclical factors. It tackles, also, key policy responses to be implemented by so as to grasp the opportunities associated with this type of migration.

Keys words: North South, Foreign migration, Morocco, determinants, socioeconomic integration.

Introduction

The foreign migration to Morocco, mainly Spanish and French, has deep historical roots. Being an old phenomenon that has been fueled by economic, social and even cultural reasons since the second half of the 20th century, this phenomenon has gained momentum in recent years especially in the aftermath of the 2008-2009 global economic crisis.

The latest available data shows the rise of French and Spanish migrants among migrants residing in Morocco. Many factors could explain this trend some of which are the political and social stability and the economic dynamism in which the country is evolving in the last two decades.

Alongside these factors, Morocco's geographical proximity, culture of tolerance and affordable cost of living compared to European standards stand as key determinants for some French and Spanish citizens to migrate to Morocco.

This paper will emphasize the key features of this new pattern of migration in the Mediterranean region, which shows that migration flows are not exclusively in one way, i.e., South-North. This new form of migration may be of great value added to host countries such as Morocco at various level: reinforcement of local demand in the case of retired migrants; setting up of new businesses that create jobs at the local level; a source of expertise to local firms actually challenged by the shortage of skills and competencies.

Approach and Methodology

The paper has shed light on this new form of migration North-South, taking Morocco as a case study. Various aspects have been examined in connection with cultural and socioeconomic determinants behind French and Spanish Migrants preference for Morocco as a country of residence.

With the view to the complexity of issues to be covered in this paper, the approach adopted combines various dimensions and relies both on qualitative and quantitative tools to assert the key findings. The paper has a policy-oriented feature as it is intended to enrich Morocco's options to promote this type of migration and take the best advantage from it.

The main research questions addressed in this paper are set below:

- How migration to Morocco from the North has evolved throughout the history?

- What are its features and determinants and to what extent it is due to structural or cyclical factors?

- How about the cultural and socioeconomic integration of French and Spanish Migrants and how this could be used as a strong argument to pledge for a new paradigm of migration within the Mediterranean region?

- What is the overall impact of this migration on Morocco's economy?

Various sources have been used to grasp this multidimensional topic: primary and secondary data from different ministerial department and public offices, published reports and books as well as scientific articles.

Literature review

The literature review on international migration revealed that most of the theories have focused either on South-North or South-South migrations, apprehended from different angles of analysis (micro-level, meso-level, macro-level). However, the last decade has witnessed an interest in North–South migration, a new pattern of migration whose occurrence coincides with the surge of economic difficulties of developed countries in the Global North. if the literature review has revealed that income, proximity, and networks are the major drivers of migration from developing to industrial countries, these drivers are paradoxically the same as North South migration.

The foreign migration to Morocco throughout the history

The foreign migration in Morocco has gone through major three periods: **a precolonial period**, **before the independence** and in the **aftermath of independence**.

During the precolonial period, the first European migrations to Morocco started in the 16th century where new shipbuilding techniques had been introduced in Morocco mainly at Salé, an Atlantic city of 16000 inhabitants considered as the only private port in Africa. An important maritime and administrative jobs with substantial transfer of know-how in the shipbuilding sector but also from other sectors such as the metallurgy and armaments sectors.

The Economic migration started after signing the treaty with Spain in 1767[1] which allows the Settlement of Spanish as merchants or as representatives of trade chambers throughout the Moroccan territory (Tangier, Larache, Tetouan and other ports). The treaty of peace of Wad Ras 1860 which ended the War between Spain and Morocco was advantageous to Spanish State with trade privileges that were extended to other European countries like Great-Britain and France. The Spanish presence represented 69% the European population living in Morocco in 1893.

Before the independence, Morocco remained more a country of immigration for work but also for settlers mainly from France and Spain. In 1952, there were 529,000 foreigners in Morocco (more than 5% of the Moroccan population) including nearly 300,000 French nationals while the Spanish presence was shared between the Saharan provinces and was almost exclusively reduced to military garrisons and in the northern zone. In 1956, the Spanish counted for 150,000residents, 37% of whom were

---

[1] Eloy Martín Corrales : Les Espagnols au Maroc (1767-1860) : le défi de travailler avec l'autre. Cahiers de la Méditerranée 84/2012

settled in Tétouan (16000 Spanish in the same area in 1923)[2]. In fact, many political exiles fleeing the Franco regime (nearly 50,000) had also found refuge in the Area of the French Protectorate, sometimes even using "pateras" to transport Spanish illegal migrants off the city of Salé.

After the independence, the number of foreign residents declined from 529,000 in 1952 to 396,000 in 1960 (27% in 8 years) due to the massive departure of the French and Spanish, reaching a rate of 72% between 1960 and 1971, then 45% between 1971 and 1982. In 1980, there were only 10,000 Spanish living in Morocco and 8,500 in 1986, settled mainly in Tangier, Casablanca and Tétouan. The downward trend continued but at a slower pace (19% between 1982 and 1994). However, the global financial crisis of 2007-2008, particularly affecting Spain, pushed many Spanish to settle in Morocco (an increase by 32% between 2008 and 2012).

Based on the last census of population in 2014, foreigners' residents in Morocco represent 0.25% of the total Moroccan population (Out of a population of 33.8 million inhabitants in 2014)[3].

Determinants, characteristics and main categories

The main determinants of European and North American migrants are related to employment, economic or cultural opportunities, retirement[4][5], climate, desire for change & proximity to Europe.

51.2% of males and 48.8% of females are estimated for an average of 56.5% and 43.5% of the total foreign population. Generally, this foreign population is highly educated, 47% of Europeans have a university degree; for the French, Spanish, Belgian and German at least one person in two has a higher education level, a little less than half among Italians and only 6.6% are without a diploma.

Six main categories of migrants can be outlined:

Lifestyle migrants: Installed in the ancient Medinas of the historic cities of Morocco, creating closed spaces, and reserved for their community. They have limited relations with the local environment to meet their daily needs, made more often by their domestic employees.

Migrants for economic reasons: The economic reforms undertaken by Morocco encourages many foreigners to settle down in the country. Generally, they are enjoying a high level of salary and good living conditions compared to local population.

Immigration over time or western "winterers" in Morocco: they are mainly French (80%), with a length of their stay varies between 3 and 6 months a year. This category is closed to tourist mobility rather than migration but the frequency and the relations with the Moroccan environment can evolve from itinerant to a relative sedentary lifestyle with the acquisition of houses or requesting a residence permit.

Fake tourists or illegal workers: they are tourists who have decided to stay in Morocco to set their business or to seek job opportunities and are mainly involved in sectors such as catering, guest houses, agriculture, architecture, decoration, consulting and real estate agency... they enjoy administrative flexibility either for tax reasons or for freedom of movement, they do not register either with the consular authorities of their country or with the administrative authorities of Morocco. Every six

---

[2] Service central de statistique, population non marocaine 1954.
[3] General Population and Housing Census (2014), Morocco
[4] 60,000 retirees in Morocco out of the 1.3 million French retirees are present in more than 50 localities. Attracted by the quality of life, mild climate and the warm welcome of Moroccans often French-speaking. The cost of living 40 to 60% cheaper than Europe.
[5] Migrants au Maroc – Cosmopolitisme, présence d'étrangers et transformation sociales 2015 p : 32. Le chiffre ressort de l'estimation de M. LE BOGOT Brenda faite sur la base de l'enquête de terrain réalisée à Agadir en 2014.

months, they renew their status as tourists by going to Ceuta, Melilla or Algeciras.

Expatriates: It is a term used today to designate all the French of Morocco: employees, investors or retirees. For convenience, this study expands the term to cover all Western foreigners working in Morocco on a fixed-term contract basis. They are often settled in Morocco under bilateral or multilateral conventions and experience their immersion in Moroccan society in an almost identical way, except for some the problem of language.

Mixed couples: A frequent tendency between Moroccans and Europeans with wide range of situations in terms of integration going from a situation of total assimilation of the European spouse by the host environment (cultural, economic and social) or a situation of a western family relocated, living at the European pace while being on Moroccan soil.

The legal & institutional framework

Many ancient texts regulating migration were replaced by new texts, including the 2011's Constitution, the international conventions ratified by Morocco. As stated in the article 30 of the Moroccan constitution, the legal status of foreigners in Morocco holds no distinction between nationalities or countries of origin, in compliance with universal human rights.

The main legal issues are related to the Mobility of capital, taxation and family succession. The mobility of capital was clearly stated in the investment's charter which allows any person settled in Morocco and wishing to bring their money back must declare and register any assets acquired or inherited in their country of origin, at the Foreign Exchange Office. Only capital that has been officially transferred by the Bank, may leave the country with their profit. Foreign residents in Morocco are not obliged to declare to the Moroccan tax authorities the assets they hold abroad.

The Moroccan French Tax Convention of 1970 was signed to avoid the double taxation (entry into force on 5 March 1975). Pensions are subject to the law of the country of residence. This measure has encouraged French retirees to settle down in Morocco.

The family law has stated that "Any child born to a Moroccan father or a Moroccan mother is Moroccan "(Article 6). Some restrictions still prevail with regard to marriage:

- The obligation to convert to Islam for non-Muslim foreign residents,
- Loss of important family rights for unconverted Christian wives (inheritance),
- Polygamy that cannot be ruled out.

The Chapter V (employment of foreign employees) of Act No. 65.99, on the Labor Code, stipulate that "any employer wishing to recruit a foreign employee must obtain authorization from the government labor authority. This authorization is granted in the form of a visa affixed to the employment contract." (Article 516). Other laws apply without distinction to nationals like the criminal law who are living in Moroccan territory (art. 10) and the law of public freedoms which allows foreigners in Morocco to enjoy the same public freedoms as nationals more particularly freedom of the press, freedom of meeting and assembly, and freedom to form or belong to an association.

Besides the legal framework, there are a set of institutions and bodies responsible for monitoring, controlling and cooperating on migration, and for collecting data and producing documents on foreign migration, whether from economically advanced countries (expatriates, residents, investors, etc.) or legal migration from economically less developed countries or illegal migration.

A considerable contribution to employment and foreign investment.

Morocco's implementation of sectoral strategies since 2005 had a considerable impact on the flow of foreign investments (hotels and restaurants, automotive, aerospace, offshoring…) and consequently on the recourse to foreign employees. The subprime crisis of 2007 has triggered as well an interest for Morocco. Many foreigners had sought job opportunities in various sectors, especially those requiring skilled labor and qualified profiles. It was estimated that 10,000 Spanish citizens were employed in the northern provinces of the Kingdom.

The data on employment is controversial depending on public official sources. If it has revealed that 26283 employees mainly French, Senegalese and Spanish were registered in 2017[6] due to the dynamics of investment projects implemented by Morocco in services, industry and construction. The official data of the Ministry of Employment and Vocational Training between 2016 and 2019 reached cumulatively 6541 for European employees and 6511 for those from Asian countries. Even though a diversification of foreign employees in Morocco was observed, still European citizens count for the majority of the foreign workforce in Morocco, 50% among them are French, followed by Turkish and Spanish employees.

Conclusion

In parallel to the so-called illegal migration from the South to the North, we witness recently the emergence of a north-south migration designated by many expressions such as: "second home mobility", "residential tourism", "leisure migration" or "life style migration"[7].

Over the past fifteen years, Morocco has become the theatre of these two phenomena: a country of migration and transit for illegal migrants seeking Europe, and an attractive destination for Migrants from Spain and France.

We are talking here about new categories of "migrants": tourists or seasonal migrants or expatriates[8]. The word of expatriates tends to fall into disuse in favor of resident or migrant or immigrant, it is, in fact, a foreigner subject to rules of entry and stay according to the country of origin, as to the exercise of civil rights reserved to nationals and special authorizations as to the exercise of commercial and wage activity.

Nevertheless, the rules of public law are applied to them as to everyone else with derogations that can be established by conventions and reciprocity.

But expatriates/residents quickly find themselves entangled in Moroccan assimilative legal rules as soon as they start a family with a Moroccan spouse or husband.

Therefore, the question of the integration of European migrants into Moroccan society is difficult to apprehend. It is not expressed in black or white colors but in very varied shades or even in the colorful range of rainbows. Its assessment and appreciation are very different from that of other migrants.

---

[6] National Social Security office

7 Benson, O'Reilly, 2009 cité par B. Le Bigot : Les migrations hivernales des européens vers le Maroc : circulations et constructions des espaces de vie. Presses de Sciences Po | « Autrepart » 2016/1 N° 77 | pages 51 à 68 https://www.cairn.info/revue-autrepart-2016-1-page-51.htm

8 M. Peraldi, L.Terrazzoni : Nouvelles migrations ? Les français dans les circulations migratoires européennes vers le Maroc. Presses de Sciences Po | « Autrepart » 2016/1 N° 77 | pages 69 à 86https://www.cairn.info/revue-autrepart-2016-1-page-69.htm

DETERMINANTS OF MIGRATION FROM RURAL HOUSEHOLDS IN INDIA: AN EMPIRICAL INVESTIGATION

Shreya Nupur[1] and Meghna Dutta[2]

Abstract

Using India Human development survey (IHDS), unique nationally representative dataset of Indian households, this study aims to examine the determinants of migration from 'rural poor households' in India. Migration is an important livelihood diversification strategy to mitigate potential risks, such as crop failure, major illness, job loss etc., in rural areas. The result from binary logistic regression suggests that household demographic characteristics, household resources, debt, caste group, education level, shock such as marriage or major illness in the household and public transfers are major factors to determine the migration from rural poor households. The possible implication would be to focus on the migration strategy taking by poor households, as poor migrants work in vulnerable and exploitative condition at destination place, so they require especial attention and need to be covered in social security scheme.

Introduction/Background

Migration is an integral part of development of individual as well as nation (United Nations, 2009). In the wake of economic reforms in 1991, Indian economy in recent years have witnessed the population mobility at rapid pace. The novel corona cataclysm has, for the first time, brought the magnitude of migration to the centre stage. The unplanned lockdown has exposed the deep fault lines in India's labour market, especially poor migrant workers. Rural to urban migration is an important and integral livelihood strategy for rural poor households to get away from poverty trap in developing nations (Chandrasekhar, 2018). Migration is an important livelihood diversification strategy to mitigate potential risks, such as crop failure, major illness, job loss etc., in rural areas (Katz and Stark, 1986). Migration and remittances acts as an insurance against these risks and save poor people from falling into extreme poverty. According to recent Census, 2011, there are near 450 million internal migrants in India and most prevalent reason for this mobility is for the purpose of employment. Meanwhile, the literature dealing with migration in India have devoted little attention to the particular group of 'rural poor population' in rural to urban streams (Tang, 2019). Nevertheless, these studies have focused on rural to urban migration in general, 'poor population from rural area' in particular has been remain neglected. In that too literature has extensively focused on migration decision as an individual's decision, which is surprising because the New Economics of Labour Migration has focused on the fact that it is household rather than individual in isolation decides about migration. The scholars such as Stark (1991), Chandrasekhar (2018) have emphasized on the role of household in migration decision as oppose to Todaro (1969) which focused on Individual role. It is argued that migration strategy is a mutual contract between individual migrant and their family to avoid risks such as drought, flood crop failure etc.

---

[1] Research Scholar, Department of Humanities and Social Sciences, Indian Institute of Technology Patna, 801106, Bihar, India
[2] Assistant Professor, Department of Humanities and Social Sciences, Indian Institute of Technology Patna, 801106, Bihar, India

Given this backdrop, using the IHDS-2, a nationally representative data, this study makes an attempt to add into the migration literature by examining the factors that determines migration decision in 'rural poor households' in India. Considering its usefulness to understand the nexus between migration mechanism and poverty in rural households in India. There is need to extend the migration policies by giving special focus to the 'rural poor households' groups among general rural to urban migration groups in developing countries.

Objective: To examine the determinants of migration decision in 'rural poor households' in India considering household as a decision making unit.

Data and key variables for the present study

The data used in the present study derived from India Human Development Survey, a nationally representative multi-topic panel survey of Indian households, conducted jointly by NCAER, New Delhi and University of Maryland, USA in 2004-05 and 2011-12 (two waves). This data includes all the states and union territories of India, except for Andaman Nicobar and Lakshadweep (Desai and Vanneman, 2015). For this study we will use the second round of IHDS (2011) which is collected in between November 2011 to October 2012. Moreover, we only consider the subset of sample of this survey to answer our research question which is 5,427. Since we want to examine the determinant of migration from 'rural poor households' so, we restricted our subset of sample to poor households of rural India. IHDS being the first large scale household survey in India provides detailed information on various socio-economic variables. Thus, this data allows to study migration mechanism at household level.

For the present study, we consider our dependent variable as 'probability of migration in rural poor households'. This is a binary variable takes '1' if 'rural poor household has sent at least one migrant' and '0' otherwise. The key explanatory variables are Household composition, caste groups, education, resources, debt and major events or shock.

Empirical Model

The analysis strategy for this study will be based on binary logistic regression

$$z_i = \beta_0 + \beta_i(X_i) + e_i \quad (1)$$

Equation (1) is binary logistic regression model where z_i is the binary dependent variable, and X_i represents ith explanatory variable

Result and discussion

Table 1. describes the results. The findings of this study indicates that probability to send migrants from poor rural households is likely to **trigger in presence of debt** in the household.

Households that have **faced major shocks** or events in form of **illness** and **marriage** are more likely to send out at least one of the member. Migration involves cost while the course of moving and getting employment at destination area. In poor rural household, resources in form of income, land and livestock plays an important role in financing migration. Hence intensifies the probability to send migrants.

Table 1. Estimates of Logistic regression for migration decision in rural poor households

Variables	Coefficients	Standard error
Household composition and characteristics		
Dependent elders	.3158809***	.056820
Dependent child	.0.263395	.023955
Dependent adult	-.2172251***	.041697
Teen male	-.2112623***	.069359
Teen female	.1436362**	.057189
Caste Groups		
Brahmin (= ref.)		
Forward/General	.1700742	.5314345
Other Backward Castes (OBC)	.3552674	.5116792
Scheduled Castes (SC) and Scheduled Tribe (ST)	.0613388	.5093173
Highest Education	.0508728	.0507429
Caste Groups # Education		
Brahmin (= ref.)		
Forward/General	-.0993111*	.0555954
Other Backward Castes (OBC)	-.1031238**	.0520432
Scheduled Castes (SC) and Scheduled Tribe (ST)	-.0864941*	.0518602
Household Resources		
Land holding any type (no=ref.)	.3488361***	.0918936
Own livestock (no=ref.)	.2146343***	.0815538
Irrigated land possession		
No holding (=ref.)		
Small	-.541399***	.2046881
Large	-.829769	.5480154
Irrigated land possession # adults		
No holding # adults (=ref)		
Small# adults	.2285405***	.0562817
Large# adults	.280484***	.1012548
Government benefit transfers (log)	-.0137551	.0099554
Debt (log)	.0405989***	.0078403

Income per capita quintile

1st quintile (=ref.)		
2nd quintile	.2969173***	.1098849
3rd quintile	.3624646***	.1103681
4th quintile	.20694**	.115442
Highest quintile	.1779073	.1197628
Household level Shocks		
Major illness	.2736968***	.0870505
Drought, fire or flood	-.1923959	.1226518
Marriage	.41731***	.0770035
Crop loss	-.0610768	.093458
Death	-.1254567	.0911532
Constant	-.6105706**	.2816923
Chi-square	292.23***	
Log likelihood	-2566.237	
Pseudo R^2	0.0539	
Observations	5427	

Note: *p < .10; **p < .05; and ***p < .01

The association between number of adults and probability of sending migrants are negative and highly significant. But as it interacts with acres of irrigated land possession by households the impact becomes positive and highly significant with increasing acres of irrigated lands. Households with elder dependent members and teen females are more likely to send migrants. Highest years of education in household has positive effect on the probability of being a migrant sending household. However, when years of education gets interacted with caste groups it becomes negative and significant.

Conclusion

This paper attempts to examine the probability of migration decision of a particular group 'poor rural household' from household perspective. And arrived at the conclusion that migration is one of the most important strategy in rural poor household to tackle poverty. Scholars have tried to examine rural to urban migration in general, but 'rural poor household' group in particular has remain neglected in literature. However, the existing studies on rural households in India is relatively scarce. This paper attempts to examine the probability of migration decision of a particular group 'poor rural household' from household perspective. The findings of this study asserted that migration is an important livelihood strategy for rural poor households. It is been triggered by debt, presence of reasonable amount of asset and livestock. In addition to that households that have faced major shocks in form of illness and marriage has high probability of sending one of the member so that they could tackle these shocks. The findings also reveal that not all poor people are in position to migrate because they cannot bear migration cost. The findings from this study will be useful to understand the nexus between migration mechanism and poverty in rural households in India. In addition to that, findings from this study is of particular importance because in the current pandemic it is the poor migrants who hit hardest therefore, it will also help in informed policymaking related to poverty alleviation.

References

Chandrasekhar, S., & Sahoo, S. (2018). Short-term Migration in Rural India: The Impact of Nature and Extent of Participation in Agriculture (Working Paper No. 2018–016).

Desai, S., & Vanneman, R.National Council of Applied Economic Research, New Delhi. (2012). India Human Development Survey-II (IHDS-II), ICPSR36151-v2. Ann Arbor, MI: Inter-university Consortium for Political and Social Research. doi:10.3886/ICPSR36151.v2

Katz, E., and Stark O. 1986. "Labor migration and risk aversion in less developed countries." Journal of Labor Economics 4: 131-149.

Stark, O. (1991). The Migration of Labour, Basil Blackwell, Oxford

Tang S. (2019). Determinants of migration and household member arrangement among poor rural households in China: The case of North Jiangsu. *Population Space Place.*

Todaro, M (1969). A Model of Labour Migration and Urban Unemployment in LDCs. *American Economic Review*, 59: 138-48.

United Nations. 2009. *Human Development Report 2009:* "Overcoming Barriers: Human Mobility and Development." United Nations Development Program, New York.

REFRAMING MIGRANCY THROUGH INTERSECTIONAL ANALYSIS: CONCEPTUALIZING THE EMBODIMENT OF MIGRATION EXPERIENCE FROM THE MEXICAN-UNITED STATES MIGRATION FIELD FRAMEWORK.

Renato de Almeida Arão Galhardi

Abstract

Mexico-United States migration research rarely use the concept migrancy and migration analysis has often used migrancy "out of context". By reviewing the usages of migrancy, I argue that migrancy is better understood as the embodiment of the experience of migration. I reason that the experience of migration is best captured through intersectional analysis. By addressing gender, ethnicity and class, migrancy can recapture migrant agency and bridge the gap between micro and macro analysis. Within the Mexico-United States migratory field, I argue that migrancy is a powerful concept that addresses the structuring forces that shape migrant experiences without sacrificing migrant agency.

Introduction

Since its introduction at the beginning of the 1960s, migrancy has been used to describe something related to the process of migration but remains a rather murky concept. Building on critical literature review of the usages of migrancy, I propose a closer approximation to the social process that embodies migrancy, by framing migrancy through the experience of migration. I argue that migrancy is indivisible from the experience of migration, and further reason that migrancy is an "entangled" property best captured through intersectional analysis. I demonstrate how intersectional analysis can capture and describe the structural and embedded geometries of power of migrancy embodied in the experience of the Mexican-United States migration field. I frame migrancy as a migrant-habitus demonstrated through the example of the mexican migrant and that migrancy occupies a *migrancy-scape* and finally, I argue that reframing migrancy through intersectional analysis allows migration research to recapture the agentic subjectivity and bridge the gaps between micro and macro analysis of migration and embed migration research in the human experience it reports.

Migrancy "out of context"

Since its introduction at the beginning of the 1960s, migrancy has been used to describe *something* related to the process of migration, but remains a rather murky concept. Migrancy is often used, I argue, "out of context", that is, as a signifier for something to do with the process of the migration but failing to articulate the social dimensions it tacitly references. What, exactly, do we mean when we say *migrancy*?

As one point of departure, we can look at Merriam-Webster dictionary's definition of migrancy, conceived as "the fact, condition, or phenomenon of habitual movement from one place of residence to another" specifically as the "habitual migration from one area to another in search of seasonal work" (Merriam-Webster., n.d.). This definition is grossly misleading and would merit its own critique in another space. Suffice to say that encapsulating migrancy as "habitual movement" and limiting its associating to "season work" is enough to discard this definition as an inaccurate and ineffective determination of the properties of migrancy. Migrancy, I argue, *is something different.*

Migrancy was first introduced in Phillip Mayer's 1962 research article, on South African Xhosa migration to East London during the first half of the twentieth century. Mayer (1962) observes how the transition from a tribal and rural environment, into the structural imposition of new urban environments, is met with reflexive negotiation of "active place-markers" (Jacobs, 2002). This "clash of culture"[1] creates what Mayer (1962) alludes to a "migrancy field", where the semantic values are reorganized in reference to the points of the migration field. It would be within the "mobility turn" (Glick Schiller & Salazar, 2013), almost three decades later, that a renewed considerations of the properties of migrancy would appear.

Building on displacement of methodological nationalism[2], and situating the discussion within the contours of transnationalism, globalization, and postmodernism, Iain Chambers reframes migrancy through the symbolic implication for subjectivity by shifting its position in *semantic space*[3] capturing the implications and complications of the experience of migration as embedded in an *entangle history*[4]. Thinking through feminist, deconstructionist, postmodern and postcolonial theories, Chambers (1994) articulates migrancy through "the repressed, the subordinate and the forgotten"[5] by considering migration as an ontological displacement of one who "is perpetually required to make herself at home in an interminable discussion between a scattered historical inheritance and a heterogeneous present" (p. 6). Chambers is effectively repositioning the agency of the subaltern subject by recognizing his "in-between-ness" in the power structures of world-system positionality. With migrancy, the biopolitical structures of power relations are made visible, highlighted by the conditions of the undocumented, the "illegal", the asylum seeker, the refugee. Migrancy, then, is more than a metaphor of equivalency of migration. *The experience of migration is an embodied act. An act that carries and expresses notions of gender, ethnicity and class.*

This regained reflexivity of the *migrant-as-other* is not a new concept and is arguably the most asserted claim of the migrant condition. However, by emphasizing the "stranger" in the migrant, Chambers is repositioning subjectivity within migration analysis, seeking its reaffirmation as a *social agent of migration.* Migrancy, then, seems to be just as important as other structuring factors of social reality -such as gender, ethnicity and class- as observed by finish sociologist, Lena Näre, in the following passage:

> Although the boundaries of migrancy are fluid and contingent, as a social category it has very real effects on people's lives. In fact, it can be argued that migrancy has become as important a social category as those classics of the modern era: gender, social class, 'race' and nationality. (Näre, 2013, p. 605).

Looking through the migrancy-scape

Reframing migrancy as the experience of migration suggests placement within Appadurai's "scapes" of cultural engagement, within the "work of the imagination". To be in a scape is to bring the social construction of the body -*the visible body* (Merleau-Ponty, 1981) -into the dialectical relationship of social organisation and enter a process of hermeneutical engagement with the embodied social dimensions and "cultural meaning inscribed in the body" (Conboy *et al.*, 1997)[6]. Butler (1997) has argued that the body a performative act forged as a historical institution and replied to within the scope of its historical

---

[1] See Ruwet, C. (2017).
[2] See Glick Schiller & Salazar (2013).
[3] see Chapter 3 in Hannan, M. T., et al., (2019). *Concepts and categories: Foundations for sociological and cultural analysis.* Columbia University Press.
[4] See Haup and Kocka, 2009.
[5] p. 3.
[6] p.1

understanding. This makes the body a semiotic landscape whereby ethnicity and class are earmarks for social engagement, interpretation and perception (Merleau-Ponty, 1981).

Given the properties of a 'scape' -the symbolic and phenomenological constitution of the biographical Self- it seems appropriate to consider the placement of migrancy within its own scape: a *migrancy-scape*. The *migrancy-scape* would embody the particular expressions of present, past and future re-memories, considerations, and situate agentic aspirations. Furthermore, addressing a *migrancy-scape* is a recognition of the structuring effect of the experience of migration on the ontological configurations of the subject acting as a *social fact* through *habitus*.

Migrancy as a social fact, nurtured by habitus

Social fact, argues Durkheim, are shared social "beliefs, tendencies and practices"[7] undertaken by a social group with coercive properties and effects. The body, then, embodies social facts within each "scape" that become horizons for interaction and relations, through ideologies and perceived representations Guillaumin (1995). As a social fact, a migrancy-scape can be construed as a space for the situated perspective of the experience of migration; the space and place in which the social organisation of reality is seen through the experience of migrancy; a *migrancy space through migrancy*. Given this, I posit that the embodiment of migrancy, as a social fact, becomes nurtured through *habitus*.

Habitus, argues Bourdieu (1990), are an internalization of regular practices that organize the social body of any given individual. *Habitus* is "embodied history" (Bourdieu, 1990, p. 56) that stretches through the fields of relationships created among and through individuals, acting as semiotic scapes for referential reasoning and agency (Sayer, 2018). Migrancy can then be seen as *habitus* of the embodied condition articulated in and through a *migrancy-scape*.

By addressing the relationships with, at least, ethnicity, gender and class in situated world-system positionality of the migrant, it is possible to situate experience in what Doreen Massey has called *power geometry*. Gender, ethnicity and class each create different engagements with the space of power relationships giving shape to the relationships between the dominant and the dominated, between the asserted and the denied[8]. Migrancy, then, is a place in the geometry of power as the entangled property of the process of migration. Intersectional analysis allows, above all, to engage with the experience of migration, and place migrancy in relationship with the migration field while maintaining the migrant agency within micro and macro analysis.

Finding migrancy and looking for *migrancia* in mexican migration to the United States

The literature on Mexican migration to the United States seems to indicate that the experience of migration -*migrancy*- is a structuring aspect of the ontological construction of social reality. The expanding migratory field between Mexico and the United States has positioned immigration as an embodied aspect of the fabric of social and cultural imagination (Massey, 1987), however, it is surprising to see scarce mention and usage of the term migrancy, in any of its variations, when attending to the migration phenomenon between Mexico and the United States. Where then is migrancy in mexican migration analysis and, maybe more importantly, where is *migrancia* -its equivalency in Spanish, in the literature? The simple answer to this question, is that migrancy is "everywhere".

The history of the border management and the construction of legality has shaped the migration field

[7] p. 54
[8] Massey, 1994, p. 149.

between these two countries placing migrancy as a cultural facet of this entangled history. Since the first researchers on mexican migration to the United States[9], migrancy has been referred to without "being referred to" explicitly. With no mention of the term "migrancy", the research on mexican migration has sought to capture this intersectionality by framing its constitution in diverse set of concepts and terminology. This conceptual dispersion does so without engaging in the limitations of conceptual constraints in terms such as migrancy.

By reframing migrancy, it becomes possible to readdress discussion within the mobility turn of migration analysis. Specifically, within the Mexican-United states migratory field, migrancy becomes exacerbated with the narratives of riskier border crossings and border deaths in the last three decades. Despite the historical role male migrants have occupied in the development of the migration field between these two countries, the story of mexican migration is not a story about men, but a story involving diverse web of people in complex stories in diverse and heterogeneous narratives intertwined within dynamic social institutions, cultural convictions among other aspects of the "social process" of migration (Minian, 2018). The reframing of undocumented mexican migrants to "illegal" migrants during the second half of the twentieth century becomes driving narratives of their migrancy within a border history forged on necropolitics[10]. Gender, ethnicity and class are prevalent in understandings and addressing migrancy of mexican migration especially when position with what Jason de León has called "Land of open graves", the alternative spaces used by migrants to enter the United States of Necessity as Manuel Gamio once described.

Conclusion

I have argued that migrancy emerges as an embedded social property of the migration experience -a *habitus*- and its articulation makes visible micro-level negotiations alongside macro-level structural influences that ultimately shape the flows and characteristics of migration. The meso properties of migrancy allow it to dialogue with structuralist positions and configurations without removing the agentic properties of the migrant.

Given the history of racialized and racist migration policies of the United States, I argue that migrancy should (re)occupy a central position in the analysis of mexican migration, as it is an indivisible property of the migration phenomenon and shines a necessary light into the embodied construction of realities. Mexican migration is a story of mexican migrations and migrancy features differently with the relationships of categories juxtaposed. By bringing gender, ethnicity and class, is to add the "necessary complexity" to seeing, analysing migrancy in migration analysis. Although the last decades has seen a dramatic increase in research on non-male and non-heteronormative migrants, there is still a lack of analysis of the patriarchal and heteronormative privileges and constitution that shape the migration forces and migration analytical lenses.

Addressing migrancy can allow for a more balanced approach by insisting in making visible the structuring forces of patriarchal, gendered, classist and ethnicized constructions of social spaces, relations and ontological forms of being and seeing the word as well as bringing a reflexivity on the role and position of the researcher within these structures. By reframing migrancy -and introducing *migrancia*- through intersectional analysis as the embodiment of migration experience, I believe we can build narratives that address multileveled dimensions of migration phenomenon without sacrificing migrant agency. I also believe that embodying migrancy with intersectional categories seeks to increase reflexive sensibilities of the power-relations that occupy the spaces of research and also bring feminist

---

[9] see Gamio (1930).
[10] see Mbembe (2019).

theories to a more central role in migration studies. Paraphrasing Theresa Alfaro-Velcamp presentation earlier this week, "telling the truth about one's experience, is about respect and resistance" and I believe migrancy and *migrancia* work toward this principle.

References

Appadurai, A. (2001). *Modernity at Large: Cultural Dimensions of Globalization*. The University of Minnesota Press.

Bourdieu, P. (1990). *The logic of practice*. Stanford university press.

Butler, J., (1997). Performative Acts and Gender Constitution: An Essay in Phenomenology and Feminist Theory. In Conboy, K., Medina, N., & Stanbury, S. (eds.). *Writing on the body: Female embodiment and feminist theory*. Columbia University Press

Chambers, I. (1994). *Migrancy, culture, identity*. Routledge

Conboy, K., Medina, N., & Stanbury, S. (1997). Introduction. In Conboy, K., Medina, N., & Stanbury, S. (eds.). *Writing on the body: Female embodiment and feminist theory*. Columbia University Press.

De León, J. (2015). The land of open graves: living and dying on the migrant trail. University of California Press.

Durkheim, E.; [1897] (1982), *The Rules of Sociological Method*. [translation of: *Les regles de la methode sociologique* by Lukes, Steven]. The Free Press, New York.

Gamio, M. (1930). Mexican Immigration to the United States. A study of Human Migration and Adjustment. The University of Chicago Press.

Guillaumin, C. (1995). *Racism, sexism, power and ideology*. Routledge.

Hannan, M. T., Le Mens, G., Hsu, G., Kovács, B., Negro, G., Pólos, L., Pontikes, E. G., & Sharkey, A. J. (2019). *Concepts and categories: foundations for sociological and cultural analysis*. Columbia University Press.

Glick Schiller, N., & Salazar, N. B. (2013). Regimes of mobility across the globe. *Journal of ethnic and migration studies, 39*(2), 183-200. https://doi.org/10.1080/1369183X.2013.723253

Jacobs, J. M. (2002). *Edge of empire: Postcolonialism and the city*. Routledge. https://doi.org/10.4324/9780203430903

Massey, D. B. (1994). *Space, place, and gender*. University of Minnesota Press.

Massey, D. S. (1987). Understanding Mexican Migration to the United States. American *Journal of Sociology, 92*(6), 1372–1403. https://doi.org/10.1086/228669

Mayer, P. (1962). Migrancy and the Study of Africans in Towns. *American Anthropologist, 64*(3), 576-592 https://doi.org/10.1525/aa.1962.64.3.02a00070

Merleau-Ponty, M. (1981). *Phenomenology of perception*. Routledge & Kegan Paul.

Merriam-Webster. (n.d.). Migrancy. In Merriam-Webster.com dictionary. Retrieved June 18, 2021, from https://www.merriam-webster.com/dictionary/migrancy

Minian, A. R. (2018). Undocumented lives: the untold story of Mexican migration. Harvard University Press.

Mbembe, A. (2019). *Necropolitics*. Duke University Press.

Näre, L. (2013). Migrancy, gender and social class in domestic labour and social care in Italy: An intersectional analysis of demand. *Journal of Ethnic and Migration Studies, 39*(4), 601-623. https://doi.org/10.1080/1369183X.2013.745238

Ruwet, C. (2017) The Cities of Robert Ezra Park: Toward a Periodization of His Conception of the Metropolis (1915–39), in Kivisto, P. (ed) *The Anthem Companion to Robert Park*. Anthem Press.

Sayer, A. (2018). Pierre Bourdieu: ally or foe of discourse analysis? In Wodak, R., & Forchtner, B. (Eds.). *The Routledge handbook of language and politics*. Routledge.

'HOME' AND 'HOMELAND' AS MOBILE PLACES: RE-EXAMINING THE TERM COUNTRY OF ORIGIN IN MIGRATION STUDIES

Maria Panteleou[1]

Abstract

The following presentation examines how the perception of 'home' and 'homeland' is not related to the country of origin in migration studies, if we take into account the temporal and subjective factor that migrants themselves attribute to these perceptions. Using material from anthropological fieldwork with Albanian migrants, who lived and worked in Greece since the 1990s, moving temporally to Albania in the 2010s, it demonstrates, on the one hand, how they express their perspective regarding their 'home' and 'homeland' as a foreign place. On the other hand, it shows how the temporal family visits that Albanians welcome in Greece bring the sense of 'home' itself together in Greece. The presentation concludes that the term country of origin defines migrants in advance by a spatial notion, whereas the subjective conceptualizations of the 'home' and 'homeland' show primarily that they are mobile, secondly that they make sense for Albanians through the temporal, relational and experiential dimension of the place.

Keywords: home, homeland, Albanian migrants, mobilities

Introduction

In the modern globalized world, migration is no longer a linear movement from the country of origin to the country of destination but a continuous and complex process. This process involves multiple temporalities and spatialities: from pre-migratory and post-migratory forms of mobility (internal, external, temporary, socio-economic) that "they may precede, intersect with, and shape trajectories of internal and international migration" (Camenisch & Müller, 2017, p. 45, 55), travel plans that change over time, transforming transit places into places of settlements and vice versa (Schapendonk, 2012, p. 580) to periods of 'waiting' and forced physical immobility caused by the political system of the nation-states that regulates and controls migrants' (im)mobilities through issuance procedures and/or renewal of appropriate legalization documents (Anderson, 2019, p. 6). This understanding of the migratory experience as a temporally and spatially structured process of mobility is interpreted differently, depending on the cultural context of the people who migrate, has been described mainly in relation to the places of migration and settlement. This presentation raises the following question: Given that the migrants' temporary returns to their place of origin in order to visit relatives and friends have been described in migration literature as a key "constitutive of the very essence of migration" (King, Lulle, Mueller, & Vathi, 2013, p. 9), do temporary and spatial processes that construct migration experiences during these short-term mobilities to the 'homeland', similar to those during their stay and / or settlement in their places of migration, also exist?

Anthropological studies have examined critically the 'home', away from the sedentarism, emotional approach, where it is understood as "a unique, stable location, a place of birth, connected with parents,

---

[1] PhD Candidate, Department of Social Anthropology and History, University of the Aegean, Greece. Email: pantmaria@hotmail.com.

childhood and the past" (Van Boeschoten & Danforth, 2015, p. 290), claiming that if we consider not only the spatial but also the temporal dimension, the cultural notion, that is attributed to specific places, changes over time. At the same specter, the notion of the one and unique homeland, which is to some extend invented by the imaginaries of deterritorialized groups (Appadurai, 2014, p. 78), has been questioned and replaced by the viewpoint of a 'mobile homeland', that permit people to "feel like home in more than one places" (Van Boeschoten & Danforth, 2015, p. 290-291).

I draw on data collected during my fieldwork (2015-2017) through participant observation and semi-structured interviews with Albanian immigrants aged between 38 and 50 years, who have been living and working in the city of Corinth and two nearby villages since 1998 moving temporarily to Albania, especially during holidays, in order to highlight the importance of the temporal and subjective dimension for the purpose of understanding the term country of origin and specifically the concepts 'home' and 'homeland' in migration studies.

Aspects of foreignness in 'home' and 'homeland'

Albanian migrants express two dimensions of the sense of foreignness upon their return to Albania. The first dimension relates to the unfamiliar wider social context in post-socialist Albania. Artan, a 45 year old man from Kruja, says:

> We feel more like home here [in Corinth], because we are living here for twenty years, they know us better here. In Albania we feel like home only when we enter our house with our relatives. When we go out on the streets, we are strangers to everyone. They do not know us, because let's say we go there for ten or fifteen days at most. We know five, six relatives and a few friends. I do not know my neighbours, nor do they know me (…) Here I have the acquaintances [with Greek employers] I have many friends and we go often to the coffee shop. On the other hand, there [in Kruja] I go there for ten days. Whom do I meet there?

The sense of the 'home' of Albanian migrants both in Greece and in Albania is not related to the home itself but to the network of social relations that they have in both countries. In Greece, they feel like 'home' because of the social and labour relationships, which they have established with Greek employers during their long-term presence and work in the area of Corinth. Also, although they now consider their co-nationals as potential competitors due to the lack of job offers, they still socialize with them mainly in the Albanian Coffee Shop in the city of Corinth. On the contrary, in Albania this intimacy is found only within their own home, when they are close to their family members, few relatives and 'friends'. The wider social context, that is, the locals who live in their birth place are unknown to them. The short duration of their visits to Albania is not enough to develop their network.

The second dimension of Albanians' sense of foreignness is expressed by Fatos, a 40- year old informant from Lushnja, who describes his temporary return as follows:

> I saw one hundred percent changes in Albania, but it was indifferent to me. I am a stranger here and a stranger there. [Why? I asked him] because if you go back somewhere after twelve years, I mean if you go back home. My home is still there but it is empty. I do not have my family there, because my parents live in Italy. My brother has gone to Belgium. I have no relatives there [in Albania]. I have my uncles who live in other countries.

The Albanians' lack of interest in the 'home' and 'homeland' is explained by the absence of their parents and close relatives who have also migrated abroad. Voutira (2007, p. 338-339) states that the idea of the 'heart', that is the home as a protection space, constitutes the sense of 'belonging'. Using the example of a Russian migrant woman, who lives in the United States, she argues that her longing is not about the Russian nation or the state, but about the 'experiential' place, that is the home, where she grew up. Similarly, the 'home' in the case of Fatos and the rest of my informants refers to the past lived relationships and experiences within the home. Now, the 'home' is literally 'empty' due to the absence of family and relative members, who constitute the sense of 'home', but also metaphorically 'empty' due to the lack of these relationships. So, Albanian migrants are unrelated to the radical social changes that have taken place during their absence. 'Home' and 'homeland' are more like 'non-home' and 'unknown' in the sense of Al - Ali and Koser (2002). The latter argue that perceptions of the 'home' have a symbolic dimension and refer to the relationships between members of every household. These perceptions are also defined by their relation to the 'outside'. "Fear, danger, the unknown, foreign and alien places (…) are all part of what is not the 'home'" (Al - Ali & Koser, 2002, p. 7). For Albanian migrants the 'here' and 'there', 'home' and 'non-home' are obscured in the context of their temporary returns to Albania and the boundaries between them become blurred.

Furthermore, many Albanian migrants argue that they no longer visit their 'homeland' so often because of the precarious labour situation in Greece in the 2010s, which requires their continual presence in order to search employment opportunities in Corinth. As Afrim, a 40, year old man from Berat, who lives in Corinth, states:

> Now, with the economic crisis in Greece, you have to chase the job, otherwise the daily wage and the month do not come out. You have to run. Today you work, tomorrow you do not. If I go there [in Albania] how will I pay the bills, the expenses?

In order to cope with the current economic conditions in Greece, Albanian migrants have developed a new strategy, which allows them to maintain bonds with their family members and not to lose employment opportunities at the same time. This strategy is about the temporary mobility. That is the Albanian migrants' parents and rarely other relatives do frequently travel from Albania or other countries to Greece and specifically to Corinth to visit them. My informants report that along with the temporary parental mobility, the feeling of their 'home' 'moves' as well, highlighting that the 'home' can be as mobile as the people who constitute the 'home'. Thus, the sense of 'homeland' becomes equally mobile, as people feel 'at home' where the people who make the sense of their 'home' are, highlights the importance of the temporal dimension beyond the spatial for the way, which people conceptualize the places and in particular their 'home' (Van Boeschoten & Danforth, 2015, p. 290-291).

Voutira (2007, p. 339) states that the ambiguity of the term 'homeland' as an ideological notion, that includes not only a person because of his/her specific national attribute but also the 'homeland' as the hearth where he/she grew up and constructed his/her memories, constitutes one of the crucial features that emphasize the ambiguity of the term 'repatriation' as well. In this light, a reconsideration of the term country of origin as an ideological category is required, as it places in advance immigrants in a particular place in the spatial sense for analytical purposes, marginalizing the fact that immigrants themselves may interpret this place as 'foreign' and unfamiliar. The case study of Albanian migrants proves that on the one hand, places, and in particular the sense of 'homeland' and 'home' can be mobile. On the other hand, they can make sense not only through their spatial dimension but through its temporal, symbolic, relational and experiential dimension.

References

Al – Ali, N., & Koser, K. (2002). Transnationalism, international migration and home. In: N. Al – Ali & K. Koser (eds.) *New approaches to migration? Transnational communities and the transformation of home*. London, New York: Rutledge, 1-14.

Anderson, B. (2019). New directions in migration studies: Towards methodological de-nationalism. *Comparative Migration Studies*, 7(36), 1-13.

Appadurai, A. (2014). Modernity at large: Cultural dimensions of globalization. Athens: Alexandria.

Camenisch, A., & Müller, S. (2017). From (e)migration to mobile lifestyles: Ethnographic and conceptual reflections about mobilities and migration. *New Diversities*, 19(3), 43-57. Retrieved from: https://newdiversities.mmg.mpg.de/?page_id=3312

King, R., Lulle, A., Mueller, D., Vathi, Z. (2013). *Visiting friends and relatives and its links with international migration: A three-way comparison of migrants in the UK*. Willy Brandt Series of Working Papers in International Migration and Ethnic Relations 4/13. Malmö Institute for Studies of Migration, Diversity and Welfare. Retrieved from: https://muep.mau.se/handle/2043/16753

Schapendonk, J. (2012). Migrants' im/mobilities on their way to the EU: Lost in transit?. *Tijdschrift Voor Economische En Sociale Geografie*, 103(5), 577–583.

Van Boeschoten, R., & Danforth, L. M. (2015). Children of the Greek Civil War: Refugees and the politics of memory. Athens: Alexandria.

Voutira, E. (2007). Refugees, returnees, and migrants: The meaning of 'home' in post-soviet Russia. In: E. Voutira & R. Van Boeschoten (eds.) *Between past and present: Ethnographies of the post-socialist world*. Athens: Kritiki, 323-345

GIVING A VOICE TO IMMIGRANTS.
TENSIONS AND PARADOXES IN PARTICIPATORY THEATRE
(TURIN, ITALY)

Francesca Quercia

Abstact

Over the last thirty years, with the redefinition of cultural and urban policies, artists have been assigned social missions: strengthening social ties, contributing to breaking down barriers in working-class neighborhoods, and integrating immigrants. This process has taken place in many European countries, including Italy. As part of urban renewal programs, many theatre associations have become involved in working-class neighborhoods. They have created art projects involving immigrants, with a dual purpose of "integration" and "empowerment". Based on an ethnographic study in a theatre association, this article illustrates how its director tried to empower immigrants, but was faced with a set of contradictions. Despite her antiracial beliefs, she ended up contributing to the minoritization of immigrants. This process confines minorities to a radical otherness over which they have little power.

Key-words: cultural and urban policies, working-class neighborhoods, minoritization, ethnicization, culturalization.

Introduction

Over the past thirty years[1], a set of national and European urban renewal programs[2] have been established in working-class neighborhoods throughout Europe. They have not only taken care of building renovations, but have also funded socio-cultural projects. These projects all have social missions: strengthening "social cohesion," "improving the image" of these neighborhoods, or promoting "participation among the population". Establishing these programs has opened up new funding opportunities for artists, while transforming their work. Arts associations have not only been assigned social missions, but they have also been required to involve specific target audiences in their creations: e.g., the inhabitants of working-class neighborhoods. However, if the term "inhabitants" seems at first glance to designate all residents of a given territory, more often than not it is a euphemism used to designate immigrant populations (Tissot 2007). In order to be part of local policies, artists are therefore called upon to work with these populations and to adjust their professional activities to that target audience.

That process has been taking hold in many European countries, including Italy. As part of urban renewal programs, a number of theatre associations have taken over working-class neighbourhoods. They have created projects involving immigrants and have had a goal of fostering "empowerment" for the participants (Pontremoli 2005). They aim to give a voice to minorities, but face a set of contradictions.

---

[1] I would like to thank Carole Hoon for her thorough re-reading of this article.
[2] Urban community initiative programs (Urban I, II and III) aimed at the economic and social revitalization of European towns and their working-class neighborhoods.

Often, the missions assigned to theatre projects by local institutions do not completely align with the way in which socio-cultural workers conceive their role. While most of them show their willingness to "give a voice" to immigrants, they also receive funding toward the goal of achieving "integration" and "social cohesion". This paper illustrates how the director of an Italian theatre association seeks to manage these contradictions.

This article is based on my PhD research, which was an ethnographic study of six theatre associations located in two working-class neighborhoods in France and Italy (Quercia 2020). However, this paper will focus only on an Italian association named "*Lotros*" in which I conducted biographical interviews with its director (N=3), with trainees (N=8) and participants (N=8). I also had many informal discussions with immigrant participants, and a number of interviews with elected representatives and local public servants (N=10). Participant observations took place in a variety of settings (rehearsals, performances, meetings, etc.).

After presenting urban local policies (a), this paper will show that the director needed to adapt her language to meet the expectations of public authorities (b), which ultimately contributed to a minoritization of immigrants.

Following a set of works focusing on "ordinary ethnicizations" (Jounin, Palomares, Rabaud, 2008, p. 8), this paper proposes to help us understand the role of theatre by re-embedding it in a set of "social, economic and institutional logics, sometimes driven by the best of intentions" *(Ibid.)*. Theses logics have concrete effects on the daily experience of minority groups. To do this, I will use the term "minoritization" over other terms such as "oppression", "domination" or even "exploitation". These notions refer to material configurations, whereas the term "minoritization" refers to a relationship which "has two sides: a concrete side and an ideological-discursive one" *(Ibid.,* p. 135). The minority group is therefore not only dominated from a socio-economic point of view, but it is symbolically confined to particularism (Guillaumin, 1972).

The urban renewal program: a more or less veiled ethnicization

Since 1960, the neighborhood in which I carried out this research was first inhabited by a working-class population from southern Italy[3], and then by extra-European immigrants.

Between 2011 and 2015, an urban renewal program was undertaken, providing not only for urban renovation, but also for economic and socio-cultural development. In this context, a call for projects was published in order to fund community-centered projects. These projects had to promote "living together," "active participation" of the "inhabitants," as well as "integration between different communities."[4]

In official documents, the general terms "communities" and "inhabitants" were used even though those terms referred to a process of ethnicization of urban policies. The term "community" was used in the plural and it was preceded by the adjective "different," so that it meant "foreign communities." By underlining the necessary "integration" between these "different communities," the public authorities contributed to their social construction as specific groups, different from the (Italian) majority population.

In addition, in many institutional discourses, the neighborhood was described as inhabited by many "foreign communities" that were in a "precarious socio-economic situation" and by an "elderly and

---

[3] FIAT Headquarters, Turin has experienced strong immigration from southern Italy.
[4] http://www.comune.torino.it/urbanbarriera/progetto/index.shtml, consulté le 23 mai 2017 à 15h.)

isolated" Italian population[5]. Because of their "social and cultural differences," these populations were presented as being "at odds" with each other. This "social mix" among "parts of society that don't naturally interact with each other" would "be at the origin of a disintegration of the local community."[6]

In this context, socio-cultural associations had a dual mission. They had to both promote "participation" among these "new citizens" and embrace their "diversity," but also aim at pacifying the neighborhood. Public authorities were confronted with a contradiction: they wanted to embrace diversity and foster participation, but they also considered the immigrants as a source of social tensions.

This kind of discourse contributed to a stigmatization of immigrants, which led to blaming them for the "social divide" (Castel 1995). It also contributed to a double process of ethnicization and culturalization of these populations. The term "ethnicization" is the process of ascribing racial or ethnic identities to a group of common origin (Poutignat, Streiff-Fenart, 1995). The term "culturalization" is the process of ascribing specific cultural traits to minorities (De Rudder, Poiret, Vourc'h, 2000). In institutional discourses, immigrants were defined as "foreign communities" that were considered culturally different from the majority. This contributed to the "othering" of immigrants (Guillaumin 2002).

Minoritization in association discourse

Lotros Association[7] offered participative theatre in the district that I studied. This association was created in 2001, thanks to funding obtained from European urban renewal programs. It was staffed by its director (Anna Maria) and eight trainees.

Since 2011, this association has led workshops with immigrants based on a methodology called "community theatre" (Pontremoli 2005): the director interviewed some inhabitants, then invited them to share their biographical stories with other participants in a set of workshops. Later, the director created a scenario from these testimonies and participants played their own stories on stage.

Most participants were from non-European countries (Columbia, Peru, Morocco, Egypt, Albania, Romania, Pakistan, Afghanistan, Senegal, and Congo).

When the director presented the project (when she spoke with sponsors or with her trainees, for example), she said that she had an empowerment goal: she wanted to empower these people by giving them the opportunity to speak about their life.

However, contradictions emerged in the director's approach. On the one hand, she often emphasized how the theatre could be an empowering venue for these people, but on the other hand, she also tried to use the theatre as a way of integrating immigrants into Italian society.

The term "integration" perpetuates a relationship of domination between the majority and minority groups, because "it is generally the dominant group that thinks the dominated groups are not integrated enough" (Lapeyronnie 2003). Thus, this term contributed to define foreigners as minorities.

In addition, when the director presented the target group, she referred to the participants as "foreigners." In her talks, this term referred not only to the legal status of non-nationals, but also to other characteristics they had. According to the director, "foreign participants" compounded social

---

[5] The terms in quotes are used by the elected representative for culture, the elected representative for education and the president of the district in a variety of settings (debates in the district council, presentations of the season in the neighborhood theatre, community-centered events, sociological interviews, etc.).
[6] Ibid.
[7] I anonymized this name in order to ensure the confidentiality of data.

and psychological difficulties, as well as relationship problems. These people were from "a very low cultural background" and "they never imagined being on stage."[8]

In the director's talks, the term "foreigners" implied "miserabilist" in the sense given to it by Grignon and Passeron (1989): participants were defined by what they lacked and how different they were from the dominant culture. This term also implied ethnicizing (Poutignat, Streiff-Fenart 1995) and culturalist (De Rudder, Poiret, Vourc'h 2000): the director targeted foreigners because she thought that they had a set of problems linked to their origins and their "culture."

This study exemplifies a trend that characterizes social work today. The individual dimension of empowerment is becoming more important than the collective and radical ones (Bacqué, Biewener 2013). In this specific case, the emancipatory aim of the theatre has been set aside to make way for the goal of integrating immigrants into Italian society.

This trend was meeting expectations of public donors. Local public policies valued "cultural diversity" and participation, but they also wanted to guarantee social peace in working-class neighborhoods (between immigrants and natives).

This study highlights a process of minoritization of immigrants with several closely-linked dimensions.

In her talks, the director often refers to the problems participants face due to their cultural specificities and their origins (in a culturalist and ethnicizing logic).

These categorizations contribute to the "othering" of immigrants. Whether or not they are brought back to their cultural differences or supposed ethnic origins, participants were not altered on the basis of what they accomplished. They were assigned to "astrictive statuses" which "preceded their birth"(De Rudder, Poiret, Vourc'h 2000, p. 32).

This process wasn't intentional. The director tried to emancipate immigrants, but she also needed funding from public authorities. Despite her antiracial beliefs, she ended up causing a minoritization of immigrants (Guillaumin 2002).

This research shows that minoritization does not manifest itself only in violent practices, but also in everyday life. In spite of their antiracial principles, the majority population can contribute to perpetuating the idea that "human beings are naturally different" (Guillaumin 2016).

References

Bacqué Marie-Hélène, Carole Biewener. 2013. *L'empowerment, une pratique émancipatrice*, Paris : la Découverte.
Castel Robert. 1995. Les métamorphoses de la question sociale. Une chronique du salariat, Paris : Fayard.
De Rudder Véronique, Christian Poiret, et François Vourc'h. 2000. *L'inégalité raciste*. Paris : Presses Universitaires de France.
Grignon Claude, Jean-Claude Passeron, Le savant et le populaire. Misérabilisme et populisme en sociologie et en littérature, Paris, Gallimard/Seuil, 1989
Guillaumin Colette. 2002. *L'idéologie raciste. Genèse et langage actuel*. Paris: Gallimard.
———. 2016. *Sexe, race et pratique du pouvoir*. Donnemarie-Dontilly: Editions iXe.
Jounin Nicolas, Élise Palomares, and Aude Rabaud. 2008. « Ethnicisations ordinaires, voix minoritaires ». *Societes contemporaines* n° 70 (2): 7-23.
Lapeyronnie Didier. 2003. « Quelle intégration? », *in* Loche (B.), Martin (C.), dir., *L'insécurité dans la ville. Changer de regard*, Paris : L'Oeil d'or.
Pontremoli Alessandro. 2005. *Teoria e tecniche di teatro educativo e sociale*. Torino: UTET Libreria.
Quercia Francesca. 2020. *Les mondes de l'action théâtrale dans les quartiers populaires en France et en Italie*. Paris: Dalloz.
Tissot Sylvie. 2007. *L'État et les quartiers. Genèse d'une catégorie de l'action publique*, Paris: Seuil.

---

[8] All the terms in quotes were used by the director in a variety of settings (interviews, meetings, rehearsals, etc.).

THE FUTURE OF DIFFERENCES IN A WORLD OF MIGRATIONS

Orazio Maria Gnerre

1. Talking about differences with respect to the migration issue could be, for the same reasons, taken for granted or confusing, since we are used to considering the migratory phenomenon as one of those events that relate various human groups, thus promoting not only the encounter between cultures, but also their hybridization and resulting in the flowering of differences. It is also known to most that migrations are often a product of huge economic differences that occur in various sectors of our planet and that cause the displacement of human masses. However, it is not only the intranational differences that produce the displacement of these masses, but also the international ones within what Wallerstein called the *economy of the world-system*[1]. Finally, migrations also produce and multiply the internal differences within the host countries: they can both affect the fragmentation of the social-cultural fabric, which is divided into enclaves and cultural groups that are not very communicating, and, once again, the increase in economic differences.

However, this is only one aspect of the migratory phenomenon with respect to the problem of differences. Another result, in generic terms, is also that of standardization, as a product of the policies applied by states and government institutions towards the people administered in their own territories. These standardizing processes develop on various vectors, both assimilationist and non-assimilationist, and yet they often produce disorienting effects, both on the citizens heirs of the previous generations and on the "newcomers".

Three problems emerge from all this: the first is that of producing a definition of what diversity is and how many "diversities" exist; the second is to understand all the vectors of production of diversity or equality and clearly distinguish them in their specific manifestation; the third is to suggest and imagine political practices for the promotion of a different administration of the migratory phenomenon on the basis of an ethical determination with respect to the question of diversity.

2. First of all, the question of defining models of diversity must be addressed. The concept of diversity is, of course, the opposite of that of equality, and both reproduce different conditioned reflections within world cultural history in general, and Western in particular. The principle of equality was definitively sanctioned during the Enlightenment era, and today it still constitutes one of those cardinal ideas on which most political systems are based. Since the Enlightenment era (which in any case did not invent it but covered it with a whole stratification of political-social meanings, as opposed to the historical period of the so-called *Ancien Régime*) the fate of the concept of equality has historically unfolded in plurality directions, even politically conflicting with each other. One of the most repeated theoretical points in the so-called "reactionary" school of thought is precisely the coexistence of the principle of equality both in liberalism (and therefore in capitalist economic systems) and in socialism. This is the reason why most of the political systems in force today adopt the concept in question as a non-negotiable principle, from the United States of America, to the European Union, to the People's

---

[1]Terence K. Hopkins, Immanuel Wallerstein et al., *Worls-System Analysis: Theory and Methodology*, Sage, Beverly Hills 1982.
Terry-Ann Jones and Eric Mielants, *Mass Migration in the World System: Past, Present and Future*, Routledge, London 2011.

Republic of China, up to the Democratic People's Republic of Korea.

Yet this does not mean that the concept of equality – which as we have said directly informs its opposite, which is the concept of difference – is equally interpreted by every political ideology. It is precisely with Marx that we have the beginning of a new critique of the concept of liberal equality, that is, what is expressed in capitalist societies[2]. Far from accepting the general meaning, of a sentimental nature, which is imparted to the concept of equality, the famous thinker from Trier conducted a critique of it starting from the political-economic bases according to a method he defined as "materialistic". It would be interesting to note how the Marxist critique of the concept of liberal equality also had many points in common with that of the reactionary school, with authors such as Maistre[3] or Bonald[4], who already highlighted how individuals in a liberal society were only equal economic actors in front of the boundless level of the market. Nonetheless, it was with the concept of equality, conveyed by another fundamental political concept, that of democracy, that the western capitalist sphere and the eastern socialist one faced and defeated Nazi-fascism in the first half of the last century, redefining the international balance in the spheres of influence decided in Yalta which, in fact, drew two large blocks in which the concept of equality, with different meanings, was predominant.

Still, this is only one side of the coin. The liberal democracies and the Soviet Union, which in the meantime was promoting the founding of a whole series of "Democratic Republics", had fought for the concept of equality, but also for that of difference. One of the accusations that were leveled at Hitler's Germany was related to the desire to found a new standardizing world political order, which would have flattened national and cultural differences in subjection to a global German Reich. One of the rhetorical arguments directed against Hitler and his politics was precisely that of the defense of national and ethnic difference in the face of the hierarchization of ethnicities and genocide.

Returning instead to the Marxian accusation against the liberal concept of equality, this was naturally borrowed from all the political systems belonging to the so-called real socialism. According to this thesis, liberal and capitalist equality would have allowed an abstract equality of every person in society, but in practice the power of money and capital would have created a social pyramid of differences even worse than those of the feudal system[5].

The latter case therefore makes clear the real great distinction to be made, whenever we talk about differences: there are cultural differences and economic differences. Although the current heirs of the materialistic school of thought often tend to vulgarize the problem, tracing every cultural specificity to economic reasons, obviously this is not founded with respect to the national and ethnic cultural dimension, and most of the classical authors of the Marxist canon were largely aware.

3. Ultimately we can therefore discriminate between the difference that exists between social groups with different cultural attributes, whether they are of a religious nature or social practices deriving from different national histories, and the difference that exists between human subjectivities with different dispositions of wealth. Only in this sense can we analyze the production of difference or equality (which we have already said are two opposite polarities of the same substance) that is generated by the contemporary migratory phenomenon.

Starting by analyzing the economic profile of difference, we have already underlined how migration is

---

[2]Cf. Karl Marx and Friedrich Engels, *The Communist Manifesto*, Penguin, New York 2002.
[3]Cf. Joseph de Maistre, *Consideration on France*, Cambridge University Press, Cambridge 1995.
[4]Cf. Louis-Gabriel de Bonald, *Teoría del poder político y religioso*, Tecnos, Madrid 1988.
[5]Cf. Karl Marx and Friedrich Engels, *The Communist Manifesto*, Penguin, New York 2002.

often a product of economic differences, both intranational and international. Intranational economic differences often depend on international ones, within a system of domination and appropriation of resources by internationally operating subjects. Many countries, even today, are victims of forms of resource dispossession and economic exploitation, and these conditions do not allow for a positive and in this sense egalitarian development of their society. This is the case of many of those countries that once fell within the sphere of the so-called "third world" and of those countries that experienced the collapse of their economic and social systems with the collapse of the Eastern Bloc at the end of the Cold War.

Often, however, it is also the countries of the so-called "first world" that export labor[6], in the face of conditions of economic imbalance between social systems of the transatlantic sphere. This also happens thanks to the economic system that has developed in the West in recent centuries, in which the workforce is considered a marketable commodity like others, and which, like the other factors of production, assumes greater usability with the possibility of disposing of it freely, also through its displacement and certainly thanks to the collapse of its price resulting from highly competitive regimes. It is no mystery that migrations produce a lowering of the cost of the labor market in the host states, the phenomenon had already been analyzed by Marx in the pages of Capital on Irish migration. This leads us to the third factor concerning the economic differences with respect to the phenomenon of human migration: the increase in the gap between rich and poor in countries that welcome migration, even in the face of an improvement in the standard of living of the "newcomers".

4. Secondly, we have the question of cultural differences. The situation in this case is more complex, since the substantial nature of human culture is that of existing in plurality. Cultures can only be evaluated on the basis of differences, and one is aware of them thanks to the difference between one and the other. On the other hand, another of the factors that make a culture such is a certain degree of homogeneity in the habits and customs of those who participate in it. The factors of maximum cultural cohesion have always been those of ethnic, religious and national affiliations. The question here becomes complicated given the fact that migration is one of those phenomena that produces and produced by the conditions of contemporary capitalist globalization. One of the effects of contemporary globalization is that of the loss of particularistic identities. This happens for various reasons, but it would be simplistic to ascribe this thing solely to the contact between different cultures. Obviously, the approach of previously distant cultural elements produces a certain amount of identity loss, but it is a common factor of the human species to be a producer of culture. From the meeting of different cultures something else or something more has always been born, and the most important human civilizations are in turn the result of the fusion of differentiated groups.

In this case the element that intervenes decreeing the definitive suppression of cultural differences is the governmental one of the apparatuses that manage the flows of social life, through the normative systems.

There are basically two models towards which this system operates. The first is undoubtedly the assimilationist one, typical of the modern national state. The principle with which this model is applied is that according to which within the borders of the nation state it is necessary to share its dominant culture and customs in order to possess citizenship, which is the guarantee of all political rights. This model, beyond the preservation of the national culture that substantiates it, produces the annihilation

---

[6]As an example of this pattern: AA.VV. (a cura di Iside Gjergji), *La nuova emigrazione italiana. Cause, mete e figure sociali*, Edizioni Ca' Foscari, Venezia 2015.

of the particular culture of those who must adhere to it, having migrated. All this is now being called into question by the overt crisis of the nation state, exposed to the politically centrifugal and economically centripetal trends of the global market. Many forces are arising in this world and questioning the balances founded on statehood. The second model, on the other hand, is that which operates from the neutralization of identity elements of any kind, including that of a nationalistic type. It proceeds from the identification of the world precisely with that boundless economic level of the market of which Marx spoke, and with respect to which every properly political element, that is not governmental but ideological, is a brake. The neutralization of differences is necessary in a governmental society that needs the quantitative agglomeration of as much space as possible, but which no longer requires an ideological engine of an identity type, as was for example in the era of imperialism described by Lenin in his famous text on the topic[7].

In this sense, migration is often a candidate to be an engine for accelerating the creation of differences, when the "newcomers" respond with closure to the difficult integration, but it is quickly turning into a factor for creating cultural equality facing the phenomena of national assimilation (model now in retreat) and global governance of the Western kind (predominant model).

5. In this regard, we must not prevent ourselves from asking ourselves serious questions about the paradigm with which we are facing migration. While it is true that contemporary migrations often have roots in structural or systemic economic issues, even when they are produced by regional conflicts[8], it is equally true that there are many reasons why humanity has often migrated from one place on the earth to another. Even from this point of view, however, the issue of climate migration could find a solution in the economic and political root of the problem[9].

In any case, considering the phenomena in motion and on which the institutional and political sphere must constantly intervene, a reformulation of the general approach to the question seems necessary, as long as it is done in relation to a whole series of guiding principles to be kept in mind.

It is on the basis of what is called "sustainable development" that the importance of reducing economic differences has been stated at the UN[10]. Here clearly a sphere is involved, the economic one, which sees many different ideas opposing each other, and this cannot be the place to face a categorical debate of this type. There are many theses on the function of economic differences and the freedom of individual subjects to operate on the market. Here we simply want to emphasize the importance of creating greater conditions for collective well-being. To do this, a reduction in economic differences is necessary. In this sense, it is important to understand the role of migration within a system of global appropriation, in order to defuse the distortions of an more and more interconnected world economic system in which value chains are increasingly transnational. In this sense, a prominent role of the public sector is all the more necessary, but questions are raised about the level from which to operate.

---

[7]Vladimir Ilyich Lenin, *Imperialism: The Highest Stage of Capitalism*, Penguin, New York 2010.
[8]"At the beginning of the twentieth century, the ratio of combatants to civilians killed in war was 8:1—eight combatants for every civilian. At the beginning of the twenty-first century, the figures were reversed; the ratio was 1:8—eight civilians were killed for every combatant. In the space of a hundred years, war itself had been redefined—people with weapons of war now kill unarmed civilians, not each other. Today you are safer being a soldier in one of the competing armies or militias than being a civilian. Armies no longer "fight" on behalf of people; they kill people and the people flee. [...] Each conflict results in migration. Smart phones have collapsed distances, become instruments of navigation and information sharing, relaying which routes are most desirable, which are to be avoided, where borders are porous and where they are walled off, and which destinations are paths to safety. These innovations in technology have facilitated both conflict and migration."
Padraig O' Malley, *Migration and Conflict*, in *New England Journal of Public Policy*, Year 2018 Vol. 30 Iss. 2.
[9]Anthony Giddens, *The Politics of Climate Change*, Polity Press, Cambridge 2011.
[10]Cf. Stephen Browne, Sustainable Development Goals and UN Goal-Setting, Routledge, London 2017.

6. Turning to the question of cultural differences, it must be affirmed that the impoverishment of cultures and identities of various kinds is certainly an overall loss for the human species. Humanity was formed in a slow process of sedimentation and cultural development that has distinguished its contours and interactions between groups. However, it is necessary to rethink the coexistence model not only to guarantee a conservationist approach to human culture, but to preserve the possibility for it to develop organically and without the interference of governmental control devices placed at the service of mere market mechanics. While it is true that it is not possible to completely abstract the sphere of cultural development from that of the economy, it is however necessary to establish ethical boundaries and priorities in an era in which the great technological revolutions are producing a surplus of power that could annihilate hundreds of thousands of years of collective traditions and experiences. The link between technology and its use for economic purposes could redesign the face of the planet and the humankind in a more problematic way than one might imagine at first sight, and ethical evaluations are therefore of great urgency in this historical period. An important contribution towards this perspective could be that of Karl Polanyi with his description of the economy as a *total social fact* (concept by Marcel Mauss[11]) as it was conceived when it was subordinated to the sphere of collective culture and was the product of collective values, beliefs and ways of life[12].

To do this, however, a complete revolution in the concept of the human being would be needed, to be understood not as a productive factor or citizen of a neutral institution, but as the bearer of a complex culture and history. An analogous approach should reject the annihilation of particularities, and find new ways to reproduce their existence, certainly in a context that is as peaceful and harmonious as possible. History has shown that the phenomena of suppression of cultural differences, far from neutralizing the conflict, generate new ones: the increase of the social differences and of poverty is here to show us how the direction taken by most advanced countries presents many problematic elements.

---

[11]Marcel Mauss, *The Gift*, HAU Books London 2016.

[12]"Polanyi [...] does not deny that markets also existed in ancient economies, but emphasizes in the most incisive way how their social significance was profoundly different from the current one. The markets of the pre-capitalist era were constitutively inserted [...] in a network of social relations, such as religion, politics and social hierarchies, and therefore it ignored the device of self-regulation which is the characteristic product of the modern order. All forms of social integration [such as] reciprocity, redistribution and exchange [...] were part of a system of relationships that determined their structure and meaning. [...] This condition changed radically in the nineteenth century due to the commodification of land, labor and money and the advent of the self-regulating market system."
Giorgio Resta, *L'istituzionalismo di Karl Polanyi e il suo valore attuale*, in *Politica & Società*, Year 2020 Iss. 2, pp. 288-289 [translated from Italian].

MIGRATION DIPLOMACY: A NEW WAY TO BARGAIN

Melek Özlem Ayas[1]

Abstract

The concepts of migration and diplomacy are frequently in connection with each other. This study, which focuses on the concept of migration diplomacy, has been prepared primarily to reveal the principals of this concept. In order to properly explain its principals, firstly, following questions were asked: "What is migration diplomacy?" and "Is migration diplomacy useful as a tool in international relations?" A comprehensive literature review was conducted to answer these questions. It is aimed first to define the concept in question and then to determine its place in the international relations.

Key Words: International Migration, Diplomacy, Migration Diplomacy.

Introduction

At several levels, the communication between migration and diplomacy effects both domestic and foreign policies. The relevance of migration and asylum policies in states' diplomatic practices explains the link between migration and diplomacy. Both diplomacy and migration diplomacy emphasize the governments' ability to negotiate and communicate, as well as their ability to persuade and influence one another. These two concepts combine to provide a useful tool for understanding some of the trade-offs that take place between international players in relation to migration and the different aims and demands that must be met.

Although there hasn't been much research into migration diplomacy, it's always feasible to discuss studies on diplomatic exchanges including migration. It is conceivable to argue that the novelty of the notion of migration diplomacy makes scanning the literature harder, but it also provides the work freedom by offering uniqueness. Various studies on the relationship between migration and diplomacy have been carried out by Nazl Choucri (1977), Michael S. Teitelbaum (1984), Myron Weiner (1992), Kelly M. Greenhill (2010), Helene Thiollet (2011), Donna R. Gabaccia (2012), and Meredith Oyen (2015). Adamson and Tsourapas were able to theorize migration diplomacy as a result of studies.

Migration Diplomacy

In its most basic sense, migration diplomacy is the employment of diplomatic tactics in connection to migration to achieve various goals. Migration diplomacy has given a favourable space for states to pursue various policies linked to political and economic objectives by using migration policies as a strategic instrument. Migration policies can be regarded an indirect type of foreign policy. As a result of this treatment, the notion of migration and asylum policies has become the topic of diplomacy (Thiollet, 2011).

Another reason why the terms migration and diplomacy are frequently used interchangeably is that diplomacy has the ability to influence policy-making in the target country via other states or international organizations (Norman, 2020). It is conceivable to argue that the notion of migration,

[1] Research Assistant, Beykent University, melekozlemayas@outlook.com, https://orcid.org/0000-0002-4594-5011.

which has become a diplomatic hot topic, may be exploited by international players as a political pressure or solution tool. Although official and informal policies, agreements, and practices are considered as the beginning point of migration diplomacy, it may also be viewed as the development of a regulatory and informational international negotiating system (Seeberg, 2020).

Migration diplomacy has been modelled in this negotiating process by strategically exploiting migration flows, relying on the governments' negotiation and communication skills, and turning them into a tool.

Although the concept of migration diplomacy is relatively new, the idea of using migration as a tool in the international arena is not. Greenhill (2003), who conducted one of the early studies on the idea of migration diplomacy, also examined the benefits and drawbacks of migrant mobility and migration policy. Greenhill preferred to assess migration in terms of security issues, using the threat of "displacement" employed by Slobodan Milošević during the Bosnian War as a case study.

Apart from the idea of diplomacy, according to Tsourapas (2017), there are two other concepts with which migrant diplomacy is intimately linked. The first of these concepts is coercive migration diplomacy. The use of political actors' migration flows or migrant stock as a threat or a means of punishment is known as coercive migration diplomacy, and it employs the same tactics as coercive diplomacy. Another idea Tsourapas mentions is collaborative migration diplomacy, which involves converting migrant flows or stock into a political or economic incentive.

Adamson and Tsourapas built the theoretical framework of migration diplomacy on these studies. It is possible to say that the scope of the idea was established by Adamson and Tsourapas (2018). Adamson and Tsourapas (2018), aiming to identify the situations that the concept includes and excludes, are based on three main situations: the relationship between state actions and migration diplomacy, the harmony between the state's general migration policy and migration diplomacy, and the reciprocity between migration mobility and migration diplomacy.

Adamson and Tsourapas emphasized the relationship between population movement and the state's different goals and diplomatic endeavours, claiming that state actions have a direct impact on migration diplomacy. The overall concordance between migration diplomacy and the state's migration policy is the second instance mentioned. According to Adamson and Tsourapas, there is no need for a state's migration policy and international migration diplomacy to be in sync. A state that permits or chooses to be totally restricted of migrant movements is not required to adjust its domestic policy decisions to its foreign policy. The reciprocity between migration diplomacy and migration mobility is the third instance. Migration diplomacy has been closely related to issues like as displacement, relocation, regulation of migrants' citizenship status or access to rights, customs regulations that govern what products migrants may carry, diaspora policies, and refugee welfare. At the same time, these concerns have the potential to impact and be the topic of interstate relations (Adamson & Tsourapas, 2018).

Many diverse tools are used in migration diplomacy. Migration laws, bilateral or multilateral readmission agreements, diaspora policies, and deportation regulations are examples of these instruments (Tsourapas, 2017). These instruments are employed by recipient, source, and transit countries to achieve their economic and political goals, whether they are connected to migration or not. The theoretical framework created by Adamson and Tsourapas helps to make sense of the use of these tools (Adamson & Tsourapas, 2018).

Conclusion

In terms of structure, the notion of migration is inextricably linked to people. Reducing the notion to simply humans, on the other hand, would be a limited approach. The idea of migration, which in its most basic sense refers to human mobility, affects both states and individuals, whether inside or across borders.

Adamson and Tsourapas' approach is primarily concerned with state capacity. This framework, which establishes the boundaries of migration diplomacy, attempts to demonstrate a state's ability to employ diplomatic instruments and procedures connected to migratory movements, as well as its overall strength and capability to use its available resources.

Migration diplomacy is a notion that will assist to clarify the relationships between states that have a part in the migration process as a source, a receiver, or a transit country at times. States that understand their capacity will continue to utilize migration as a tool, with the goal of getting the most out of it. As a result, proper examination of the idea of migration diplomacy will be critical in the future for both nations and individuals.

References

Abourabi, Y. and Ferrié, J. N. (2019). La politique migratoire du Maroc comme instrument de sa diplomatie africaine. *Afrique (s) en mouvement, 1,* 68-80.

Adamson, F. B. and Tsourapas, G. (2018). Migration diplomacy in world politics. *International Studies Perspectives, 20*(2), 113-128.

Adamson, F. B. and Tsourapas, G. (2019). The Migration State in the Global South: Nationalizing, Developmental, and Neoliberal Models of Migration Management. *International Migration Review,* 1-30.

Ahlborn, F. (2019). The Role(s) of Migration Diplomacy: The concept of migration diplomacy from a role theory perspective and the case of Morocco's "migration roles".

Akçapar, Ş. (2017). International Migration and Diplomacy: Challenges and Opportunities in the 21st Century. *PERCEPTIONS: Journal of International Affairs, 22* (3), 1-34 .

Baldwin, D. A. (1971). The power of positive sanctions. *World Pol., 24,* 19.

Castles, S. and Miller, M. J. (1998). *The age of migration: International population movements in the modern world.* Macmillan International Higher Education.

Düvell, F. (2017). The EU's International Relations and Migration Diplomacy at Times of Crisis: Key Challenges and Priorities. *PERCEPTIONS: Journal of International Affairs, 22*(4), 35-54.

Greenhill, K. M. (2003). *The use of refugees as political and military weapons in the Kosovo conflict.* In Yugoslavia Unraveled: Sovereignty, Self-Determination, Intervention, edited by Raju G.C. Thomas, 205–42. Lanham, MD: Lexington Books.

Greenhill, K. M. (2010). Weapons of mass migration: Forced displacement, coercion, and foreign policy. Cornell University Press.

İskit, T. (2018). *Diplomasi: tarihi, teorisi, kurumları ve uygulaması.* İstanbul Bilgi Üniversitesi Yayınları.

Oyen, M. (2016). The Diplomacy of Migration: Transnational Lives and the Making of US-Chinese Relations in the Cold War. Cornell University Press.

Perea, J. F. (Ed.). (1997). Immigrants out!: the new nativism and the anti-immigrant impulse in the United States. NYU Press.

Schwenken, H., Russ, S., ve Ruß-Sattar, S. (Eds.). (2014). New border and citizenship politics. Springer.

Seeberg, P. (2018). Citizenship and migration diplomacy: Turkey and the EU. In *The Middle East in Transition.* Edward Elgar Publishing.

Thiollet, H. (2011). Migration as diplomacy: Labor migrants, refugees, and Arab regional politics in the oil-rich countries. *International Labor and Working-Class History, 79*(1), 103-121.

Thiollet, H. (2016). Gérer les migrations, gérer les migrants : une perspective historique et transnationale sur les migrations dans les monarchies du Golfe. *Arabian Humanities. Revue internationale d'archéologie et de sciences sociales sur la péninsule Arabique/ International Journal of Archaeology and Social Sciences in the Arabian Peninsula,* (7).

Tsourapas, G. (2017). Migration diplomacy in the Global South: cooperation, coercion and issue linkage in Gaddafi's Libya. *Third World Quarterly, 38*(10), 2367-2385.

THE PATH OF REMITTANCES TO CONSUMPTION OR SAVING! ALBANIA CASE STUDY

Nevila Mehmetaj

Abstract

Since the change of the political systems in the 1990-s in Albania, massive emigration has been a continuous phenomenon of different scales in Albania. The outflow migration phenomenon is associated with inflow of financial resources to the origin families. Remittances have been a vital financial source of living for a considerable number of households. Therefore they constitute an important financial mechanism for the funding of the country's economy. Empirical studies perform in the field suggest contradictory results as remittances do not have uniform macroeconomic effects from country to country or across time. Empirical regression analysis on emerging economies, with long-period data, suggest both that there is a positive impact of remittances on country economic growth; while others confirm a negative relation effect of remittances on the country's economic development. The analysis further reveal that remittances diminish macroeconomic volatility through smoothing aggregate consumption.

Based on this, naturally, it is raised the question: is any impact of remittances in the macroeconomic gears of Albania country? Therefore it is the purpose of this paper to analyze the effect of the Albanian emigrant' remittances on the country-specific macroeconomic variables such as aggregate consumption, national saving (by real variables, in % of GDP), and economic growth rate.

Migration and Remittances in Albania

Emigration has been a continuous phenomenon of Albania for a long time. During half a century of the communist regime, Albania was a blind spot in the eyes of Europe and the world. Only in 1991, it was massively presented, when media all over the world showed remarkable pictures of overcrowded ships embarking impoverished and desperate Albanian people emigrating in southern Italy. At the 1990s, due to the damage of industrial fabrics and high unemployment rates, massive labor migration took place. The migration of Albanians cannot be reduced simply to such key moments; it has been going later on for almost 30 years. An exact figure of the Albanian emigrants is still not calculated due to the complexity that characterizes this phenomenon. In 2019, according to indirect estimates, the number of new Diaspora (emigrants leaving the country after the 1990-s) is estimated to be about 1.64 million citizens abroad or about 36% of total Albanian population (Instat, The diaspora of Albania, in figures., 2019). In 2021, the population of Albania is estimated at 2.83 million, decreasing from the previous census in 2011 by 2.7%. This is due to a decrease in fertility rates and emigration of population (Instat, 2021).

Historically, Albanians have emigrated towards more developed countries, but mostly to Italy, Greece, and other countries in Europe and North America. During the last decade period, the spatial distribution of emigrants to developed economies is dominated by destinations as Italy, Greece, Germany, United States, United Kingdom, and France (IOM, 2020). The emigrant's outflow according to the destination country during the last decade continues to be dominant in the neighmbour countries Italy and Greece.

Figure 1. Emigration outflow by destination countries during 2011- 2019.

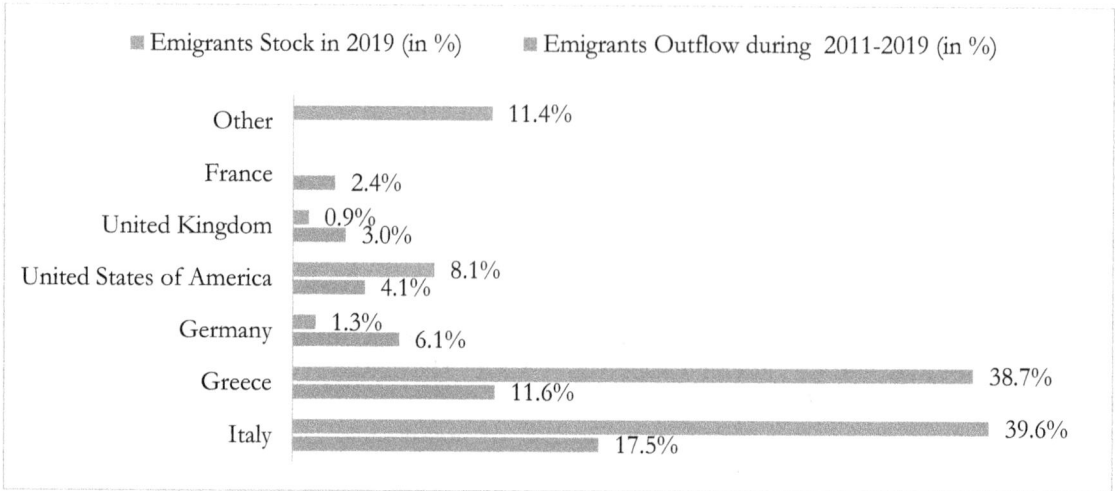

Source : IOM, National Households Migration Survey in Albania, 2020, pg 25.
Instat, Diaspora of Albania in figures, 2019, pg 11.

Emigration was dominated by a relatively young and working-age population, observed for both genders, who emigrated mostly for employment reasons. Albanian emigration has been dominated by economic factors. The main reasons for emigration include better opportunities for work, education, and health care. According to the Labor Force survey, 2018, the main reason for leaving Albania is employment opportunities by 77.0%, followed by family reunions, another form or tendency of households emigration. The wives together with their children follow their husbands to the destination country.

Figure 2. Reasons of Emigration

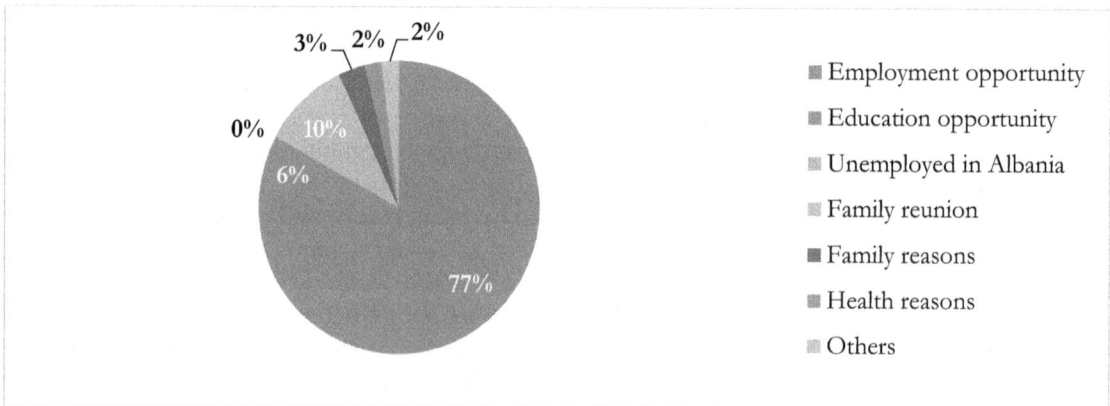

Source: Instat, Diaspora of Albania in figures, 2019, pg 21.

The phenomenon of **outflow of emigrants** is associated with inflows of remittances in the origin country. The contribution of migrants sending remittances to their families in Albania has been extremely helpful for their micro-economies. This especially during the 1990-s and in the rural and urban areas characterized by extreme poverty. Many families in Albania had been having remittances from their emigrating family members, as the only financial source for their existence. Remittances have injected a lot of money into the national economy of the country, contributing to the increase of national statistics as consumption, saving, and economic growth.

Figure 3. Annual GDP growth rates and Remittances rates (% of GDP) - Albania

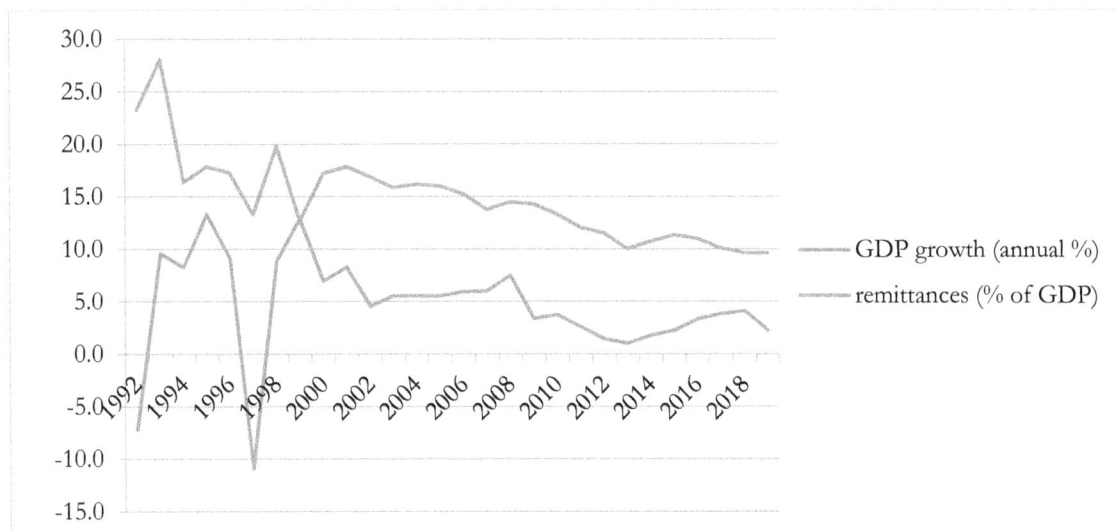

Source: Instat, Economic growth rates and remittances rates. Statistics 1992-2019.

The trend of remittances from the 1990-s has been declining during the years. It reached a maximum of 28% in 1993 and 9.6 5 of GDP in 2019. Due to the injecting money into the economy remittances have given an impact the aggregate consumption. In the early 1990-s, the fall of the communist era regime and the detriment of the public-owned fabric diminished the GDP to the lowest levels. Country aggregate consumption, in 1992, dimidiated from 186.9% to 91.8% of GDP in 2019.

Figure 4. Aggregate Consumption and Remittances (% of GDP) - Albania

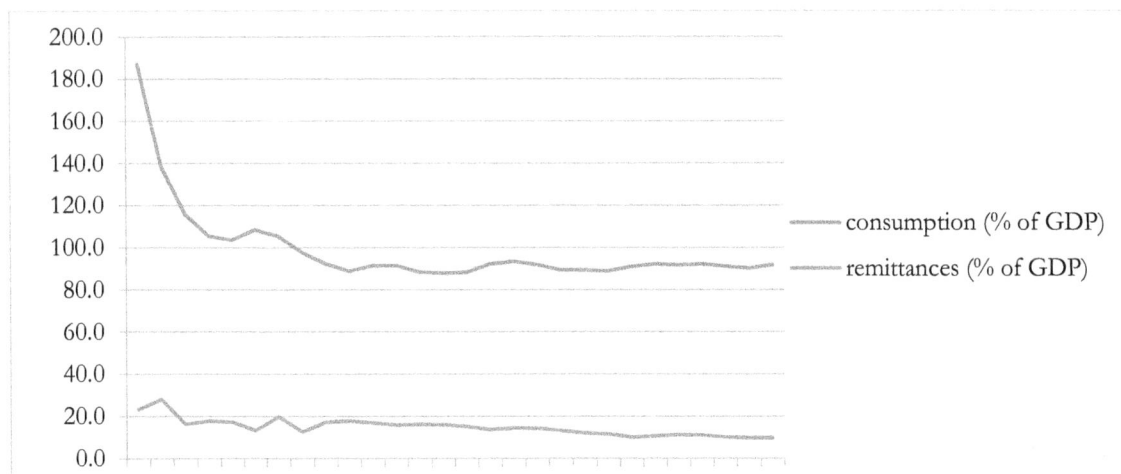

Source: Instat. Consumption rates and remittances rates. Statistics 1992-2019.
National saving during the last decades has had its cycles, with its minimum value of 9.43 % in 1992 to its maximum value of 29.59 in 2006.

Figure 5. National Saving and Remittances (% of GDP) - Albania

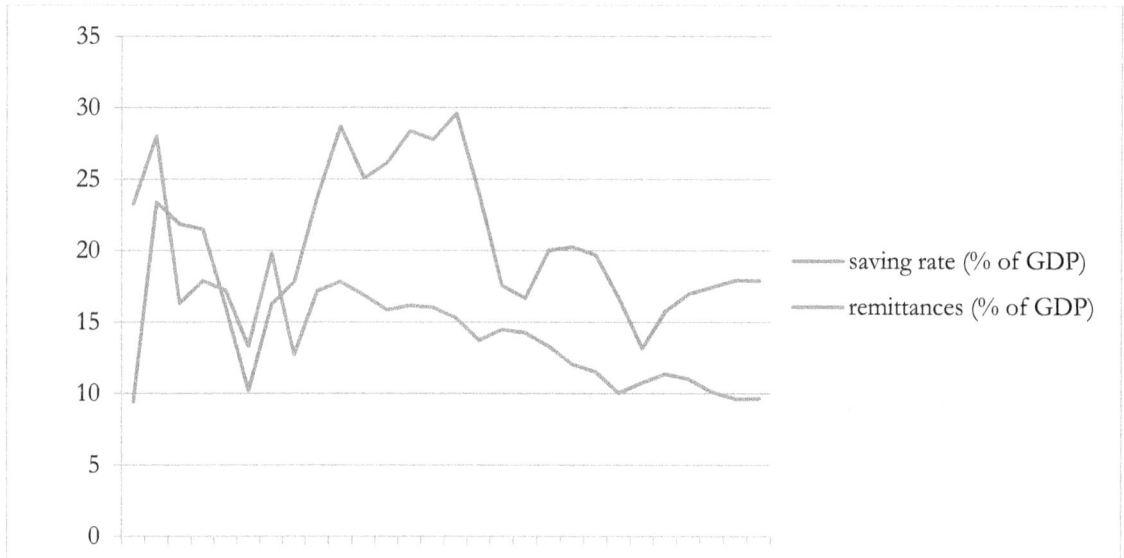

Source: Instat. Saving rates and remittances rates. Statistics 1992-2019.

Literature Review

The role of remittances is studied by many authors. Gedeshi presented that remittances are an important source of employment and income for many Albanian households (Gedeshi, 2002). In the years following the collapse of communism, remittances were an important factor in the Albanian economy. They played a significant role in maintaining standards of living in times of economic turbulence and providing capital for business development (Konica & Filer, 2005).

Many studies are performed in different developing countries presenting different results. Some studies show a positive impact of remittances on economic growth (Fayissa & Nsiah, 2010; Shera & Meyer, 2013). While other empirical regression analyses on emerging countries with long-period data confirm a negative relation effect of remittances on the country's economic growth or development (Sutradhar, 2020). Empirical evidence analyzed the yearly data of 22 developing countries for the period 1960 - 2010, showing that remittances do not have uniform macroeconomic effects through countries or across time. The results suggested that remittances diminish macroeconomic volatility mainly through smoothening aggregate consumption (Mishi & Kapingura, 2013).

Recent studies in the field for central European countries conclude a validation of the hypotheses of remittances on economic growth for all the countries (Bulgaria, Czech Republic, Estonia, Hungary, Lithuania, Latvia, Czech Republic, and Lithuania) except Romania economy (Cismaş & Curea-Pitora, 2020).

Analyses of panel set data of 10 former post-Soviet countries presented that a 1% increase in remittance flows provokes about a 0.25% rise in per capita GDP. Remittances seem to produce significant effects on increasing income and smoothing consumption levels (Abduvaliev & Bustillo, 2020).

Methodology

The general objective of this study is to describe the migration in Albania and the remittances effect on the country macroeconomic variables associated with this phenomenon. Quantitative method is used to analyze the effect of emigrant remittances (the independent variable) to the country economic growth, national saving and aggregate consumption (the dependent variables). Econometric model based on the ordinary least squared method (OLS) is performed to highlight the correlation and the causality between the macroeconomic variables. The variables are in real terms and are expressed in % of GDP. The empirical research is focused on three directions: first, the effect of remittances on economic growth rate; second the effect of remittances on the country aggregate consumption rate; and third, the effect of remittances on the country aggregate saving rate. Time series data of Albania are used from the World Bank and Institute of Statistics of Albania database for the period 1992-2019. The econometric analysis is performed through R software.

- Y Consumption (in % of GDP) = a + X Remittances (in % of GDP)

Coefficients: Estimate Std. Error t value Pr (>|t|)

Remittances rate 3.2336 0.6971 4.639 8.72e-05 ***

- Y National Saving (in % of GDP) = a + X Remittances (in % of GDP)

Coefficients: Estimate Std. Error t value Pr(>|t|)

Remittances rate 0.2761 0.2407 1.147 0.261810

(Signif. codes: 0 '***' 0.001 '**' 0.01 '*' 0.05 '.' 0.1 ' ' 1)

- Y GDP growth rate = a + X Remittances (in % of GDP)

Coefficients: Estimate Std. Error t value Pr (>|t|)

Remittances rate 0.2749 0.2270 1.211 0.237

The model results of the study show that the majority of remittance income is consumed from the recipient families contributing to the aggregate demand. According to the model 1 percent increase of remittances contributes to a 3.2336 percent increase in the aggregate consumption in the economy. While according to the second and third model, there are positive relationship of remittances with national saving and economic growth rate of the country, but both model show not significant results.

Conclusion

Migration is a phenomenon from an economic effect point of view. It is very often suggested that emigrants will contribute economically to the development of their country of origin. Albania in its history has been having a high net outflow of emigrants. It has been and continues to be economic reasons that push most of Albanians to leave the country. The economic literature has focused high attention on the influence of remittances of the origin country of migrants. The data analyses results reveal different and often contradictory results. This study results are in accordance with the recent studies in the field and conclude that remittances of emigrants injected into the Albanian economy have a significant effect on the country's aggregate consumption. While remittances have neither a significant effect on a country's national saving nor the country's economic growth rates.

The article contributes to the development of knowledge in the economic field by offering another empirical analysis of the literature regarding the positive effect and the negative effect of the remittances on the receiving country macroeconomic real variables. This empirical analysis focused on the recent data of Albania, adds value to the existing empirical studies on developing countries.

Bibliography

Abduvaliev, M., & Bustillo, R. (2020). Impact of remittances on economic growth and poverty reduction amongst CIS countries. Post-Communist Economies, 32:4, 525-546, DOI: 10.1080/14631377.2019.1678094.

Cismaș, L. M., & Curea-Pitora, R. I. (2020). The impact of remittances on the receiving country: some evidence from Romania in European context. Economic Research-Ekonomska Istraživanja, 33:1 , 1073-1094, DOI: 10.1080/1331677X.

Fayissa, B., & Nsiah, C. (2010). The Impact of Remittances on Economic Growth and Development in Africa. The American Economist 55(2), 92-103. doi:10.1177/056943451005500210.

Gedeshi, I. (2002). Role of Remittances from Albanian Emigrants and Their Influence in the Country's Economy. Eastern European Economics, 49-72. Retrieved August 10, 2021, from http://www.jstor.org/stable/4380312.

Instat. (2020). Statistics in years: Remittances, Consumption (in % of GDP), National Saving (in % of GDP). Tirane: Institute of Statistics.

Instat. (2019). The diaspora of Albania, in figures. Tirane: Instat.

Instat. (2021). The population of Albania. Tirane, found at http://www.instat.gov.al/en/statistical-literacy/the-population-of-albania/: Instat.

IOM. (2020). National Households Migration Survey in Albania. 25.

Konica, N., & Filer, R. K. (2005). Albanian Emigration: Causes and Consequences. Prague: CERGE-EI Working Paper 181.

Mishi, S., & Kapingura, F. M. (2013). Macroeconomic significance of remittances in developing countries. Int. J. Economic Policy in Emerging Economies, Vol. 6, No. 3 , 238-253.

Shera, A., & Meyer, D. (2013). Remittances and their impact on Economic Growth. Periodica Polytechnica Social and Management Sciences 21/1 , 3-19. doi: 10.3311/PPso.2152.

Sutradhar, S. R. (2020). The impact of remittances on economic growth. International Journal of Economic Policy Studies 14 , 275–295. https://doi.org/10.1007/s42495-020-00034-1.

WorldBank. (2012). Profile of migration and remittances : Albania (English). Profile of Migration and Remittances. Washington, D.C. Retrieved at http://documents.worldbank.org/curated/en/537441467998819718/Profile-of-migration-and-remittances-Albania: World Bank Group.

LITERATURE REVIEW ON REMITTANCES UTILIZATION IN MIGRANTS HOME COUNTRIES

Eugene Terungwa Agoh and Vilmantė Kumpikaitė-Valiūnienė

Abstract

The Philippines is the highest labour exporter among its neighbours in East and South-East Asia (Pratt, 2018). Consequently, diaspora Filipinos send the equivalent of 34 billion USD as remittances from around the world making the Philippines the third highest remittance receiver in the world just behind India and Mexico (Bank, 2019). These remittances are utilized in various ways proven to positively impact the migrant's receiving households. Conclusively, remittances play an important role in Philippines households as shown in 17 papers, which focused on evaluating the positive and negative sides of remittances; to the Philippines households are highlighted. Though the case of the Philippines is unique, several other studies show similar results in countries such as Mexico, Nigeria, Pakistan, India, Vietnam, Ghana, South Africa, Lithuania, Germany, Estonia, Poland etc. This wide variety of remittances utilization motivated this literature review.

Keywords: Remittances, Migration, Remittance's utilization.

Introduction

Remittances are utilized in various ways according to evidence presented in many works of literature. According to the world bank report of 2019, low- and middle-income countries (LMICs) received $554 billion in remittances (World Bank, 2019). Largely, remittance inflows to (LMICs) experienced a little decline due to Covid-19 after many years of consistent growth. However, it hits a record of $540 billion in 2020, just 1.6 percent below the 2019 total of $554 billion (World Bank, 2020).

 In some migrant home countries, remittances (REM) are utilized more for consumption, savings and productive investment purposes. While in others, remittances are spent more on education, health, agriculture and housing. These vary from country to country and are mostly influenced by the number of remittances and the socio-economic status of the remittance's recipient households.

Given the importance of remittances and how it's utilized in various recipient countries, the purpose of this study is to present a systematic literature review of the utilization of remittances in various migrant home countries and to highlight how these studies are done in different countries focusing on remittances utilization while taking into account, the data used, countries socio-economic factors and how it influences REM utilization.

Remittances Utilization Classification in Migrants home countries

According to Durand's (1994) (cited by Goldring, 2004), REM could be classified into three groups according to their utilization:

1. Remittances as wages or compensations

2. Remittances as investments

3. Remittance as capital

Remittances as wages or compensations include spending of REM for everyday life such as food, education, health care, etc. Each of these categories is discussed below, under the umbrella of their main phenomenon. Jena (2017) and Simiyu (2013) stated the durable and physical investment of REM is for the wellbeing of the families in low/middle-income countries, under altruistic behaviour relating to the altruism theory of remittances. REM has the tendency to decrease the poverty level of REM recipient families in low/middle-income countries. As stated by Acosta (2007), REM is under negative connotation towards inequality distribution of income.

Remittances as a source of investment are for the purpose of spending REM on different types of investments, for example, housing or financial loans. These REM could be sent during a stay in a foreign country or brought back when they return to their home countries. They were related to workers, remitters who made a couple of journeys with a particular goal, for example, setting aside cash to purchase land or build a house.

Remittances as capital could be described as cash spared explicitly to put resources into a beneficial endeavour and productive investment.

Method

This study focuses on scientific articles that aim at exploring the utilization of remittances and their social-economic impact in 156 countries and regions spanning over 35 years. A combination of theoretical and empirical studies consisting of 214 articles aimed at studying remittances utilization in migrants home countries were analysed to present various ways remittances are utilized in various countries and regions.

MAXDQA software program was used for analysis and to elaborate a map of remittances utilization and country grouping based on analysed literature.

Results

After analysis of literature, the main subgroups in the main three groups of remittances were revealed.

Remittances as wages or compensations

Many migrants send money to their families and their everyday consumption in the home county. Generally, these remittances are used in several ways. Firstly, it could be used for self-utilisation (Petreski et al., 2018; Zhang and Lin, 2019). Several authors have shown a positive relation between remittances and poverty reduction (Adams and Page, 2003; Azam et al., 2016; Bang et al., 2016; Pekovic, 2017).

Secondly, remittances are used for education (Lopez, 2004; Davalos, et al., 2017; Bhadra, 2007). Education is the direct and indirect channel through which REM positively affects growth, development and performance. Children of migrants' families get more education through the REM they receive.

Thirdly, remittances in the home country are used for food (Regmi and Paudel, 2016; Kumar et al., 2018; Seidu et al., 2018). Studies demonstrate food consumption security is increased by the increased flow of REM for the poor families in Bangladesh (Regmi and Paudel, 2016; Kumar et al., 2018), Albania (Seidu et al., 2018) and other countries.

Finally, analysed studies revealed that remittances are used for health care (Wang et al., 2019; World Bank, 2019; McKenzie, 2006; Petreski et al., 2018). For example, recently, Wang et al. (2019)

ascertained the usage of REM in households on hospitalization and healthcare, more than on food in Kyrgyzstan. In the report of World Bank (2019), Kyrgyzstan is the poorest country in Asia and ranked second in being REM dependent in the world.

Remittances as investments

In Argentina positive integration is found between private investments and REM, for data 1956-1996 (Acosta and Loza, 2005). An empirical study in five major South Asian countries, i.e., India, Sri Lanka, Pakistan, Nepal, and Bangladesh, for data from 1990 to 2016 also showed long and short-run associations of private investments and REM flows (Khan et al., 2019). For the time period of 2007 to 2010 in Peru, families receiving REM do venture investments (Salas, 2014). Maphosa (2007) found a positive connection between REM and investment in Zimbabwe.

Summarising analysed literature, Investments could be used for housing (Quashie, 2019; Sunny et al., 2020; Hamouri, 2020, Ahmed et al., 2020), ICT (Tazanu, 2018; Coly and Cabral, 2020; Pradhan et al., 2017; Asongu and Odhiambo, 2019), (Jayaraman et al., 2019), agriculture (Kapri and Ghimire, 2020; Liu et al., 2019; Jokisch, 2002), Crisis management (Wu, 2006; Manandhar, 2014; Fagan, 2006) or financial investments and savings (Coly and Cabral, 2020; Munir et al., 2011).

As explored by Adams and Cuecuecha (2013) in a study led in Guatemala showed a significant investment of REM on housing. 37.1 % and 39.5% is spent on internal and international housing. This later was authenticated in Ghana as it depicted the physical investments as REM utilization (Adams and Cuecuecha, 2013; Asiedu, 2003). Agriculture investments are observed in Central America (Davis and Lopez-Carr, 2014).

Githaiga and Kabiru (2014) conducted a study on 31 countries for the data from 1980 to 2012 and found a highly significant impact of REM on shares investments. Further, 39 Latin America and Caribbean countries evidently sing RM on shares, for the data from 1970 to 2002 (Mundaca, 2009).

As discovered by Tazanu (2018) in Cameroon, REM received by remitters' relatives is used in communication technologies, such as the internet, mobile, laptop, etc. Further, a study conducted in Burkina Faso and Senegal showed a 30% increase in saving of REM by the families receiving it (Coly and Cabral, 2020). In Vietnam, from 1980 to 2012, REM has developed ICT investment in the long run (Kumar and Vu, 2014).

Finally, REM plays a vital role if any natural disaster occurs. Just in the case of Pakistan, after the hit of the earthquake in NWFP (North Waziristan Frontier Province), the inflows of REM increased to 95%. REM was utilized after the wake of the earthquake in crises investment (Suleri and Savage, 2006).

Remittance as capital

REM is invested in migrants home countries in the form of R & D or education funds; thus, making people more productive and contributing towards the overall productivity and subsequently rise in GDP and economy (Ediri & Okonkwo, 2019). Moreover, remittances could be used for energy consumption (Abdin and Erdal, 2016; Shahbaz et al., 2013; Rahman and Amin. 2018; Akcay and Demirtas, 2015) or democracy development in particular countries (Issifu, 2018; Kevin, 2017; Abbas et al., 2017).

The summary of explored literature is presented in Figure 1, where all remittances utilization groups are divided into depicted subgroups and indicates a number of countries, found in explored literature.

Figure 1. Remittances utilization in explored literature

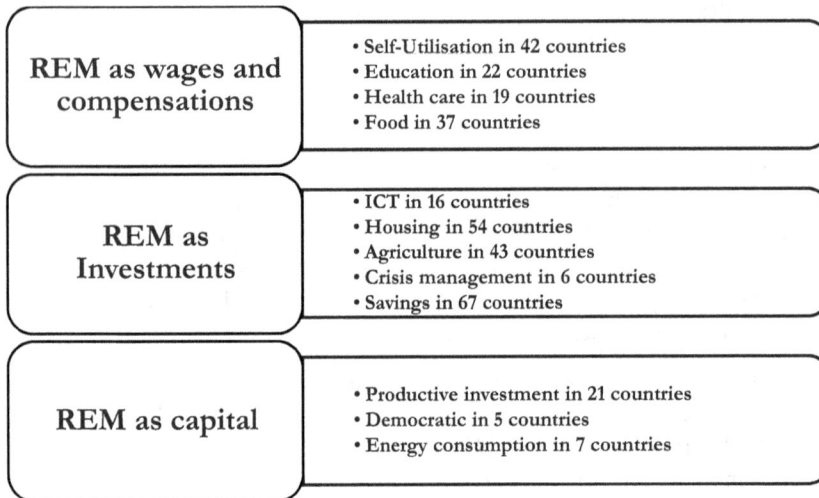

REM as wages and compensations	• Self-Utilisation in 42 countries • Education in 22 countries • Health care in 19 countries • Food in 37 countries
REM as Investments	• ICT in 16 countries • Housing in 54 countries • Agriculture in 43 countries • Crisis management in 6 countries • Savings in 67 countries
REM as capital	• Productive investment in 21 countries • Democratic in 5 countries • Energy consumption in 7 countries

Conclusions

A grouping of countries based on remittances utilization under the above-listed remittances utilization classification was shown to present a pictorial and easier understanding of remittances utilization in receiving migrant countries. Analysis was done using the MAXQDA program.

Studies on remittances utilization in different countries demonstrate variety in REM utilization. We provide a map of REM utilization and groups of countries based on existing studies. We cannot state that REM is utilized just for highlighted purposes in analysed countries and are not used for other purposes. However, we provide a picture of REM utilization purposes in grouped countries according to analysed studies.

References

Abbas, F., Masood, A., & Sakhawat, A. (2017). What determine remittances to Pakistan? The role of macroeconomic, political and financial factors. Journal of policy modeling, 39(3), 519-531.

Abdin, Z. U., & Erdal, M. B. (2016). Remittance-sending among Pakistani taxi-drivers in Barcelona and Oslo: Implications of migration-trajectories and the protracted electricity crisis in Pakistan. Migration and Development, 5(3), 378-393.

Acosta, P., Calderón, C., Fajnzylber, P., & López, H. (2006). Remittances and development in Latin America. World Economy, 29(7), 957-987.

Acosta, P., Fajnzylber, P., & Lopez, J. H. (2007). The impact of remittances on poverty and human capital: evidence from Latin American household surveys (Vol. 4247). World Bank Publications.

Adams Jr, R. H., & Cuecuecha, A. (2013). The impact of remittances on investment and poverty in Ghana. World Development, 50, 24-40.

Adams, R. H., & Page, J. (2003). International migration, remittances, and poverty in developing countries (Vol. 3179). World Bank Publications.

Ajaero, C. K., Nzeadibe, C. T., Obisie-Nmehielle, N., & Ike, C. C. (2018). The linkages between international migration, remittances and household welfare in Nigeria. *Migration and Development*, 7(1), 40-54.

Akçay, S., & Demirtaş, G. (2015). Remittances and energy consumption: evidence from Morocco. International Migration, 53(6), 125-144.

Al Mamun, M., Sohag, K., Uddin, G. S., & Shahbaz, M. (2015). Remittance and domestic labor productivity: Evidence from remittance recipient countries. Economic Modelling, 47, 207-218.

Anarfi, J., Kwankye, S., Ababio, O. M., & Tiemoko, R. (2003). Migration from and to Ghana: A background paper. University of Sussex: DRC on Migration, Globalisation and Poverty.

Asongu, S. A., & Odhiambo, N. M. (2020). Remittances, the diffusion of information and industrialisation in Africa. Contemporary Social Science, 15(1), 98-117.

Azam, M., Haseeb, M., & Samsudin, S. (2016). The impact of foreign remittances on poverty alleviation: Global evidence.

Economics & Sociology, 9(1), 264.

Bang, J. T., Mitra, A., & Wunnava, P. V. (2016). Do remittances improve income inequality? An instrumental variable quantile analysis of the Kenyan case. Economic Modelling, 58, 394-402.

Bhadra, B. (2017). Precarity and surrogacy: The invisible umbilical cord in the digital age. In Precarity within the Digital Age (pp. 31-68). Springer VS, Wiesbaden.

Coly, S. M., & Cabral, F. J. (2020). Consumption-Savings Trade-Off in the Allocation of Migrants' Remittances and Economic Growth: The Cases of Burkina Faso and Senegal.

Dávalos, J., Karymshakov, K., Sulaimanova, B., & Abdieva, R. (2017). Remittances and labor supply of the left-behind youth: Evidence from Kyrgyzstan. Asian and Pacific Migration Journal, 26(3), 352-380.

Davis, J., & Lopez-Carr, D. (2014). Migration, remittances and smallholder decision-making: Implications for land use and livelihood change in Central America. Land use policy, 36, 319-329.

Fagan, P. (2006). Remittances in crises: a Haiti case study. Overseas Development Institute.

Ghimire, S., & Kapri, K. P. (2020). Does the source of remittance matter? Differentiated effects of earned and unearned remittances on agricultural productivity. Economies, 8(1), 8.

Githaiga, P. N., & Kabiru, C. G. (2014). Remittances as a determinant of financial sector development. Journal of business economics and finance, 3(4).

Goldring, L. (2004). Family and collective remittances to Mexico: A multi-dimensional classification. *Development and change*, *35*(4), 799-840

Green, S. H., Wang, C., Ballakrishnen, S. S., Brueckner, H., & Bearman, P. (2019). Patterned remittances enhance women's health-related autonomy. SSM-population health, 9, 100370.

Gurung, G., Reddick, M., Bhandari, D., Manandhar, B., Trusilo, D., & Congi, G. (2014). Understanding the Role of Remittances in Reducing Earthquake Risk.

Hamouri, Q. (2020). Reflection of Remittances on Advancement of REM & ICTs sectors in developing countries.

Issifu, I. (2018, March). The impact of remittance on domestic investment: The role of financial and institutional development in five countries in Sub-Saharan Africa. In Forum of International Development Studies (Vol. 48, No. 9, pp. 1-20).

Jayaraman, T. K., & Makun, K. (2019). Information and Communication Technology as a Contingent Factor in India's Economic Growth–Remittances Nexus. In Advances in Management Research (pp. 71-90). CRC Press.

Jokisch, B. D. (2002). Migration and agricultural change: The case of smallholder agriculture in highland Ecuador. Human ecology, 30(4), 523-550.

Khan, Z., Rabbi, F., Ahmad, M., & Siqun, Y. (2019). Remittances inflow and private investment: a case study of South Asian economies via panel data analysis. Economic research-Ekonomska istraživanja, 32(1), 2723-2742.

Khanal, K., & Todorova, Z. (2019). Remittances and households in the age of neoliberal uncertainty. Journal of Economic Issues, 53(2), 515-522.

Khatri, B. B. (2017). Utilization of remittance at household level: A case of Khanigaun Village of Resunga Municipality, Gulmi District. *Nepalese Journal of Development and Rural Studies*, *14*(1-2), 12-20.

Kumar, R. R., & Vu, H. T. T. (2014). Exploring the nexus between ICT, remittances and economic growth: A study of Vietnam. Journal of Southeast Asian Economies, 104-120.

Kumar, R. R., Stauvermann, P. J., Patel, A., & Prasad, S. (2018). The effect of remittances on economic growth in Kyrgyzstan and Macedonia: Accounting for financial development. International Migration, 56(1), 95-126.

Kumar, R. R., Stauvermann, P. J., Patel, A., & Prasad, S. (2018). The effect of remittances on economic growth in Kyrgyzstan and Macedonia: Accounting for financial development. International Migration, 56(1), 95-126.

Lin, J., Zhang, Z., & Lv, L. (2019). The Impact of Program Participation on Rural Household Income: Evidence from China's Whole Village Poverty Alleviation Program. Sustainability, 11(6), 1545.

Mabrouk, F., & Mekni, M. M. (2018). Remittances and food security in African countries. *African Development Review*, *30*(3), 252-263.

Maphosa, F. (2007). Remittances and development: the impact of migration to South Africa on rural livelihoods in southern Zimbabwe. Development Southern Africa, 24(1), 123-136.

McKenzie, D. J. (2006). Beyond remittances: the effects of migration on Mexican households. International migration, remittances, and the brain drain, 123-147.

Mundaca, B. G. (2009). Remittances, financial market development, and economic growth: the case of Latin America and the Caribbean. Review of development economics, 13(2), 288-303.

Munir, R., Sial, M. H., Sarwar, G., & Shaheen, S. (2011). Effect of Workers' Remittances on Private Savings Behavior in Pakistan. Asian Economic and Financial Review, 1(3), 95.

Odipo, G., Olungah, C. O., & Omia, D. O. (2015). Emigration and remittances utilization in Kenya. *Journal of Research on Humanities and Social Sciences*, *5*(14), 163-172.

Pant, B. (2011). Harnessing remittances for productive use in Nepal. *Nepal Rastra Bank Economic Review*, *23*, 1-20.

Peković, D. (2017). The effects of remittances on poverty alleviation in transition countries. Journal of international Studies, 10(4), 37-46.

Petreski, B., Tumanoska, D., Dávalos, J., & Petreski, M. (2018). New light on the remittances-poverty-health nexus in Macedonia. International Migration, 56(5), 26-41.

Pradhan, N. S., Fu, Y., Zhang, L., & Yang, Y. (2017). Farmers' perception of effective drought policy implementation: A case study of 2009–2010 drought in Yunnan province, China. Land use policy, 67, 48-56.

Quashie, N. T. (2019). Social Welfare and Remittances to Older Adults in Two Caribbean Cities. International Migration, 57(5), 71-88.

Rahman, B., & Amin, S. B. (2018). An empirical investigation on the relationship between remittance and energy consumption towards Bangladesh economy. World Rev Bus Res, 8(3), 86-103.

Regmi, M., & Paudel, K. P. (2017). Food security in a remittance based economy. Food Security, 9(4), 831-848.

Salas, V. B. (2014). International remittances and human capital formation. World development, 59, 224-237.

Seidu, A., Onel, G., & Moss, C. B. (2020). Do international remittances accelerate out-farm labor migration in developing countries? A dynamic panel time-series analysis. Journal of Agribusiness in Developing and Emerging Economies.

Simiyu, C. N. (2013). Remittance and household expenditures in Kenya.

Suleri, A. Q., & Savage, K. (2006). Remittances in crises: a case study from Pakistan. London: Sustainable Development Policy Institute.

Sunny, J., Parida, J. K., & Azurudeen, M. (2020). Remittances, investment and new emigration trends in kerala. Review of Development and Change, 25(1), 5-29.

Tazanu, P. M. (2018). Communication technologies and legitimate consumption: making sense of healthcare remittances in Cameroonian transnational relationships. Africa, 88(2), 385-403.

Ugherughe, J. E., & Jisike, J. O. DIASPORA REMITTANCES AND THE NIGERIAN ECONOMY: AN EMPIRICAL ANALYSIS (1977–2017).

Williams, K. (2017). Do remittances improve political institutions? Evidence from Sub-Saharan Africa. Economic Modelling, 61, 65-75.

Yi, F., Liu, C., & Xu, Z. (2019). Identifying the effects of migration on parental health: Evidence from left-behind elders in China. China Economic Review, 54, 218-236.

THE REFLECTION OF DISCRIMINATION AND GENDER ON LABOUR RIGHTS: SYRIAN WOMEN IN TURKEY- A COMPARATIVE ANALYSIS

Aysel Ebru Okten[1] and Itir Aladag Gorentas[2]

Turkey has been home to displaced Syrians since April 2011. Today Syrian community in Turkey is close to 4 million and women generate 45 % of it. In time, expected temporariness has begun to evolve to permanency and each individual has to find their way through the crisis. Though legal regulations such as Law on Foreigners and International Protection and its Temporary Protection Regulation, European Convention on Human Rights and dubious EU- Turkey Statement of 2016 confer labour rights to some extent, it is of common knowledge that Syrians generally work undocumented and this situation make them even more vulnerable.

This study focuses on lived experiences of Syrian women in Turkey regarding working rights. First, the research will focus on legal regulations in Turkey on foreigners' labour rights and discrimination. Afterwards, by in-depth interviews and surveys in Kocaeli, İstanbul, İzmir, Hatay and Gaziantep we will analyse possible discriminative experiences Syrian women might come across, comparatively. The current research shows Syrian women face difficulties in accessing employment opportunities. Only 15 % of women are employed (Yucel et al., 2018). Yet once they are employed (or the ones employed), they go through other kinds of obstacles. The aim is to evaluate if legal rights reflect in real life experiences. The study also proposes a gendered analyse of changing roles in Syrian families and its sociological effects.

Introduction

As a result of open door policy since the beginning of Syrian civil war, Turkey has been the recipient of the most crowded refugee population in the world. As of 2021, according to official data from Government of Turkey, Syrian population in Turkey 3,696,919 and this number makes 65, 7 % of all displaced Syrians around the world. Turkey, like every other country in the world should be, by no means ready for this amount of migration demand so accordingly, Syrians access to basic needs such as education, accommodation, labour rights, access to healthcare and social services and legal aid have been a part of struggle from time to time and these issues have been hot on the public agenda.

Among above mentioned rights, labour rights are especially important for integration and sustainability of an independent livelihood. Being active in labour life is also very vital for women's place in society. To this end this paper will focus on Syrians women's labour rights. First we will present a perspective of legal regulations on the subject and then give brief information about general conditions of Syrians in Turkish labour market. Finally the study will focus on Syrian women's employment and their conditions in Turkey. At this part of the study we will address the issue with the help of in- depth interviews.

---

[1] PhD Candidate, Kocaeli University Migration Studies Programme ayselebruokten@gmail.com
[2] Assistant Professor, Kocaeli University Department of International Relations The Chair of International Law itir.aladagg@gmail.com

Legal Regulations on Labour Rights of People under Temporary Protection

In Turkish national legislation there are three main documents regulate the labour rights (in addition to others) of people under international protection and people under temporary protection. The main document is Law on Foreigners and International Protection of 2013 which is followed by Temporary Protection Regulation of 2014 with an apparent need to detail and identify rights and principles going to apply to people under temporary protection. Yet these two documents do not provide strict road map for labour rights, in 2016 the Turkish Council of Ministers adopted the Regulation Concerning the Work Permits of Temporary Protection Beneficiaries.

In line with the Temporary Protection Regulation Article 29, the conditions apply to people under temporary protection is ruled to be determined by the Presidency of the Republic of Turkey according to the recommendation of the Ministry of Family, Labour and Social Security (TPR, Article 29). In the initial version of the Regulation, these decisions were on the Turkish Council of Ministers and in 2016 the Council adopted the Regulation Concerning Work Permits of Temporary Protection Beneficiaries (Resmi Gazete, 2016/ 8375). While Article 89 of Law on Foreigners and International protection allows application for work permit after 6 months following the lodging date of an international protection claim (LFIP, Article 89), for people under temporary protection, in current case for Syrians, article 5 line 1 of the Regulation Concerning the Work Permits of Temporary Protection Beneficiaries rules that individuals who have been granted temporary protection in Turkey for more than six months can apply for work permits (RCWPTPB, Article 5). The same Regulation concludes temporary protection beneficiaries with work permits will not be paid under minimum wage (RCWPTPB, Article 10).

Even with these positive regulations labour rights of people under temporary protection is still quite restricted and *in no way absolute* (İneli- Ciğer, 2017: 561). For example, according to Article 7 of the Regulation Concerning Work Permits of Temporary Protection Beneficiaries, work permits will be based on the residence permit of the temporary protection beneficiary. In other words, the temporary protection beneficiary will only be allowed to work in the city where he/ she is registered (RCWPTPB, Article 7). The Regulation also restricts the number of temporary protection beneficiaries to a maximum of 10 % of the Turkish citizen total staff in a workplace (RCWPTPB, Article 8; İneli- Ciğer, 2017: 561). The same article in its second line rules, businesses with less than 10 employers can only hire one temporary protection beneficiary (RCWPTPB, Article 8 Line 2). Temporary protection beneficiaries who apply to work in the health or education sectors first need to apply for a prior authorization from relevant ministry or the High Council of Universities (RCWPTPB, Article 6).

The General Conditions of Syrians in Turkish Labour Market

As mentioned above Turkey passed a regulation in January 2016 for Syrians' work permits (Del Carpio et al., 2018: 10) accordingly Syrians in Turkey have right to work and access to labour market in theory. Yet the conditions to obtain a work permit is still complex, for example temporary protection beneficiaries cannot apply for work permit of their own, this burden is on the employers (İneli- Ciğer, 2017: 563). This puts formal employment rights of the Syrians dependent to the employers' sole discretion. Syrians' inability to obtain work permits individually seems to force them towards informal market. To reverse this tendency, skill building programs for refugees are quite important for their integration in labour market (İçduygu & Diker, 2017). With this being said, the effect of Syrian's in Turkish labour market is multi-faceted. For example, the price of goods which production process is mostly lean on informal workers has declined as a result of Turkish informal workers to Syrian informal workers with lower wages (Caro, 2020: 1; also Konun & Tümen, 2016; Tümen, 2016). According to Caro's report besides a certain degree of substitutability between Turkish workers and Syrian workers in informal jobs, Syrians are employed in jobs that natives are not willing to do (Caro, 2020: 1). In a similar study, Del Carpio & Wagner (2015) stresses the displacement of women and the low educated away from the labour market as a result of Syrians' arrival which can be interpreted as a deficit for the employment of Turkish women and goes beyond the scope of this study.

Caro's report for International Labour Organization (ILO) reveals the average age of Syrian refugees living in Turkey is 23 years old while Turkish natives average stands on 33 (Caro, 2020: 4). This means in the near future a large number of young Syrians are expected to crowd labour market and this prospect should initiate skill development programs and job creation to avoid possible social tensions (Caro, 2020:5). Even today, though official number is still a mystery, summed from the statistical data from Turkey's Disaster and Emergency Management Agency, the Ministry of Health and the World Health Organization there are over two million working Syrians (Del Carpio et al., 2018: 11). That is nearly half of the Syrian population in Turkey. Within these two million half of them work informally and among these women make up a really low portion (Del Carpio et al., 2018: 11).

Notwithstanding their status, formal or informal, employment rates are very high among Syrian men (Caro, 2020: 6). This is especially striking regarding teens. There are three main reasons behind this statistic. First, schooling rates are very low among teen boys so they need jobs to occupy themselves. Second, the most Syrians work informally earns less than the minimum wage so they look for income increase. Third reason is cultural background placing men at the position of income earner while positioning women as homemaker (Caro, 2020: 6).

The Employment of Syrian Women

Especially after 2015, the number and variety of studies focusing on Syrians conditions in general highly increased, yet studies addressing individual experiences of refugee women in labour market are still in need of development and attention. In fact, as Üstübici and İnce draw attention a gender- based perspective on forced- migration is at least left- behind (Üstübici & İnce, 2020).

The Syrian women's employment rates are quite different from men; 11.2 % of aged 15- 65 work compared with 71.0 % of men of then same age range (Caro, 2020: 6). These unfavourable employment rates of Syrian women reflect favourable in schooling rates. Yet comparing to natives schooling rates of young Syrian women is still low.

Both Syrian and Turkish women have higher unemployment rates than their gender counterpart (Caro, 2020: 8). It seems women have fewer chances than men in the labour market, men's working lowers the women's pressure to find a job and also culturally women are expected to fulfil household duties (Caro, 2020: 8). Regarding percentage of young person's not engaged in education, employment or training Syrian women in Turkey have the highest rates in the world (Caro, 2020:8). Yet, the formal employment of Syrian women is quite low (del Carpio et al., 2018). As Üstübici and İnce stresses the most of Syrian women earn less than the minimum wage and they are less paid comparing to Syrian men (2020). In addition to economic factors, one of the reasons behind Syrian women's low employment rates lies on the cultural principle that women should not work outside their homes (Üstübici and İnce, 2020).

The Perspective of Syrian Women

Academic studies conducted in Turkey since the start of the migration movement which is now in its 10th year, have revealed a picture of how Syrians living under temporary protection status live and access to basic rights such as education, health, housing, and their working conditions. As mentioned above in migration literature after the Syrian humanitarian crisis still lacks attention to a gendered perspective while evaluating access to basic rights. In this study we wanted to address this gap in terms of labour rights. Accordingly we conducted field study to reveal if there are any forms of discrimination Syrian women face in their working experience. Surveys and interviews questions were designed to evaluate the integration of Syrian women living in Kocaeli, Istanbul, Izmir and Gaziantep to social life, working life and the impact of all this on family life. Due to the fact that this is a study conducted during the pandemic process, participants were also asked questions in this direction. This has been said; also due to pandemic conditions the study has not reached planned number of participants. The readers should know this study is a part of an ongoing project. When pandemic conditions loosen, we aim to extend our study to a more comprehensive group.

Returning to field study, all of the participants worked periodically or continuously in a job after arriving in Turkey, and accordingly specific questions were asked to describe the change in working life that they created. For example, as you will find below in detail, Z.'s experience in textile sector states that working as a Syrian woman in workplaces places individuals at bottom of the ranking, and the attitude of the employer also changes in accordance with this ranking. Discrimination can be made against women by men, by their employers, or by women who are members of the host community. We believe understanding these lived experiences is vital to develop policies against this discriminative practices and build a future together. As you can follow from the interviews not all workplace experiences are negative yet it is common that Syrian women are paid the lowest wages. Due to low wages, discriminative narratives and insecure working conditions, most of the participants compare working conditions of Syria (wages, working hours, etc.) as better than the working conditions of Turkey. To detail these experiences, below you will find some of the testimonials of Syrian women.

Z.- İstanbul

Z. is a 39-year-old, undergraduate, married woman with 3 children. She has been living in Turkey since 2013. After staying in Hatay for 2 years, she has been living in Istanbul for 6 years. She says that the reason she came to Istanbul from Hatay is prospective job opportunities. She sees the life in Istanbul as challenging and she does not feel accepted. Z. thinks Syrians in Turkey are generally welcome, but this does not comprise to everyone. She says *"If 70 percent of Turkey accepts us, 30 percent does not"*. Z. is aware that Syrians in Turkey are under temporary protection status, yet she thinks the rights attached to this status are not sufficient. Z. acknowledges The European Union and the United Nations High Commissioner for Refugees as policy makers regarding the situation of Syrians in Turkey. *"The EU gives 100 euros for us to the government on a monthly basis, but these assistance does not reach us, we can only receive 155 Turkish Liras given by the Red Crescent,"* she adds.

Z. evaluates housing as the most important need. She stresses that house rents in Istanbul are expensive, but extra expensive for Syrians. Z. thinks Syrians are integrating to Turkey, but yet there are still some obstacles remain such as language barrier, the restriction of their ability to work and the bias in society. She sees a future in Turkey, yet she wants to return to Syria if conditions improve in Syria. The participant evaluates living in Hatay as more comfortable than living in Istanbul, since there were no job opportunities there; she and her family have to immigrate to Istanbul. She states that she would like to emigrate from Turkey to Canada, where she has relatives, if she were allowed.

Z. was a nurse in Syria, now works in textiles in Turkey. Because of her asthma she had hard time working in this section which extends up to 11 hours of work daily. Mentioned above she stresses working conditions in Syria were better than Turkey. Her weekly salary 900 Turkish Liras and accordingly her current job only satisfy the minimum wage, her working hours are too long, and she does not receive an extra fee for the uninsured, road and food costs. Comparing to even Syrian men,

Syrian women still have the worst conditions. Syrian men receive 1,500 TL per week, while Syrian women receive 900 TL. Meanwhile Turkish women are paid 1,100 TL per week. In this respect, Turkish women are paid more than Syrian women, Syrian men are paid more than Turkish women, and Turkish men are paid more than anyone else. Syrian women are the lowest paid in this hierarchy.

Z. finds employers very nervous and bad when working hours start, they tend to behave themselves well at the end of work. Z. thinks starting work negatively affects her life due to the long hours work in Turkey. While she is working under hard conditions, her husband is unable to work because of his heart condition. Being under the necessity of work, Z. had to leave her 8-month-old child behind. This obviously affects her family life negatively. On an additional note, Z., also have prior work experience from Syria, noted that the length of her working hours in Turkey also negatively affected her relationship with men in the family.

S.- İstanbul

S. is a 35-year-old married woman with 2 children. She was working as a teacher in Syria, now she does not have a work permit. She is working undocumented.

S. came to Turkey in 2013 for job opportunities and also some of her relatives including her mother-in- law are here. She recalls the first time she came to Istanbul with good memories and adds the neighbors being so helpful. The problems occurred after a while. She lives in Topkapi neighborhood of Fatih district. According to her experience, Turkish society does not accept Syrian people as it is supposed to be. Contrary to this opinion, she believes the Government of the Republic of Turkey and the European Union are producing policies on the situation of Syrians in Turkey.

According to S. the most important need for Syrians in Istanbul is employment and lack of job opportunities hinder integration of Syrians to the Turkish society. Under the current conditions she finds long working hours unbearable and evaluates working conditions in Syria were much better. Her current job covers the minimum wage, beyond reasonable working hours and the employer does not cover travelling or aliment costs. Different from other participants, she says the working conditions are the same with Syrian men and women; there is only a difference of 200 TL on men's favor. One way or another, working in the bead- stringing line, S. thinks the attitude of the employer and her colleagues to her is good and she feels accepted.

Originally S.'s husband is a civil engineer, but he cannot find long term job in Turkey. Similar to other participants, S. mentions difficulties she had in her family life after she started to work. She feels like she does not devote enough time to her family because of long hours work. S. could not get paid for the days she did not work during the pandemic outbreak, for about 5 months, so she received financial support from her brother, who lives in France. During her years in Turkey, she only received stationery assistance for her young child and received no other assistance from any institution. Yet, she sees her future in Turkey since her children are getting education here.

K.- İstanbul

K is 38-years-old, primary school graduate and married with 5 children. She lives in Istanbul. In 2013 she decided to move to Istanbul for living since she has relatives here. She believes the Turkish society in general and her neighborhood in special accepted Syrian people. Yet she thinks Syrians are not fully integrated in the society and one of the reasons behind that is still existing prejudices in the society. She is unaware of civil society organizations work in the field. She adds if such efforts exist, it is insufficient, she notes that they do not reach out who needs.

K. worked as an agricultural worker in Syria, worked in a ladder wiping business when she came to Turkey, as well as working in daily jobs without insurance. Similar to other participants, K. finds working conditions in Syria better. Nevertheless she feels better in Turkey as being someone who makes her money in society. Working in Turkey does not have a big impact on her family life, she adds. From her perspective, the women she works with treat her well while the employer's attitude is negative.

E.- Kocaeli

E. is 22 years old, a secondary school graduate and married with no children. She lives with her husband and brother. She came to Kocaeli in 2018 because her relatives are in Kocaeli, believes that they are accepted by the Turkish society within the temporary protection status. E. is aware of municipality's language courses; she believes teaching Turkish and creating job opportunities is the most important works of civil society. Like other participants, she thinks the most important need for Syrians is employment. While she did not have a job in Syria, now she works as a hairdresser in Kocaeli. She is in charge of the whole process herself because she does her own work. E. thinks being employed has a positive impact on family life and social environment. Pandemic slightly affected her; she did not open her shop during pick of the crisis to avoid coronavirus.

E. thinks Syrians are unaware of the need to their integration to Turkish society and she thinks the burden of integration is mostly on local government. She thinks the biggest obstacle to adaptation is the language barrier; explains that no connection can be established with anyone if they do not know the language.

Conclusion

Even after ten years of presence in Turkey, Syrians fundamental rights are still a topic of discussion. According to the authors of this paper, among these rights labour rights are of highest importance since it is vital for integration. Data shows half of the Syrians work actively yet among them only half work officially. The unemployment rate in Turkey is already high among Turkish citizens (İneli- Ciğer, 2017: 563) and this obviously affects the employment rate and the number of work permits issued to the Syrians. This atmosphere negatively reflects on Syrian women's working conditions. They are paid less than their peers if they are lucky enough to find a job but usually they are expected to fulfil household duties as a result of cultural principle. Due to low wages, discriminative narratives and insecure working conditions, most of the participants compare working conditions of Syria (wages, working hours, etc.) as better than the working conditions of Turkey. What we understand from our field stud and testimonials when Syrian women work they become a facilitator of the integration of the whole family. Accordingly creating job opportunities for temporary protection beneficiaries is important but it is important for especially women to build a life outside the house and create a bridge between the Syrians and the host community.

In our study, we wanted to reflect the conditions of Syrian women in the job market. From the literature review it is clear that the topic is still understudied, much more effort to develop rights based analysis is needed. As mentioned above, due to pandemic conditions the study has not reached planned number of participants. The readers should know this study is a part of an ongoing project. When pandemic conditions loosen, we aim to extend our study to a more comprehensive group.

References

Caro, Luis Pinedo (2020). "Syrian Refugees in the Turkish Labour Market", ILO (Turkey Office Report), pp.1- 57. https://www.ilo.org/wcmsp5/groups/public/---europe/---ro-geneva/---ilo-ankara/documents/publication/wcms_738602.pdf (Accessed 13.08.2021)

Del Carpio, X. V. & Wagner, M. (2015). The impact of Syrian refugees on the Turkish labor market. Policy Research Working Paper 7402, World Bank Group, August 2015. http://hdl.handle.net/10986/22659 (Accessed 16.08.2021)

Del Carpio, X. V. & Demir Şeker, S. & Yener, A. L. (2018). "Integrating Refugees into the Turkish Labour Market", Forced Migration Review, Issue 58, pp. 10- 13.

Konuk, B. B. & Tümen, S. (2016). Immigration and prices: Quasi-experimental evidence from Syrian refugees in Turkey. Central Bank of Turkey Working Paper No 16/01. https://www.tcmb.gov.tr/wps/wcm/connect/778bac8a-d196-4098-9448-667251bb8dcd/wp1601.pdf?MOD=AJPERES&hx0026;CACHEID=ROOTWORKSPACE778bac8a-d196-4098-9448-667251bb8dcd (Accessed 18.08.2021)

İçduygu, Ahmet; Diker, Eleni (2017). "Labor Market Integration of Syrian Refugees in Turkey: From Refugees to Settlers". *Göç Araştırmaları Dergisi*. Cilt: 3, Sayı: 1. pp. 12- 35 (h).

İneli- Ciğer, M. (2017). "Protecting Syrians in Turkey. A Legal Analysis", International Journal of Refugee Law, Volume 29, No 4, pp. 555- 579.

Üstübici, Ayşen; İnce, H. Berra (2020). "Syrian Refugees in Turkey: What Existing Data Implies for Gender and Displacement", KOÇKAM Blog, https://kockam.ku.edu.tr/syrian-refugees-in-turkey-what-existing-data-implies-for-gender-and-displacement-aysen-ustubici-h-berra-ince/ (Accessed 18.05.2021).

Tümen, S. (2016). The economic impact of Syrian refugees on host countries: Quasi-experimental evidence from Turkey. American Economic Review, 106 (5), 456–460.

The Republic of Turkey (2013): "Law on Foreigners and International Protection", https://www.mevzuat.gov.tr/MevzuatMetin/1.5.6458.pdf (accessed 04.08.2021).

The Republic of Turkey (2014): "Temporary Protection Regulation", https://www.goc.gov.tr/kurumlar/goc.gov.tr/evraklar/mevzuat/Gecici-Koruma.pdf (accessed 04.08.2021).

The Republic of Turkey (2016): "The Regulation Concerning the Work Permits of Temporary Protection Beneficiaries", https://www.resmigazete.gov.tr/eskiler/2016/01/20160115-23.pdf (accessed 04.08.2021).

PRINCIPIOS DE UNA ARQUITECTURA ACERTADA A LAS NECESIDADES DE LOS MIGRANTES

Estefany Hernández Gutiérrez

Abstract La arquitectura se considera como una de las disciplinas más completas, ya que se abordan en ella aspectos de arte, ciencias y humanidades. Esta última, la convierte en algo sumamente empático (García, 2018, p.11). Es por ello que suele tomarse en cuenta al cliente, con la finalidad de que sus peticiones sean atendidas y acertadas. El término acertado, en la arquitectura, implica realizar el diseño y construcción de manera adecuada para que este tenga un buen efecto hacia el usuario, además, de ser conscientes de que el ser humano tiene necesidades personales. Sin embargo, este conocimiento, que se considera como "default" en la arquitectura, parece ser ignorado o irrelevante en algunos casos, específicamente, en los módulos de emergencia. La arquitectura efímera por emergencia, debe garantizar calidad y capacidad de proporcionar refugio en el menor tiempo posible. En particular, estas soluciones arquitectónicas, están destinadas a albergar, durante un tiempo limitado, a una masa de personas que han migrado debido a una crisis humanitaria o ambiental(Consuegra, 2020). Dicho lo anterior, es relevante cuestionar sobre la existencia de módulos de emergencias que hayan considerado en el proceso de diseño al usuario y su relación con el entorno,y que respetaran la premisa de la arquitectura (sobre cubrir las necesidades personales) junto con la rapidez y urgencia que se le debe dar al mismo. Ahora bien, se plantea una interrogante: ¿Cuáles fueron las experiencias de diseño más acertadas de los módulos de emergencia? Para responder esta pregunta, se llevó a cabo una recolección de datos en la que se investigaron como casos de estudios varios proyectos de arquitectura modular por contextos de emergencia. Posteriormente, se clasificaron y analizaron los datos según indicadores clave que deben tener por ser arquitectura efímera por emergencia (Equipo Editorial, 2017). Para corroborar estos indicadores, se realizaron dos entrevistas, acerca de la migración, sus razones y posibles alternativas, a expertos que han presenciado el fenómeno de la migración desde el puesto de director de una Casa del Migrante en Ciudad Juárez, y una arquitecta y cofundadora de un taller donde son partícipes migrantes, en su mayoría africanos, en Berlín. En conclusión, la arquitectura, además de poder ofrecer un módulo efímero funcional y seguro, tiene la capacidad de aportar a la restauración de la dignidad y bienestar físico-emocional de refugiados y migrantes. Por esto, es indispensable desarrollar proyectos que cumplan con los principios de protección, que atiendan las necesidades básicas de manera higiénica, que respeten la diversidad cultural y que establezcan un diálogo tanto con la población refugiada y migrante, como con el lugar.

Keywords: diseño empático, arquitectura efímera, migración, refugios

Introducción

La arquitectura tiene como objetivo transformar el mundo natural y social, y con ello satisfacer necesidades y albergar diversas actividades humanas (Estany,2013, p.47). Rúa García afirma en Arquitectura Empática: "Entre las múltiples capacidades que posee la Arquitectura, una de las más intensas y distintivas es la de imbuir estados de ánimo en las personas"(2018, p.11). Por lo cual, cuando se diseña una vivienda, se busca que ésta de una sensación de placer al usuario, y así incitar a habitarla.

Se consideran algunos factores, como que la residencia debe ser útil, segura y estética. Además, se está consciente de que el ser humano tiene necesidades por lo que, el inmueble debe tener en su interior espacios para dormir, comer y realizar el aseo, así como contar con sistemas de luz, agua, drenaje y gas. Sin embargo, estos aspectos parecen ser ignorados o irrelevantes en los módulos de emergencia. La arquitectura por emergencia es un tipo de arquitectura efímera, pues consiste en dar respuesta a las necesidades de un determinado momento, sin necesidad de permanecer en lugar. La arquitectura efímera por emergencia debe ser de calidad y capaz de ofrecer refugio en el menor tiempo posible (Consuegra, 2020). Dicho tipo de arquitectura es muy solicitada, ya que es una herramienta clave para atender y albergar a las personas que se desplazan durante un periodo de tiempo limitado, generalmente con la intención de buscar trabajo o nuevas oportunidades económicas, reunirse con familiares o para estudiar (INEGI, 2020). Incluso, unos huyen de conflictos, terrorismo, violaciones o abusos los derechos humanos, mientras otros buscan un lugar estable ante efectos del cambio climatico, desastres naturales u factores ambientales (Naciones Unidas, 2020). Las situaciones mencionadas anteriormente son detonantes de estrés y ansiedad, debido al peligro inmediato e impredecible que representan para la integridad de las personas involucradas. Las tragedias desencadenan una sensación de vulnerabilidad al sobreviviente por sus pérdidas, por lo que es probable que termine con traumas (Paranhos & Werlang, 2015). Ahora bien, es preocupante cómo se aborda el diseño de los módulos de emergencia con una idea tan drástica de funcionalidad, que no siempre resulta con productos eficaces; y fragmentan lo funcional y lo emocional, envés de trabajarlos en conjunto durante el proceso, lo que desencadena, por cuestiones de emergencia, establecer como prioridad la función, a tal grado que lo emocional eventualmente se vuelve un aspecto inexistente en el producto final. En otras palabras, algunos módulos solucionan de manera superficial la problemática o solo una parte de ella, pero se muestran indiferentes a lo emocional y experiencias psicológicas que estos puedan provocar de manera positiva o negativa. Por todo lo anterior, la pregunta que se formula en esta sección se dirige a discutir lo siguiente:¿Cuáles fueron las experiencias de diseño más acertadas de los módulos de emergencia? Para responder la interrogante, se empezó con comprender la función de la arquitectura y el término de la migración, junto con sus causas y consecuencias. Luego, se llevó a cabo una recolección de datos que consistió en investigar en literatura y artículos de investigación sobre arquitectura emergente, diseños empáticos y refugios de migración. Posteriormente, se hizo uso de artículos de divulgación publicados en el sitio web de arquitectura, ArchDaily, con la finalidad de encontrar diversos casos de módulos emergentes y efímeros. Así pues, con la información recabada se procedió a generar dos tablas, en las que se registraron, clasificaron y organizaron dichos datos, para poder analizar los siete casos de estudio encontrados, de una manera más efectiva y precisa.

La primera tabla engloba datos generales como: nombre del proyecto, autor, emergencia que atendió/para la que fue diseñada, país de origen del módulo, usuario, material, capacidad, medidas y año. En algunos proyectos, no se cuenta con el dato de país/usuario dirigido, siendo que no tienen una ubicación específica pues su lugar de destino está determinado por factores climáticos y antropológicos que se presentan inesperadamente. Por otro lado, se determinaron 12 indicadores que se consideran clave para que un diseño sea empático y realizado de manera acertada, y por ende, exitoso (Equipo Editorial, 2017).

- Sistema Modular
- Prefabricado
- Adaptabilidad situacional
- Diferentes opciones de uso

- Fácil instalación

- Ligero

- Transportable

- Sistema de servicios

- Cualquier Clima

- Alta resistencia

- Relación cultura/contexto

- Pensó en las necesidades del usuario

Sin embargo, solo 9 indicadores fueron relevantes, ya que se consideró que para ser caso de estudio válido en la presente investigación debían tener tres características como: tener un sistema modular, prefabricado y adaptabilidad situacional. Todos los indicadores se depositaron en una segunda tabla y se acentuaron los proyectos de módulos de emergencia que cumplían con dichas cualidades. Para complementar la información recabada, se realizaron dos entrevistas acerca de la migración, y se preguntaron sobre las maneras de mejorar la experiencia ante dicho fenómeno. Se realizó una entrevista al Padre Calvillo, director de una casa del migrante en Ciudad Juárez, ya que ha presenciado varios escenarios en su refugio y ha escuchado testimonios de los migrantes. Mencionó que a pesar de que los albergues probablemente nunca lleguen a igualar la esencia de su residencia original con su familia; dicha organización no gubernamental está comprometida en apoyarlos, y darles las oportunidades y recursos necesarios para desarrollarse como persona. De esta manera, los migrantes mejoran su situación física y emocional en la menor cantidad de tiempo posible. Igualmente, se entrevistó a Corinna Sy, arquitecta y cofundadora de CUCULA, taller de diseño para refugiados fundado en 2014. El proyecto consiste en un espacio de diseño experimental en el que los desafíos sociales se enfrentan con acciones pragmáticas y orientadas a soluciones. Así pues, al observar que la Arq.Corinna le da mucha atención al bienestar emocional y busca que los migrantes tengan una buena experiencia junto con la sensación de crecimiento personal, fue óptimo preguntar qué cualidades considera que un refugio debería tener. Explicó la relevancia de entender la situación del migrante y de tratar de aminorar su vacío emocional, por ejemplo que el refugio tenga una conexión con el lugar y el contexto, que cuente con sus propios espacios, por cuestiones higiénicas; y con áreas para desenvolverse, con el fin de que el usuario pueda sentirse identificado. La relación diseño-usuario es manifestada por la manera en que se recupera la brecha entre los objetivos de la persona, definido en términos psicológicos; y el sistema físico, expresado en variables físicas. A esta situación sobre la relación diseñador, usuario y sistema físico, se enfoca el modelo de Donald Norman, conocido profesor de ciencia cognitiva. En el libro Diseño Emocional, Norman introduce a las emociones como un elemento a considerar en el diseño de cualquier objeto cotidiano, y la arquitectura no es la excepción, ya que se puede buscar sus equivalentes en la arquitectura al abordar dos tipos de diseño (visceral y conductual). El diseño visceral debe corresponder a los sentidos, es decir, afectan a la sensación de bienestar o malestar y coincide con la luz, el sonido, la temperatura y el espacio. Aun así, se pueden observar ciertos desajustes en el caso de la arquitectura, ya que los sentidos tienen una doble vertiente: una está relacionada con el diseño visceral y otra que se puede relacionar más con la funcionalidad, o como Norman lo etiqueta, diseño conductual. Ocasionalmente interaccionan los dos tipos de diseño, lo cual es difícil tratarlos aisladamente, pues no permiten tomar en cuenta varios criterios valorativos en el mismo grado. El objetivo de una ciencia de diseño como la arquitectura es saber hacer compatible o balancear varios valores que pertenecen a distintos niveles del cerebro. A modo de resumen, la cuestión en la arquitectura comúnmente será qué prioridad se da a cada uno de los distintos tipos de diseño y elementos, y en qué grado (A. Estany, 2013, pp.55-57). Por otro lado, el Manual para situaciones de Emergencia Operaciones, creado por ACNUR, tiene la finalidad de que la ubicación sea apropiada, bien seleccionada y que los asentamientos de refugiados sean firmemente planificados, con buenos alojamientos y una infraestructura bien incorporada (ACNUR, 2012, pp. 1-3). A continuación, se muestran algunos principios ante la respuesta y medidas concretas para la Elección del Lugar, Planificacion y Alojamiento:

- Utilizar principios de planificación a largo plazo, incluso cuando se crea que la situación de los refugiados va a ser sólo temporal.

- Evitar las altas densidades de población en los asentamientos y los alojamientos.

- Hacer participar a los refugiados en todas las fases del asentamiento y de la planificación y construcción de los alojamientos.

- Desarrollar un plan maestro completo, diseñando el asentamiento alrededor de las instalaciones sanitarias y otros servicios, y dejando espacio para futuras ampliaciones.

- Evaluar las necesidades más inmediatas de los refugios de emergencia y proporcionar los materiales necesarios que no pueden conseguirse a nivel local.

En este sentido, el conjunto de obras seleccionadas muestran un interesante repertorio de aspectos, que son base desde las primeras etapas de ideación y elaboración de proyectos arquitectónicos efímeros para emergencias. Se refiere más concretamente a: la funcionalidad y eficacia del módulo de emergencia, y a la sensación de pertenencia o relación con el lugar que este pueda ofrecer. Entendiendo lo anterior, se procedió a rescatar la información más relevante de cada proyecto y analizar en dos tablas los atributos de cada uno de los módulos de emergencia seleccionados para conocer los resultados, y con ello saber cuáles de los proyectos tienen un diseño acertado y exitoso.

Tab. 1. Datos generales de los casos de estudio sobre módulos emergentes.

Proyecto	Despacho	Emergencia Atendida	País	Dirigido	Material	Capacidad	Medidas	Año
TENTATIVE	Designnobis	Desastres naturales	Ankara, Turquía		Perlita, aluminio y material compuesto reciclable	2 adultos y 2 niños	8m²	2015
Living Capsule	César Oreamuno	Emergencia o desastre natural	Costa Rica		Acero y hierro	6 personas	13.7m²	2015
Shiftpod (Refugios ASSI)	Christian Weber	Migración por guerra o política y desastres naturales	Desierto Black Rock, Nevada	Haití, Japón, Nepal, Grecia, Florida, Hawaii	Carpa tela	4 personas	2.5m²	2015
Weaving A Home	Abeer Seikaly	Dsiturbios políticos o desastres naturales	Japón		Tela y tubos de plastico	3 personas	10m²	2015
Promesa al Amanecer	AIR, Moon Architecture	Homeless	Paris, Francia	Personas sin hogar en el Bois de Boulogne, al lado del barrio más caro de Paris.	Madera	200 personas	260-352m²	2016
Transient Elements	Zarith Pineda + Juligon y WXY Architecture + Urban Design.	Migración por política	Bogota, Colombia	Migrantes venezolanos en Colombia		30 personas		2018
Refugios ACNUR	Juliana Coelho	Centros de tránsito y centros de recepción / documentación para refugiados y migrantes. Y ahora COVID 19	Brasil	Migrantes venezolanos en Brasil, Colombia y en proceso en Venezuela	Plástico	4 personas	10m²	2020

Tab. 2. Indicadores clave para determinar si el proyecto es funcional, práctico y tiene un diseño empático.

Proyecto	Sistema Modular	Prefabricado	Adapt. Situacional	Dif. Opciones de uso	Fácil Instalación	Ligero	Transportable	Sistema de servicios	Cualquier Clima	Alta resistencia	Relación Cultura / Contexto	Pensó en el usuario
TENTATIVE	X	X	X		X	X	X		X			
Living Capsule	X	X	X	X	X	X	X	X	X	X		X
Shiftpod (Refugios ASSI)	X	X	X		X	X	X		X	X		X
Weaving A Home	X	X	X	X	X	X	X	X	X		X	X
Promesa al Amanecer	X	X	X	X				X	X	X	X	X
Transient Elements	X	X	X	X	X		X			X	X	X
Refugios ACNUR	X	X	X			X	X	X		X		X

Lo que dio como resultado a 3 módulos de emergencia que destacaron por sus cualidades y la experiencia que ofrecieron a los refugiados. Estos fueron:

• Living Capsule: En el 2015, el arquitecto César Oreamuno diseñó un módulo que se acomoda a las necesidades básicas de una comunidad tras una emergencia o desastre. El tema principal del proyecto se enfoca en mejorar la calidad de la atención para las víctimas, así como el estímulo al desarrollo de la comunidad. Ver Figura 2.

Fig. 2. La razón de dividir el espacio es para incluir un amplio programa arquitectónico en la menor área posible.

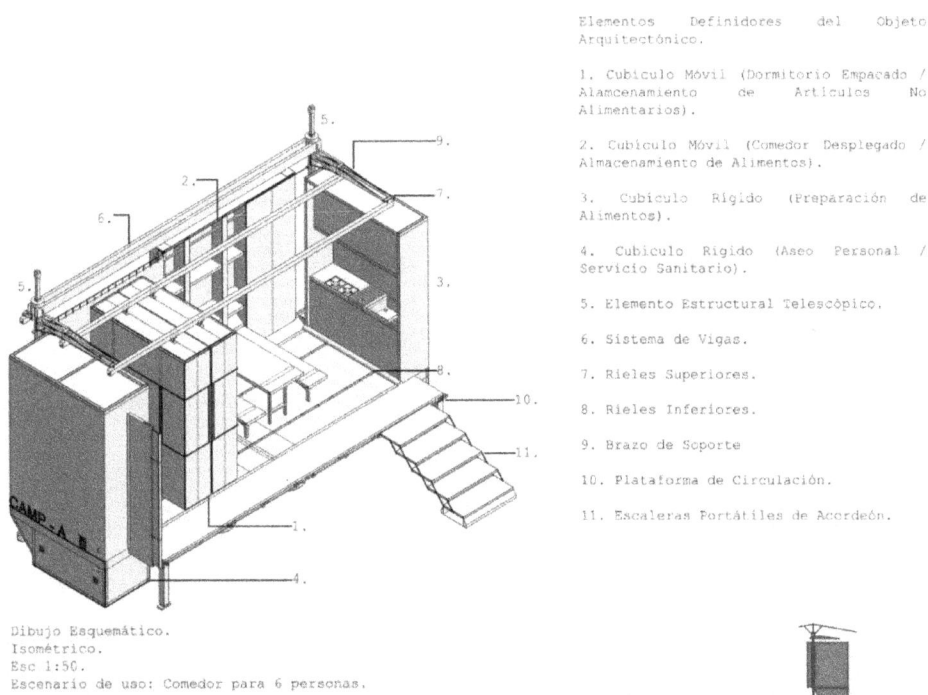

Elementos Definidores del Objeto Arquitectónico.

1. Cubículo Móvil (Dormitorio Empacado / Almcenamiento de Artículos No Alimentarios).

2. Cubículo Móvil (Comedor Desplegado / Almacenamiento de Alimentos).

3. Cubículo Rígido (Preparación de Alimentos).

4. Cubículo Rígido (Aseo Personal / Servicio Sanitario).

5. Elemento Estructural Telescópico.

6. Sistema de Vigas.

7. Rieles Superiores.

8. Rieles Inferiores.

9. Brazo de Soporte.

10. Plataforma de Circulación.

11. Escaleras Portátiles de Acordeón.

Dibujo Esquemático.
Isométrico.
Esc 1:50.
Escenario de uso: Comedor para 6 personas.

Living Capsule está conformado por 5 cubículos, de los cuales tres son móviles, con mobiliario interior y dos son rígidos, pues son usados como soporte estructural. En el primer cubículo se puede preparar para ser un comedor de 6 personas; el segundo consta de un espacio para preparar y almacenar alimentos; el tercero además de ser usado para guardar la vestimenta y artículos de limpieza, se localizan dos camas; el cuarto cubículo tiene la capacidad de almacenar artículos de higiene y limpieza, ropa de cama y dos camas; El quinto cubículo es una área para aseo personal con servicio sanitario (Equipo Editorial, 2017).

• Weaving a Home: Los disturbios políticos, desastres naturales y las crisis de refugiados en el mundo inspiraron al diseñador Abeer Seikaly a crear "Weaving A Home" en 2015. El refugio de tela estructural plegable brinda las comodidades de: calefacción, agua corriente y electricidad, por lo que puede adaptarse a varios climas. Ver Figura 5.

Fig. 5. Representación de Weaving a Home en relación al contexto social y geográfico.

Weaving a Home está compuesto por tubos de plástico de alta resistencia y una membrana de tela elástica, de esta manera, el sistema estructural logra que este se expanda para habitarlo y se contraiga para transportarlo. Los segmentos se pueden abrir para crear puertas o ventanas para promover la circulación de aire en climas cálidos, o se pueden mantener cerrados para conservar el calor en climas fríos. Ver Figura 6.

Fig. 6. Estructura y movimiento de Weaving a Home durante invierno y verano: Vista Isométrica.

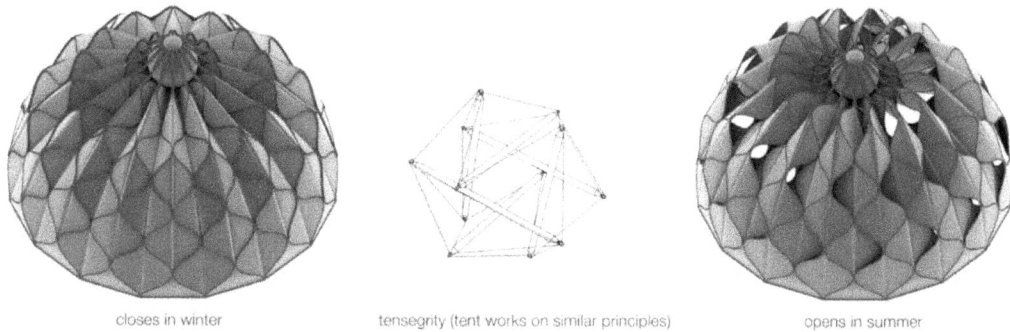

closes in winter   tensegrity (tent works on similar principles)   opens in summer

Para aportar energía al refugio, el diseñador planificó que el tejido de la estructura pudiera convertir la radiación solar en electricidad y asimismo, recargara una batería integrada en el sistema. De la misma manera, en el domo se encuentra un tanque de almacenamiento de agua que proporciona agua dentro de la unidad, la cual es suministrada por la recolección de agua pluvial o de una fuente en el sitio, y se traslada al tanque de almacenamiento (D. Douglass-Jaimes, 2017). Ver Figura 7.

Fig. 7. Los componentes del módulo: Ventilación e iluminación; drenaje de agua y agua pluvial; sistema de agua caliente y almacenamiento de agua; y electricidad por medio de radiación solar.

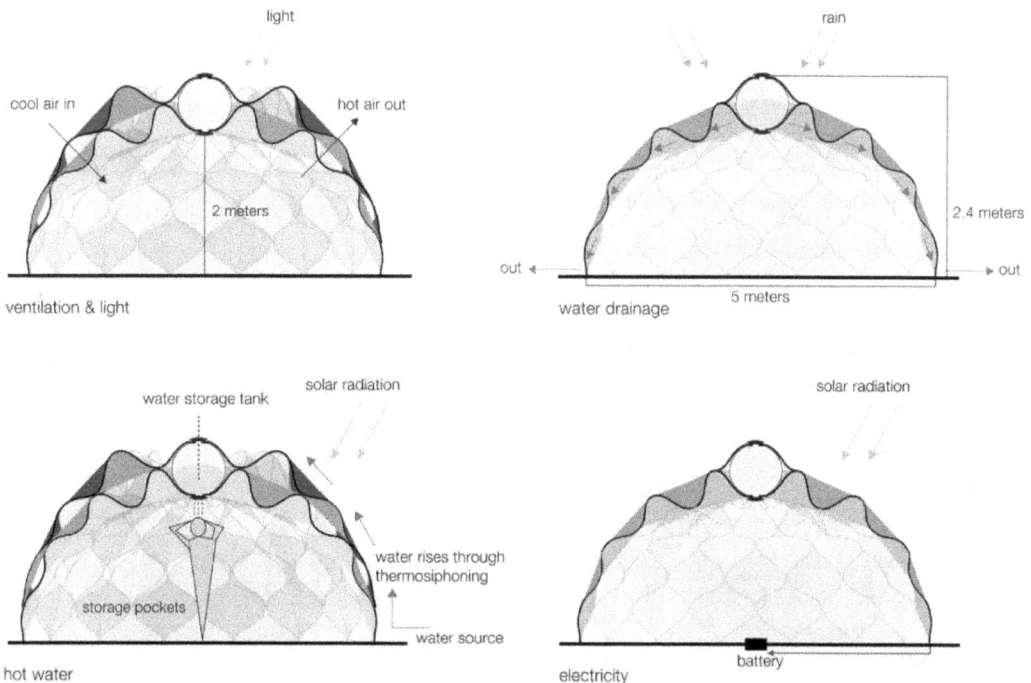

• Promesa al Amanecer: Los arquitectos de AIR, Cyrille Hanappe y Olivier Leclercq crearon en 2016 un Centro de hospedaje de emergencia para personas sin hogar en el Bois de Boulogne, al lado del barrio más caro de París. Se planeó como temporal, por lo que existió solo por tres años. Sin embargo, el proyecto fue construido como si fuera permanente, lo cual fue relevante ya que los arquitectos querían que el edificio se incorporara totalmente en la ciudad y en el vecindario, sin evidenciar su estado temporal, para que los usuarios no se sintieran diferentes de los demás ciudadanos de los alrededores. Ver Figuras 8 y 9.

Fig. 8. Módulos con revestimiento de madera acompañado de una variedad de colores en los muros y con los árboles circundantes.

Fig. 9. Centro de hospedaje de emergencia para personas sin hogar en el Bois de Boulogne, al lado del barrio más caro de París.

El edificio fue prefabricado y se entregaron 117 módulos de madera para ofrecer 200 alojamientos, entre ellos habitaciones individuales o familiares y habitaciones compartidas. Se formaban nueve bloques con los módulos ya ensamblados y creaban vistas hacia el Bois de Boulogne (P. Caballero, 2020).

La presente investigación ha mostrado que el diseñador de cualquier tipo de construcción que atienda o albergue a personas excluidas tales como inmigrantes, personas sin hogar y refugiados, debe estar consciente de la gran responsabilidad que tiene, pues aún existe la posibilidad de afectar de manera positiva o negativa el bienestar del usuario, a pesar de haberle ofrecido una estructura funcional que le brinda protección. Dicho lo anterior, se considera importante brindar una imagen de sostenibilidad al módulo de emergencia dedicado a las personas que necesitan estabilidad, e incluso, darle el mismo nivel de atención que la vivienda permanente, e incluir infraestructura de servicios básicos. También, es relevante el que el hábitat efímero llegue a tener un aspecto "camaleónico", como se hace referencia Valle Gonzalez en "De, por, para… la arquitectura.", y así logre la máxima integración con el entorno al tomar su color de los materiales del lugar (2013, p.109). Es conveniente subrayar que la arquitectura llega a conmover porque establece una empatía directamente vinculada al hemisferio derecho del cerebro, hemisferio conocido por ser intuitivo (García, 2018, p.11-13). Dicha relación de empatía marca una gran diferencia en el producto, ya que está basada en un grado extremo de comunicación entre obra y usuario, y sobre todo, sólo puede ser expresada por quienes han experimentado ese espacio. A modo de conclusión, la arquitectura además de poder ofrecer un módulo efímero funcional y seguro; tiene la capacidad de aportar a la restauración de la dignidad, y bienestar emocional y físico de refugiados y migrantes, por medio de proyectos que cumplan con los principios de protección, atiendan las necesidades básicas de manera higiénica, respeten la diversidad cultural y establezcan un diálogo con la población refugiada y migrante, y con el lugar.

Bibliografía

ACNUR. (2012). Manual para situaciones de emergencia (2.a ed.) [Libro electrónico]. https://www.acnur.org/fileadmin/Documentos/Publicaciones/2012/1643.pdf

Baraya, S. (2020, 27 mayo). Territorial Empathy propone intervenir Plaza de Bolívar para atender la crisis de migrantes Venezuela-Colombia. ArchDaily México. https://www.archdaily.mx/mx/940397/territorial-empathy-propone-intervenir-plaza de-bolivar-para-atender-la-crisis-de-migrantes-venezuela-colombia?ad_source=searc h&ad_medium= search_result_all

Buckley, S. (2017, 10 diciembre). Prefab Pop-Up Shelter Designed for Burning Man and Perfected for Disaster Relief. ArchDaily. https://www.archdaily.com/883389/prefab-pop-up-shelter-designed-for-burning-ma n-and-perfected-for-disaster-relief?ad_medium=bookmark-recommendation&ad_na me=iframe-modal

Caballero, P. (2020, 5 agosto). Centro de hospedaje de emergencia «Promesa al amanecer» / AIR + Moon Architecture. ArchDaily México. https://www.archdaily.mx/mx/945054/centro-de-hospedaje-de-emergencia-promes a-al-amanecer-air-plus-moon-architecture?ad_source=search&ad_medium=search_r esult_all

Consuegra, J. (2020, 11 noviembre). ¿Qué es la Arquitectura Efímera? Reto KÖMMERLING. https://retokommerling.com/arquitectura-efimera/

Douglass-Jaimes, D. (2017, 14 septiembre). Abeer Seikaly's Structural Fabric Shelters Weave Refugees' Lives Back Together. ArchDaily. https://www.archdaily.com/778743/abeer-seikalys-structural-fabric-shelters-weave-refugees-lives-back-together?ad_medium=bookmark-recommendation&ad_name=ifr ame-modal

Equipo Editorial. (2017, 14 septiembre). Living Capsule Offers Shelter From Disasters. ArchDaily. https://www.archdaily.com/801540/living-capsule-offers-shelter-from-disasters?ad_medium=bookmark-recommendation&ad_name=iframe-modal

Estany, A. (2013). La arquitectura, ¿una ciencia de diseño?: Factores científicos, cognitivos y sociales. Arquitectonics, (25), 43-61,7. Retrieved from https://0-search-proquest-com.biblioteca-ils.tec.mx/trade-journals/la-arquitectura-u na-ciencia-de-diseño-factores/docview/1503684291/se-2?accountid=11643

Ghisleni, C. (2020, septiembre 4). El papel de la arquitectura en el tema de los refugiados y migrantes latinoamericanos. ArchDaily México. https://www.archdaily.mx/mx/947087/el-papel-de-la-arquitectura-en-el-tema-de-los-refugiados-y-migrantes-latinoamericanos?ad_source=search&ad_medium=search_r esult_all

INEGI. (2020). Población. Migracion. http://cuentame.inegi.org.mx/poblacion/migracion.aspx?tema=P

Naciones Unidas. (2020, 15 septiembre). Migración. https://www.un.org/es/sections/issues-depth/migration/index.html#:%7E:text=La%20Organizaci%C3%B3n%20Internacional%20para%20las,2)%20el%20car%C3%A1cter%20voluntario%20o

Oh, E. (2017, 14 septiembre). Designnobis' "Tentative" Provides Compact, Individual Living Spaces for Disaster Victims. ArchDaily. https://www.archdaily.com/772497/designnobis-tentative-provides-compact-individ ual-living-spaces-for-disaster-victims

Paranhos, M. E., & Werlang, B. S. G. (2015). Psychological emergencies: A new practice to be discussed. Psicologia : Ciencia e Profissao, 35(2), 557-571. doi:http://0-dx.doi.org.biblioteca-ils.tec.mx/10.1590/1982-370301202012

Rúa García, M. (2018). Arquitectura con empatía. Oviedo, España, Síntesis Arquitectura. Recuperado de https://0-elibro-net.biblioteca-ils.tec.mx/es/ereader/consorcioitesm/103024?page=1 1.

Valle González, R. D. (2013). De, por, para… la arquitectura. Buenos Aires, Argentina: Editorial Nobuko.Recuperado de https://0-elibro-net.biblioteca-ils.tec.mx/es/ereader/consorcioitesm/77955?page=10 9

LA INFLUENCIA DEL DISEÑO ARQUITECTÓNICO EN EL BIENESTAR DE LOS MIGRANTES REFUGIADOS

Laura Martínez

Abstract

A lo largo de los años, se han buscado soluciones de viviendas y sistemas para los campos de refugiados, sin embargo, ninguna ha resultado exitosa del todo. Lo que lleva a cuestionarse ¿cómo el diseño arquitectónico influye en el bienestar de los migrantes? Para esto se realizó una investigación basada en casos de estudio del campo de la Ciudad de Kakuma y el campo de refugiados en Zataari, Jordania. Estos campos serán calificados según los indicadores establecidos por la Organización para la Cooperación y Desarrollo Económicos. Los resultados del análisis evidenciaron que los ámbitos urbanos, económicos y sociales son de gran valor para su bienestar.

Introducción

La migración es un evento que experimentan las personas por múltiples razones, entre estas políticas, sociales, económicas o ambientales. A lo largo de los años, se han buscado soluciones de viviendas y sistemas para campos de refugiados, sin embargo, ninguna ha resultado exitosa del todo. Lo que lleva a cuestionar cuáles son los factores que contribuyen a que los migrantes pasen de sentir incertidumbre sobre sus futuros, a sentir pertenencia de sus alrededores, llegando a una pregunta más específica, ¿cómo el diseño arquitectónico influye en su bienestar?

Metodología

Para responder a esta cuestión se tomaron dos casos de estudio de algunos de los más grandes campos de refugiados en el mundo. Los campos a evaluar son el campo de la Ciudad de Kakuma en Kenia, y el campo de refugiados de Zaatari en Jordania. El primero alberga a 182,000 refugiados, principalmente provenientes de Sudán, Somalia y Etiopía, ha existido desde 1992, a pesar de ser pensado como temporal (IAAC, 2019). Por otro lado, el campo de Zaatari ha existido desde el 2012 y alberga a un total de 80,000 refugiados que han sido obligados a huir de Siria (Schön, Al-Saadi, Grubmueller y Schumann-Bölsche, 2018, pp. 346-373).

Ambos casos serán evaluados según los indicadores establecidos por la Organización para la Cooperación y el Desarrollo Económicos, los cuales ayudan a definir el bienestar de los migrantes. Los indicadores consisten de dos categorías: Calidad de Vida y Condiciones Materiales. En la primera categoría se tomarán en cuenta Estatus de la Salud, Educación y Habilidades, Conexiones Sociales, Calidad del Medio Ambiente y Seguridad Personal. Para la segunda categoría se tomarán en cuenta Ingreso y Riqueza, Trabajos y Ganancias, y Alojamiento. No se encontró información relevante para la investigación sobre los indicadores de Balance Trabajo-Vida, Compromiso Cívico y Gobernanza, y Bienestar Subjetivo, por lo que no serán tomados en cuenta (OECD, 2018).

Tab. 1. Evaluación de los campos escogidos según los indicadores de la OECD.

	PROYECTOS	Ciudad de Kakuma	Campo de Refugiados Zaatari
C A L I D A D D E V I D A	Estatus de la Salud	Hay ocho hospitales disponibles.	Hay dos hospitales y nueve centros de salud disponibles.
	Balance Trabajo-Vida		
	Educación y Habilidades	Existen 52 escuelas en el campo, donde el 87% de los maestros son refugiados.	Existen 24 escuelas, de las cuales, nueve son formales, donde en cada una estudia un promedio de 865 niños.
	Conexiones Sociales	El 59% de los refugiados confían en la comunidad hospedadora y el 82% confía en sus vecinos.	Las personas se identifican con uno de tres grupos culturales basados geográficamente (As Sanamayn, Izra', Dara) por lo que buscan mudarse a las áreas que se identifican con su cultura.
	Compromiso Cívico y Gobernanza		
	Calidad del Medio Ambiente	Está localizado en el desierto, por lo que no hay bosques ni fuentes de agua locales. La gran población acelera la erosión y vuelve a las áreas grandes campos de polvo.	Está localizado en el desierto, por lo que no hay bosques ni fuentes de agua locales. La gran población acelera la erosión y vuelve a las áreas grandes campos de polvo.
	Seguridad Personal	Las percepciones de seguridad de los migrantes son generalmente positivas. El 93% se siente seguro al caminar por el campo de día y el 21% al caminar de noche.	Hay una estación de policía. El 80% de los habitantes tiene una buena percepción de seguridad.
	Bienestar Subjetivo		

C O N D I C I O N E S M A T E R I A L E S	Ingreso y Riqueza	La ciudad necesita ser económicamente autosuficiente para reducir el apoyo de la UNHCR. 7,060 familias reciben un apoyo económico para Asistencia Básica.	A pesar de que los refugiados sirios registrados reciben un ingreso mensual por parte del Programa Mundial de Alimentos, solo para el 60% es suficiente para abastecer sus necesidades básicas.
	Trabajos y Ganancias	Las leyes de Kenya hacen casi imposible que los refugiados obtengan empleo, por lo que no existe este balance. Solo el 20% de los refugiados están empleados. Existen alrededor de 2,500 negocios informales.	Solo el 10% de los refugiados tienen permiso para laborar.
	Alojamiento	Las viviendas se conforman de paredes de bambú, lonas de plástico y techos de metal corrugado. Estas están sobreocupadas y no protegen del calor, inundaciones, radiación y tormentas de arena. El 5% de la población cuenta con electricidad.	Existen tres formas de refugio individual: la unidad modal, la carpa y la pared de block de conereto. Las familias usualmente son asignadas a la unidad o a la carpa, en las que el número promedio de personas que habitan son seis. Con el paso del tiempo les van agregando cuartos.

En la Tabla 1 se puede observar que al comparar ambos campos en base a los indicadores de la OECD, existen muchas similitudes entre ellos. Para comenzar, ya que ambos campos se encuentran localizados en países Africanos, estos comparten características ambientales perteneciente al desierto como son las temperaturas extremas de días y noches, la falta de recursos como árboles y agua, la exposición a vientos y campos de polvo. Todos estos eventos ambientales afectan naturalmente la vida de los migrantes, por lo que deberían ser tomados en cuenta en la planeación urbana y el diseño arquitectónico, sin embargo, no lo están. Los migrantes sufren inundaciones e incendios en sus hogares, pues aunque se intentan aplicar medidas como sistemas anti-incendios de acomodo urbano, estos se ven obstaculizados gracias a factores como la llegada de nuevos migrantes que ocupan con sus hogares estos espacios designados (IAAC, 2019) (Slater, 2014).

Las viviendas de la Ciudad de Kakuma están conformadas más que nada por recursos locales, bambú, lonas de plástico y techos de metal corrugado, por lo que no están del todo equipadas para soportar los eventos climáticos y pertenecientes a la zona como es la radiación, tormentas de arena, temperaturas extremas, inundaciones e incendios. También, gracias a las frecuentes llegadas de más migrantes al campo, las viviendas suelen estar sobrepobladas (IAAC, 2019). Por otro lado, en el campo de Zaatari las viviendas funcionan con un sistema algo distinto, pues se conforman de tres tipos de refugios individuales: la unidad modal, la carpa y la pared de block de concreto. Las familias usualmente son asignadas a la unidad o carpa, en las que el número promedio de personas que habitan son seis, pero al buscar expandir su vivienda, suelen juntarse con otras familias para lograrlo (Slater, 2014).

Actualmente, en la Ciudad de Kakuma hay 52 escuelas donde el 87% de los maestros son refugiados, sin embargo sigue habiendo una escasez de maestros, por lo que las clases están sobrepobladas, reduciendo así la calidad de la educación (UNHCR, 2019). De igual manera, en Zaatari hay solo nueve escuelas formales, a las que asisten un promedio de 865 alumnos (Schön, Al-Saadi, Grubmueller y Schumann-Bölsche, 2018, pp. 346-373). A pesar de que con los años, la cuestión educativa ha mejorado bastante en ambos campos, aún existen fallas en el sistema, que por suerte ya se están trabajando, pues poco a poco se reconoce más la importancia de la información, la educación, y los efectos que tienen en el funcionamiento de los campos, donde en un futuro, si aplicada correctamente, ayudará al sistema autosuficiente al que se busca llegar para reducir el apoyo proveniente de la UNHCR y así acercarse a la independencia (IAAC, 2019).

Fig. 1. Campo de la Ciudad de Kakuma

PHOTO: REUTERS/THOMAS MUKOYA

Continuando con el ámbito económico y su gran impacto a la resolución de la cuestión planteada, la empleabilidad es aún un problema grave para los migrantes. En el campo de la Ciudad de Kakuma los refugiados se enfrentan a la leyes locales pues los limitan de obtener empleos, tanto en el campo como en la ciudad hospedadora, solo el 20% de los refugiados tienen un empleo formal, el 9% está desempleado y la mayor parte del 71% no tiene capacidades para obtener un empleo, por lo que están desempleados o solo obtienen trabajos temporales, de los que no pueden depender para traer un ingreso fijo a su hogar (UNHCR y WBG, 2021). Existe un cierto grupo de personas en este campo, conformado por 7,060 familias, que recibe un apoyo económico cada dos meses por parte de la UNHCR (2019). De manera similar en el campo de Zaatari, el Programa Mundial de Alimentos provee a los refugiados un ingreso mensual, sin embargo, solo el 60% de los migrantes puede abastecer sus necesidades básicas con este. En este mismo campo, solo el 10% de los refugiados tiene permiso para laborar y el 7% se resiste a obtener un empleo aunque exista la oportunidad, esto por razones de género más que nada. De modo que, un 83% de los migrantes, al igual que en Kakuma, solo obtiene empleos informales e inseguros (Schön, Al-Saadi, Grubmueller y Schumann-Bölsche, 2018, pp. 346-373).

Existe una conexión directa entre el ingreso económico de los migrantes y sus viviendas, pues al tener la libertad de invertir este apoyo, en lugar de obtener bienes obligados, como comida que probablemente no sea de su agrado, ellos pueden dedicar una parte del dinero hacía su vivienda, comprando materiales que ayuden a ampliarla o mejorarla (Schön, Al-Saadi, Grubmueller y Schumann-Bölsche, 2018, pp. 346-373).

Fig. 2. Campo de Refugiados de Zaatari

En cuanto a Seguridad, los migrantes de la Ciudad de Kakuma tienen una percepción generalmente positiva, donde el 93% de los refugiados se siente seguro al caminar por el campo de día y el 21% al caminar de noche (UNHCR y WBG, 2021). De igual forma, en Zaatari, el 80% de los residentes del campo tienen una percepción positiva de seguridad (Schön, Al-Saadi, Grubmueller y Schumann-Bölsche, 2018). Sin embargo, en cuanto a Salud, aquí solo hay disponibles dos hospitales y nueves centros de salud, por lo que existe un hospital por cada 40,000 habitantes (Schön, Al-Saadi, Grubmueller y Schumann-Bölsche, 2018, pp. 346-373). Mientras que, en Kakuma hay ocho hospitales disponibles, por lo que hay uno por cada 25,000 habitantes (UNHCR, 2019). En general, en ambos se procura mucho tanto la salud física como la mental, por lo que estos números no son del todo preocupantes.

Por último, el ámbito social, factor que es enormemente afectado por la planeación urbana pues esta define el acomodo de las viviendas e instalaciones, estableciendo así las relaciones más cercanas. En

Zaatari, las personas se identifican con uno de tres grupos culturales basados geográficamente (As Sanamayn, Izra', Dara), como se puede observar en la figura 3, por lo que buscan mudarse a áreas que se identifican con su cultura para encontrar un sentido de comunidad cercano a lo que tenían anteriormente (Slater, 2014). Por el otro lado, el campo de Kakuma tiene una interacción más recurrente con la comunidad hospedadora por lo que es importante valorar que el 59% de los refugiados confía en esta, pero es un número algo bajo comparado al 89% que confía más en sus vecinos, pues existe una conexión más fuerte entre ellos y aún existe mucha segregación hacía ellos por parte de los hospedadores (UNHCR y WBG, 2021).

Fig. 3. Acomodo cultural de Refugiados en el Campo de Zaatari

As Sanamayn

Izra'

Dara

Conclusión

Todos los aspectos evaluados por los indicadores se conectan de una forma u otra, la seguridad originada de las conexiones sociales creadas gracias al acomodo urbano, las viviendas conjuntas, provenientes de las organizaciones, el ingreso económico de las familias y el crecimiento a una comunidad económicamente autosuficiente gracias a los recursos académicos que se les está brindando en las instituciones educativas, lo que demuestra el gran valor de todos estos factores para el bienestar comunal y el individual.

De esto se concluye que todo se puede trazar devuelta al diseño urbano, responsable de establecer las conexiones sociales entre los migrantes, y la vivienda, especialmente considerando que este es el único bien del que son propietarios y que es donde pasan la mayor parte de su tiempo. La vivienda es el centro del individuo, por lo que dar la libertad de diseñarla, tiene efectos positivos en los migrantes, pues es la forma en la que expresan su individualidad, en la que resaltan sus necesidades y deseos, en la que se sienten involucrados con sus alrededores, y es el cómo encuentran una manera de seguir sintiéndose conectados a las tierras que fueron obligados a abandonar.

References

Instituto de Arquitectura Avanzada de Cataluña. (2019, febrero 23). Kakuma City. IAAC Blog. http://www.iaacblog.com/programs/kakuma-city/

Organización para la Cooperación y el Desarrollo Económico. (2018, enero). Measuring migrants' well-being. https://www.oecd.org/migration/forum-migration-statistics/3.Kate-Scrivens.pdf

Schön, A.-M., Al-Saadi, S., Grubmueller, J., & Schumann-Bölsche, D. (2018). Desarrollo de un sistema de indicadores de rendimiento del campamento y su aplicación a Zaatari, Jordania. Journal of Humanitarian Logistics and Supply Chain Management, 8(3), 346-373. https://doi.org/10.1108/jhlscm-10-2017-0047

Slater, J. (2014). Urban Systems of the Refugee Camp (Architecture Thesis Prep. 272. Recuperado de https://surface.syr.edu/architecture_tpreps/272

UNHCR. (2019, mayo). KAKUMA CAMP AND KALOBEYEI SETTLEMENT. https://www.unhcr.org/ke/wp-content/uploads/sites/2/2019/06/Briefing-Kit_May-2019-approved.pdf

UNHCR & World Bank Group. (2021). Understanding the Socioeconomic Conditions of Refugees in Kenya. http://documents1.worldbank.org/curated/en/443431613628051180/pdf/Understanding-the-Socio-Economic-Conditions-of-Refugees-in-Kenya-Volume-B-Kakuma-Camp-Results-from-the-2019-Kakuma-Socioeconomic-Survey.pdf

LA ARQUITECTURA BIOCLIMÁTICA COMO ALIADA PARA EL BIENESTAR DE MIGRANTES:ESTUDIO EN CLIMAS ÁRIDOS Y FRONTERIZOS (CHIHUAHUA, MÉXICO).

Jacqueline Beltrán Palomares

Resumen:

De 100 personas que llegan a Chihuahua, 93 pretenden cruzar a Estados Unidos (INEGI).

¿Cómo puede la arquitectura bioclimática ayudar a casas de migrantes en Chihuahua aofrecer mejores soluciones de hospedaje?

Se analizaron dos edificaciones bajo: el aprovechamiento solar de los edificios, cuánto seinvierte en ellos y los termopreferendums de los migrantes.

Se evidenciaron las pocas o nulas estrategias bioclimáticas en ambas edificaciones. A pesar delesfuerzo de los administradores, se expone el por qué se logran parcialmente los niveles de confort de los migrantes y que la gestión financiera de la casa se ve afectada intentando alcanzarlos.

Palabras Clave: Calidad de vida, estrategias, servicios.

Planteamiento del problema

En 2020 se tuvo un crecimiento del 34% de solicitudes de refugio en México, llegandoa más de 80,000 solicitantes (Monroy, J. 2020). Miles de personas llegan a México con la esperanza de poder restablecerse aquí o pasar a Estados Unidos. ¿Cómo es el lugar donde pasan su día a día?

El siguiente ejemplo a exponer es una propuesta de un albergue bioclimático efímero propuesto para ubicarse en Santa Ana, Sonora, México, donde la temperatura varía de 5°C y enpocas ocasiones baja a menos de 0°C o rebasa los 41°C (Weather Spark, s.f). Ese trabajo fue analizado -por quienes lo realizaron- bajo un enfoque medioambiental, económico y social, encaminado hacia la problemática de la migración en México.

Con el fin de asegurar el bienestar social, reducir el impacto del daño al medio y cuidarel gasto monetario, el diseño bioclimático busca brindar confort y un espacio digno para residirpor un tiempo indefinido. Tras hacer los análisis, se concluyó que el edificio cumple con los requisitos energéticos y lumínicos para comprenderse como un exitoso diseño bioclimático (Cervantes, C. & Rosalía, I., 2006).

La arquitectura es un elemento clave en el desarrollo de toda sociedad y una herramienta de inclusión bastante poderosa. Los diseños arquitectónicos pensados para losmigrantes muchas veces sólo se piensan para dar soluciones rápidas. *¿Cómo puede la arquitectura bioclimática ayudar a las casas de migrantes y albergues en el estado de*

Chihuahua a ofrecer mejores soluciones de hospedaje?

Marco Teórico

Las fuentes primarias de este documento son; la entrevista con el agente clave de la Casa Migrante en ciudad Juárez, y la realizada el 13 de Octubre de 2020 con la directora de la Casa Migrante San Agustín en la ciudad de Chihuahua. Ambas dan a conocer de dónde vienenlos migrantes, razones por las cuales migran, y aspectos con los que cuentan las casas.

Este trabajo se enfoca en la arquitectura "bioclimática" debido a su enfoque en aprovechar las opciones del medio, con el propósito de disminuir el consumo energético y elimpacto ambiental (Seguí, P. sf).

Estado de la cuestión

Según un informe del Ihobe - Sociedad pública enfocada en la gestión ambiental en losámbitos en los que se desarrolla la actividad humana-, el 40% de las emisiones de dióxido de carbono, el 30% del consumo de materias primas, el 20% de consumo de agua y el 30% de la generación de residuos proviene del sector de edificación (Espino, A. 2018).

De acuerdo con los oradores de la plática "Good Design for a Bad World" durante la "Dutch Design Week" en 2017, se "*debe*" cambiar la narrativa de los movimientos migratoriosy apoyar a que las ciudades tengan mejor y mayor capacidad; Kilian Kleinschmidt, experto en ayuda humanitaria, comentó: "No diseñes otro refugio para refugiados, no son una especie. Porlo tanto, no hay necesidad de tecnología, diseño o arquitectura para los refugiados" (Fairs, M. 2017).

A pesar de la diversidad cultural en los albergues de refugiados, la idiosincrasia y aspectos etnográficos; la arquitectura tiene el arma de ser incluyente, este es un tema donde el diseñoespacial es clave.

La arquitectura bioclimática, además de hacerse a base de análisis climáticos, solares, recursos disponibles y otros; también toma en cuenta aspectos como el termopreferendum y el confort acústico de los usuarios. Dichos aspectos están relacionados directamente con el lugar de donde provenimos.

Objetivo de la investigación

El objetivo de esta investigación es responder a cómo la implementación de la arquitectura bioclimática ayudaría a desarrollar espacios que contribuyan al bienestar físico yemocional en el camino del migrante y ayudar a las asociaciones a proporcionar espacios dignos y acogedores aprovechando los recursos que el ambiente de Chihuahua ofrece.

Metodología

Esta investigación se enfoca en Chihuahua, por su diversidad de flora, por el hecho de es estado fronterizo con Estados Unidos de América y por su gran capacidad de recepción solar. Su temperatura media anual oscila entre 18 y 22 °C, con lluvias en verano, y régimen delluvias invernales <5 % de la anual (Tercera actualización del Plan de Desarrollo urbano de laCiudad de Chihuahua: Visión 2040).

El clima de Chihuahua es un factor que afecta a la economía directamente aunque no sepercate fácilmente, pero a largo plazo se invierte muchísimo dinero en instalaciones de clima. La arquitectura puede cambiar esto.

Se analizarán 2 diferentes lugares en el estado de Chihuahua, uno en la capital y el otroen el municipio de Juárez; teniendo en cuenta las diferentes nacionalidades que llegan; este factor es de suma importancia, ya que es necesario conocer sus *termopreferendums*, es decir, "la temperatura ideal para poder moverse dentro de un gradiente térmico" (S.a, 2017).

Según el informante clave de la casa Migrante Juárez, se recibieron personas de África,Haití, Cuba, Brasil, Nicaragua, El Salvador, Venezuela, Chile y de la misma República Mexicana. También comentó que las 3 razones principales por las cuales las personas llegan a la Casa del migrante son las siguientes:

1. Inseguridad y violencia.

2. Política.

3. Superación

Casa Migrante San Agustín, Chihuahua, Chih.

La Casa Migrante San Agustín está ubicada en la zona aeropuerto de la ciudad deChihuahua (imagen 1.1-1.3).

Imagen 1.1.- Ilustración: Localización general. Fuente: IMPLAN Chihuahua. Segunda captura de pantallarecuperada de Google maps.

Imagen 1.2.- Fachada frontal de Casa Migrante San Agustín, Chihuahua, Chih.

Imagen 1.3. -Plano arquitectónico de Casa Migrante San Agustín, Chihuahua.

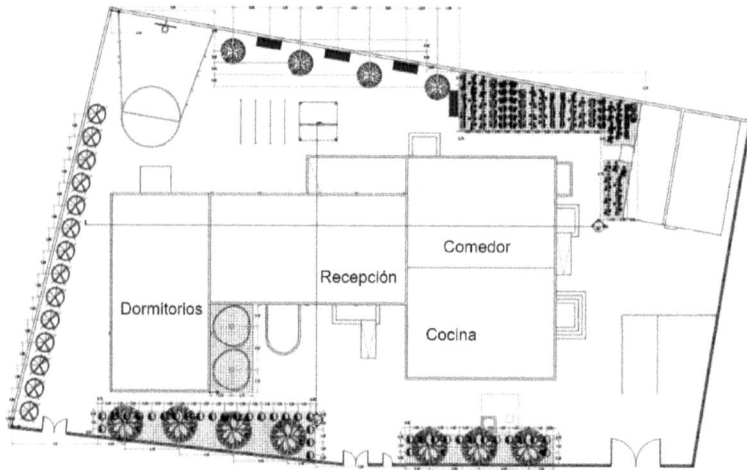

El análisis solar (imagen 1.4) nos indica que el sol llega principalmente por la fachada principal, pues ésta da hacia el Este, provocando que se ilumine principalmente la recepción dela casa (imagen 1.3), pero no los dormitorios ni la cocina debido a que no existen ventanas hacia ese sentido. Las ventanas de los dormitorios dan hacia el sur, y las ventanas del comedorhacia el norte.

Imagen 1.4.- Análisis solar de la Casa del Migrante San Agustín. Chihuahua, Chih.

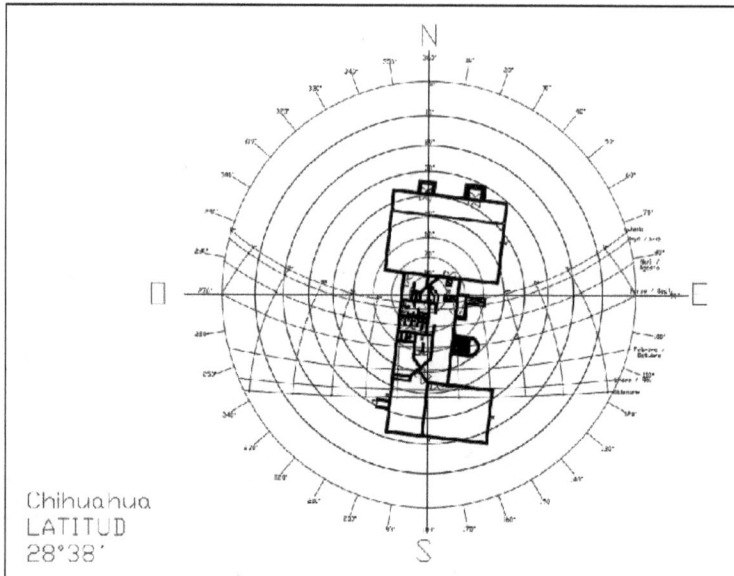

Aquí se reciben personas de Honduras, Haití, Guatemala, Brasil, El Salvador, Ecuador, Cuba y Nicaragua. Sus termopreferendums varían, si hacemos un promedio de la zona de confort de las personas de distintas nacionalidades que llegan a la casa, es de 23°C. La zona deconfort Szokolay para los 8 países en promedio es de 22°C-27.5°C.

En la Casa del Migrante San Agustín decidieron enfocarse en tener calefacción; eninvierno se pagan entre $7,000.00 - $8,000.00 pesos para el gas. Durante el verano, con unaforo de 50 personas se tuvieron que pagar $8,000.00 pesos mensuales de agua.

Esta casa mantiene el diseño Norte a Sur, lo cual no es favorable si lo que se pretendees captar la radiación solar en tiempo de invierno; lo cual se confirma al momento en que se compartieron las cantidades que se deben pagar en servicios.

Imagen 1.5.-Cuartos del dormitorio para mujeres de la Casa Migrante San Agustín, Chihuahua, Chih.

Casa Migrante Cd Juárez, Chihuahua.

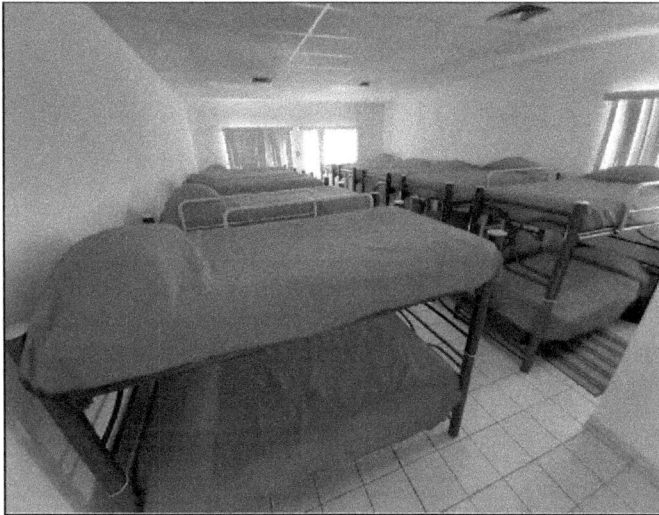

El segundo lugar a analizar, es la Casa del Migrante en Ciudad Juárez. Se encuentra en lafrontera con Estados Unidos de América.

Imagen 1.6.- Ubicación de la Casa Del Migrante en Ciudad Juárez. Ilustración: Carta urbana Cd. Juárez.Asociación de Ingenieros y Arquitectos de Cd. Juárez. A. C. Segunda captura de pantalla recuperada de Google Maps.

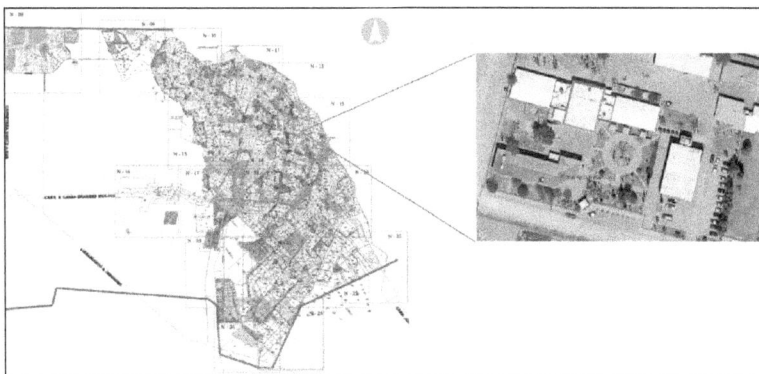

En este documento se analizará únicamente el edificio principal de la Casa del MiganteCd. Juárez.

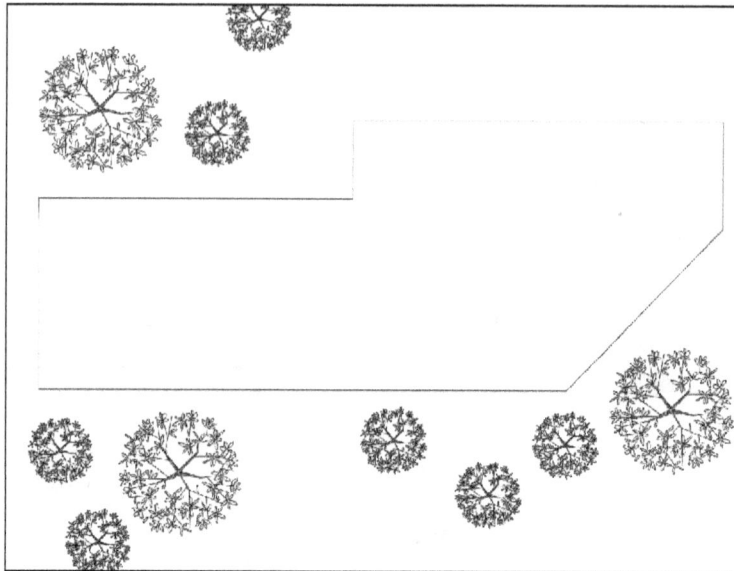

La entrada de la casa está dirigida hacia el Sureste (imagen 1.7), de modo que el sol pega directamente en las mañanas hacia esa parte de la casa durante las mañanas. A partir de las 11:30 am, el sol pega directamente en todo el techo de la casa y así permanece hasta las 3:30pm, después se empieza a crear la sombra del lado de la fachada principal (imágenes 1.8,1.9 y 1.10).

Imagen 1.7.-Edificación representada en la gráfica solar del estado de Chihuahua.

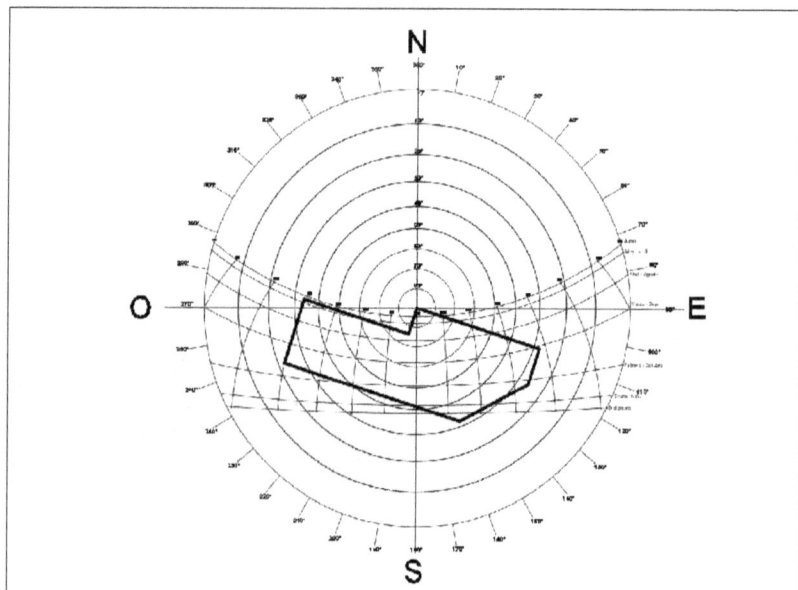

Imagen 1.8. - Representación solar a las 8:45 am.

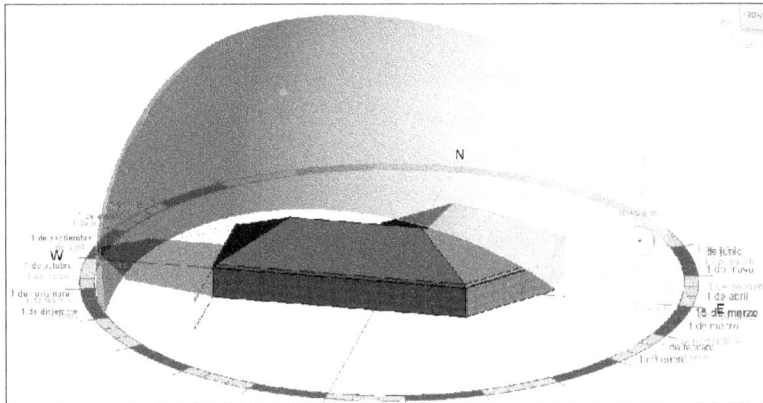

Imagen 1.9.- Representación solar a las 11:15 am.

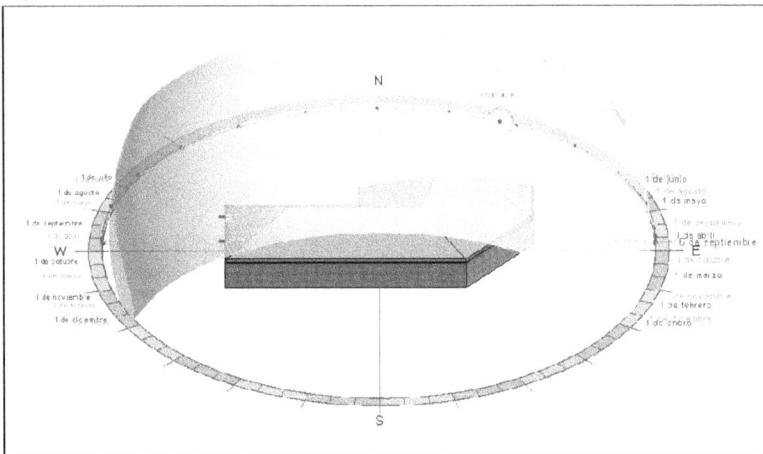

Imagen 1.10.- Representación solar a las 3:15 pm.

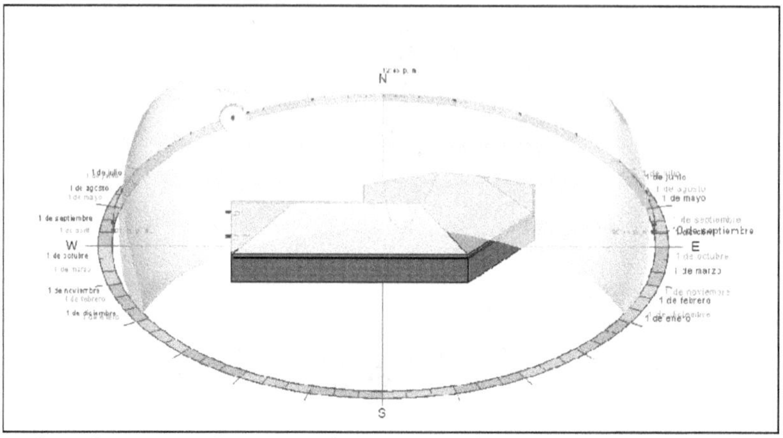

Según el informante clave, la casa se planeó con la intención de que los migrantes tengan sus cuartos, áreas recreativas, atención profesional y acceso a teléfono y wifi. Se puededar cupo de 600 personas.

Uso de los resultados obtenidos

Los usuarios que llegan a ambas casas están acostumbrados a climas más calurosos que fríos, lo cual indica que la arquitectura debería favorecer a la captación solar para el mejor aprovechamiento: tanto para que la casa esté más cálida en invierno y en verano la captación de energía sea óptima sin sobrecalentar el edificio.

Tabla 1.0. Resumen de resultados y similitudes entre ambas casas.

CIUDAD CHIHUAHUA	SIMILITUDES	CIUDAD JUÁREZ
Casa Migrante San Agustín		**Casa del Migrante**
La nula vegetación alrededor deledificio no da lugar a que haya humedad en el ambiente	–	Sí existe vegetación rodeandola edificación, ésto humidificael ambiente y proporciona un lugar más agradable para los usuarios
No existen áreas verdes recreativas	–	Sí existen áreas verdes recreativas
Orientación de la casa hacia el norte: este factor dificulta que lacasa se caliente durante la temporada más fría, provocandoque los gastos en servicio de electricidad aumenten.	Desaprovechamiento de energíasolar	Orientación de la casa de Estea Oeste, permitiendo que la casa se caliente con mayor facilidad. Además, su captación solar es excelente.
Países: Honduras, Haití, Guatemala, Brasil, El Salvador,Ecuador, Cuba y Nicaragua.	Los usuarios están acostumbrados arangos de temperaturas cálidas. Específicamente entre los 22°C alos 27°C.	Países: África, Haití, Cuba, Brasil, Nicaragua, El Salvador,Venezuela, Chile y de la misma República Mexicana.

Gastos:		Gastos:
$8,000.00 pesos mensuales de aguadurante el verano.	Altos costos monetarios para dar abasto de servicios tales como aguay gas a los usuarios.	El agente clave únicamente proporcionó un estimado de $8,000.00 pesos mexicanos destinados a electricidad.
$7,000.00 - $8,000.00 pesos parael gas en invierno.		

Conclusión

Si tomamos la arquitectura bioclimática como aliada, Chihuahua podría ofrecer una increíble estancia a los migrantes por el aprovechamiento de recursos naturales y clima con elque cuenta, se pueden crear estrategias con el mismo diseño bioclimático y añadir el uso energías renovables; según la CEPAL, México es el segundo país con menor participación enellas en Latinoamérica; y además, según la CONAGUA, México muestra un aumento de temperatura de 1.4 grados centígrados mientras que el resto del planeta promedia 0.98°C (GreenPeace México, 2021).

Si los albergues para migrantes fueran construidos de forma consciente, a base de una Arquitectura Bioclimática, el impacto no sólo estaría en el bolsillo de los encargados de pagar por servicios, sino que también contribuiría a un mejor desarrollo integral de los migrantes, yaque el poder ser parte de un ambiente sostenible ayuda a que sus tareas puedan tener un enfoque diferente y haya mayor aprovechamiento de recursos y de espacio. Además, se podríagarantizar una mejor sensación térmica en aquellos lugares donde pasan más tiempo: comedor,salas de estar y dormitorios.

El papel principal del arquitecto es garantizar el bienestar de los usuarios por medio del diseñode la estructura. Es imprescindible que nuestros proyectos (1)sean de ayuda para las comunidades vulnerables y (2) que favorezcan y aporten valores a nuestra sociedad.

Referencias Bibliográficas

Cervantes, C. & Rosalía, I. (2006). Albergue bioclimático para migrantes "Saayi". Febrero 22, 2021, de UAM Sitio web: http://zaloamati.azc.uam.mx/handle/11191/6186

Fairs, M. (2017). "Don't design yet another shelter" for refugees, say experts. Febrero25, 2021, de Dezeen Sitio web: https://www.dezeen.com/2017/12/18/dont-design-shelter-refugees-kilian-kleinschmidt-rene-boer-good-design-bad-world/

Green Peace México. (2021). .. Marzo 13, 2021, de Instagram Sitio web: https://www.instagram.com/p/CMYbx3AhYGl/?utm_source=ig_web_copy_link

Maiztegui, B. (2021). Arquitectura bioclimática en Latinoamérica: Técnicas naturales para economizar energía. [Imagen]. Marzo 20, 2021, de ArchDaily Sitio web: https://www.archdaily.mx/mx/956847/arquitectura-bioclimatica-en-latinoamerica-tecnic as-naturales-para-economizar-energia/602a1e95f91c81e513000034-arquitectura-biocli matica-en-latinoamerica-tecnicas-naturales-para-economizar-energia-imagen

Monroy, J. (2020). Solicitudes de refugio en México crecen 34%; prevén oleada para 2021. Febrero 22, 2021, de El Economista Sitio web: https://www.eleconomista.com.mx/politica/Solicitudes-de-refugio-en-Mexico-crecen-3 4-preven-oleada-para-2021-20200724-0042.html

Noticias Passivhaus. (s.f). Diferencia entre casa pasiva, sostenible, bioclimática. Marzo02, 2021, de Madrid Arquitectura Sitio web:
https://madridarquitectura.com/casa-pasiva-sostenible-bioclimatica/#:~:text=Una%20ar quitectura%20sostenible%20es%20la,clima%2C%20la%20radiaci%C3%B3n%20solar %2C%E2%80%A6

Olgyay, V. (2019). DESIGN WITH CLIMATE. Bioclimatic approach to architectural regionalism. Barcelona, España: Editorial Gustavo Gili, SL.

S.a. (2017). Termopreferendum. Marzo 20, 2021, de Glosarios Sitio web:https://glosarios.servidor-alicante.com/ ecologia/ termopreferendum

Seguí, P. (s.f). Arquitectura bioclimática principios esenciales. Febrero 24, 2021, de Ovacen Sitio web: https://ovacen.com/arquitectura-bioclimatica-principios-esenciales/

WeatherSpark. (S.f.). Clima Promedio en Santa Ana. Marzo 12, 2021, de WeatherSpark Sitio web: https://es.weatherspark.com/y/2577/Clima-promedio-en-Santa-Ana-M%C3%A9xico-durante-todo-el-a%C3%B1o#Sections-Humidity

WeatherSpark. (S.f.). Clima Promedio en Chihuahua. Marzo 12, 2021, de WeatherSpark Sitio web: https://es.weatherspark.com/y/2577/Clima-promedio-en-Santa-Ana-M%C3%A9xico-durante-todo-el-a%C3%B1o#Sections-Humidity

Anexos

Ejemplo de una arquitectura bioclimática. Fuente: ArchDaily

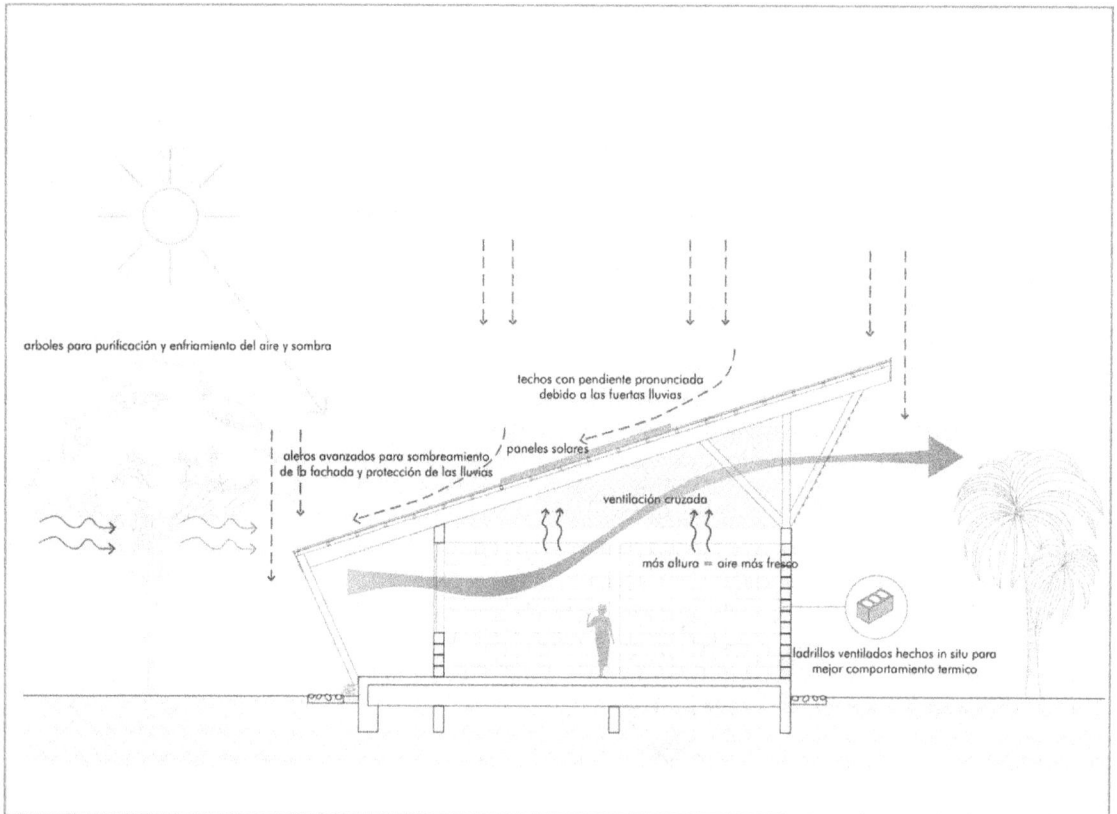

arboles para purificación y enfriamiento del aire y sombra

techos con pendiente pronunciada debido a las fuertas lluvias

aleros avanzados para sombreamiento de la fachada y protección de las lluvias

paneles solares

ventilación cruzada

más altura = aire más fresco

ladrillos ventilados hechos in situ para mejor comportamiento termico

Magdaleno, M. 2018. Imagen de la Casa del Migrante en Ciudad Juárez. Recuperado de Google Maps.

Magdaleno, M. 2018. Imagen de la Casa del Migrante en Ciudad Juárez. Recuperado de Google Maps.

Ríos, J. 2018. Imagen de la Casa del Migrante en Ciudad Juárez. Recuperado de Google Maps.

RELIGIOUS CONSCIOUSNESS IN THE CONTEXT OF THE MIGRATION SITUATION: CASE OF RUSSIA

Irina Savchenko

Introductiom

The largest share of the immigrant community in the regions of central Russia is formed by immigrants from post-Soviet states where Islam is the traditional religion. The shared Soviet past facilitates the mutual integration of immigrants and members of the host community (Taran et al 2016). However, there are significant contradictions in the religious consciousness of migrants and one of the citizens of the host community. The author conducted a survey study and found some trends that are typical not only for Russia, but also for many immigrant countries (Collins-Mayo 2012), (Horwath et al 2008), in the history of which Christianity played a leading role in previous eras.

Background of the issue

In the Russian Empire (before 1917) free people had passports and there was a count of religion: Orthodox, Lutheran, Catholic, Mohammedan, Buddhist, Jew... In the Soviet Union, which replaced the Russian Empire, the ideology changed. The column about religious affiliation disappeared from the passport. There was now a column about the nationality and criminal record.

In 1926, a census was held, and more than half of the population of the Soviet Union could not say who they were by nationality, but they still pointed out their religious affiliation. At that time, this applied equally to Christians, Muslims and representatives of other religious movements. However, the situation was beginning to change rapidly.

The cultural identity of those whose ancestors considered themselves Orthodox Christians was changing especially rapidly. In the Soviet Union churches were blown up, other church buildings were turned into warehouses. Church property was seized, holy places were desecrated, church utensils were destroyed, priests were persecuted. An active religious position was fraught with great problems at work and, especially, at an educational institution (for students). Most of those who are now over 65 years old were baptized, but they were baptized secretly.

Not only Christians, but all religious movements were under pressure. However, it was the Orthodox Christians who experienced the most serious pressure. It was Orthodoxy that was once considered the antipode of communist ideology.

As for the southern native Muslim republics of the USSR (Tajikistan, Kazakhstan, Uzbekistan, Kyrgyzstan, Azerbaijan), the Soviet government there relied on local elites representing certain clans. And these elites were in no hurry to conflict with the population and destroy the traditional religious way of life.

Meanwhile, the attitude of Russians to Orthodoxy has changed dramatically over the past century. While in the minds of millions of Orthodox Russians the religious component became less and less significant, Soviet Muslims preserved their religious identity. Apparently, there is still a complex of reasons here. The Orthodox regions have experienced more violence in the USSR. Besides, Orthodoxy, like all Christianity, was in a state of crisis already at the beginning of the 20th century. Finally, Islam today really has a passionate charge – the same as Christianity possessed in the Middle Ages. However, the attitude of Russians to Orthodoxy has changed dramatically over the past century.

After the collapse of the Soviet Union, as it always happens, people from the outskirts of the empire rushed to the metropolis. Natives from traditionally Islamic territories began to arrive in huge numbers in the native Orthodox Russian regions.

Data source and method

Against the background of the current situation, the author conducted an empirical study, the **purpose** of which was to reveal some significant contradictions in the youth religious consciousness of migrants and one of the citizens of the host community on the example of Russia.

The survey (2019-2020) was conducted in the following Russian cities: Nizhny Novgorod, St. Petersburg, Vladimir, Kirov, Ivanovo, Penza, Perm, Ryazan, Irkutsk, Michurinsk, Shuya. The age of respondents was from 18 to 35 years. The sample was represented by migrants (n =173) from the Muslim republics of the former Soviet Union and by indigenous residents (n = 947) of Russian cities. The statistical error of the data is no more than 4.7%.

Survey results

The author interviewed young native inhabitants and young Muslim migrants and found a number of surprising moments concerning the attitude of young people to religion. It is important to study the religious consciousness of today's youth (Fedorova, Rotanova, Boryshneva 2017). After all, it is in the youth environment that the ethno-confessional atmosphere of the future is formed. The respondents were asked a number of questions, the answers to which allowed to shed some light on the problem posed.

Figure 1. *"Do you believe in God?"*: responses from residents and Muslim immigrants

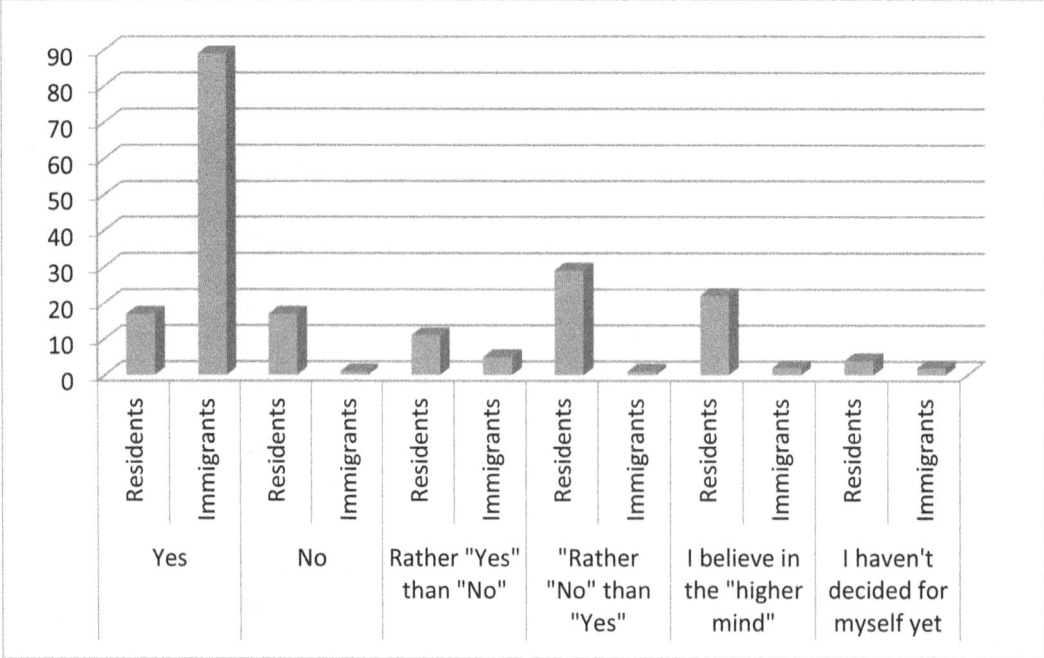

First of all, the author asked the respondents whether they believe in God. It turned that almost 90% of Muslim migrants believe in God. Of the Russians, only 17% admitted believing in God (Figure 1).

Figure 2. *"Are you a religious person?"*: responses from residents and Muslim immigrants

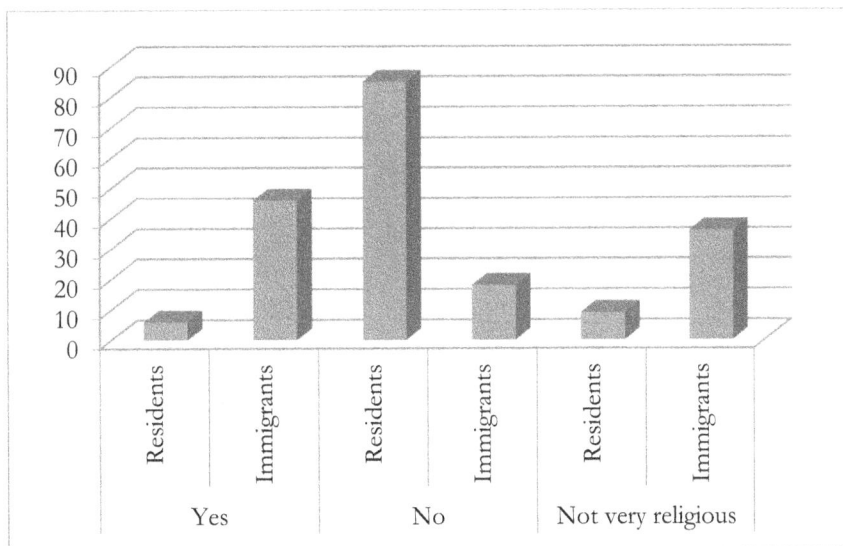

However, almost half of migrants and only 6% of Russians consider themselves religious (Figure 2).

Figure 3. "What is your attitude towards Orthodox religious (believers) people?": responses from residents and Muslim immigrants

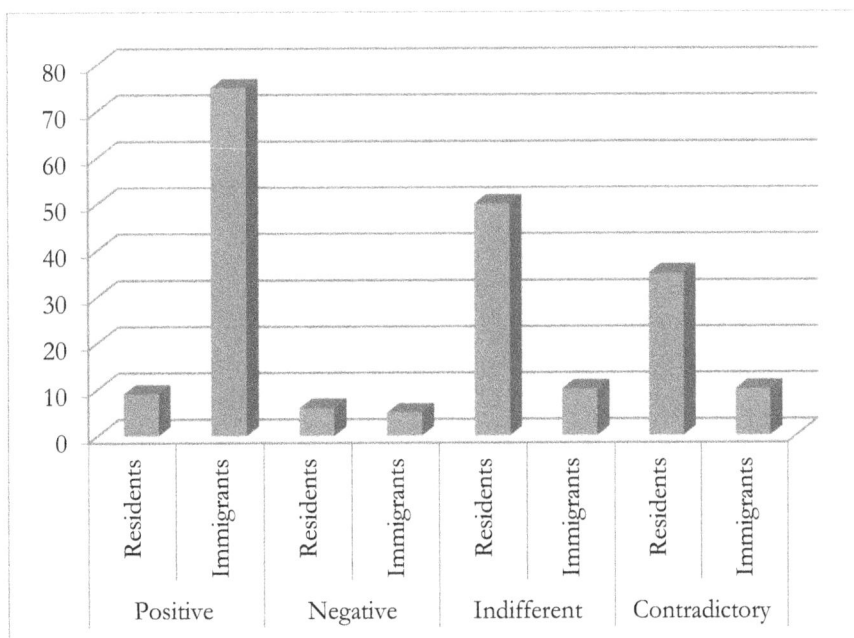

According to the respondents' answers, 75% of migrants are well-disposed towards Orthodox believers, while the majority of Russians clearly dislike people who regularly go to church, or try to stay

away from them (Figure 3).

Figure 4. "Do you differentiate between the Orthodox Church and the Orthodox religion?": responses from residents and Muslim immigrants

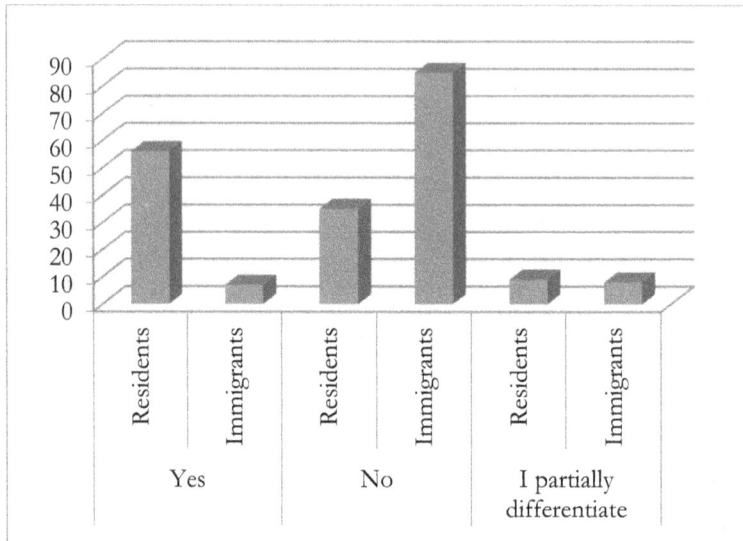

At the same time, it is quite expected that for most migrants, the Orthodox religion and the Orthodox Church are practically the same, while Russians tend to differentiate these concepts. Russians definitely have a more positive attitude to the religion as a whole than to the church (Figure 4).

Figure 5. "*What is your attitude towards Christianity?*": responses from residents and Muslim immigrants

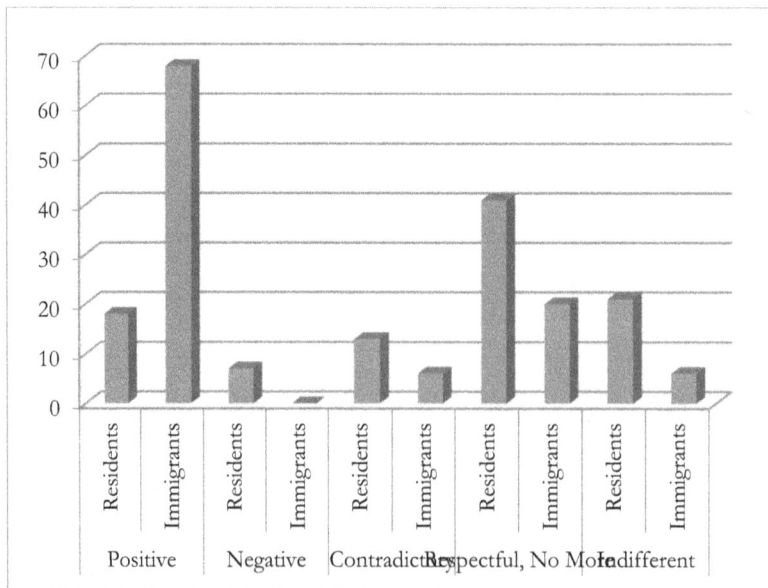

Immigrants (68%) have a positive attitude to Christianity, that cannot be said about residents (only 18%). Russians (41%) are more likely to treat Christianity with respect, but no more (Figure 5).

Figure 6. "*What is your attitude to the Russian Orthodox Church?*": responses from residents and Muslim

immigrants

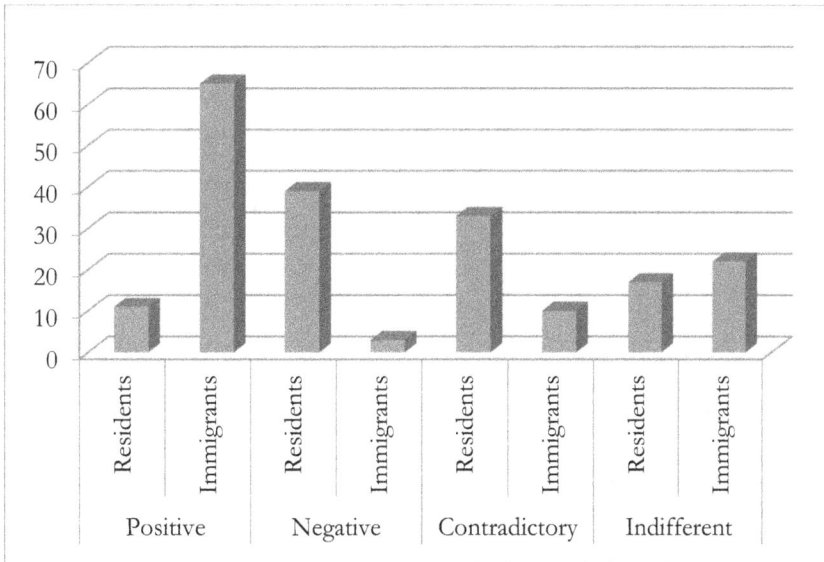

Russians do not have particularly warm feelings towards the Russian Orthodox Church as a social institution, while migrants think quite differently and treat this institution rather positively (Figure 6). The trend persists with regard to Orthodox clergy (Figure 7).

Figure 7. *"What is your attitude towards the Orthodox clergy?":* responses from residents and Muslim immigrants

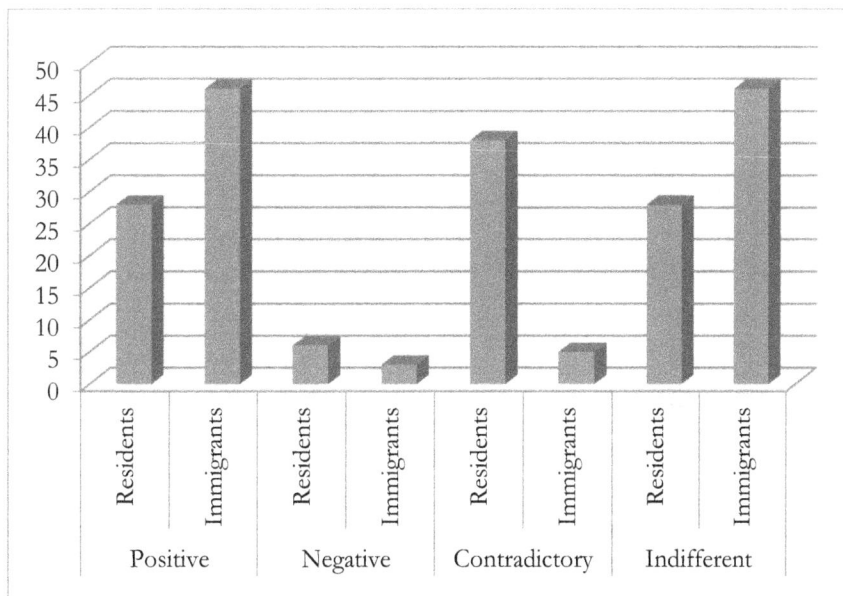

Figure 8. *"What is your attitude to Islam?":* responses from residents and Muslim immigrants

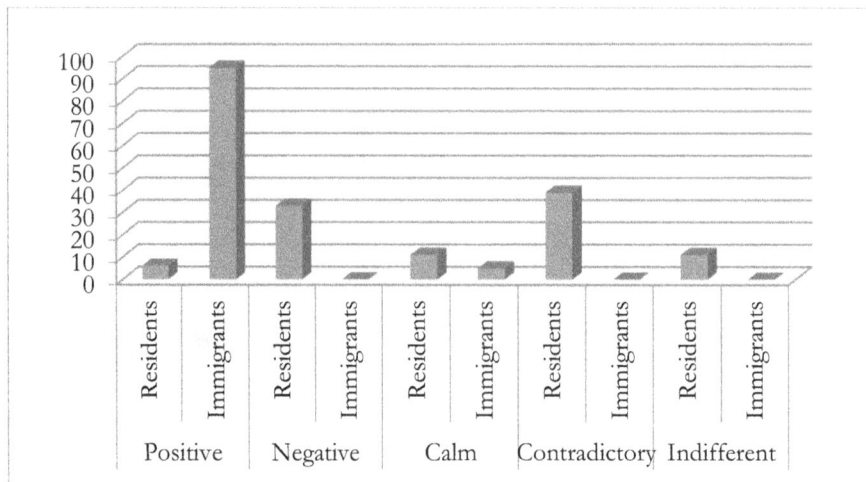

We couldn't help but ask a question about Islam. Clearly, 95% of migrants perceive it positively (5% are "calm" about Islam). And only 6% of residents have a positive attitude to Islam. Among Russians, the answers are "negative" (33%) and "contradictory" (39%) (Figure 8).

Figure 9. "What is your attitude to other religious movements (Buddhism, Judaism, Hinduism (including Krishnas and Zen Buddhists), etc.)?": responses from residents and Muslim immigrants

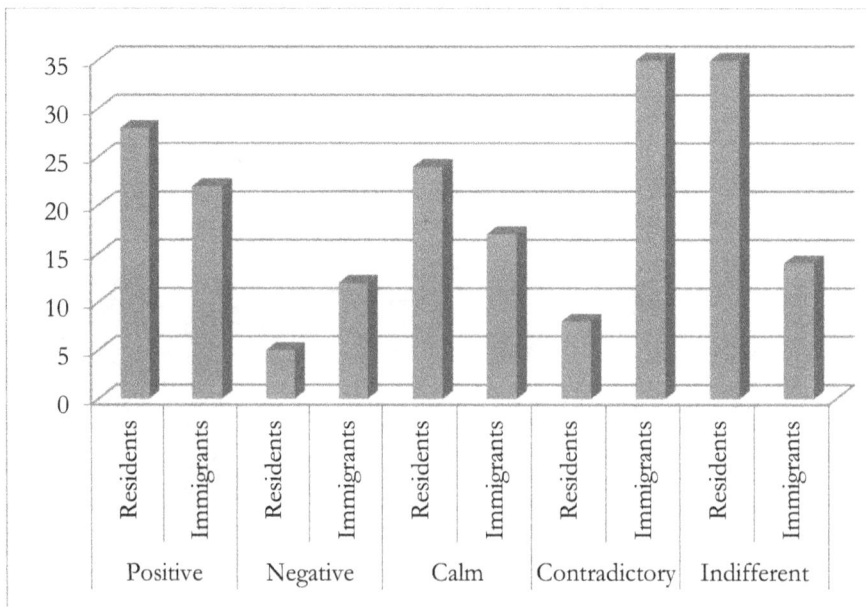

As for the attitude of local residents and migrants to other religions (in addition to Islam and Christianity), Muslims here are more wary and suspicious (Figure 9).

The survey allows to get some idea of the religious situation in modern Russian society, which today, of course, is an immigrant one. Moreover, it is likely that the trends in the development of religious consciousness among the youth of most modern immigrant communities are similar.

Conclusion

When a migrant from a Muslim country or region comes to central Russia, he sees an unusual picture. He sees a rather cool attitude of the host community towards their elderly people, their own culture and their own religion. When it comes to adaptation, the migrant faces a natural question: what exactly should he adapt to? The immigrant gets the impression that the host society can not transfer anything to him, except for the workplace, although here, of course, there are considerable difficulties (Khattab, Sirkeci, Johnston, Modood 2011). What is acculturation, in addition to language acquisition (Savchenko, Barseghyan 2021)? It is no coincidence that many immigrants have told that they feel an inner "spiritual" superiority over the locals, who "do not believe in anything", who "have forgotten who they are" and "where they come from". Nevertheless, even among Muslim migrants, spiritual transformations are beginning. A certain part of them tries to match the way of life of local residents and is quickly marginalized.

At the beginning of my article, I spoke about the destruction of religion and the church in the Soviet Union. Therefore, the current picture can be considered as a consequence of the events of the Soviet period. But is it so? We cannot deny that there are some tendencies that are peculiar only to Russian society but also to for majority of societies whose historical development was associated with any of the branches of Christianity. In completely different ways, Russia and the West came to about the same situation. I would call this situation a cultural crisis, since no culture has emerged and reached heights outside of religion.

References

Collins-Mayo, S 2012 'Youth and religion. An international perspective', *Theo-Web. Zeitschrädaift für Religionspgogik, no. 11, h.1*, pp. 80-94.

Horwath, J, Lees J, Sidebotham, P, Higgins, J & Imtiaz, A 2008 'Religion, beliefs and parenting practices. A descriptive study', *Sheffield: University of Sheffield,* 66 p.

Khattab, N, Sirkeci, I, Johnston, R, and Modood, T 2011 'Ethnicity, religion, residential segregation and life chances'." *In: T. Modood and J. Salt (eds.) Global Migration, Ethnicity and Britishness, Palgrave Macmillan, pp.153-176.*

Taran, PA, Neves de Lima, G, Kadysheva, O & Vardinoyannis, MV 2016 'Cities welcoming refugees and migrants: enhancing effective urban governance in an age of migration', *UNESCO. Director-General, 2009-2017 (Bokova, I.G.).* 87 p.

Savchenko, IA, Barseghyan, SS 2021 'Bilingualism as a phenomenon of transcultural communication in foreign language teaching', *Tomsk State University Journal, 2021, no 463, pp. 188-195.*

Fedorova, M. Rotanova, M, Boryshneva, N 2017 'Religious values of Russian youth', 4th international multidisciplinary scientific conference on social sciences and arts SGEM2017 : conference proceedings, Albena, Bulgaria, P. 585-592.

UNDERSTANDING THE ENABLERS AND BARRIERS IN HEALTH SERVICE ACCESS AMONG COVID-19-INFECTED REFFUGEES IN TURKEY

Seyda Eruyar[1], Hatice Betül Yücekaya[2], Gökçe Baydoğan[3], Huriye Tak[4], and Rabia Olucak[5]

This study provides insights on the experiences of Covid-19 Infected refugees in accessing health services in Turkey. Semi-structured interviews were conducted online with 17 adult refugees who were diagnosed with COVID-19 from three distinct of Turkey, i.e. İstanbul, Kahramanmaras, and Konya. Data were analysed through a thematic approach. The results revealed two themes: enablers and barriers. Most participants highlighted that they have no difficulty accessing health services, including having tests, medication, and in-patient care. Fewer participants had difficulty in accessing health services because of registration issues, language barrier and limited knowledge about service utilisation.

Keywords: refugee, health service access, enablers, barriers, disease awareness, Covid-19 pandemic

Introduction

A total of 4 million migrants, consisting in 3.6 Million Syrian citizen, and approx. 330,000 other Migrants and migrants of other nations is living in Turkey (Directorate General of Migration Management, Date of Data: 28.07.2021). Taking the unregistered individuals into account, this figure is estimated to be over 4 million.

Migrants living in Turkey are able to get primary and secondary health services. In addition to primary and secondary healthcare services, Migrant Health Centers and family doctors offer internal medicine, child, gynecology, oral and dental health and psychosocial support services (Migrant Health Centers, 2017). Nevertheless, migrants living in Turkey encounter certain restrictions and barriers in accessing healthcare services.

Firstly, obligation of registration and complicated registration process is the major challenge for migrants. According to rules of health services to be given to Syrian, those who have not completed registration can only benefit from contagious and epidemic prevention services and emergency (İlhan et al., 2016).

Mobility of the migrants is another obstacle to sustaining access to health services. According to the regulations, it is essential that those under temporarily protection (TP) receive health services in the province they have been registered. Syrian who are under TP frequently change places in order to find work. Meanwhile, they lost their access to health services. More important physical obstacle to increase accessibility of vulnerable groups is low health literacy. Comprehensive Health Literacy (CHL) refers to "literacy and entails people's knowledge, motivation and competences to access, understand,

[1] Department of Psychology, Necmettin Erbakan University, Turkey
[2] Turkish Red Crescent, Community Based Migration Programmes, SPSS Programme, Turkey
[3] Turkish Red Crescent, Community Based Migration Programmes, Mersin Community Center, Turkey
[4] Turkish Red Crescent, Community Based Migration Programmes, İstanbul Community Center, Turkey
[5] Turkish Red Crescent, Community Based Migration Programmes, Kahramanmaraş Community Center, Turkey

appraise and apply health information in order to make judgements and take decisions in everyday life concerning health care, disease prevention and health promotion to maintain or improve quality of life during the life course" (Sørensen et al., 2015). In a study conducted among 513 refugees speaking Arabic, Dari, and Somali, it was founded that Limitation in CHL was associated with having reported poor health and having refrained from seeking healthcare (Wångdahl et al., 2018).

In addition to the challenges associated with being included in the health system, refugees also face some difficulties within the health system. The most prominent difficulty is the language barrier. Hospitals in Turkey, the language of the appointment system and call centres are in Turkish. Although Syrians make an appointment on their own or with someone's assistance, they have difficulty in describing their physical or mental problem or understanding treatment that the doctor prescribe (Bilecen & Yurtseven, 2018).

Access to Health Services of Migrants in Turkey During Covid-19 Pandemic

Migrants face with difficulties in accessing healthcare services under the conditions of the Covid-19 pandemic in addition to registration issues, language barrier and low health literacy. Fear of deportation, stigmatization and socioeconomic challenges such as living in crowded households, losing the job and living rural areas are other difficulties for migrants, which emerges in pandemic conditions (Özvarış et al., 2020).

COVID-19 pandemic has been resulting in unprecedented economic and social consequences across the World. Where measures to prevent the disease and health service provision fell short in many countries during the pandemic, refugees became among the most vulnerable groups as they have preexisting adverse living conditions such as crowded households, poor living conditions, limited access to services and economic hardships (Brickhill-Atkinson & Hauck, 2021). Yet, little is known about the constituents of health service access among migrants resettled in the Majority World Countries and especially experiences of migrants infected Covid-19. Thus, this study aimed to understand the experiences of refugees in Turkey and diagnosed with Covid-19 in terms of their access to health-care system and the challenges they faced in this course.

Method

Paticipants: 17 adult migrant diagnosed with COVID-19 were recruited using a purposive sampling approach from 3 distinct provinces of Turkey (İstanbul, Konya and Kahramanmaraş). Two of participants were Turkmen and rest of them were from Syrian. The sample size was determined by thematic saturation.

Procedure: Semi-structured interviews were carried out between 2 November 2020 and 30 December 2020 in the participants' preferred language (in Arabic). During these months, number of new cases increased to 30.000. Interviews are carried out by psychologists who have master degree in clinical psychology through a video communication application with assistant of a professional interpreter.

Data Analysis: All interviews were transcribed and translated by an interpreter. Data were coded using a Thematic analysis approach through CATMA. The authors read 17 transcripts independently in order to generate main and sub codes and then, held discussions to reconcile discrepancies in the assignment of codes and their interpretation.

Results

The demographic information of the participants and the disease symptoms they describe are presented below (see Table 1).

Table 1. Demographic Information and Symptoms

Participant No	Gender	Age	Occupation	Symptoms (Stated)
P1	Male	27	Laborer	Aches, fever
P2	Male	23	Laborer	Ache, fatigue, loss of taste and smell
P3	Male	21	Laborer	Cough, mild fever
P4	Female	21	-	Aches, fatigue, loss of teste and smell, difficulty breathing
P5	Male	24	Laborer	Fatigue, fever, diarrhea
P6	Female	43	-	Headache
P7	Male	40	Laborer	Fatigue, fever, cough, diarrhea
P8	Female	21	-	Cough, loss of taste and smell, difficulty breathing
P9	Male	27	Laborer	Fatigue, loss of taste and smell
P10	Female	32	-	Fatigue, loss of taste and smell
P11	Female	60	-	Fatigue, fever, aches
P12	Female	32	Teacher	Fatigue, difficulty breathing
P13	Female	43	-	Fatigue, fever, difficulty breathing
P14	Female	40	Teacher	Aches, fever, loss of taste and smell
P15	Female	27	-	Aches, loss of taste and smell
P16	Male	21	Student	Sore throat, fatigue, aches
P17	Male	25	Skilled Laborer	Aches, fever, difficulty breathing

The results revealed two themes: enablers and barriers. The enablers theme consisted of two sub-themes and the barrier theme consisted of three sub-themes (see Tablo 2).

Tablo 2. Themes

Results	Themes	Sub-themes
1	**Enablers**	• Good level of knowledge about the disease and related symptoms
		Having preexisting chronic disease
2	**Barriers**	• Being registered in another city • Language Barrier
		Limited knowledge about service utilisation

Discussion

The first theme, "the enablers in accessing health services" included high awareness of disease and transmission. Good level of knowledge about the disease and related symptoms, and having preexisting chronic disease prompted participants to apply to the hospitals. Most participants highlighted that they have no difficulty accessing health services, including having tests, medication, and in-patient care. They also reported that family practitioners made calls to check their health status after diagnosis. Moreover, participants with high awareness of transmission took precautionary measures before applying to hospitals, including wearing masks, applying hygiene practices and self-quarantine. Social media was reported as a source of knowledge, although the misinformation spread through the media regarding the disease caused anxiety in some participants. In the study conducted by SGDD-ASAM (2020), it is found that 85% of the survey participants who felt the necessity to benefit from health-care services in the course of Covid-19 had an access to the health-care services.

The second theme, 'the barriers', identify the difficulties in accessing health services. Fewer participants had difficulty in accessing health services because of registration issues. A participant stated that he had to apply private hospital as he was registered in another city. In the survey conducted by Relief International (2020) on the access to health-care services involving 879 Migrants in 6 cities, 71% of the it is found that 71% of the participants (especially metropolises such as Istanbul and Izmir where the access to services are relatively harder) cannot access the health-care service. Likewise, the survey of Care (2020) involving 426 Syrian migrants in Gaziantep, Şanlıurfa and Kilis demonstrated that 63% of the participants (especially elders and persons with disabilities) have reduced access to health-care services due to Covid-19 pandemic. Survey of MUDEM (2020) involving 385 migrants from 19 cities of Turkey showed that 26% of the participants who applied to the hospital units could not benefit from the health-care services, compared to 74% who could access the health-care services. Most of the individuals who said that they could not access the health-care service stated that they could not benefit from the health-care services due to the lack of appointment or going hospital without wearing a mask (Küçükşen, & Sayın 2020). In addition, it is known that during pandemic, the capacities of the pandemic services have been increased and accordingly the service capacity in other departments of the hospitals has been reduced.

The language was another barrier for some participants as it causes communication problems with health workers and made it difficult for them to express related symptoms. Turkey has been trying to solve this problem by employing translators, but the number of translators is not enough to serve all the needy one (Ekmekçi, 2016; İlhan et al., 2016).

Another barrier to access the health-care services is limited knowledge about service utilisation. Syrian refugees under TP constitutes approximately 4.40% of the total population of Turkey; this has been an unexpected increase the need in the health system (Ekmekci, 2017). Therefore, Turkish healthcare system is going through a general transformation process. Although healthcare services were standardized for individuals under TP by including them in the public health insurance system via the introduction of new laws and regulations, regulations and rules related to individuals under TP is still the most dynamic part of this transition process (Bilecen & Yurtseven, 2018). Therefore, the first difficulty encountered by Syrians in Turkey is their adaptation to the health care system including making appointments with clinics and the referral system used by doctors and healthcare personnel (Destek, 2016) and accessing correct information in accessing public services in the local community (Önder, 2019).

Conclusion

Understanding the refugees' experiences is essential in establishing their needs and increasing health service access. These findings suggest that the refugee population needs to be informed about the COVID-19, transmission and service usage, and language support should be provided by having interpreters presented at hospitals to increase the health service access.

References

Bilecen, B., & Yurtseven, D. (2018). Temporarily protected Syrians' access to the healthcare system in Turkey: Changing policies and remaining challenges. *Migration Letters, 15*(1), 113-124.

Brickhill-Atkinson, M., & Hauck, F. R. (2021). Impact of COVID-19 on resettled refugees. Primary Care: Clinics in Office Practice, 48(1), 57-66. https://doi.org/10.1016/j.pop.2020.10.001

Care. (May 2020). COVID-19 Impact Assessment, South East Turkey. Retrieved from https://reliefweb.int/report/turkey/

covid-19-impact-assessment-south-east-turkey-may-2020

Destek, H. (2016). İstanbul'daki suriyeli mültecilere ilişkin zarar görebilirlik değerlendirme raporu. Retrieved from https://www.hayatadestek.org/wp-content/uploads/2019/06/istanbuldaki-suriyeli-multeciler-zarar-gorebilirlik-raporu.pdf

Ekmekci, P. E. (2017). Syrian refugees, health and migration legislation in Turkey. *Journal of immigrant and minority health*, *19*(6), 1434-1441.

Göç İdaresi Genel Müdürlüğü - İstatistikler. (2021). (Directorate General of Migration Management – Statistics). Retrieved from https://www.goc.gov.tr/gecici-koruma5638

Güleç G., Erdoğan Taycan S., Başar K. (2020). Covid-19 ve mülteciler. (Covid-19 and Refugee) Türkiye Psikiyatri Derneği Ruhsal Travma ve Afet Çalışma Birimi. (Psychological Trauma and Disaster Working Unit of Psychiatry Society of Turkey)

İlhan, M. N., Gözlü, M., Atasever, M., Dündar, M. A., Büyükgök, D., & Barkan, O. B. (2016). Göç ve halk sağlığı. *SASAM Enstitüsü Analiz*, *2*(7), 1-24.

Küçükşen D., & Sayın N. G., (2020) Covid-19'un Mülteciler Üzerindeki Etkisine İlişkin Raporlara Dayalı Sistematik Bir Derleme. (A Systematic Compilation on Reports on Effects of Covid-19 on Refugees). Sığınmacılar ve Göçmenler Dayanışma Derneği. (Refugges and Migrants Solidarity Society)

Migrant Health Centers (2017). Retrieved from https://hsgm.saglik.gov.tr/tr/g%C3%B6%C3%A7men-sa%C4%9Fl%C4%B1%C4%9F%C4%B1-merkezleri.html

MUDEM. (2020). "COVID-19 Krizi Sürecinde Türkiye'deki Mültecilerin Durum Analizi". (Situational Analyis on Refugees in Turkey During COVID-19 Crisis)

Önder, N. (2019). Türkiye'de Geçici Koruma Altındaki Suriyelilere Yönelik Sağlık Politikalarının Analizi. *Göç Araştırmaları Dergisi*, *5*(1), 110-165.

Özvarış, Ş. B., Kayı, İ., Mardin, D., Sakarya, S., Ekzayez, A., Meagher, K., & Patel, P. (2020). COVID-19 barriers and response strategies for refugees and undocumented migrants in Turkey. *Journal of Migration and Health*, *1*, 100012.

Relief International. (2020). "Impact of the COVID-19 Outbreak on Syrian Refugees in Turkey-Results from Rapid Needs Assessment Conducted in Istanbul, Izmir, Manisa, Gaziantep, Kilis and Reyhanli".

SGDD-ASAM. (May 2020) "COVID-19 Salgınının Türkiye'de Mülteciler Üzerindeki Etkilerinin Sektörel Analizi". (Sectoral Analysis of Effects of COVID-19 Pandemic on Refugees in Turkey.)

Sørensen, K., Pelikan, J. M., Röthlin, F., Ganahl, K., Slonska, Z., Doyle, G., & Falcon, M. (2015). Health literacy in Europe: comparative results of the European health literacy survey (HLS-EU). *European journal of public health*, *25*(6), 1053-1058.

Wångdahl, J., Lytsy, P., Mårtensson, L., & Westerling, R. (2018). Poor health and refraining from seeking healthcare are associated with comprehensive health literacy among refugees: a Swedish cross-sectional study. *International journal of public health*, *63*(3), 409-419.

RIVER AND MEMORIES: MIGRATION, ECOLOGY AND LANDSCAPE IN THE NARRATIVES OF INDIA'S PARTITION

Anuparna Mukherjee

Keywords: Migrants' Literature, Memory, Landscape, 1947-Partition

(1)

The creative literature that grew out of the event of India's Partition in 1947, which resulted in the uprooting of nearly twelve million people across the borders not only embodies one of the most significant sites of mourning but also explores the variegated responses to the violence through spatial memories associated with trauma and nostalgia. In *Partition Dialogues*, Alok Bhalla purports that India's vivisection into two nation-states, and the subsequent exchange of population based on their religious identities not only dislocated the migrants from their homes but also from their sensory world rife with words like "friendship", "neighbourhood" with which they had forged strong emotive bonds. So, nostalgia became a cardinal affect underpinning migrant narratives and aesthetics, replete with allusions to the life of abundance amidst the natural environment in the former home(land), as opposed to the cramped spaces of the refugee ghettos that severely ruptured the everyday rituals which gave shape and meaning to home.

 The memories of the landscape, weaving itself in the syncretic social and cultural life of the migrants is repeatedly evoked in literature, oral poetry, songs and other artefacts of folk culture. Some of the most vivid pictures of such an idyllic village are found in poets such as Jibanananda Das, especially, in his collection of pre-Partition sonnets, *Rupashi Bangla* (*Bengal Beautiful*) composed around 1934 and published posthumously in 1957. In one of the better-known poems of the anthology, Das writes:

> I have looked on the face of Bengal: nowhere else shall I go to see
>
> the loveliness of the Earth; waking in dark I discover
>
> dawn's *doyel*-bird in a fig-tree; above it I see hover
>
> a large leaf like an umbrella—and mounds of tree-greenery,
>
> *jaam bat, kanthal, hijal ashwattha* on all sides silently
>
> over cactus-thicket and shati-bush throw shadow-cover;
>
> but when did Chand from his bee-boat near Champa look out over
>
> that blueish shade? —*hijal bat tamal*—Bengal past loveliness…
>
> (Trans. Joe Winter; 2)

Here, Das's poetry restores nostalgia to the mundane life with such phrases, metaphors, names and idioms that are deep-set in the spatio-cultural memory of his land. The language, which is an important conduit for sustaining this reality, is loaded with myth, history and tradition, and is almost conceptualised as flowing out of the body of "mother Bengal" in its intimacy with the earth and earth-born creatures.

Alison Hui in her essay, *Placing Nostalgia* explores such affective attachment to places by "thinking about place and affects as not static states or entities but rather mobile processes that are practised repeatedly. People can return home through imaginative mobilities to their places of memory, and these imaginative mobilities are unhindered by financial resources or temporal constraints" (81). And nostalgia is one such affect which facilitates this "imaginative mobility" that is vividly articulated in migrant literature and art to resuscitate the vital links between the "self-in-present" and the "self-in-past", fractured by the Partition.

When the Partition refugees relocated to distant and inhospitable places in their adopted country, they missed the familiar surroundings, especially the landscape of undivided Bengal around which the communities constructed their everyday histories and identities. The sudden transformation wrought by the catastrophe of Partition irrevocably altered their cultural, linguistic and economic environments, along with food habits that heavily incorporated pescatarian meals, compounding their sense of bewilderment and loss. Thus, there are constant evocations of the water-bodies, transports and livelihoods in songs (the musical traditions of India and Bangladesh— *bhatiyali, Majhigaan* —are noteworthy in this respect), demotic performances, oral and written recollections of the migrants whose humdrum, habitual practices were rooted in the riverine ecology of lower Bengal. In the short story, *The Road* by Ritwik Kumar Ghatak, for instance, all the memories of land left behind are attached to the river that recurs in the young refugee boy's song filled with yearning:

> The river is red where rises the red run
>
> Blushing with love at the red sky
>
> Follow the course of the red river as it flows into its estuary
>
> O the boat of my soul, driven by desire. (16)

To these lines, expressive of the refugees' powerlessness and desire, the narrator observes that "the abounding immensity of the Padma carried aloft by the strains of that melody entered our souls while we stood under the reddening dawn there. (16-17)" The affective content of such memories, both collective and individual, profoundly impacted the resettlement pattern of the migrants in their host country. The next section will particularly focus on these rivers and their entanglements in literary narratives by delving into the fluvial memories of deltaic Bengal in the inscriptions of space and identity.

(2)

The overwhelming emphasis on the natural surroundings in the literary corpus on the Partition memories is partially due to the sudden breakdown of intimacies between communities owing to the escalating religious tension which eventually led to the riots and mass migration. Thus, one obverses a subtle displacement of emotions from man to nature in various manifestations of nostalgia and trauma. And Bengal being situated in the largest delta of the world surrounded by rivers, marshes and estuarine bodies, fluvial imagery saturated the spatial memories of the dispossessed in their new habitats. Tarashankar Banerjee in his renowned novel, the *Tale of the Hansuli Turn (1951)* calls Bengal "a river country" which is followed by a heady narration of the Bengal's aqueous, riverine landscape:

Water and land all mixed up. Rivers running full a twelvemonth; tide comes in, water pours over

riverbanks, brimming in green fields; flow tide then ebb tide...when the river course empties, banks surface....Like the flow of Ganges-Jamuna, dark and eerie; their folks get the shakes setting off to cross from one side to the other. And just one stream? Where one stream comes and joins from, where the flows split and go—can't tell. It's like a seven-stranded water necklace—not a hansuli! River bends ever end over there? "Eighteen Bender," "Thirty Bender," river looks different every turn (Bandyopadhyay 4, *trans.* Ben Conisbee Baer).

However, this locational dynamic also exposed a large cross-section of the community to natural disasters ranging from cyclones, the erosion of embankments, formation and sudden disappearances of silt-beds to recurrent floods of varying intensity, thereby, reminding us of the proverb "Life by a river, year-long worry-giver" (Bandyopadhyay 4). This became the mainstay of a genre of "river-centric literature" in Eastern India where geography and spatial identity shaped the intimate, regional lifeworlds of the riverine population of anglers, boatmen, small farmers, and fishing communities within the novelistic form through an "enmeshment" of the human and the natural in the literary aesthetics. Many of these works coming from prominent writers such as Manik Bandopadhyay, Debesh Roy, Samaresh Basu, Advaita Mallabarman and Tarashankar Bandyopadhyay, captured the beauty and the terror of this precarious environment of deltaic Bengal through the struggle of the indigent subaltern classes for survival against natural calamities and the oppression of river bandits, big merchants, landlords and moneylenders. Sourit Bhattacharya in his essay on "peripheral aesthetics in Indian Literature" analyses Tarashankar Bandyopadhyay's *Hansuli Banker Upakatha* to unpack how divergent "regional narratives have repeatedly demonstrated the complex links between social dynamics, tribal cultural and ecological beliefs, and diverse negotiations of the traditional-rural and the urban-modern – aspects" (1-2), which Bhattacharya reads together as "regional ecologies". Here, I will briefly dwell on this assertion by alluding to Advaita Mallabarman's *A River Called Titash* which was later made into a film by Ritwik Kumar Ghatak. It chronicles the gradual decline and dispersion of the *Malos*, the native fisherman community residing on the banks of Titash—a "150- mile long channel" that loops away from the *Meghna* River. Right at the outset, the author crafts the singular, albeit tragic lifeworld along the river-steam. In a land of proliferating water-bodies, it is almost a customary practice in all the riverine novels to set apart its river from the other streams in the introductory chapter by evoking the differential cultural geographies, forms, practices and beliefs. So, every river is known by its singularity, and Titash is no exception to the rule:

Titash is the name of a river. Its banks brim with water, its surface is alive with ripples, its heart exuberant.

It flows in the rhythm of a dream....

... The river Titash does not hold the awesome terror of the Padma and the Meghna....It is a medium-size river....

On the banks of so many rivers once rose the ramparts of the indigo merchants' estates; their ruins still meet the searching eye. So many rivers saw the armies of the Pathans and the Mughals pitch tents on their banks....How the waters of those rivers ran red with the blood of people and of horses and elephants. Perhaps some of those rivers are dry today, but they have left their marks in the pages of scholarly books. Titash holds no such grand history in its bosom. It is simply a river…(Mallabarman 11, *trans Kalpana Bardhan*)

Of course, despite its nondescript, tranquil appearance, Titash is not "simply a river". Its trajectory is deeply entwined with the evolution of the *Malo* fishing community, whose quotidian life pulsates with the rhythm of the stream. To start with, the river bolsters their economy and identity, but in course of the novel, as it slowly dries up altering its terrain, the close-knit and brittle universe of the fishermen falls apart. With the shrinking of their lifeline, people are reduced to penury and starvation. The narrative ends on a poignant note signalling the dispersion and gradual disappearance of the inhabitants, whose local world is erased unceremoniously from history. What is captured as literary and cinematic memory on celluloid finds a parallel in the context of post-Partition India and Bangladesh. The fraught issues of water-sharing, environmental justice and survival had their bearing on the bilateral relationship between the two countries at different historical junctures.

The drying of riverbeds, inundation of banks or the chocking of the channels due to heavy deposition of silt or alluvium by the big rivers are common challenges in the deltaic regions. Their impacts are intensified in this context by the transnational or transboundary distribution of water resources between the two neighbours. It brings up the knotted problem of apportioning the geopolitical landscape to different countries in a manner that supports a neat or discrete division since the rivers constantly alter their borders with new sedimentations, seasonal flooding and the change of courses. In overt and implicit ways, the legacy of the Partition has, thus, engendered new precariats whose lands and livelihoods are affected in the vulnerable tidal lowlands.

Culminating with the thought of how the partitioning of the ecological resources with the etching of new geopolitical borders impacted the marginal riverine communities whose material and spiritual worlds are imbricated in their relationship with the physical environment, the paper, created a framework to argue the ways in which the rivers imbue local, political and mythical values to the human sense of place that ripens in our everyday experiences and transmits as a memory when individuals move and negotiate with their manifold "social relations" across time-space.

Work Cited

Bandyopadhyay, Tarashankar. *The Tale of Hansuli Turn*. Translated by Ben Conisbee Baer. Columbia UP, 2011.

Bhalla, Alok. Partition Dialogues: Memories of a Lost Home. Oxford UP, 2006, p.7.

Bhattacharya, Sourit. "Regional Ecologies and Peripheral Aesthetics in Indian Literature: Tarashankar Bandyopadhyay's *Hansuli Banker Upakatha*". *South Asian Review,* 2021, pp. 1-16.

Das, Jibanananda. *Bengal the Beautiful*. Translated by Joe Winter, Anvil P, 2006.

Ghatak, Ritwik Kumar. "The Road". Translated by Rani Ray. *Mapmaking: Partition Stories from Two Bengals*. Srishti, 2003, (pp. 23-39), p.25

Hui, Allison. "Placing Nostalgia: The Process of Returning and Remaking Home." *Ecologies of Affect: Placing Nostalgia, Desire, and Hope*. Edited by Tonya K. Davidson and, Ondine Park, Wilfrid Laurier UP, 2011, pp. 85-104.

Mallabarman, Adwaita. *A River Called Titash*. Translated by Kalpana Bardhan. U of California P, 1993.

GENDER, AGENCY, AND THE SOCIAL IMAGINARY IN JAPANESE LIFESTYLE MIGRATION TO EUROPE

Yana Yovcheva

Abstract

Gender, agency, and the social imaginary all feature prominently in lifestyle migration, but their relationship with one another has hardly been explored. This paper examines the impact gender has on Japanese lifestyle migrants' engagement with the social imaginary about European destinations and the exercise of agency in subsequent migration decisions. The research finds that Japanese women generally indulge in imagining a life abroad and act on the imagined (i.e., exercise agency) much more freely and resolutely than men do. Also, that imagining a life in (Western) Europe in particular is characteristic of Japanese women, rather than men.

Introduction

Lifestyle migration has been a growing phenomenon in the last few decades – both in the West and in the richer parts of Asia, including Japan. By definition, "lifestyle migrants are relatively affluent individuals of all ages, moving either part-time or full-time to places that, for various reasons, signify, for the migrant, a better quality of life" (Benson & O'Reilly 2009: 609). Their stories are typically ones of escape – from undesirable circumstances in their countries of origin into a new life (often abroad) where they can 'make a fresh start', which may include the re-negotiation of the work/life balance, achieving better quality of life and/or freedom from prior constraints (ibid.).

So far, scholars of lifestyle migration have made various contributions to the literature. The exercise of agency and the role of the social imaginary in lifestyle migration have been examined at length. The gender dimension in the migration decisions and experiences of Western migrants has also been explored. Studies on Japanese lifestyle migration to the non-European West have also discussed gender and the social imaginary, separately. Yet, the link between gender, agency, and the social imaginary has not been explicitly addressed neither with regard to Western nor to Japanese lifestyle migration. Japanese lifestyle migration to Continental Europe has also not been studied. This paper aims to fill that gap by taking a look at the impact gender has on Japanese lifestyle migrants' engagement with the social imaginary about European destinations and how that affects the exercise of agency in subsequent migration decisions.

While in traditional, economic, migration, it has been acknowledged that the financial motivation is always primary to female migrants and that 'side benefits' – such as freedom from oppressive gendered social norms – remain secondary (at least officially), in lifestyle migration, freedom from socially imposed gender constraints appears to be of utmost importance to female migrants (Croucher 2013). In order to escape from such constraints, women first need to imagine what life abroad could be like and, to do that, they engage with the social imaginary.

The social imaginary is of paramount importance to lifestyle migration – "a migration seeped in imaginings and romanticism" (O'Reilly 2014: 211). While there have been arguments that there is no such thing as a *social* imaginary, that only individuals imagine, not societies (Strauss 2006), a number of studies (see Griffiths & Maile 2014, Korpela 2010, etc.) reveal that personal migration decisions are very much influenced by collectively-shared ideas about destinations and what they offer. As O'Reilly (2014: 212) points out, "[t]he imaginary is not (necessarily) a reflection of reality or a figment of the imagination, but acknowledges that places come to have shared, collective meanings, mediated through language, symbols, and other significations, and that these meanings have the power to shape reality through the actions of individuals and groups." Also, "[i]maginaries are both actions and structures, shaped by and shaping of agency, and are central to understanding lifestyle migration as an ongoing process. The concept acknowledges both the creative aspects of agency and the role of collective representations in the practice of daily life" (ibid.: 213).

A quick overview of studies conducted on Japanese lifestyle migration in the non-European, English-speaking West reveals how the West is imagined by Japanese people. Both men and women potential lifestyle migrants tend to see the West as a place where they can escape from restrictive Japanese social norms and enjoy a better quality of life – more time for themselves, a better work/life balance, more living space, fewer obligations, free communication etc. (Nagatomo 2014). Gender inequality in Japan is also something that prompts women in particular to indulge in imagining a life in the West (ibid.) and seek what some scholars call 'gender liberation' (Igarashi 2015). This gender liberation may or may not lead to a career in the host country, but is certainly imagined as offering freedom from gendered expectations in Japan – about looks, romance, marriage, motherhood, wifehood, family and social obligations etc. And last but not least, Western men have been an object of desire for Japanese women since at least the 1980s, as they are imagined as both physically attractive and offering the kind of romantic relationships that Japanese women want but Japanese men are seen as unable to provide (Kelsky 2001).

Data and methodology

This paper is based on the accounts of twenty-nine Japanese people living in Austria and Bulgaria who can be described as lifestyle migrants, as well as several Japan experts in the two countries. They were interviewed between November 2012 and January 2017, as part of a larger research project. Interviews with migrants were unstructured – allowing respondents to share their life and migration histories at their own pace, while occasionally interjecting with open-ended questions. Interviews with experts were semi-structured, following the themes that had emerged in interviews with migrants. Respondents were approached through a number of channels – Japanese diaspora organizations, universities, Japanese restaurants, websites of Japanese living in the host country, but mostly through introductions within respondents' networks (i.e., snowball sampling).

In terms of age, respondents ranged from their early 20s to their late 80s, although most were between 35 and 70. The youngest participants were university students who declared their interest in living in the host country for lifestyle reasons (rather than, say, career) once their studies are over, and are thus considered 'potential' lifestyle migrants. The majority of respondents, however, were 'actual' lifestyle migrants who either moved to the host country already with the intention to enjoy a different lifestyle or initially with the intention to study and/or have a career, but later changed their minds.

Results and discussion

In line with what is already known about the way Japanese people imagine the West, this research confirmed that the West is collectively seen as a place where one can escape from prescribed social interactions in Japan, the toxic work culture, and gender inequality. While the first two are relevant to men and women alike, the latter is definitely more important to women. Looking at the numbers of

Japanese migrants in the West, it is obvious that Japanese women are more interested in a life outside Japan – they outnumber men in all Western destinations by at least 52% to 48%. This may have to do not only with Japanese women's desire to leave social constraints (including gendered ones) behind, but also with their perceived 'freedom' to quit the Japanese labor market (as they were not expected to be part of the labor force in Japan beyond marriage and/or giving birth anyway), and instead pursue their interests, even if that takes them abroad.

But why choose Europe over the USA or Australia? Based on respondents' accounts of what they thought about various European destinations prior to migration, it appears that (Continental) Western Europe is imagined as offering everything that the non-European West does – minus English, plus 'culture'.

As English is the only foreign language taught in Japanese high schools, it is mostly those Japanese who have had access to university-level education in other foreign languages (either in Japan or in the host country) that are in a position to imagine themselves living in non-English speaking countries. And the interest in studying other foreign languages often comes via an interest in the respective country's art, music, literature, fashion, architecture, philosophy, etc.

This is where the term 'culture' comes into play. Respondents often talked about 'the culture of Europe' – in the sense of 'the art, music, literature, fashion, architecture, philosophy etc.' – as the thing that distinguishes Europe from the non-European West. While the USA, Canada, Australia, and New Zealand are certainly recognized as belonging to the Western civilization, Europe is perceived as the place of its roots and the majority of its achievements. For those Japanese who want to experience those achievements on a regular basis, not just as tourists, Europe seems to be the preferred destination for migration.

The question is, who are those Japanese who seek to settle in Europe for lifestyle reasons? By all means, the fascination with something comes with exposure to it. In the case of the Japanese fascination with European culture, this typically happens by means of reading books, watching films, listening to music, or looking at art/fashion/architecture, but also by means of travel and/or hearing travel-related stories. While an interest in foreign culture may or may not be the result of upbringing, more often than not it is people who grew up middle-class that were prompted by their parents and/or social circle to read, watch, listen, and look at the achievements of European culture. Many of them also had access to travel opportunities and/or heard stories from well-traveled relatives/acquaintances as children. Respectively, it is the Japanese middle class that has developed a taste for Europe.

Within the middle class, however, it is women, and not men, who are encouraged to dabble in, study, or even have a career related to European culture. On the one hand, this has to do with a tendency to value being knowledgeable about this culture – and even practicing it in some form, such as playing a musical instrument or speaking languages – as a particularly desirable trait for women. That is, (some) Japanese women are socialized to have an affinity for Europe and its culture beyond the standard middle-class fascination. On the other, with the aforementioned 'freedom' to quit the Japanese labor market. This – in combination with a desire to leave restrictive social norms (including gendered ones) behind – makes it more likely for Japanese women to engage with what is collectively imagined about Europe and picture a life there.

As a result, considering a life in (Western) Europe in particular, as opposed to the non-European West, is more characteristic of women than of men. Just for reference, the share of women among Japanese migrants in Europe is more than 60%. It should also come as no surprise that Japanese women seem to indulge in imagining a life abroad and act on the imagined (i.e., exercise agency) much more freely and resolutely than men do. As several of the respondents suggested, this likely has to do with the fact that women tend to have 'less to lose' in Japan – only freedom, romance, and expanded cultural horizons to gain (once abroad).

Conclusion

It can be concluded that gender clearly affects Japanese people's exercise of agency and engagement with the social imaginary, and that this likely is a function of the existence of unique gendered social norms within Japanese society. Social expectations towards women may place them at a disadvantage in Japan, but simultaneously give them a license to imagine a life abroad and to act on the imagined which is informed by the social imaginary.

References

Benson, M., & O'Reilly, K. (2009). Migration and the search for a better way of life: a critical exploration of lifestyle migration. *The sociological review, 57*(4), 608-625.

Croucher, S. (2013). The gendered spatialities of lifestyle migration. In *Contested spatialities, lifestyle migration and residential tourism* (pp. 31-44). Routledge.

Griffiths, D., & Maile, S. (2014). Britons in Berlin: Imagined cityscapes, affective encounters and the cultivation of the self. In *Understanding lifestyle migration* (pp. 139-159). Palgrave Macmillan, London.

Igarashi, H. (2015). Privileged Japanese transnational families in Hawaii as lifestyle migrants. *Global networks, 15*(1), 99-117.

Kelsky, K. (2001). Women on the verge: Japanese women, Western dreams. Duke University Press.

Korpela, M. (2010). A postcolonial imagination? Westerners searching for authenticity in India. *Journal of Ethnic and Migration Studies, 36*(8), 1299-1315.

Nagatomo, J. (2014). Migration as transnational leisure: The Japanese lifestyle migrants in Australia. Brill.

O'Reilly, K. (2014). The role of the social imaginary in lifestyle migration: employing the ontology of practice theory. In *Understanding lifestyle migration* (pp. 211-234). Palgrave Macmillan, London.

Strauss, C. (2006). The imaginary. *Anthropological theory, 6*(3), 322-344.

TYPOLOGY OF REMITTANCES AND TRANSNATIONAL TIES: STUDY OF PUNJABI FAMILIES IN NETHERLANDS, GULF AND PUNJAB (INDIA)

Atinder Pal Kaur

Abstract: Migration gives birth to societies in which families are staying across the borders, resultant growth of transnational families. In these scenarios, remittances play a positive role to overcome economic hardship and improve the social wellbeing of the families left behind. Remittances are usually perceived in economic terms but it has various interpretation according to sender and receivers' point of view. Sender share an emotional bond that are the foundations of these transactions. Remittances are also a way to maintain sense of belongingness with the families and at the same time to show the identity of being money provider. With this the sender tried to show their presence and maintain strong relation with their families.

I. Introduction: In the development discourse related to remittances, several meanings are attached as an active stock of human and financial capital and as assets used to alleviate poverty, a way to develop and to improve household economies and survival strategies (Lo, 2008). India remains one of the main labor sending countries all over the world. India comprises 17.5 million large Diaspora all over the world (IOM, 2020) and received the highest remittance that is US $ 78.6 billion. Dusenbery and Tatla (2009) also stressed that India, one of the world's largest beneficiaries of migration has started paying heed to its Diaspora populations and Punjab is one of the Indian states with the highest proportion of NRI's.

It is estimated that about 33% of the total remittances to Punjab come from North America and Europe, while Gulf countries contribute 15%. South America, Africa, and East Asia contribute 13% of the total remittances (Rajan et al., 2015). In Punjab, the *Doaba* region has dominated in migration in the 20th century and people started the migration to all parts of the world to earn their livelihood. But these remittances include various types of monies that are sent on different occasions to their extended kin to maintain transnational relations. But the question that remains unanswered is how remittances are perceived by sender and receiver points other than economic meaning attached to it.

II. Justification: Punjab shares a long history of migration that is before 1947 (Independence of India) but earlier studies focused on the migration of Punjabi, their destination countries, and employment opportunities. Although few attempts were made to define remittances used in Punjab; studies on the use of remittances and typology of remittances in Punjab from sender and receiver points of view in transnational settings are negligible. So, the present study was initiated to shed light on this area with the help of empirical research.

III. Objective: The utilization of remittances in different settings that include the flow of remittances from migrants to their home country. The context of sending remittances is in a particular time and situation.

IV. Review of Literature: Studies have given economic interpretations of remittances (Semyonov& Gorodzeisky, 2005) in which major share of the remittances are used for household budgets (Canales, 2000; Adams & Cuecuecha, 2013), children's education (Edward &Ureta, 2003, Kaur, 2016; 2019;

2020), investment in agricultural land, property, health (Nguyen et al., 2007) and rebuilding of old houses (Roy et al, 2015). Singh et al (2010) defined remittances are also used by migrant families as a care economy.

V. Data and Methods: The data was collected through longitudinal survey from 2016-2019 via open-ended interviews and participant observation in different settings. 27 case studies were collected from Punjabis staying in the Netherlands (via visiting gurudwara, Sikh Temple); attending daily morning prayers and having langer (afternoon meal). 48 case studies were conducted with Punjabi left behind families staying in the Doaba region of Punjab and lastly, interviews were also conducted with 6 Gulf migrants during their holiday visit to their homeland Punjab. An attempt is made to understand the hidden meaning of remittances from the sociological approach in which the sender/receiver's emotions are attached and money is used as a medium of maintaining the relationship, care, and love in transnational settings.

VI. Result and Discussion

Remittances Beyond Economic Transfers: Remittances are the way to maintain transitional relations that connect people to one's geographical locations and around cultural diversities. Generally, perceived remittances are defined as a survival strategy and to maintain healthy savings to overcome poverty and market constraints. Thus migrants, generally viewed remittances in economic terms but remittances include different types of monies (Fig.1) that flow from migrants to their families or communities.

Figure 1. Typology of Remittances

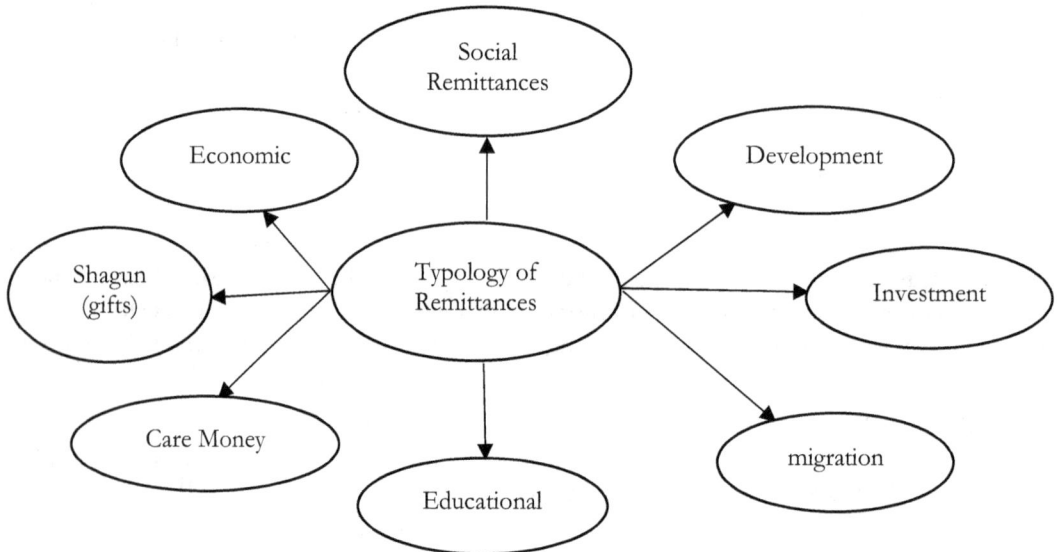

Economic Remittances: The major share of remittances is used to fulfil the basic needs of the households (Lipton,1980) and the amount usually sent to maintain household budgets (Gulati, 1987). Results from Turkey (Toepfer,1985) and Yemen (Swansan, 1979), and Sub-Saharan Africa (Adepoju, 1988) showed that international remittances are spent on consumption rather than production.

Shaguns (Gifts): Migrant has multiple relations with his family; he is a brother, husband, Son, and uncle also. While relatives always seek migrants as a gift provider, believing that migration is the place of high earning. Culturally India is a country of festivals that include ceremonies related to Birth, death, marriage, Diwali, Holi, New Year, Rakhi, etc. So, the shaguns are either given in cash or kind (gift) to show love and care to their beloved ones. Except for sending regular remittances, sometimes money and gifts were sent according to the occasion at the homeland. Harjeet Singh mentioned that "during his visit to Punjab from the Netherlands, he gifted watches and perfumes to his relatives as well as gifts to close relatives as a token of love". Rani mentioned that "she tried to give best shagun gifts during Rakhi to her sisters-in-laws. So that they never think, their brother didn't send money for them after migration".

Care Money: Usually remittances are sent for household consumption but one part of the remittances also includes care money in which money is sent to loved ones for their care and show to love. Generally, in India or Punjab after the marriage of a daughter, she becomes a member of the in-law's family and parents never accept money from her. But Harpinder from Netherland told us that "she sometimes sends money to her parental house for care and love. While Avtar Singh a gulf migrant also mentioned that "he sends a major share of his wages to his wife and children so that they can live a good life".

Educational Remittances: Remittances are used to provide better education to left-behind children. The Gulf migrants usually try to send remittances for the education of younger siblings and children. With the change, money was also invested in daughter education and special emphasis is given to get professional education for daughters.

Migration: With time when children are grown up and observe their kin, father, and siblings' successful years of migration in the host country. They also want to follow in similar footsteps. Harjeet mentioned that "she was sending her son to Canada for his bright future because, after years of his father's migration, they were able to provide a good education that can help his son in further studies and also settle permanently" (Left behind wife). Daughters of migrant families were also migrating to the developed countries with the help of parents and the majority of migration took place from migrant families. Fathers, especially Gulf migrants, were investing their money in their children's migration.

Investments: The migrants usually spend money to open small businesses and entrepreneurial activities. What we found is that in Punjab, remittances investments to purchase agricultural land because of being an agrarian family setup and having land means izzat or Honor (status) in the village. Secondly, money is also invested to construct big houses as a symbol of success after years of migration. Ram mentioned that "he constructed a house with the name Holland House in his village that symbolizes his success story in the Netherlands".

Development: The attachment with the motherland and emotional bond always plays a vital role in the migrant's life. Many times, migrants and diasporic communities send remittances for the construction of religious places, construction of roads, community hall and lastly philanthropic work is also included. The caste-based separate gurudwaras to maintain identity and Honor were constructed in villages. So, within the village, more than one gurudwara was constructed by different castes after getting funding from village migrants. More than that another way to show status of caste is with the construction of houses.

Social Remittances: Peggy (2001) defined social remittances that were usually transformed during their visits to their homeland country. The use of mobile phones and wearing t-shirts with the country flag of migrants have become common in villages. More than that houses, cars, or motorcycles also used the flag of the country of migrants to show their links. Even women's mobility increased outside their home and participation in family decision-making. While houses of migrants become a replica of western houses that in some cases, they referred to as the white house.

VII. Conclusion: The remittances sent to left-behind families in Punjab are generally to show their emotional bonds. The migrants share their bond not with their families but with their motherland also. After migration that bond becomes more intense and they always tried to remit more in different forms. Secondly, the sense of belongingness is another reason for sending remittances. The Punjabi diaspora in the Netherlands, generally maintaining land holdings and sending money for philanthropic work, tried to show their belongingness with the motherland. Thirdly to show their presence and maintain relationships with their extended families; the money is usually sent as remittance. So that they are always remembered and relationships remain strong. Fourthly, they want to maintain their identity of being money providers so that they should have a special place in the family as well as the community. Other than that caste identity also played a big role. The nexus between the higher (Jat) caste that is a land owing caste and the lower (Dalit) caste that is the labor caste on Jat land holding become more intense after migration. Both castes tried to maintain their identity at the village level by constructing religious places and also big dwellings. Thus, the remittances that are studied in economic terms have various hidden meanings that are attached according to the sender and receiver point of view.

References

Adams, R. H., &Cuecuecha, A., (2013). The impact of remittances on investment and poverty in Ghana. World Development, 50, 24-40.

Adepoju, A., (1988). Links between internal and international migration: the African situation. Pp. 34-45 in Charles W. Stahl, ed., *International Migration Today*, Volume 2: Emerging Issues. Paris: United Nations Education, Scientific and Cultural Organization.

Dusenbery, V., & Tatla, D. S. (2009). NRIs are the new VIPS. *Sikh diaspora philanthropy in Punjab: Global giving for local good*, 3-29.

Edwards, Alejandra Cox, and Manuelita Ureta., 2003. International migration, remittances, and schooling: evidence from El Salvador. *Journal of development economics* 72 (2): 429-461.

Gulati, L. (1987). Coping with male migration. *Economic and Political Weekly*, WS41-WS46.

International Organization for Migration (2020). World Migration Report 2020.Geneva; IOM. Retrieved on 14April 2020 from https://publications.iom.int/system/files/pdf/wmr_2020.pdf.

Kaur, A. P (2016). Migrant father and consequences on children's education: A study of rural Punjab. *International Journal of Education and Management Studies*, 6(2), 139.

Kaur, A.P. (2019). "International Migration and Impact of remittances on left behind wives: a case study of Doaba Region of Punjab". In S.I Rajan and N. Neetha (eds) *Migration, Gender and Care Economy*, New York: Routledge.

Kaur, A. P., (2020). Impact of migration on gender roles: Study of left behind wives in rural Punjab. *Indian Journal of Health and Wellbeing*, 11(7-9), 407-411.

Levitt, P. (2001). *The transnational villagers*. University of California press.

Lo, Marieme S., (2008). Beyond instrumentalism: Interrogating the micro-dynamic and gendered and social impacts of remittances in Senegal. *Gender, Technology and development* 12(3): 413-437.

Rajan, S.I and Nanda,A.K (2015). Transnational World and Indian Punjab: Contemporary Issues. In *Migration, Mobility and Multiple Affiliations*. Edited by Rajan, S. I.,Varghese, V. J.,and Nanda, A. K, 1-19. Delhi: Cambridge University Press.

Semyonov, Moshe, and Anastasia Gorodzeisky., 2005 Labor Migration, Remittances and Household Income: A Comparison between Filipino and Filipina Overseas Workers 1. *International Migration Review* 39 (1): 45-68.

Singh, S., Cabraal, A., & Robertson, S. (2010). Remittances as a currency of care: A focus on 'twice migrants' among the Indian diaspora in Australia. *Journal of Comparative Family Studies*, 41(2), 245-263.

Swanson, Jon C., 1979a. Emigration and Economic Development: The Case of the Yemen Arab Republic. Boulder, CO: West view Press.

Toepfer, Helmuth., 1985. The economic impact of returned migrants in Trabazon, Turkey. In *Uneven Development in Southern Europe: Studies of Accumulation, Class, Migration and the State*, edited by Ray Hudson and Jim Lewis, pp. 76-100. London:

MY GRATE IN MIGRATE: INTERROGATING THE SHADES OF MULTI– IN MULTICULTURALISM

Sukhpreet Bhatia

Multiculturalism has been defined by the International Federation of Library Associations and Institutions (IFLA), as the co-existence of diverse cultures, where culture includes racial, religious, or cultural groups and is manifested in customary behaviours, cultural assumptions and values, patterns of thinking, and communicative styles. As the title suggests, the topic of my paper is to investigate the actual picture of the policy of Multiculturalism that has been theoretically adopted by most of the nations of the world, especially the western countries and its impact on the migrants. Earlier these countries had been popularizing the homogenizing notion of "assimilationism", inherent in the idea of West as a melting pot, but that entailed the view of urban society as a racial hierarchy, giving only the option of conformity to the so-called inferiors and outsiders. This idea had been well-established and widely documented till the 1970s. Since then, various countries had been proposing ways and policies to accommodate ethnic diversity in a liberal atmosphere and projecting themselves as truly multicultural nations.

As Will Kymlicka puts it in his report titled "Multiculturalism: Success, Failure and Future" compiled under an initiative of the Migration Policy Institute, Europe, "multiculturalism was characterized as a feel-good celebration of ethnocultural diversity, encouraging citizens to acknowledge and embrace the panoply of customs, traditions, music and cuisine that exist in a multiethnic society." (Kymlicka72). This multiculturalist model, which was touted as a decided progress over the melting-pot philosophy, was expected to allow various ethnic groups, the freedom, to preserve their cultural markers and retain their native identities in a mutually respectful atmosphere. For the European Union generally and Britain specifically, it appears, that the transition from the Empire in which the sun never sets to an accommodating multicultural nation, sensitive to the individual needs of its diverse ethnic minorities, is a gradual and arduous journey marked by what Paul Gilroy calls a 'melancholia' in his 2004 book *After Empire: Melancholia or Convivial Culture?*

In spite of its ostensible claims of providing religious freedom and respect to the ethnic customs and practices of the minorities, multiculturalism seems to have moved only in the direction of a coercive national culture into which the immigrants are expected to integrate, more like the earlier hierarchical assimilation because it is the native culture that reigns supreme. Rather than being seen in the hype created by the government, it is in the everyday goings-on on the streets that the reality of multiculturalism becomes visible. With the increased intermingling of diverse ethnicities in the globally connected world of today, the earlier hierarchical and ideological East-West confrontation of the 20th century has been taken over by a cultural self-awareness and with it, an increased cognizance of the cultural differences.

It is out of the realization, of these conspicuous and inerasable differences, that the culture which Joel S. Kahn terms 'street cred' comes into being. He quotes Anderson in *Culture, Multiculture Postculture* to bring forth this point:

Street cred grows up in the shadow of, and then directly challenges, the hypocritical liberalism of a hegemonic discourse: street culture has evolved what may be called a code of the streets, which amounts to a set of informal rules governing interpersonal behavior, including violence. . . .The code of the streets is actually a cultural adaptation to a profound lack of faith in the . . . system. (Kahn 105)

The complete lack of social acceptance and a feeling of incapability at not being able to do anything about it, makes the individual interrogate his 'patchwork identity', to use Thomas Meyer's expression in *Identity Mania*. In order to be a socially responsible and acceptable being, a person needs to be clear about how he is perceived by the 'others' in terms of his behavior, belief system and ethnicity. Members of racial minorities appear to be in a state of confusion regarding who they really are and where they belong.

Here, begins an individual's earnest quest for his true identity which according to Meyer is fueled by the politicization of cultural differences in a multicultural scenario where divergent identities are expected to be preserved. Rootedness in one's native identity and establishment of its supremacy over foreign cultures is viewed as empowering and attracts the fragmented psyche of the migrant individual. Meyer cites empirical evidence in support of this view:

A comprehensive overall survey with fourteen empirical case-studies for seven different sets of civilizations from five continents has revealed that language, religious, ethnic and cultural differences are being deliberately politicized in all civilizational groupings in order to create animosities and play off one side against another. (Meyer, 7).

We should not allow the political players of the world to do this to the humankind. In his autobiographical book *Balti Britain*, Ziauddin Sardar expresses the same sentiment:

As we the Asian community, became more British, we also needed to build more barricades against losing touch with where our parents came from. We needed barricades to protect us from the increasing sense of rejection by the British society.... We wanted respect for our cultures and religions and space for them to breathe. (Sardar 88)

A return to fundamentalism, thus, is reinvigorating as it gives an individual the air of importance, a feeling of determined identity and an empathetic understanding of his sense of loss. In that state, it can choose to impose on him, any interpretation of tradition and religious beliefs to justify its means, to claim supremacy over his detractors. In this manner, the use of violence and militancy are legitimized. However, fundamentalism is certainly, not the answer, as it does not satisfy the quest for identity, which to use Meyer's words "is not a possession but a social process of achieving an equilibrium between conflicting expectations". (Meyer15) It is a deliberation between the individual's image of himself, his past and his present, and the anticipation that the society has from him, none of which remains static. It requires that the individual possesses the requisite strength to deal with contradictory social demands and create an identity indomitable enough to handle divergent social pressures and not feel threatened or insecure.

A truly multicultural society, would be one, that is conducive to the forging of such fearless identities and liberal enough to allow them to flourish simultaneously and collectively. As Will Kymlicka, the diehard advocate of multiculturalism, quotes from The International Comparative Study of Ethnocultural Youth:

Immigrants do best, both in terms of psychological well-being and socio-cultural outcomes, when they are able to combine their ethnic identity with a new national identity. Scholars often call this an "integration orientation," as opposed to either an "assimilation orientation" (in which the immigrants abandon their ethnic identity to adopt a new national identity) or a "separation orientation" (in which immigrants renounce the new national identity to maintain their ethnic identity) …. Members of immigrant minorities will be more likely to identify with a new national identity if they feel their ethnic identity is publically respected. (Kymlicka, 12)

So, whatever we are observing, taking place in the world around such as the recent 'Black Lives Matter' movement in the US, or racial and religious alienation in the UK or even closer home in the form of enhanced communalism, needs to be addressed from this perspective. Therefore, rather than pronouncing multiculturalism dead, this paper proposes, that let us learn from the Canadian example and make efforts to revive it and sustain it in its true spirit of liberal and democratic multiplicity. The differences have to be retained, but neither commodified nor asserted.

Peter van der Veer, who is Professor of Comparative Religion and Director of the Research Centre for Religion and Society at the University of Amsterdam and the author of *Gods of the Earth* and *Religious Nationalism* underscores that the celebration of hybridity, multiculturalism and syncretism in Cultural Studies is a smugness of the elitist world of litterateurs, a world in which literary texts become the sites of "self-fashioning in modern bourgeois culture". He criticizes the modern tendency to relegate religious expression to the private sphere and affirms that religious faith and other forms of cultural difference are not obliterated but transformed and comfortably accommodated by urban consumer capitalism. Pnina Werbner, the Professor Emerita in Social Anthropology at Keele University, also reiterates that there are innovative and creative dimensions to religious discourses:

> "A truly comprehensive study of migrant culture would need, therefore, to go beyond migrant literary texts, such as those by Naipaul and Rushdie, to examine a wider range of textual interventions including those articulated by migrant-settlers in a religious idiom, as these are played out in the West. (Werbner 104)

A reinvention and revival of the religious concepts is advocated by many postcolonial theorists such as Ziauddin Sardar (2013), Alberto Melucci (1996), Pnina Werbner (1997) and Peter Van Der Veer (1994). Sikhism, the youngest of the world religions, for instance was founded at a time and a place where several faiths and religious traditions co-existed. It was conceived as a revolutionary way of life to purge the prevalent religions of the corrupt practices and degenerative rituals that had crept into those. It exhorted the people to give respect to the diverse traditions and in a cosmopolitan spirit, urged all to pursue their own path with complete devotion, in a harmonious atmosphere of mutual space and democratic autonomy. Revisiting the past and comprehending that multi-religious scenario for its lessons on co-existence and strategies of identity negotiation, might prove beneficial in framing the global multicultural policies. Something like, what Guru Granth Sahib, the sacred text of the Sikh religion, the essence of which was and is indubitably egalitarian, states:

> *"Awwal Allah noor upaya, kudrat ke sab bande*
>
> *Ek noor te sab jag upjya, kaun bhale kaun mande."* (SGGS 1349)
>
> which means that
>
> It is the same divine light that manifests in all humanity.
>
> We are all sparks of the same celestial light and no one is superior or inferior. (My

trans.)

References

Brah, Avtar. Cartographies of Diaspora: Contesting Identities. Routledge, 2005.

Gilroy, Paul. *The Black Atlantic*. Verso, 1999.

Kahn, Joel S. *Culture, Multiculture, Postculture*. SAGE Publications, 1995.

Kymlicka,Will. Multicultural Citizenship: A Liberal Theory of Minority Rights. Clarendon Press, 1996.

Lewis, Richard. Multiculturalism Observed: Exploring Identity. ASP-VUB Press, 2006.

Lott, Bernice. Multiculturalism and Diversity: A Social Psychological Perspective. John Wiley and Sons, 2009.

Madood, Tariq. *Multiculturalism*. John Wiley and Sons, 2013.

Meyer, Thomas. Identity mania: Fundamentalism and the Politicization of Cultural Differences Zed Books, 2001.

Sardar, Ziauddin. *Balti Britain*. Granta Publications, 2009.

Singh, Gurbhagat. *Sikhism and Postmodern Thought*. Naad Pargass, 2016. *Sri Guru Granth Sahib Ji*. Sainchi 1. Bhai Chatar Singh Jiwan Singh Publishers, Sri Damdami Birh, Bikrami 1765.

COMPLEMENTARY PROTECTION BETWEEN HUMAN RIGHTS OBLIGATIONS AND HUMANITARIAN MOTIVES: ITALIAN CASE STUDY

Gabriella Morrone, Maria Teresa Rovitto, and Mariella Crisci

Complementary protection has emerged over the last decades as a generic label including all such forms of protection used by States to avoid the return of asylum seekers who have failed their claim under the 1951 Geneva Convention but cannot be returned to their countries of origin for various reasons, and in order to comply with their *non-refoulement* obligation under international law. It may be interpreted as the result of a protection gap deriving from the fact that the Geneva Convention definition of a refugee does not cover the protection needs of all persons – and there might be people needing protection, who nevertheless fall outside the scope of the Convention. There are large discrepancies in States' understandings of who should benefit from complementary protection: many countries grant complementary protection to those persons who do not qualify for international protection, but cannot be returned to their countries because of binding human rights obligations. Some others allow persons to remain in their territories, on the basis of compassionate or humanitarian grounds. The significance of these humanitarian reasons is discretional and varies from state to state (Feijen, 2021).

Although the term "complementary protection" itself is not specifically defined in any international instrument, it nevertheless arises from international human rights obligations that are based not only on the principle of *non-refoulement* set out in article 33 of the Geneva Convention, but also more widely on various international human rights instruments – to name a few: art. 3 of the Convention Against Torture, art. 7 of ICCPR, art. 3 of ECHR (McAdam, 2007; Hathaway, 2005). There is also an emerging case law from the Strasbourg Court on the application of art. 8 to protect the rights of third country nationals who have family ties in the host country, of long-term stayers and second-generation immigrants. In the Common European Asylum System, Considerandum 15 of the Recast Qualification Directive 2011/95 establishes the possibility for member states to allow third country nationals to remain in their territories on a "discretionary basis on compassionate or humanitarian grounds", therefore falling outside of the scope of the Directive.

In Italy, complementary protection was introduced in 1998, within a new immigration law that established the possibility for a third country national to obtain "humanitarian protection". The new law introduced the concept of humanitarian protection in article 5.6, that establishes that a person who does not obtain a permit to stay can be expelled *"unless there are serious reasons, in particular of a humanitarian nature or resulting from constitutional or international obligations of the Italian State."* (Durante Viola, 2019). In this article there was a specific reference to both international human rights obligations (principle of *non-refoulement),* and to humanitarian reasons per se. This new type of protection was set out as an open catalogue, and the contents of such "serious reasons" has evolved with time – with the evolving interpretation of Territorial Commissions and Courts. Among the instances in which humanitarian protection was recognized there were, for instance: a context of widespread human rights violations; political instability in the country of origin, or a situation of humanitarian crisis; internal or international conflict that did not meet the threshold for the recognition of subsidiary protection (art. 15 let. c of the Qualifications Directive);a condition of vulnerability of the applicant, that could refer to age, health, disability, etc.: cases in which a hypothetical return could lead to a breach of the dignity and fundamental rights of the applicant; integration of the applicant in the host country.

In 2018, the landmark judgement of the Court of Cassation n. 4455/2018 clarified what criteria must authorities uphold when assessing humanitarian protection: the principle set out in this judgement is that the level of social integration reached in the host country cannot *per se* constitute the entitlement to humanitarian protection, which requires a specific situation of vulnerability of the applicant: authorities must engage in a comparative evaluation of the situation in the country of origin of the applicant, and the prospective consequences of their return – and their subjective situation.

Territorial Commissions for International Protection are the local governmental bodies in charge of first examination of asylum requests and interview of asylum, and their decisions can be appealed in Specialized Courts for Migration and International Protection. Interviews conducted by the Commissions are, indeed, the main sources of relevant indicators as well as the first context in which vulnerabilities emerge. The techniques used during the asylum interview in order to acquire useful elements related to humanitarian needs include both open-ended and specific questions on the applicant's "personal circumstances" (i.e., age, education, background, family relationships in the country of origin), but also on the migration journey, its route and financing as well as the experiences in transit countries. An important part of the interview also consists of questions related to living conditions in Italy, that can be used in order to acquire information on the level of social integration of the claimant - one of the two fundamental aspects of the comparative evaluation approach to humanitarian protection built by national case law. As a consequence, the asylum officer investigates the presence of family members of the applicant on Italian soil, their knowledge of Italian language, their work experience and health conditions. This list is certainly not exhaustive: this approach sees vulnerability as a multidimensional and dynamic concept, based on the interaction of cumulative factors, and as a consequence, it continuously needs to be reassessed. Commissions have a fundamental role in such a process as well as in interpreting, implementing and somehow shaping the "rules" of complementary protection, either adhering strictly to the indications coming from the policy and legislation level - which in turn are influenced by politics and by what is perceived each time as the superior interest of the State - or trying to stretch those limits by means of interpretation and compliance to national constitutional values, international instruments and case law.

Such framework of complementary protection was subjected to profound changes in 2018, the adoption of D.L. n. 113/2018, converted with modifications in Law n. 132/2018. Humanitarian protection was in fact abolished and replaced with "special protection", which only applied in cases where the criteria for refugee status and subsidiary protection were not met, and yet the authorities believed that the applicant could not be returned to their country of origin because they risk facing persecution or torture – notwithstanding the vulnerability or level of integration of the applicant in the host country.

In 2020, lastly, there was one final reform of the protection system: D.L. n. 130/2020 reformed the definition of the "special protection": in addition to the non-refoulement clause, the new law also introduced the prohibition of expulsion or refoulement of the non-citizen to a State "*if there are justified reasons to believe that the expulsion from the national territory involves a violation of the right to respect for his/her private and family life*" (with a clear reference to art. 8 ECHR): the assessment has to take into account, once again, elements such as family ties and integration. This way, the present-day Italian form of complementary protection has tried to connect the "compassionate grounds" to specific human rights – namely the right to private and family life – in order to bridge the gap between protection granted on the basis of *non-refoulement* and for humanitarian reasons.

The changes in law and the evolution of case law have undoubtedly impacted the reality and implementation of complementary protection in Italy, changing not only the numbers but also the lives of many, which is clear when comparing statistical data. The figures released by the National Commission for the Right to Asylum (CNDA) in recent years, show that 20.166 permits for humanitarian protection were issued in 2017 versus 20.014 in 2018, accounting for 25% and 21% of asylum requests processed each year, respectively. Such percentages are consistent with those of the previous years: in 2015 and 2016 the share of positive decisions granting humanitarian protection accounted for 21% and 22% of the processed requests respectively. In order to better understand these data, it is worth noting that over the considered timeframe, the share of permits issued for refugee status compared to the total number of processed asylum requests, fluctuated between 5% (2015) and 8% (2018), whereas the permits granted for subsidiary protection accounted for 14% in 2015 and dropped to 5% in 2018. The rejection rate remained stable around 60-65%. Thus, humanitarian protection represented the main type of protection granted to asylum seekers in Italy up to 2018.

The modifications introduced with the D.L. n. 113/2018 had a significant impact on the framework described: of the total 95.060 asylum requests processed during the year, 11% of the applicants were granted refugee status, 7% received subsidiary protection and only 1% received the new "special protection", which in the new formulation only covered the most stringent hypothesis of violation of the non-refoulement clause set in art. 3 ECHR. Conversely, 81% of the decisions were negative, the highest percentage ever so far. According to an estimate by ISPI, more than 37,000 people have become undocumented since 2018 because of the abolition of humanitarian protection, with significant restrictions in terms of access to basic rights and services in Italian territory (Sunderland, 2020). The legislative change also resulted in a huge increase in litigation rate, with a significant overload for local Courts and for the Supreme Court. The year 2020 was characterized by a similar trend. In the first 10 months of 2020, 77% of asylum claims were rejected, just a slight decrease from 2019 (81%), meaning that the number of negative decisions was still greater than it was before humanitarian protection permits were abolished in 2018. Special protection permits were then still uncommon, as they accounted for only 2% of all applications processed in 2020, with refugee status and subsidiary protection accounting for 11% of all asylum claims processed.

The situation just described underwent further modifications with D.L. n. 130/2020 and its new "special protection". It is still too early to fully understand how and to what extent the amendments introduced with the protection of the right to private and family life (art. 8 EHCR), will impact the asylum system. However, the year 2021 began with an interesting trend towards an increase in the number of complementary protection decisions adopted. The figures provided by the CNDA relating to the first three months of this year show that the recognition rate of special protection permits rose to 8%, whereas the share of rejected applications decreased to around 60%, a possible indication of a resurgence of the vulnerability and human rights approach in place until 2018.

The analysis of the Italian complementary protection system confirms, on the one hand, the discretionary nature of humanitarian protection, due to a still rooted perception of an instrument to govern the exceptionality but also to the absence of a formal and homogenous legal framework at the international and European level. The Italian humanitarian protection system has been entirely shaped by this never-ending conflict between state's prerogatives on one side, and the imperatives of humanitarianism and human rights protection on the other. Nonetheless, the legislative evolutions we have discussed tell us that the latest Italian interpretation of complementary protection implies more than a negative obligation to protect from *refoulement*, as it rather tends toward a positive idea of preserving human dignity and the effective enjoyment of fundamental human rights. There has been an effort to fill this gap with the latest reform, and through the implementation of article 8 ECHR, complementary protection has been pushed even beyond the principle of *non-refoulement* and the main human rights obligations, thus creating an instrument that is able to cover the wider principle of human dignity.

References

Feijen, L. (2021). The Evolution of Humanitarian Protection in European Law and Practice. Cambridge University Press.

Hathaway, J.C. (2005). The Rights of Refugees under International Law. Cambridge University Press.

McAdam, J. (2007). Complementary Protection in International Refugee Law. Oxford University Press.

Durante Viola, L (2019). *Asylum in Italy between human rights and the Constitution.* Retrieved at:https://repository.gchumanrights.org/bitstream/handle/20.500.11825/1087/Durante.pdf?sequence=1&isAllowed y.

Commissione Nazionale per il Diritto d'Asilo – CNDA. *Quaderno statistico 1990-2020.* Retrieved at: http://www.libertacivili immigrazione.dlci.interno.gov.it/it/documentazione/statistica/i-numeri-dellasilo.

Sunderland, J (2020). Finally, Good News for Asylum Seekers in Italy. Retrieved at: https://www.hrw.org/news/2020/10/07/finally-good-news-asylum-seekers-italy.

SIBERIA'S ATTRACTIVENESS FOR MIGRANTS EVALUATED BASED ON THE HUMAN CLIMATIC NICHE

Amber J. Soja, Elena I. Parfenova, Nadezhda M. Tchebakova, and Susan G. Conard

Introduction

Past human migrations have been associated with climate change. As our civilizations and infrastructure developed, humans depended less on the external environment. Asian Russia is currently sparsely populated, with most of the population in southern regions of forest-steppe where fertile soils support agriculture and climate is reasonably temperate. We used current and predicted climate scenarios from 20 CMIP5 general circulation models to evaluate the potential comfort of climate for human settlement in various landscapes throughout the 21st century. We applied two CO2 Representative Concentration Pathway scenarios, RCP 2.6 representing mild climate change and RCP 8.5 representing more extreme changes, across Asian Russia. We used three climate indices that relate to human well-being: Ecological Landscape Potential, winter severity, and permafrost coverage. Climates predicted by the 2080s over Asian Russia would be warmer and milder without excessive aridity. The permafrost zone is projected to shift to the northeast. Ecological Landscape Potential in the current permafrost zone would increase from 'low' to 'relatively high' with a resulting higher capacity for human populations across Asian Russia. Understanding ecological landscape potential is crucial information for developing viable strategies for long-term economic and social adaptation to changing climate. We also conducted a GIS analysis of population density with climatic layers of warmth, water resources and climate severity. The resulting bioclimatic model Russia explained 38% of current variation in population density. We applied this population model to the RCP 8.5 scenario. Over most of the country, the potential population density would increase, but it would remain low in permafrost regions in Siberia and the Far East by 2080. This contrasts with demographic projections that the population in Russia may decrease by the mid-century from the present 146 million to 92-120 million people. Thus there will be much more suitable habitat than the expected population. This leaves open the possibility for migration from more southern areas where climate has become less tolerable.

Our goal was to quantitatively estimate climatic distances between climates in which migrants live in their homeland and in some regions of the Krasnoyarsk Territory (central Siberia) where they settle.

Data and Methods

Data on the origins of migrants who arrived in the Krasnoyarsk Territory were derived from the Krasnoyarsk Statistic Department (http://krasstat.gks.ru/wps/wcm/connect/rosstat_ts/); most migrants arrive from Armenia, the European Part of the Russian Federation (EPR), Ukraine, Kazakhstan, Kirgizia, Uzbekistan, Tajikistan, Azerbaijan, the Korean People's Democratic Republic, China, and Georgia.

Climates of migrant places of origin were approximated by using climate data from the capitals or big cities of these countries (which are mostly small countries) and were derived from (www.pogodaiklimat.ru) (Table 1). Three big industrial cities of the Krasnoyarsk Territory were taken as places for migrant labor activities (south-to-north): Minusinsk, Krasnoyarsk, and Norilsk. Climate data for these cities were derived from (www.meteo.ru). Two foremost temperature variables that characterize living conditions in winter and summer were used: mean January and July temperatures for the last 60 years. Then the differences in both temperatures between places where migrants currently live in the Krasnoyarsk Territory and the places of their origin were calculated, and the portraits of the labor migration across the Krasnoyarsk Territory were plotted on the axes of July temperature (axis Y) and January temperature (axis X) for two big cities of current migrant residence (Fig. 1 a, b).

Results

When arriving from the place of origin to the place of permanent residence (for work, study, etc.), labor migrants not only cover large geographic distances and get into unknown culture environments, but also as a rule get into untried climate environments.

As seen from Fig 1, the null point in each portrait indicates living conditions for the locals in each region, and the distance from the migrant origin to the null demonstrates the difference which a migrant would physiologically and psychologically need to overcome after arrival in a new land (Fig. 1). As Fig 1 illustrates, a distinct difference in climates between the origin and present residence is inevitable especially in winter conditions which migrants, who are usually from warm countries, may not expect and for which they are likely unprepared. a. b.

Fig.1. Places of the migrant origin in the axes of January and July temperatures differences between the place of labor and the place of origin in two industrial regional centers: Minusinsk (a), Norilsk (b).

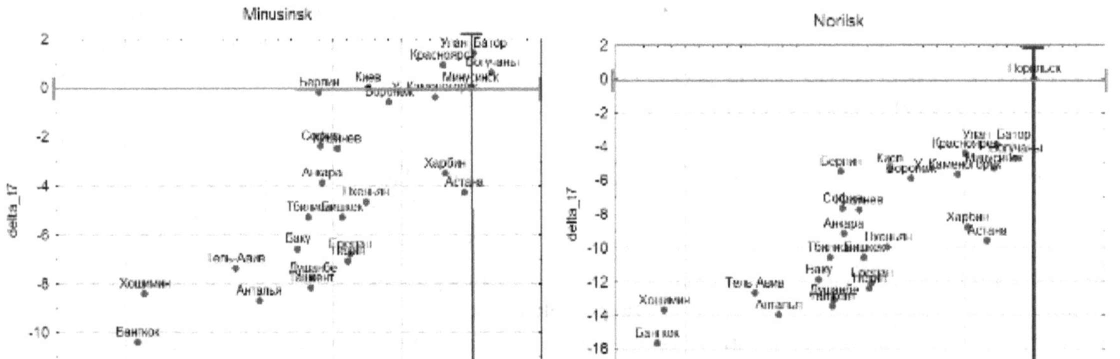

Fig. 2. Distribution of annual temperature over Russia under baseline climate (left), RCP 2.6 scenario (center) and RCP 8.5 (right): 1 <-10; 2 -10/-5; 3 -5/ 0; 4 0/ 0.01; 5 0.01- 5; 6 5-10; 7 10-15.

The annual temperature distribution was mapped in current and future RCP 2.6 and RCP 8.5 climates (Fig. 2.). The relationship between the gross regional product per capita (GRP) and the population density was constructed based on data of the subjects of the Russian Federation (Fig. 3). The relationship between income and January temperatures in various countries (Fig. 4).

Fig. 3. Dependence of GRP on the population density

Fig. 4. Dependence of income in the subjects of the Federation on January temperature

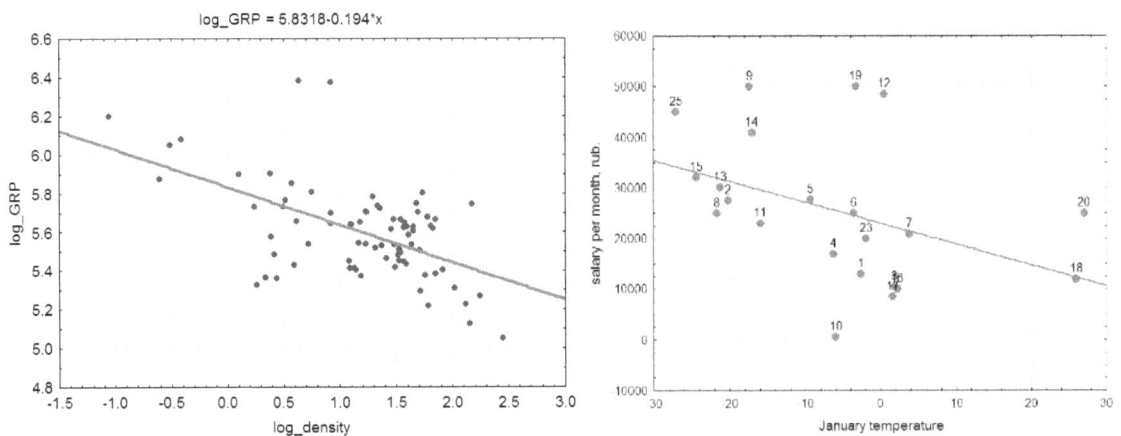

Discussion and Conclusions

Some assumptions were adopted in our study. Climates of places of migrants' origins were approximated by using the climates of big cities despite differences in climate variables distributions across each country. Such an approach was developed and applied by Zorkaltsev and Khazheev (2015) in which they related the country's population density to the annual temperature in its capital. In biological and ecological sciences, a method of transfer functions is widely used (Rehfeldt et al., 2002) whose essence is to estimate the distance (difference) between conditions of places of origin and to places of migration as an adjustment rate. In our study we estimated the distance between climates in places of origins and settlements as a rate of comfort/discomfort for migrants who arrive to untried climates. For doing such a study, data on migrants adapting to a new life were needed. These data may be multi-year data from surveys of migrant respondents on the number of years that they have lived in a given new place, their perceptions of living conditions, and their subjective feeling of life satisfaction. This survey method, including questions regarding climate change perceptions, is currently widely used globally by people (Rehdanza and Maddison, 2005). Based on Fig. 1, seasonal work for migrant workers from certain regions of the Russian Federation and abroad may be recommended.

Our bioclimatic model of the human niche provided a prospect for predicting the niche capacity based on future changing climates (Parfenova, Tchebakova, 2020). The future IPCC climates (2014) predicted for Russia will become more favorable for human well-being. By the end of the current century, the population density would increase over most of Russia, though it would remain invariably low over the permafrost zone and in some small southern border regions likely related to climate aridization.

In the future climates in Russia, regions would emerge whose annual temperatures would match high global GRP (Fig. 2). However, in the current climate we found an opposite relationship: that the GRP increased with decreasing annual temperatures (Fig. 3).

Demographers, in turn, draw less optimistic pictures (Vishnevsky, Andreev, 2001; Manakov, Suvorkov, 2018). From their estimations, the population in Russia would decrease to 92-120 million people by the middle of the century; thus "the only source of the population growth in the near future may be due to in-migration" (Vishnevsky, Shcherbakova, 2018). Automation and robotization in industries and services may be considered as an alternative to this in-migration especially in regions with severe climates and low population densities.

Additionally, an interesting was discovered: GRP in federal subjects was inversely correlated with its population density (Fig. 3). Evidently, this irregularity may be explained by the distribution of mineral that are located in the Asian portion of Russia and beyond the Polar Circle territories which have severe climates and low population densities.

Acknowledgements. The reported study was supported by RFBR, project number 19-45-240004 («Predictions of the ecological-economic potential for possible "climatic" migrations in the Angara-Yenisei macroregion in a changing climate of the 21st century») funded by Russian Foundation for Basic Research, Government of Krasnoyarsk Territory, Krasnoyarsk Regional Fund of Science.

References

Burke M., Hsiang S.M. & Miguel E. 2015. Global non-linear effect of temperature on economic production. - doi:10.1038/nature15725

Isachenko A.G. and Shliapnikov A.A. Landscapes. Nature of the World. 1989. Moscow, Mysl. 504 pp.

Krasnoyarsk Rosstat Department. http://krasstat.gks.ru/wps/wcm/connect/rosstat_ts/krasstat/resources

Parfenova E.I., Tchebakova N.M., Soja A.J. 2019. Assessing landscape potential for human sustainability and 'attractiveness' across Asian Russia in a warmer 21st century. - Environ. Res. Lett. 14 (2019) 065004 https://doi.org/10.1088/1748-9326/ab10a8

Parfenova, E., Tchebakova, N. 2020. Potential human population redistribution in Russia in a warmer 21st century as predicted by a bioclimatic population model. International Multidisciplinary Scientific GeoConference Surveying Geology and Mining Ecology Management, SGEM, 2020, 2020-August(5.2), 381–388 p.p. DOI: 10.5593/sgem2020/5.2/s21.047

Reference books on Climate of USSR. Iss. 24. part 2. Temperature of the air and soil. 1967. Λ. Hydrometeoizdat. 504 c.

Rehdanza K. and Maddison D. 2005. Climate and Happiness/ Ecological Economics. Volume 52, Issue 1, Pages 111-125. https://doi.org/10.1016/j.ecolecon.2004.06.015

Rehfeldt G. E., Tchebakova N. M., Parfenova E. I., Wykoff W. R., Kuzmina N. A., Milyutin L. I. Intraspecific responses to climate in Pinus sylvestris // Global Change Biology. - 2002. - Vol. 8. - P. 912-929.

Vishnevsky A., Shcherbakova E. 2018. A new stage of demographic change: A warning for economists. - Russian Journal of Economics 4 (2018) 229–248 DOI 10.3897/j.ruje.4.30166

Xu C., Kohlerb T., Lenton T., Svenning J.-C., and Scheffer M. 2020. Future of the human climate niche. - www.pnas.org/cgi/doi/10.1073/pnas.1910114117

Zorkaltsev V.I and Khazheev I.I. How climate impacts the economics. 2015. ECO. 7: 147-162

Supplementary 1.

Table 1. Climatic variable of places of migrant origin and labor in the Krasnoyarsk Territory

Place of Origin	January temper.	July temp.	Minusink		Krasnoyarsk		Boguchany	
			Δ Jan. temp	Δ Jul. temp	Δ Jan. temp	Δ Jul. temp	Δ Jan. temp	Δ Jul. temp
Bishkek	-2.6	24.9	-18.6	-5.3	-14.5	-6.2	-21.7	-5.9
Astana	-20.2	23.9	-1.0	-4.3	3.1	-5.2	-4.1	-4.9
Tashkent	1.9	27.8	-23.1	-8.2	-19.0	-9.1	-26.2	-8.8
Kiev	-6.3	19.6	-14.9	0.0	-10.8	-0.9	-18.0	-0.6
Voronezh	-9.3	20.2	-11.9	-0.6	-7.8	-1.5	-15.0	-1.2
Erevan	-3.6	26.4	-17.6	-6.8	-13.5	-7.7	-20.7	-7.4
Baku	3.9	26.2	-25.1	-6.6	-21.0	-7.5	-28.2	-7.2
Ulan-Bator	-21.6	18.2	0.4	1.4	4.5	0.5	-2.7	0.8
Harbin	-17.4	23.1	-3.8	-3.5	0.3	-4.4	-6.9	-4.1
Pyongyang	-6.0	24.3	-15.2	-4.7	-11.1	-5.6	-18.3	-5.3
Ust-Kamenogorsk	-16.0	20.0	-5.2	-0.4	-1.1	-1.3	-8.3	-1.0
Sofia	0.5	22.0	-21.7	-2.4	-17.6	-3.3	-24.8	-3.0
Ho Chi Minh City	26.0	28.0	-47.2	-8.4	-43.1	-9.3	-50.3	-9.0
Peking	-3.3	26.7	-17.9	-7.1	-13.8	-8.0	-21.0	-7.7
Bangkok	27.0	30.0	-48.2	-10.4	-44.1	-11.3	-51.3	-11.0
Ankara	0.3	23.5	-21.5	-3.9	-17.4	-4.8	-24.6	-4.5
Berlin	0.7	19.8	-21.9	-0.2	-17.8	-1.1	-25.0	-0.8
Kishineu	-1.9	22.1	-19.3	-2.5	-15.2	-3.4	-22.4	-3.1
Tel Aviv	13.0	27.0	-34.2	-7.4	-30.1	-8.3	-37.3	-8.0
Antalya	9.6	28.3	-30.8	-8.7	-26.7	-9.6	-33.9	-9.3
Tbilisi	2.3	24.9	-23.5	-5.3	-19.4	-6.2	-26.6	-5.9
Dushanbe	1.7	27.4	-22.9	-7.8	-18.8	-8.7	-26.0	-8.4
Norilsk	-27.0	14.3	5.8	5.3	9.9	4.4	2.7	4.7
Minusinsk	-21.2	19.6	0	0	4.1	-0.9	-3.1	-0.6
Krasnoyarsk	-17.1	18.7	-4.1	0.9	0	0	-7.2	0.3
Boguchany	-24.3	19.0	3.1	0.6	7.2	-0.3	0	0

GLOBAL WARMING AND CLIMATE REFUGEES OF 21ST CENTURY: A THREAT ASSESSMENT OF SEA LEVEL RISE FOR THE LOOMING HUMANITARIAN CRISIS

Ismail Utku Canturk

Abstract

Realism is the International Relations (IR) theory that still has the biggest influence over the discipline and policymaking processes. However, trivializing existential threats to states that have non-military origins causes realism to overlook the connections between national, human and environmental security. Focusing its empirical research on "future climate refugees due to sea level rise", this work asserts the necessity of an eco-centric paradigm shift in realist IR theory in order to propel global policymaking towards taking climate action. The novel discourse of "planetary realism" is presented as a pathway to increase state resilience during the Anthropocene.

Introduction

Mainstream International Relations (IR) literature, particularly Realist IR theory (that dominated the IR discipline throughout most of 20th century and still has the biggest impact in IR literature), mostly defines external threats toward state within the paradigm of "low politics-high politics" dichotomy. Realism defines any external threat that may endanger the survival of states as a "high politics" issue, categorizing the rest of the issues under "low politics". According to the realist paradigm, these "high politics" issues are state-centered military threats that have conventional origins. This definition trivializes existential threats to the states that are born out of economic, sociological, political and environmental sources by defining them as "low politics" issues. However, contemporary threats we face in 21st century that endanger the survival of the states are not only of military origin. In fact, current empirical data allows us to have an exact opposite claim. Many threats brought by the environmental crisis, especially climate change, endanger the existence of both the level of analysis (international system) and the unit of analysis (states) of realist IR theory.

As one of the most complex issues that threaten the international security in the 21st century, global warming stems from the rapid anthropogenic deterioration in the structure of the athmosphere. The depletion of ozone layer in the athmosphere is caused by the excessive industrial production (fossil fuels, industrial agriculture and husbandry) and consumption during the Anthropocene; due to the exponential increase in greenhouse gas density within the athmosphere, global temperature levels have increased by approximately $1°C$ relative to the pre-industrial levels. According to the Intergovernmental Panel on Climate Change (IPCC), this increase is expected to be exacerbated to $1.5°C$ between 2030-2052. Many newer simulations using advanced AI suggest far worse outcomes, asserting that IPCC's predictions are quite optimistic. This brings with it the possibility of one of the worst humanitarian crises in human history: climate refugees of 21st century. According to Myers, there were at least 25 million "environmental refugees" globally in 1997; the total number of recorded conventional refugees in the same year is only 22 million. The majority of the climate refugees reside in sub-Saharran Africa, Indian subcontinent, China, Mexico and Central America. Myers' famous prediction suggested that rising global sea levels, draughts and disruption of rain patterns is likely to cause existential and agricultural migrations that will increase the number of "environmental refugees" up to 200 million within 21st century. According to Brown, however, Myers himself admitted his famous estimate required "heroic extrapolations" even though it was calculated using the best contemporary data available to him. Despite this, Myers' attempt at bringing the possibility of a climate refugee crisis under academic and institutional spotlight has been successful.

This work adopts the term "climate refugees" over other variations such as "climate migrants" for two main reasons. One, "climate refugees" as a political label can serve as a "call to arms" both to highlight the possibility of mass environmental migrations abroad and to advocate for a protection-focused response against the environmental crisis. Two, promoting "climate refugee" as a legally recognized term can better equip international law in responding to a possible climate refugee crisis throughout the century. However, such proposed terminological shift is one that requires utmost delicacy; expanding the definition of the term "refugee" to make it also encompass people that have to migrate to another country due to climate change must not degrade the political strength of the term itself. This could do more harm than good, as taking away from the political meaning of the term "refugee" may reduce the international action taken for conventional refugees.

To Turn Back The Tide: Resilience in the Anthropocene

This work has two main objectives. The first is to focus specifically on the threat of global sea level rise and to demonstrate its consequences for coastal and island communities, using various data acquired from contemporary research and simulations that are based off of multiple scenarios in global temperature rise. The rapid thawing in Arctic and Antarctic ice sheet and Greenland's glaciers due to the global climate change is causing the global sea levels to rise; the world's oceans and seas have risen by approximately 15 to 20 cm in the last 100 years. Global warming itself is exacerbating the speed of sea level rise: global sea temperatures are rising in parallel with global temperatures, causing water bodies to expand and take up more space. Almost all coastal communities and island nations on the planet are subject to the destructive effects of sea level rise to an extent. The importance of tackling the threat of sea level rise can be assessed under two different approaches: "human security" and "national security". This makes it easier to convince policymakers to take necessary steps for climate adaptation policies. How sea level rise poses an existential risk to "human security" is empirically clear: Kulp and Strauss observed that currently, over 60 million people living in China, Bangladesh, India, Vietnam, Indonesia, Thailand, Philliphines and Japan are facing the destructive consequences of the rising sea levels. A recent simulation shows that even in a scenario in which the greenhouse gas emissions are radically reduced, the rising sea levels will result in coastal areas that consist of 19%, 26% and %17 of the populations of Bangladesh, Vietnam and Thailand respectively to be completely submerged underwater. Kulp and Strauss argues that, under a global warming scenario of 2°C relative to pre-industrial levels, sea level rise and annual flood levels will threaten terrestrial land that is housing 140 to 170 million people by 2050 and 310 to 420 million people by 2100. Developing or small countries are not the only ones that are going to be affected by sea level rise; many developed coastal regions around the world, including some of the most significant financial hubs such as New York, San Francisco, London, Brugge, Delft, Ribe, Bangkok, Shanghai and Port Douglas are under severe risk. To demonstrate such risk, this work uses flood data from CoastalDEM, one of the most accurate coastal risk assessment tools with algorithms that build on NASA's Shuttle Radar Topography Mission (SRTM) data, "cutting SRTM's error scatter nearly in half." It is important to note here, however, that data collected from algorithm and simulation-based methods have a much wider spectrum of results that don't account for human modifications to coastlines. These results can only be narrowed down and be made more accurate by localized field research and data collected from local / indigenous communities.[1] On the other hand, the correlation between sea level rise and "national security" is a topic that requires a more elaborate answer, supported by case studies and foreign policy analyses. In this work, India-Bangladesh Border Dispute is used to demonstrate possible national security threats states might perceive –or create- under rhetorical premises. It is clear that by antagonizing the anthropogenic factors that cause the sea level rise -not the climate refugees from Bangladesh- India and other major carbon actors can contribute to slowing down climate change and pursue climate adaptation policies.

Secondly, the work utilizes "planetary realism"[2] as a political tool that reforms realist IR theory to make it optimally effective in policymaking towards climate action. Acknowledging the current existential crisis and its inevitable effects –or rather, embracing the grim reality as it is- planetary realism strives towards preparing the states for surviving in the Anthropocene. It provides the optimal theoretical framework for climate change politics with practical tools that can efficiently be integrated into policymaking. It stresses that both minimizing the amount of damage coastal communities will have to suffer and tackling the issue of sea level rise requires "making states and communities of the world more resilient against the evolving risks of climate change". Using "resilience" as a policy model, planetary realism offers two vitally important practical mechanisms in order to successfully adapt to changing conditions of climate change. First mechanism is the harmonization of central and local policies. Planetary realism argues that no top-down, centralized adaptation policy is possible or desirable for the goal of planetary resilience. Issues caused by climate change, such as sea level rise, affect each region of the world differently. Hence, harmonizing local and central policies by guiding central planning according to local empirical data has vital importance. As IPCC holds and Rothe points out, "only the vulnerable communities themselves would possess the appropriate forms of tacit knowledge required for successful adaptation." Second mechanism is gathering information from indigenous populations throughout resilience policymaking. Planetary realism defines indigenous populations as communities that are "perfectly adapted to local ecosystems and their various rhythms, patterns and cycles". The UNESCO report titled *Weathering Uncertainty: Traditional Knowledge for Climate Change Assessment and Adaptation* supports this notion by pointing out that "indigenous peoples and local communities are actively responding to changing climatic conditions and have demonstrated resourcefulness and resilience in the face of climate change".

Wielding the mechanisms provided by planetary realism, this work concludes by returning to the threat of sea level rise and discussing resilience policymaking for both short-term and long-term mitigation strategies. For short-term, it discusses the reliability of human modifications to coastlines as a means to mitigate flood risk. Kelman points out that these modifications, "such as sea walls tend to modify floods so that apparent flood risk decreases in the short-term but actual flood risk increases in the long-term."[3] For long-term, the only feasible option to *turn back the tide* is making sure governments of the world –especially the major carbon actors such as China, United States, India, Russia, Japan and Germany- cut back on carbon emissions and reach "carbon neutrality" as soon as possible. Thanks to a theoretical framework that combines *realpolitik* of IR realism and the *reality* of the Anthropocene, planetary realism provides an effective pathway for convincing policymakers into taking definitive

---

[1] Further theoretical and practical discussion about the importance of local data is available within the rest of this full short paper.

[2] Named by Rothe and defined by him as the *realpolitik of resilience,* planetary realism is one of the three main political discourses over the Anthropocene.

[3] Personal communication with Professor Ilan Kelman.

climate action.

References

Brown, O. (2008). Migration and Climate Change. Geneva: International Organization for Migration, 11.

Climate Central. CoastalDEM: Better elevation data for better flood risk assessment. https://go.climatecentral.org/coastaldem/ (26.08.2021).

Etkin, D. (1999). Risk transference and related trends: driving forces towards more mega-disasters. *Global Environmental Change Part B: Environmental Hazards*, 1, 69-75.

Intergovernmental Panel on Climate Change (IPCC). (2018). Global Warming of 1.5°: Summary for Policymakers. Geneva: IPCC, 4-10.

Kelman, I. (2018). Islandness within climate change narratives of small island developing states (SIDS).

Kulp, S. A., & Strauss, B. H. (2019). New elevation data triple estimates of global vulnerability to sea-level rise and coastal flooding. *Nature Communications*, 10(4844), 3-4.

Myers, N. (1997). Environmental Refugees. Population and Environment: A Journal of Interdisciplinary Studies, 19(2), 167-182.

Nakashima, D. Et al. (2012). Weathering Uncertainty: Traditional Knowledge for Climate Change Assessment and Adaptation. Paris & Darwin: United Nations Educational, Scientific, and Cultural Organization and United Nations University, 8.

Rothe, D. (2020). Governing the End Times? Planet Politics and the Secular Eschatology of the Anthropocene. *Millenium: Journal of International Studies*, 48(2), 143-164.

Yamamoto, L., & Esteban, M. (2010). Vanishing Island States and sovereignty. *Ocean & Coastal Management*, 53(1), 1-9.

CATALYZING DECISION MAKING FOR MIGRATION AND SUSTAINABLE WATER-ENERGY-FOOD SYSTEMS - THE TEXAS CASE STUDY

Konstantinos Pappas

Introduction

Water, energy, and food are vital resource systems for human well-being and sustainable development. Pressures on these resources is projected to increase due to population growth, economic development, international trade, urbanization, diet shifts, cultural and technological changes, and climate variability. These societal megatrends continue to pressure already scarce or depleted natural resources, threatening their sustainability and undermining community resilience.

Migration trends are expected to grow in the US and globally, for different reasons (economic, climate, war-related, etc.). As the US hosts more immigrants than any other country, with one million people landing each year, it becomes important to better understand these migration trends, their root causes, and the anticipated impact they might have on the interconnected resource systems in host regions.

While a large body of work has explored the interconnections between water, energy, and food (WEF) systems during the past decade, with different tools being developed at different scales, little progress has been done on better integrating migration models with these WEF integrative assessment tools. Migration is connected directly and indirectly through basic resources, water, energy and food where there is hardly any literature found which has leveraged these interconnections to provide multi-dimensional framework.

Figure 1. Interconnections among water, energy food and migration

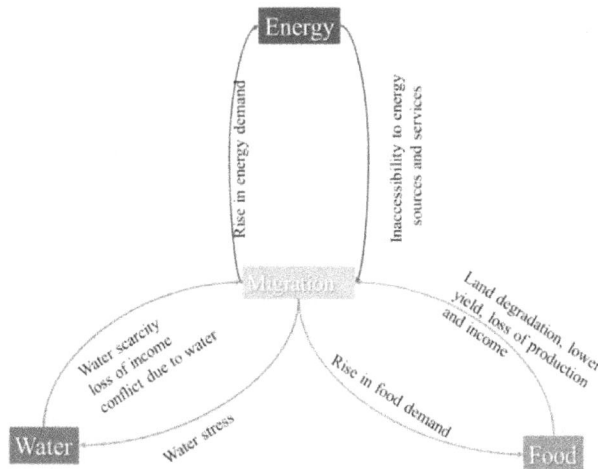

As WEF nexus framework is concentrated on understanding the key resource interactions, the nexus analysis offers an opportunity to realize the magnitude of resource insecurity surfacing from migration, identifying the critical issues when it happens and develop resilient planning in managing resources to reduce vulnerability and safely manage migration. The analysis can be extended to understand the resource insecurity in migrating communities and the resource pressure in hosting communities.

With growing population and increasing resource demand, such analysis is critical in planning sustainable, effective, and safe management of resources for migrants in future. Fig. 1 summarizes the discussed interconnections among water, energy food and migration.

The purpose of this paper is to provide a model of the WEF Nexus framework that can measure the impact of migration on WEF Nexus components, interconnections, and associated externalities, highlighting the case of Texas. Multi-sectoral decision makers lack the tools for quantifying the impact of anticipated migration flows on these interconnected resource systems and on economic, social, and environmental indicators. Such tools could play a key-role in the development of effective policies and management strategies across sectors to minimize any anticipated pressures.

Texas WEF Nexus and migration trends

The state of Texas is known for both its agricultural variety and energy production. Texas is a major U.S. producer of cattle, dairy, and cotton, oil, and natural gas. Additionally, the state houses a number of large urban cities including Houston, Austin, San Antonio, and Dallas. Texas' population size continues to increase in coherence with its use of natural resources (Daher et al., 2019, p. 456; USDA, 2016).

Water

By 2070, the state of Texas risks a 41 percent water gap due to a projected 70 percent growth in population between 2020 and 2070 (Daher et al., 2019, p. 456; TWDB, 2017). The energy and agricultural industries utilize water resources, making Texas a highly water-intensive state in total. Water is necessary for "nearly all production and conversion processes in the energy sector, including fuel extraction and processing (fossil and nuclear fuels, as well as biofuels) and electricity generation (thermoelectric, hydropower, and renewable technologies)" (Spang et al., 2014).

Energy

According to the U.S. Energy Information Administration (EIA), Texas is the largest energy-producing and energy-consuming state in the nation, producing 43 percent of the U.S.'s crude oil and 26 percent of its natural gas in 2020. The industrial sector, including refineries and petrochemical plants, accounts for half of the energy consumed in the state, while residential purposes comprise 33 percent of the total electricity use in Texas (Texas - State Energy Profile Overview - EIA, 2020).

Agriculture/Food

Texas leads the nation for the total number of farms with over 248,000 (2017 Census of Agriculture), and it contributed nearly $25 billion to the economy in products sold in 2017 (U.S. Department of Agriculture, 2017).

The production of Texas agriculture has been exposed to recent vulnerabilities due to climate variability in the form of "increasing temperatures, longer and more intense drought periods, and more extreme precipitation events," (Steiner et al. 2017). Regardless of the location or region, water is necessary to produce food due to irrigation requirements and livestock farming, while energy production is necessary for the irrigation and farming practices (i.e., tillage, pumping, fertilization, planting) (Kulat et al., 2019). The interlinkages between the agricultural and energy sectors can be manifested through increased pumping during droughts, which leads to long-term regional groundwater depletion and impacts other systems (Wang et al. 2011; Steiner et al. 2017).

Drought and high temperatures are of similar concern for beef cattle and other livestock production, as they affect the availability of grazing and forage systems, lower their water supply, and lead to increased heat stress (Polley et al. 2013; Steiner et al. 2015, Steiner et al. 2017).

Demographic and migration trends

Texas is the second most populous state in the US (US Census Bureau, 2020). Of Texas' total population growth between 2010 and 2016, migration accounted for almost exactly half. The state's net domestic migration represented about 32 percent of the total increase and net international immigration accounting for 19 percent (Texas Comptroller of Public Accounts et al., 2017).

Texas depends on and is shaped by its migration flows. Out of Texas' immigrant population of 4.9 million people, one in five workers in its economy is an immigrant. Together, immigrants make up a vital 22 percent of the state's labor force in a variety of industries (U.S. Economic Classification Policy Committee (ECPC) et al., 2017). Additionally, there are an estimated 1.6 million undocumented residents (5.7 percent of the total population) (US Census Bureau, 2019; Rodríguez-Sánchez & Rice University's Baker Institute for Public Policy, 2020).

The highest shares for immigrant places of birth include Asia at 22.9 percent and Latin America at 67.5 percent. According to Kobayashi-Solomon (2019), immigrants increasingly originate from the "dry corridor" of Central America, such as El Salvador, Honduras, and Guatemala, rather than the usual historic majority of trends from Mexico. This group of countries has been hit by alternating drought and high precipitation patterns connected to climate change. The addition of social unrest combined with unstable farming economies had led to migration movements (Kobayashi-Solomon, 2019).

Domestic migration to Texas has also increased considerably recently. The recent Silicon Valley "Texodus" signifies a new trend of high-income technology companies and laborers moving to Texas, especially to Austin. Some highlight the lack of business restrictions and regulation as an incentive for companies, while others point to the lower cost of living (Farivar 2021, Agresta 2021). In 2018 and 2019, net migration to Texas from California was over 45,000, higher than any other years in the previous decade and accounting for about a third of the average yearly domestic immigration rate as found by the Texas demographic center (Fulton 2021, White et al., 2017). Although this immigration driver is at a smaller scale than international migration and involves a different demographic of migrants, it highlights that Texas is seeing population growth from many different factors.

The impacts of migration on the labor market, agricultural industry, and the distribution of resources can run large. Many immigrants in Texas work in industries affected resource strains. Additionally, immigrant groups categorized as low-income, non-English speaking, or undocumented will have an increasingly difficult time adapting to a strain in WEF resources, which is indicated by their current difficulties accessing health and human services compared to native-born residents (Pereira et al., 2012).

Conceptual Scenario Based Framework and Tool Structure

The proposed conceptual framework for this case study can serve as a foundation for transcending the relationship between migration and WEF systems. This can be represented as a cascaded framework for two different concepts: an increase in population due to migration and water-energy-food resource interactions in a host country (see Figure 2). The framework starts with simple population projection which accounts for the gradual increase in population as well as the net inflow of migrants in the projected year. Once the migration inflow is assumed, the overall resource demand is projected based on total population at the destination country.

The next step is to identify the key interactions in basic and shared resources (i.e., water, energy, food, land, and environment) and develop an integrated water-energy-food system. In this part of the framework, the major consumed food groups (crops, vegetables, fruits, and animal feeds), sources of water, and sources of energy are identified for the state of Texas. The consumption of the food groups is assumed to be dependent on the population, whereas the local production of food, as well as imports and exports, can be decided. Similarly, the available energy and water sources are identified, but the share from each of the sources in total energy and water demand are kept as decision variables. Based on a projected or assumed net migration inflow, identified food, water and energy portfolios, the feasibility and performance of any proposed scenarios can be assessed while respecting resource system interconnections with local characteristics.

Figure 2. The proposed conceptual scenario-based framework.

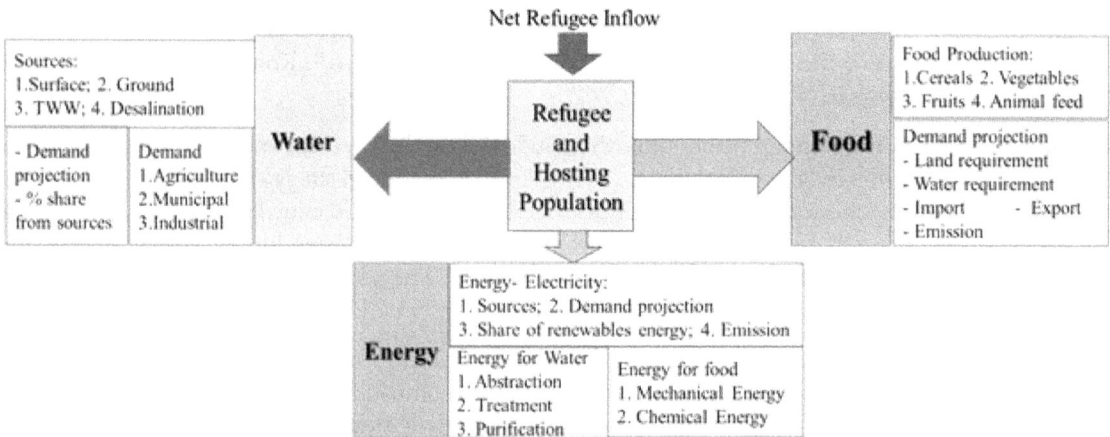

As the increase in population results from migration, subsequent resource demand and the interconnections among resources are also identified. Figure 3 represents the tool structure that allows for creation and assessments of different scenarios. It consists of inputs that reflect the integrated migration hosting, water, food, and energy strategies.

Figure 3. Tool structure for the proposed framework

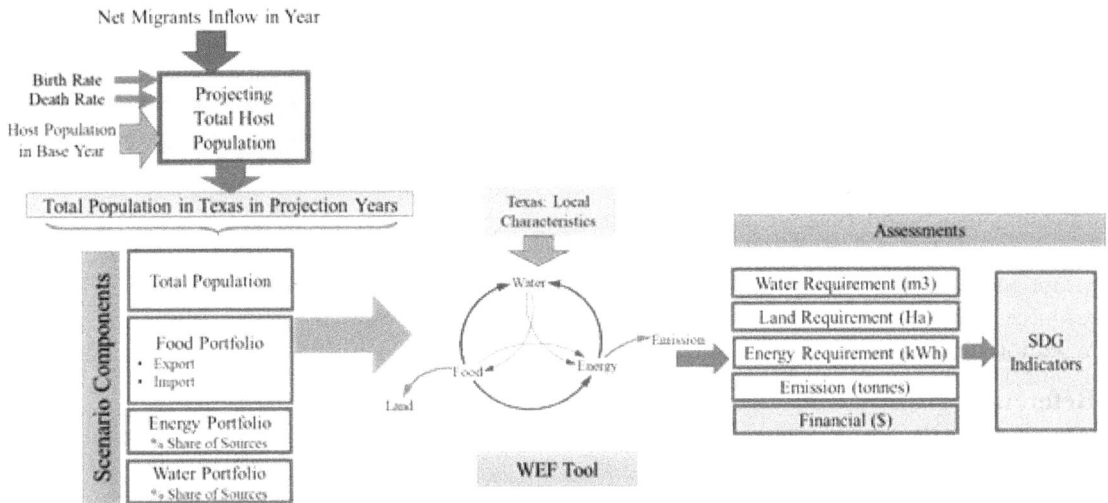

Scenarios explored

Governed by the presented methodology and tool structure, five different scenarios were developed by changing the production quantities for different types of crops, sources of water, sources of energy, and the number of migrants Texas is projected to host, in order to assess the impacts in a future year.

Year 2018 is taken as reference year for comparison. The migration rates selected are based on the migration rates of previous years (i.e., equal to average rates seen in 2000-2010, 2010-2015, 2010-2018, and 20% higher than average for 2010-2018). The resource demand is projected for years 2030 and 2050 under a *net-zero migration* condition and assumptions that have been made for assessing scenarios. Then, for the proposed scenarios, resource demand and externalities are calculated for year 2030 and 2050 using the developed tool.

Preliminary results

Preliminary assessments show how a gradual increase in population, resulting from economic migration, can impose a demand burden on food and energy, as well as on shared resources such as land and water.

The food and feed demand, water, and land requirements are found to be linearly dependent on the population growth projected in 2030 and 2050. The stress on commonly shared resource water becomes severe when the projected population increases rapidly under different annual migration rates and composition.

Different energy and food resources have diverse water and land requirements.

Alternative sources of water, such as desalination, rainwater harvesting, increasing water use efficiency and treating more wastewater at the cost of more expenditure, energy, and emission.

By changing the portfolio of energy and food as well as introducing more alternative sources for water, the stress on commonly shared resources can be decreased.

Conclusion

Lack of water and food security have driven people to change their residence, temporarily or permanently (e.g., the drought in Mexico caused migration to the U.S.). Moreover, migration inflows have caused water and food scarcity (e.g., Lebanon and Jordan). The mismanagement of water and food systems in Central America were also found to be leading drivers of migration as farmers' markets worsened (Oxfam Report). Thus, resource stress can both trigger migration or be triggered by migration and lead to the causation or worsening of associated events (Pandemics and Disease Spread).

A WEF framework built based on foresight technique can help us in assessing such stress on resources based on demand and supply. Foresight can take various forms, such as horizon scanning (identifying emerging issues and possible impacts on trends), trends analysis (analyzing factors of changes), scenarios building (testing alternative possible futures) or visions and roadmaps (identifying desired future and associated policy agendas). This analysis can be further extended to inspect and measure resource stresses and resource capacities in countries to prevent or predict forced or voluntary migration movements.

References

Daher, B., Lee, S. H., Kaushik, V., Blake, J., Askariyeh, M. H., Shafiezadeh, H., Zamaripa, S., & Mohtar, R. H. (2019). Towards bridging the water gap in Texas: A water-energy-food nexus approach. Science of The Total Environment, 647, 449–463. https://doi.org/10.1016/j.scitotenv.2018.07.398

Kobayashi-Solomon, E. (2019, April 24). Agriculture, Climate Change, And The Southern Border Crisis. Forbes. https://www.forbes.com/sites/erikkobayashisolomon/2019/04/24/climate-change-agriculture-and-the-southern-border-crisis/#524a118831c0

Kulat, M. I., Mohtar, R. H., & Olivera, F. (2019). Holistic Water-Energy-Food Nexus for Guiding Water Resources Planning: Matagorda County, Texas Case. Frontiers in Environmental Science, 7, n.p. https://doi.org/10.3389/fenvs.2019.00003

Polley, H. W., Briske, D. D., Morgan, J. A., Wolter, K., Bailey, D. W., & Brown, J. R. (2013). Climate Change and North American Rangelands: Trends, Projections, and Implications. Rangeland Ecology & Management, 66(5), 493–511. https://doi.org/10.2111/rem-d-12-00068.1

Rodríguez-Sánchez, J. I., & Rice University's Baker Institute for Public Policy. (2020, May). Undocumented immigrants in Texas: a cost-benefit assessment. Rice University's Baker Institute for Public Policy. https://www.bakerinstitute.org/files/15839/

Spang, E. S., Moomaw, W. R., Gallagher, K. S., Kirshen, P. H., & Marks, D. H. (2014). The water consumption of energy production: an international comparison. Environmental Research Letters, 9(10), n.p. https://doi.org/10.1088/1748-9326/9/10/105002

Steiner, J. L., Briske, D. D., Brown, D. P., & Rottler, C. M. (2017). Vulnerability of Southern Plains agriculture to climate change. Vulnerability of Southern Plains Agriculture to Climate Change, 146(1–2), 201–218. https://doi.org/10.1007/s10584-017-1965-5

Steiner, J., McNeeley, S., Cozzetto, K., Childress, A., & Ojima, D. (2015). Great Plains regional technical input report. Island Press.

Stillwell, A. (2010, May). The Energy-Water Nexus in Texas. University of Texas at Austin. http://www.webberenergygroup.com/publications/the-energy-water-nexus-in-texas-2/#citation

Texas - State Energy Profile Overview - U.S. Energy Information Administration (EIA). (2020, March). U.S. Energy Information Administration. https://www.eia.gov/state/?sid=TX

Texas Comptroller of Public Accounts, United States Census Bureau, McPherson, K., & Wright, B. (2017, October). Gone To Texas: Migration. Texas Comptroller of Public Accounts. https://comptroller.texas.gov/economy/fiscal-notes/2017/october/migration.php

Texas Water Development Board. (2017). 2017 State Water Plan | Texas Water Development Board. http://www.twdb.texas.gov/waterplanning/swp/2017/

U.S. Department of Agriculture. (2017). Market Value of Agricultural Products Sold Including Landlord's Share, Food Marketing Practices, and Value-Added Products: 2017 and 2012. USDA. https://www.nass.usda.gov/Publications/AgCensus/2017/Full_Report/Volume_1,_Chapter_1_State_Level/Texas/st48_1_0002_0002.pdf

U.S. Economic Classification Policy Committee (ECPC), Statistics Canada, & Instituto Nacional de Estadistica y Geografia. (2017). North American Industry Classification System Manual (NAICS). United States Census Bureau. https://www.census.gov/eos/www/naics/index.html

US Census Bureau. (2019). U.S. Census Bureau QuickFacts: Texas. Census Bureau QuickFacts. https://www.census.gov/quickfacts/TX

US Census Bureau. (2020, January 2). Population Estimates Continue to Show the Nation's Growth Is Slowing. The United States Census Bureau. https://www.census.gov/newsroom/press-releases/2019/popest-nation.html

USDA. (2016). Texas State Data. United States Department of Agriculture Economic Research Service. https://data.ers.usda.gov/reports.aspx?StateFIPS=48&StateName=Texas&ID=17854

Wang, W., Park, S. C., McCarl, B. A., & Amossen, S. (2011). Economic and Groundwater Use Implications of Climate Change and Bioenergy Feedstock Production in the Ogallala Aquifer Region. Agricultural & Applied Economics Association's 2011 AAEA&NAREA Joint Annual Meeting, Pittsburgh, Pennsylvania.

MIGRACIÓN, ACCESO A LA SALUD Y TICS APRENDIZAJES FRENTE AL COVID-19

García Zamora Pascual Gerardo, Juan Lamberto Herrera Martínez,
Dellanira Ruiz de Chávez Ramírez, Cristina Almeida Perales, Reyes Estrada Claudia Araceli, and
Christian Starlight Franco Trejo

Resumen

La emergencia sanitaria por COVID-19 ha tenido como efecto una negación sistemática de los derechos de las personas migrantes, muchos gobiernos en Latinoamérica, restringieron el movimiento de migrantes en tránsito para intentar disminuir tanto la propagación como el impacto de COVID-19. Tanto el cierre de fronteras y actividades denominadas "no esenciales" derivó en circunstancias donde los migrantes siguen perdiendo apoyos de servicios y redes, empleo, seguridad y protección social, lo que se traduce en la pérdida oportunidades para acceder a una vida digna y regresar a sus países de origen.

En este artículo se aborda y estudia la relación entre la migración internacional en el marco de la emergencia sanitaria y el uso de las tecnologías de la información y comunicación (TIC); asumidas como una herramienta empleada para empoderar a los migrantes en el acceso y ejercicio pleno de sus derechos fundamentales.

Las consecuencias políticas y económicas resultantes del cierre de actividades, así como el ambiente hostil que padece la población migrante han forzado a migrantes y refugiados a retornar por la misma ruta para huir de su contexto y regresar a las mismas condiciones de violencia, privación y peligro de las que intentaron huir en primera instancia. En este nuevo ciclo de migración revertida alentada por COVID, evidencia de nueva cuenta la vulnerabilidad por la falta de garantías en los países de tránsito y protección de los derechos humanos de las personas migrantes.

La migración es un evento decisivo en la vida de las personas, deben considerarse las diversas circunstancias en la que ocurre esta y las que delimitan este suceso, así como la integración al país de destino y los efectos que puedan generarse en conjunto, además de otros factores como su salud, que influyen en su calidad de vida. Las TIC poseen presencia, influencia y utilización por los colectivos migrantes, además de difusión de contenidos, noticias, formas de financiamiento, debates políticos entre otros grandes beneficios adicionales.

Durante la integración en el país destino, el inmigrante afronta entonces procesos de adecuación al nuevo entorno, las TIC sirven de instrumentos enfocados al contacto con familiares y/o amistades también migrantes en el país de origen qué, con apoyo de redes sociodigitales; coadyuvan en la construcción y soporte de redes migratorias en estos contextos digitales.

Abstract

The health emergency due to COVID-19 had and still has an effect of a systematic denial of the migrant rights, many governments in Latin America, restricted the movement of migrants in transit to try to reduce both the spread and the impact of COVID-19. Both the closure of borders and activities called "non-essential" resulted in circumstances where migrants continue to lose support from services and networks, employment, security and social protection, which this translates into the loss of opportunities to access a dignified life and return to their origin countries.

This article addresses and studies the relationship between international migration in the context of the health emergency and the use of information and communication technologies (ICT); assumed as a tool used to empower migrants in the access and full exercise of their fundamental rights

The political and economic consequences resulting from the closure of activities, as well as the hostile environment suffered by the migrant population, have forced to migrants and refugees to return by the same route to flee their context and return to the same conditions of violence, deprivation and danger. of those who tried to flee in the first instance. In this new cycle of reverse migration stimulated by COVID, this is the evidence of vulnerability due to the lack of guarantees in transit countries and the protection of the human rights of migrants is evidenced once again.

Migration is a critical event in people's lives; the age and circumstances in which it occurs and delimits this event, integration to the country of destination and effects that may be generated together, among other factors influencing its occurrence, must be considered. quality of life and health outcomes. ICTs have presence, influence and use by migrant groups, in addition to the dissemination of content, news, forms of financing, political debates among other benefits.

During integration in the destination country, the immigrant then faces processes of adaptation to the new environment, ICTs serve as instruments focused on contact with family members and / or friends who are also migrants in the country of origin what, with the support of ICT; They contribute to the construction and support of migratory networks in these digital contexts.

Introducción

El objetivo del presente trabajo es analizar la relación entre migración, derechos humanos y el uso de las tecnologías de la información y comunicación como una herramienta en el empoderamiento en los derechos fundamentales de los migrantes en la declaración de los Derechos Universales del Hombre en 1958, durante la pandemia de la COVID-19. La migración ha sido compañera de la especie humana desde el momento en que el Homo erectus salió de África e inició su expansión por otros continentes, en busca de alimentos y mejores condiciones de vida.

Cuando el tamaño de la población superaba los límites tolerables por la naturaleza era necesario buscar alimentos en otras partes. La sobrevivencia ha sido desde entonces el principal expulsor de los humanos del lugar de donde nacieron, con el paso del tiempo los motivos se han incrementado y el proceso migratorio se ha convertido en un fenómeno complejo y de mucho riesgo para la salud e integridad de las personas que lo realizan.

Migración ante la pandemia por COVID-19

En la actualidad podemos hablar de dos tipos de migrantes: 1) los que son forzados por: a) falta de opciones laborales y condiciones de vida dignas, b) por violencia e inseguridad en sus lugares de origen, c) por problemas de tipo político y 2) los que migran por elección, son personas con mejores condiciones socioeconómicas pero insatisfechas con las expectativas de vida y desarrollo personal que ofrecen sus lugares de origen.

En este trabajo se abordará la primera opción, por presentar las condiciones más complejas y de mayor vulnerabilidad a sus protagonistas. Según refiere García Macías P, con la contingencia sanitaria de la COVID-19 la migración se ralentizó al tiempo que se impusieron restricciones y cierre de fronteras, sin embargo, continuaron los desplazamientos masivos forzados a causa de desastres naturales como lo son: ciclos fuertes de lluvias y sequías, problemas económicos, falta de empleo, ingresos insuficientes, además de la violencia e inseguridad presentes en los países de origen. A pesar de la emergencia sanitaria, la movilidad de desplazados y/o refugiados no se ha detenido, la supervivencia ha premiado en la situación de emergencia ante el riesgo de contagio por el coronavirus[1].

El virus COVID-19 visibilizó la fragilidad y deterioro de los sistemas sanitarios del planeta, centrados en su mayoría en una atención curativa y hospitalocentrista, producto de tres décadas de políticas neoliberales orientadas al desmantelamiento del estado de bienestar y en el fortalecimiento de la oferta de servicios como la atención a la enfermedad y la educación por la iniciativa privada a fin de limitar los servicios ofertados por los gobiernos.

António Guterres, el Secretario General de la Organización de las Naciones Unidas (ONU), expresó en 2020 que para los migrantes y desplazados, la pandemia ha tomado la forma de una triple crisis: la sanitaria, la socioeconómica y la de protección. Se argumenta "crisis sanitaria" porque en las condiciones de hacinamiento a las que se enfrentan los migrantes, a menudo impide el llamado distanciamiento social, que se convierte en "un lujo imposible" y, en los campamentos que los albergan, es difícil acceder a agua, saneamiento, atención de salud y nutrición; se denomina "crisis socioeconómica" porque los migrantes y refugiados, en especial los que trabajan en la economía informal, laboran sin protección social y su pérdida de ingresos afecta las remesas vitales, que son de las que dependen sus familias, suman 800 millones de personas. La "crisis de protección" alude a la propagación del virus, que hizo que 150 países adoptasen restricciones fronterizas, en 99 se han desatendido solicitudes de asilo y, en general se avivaron la xenofobia, el racismo y la estigmatización, pasando por alto los Derechos humanos[2].

La pandemia por COVID-19 aglutina fuertes efectos en el ámbito de la salud y profundas implicaciones, tanto en el crecimiento económico como en el desarrollo social. COVID-19 arriba a Latinoamérica y el Caribe en un contexto de bajo crecimiento, en especial de alta desigualdad y vulnerabilidad, en el que se observan tendencias crecientes en pobreza y pobreza extrema, un debilitamiento de la cohesión social y manifestaciones de descontento de las poblaciones. Las medidas de cuarentena, en especial el distanciamiento físico y social, necesarios para frenar la propagación acelerada del coronavirus y salvar vidas, han generado pérdidas de empleo (en 2019 alcanzó 3.5% de la Población Económicamente Activa (PEA) respecto al 4.7% registrado en enero 2021, un incremento del 1.2%) lo que reducen los ingresos laborales de las personas y de los hogares. La pérdida de ingresos afecta sobre todo a los amplios estratos de población que se encuentran en situación de pobreza y vulnerabilidad, así como a las personas que trabajan en actividades más expuestas a despidos y reducciones salariales, en general condiciones de precariedad laboral[3].

La experiencia internacional indica que los efectos de la pandemia del COVID-19 están profundizando las desigualdades sociales. Ello, a su vez, incrementa el riesgo de que personas en situación de vulnerabilidad (especialmente las mujeres, los niños y la población migrante) sean víctimas de trabajos forzosos o de la trata de personas con fines de explotación laboral o sexual. Asimismo, miles de migrantes en América Latina corren el riesgo de ser víctimas de traficantes que aprovechan la

---

[1] Alberto Acosta, Pascual García, y Ronaldo Munck, *Posdesarrollo. Contexto, contradicciones y futuros | Observatorio Económico Latinoamericano OBELA*, Primera (Quito-Ecuador: Ediciones Abya-Yala, 2021), http://www.obela.org/recomendaciones/posdesarrollo-contexto-contradicciones-futuros.

[2] Acosta, García, y Munck.

[3] Cristian Téllez, "Tasa de desempleo se ubica en 3.5% en 2019", Noticias financieras, El Financiero, 2021, https://www.elfinanciero.com.mx/economia/tasa-de-desempleo-se-ubica-en-3-5-en-2019/.

desesperación de una población altamente vulnerable para conseguir ganancias económicas[4] [5].

Para los migrantes, el acceso a los sistemas sanitarios y a la seguridad social es deficitario a causa de la escasa información de los derechos de migrantes en tránsito, así como por su temor a ser identificados en el momento de solicitar la atención de los sistemas de salud locales. Estos problemas se agudizan en el caso de la niñez migrante —acompañada o no— en situación de desplazamiento interno y ante el posible aumento de la xenofobia y la discriminación y el racismo en contra de los migrantes[6].

En el contexto de la pandemia, el cumplimiento de las medidas sanitarias por parte de las autoridades migratorias no está garantizado, lo cual pone a los migrantes y a la población de los países receptores en riesgo. Una investigación realizada por el New York Times y el Proyecto Marshall, entre marzo y junio de 2020, reveló que el Servicio de Inmigración y Control de Aduanas (ICE) de Estados Unidos deportó a migrantes portadores del SARS-CoV-2 hacia países de Centroamérica como Haití, Guatemala y El Salvador. A finales de abril, la agencia Reuters reportó casos similares de infección por el nuevo coronavirus entre migrantes deportados de Estados Unidos hacia Colombia, Guatemala, Haití, México y Jamaica[7] [8].

Por su parte, México también deportó a fines de marzo hacia Guatemala, Honduras y El Salvador a la gran mayoría de los migrantes que se encontraban en los centros oficiales de acogida, a pesar del rechazo y el miedo al contagio que ello generó entre la población nacional de esos países. Según datos proporcionados por la Comisión Mexicana de Ayuda a Refugiados que recoge de la Agencia de la ONU, desde el pasado mes de enero de 2021, se tienen registradas más de 22,600 solicitudes, lo que representa un incremento del 31% respecto al año pasado (2020) y 77% de igual forma, respecto al período similar en 2019[9]

Este colectivo estaba afectado por los Protocolos de Protección de Migrantes (PPM) (Remain in Mexico Programme), un acuerdo entre México y Estados Unidos que permite a este último país enviar de regreso a México a los solicitantes de asilo de nacionalidad no mexicana mientras su solicitud está pendiente de resolución en las cortes estadounidenses. Sin embargo, a pesar de que este retorno está avalado por un acuerdo bilateral entre estados, no existen garantías para la salud y seguridad de los solicitantes de asilo retornados a México. Muchos de ellos no encuentran un lugar donde vivir –ya que los albergues para migrantes están reduciendo su aforo para cumplir con las normas de distancia social– y se ven obligados a retirar sus solicitudes de asilo y transitar por diferentes ciudades en busca de alojamiento y empleo, lo cual incrementa su vulnerabilidad[10].

Algunos gobiernos, en vez de cumplir con sus obligaciones de ampliar los servicios de protección y salud para las comunidades de alto riesgo en la región, aprovechan de la crisis para impulsar medidas de desalojo forzoso y deportación. La pandemia destaca así una dinámica que revierte la migración forzada sobre las personas que huyeron en primer lugar de países y comunidades afectadas por múltiples crisis en los últimos años y que ahora se ven obligados a regresar, ya sea por la pérdida de

[4] Luisa Feline Freier, "CIDOB - Movilidad y políticas migratorias en América Latina en tiempos de COVID-19", *inmigración en tiempos de COVID-19*, Anuario CIDOB de la Inmigración 2020, febrero de 2021, 15, https://doi.org/doi.org/10.24241/AnuarioCIDOBInmi.2020.50.

[5] Alicia Bárcena, "América Latina y el Caribe ante la pandemia del COVID-19 Efectos económicos y sociales", abril de 2020, https://www.cepal.org/es/publicaciones/45337-america-latina-caribe-la-pandemia-covid-19-efectos-economicos-sociales.

[6] Miguel Tonatiuh Santiago, *Los desafíos de la migración y los albergues como oasis: encuesta nacional de personas migrantes en tránsito por México*, 2018.

[7] Acosta, García, y Munck, *Posdesarrollo. Contexto, contradicciones y futuros | Observatorio Económico Latinoamericano OBELA*.

[8] GobMX Gobernación, "Movilidades. ANÁLISIS DE LA MOVILIDAD HUMANA", el 5 de noviembre de 2020, http://www.politicamigratoria.gob.mx/work/models/PoliticaMigratoria/CEM/Publicaciones/Revistas/movilidades/5/movno5.pdf.

[9] Int ONU, "Las solicitudes de asilo en México baten su récord en marzo", Organismo internacional, Noticias ONU, el 13 de abril de 2021, https://news.un.org/es/story/2021/04/1490802.

[10] Freier, "CIDOB - Movilidad y políticas migratorias en América Latina en tiempos de COVID-19".

medios para sopesar necesidades básicas ; por la limitación de cobertura y provisión de servicios de salud y protección social; o bien a causa del retorno forzado de migrantes ´irregulares´ a consecuencia de medidas gubernamentales tomadas a pesar de recomendaciones de organismos oficiales y expertos en contra de ello , incluyendo la declaración internacional[11].

Migración y Derechos humanos

La Pandemia de COVID-19 ha resultado en una negación de derechos de las personas migrantes, muchos gobiernos de América Latina, introdujeron medidas de restricción de movimiento con el objetivo de disminuir la propagación e impacto de COVID-19. Por ejemplo, Argentina, Bolivia, Paraguay, Ecuador, Perú y Colombia decretaron una cuarentena obligatoria para todos aquellos que viven dentro de su territorio. Ecuador y Perú introdujeron toques de queda; mientras que, en Chile y El Salvador, se declaró estado de emergencia, dejando la seguridad interna y la custodia de servicios de salud al control de las fuerzas armadas.

Estas estrategias son restrictivas para migrantes y refugiados en dichos países, muchos de ellos excluidos de mercados laborales u oportunidades de acceder a beneficios sociales ofrecido a connacionales. En México, con más de un millón de migrantes viviendo en el país según cifras de 2019, a muchos migrantes y refugiados se les negó la posibilidad de acceder a albergues, al tiempo que se ha incrementado la vigilancia fronteriza y deportaciones. La mayoría de los países de la región han cerrado sus fronteras a todo extranjero o no-residente[12].

El cierre de actividades no esenciales y fronteras ha creado una situación en donde los migrantes pierden el apoyo de los servicios y las redes, empleo y opciones de seguridad y protección social, y sobre todo la posibilidad de obtener una vida digna al ser obligados a cambiar la dirección de los flujos migratorios y regresar a sus países de origen, a pesar del potencial de abuso, violencia y riesgo de infección por COVID-1.9 en situación de tránsito, tal como reconoce la Organización Internacional para las Migraciones.

Esto sucede particularmente en dos rutas migratorias en América Latina: aquella que involucra migrantes provenientes de países del triángulo de América Central de Honduras, Guatemala y El Salvador hacia México; y aquella que va desde Venezuela hacia Colombia y Brasil. En ambos casos, las consecuencias político-económicas desencadenadas por el cierre de actividades y el ambiente hostil que vive la población migrante han forzado cientos de migrantes y refugiados venezolanos y Centroamericanos a retornar por la misma ruta que tomaron para huir y regresar a las mismas condiciones de violencia, privación y peligro de las que intentaron huir en primera instancia. Este nuevo ciclo de migración revertida, catalizada por COVID, evidencia la vulnerabilidad por la falta de garantía en los países de tránsito, en la protección de los derechos humanos de los y las migrantes, generando problemas por tres razones claves:

Primero. El retorno forzado extenderá las situaciones de desplazamiento prolongado en las cuales los migrantes quedarán atrapados en un ciclo de desplazamiento forzado, incluso dentro de su propio país de origen. Innumerables personas muy probablemente saldrán de nuevo de su país en el futuro y, al mismo tiempo, este periodo de desplazamiento prolongado exacerbara los factores de riesgo asociados al mismo, incluyendo la violencia física y psicológica (agresión, violencia sexual, etc.) y limitantes en el acceso a servicios de salud y protección social.

---

[11] Ana Sedas et al., "[LANCET MIGRATION] REPORTE SITUACIONAL MIGRACIÓN DE TRÁNSITO EN MÉXICO DURANTE LA PANDEMIA DE COVID-19", Migration and health, el 27 de mayo de 2020, https://doi.org/10.13140/RG.2.2.23768.32005.
[12] Santiago, *Los desafíos de la migración y los albergues como oasis*.

Segundo. La migración revertida incrementará la vulnerabilidad financiera de aquellos migrantes y personas desplazadas, para los cuales los riesgos de vivir en pobreza, explotación y abuso aumenta.

Tercero. Aquellos retornados a sus países de origen podrían enfrentar sentimientos anti migratorios y de estigmatización. Al mismo tiempo, podrán encontrarse en situaciones donde se les desconocen todos los derechos considerados en la Declaración Universal de los Derechos Humanos emitida el 10 de diciembre de 1948 en Ginebra Suiza[13] [14].

Yanapay (Yanapay es una palabra en quechua, sinónimo de la palabra contribución o ayuda) funge como los aportes de los migrantes, dentro de sus interacciones y compromisos (formales e informales, amplios y cerrados) que construyen los individuos con la sociedad en la que habitan, el compromiso que tienen de ellos para el otro y para sí.

Así, en un sentido amplio, por Yanapay migrante se entiende la acción y contribuciones que generan la construcción del bienestar en el entorno de los migrantes y los procesos sociales que dan forman y sustentan a la comunidad y sociedad migrante. Manteniendo un equilibrio y bienestar entre ellos, la cooperación recíproca, la ayuda mutua que trasciende la monetización y las remesas. Yanapay migrante se contextualiza con las prácticas socioculturales.

En su vertiente socio-cultural Yanapay migrante, puede fungir también como experiencia emancipadora o generadora de resiliencia y de cambio. Pueden ser los catalizadores en cambio de patrones (disminución del machismo, promoción del reciclaje, disminución de tasas de fertilidad, propagación del poder de la democracia, aumento de equidad de género, etc.). Coincidiendo con Giovanni Sartori en el año de 2001, respecto a los estudios de los efectos positivos de la sociedad multicultural o bien el concepto de la superdiversidad, idea basada en las realidades que viven los migrantes cuando habitan y experimentan ciudades o comunidades con un alto índice de heterogeneidad, donde las culturas se mezclan, conviven y fusionan creando cohesión social[15].

Las Tecnologías de la Información y Comunicación (TIC)

Las nuevas tecnologías deben de ser una herramienta transversal; facilitadoras para la formación de los nuevos perfiles de ciudadanía mundial, que les permita estar más y mejor informados, con una mayor integración en un mundo globalizado que garantice el acceso y disfrute a sus derechos universales; un ejemplo de ello es la Organización No Gubernamental (ONG) "Pueblo Sin Fronteras", que en su Web como: un pequeño grupo de educadores populares, organizadores, migrantes, refugiados y personas solidarias con migrantes del mundo que, durante años ha estado acompañando a las caravanas de inmigrantes de América Central a los EE UU.

Esta agrupación es apoyada por las organizaciones "Pueblo Sin Fronteras" y el "Centro de Dignificación Humana", ambas de origen mexicano y mediante el sitio que recibe donaciones llamado " Charity fundraising made easy" con el objeto de recibir financiación, donaciones para la logística, alimentación y apoyo legal a migrantes que transitan desde Centroamérica hacia los EE UU mediante la asociación "Freedom For Immigrants".

Como forma de afrontamiento por parte de los migrantes y sus familias, la comunicación es una nueva faceta, aunada a la creciente y predominante conectividad sociodigital que otorga las bondades de ofrecer la comunicación por texto, audio, multimedia y la ubicuidad, permite a las personas usuarias

---

[13] ONU CEPAL, *El desafío social en tiempos del COVID-19* (CEPAL, 2020), https://www.cepal.org/es/publicaciones/45527-desafio-social-tiempos-covid-19.
[14] Pia Riggirozzi, Jean Grugel, y Natalia Cintra, "¿Proteger a los Migrantes o Revertir la Migración? COVID-19 y los Riesgos de una Crisis Prolongada en América Latina", el 18 de agosto de 2020, 7.
[15] Acosta, García, y Munck, *Posdesarrollo. Contexto, contradicciones y futuros | Observatorio Económico Latinoamericano OBELA*.

adquirir nuevas facetas de interacción, en sus relaciones interpersonales a partir de estos medios digitales[16].

La migración es un evento crítico en el curso de vida de una persona, para el cual debe considerarse la edad en la que ocurre, las circunstancias que delimitan este suceso, la integración a el país de destino y los efectos que en conjunto pueden generarse a lo largo de la vida, entre otros factores de influencia en calidad de vida y resultados de salud. Desde esta perspectiva, la migración internacional representa en sí misma un determinante social de salud; circunstancias en las que esta tiene lugar, en particular experiencias de riesgos y vulneraciones sociales y de salud, las que pueden influenciar en forma negativa la salud.

Esto es de especial relevancia dadas las barreras que se han identificado a nivel mundial para el acceso y uso de los sistemas de salud por parte de población migrante en esta pandemia, así como respecto a las medidas impulsadas por las autoridades sanitarias a nivel global. Así, por ejemplo, la evidencia da cuenta de una falta de información generalizada respecto a COVID-19 en población migrante a nivel global. Junto con lo anterior, las medidas de distanciamiento social y mejoramiento de la higiene adoptadas por gran parte de los países no son viables para algunos grupos de migrantes. En este sentido, la evidencia sugiere asegurar que las poblaciones migrantes se acerquen a los sistemas de salud en busca de información y atención de salud relacionada al COVID-19 así como también de salud mental[17].

La evidencia de lo anterior, la encontramos en un estudio realizado en Chile en 2020, en la cual uno de cada cuatro participantes consideró no estar recibiendo información suficiente sobre el virus SARS-CoV2 y su enfermedad COVID-19 (25%), pero uno de cada tres reportó que la información que obtenía no era comprensible (33%). El 61% declaró no sentirse preparado para enfrentar esta pandemia y uno de cada cuatro migrantes internacionales indicó que ha recibido información de mala o muy mala calidad acerca del COVID-19 (25%). Nueve de cada 10 reportaron sentirse angustiados o preocupados (90%) y 7 de cada 10 tristes o deprimidos a causa de la pandemia (70%). Comparado con colombianos (referencia), los migrantes internacionales venezolanos y haitianos tienden a sentirse menos preparados respecto a migrantes internacionales que califican como buena o muy buena la información que han recibido por parte de autoridades, así como equipos de salud que también se sienten mejor preparados. Los que se han sentido angustiados o deprimidos tienden a sentirse menos preparados para enfrentar el COVID-19.

Los resultados de este estudio dan cuenta de que el recibir información sobre la pandemia y el estado anímico de las personas son factores importantes asociados a sentirse preparado para enfrentar el COVID-19 en migrantes internacionales en Chile. Ambas dimensiones son potencialmente modificables para incidir en una mejor atención en salud a migrantes en tiempos de pandemia. Estos resultados se condicen con lo que está siendo presentado por la evidencia internacional en el contexto de la situación de la población migrante internacional a frente a la pandemia de COVID-19. Existe consenso respecto a que la pandemia de COVID-19 está exacerbando la situación de precariedad de esta población[18].

---

[16] Rebeca Oroza Busutil y Yoannis Puente Márquez, "Migración y comunicación: su relación en el actual mundo globalizado", *Revista Novedades en Población* 13, núm. 25 (junio de 2017): 10–16.

[17] Riggirozzi, Grugel, y Cintra, "¿Proteger a los Migrantes o Revertir la Migración? COVID-19 y los Riesgos de una Crisis Prolongada en América Latina".

[18] Báltica Cabieses, Florencia Darrigrandi, y Alexandra Obach, "Factores asociados a sentirse preparado para enfrentar el COVID-19 en migrantes internacionales en Chile", *Revista del Instituto de Salud Pública de Chile* 4, núm. 2 (el 31 de diciembre de 2020), https://doi.org/10.34052/rispch.v4i2.103.

Las TIC tienen gran presencia, influencia y utilización por los colectivos migrantes, así como difusión de contenidos, noticias, medios de financiamiento, debate político y hasta "fake news" [19]. Los procesos migratorios implican una serie de cambios significativos, tanto en las personas como en sus familias en sus diversos contextos biopsicosociales, además del cultural y económico. Llegado el momento de migrar, desde el comienzo del viaje, este se convierte en un inmigrante, frente a profundos cambios y retos relativos a la cultura, gastronomía, idioma, entre otros, con un duelo de dejar atrás familia, seres queridos y el entorno del que era parte. Una forma de afrontamiento por parte de los migrantes y sus familias es la comunicación en una nueva faceta, la creciente y predominante conectividad sociodigital, que otorga las bondades de disponer, además de la comunicación por texto y el audio, a la multimedia y la ubicuidad, permitiendo a las personas usuarias, adquirir nuevas facetas de interacción, en sus relaciones interpersonales a partir de estos medios digitales[20].

Respecto a las circunstancias de migración como respuesta tanto a crisis humanitarias como por solicitud de refugio, el acceso a TIC durante la travesía o trayecto migratorio podría estar restringido o disminuido, no obstante, suelen existir refugios o estancias con una adecuada conectividad digital, que permite incluso realizar actividades como la captura de selfie (autofoto) o uso de comunicaciones por voz. Durante la integración al nuevo ambiente en el país destino, el inmigrante afronta un proceso de adecuación al nuevo entorno en donde las redes sociodigitales fungen como instrumentos vitales, enfocadas al contacto con familia y/o amistades tanto de quienes han migrado como quienes se encuentran en el país de origen. El resultado en general es la edificación y andamiaje de auténticas redes migratorias en y desde los contextos digitales[21].

Conclusiones

Las contribuciones de los migrantes a la sociedad de origen y destino, se ha cernido bajo una concepción cuantitativa y economicista, tomando como unidad única de medición a las remesas. Percibiendo la contribución de los inmigrantes en referencia solamente a los aportes al Producto Interno Bruto (PIB) del país que los acoge.

La migración es un evento crítico en la vida de las personas, deben de considerarse diversos factores como la edad y las circunstancias en la que ocurre y delimitan este evento, la integración al país de destino, así como los efectos que puedan suscitarse en conjunto, además de otros factores de influencia en su calidad de vida y resultados en la salud.

A partir de que las TIC gozan de una significativa influencia y utilización por los diversos grupos de migrantes, la difusión de una cantidad, cada vez más ingente de contenidos; entre ellos noticias, formas de financiamiento de actividades, debates, actividades lúdicas y otras formas de socialización, permiten que los diversos colectivos de migrantes y sus familias, independientes de su ubicación geográfica, puedan lograr y mantener lazos estrechos de interacción, que les mantiene con fuertes vínculos a través de este tipo de tecnologías

No obstante, con lo anterior, están también presentes "nuevas normalidades" en este contexto con la presencia de nuevos ciclos de migración revertida, detonadas, estimuladas y fomentadas por COVID-19; hacen evidentes y acentúan las brechas y vulnerabilidades por causas de la ausencia de garantías en

[19] Cecilia Melella y Gimena Perret, "Uso de la Internet en contextos migratorios. Una aproximación a su estudio", *Enl@ce: Revista Venezolana de Información, Tecnología y Conocimiento* 13, núm. 2 (el 1 de febrero de 2016), https://www.redalyc.org/jatsRepo/823/82349540005/html/index.html.
[20] Oroza Busutil y Puente Márquez, "Migración y comunicación".
[21] Daniela Jaramillo-Dent y Paloma Contreras-Pulido, *Migrantes y redes sociales: Entrevista semi-estructurada para explorar usos y apoyos*, 2020, https://www.researchgate.net/publication/345342590_Migrantes_y_redes_sociales_Entrevista_semi-estructurada_para_explorar_usos_y_apoyos.

los países de origen, tránsito y EE UU respecto a la protección de los derechos humanos de las personas migrantes, generando una gran cantidad de problemas y padecimientos de toda índole, en el trayecto de ida y retorno, además de regresar a las condiciones que les han expulsado en sus países de origen.

Para los inmigrantes, durante la integración en el país destino; estos afrontan procesos de adecuación al nuevo entorno donde las TIC y en particular las redes sociodigitales, sirven de instrumentos enfocados al enlace y contacto con familiares y/o amistades, que han migrado y también como instrumento para visibilizar las condiciones en que realizan su proceso migratorio e incluso violación a sus derechos humanos, las nuevas tics pueden proporcionar certeza y tranquilidad para acceder a servicios sociales cuando se requiera de forma emergente. En general, el resultado es la construcción y soporte de redes migratorias mediante las TIC en estos contextos digitales.

Referencias

Acosta, Alberto, Pascual García, y Ronaldo Munck. *Posdesarrollo. Contexto, contradicciones y futuros | Observatorio Económico Latinoamericano OBELA*. Primera. Quito-Ecuador: Ediciones Abya-Yala, 2021. http://www.obela.org/recomendaciones/posdesarrollo-contexto-contradicciones-futuros.

Bárcena, Alicia. "América Latina y el Caribe ante la pandemia del COVID-19 Efectos económicos y sociales", abril de 2020. https://www.cepal.org/es/publicaciones/45337-america-latina-caribe-la-pandemia-covid-19-efectos-economicos-sociales.

Cabieses, Báltica, Florencia Darrigrandi, y Alexandra Obach. "Factores asociados a sentirse preparado para enfrentar el COVID-19 en migrantes internacionales en Chile". *Revista del Instituto de Salud Pública de Chile* 4, núm. 2 (el 31 de diciembre de 2020). https://doi.org/10.34052/rispch.v4i2.103.

CEPAL, ONU. *El desafío social en tiempos del COVID-19*. CEPAL, 2020. https://www.cepal.org/es/publicaciones/45527-desafio-social-tiempos-covid-19.

Freier, Luisa Feline. "CIDOB - Movilidad y políticas migratorias en América Latina en tiempos de COVID-19". *inmigración en tiempos de COVID-19*, Anuario CIDOB de la Inmigración 2020, febrero de 2021, 15. https://doi.org/doi.org/10.24241/AnuarioCIDOBInmi.2020.50.

Gobernación, GobMX. "Movilidades. ANÁLISIS DE LA MOVILIDAD HUMANA", el 5 de noviembre de 2020. http://www.politicamigratoria.gob.mx/work/models/PoliticaMigratoria/CEM/Publicaciones/Revistas/movilidades/5/movno5.pdf.

Jaramillo-Dent, Daniela, y Paloma Contreras-Pulido. *Migrantes y redes sociales: Entrevista semi-estructurada para explorar usos y apoyos*, 2020. https://www.researchgate.net/publication/345342590_Migrantes_y_redes_sociales_Entrevista_semi-estructurada_para_explorar_usos_y_apoyos.

Melella, Cecilia, y Gimena Perret. "Uso de la Internet en contextos migratorios. Una aproximación a su estudio". *Enl@ce: Revista Venezolana de Información, Tecnología y Conocimiento* 13, núm. 2 (el 1 de febrero de 2016). https://www.redalyc.org/jatsRepo/823/82349540005/html/index.html.

ONU, Int. "Las solicitudes de asilo en México baten su récord en marzo". Organismo internacional. Noticias ONU, el 13 de abril de 2021. https://news.un.org/es/story/2021/04/1490802.

Oroza Busutil, Rebeca, y Yoannis Puente Márquez. "Migración y comunicación: su relación en el actual mundo globalizado". *Revista Novedades en Población* 13, núm. 25 (junio de 2017): 10–16.

Riggirozzi, Pia, Jean Grugel, y Natalia Cintra. "¿Proteger a los Migrantes o Revertir la Migración? COVID-19 y los Riesgos de una Crisis Prolongada en América Latina", el 18 de agosto de 2020, 7.

Santiago, Miguel Tonatiuh. Los desafíos de la migración y los albergues como oasis: encuesta nacional de personas migrantes en tránsito por México, 2018.

Sedas, Ana, Mercedes Aguerrebere, Luis Martinez Juarez, Luis Alba, Itzel Eguiluz, y Jacqueline Bhabha. "[LANCET MIGRATION] REPORTE SITUACIONAL MIGRACIÓN DE TRÁNSITO EN MÉXICO DURANTE LA PANDEMIA DE COVID-19". Migration and health, el 27 de mayo de 2020. https://doi.org/10.13140/RG.2.2.23768.32005.

Téllez, Cristian. "Tasa de desempleo se ubica en 3.5% en 2019". Noticias financieras. El Financiero, 2021. https://www.elfinanciero.com.mx/economia/tasa-de-desempleo-se-ubica-en-3-5-en-2019/.

LGBTQ FORCED MIGRANTS' LABOR MARKET INTEGRATION IN MEXICO CITY: PERSPECTIVES FROM MEXICAN GOVERNMENT AGENCIES, INTERNATIONAL ORGANIZATIONS, AND MEXICAN CIVIL SOCIETY

Rolando Diaz

Introduction

Mexico's increasingly diverse migration patterns, from Spanish Republicans and Ashkenazi Jews to Haitian and Black African groups, have captured the interest of researchers across disciplines. Eclipsed by the politics of Mexican migration to the US, Mexico has a long history of immigration, emigration, refuge, transit, and return migration. These realities compound Mexican migration policy and coupled with the gendered experiences of migration, generate a complicated journey for migrants, especially those pertaining to the Lesbian, Gay, Bisexual, Trans, and Queer (LGBTQ) community.

LGBTQ migration has been in increasingly researched in Western migrant-receiving states, where LGBTQ asylum laws and integration experiences are studied. LGBTQ migration towards Mexico from Central has sharply increased during the 2010s, yet LGBTQ migrants' integration experiences are understudied. Mexico City, known for its cosmopolitan culture, is home to many LGBTQ migrants, but efforts to integrate them are not well known.

This paper aims to understand how LGBTQ migrants are integrated into the city, and to understand the recent challenges in this undertaking.

Methodology

The research design is composed of 17 semi-structured interviews with individuals representing Mexican government agencies, international organizations, and Mexican civil society who are associated with the integration of migrants across Mexico. The interviews were conducted in Spanish through remote platforms during Summer 2020. Due to the COVID-19 pandemic, no interviews were possible with LGBTQ migrants. Mexico City was selected as the site over its strong diversity, history of migration and LGBTQ rights, and its proximity to migration organizations and networks.

Literature Review

Researchers in Migration Studies have inquired into gender and migration policies for decades, but those studies have fallen within confines of heteronormative understandings of migrants' journeys. Heteronormativity has long been the basis for how systems operate (Rich, 1980; Warner, 1990).

Since the 1980s, theorists like De Lauretis (1991), Berlant (1998), Butler (1999), and Sedgwick (1990) have advanced queer theory to gain better understandings of how gender inequities impact LGBTQ people. Early queer theory, however, didn't explore international migration contexts. Emerging out of the HIV/AIDS pandemic and US Immigration Act of 1990, queer migration studies became a necessary subdiscipline. Studies by Cantú (2009), Chavez (2013), Luibhéid (2008), and Manalansan (2006) advanced understandings of queer migration and impacts of migration policies on LGBTQ people. Using mostly qualitative approaches, these studies amplify LGBTQ migrant narratives and their intersecting identities. Queer migration scholars have emphasized migrants' experiences mostly in Western countries, leaving limited understanding of Latin America in this context. However, queer migration continues to diversify as research questions become decentered away from heteronormative and Western-centric presumptions.

Literature on labor market integration is also Western-centric and limited. Most of it focuses on migrants' labor integration in the US and Europe. In Mexico, the primary focus is on inter-regional migration and return migration. Very little literature exists on international forced migrants' labor integration in Mexico, much less pertaining to LGBTQ migrants. While labor integration is mainly applied to a European context, Desiderio's (2016) interpretation of labor integration can also be applied to Mexico.It should also be considered that in addition to integrating newcomers, Mexico does face challenges in integrating return migrants, for which government investment into reintegration has been a key priority in recent presidential administrations (Schmidtke & Chauyffet, 2018), (Alfaro; Hernández; Salas, 2019), (Télles-Anguiano; Cruz-Piñero; Burey-Garbey, 2013) (Lizama, 2018).

To further understand labor integration in Mexico, the country's legal framework and political geography needs to be dissected. Two main laws governed Mexican immigration law, the 1974 *Ley General de Población* and the 2011 *Ley de Migración*. Additionally, the 1984 Cartagena Declaration served as the international basis that guides Mexico's approach to refugee admissions in response to major humanitarian crises across Latin America that the 1951 Refugee Convention and 1967 Protocol did not account for. Mexico's migration policies began to advance in the 2010s, allowing migrants to access new services with less bureaucracy (Tamagno, et al., 2018). Inconsistencies in how the 2011 law is applied continues to mark the overall migration phenomenon across the country, highlighting Mexico's pattern of legislating on impulse, and not through long-term solutions (García 2018). This is especially evident as conditions across Central America for LGBTQ people become increasingly dire, all the while Mexico grapples with a heavily securitized northern and southern border.

Despite Mexico City's forward-thinking culture and the country's favorable legal framework that offers protections for LGBTQ Mexicans, the country's neighbors are not so privileged. In Honduras, for instance, 215 LGBTQ people were murdered between 2009-2015 (Tucker, 2016). Between 2007-2017, over 1,200 LGBTQ Salvadorans have sought gender-based asylum in the US (HRW, 2021). Patterns of violence have caused many to flee towards the US-Mexico border, and in 2017, many witnessed "Rainbow caravans" from Central America. In 2013, the first LGBTQ refugee claims were made in the southern border city of Tenosique, Tabasco (Kiernan; Flores; Lucero, 2017), presenting new challenges for Mexico's migration system.

Findings

Budget and operational support

A lack of adequate budget in provider's capacities to address challenges in migration and labor integration was identified as one of the most consequential factors in the lack of integration efforts. Government agencies, international organizations, and civil society all expressed similar concerns regarding budget constraints, including agencies like *Instituto Nacional de Migración* (INM), *La Unidad Política Migratoria, Registro e Identidad de Personas* (UPMRIP), *Comisión de Ayuda a Refugiados* (COMAR), the United Nations High Commissioner for Refugees (UNHCR), and *Sin Fronteras*. Mexico's top refugee authority, COMAR, reported its difficult task of processing 70,000 applications with only 150 personnel in 2019. With an annual budget of USD$1.2 million, help to fill operational voids is requested by UNHCR.

The dismal budget for refugee processing also impacts integration efforts. "Very weak budgets mean less successful integration," stated Ana with *Sin Fronteras*. Consequently, the only pragmatic approach is to introduce pilot integration programs, according to Jessica, an employee with UPMRIP. Budget limitations have also provoked competition over who's integration is more urgent. The recent Migration Protection Protocols (MPP) at the US-Mexico border, for instance, presented major challenges in how international organizations respond to the migrants' integration needs. At the same time, return migration of Mexican immigrants abroad has been a high priority of the federal government, forcing vulnerable groups like migrant seniors, children, women, LGBTQ people, and disabled people out of the federal government's purview, leaving the task to civil society and international organizations.

LGBTQ migrant data

This study revealed challenges in identifying LGBTQ migrants due to institutional practices that do not track data relating to LGBTQ people. Every stakeholder was asked if there is a tracking process for LGBTQ people. Mexico's top immigration and labor authorities like INM, COMAR, *Secretaría de Trabajo y Previsión Social*, as well as Mexico City's local *Secretaría de Inclusión y Bienestar Social*, all stated they do not track LGBTQ migration data unless sexual orientation is disclosed first. The limited data that does exist comes from INM, which reported only seven LGBTQ migrants since 2018. However, these data do not fall in line with the reality on the ground, where civil society reports a higher number of LGBTQ migrants coming through migrant shelters and stations across the country. "It comes down to prioritizing attending people on the ground versus tracking data," Jessica of UPMRIP states. Mexican government agencies and civil society in the capital are in a position where they cannot afford to quantify migrants' particularities but are instead forced to face the urgent reality of getting them processed and sheltered, that is, if they do not decide to not move to the US-Mexico border. This research was unable to identify LGBTQ migrants, who could have offered more insight, however COVID-19 restrictions limited the research.

Building awareness

This study found that building awareness and sensitivity training with immigration and labor institutions has become an increased priority by international organizations. "We conduct trainings so that we can build better understandings among public officials on sexual orientation…we want to ensure public officials can guarantee adequate responses to vulnerable migrants," says Andremar of the International Organization for Migration. Doing so, however, is easier in Mexico City than in other regions. "We do need to work towards sensibility training in key institutions that are local, state, and federal," says Florian with UNHCR. "In Mexico City, you can change your identification documents to fit your gender identity, but we know that LGBTQ migrants will be treated differently in states like Chiapas or in the northern region compared to Mexico City," says Jessica with UPMRIP. Despite efforts to build awareness of LGBTQ rights within immigration institutions, the progress is slow. "The Mexican government has had international recommendations for over a decade, but there has not been much progress," says Jessica. "Many of our LGBTQ migrants have suffered beatings from police…there have been instances of police stealing their money, telling them 'I hope they deport you,'" reported Sister Lidia Mara de Souza of the Scalabrinian Mission for Refugees based in Mexico City.

Labor integration programs

A UNHCR-led pilot program, *Reubicación, Vinculación Laboral y Acompañamiento* has shown promise in advancing labor integration for migrants. This specific program started in Saltillo, Coahulia in 2016, where labor shortages in local industry needed to be filled. In conjunction with COMAR, INM,

Secretaría de Trabajo y Previsión Social, and *Servicio Nacional de Empleo*, 38 migrants found full-time jobs in 2016, 114 in 2017, 500 in 2018, with results showing that 6 out of 10 migrant families in this program were lifted out of poverty in the first year of integration. This pilot program has been extended to other cities, including Guadalajara, Monterrey, Puebla, and León, according to Florian with UNHCR. It is unclear, however, if this program aided in LGBTQ migrants' integration as that data is not tracked by any of the agencies involved. In Mexico City, local integration efforts in civil society, such as Casa Mambré, show promising socioeconomic integration programs that offer employment to LGBTQ migrants, mainly in the cosmetology and retail. The partnership between *Casa Mambré* and employers is the only LGBTQ socioeconomic integration program in the country. More locally, Mexico City's *Programa Hospitalitaria y Movilidad Humana* led by the *Secretaría de Inclusión y Bienestar Social* offers capacity training programs and matches migrants with employment, mainly in retail and customer service industries, based on their experience. Like the national integration program, it is unclear if LGBTQ people benefit from this program as well, but it cannot be concluded that it does or does not benefit LGBTQ migrants. *Casa de las Muñecas Tiresias* is a transwomen shelter in Mexico City that also aids migrant transwomen, however founder Kenya Cuevas states that with all the integration efforts, migrant transwomen are still susceptible to less desirable work, placing them in vulnerable and dangerous positions. Labor and health education is a necessary component for LGBTQ migrants, according to Kenya, and is the least invested.

References

Anguiano-Tellez, M; Piñeiro-Cruz, R; Garbey-Burey, R. (2013). Migración internacional de retorno: trayectoras y reinserción laboral de emigrantes veracruzanos. Papeles de Población.

Berlant, L., & Warner, M. (1998). Sex in public. *Critical inquiry*, 24(2), 547-566.

Butler, J. (1990). Gender Trouble: Feminism and the subversion of identity. 1st Ed. Routledge.

Cantú, L. (2009). The sexuality of migration. New York University Press.

Chavez, K. (2013). *Queer Migration Politics: Activist Rhetoric and Coalitional Possibilities.* University of Illinois Press. Retrieved from: http://www.jstor.org/stable/10.5406/j.ctt3fh5cn

De Lauretis, T. (1991). Queer theory: Lesbian and gay sexualities. *Differences: A Journal of Feminist Cultural Studies*. Vol. 2, No. 22.

Desiderio, M. (2016). Integrating refugees into host country and labor markets: Challenges and policy options. Washington DC: Migration Policy Institute.

Lizama, M. (2018). Labor reintegration of return migrants in two rural communities of Yucatan, Mexico. Migraciones Internacionales.

Luibhéid, E. (2004). Heteronormativity and immigration scholarship: a call for change. *GLQ: A Journal of Lesbian and Gay Studies,* 10(2).

Luibhéid, E. (2008). Queer/migration. *GLQ: A Journal of Lesbian and Gay Studies,* vol. 13.

Manalansan, M. (2006). Queer intersections: Sexuality and gender in migration studies. The *International Migration Review. Vol. 40, No. 1.*

Manalansan, M. (2003). Global divas: Filipino gay men in the diaspora, Durham, NC: Duke University Press.

Schmidtke, R. & Chauyffet, R. (2018). Reintegrating Returned Mexican Migrants Through a Comprehensive Workforce Development Strategy. Wilson Center. Retrieved from: https://www.wilsoncenter.org/article/reintegrating-returned-mexican-migrants-through-comprehensive-workforce-development-strategy

Sedgwick, E. K. (1990). Epistemology of the closet. *University of California Press.*

Tamagno, C, et al. (2018). Migración Laboral, Seguridad Social y Empleo Juvenil en México. In Migración Laboral y Seguridad Social en la Alianza del Pacífico. International Organization for Migration, Internatoinal Labor Organization, Ibero-American Social Security Organization.

ACADEMIC BRAIN DRAIN: THE CASE OF NORTH MACEDONIA

Merita Zulfiu Alili, Memet Memeti, Blerta Ahmedi-Arifi and Pranvera Kasami

Abstract

Skilled labour is an important asset for any country in the development process and the emigration of skilled individuals presents a threat of a 'brain drain' which can affect growth, development and the quality of education. Brain drain in this research represents the loss of academic staff and researchers from a source country to a recipient country. Using survey data this study investigates the factors affecting academic staff's decision on migration. It critically examines brain drain in higher education institutions in North Macedonia and its implications. Most of the academic staff intends to migrate to more developed countries mainly because of low standards of living and wages, because they think that there is no future in this country, lack of promotion possibilities based on merit and political influence in universities. Based on the findings this paper proposes policy recommendations for institutions to explore strategies on how to best use the skills of academic and research staff for improving socio-economic benefits, and most importantly commitment to implementing these strategies.

Keywords: Rule of law, migration, academic staff

Introduction

North Macedonia as many other countries in the region is facing the challenge of "brain drain" for a long time and especially in the last decade. Despite the intensive migration of all categories of population, the recent research indicates an increase of the percentage of highly educated and qualified persons that are leaving the country.

This paper present the analysis related to the challenge called "brain drain", or the migration of the academic staff or skilled individuals from North Macedonia to other countries. In the recent years North Macedonia is facing an increase in the phenomenon of "brain drain". This is the case due to the fact that the the academic staff is not satisfied with the working conditions in North Macedonia and with the existings prospects for career development. In different European countries the academic staff finds better opportunities for employment and development compared to North Macedonia. This is the reason why the emigration of the population from North Macedonia includes a considerable number of the educated population, namely, the academic staff or in general the skilled individuals.

The aim of this research is to highlight the perspective of the citizens of Macedonia who work in academia and research, regarding the dilemma to continue working in their home country or to leave for another country. The data from the survey presented in more detail in the next section provide answers to the questions whether there is still an intention among North Macedonian academic staff to leave the country and which are the push and pull factors.

Republic of North Macedonia for a long time is facing the challenge of "brain drain", ie the migration of highly qualified people, despite the existence of intensive migration of all categories of the population, recent research shows that for the last few years there are increases in the number of qualified and educated people in the field of social sciences who leave the country (Dokmanoviq, 2017, p.4; Šelo Šabić and Kolar, 2019; Topuzovska Latkovikj et al., 2019). So far, the North Macedonian state institutions have fostered strong political ties and utilized the potential of the Diaspora for political mobilization primarily around questions of identity, and in this regard the economic cooperation between the two sides and especially cooperation in the field of brain gain has yet to happen (CRPM)·

In 2018, a total of 228,000 nationals of the WB6 emigrated legally to the EU in 2018, according to a recent Eurostat report andt the outflow was strongest in Albania, where 2.2% (62,000 people) of the country's overall population migrated to the EU and the situation is quite similar in North Macedonia (2.1%; 24,300 people) (Valeska, Palm, & Hansjörg, 2020).

Survey analysis

Data for this study were collected between April and June 2021 in the form of an online questionnaire sent to the main public and private universities in North Macedonia. The questionnaire was answered by 295 university professors representing all major fields of study in social and natural sciences, and humanities.

The questionnaire had 32 questions organised into four sections: biographical questions such as age, gender, ethnicity, place of residence, university, faculty, academic title, salary, followed with questions on satisfaction with their salary and opportunities for research, opportunities to progress professionally, access to research funds, government investments in research and development; intentions to migrate both virtually and physically; intended destination country and incentives and barriers thereto; and their history of migration. The aim of the questionnaire was to match the intention to migrate with a wide range of individual characteristics and different push and pull factors.

Table 1 describes the characteristics of the respondents. In this sample, the percentage of females (51.19%) is slightly higher compared to males (48.81%). The average age of the professors and researchers is 44.06 years, corresponding with the reached academic title (half of our respondents are assistant or associate professors hence in their mid-career). The questionnaire was mainly answered from Albanian ethnic background professors (63.05%), whereas 34.58% were declared as Macedonians, 1.02% as Turkish, 0.68% as Vlach, 0.34% as Bosnian and 0.34% as other. The data show that most of the respondents live in urban places (both males and females). A question about the net monthly salary was included in the questionnaire. In this regard, most of the respondents (83.56%) declared to have a monthly net salary up to 1000 euro, 13.36% have a net monthly salary from 1001 to 1500 euro, 2.40% are in the category from 1501 to 2000 euro and only 0.68% of the respondents have a monthly net salary over 2000 euro and those are males. In addition, the respondents were asked if they are satisfied with their net monthly salary and if not, how much their salary should increase so they would be satisfied. As expected, the majority (77.05%) are not satisfied with their net monthly salary, 47.08% of whom would like their salary to be increased from 20% to 50%.

Table 1. Characteristics of the respondents (all data % except age)

Characteristics of the respondents		Female	Male	Total
Gender		51.19	48.81	100
Age (mean, years)		41.23	47.03	44.06
Ethnicity	Macedonian	35.76	33.33	34.58
	Albanian	60.93	65.28	63.05
	Turkish	1.32	0.69	1.02
	Vlach	1.32	0.00	0.68

	Bosnian	0.66	0.00	0.34
	Other	0.00	0.69	0.34
Place of residence	Urban	84.77	78.47	81.69
	Rural	15.23	21.53	18.31
	Collaborator	19.21	13.89	16.61
	Assistant Professor	27.81	21.53	24.75
Academic title	Associate Professor	27.15	23.61	25.42
	Full Professor	13.91	30.56	22.03
	Other	11.92	10.42	11.19
	0-1000 euro	89.26	77.62	83.56
	1001-1500 euro	9.40	17.48	13.36
Monthly net salary	1501-2000 euro	1.34	3.50	2.40
	over 2000 euro	0.00	1.40	0.68
	Yes	18.24	19.44	18.84
Are you satisfied with your salary?	No	79.73	74.31	77.05
	Other (partially satisfied)	2.03	6.21	4.08
	10-20 %	9.70	7.32	8.56
If not, to be satisfied with your salary, the same should increase by:	20-50 %	51.49	42.28	47.08
	50-80 %	24.63	28.46	26.46
	80-100 %	5.22	13.01	8.95
	over 100 %	8.96	8.94	8.95

Source: Authors' calculations.

Determining the conditions in which professors and researchers work in North Macedonia and their impact on brain drain the questions, "Do you think that the government is investing enough in research and development?, "Do you have access to funding in your research field?" and "Do you consider that you progress in your career in your country?" were included in the survey.

In this regard, as presented in Figure 1, most of the respondents (94.88%) have given a negative response. A similar trend is presented in the part of financing their research projects. Most of the respondents (64.01%) declared that they have not obtained any kind of funding for their research projects (Figure 2). One third of the respondents have obtained funds for their research either through institutions where they work, international institutions or national agency for research. However, as shown in Figure 3, only 11.53% consider that they do not progress in their career or even regress (4.75%), whereas 31.86% have a little progress and 41.02% progress to some extent. Only 8.14% of the respondents consider that they are greatly progressing in their career and about 3% declared a full progress.

Figure 1. Do you think that the government is investing enough in research and development?

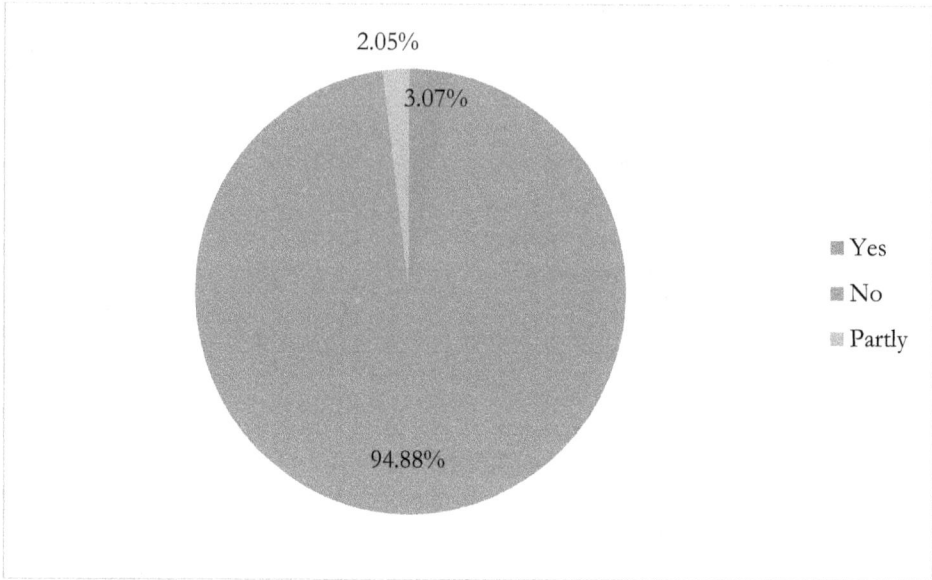

2.05%

3.07%

Yes
No
Partly

94.88%

Figure 2. Do you have access to funding in your research field?

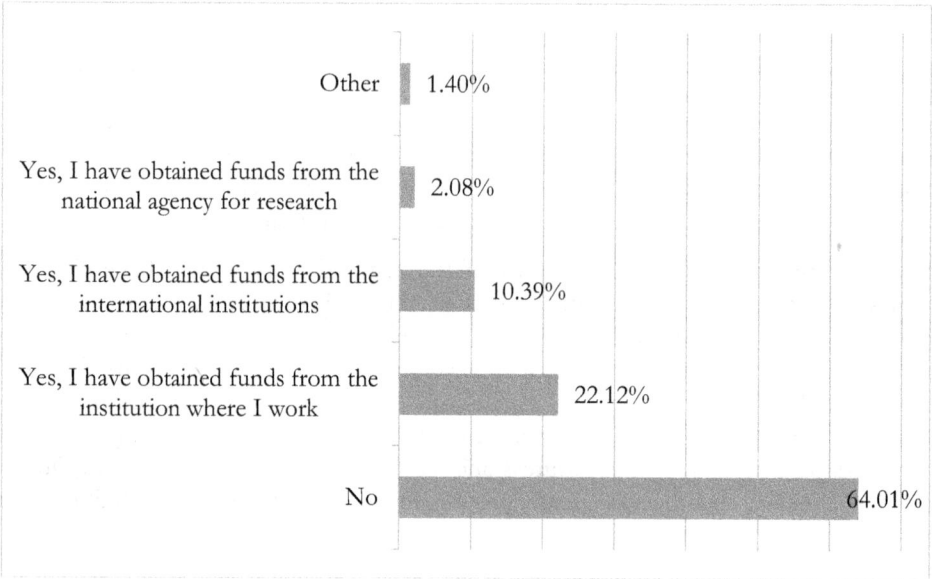

Other — 1.40%

Yes, I have obtained funds from the national agency for research — 2.08%

Yes, I have obtained funds from the international institutions — 10.39%

Yes, I have obtained funds from the institution where I work — 22.12%

No — 64.01%

Figure 3. Do you consider that you progress in your career in your country?

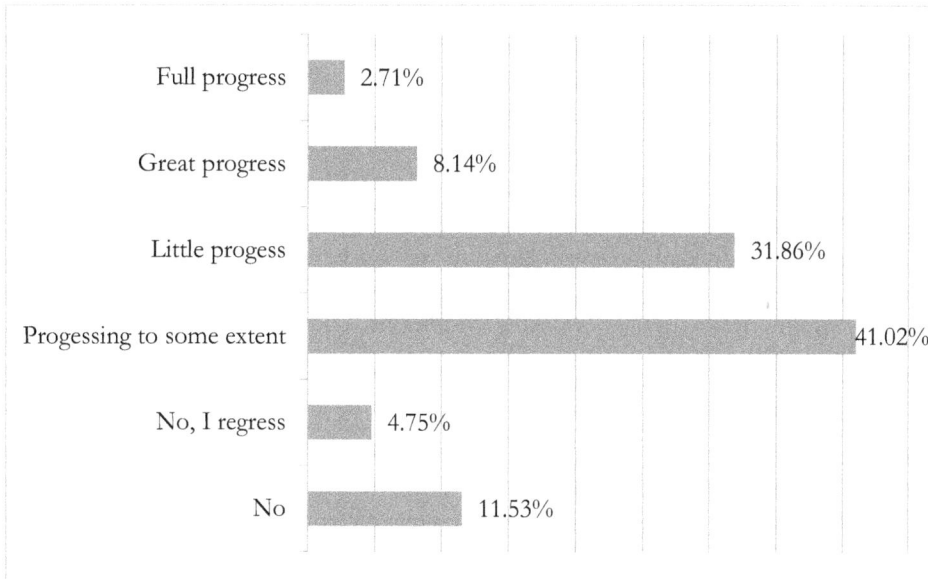

Category	Percentage
Full progress	2.71%
Great progress	8.14%
Little progess	31.86%
Progessing to some extent	41.02%
No, I regress	4.75%
No	11.53%

Source: Authors' calculations.

Given the above characteristics of the sample, we will move on the analysis of the questions on the intention to migrate. Table 2 reveals that the intention to migrate is higher in both groups, albeit higher among females, when respondents were asked the question: "If you are given the opportunity to work online (abroad), would you consider emigrating in the future from North Macedonia?". However, in the next question when asked if they intend to migrate only 38.31% answered positively. The most likely time horizon for migrating, affecting around two-thirds of respondents in both groups (males and females), is not immediately but within the next five years. Over one third of the respondents who intend to migrate would stay abroad forever.

Table 2. Likelihood of migration (all data %)

Likelihood of migration		Female	Male	Total
If you are given the opportunity to work online (abroad), would you consider emigrating in the future from North Macedonia? (Emigration = To move abroad for at least one year)	Yes	58.94	48.61	53.90
	No	21.85	31.94	26.78
	I do not know	19.21	19.44	19.32
Do you intend to migrate?	Yes	38.41	38.19	38.31
	No	61.59	61.81	61.69
When do you plan to migrate?	Within a year	15.52	25.45	20.35
	Over the next 5 years	63.79	63.64	63.72
	After more than 5 years	17.24	3.64	10.62
	Other (I do not know)	3.44	7.27	5.31

If you plan to migrate, how long would you stay abroad?	Up to 1 year	0	5.45	2.65
	2 years	8.62	21.82	15.04
	5 years	20.69	5.45	13.27
	10 years or more	24.14	34.55	29.20
	Forever	36.21	32.73	34.51
	Other (I do not know)	10.34	0	5.31

Source: Authors' calculations.

The question on the intention to migrate gave respondents various options in order to choose the most important reason, which were then divided into push and pull factors (Figure 4 and 5). It can be noted that some push and pull factors are, in practice, opposite sides of the same coin – for instance, "unsatisfactory working conditions (e.g. salary, working conditions, contracts, etc.)" versus "better job/higher income". Analysing the lists of push and pull factors, shows that economic factors, relating to income, living standards and reasons related to better education system for children and better opportunities for specialisation/qualification are the dominant ones. In addition, inability to progress on merit basis, the involvement of politics in the university and poor health services and reasons related to prior experiences of living or travel abroad are also listed among important factors. "Networking" factors with family, partners, relatives and friends and reasons related to language are not nominated as so important.

Figure 4. Main push factors for professors' intended migration (%)

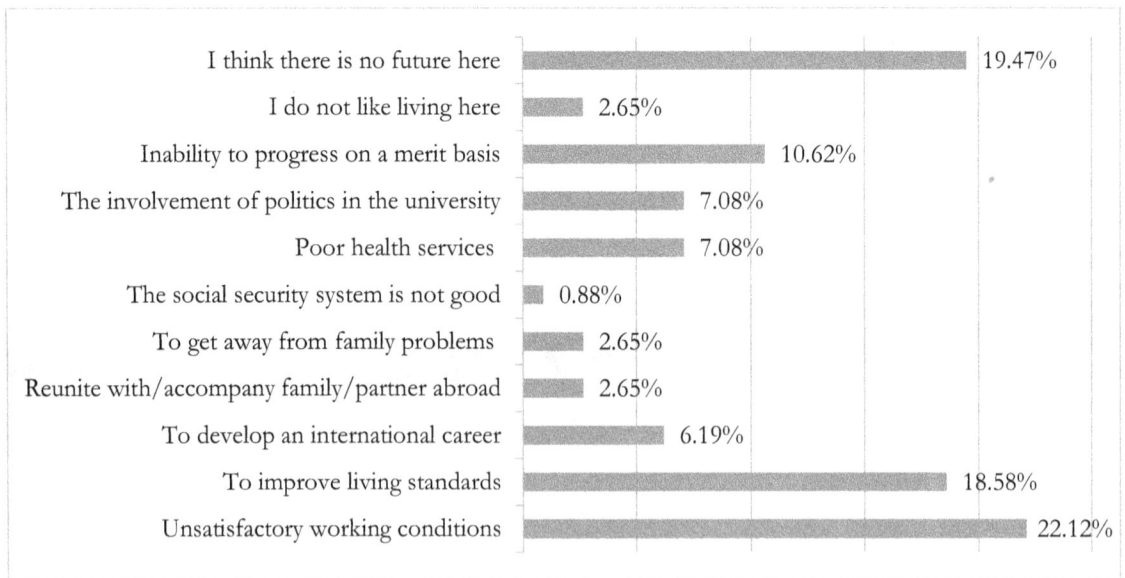

Source: Authors' calculations.

Figure 5. Main pull factors for professors' intended migration (%)

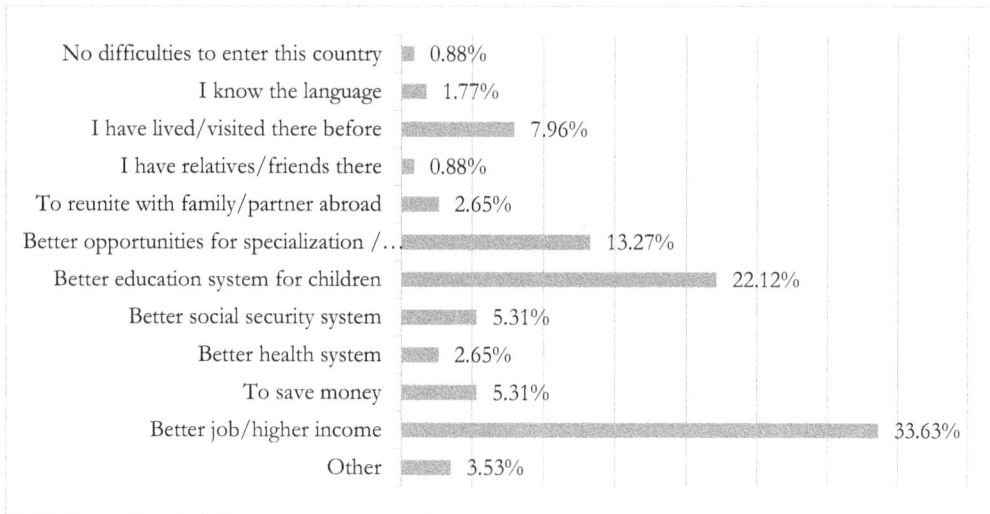

Factor	Percentage
No difficulties to enter this country	0.88%
I know the language	1.77%
I have lived/visited there before	7.96%
I have relatives/friends there	0.88%
To reunite with family/partner abroad	2.65%
Better opportunities for specialization /...	13.27%
Better education system for children	22.12%
Better social security system	5.31%
Better health system	2.65%
To save money	5.31%
Better job/higher income	33.63%
Other	3.53%

Source: Authors' calculations.

Figure 6 shows the main countries which are the preferred destinations for respondents intending to migrate. Germany, Austria, USA and Switzerland are the most common choice counties for migration.

Figure 6. Country of intended destination (%)

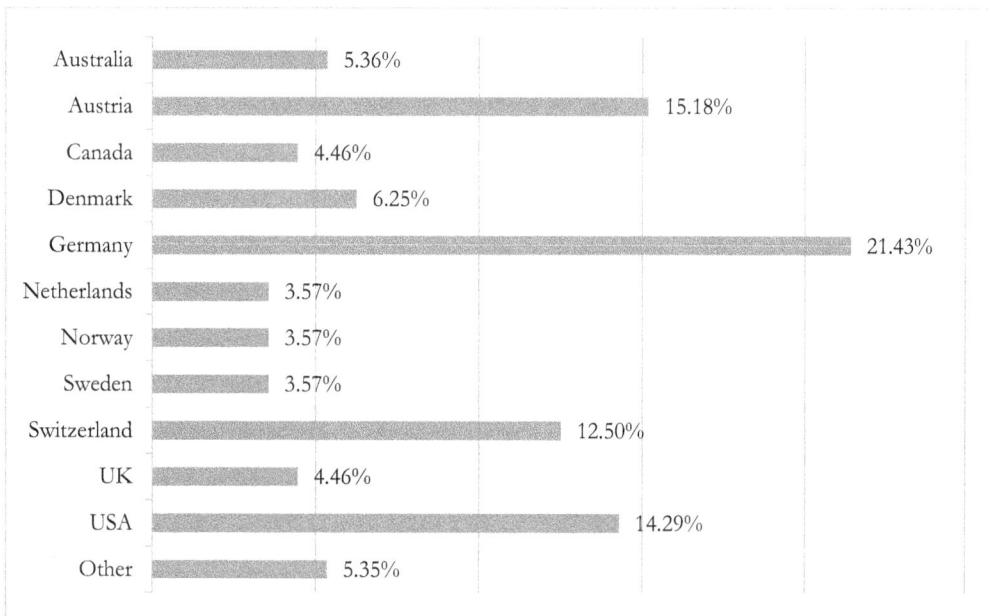

Country	Percentage
Australia	5.36%
Austria	15.18%
Canada	4.46%
Denmark	6.25%
Germany	21.43%
Netherlands	3.57%
Norway	3.57%
Sweden	3.57%
Switzerland	12.50%
UK	4.46%
USA	14.29%
Other	5.35%

Source: Authors' calculations.

Asked if they can finance their emigration, 72.07% answered positively and 80.53% declared that they have enough information on the country they intend to migrate. The main sources of information are from their previous visits to those countries and from family, friends in the country where they plan to migrate. Other sources of information are from internet, agencies, universities or other sources. An additional indicator of the mood of the respondents was the question "would you accept a job abroad that does not match your qualifications? ". To this question 37.17% gave a positive answer, 46.90% answered negatively and the remaining 15.93% answered "I do not know".

The proportion of respondents who in past have lived abroad for at least one year is 32.88%. Having previous experience with migration seems to motivate respondents to migrate again, i.e. 45.36% of respondents with previous migration experience are planning to migrate again and 34.85% of those with no previous migration experience plan to migrate.

Conclusion

North Macedonia as many other countries in the region is facing the challenge of "brain drain" for a long time and especially in the last decade. Despite the intensive migration of all categories of population, the recent research indicates an increase of the percentage of highly educated and qualified persons that are leaving the country. Using survey data this study investigates the factors affecting academic staff's decision on migration. It critically examines brain drain in higher education institutions in North Macedonia and its implications. The recent pandemic opened new possibilities of academic staff and researchers to work or emigrate 'virtually' without the need to be physically present there. These possibilities should be explored and could be attractive as well for the skilled emigrants to transfer their knowledge to their colleagues and institutions in the home country, i.e. 'virtual return'. In order to investigate the intention to migrate among professors two questions were included in the survey: "If you are given the opportunity to work online (abroad), would you consider emigrating in the future from North Macedonia?"and "Do you intend to migrate?". In the fist question more than fifty percents of the respondents answered positively. However, in the next question, when asked if they intend to migrate, about fourty percent are willing to leave the country and one third of whom would stay abroad forever. Most of the academic staff intends to migrate to more developed countries mainly because of low standards of living and wages, because they think that there is no future in this country, lack of promotion possibilities based on merit and political influence in universities. Results indicte that in North Macedonia has been created the potential for migration of highly educated people of all fields and not only for technical and medical sciences as expected.

The government in cooperation with the Ministry of Education and Science needs to revise the existing national documents that deal with the issue of migration and implement the foreseen measures in the national documents to prevent "brain drain". In this aspect, measures to improve the conditions, resources and opportunities for doing research are necessary as well as higher monthly income for the category of most educated population.

References

Šelo Šabić , S., & Kolar, N. (2019). Emigration and demographic change in Southeast Europe. Skopje: Institutite for Democracy "Societas Civilis" .

Topuzovska Latkovikj, M., Borota Popovska, M., Serafimovska, E., Cekikj, A., & Starova, N. (2019). Youth Study North Macedonia 2018/2019. Berlin: Friedrich-Ebert-Stiftung.

CRPM. (n.d.). Developing Brain Gain Policies in Macedonia: Pitfalls and Challenges. Skopje: Center for Research and Policy Making.

Dokmanoviq, Misho. (2010). Воспоставување на критериуми за квалитет во општествените науки во функција на спречување на одливот на мозоци од Република Македонија. Skopje: Институт за стратешки истражувања и едукација.

Valeska, E., Palm, V., & Hansjörg, B. (2020). Emigration from the Western Balkans. Berlin: The Aspen Institute

INTERNATIONAL MIGRATION OF HIGHLY EDUCATED, STAY-AT-HOME MOTHERS: THE CASE OF THE UNITED KINGDOM

Dr Arzu Kırcal Şahin[1]

Abstract

The purpose of this study was to explore about the experiences of highly educated mothers with at least one child who have left their jobs and have immigrated to the UK because of their spouse's job. The study investigates the barriers that these Turkish women may face in the UK. Research on immigrants has been mostly restricted to quantitative methods which rely on statistical data sets. A search of the literature revealed that qualitative studies are rarely used within the field. In order to examine this issue, in-depth interviews were held with 20 Turkish participants who met the research criteria. Integrating these findings with relevant international migration theories, this doctoral research reveals that those highly educated Turkish women with advanced career success who took part in this research have not managed to break the cycle of traditional gender roles. It also shows that these women have, not only taken care of their children, but also have established a harmonious family environment in order to assist their husbands' career. The findings of this study show that moving to the UK with their spouses inevitably has resulted in a decline in the career success, financial and social status for the participants.

Keywords: Highly educated, stay-at-home mothers, international migration, United Kingdom

Introduction

In the era of globalisation, more people are moving worldwide and migrating to other countries because the world is more connected due to advanced telecommunications, more accessible transportation opportunities and an unprecedented extension of goods and capital markets. Castles, De Haas and Miller have defined this phenomenon as the "era of immigration"[2]. Generally, people are trying to move to countries that are more developed than their own countries.

The UK has been a significant target country for immigrants for various reasons. An increase in the number of immigrants had been observed in the last fifty years, with a high growth especially in the last 15 years. Immigrants from Europe who were using their rights to move freely came to the UK. In December 2019, about 715,000 individuals had immigrated to the UK, whereas about 403,000 individuals had immigrated from the UK[3].

The preference for staying at home requires self-sacrifice at many levels. DeSimone defines the highly qualified stay-at-home mothers as ones bearing the sense of guilt by focusing only on their families instead of combining career and family commitments. According to DeSimone, these women also face

---

[1] Institute of Social Sciences, Bursa Uludag University, Bursa, Turkey

[2] Stephen Castles, Hein De Haas, and Mark J. Miller, *The Age of Migration: International Population Movements in the Modern World* (Palgrave Macmilllan: Basingstoke, 5th. Ed. 2014).

[3] Mike James, "Migration Statistics Quarterly Report," *Office for National Statistics*, 2020, August 27,
https://www.ons.gov.uk/peoplepopulationandcommunity/populationandmigration/internationalmigration/bulletins/migrationstatisticsquarterlyreport/august2020.

a conflict of roles between being a babysitter and being successful in their careers[4].

Research's Purpose and Method

The study utilised in-depth interviews conducted online due to the COVID-19 pandemic. Highly educated Turkish mothers with at least one child who have left their jobs and immigrated to the UK because of their spouses' jobs participated. Twenty women agreed to take part in the study.

Participants' Demographic Characteristics

The participants were twenty highly educated Turkish stay-at-home mothers who had immigrated to the UK due to their spouses' career commitments. The women were aged between 30-53. They were living in the UK, along with their spouses and children. Eight of these had a master's degree, one had a doctorate, and the remaining eleven had first degrees from various universities. They had professional careers before moving to the UK. Five of them were teachers, three were engineers, three were bankers, three were managers at private companies, two were academics, one was a medical doctor, another a dentist, one an architect, and one a public officer. All were highly qualified individuals who worked in successful careers in Turkey (one in Germany).

Findings

In analysing the data, the focus was on identifying common themes to help the researcher gain better insights into the participants' experiences. These included: the motive for immigration, challenges as experienced by the participants in the UK, and reasons behind mothers' preference for remaining at home.

The motive for immigration

The business of their spouses, plans for the future, and their children's education were the main reasons why these participants chose to immigrate to the UK. Fatma, one of the participants, was among those who considered her children's future. According to her:

> "I always used to feel a bit different than normal people. I felt like I didn't belong to my country much. And as I always had the problem of foreign language in my life, my dream was to ensure my children have an education in a foreign country. In this direction, we decided to come here."

Ezgi, on the other hand, was one of those who never wanted to immigrate. But she made it to England because of her spouse. According to Ezgi:

> "I'm not a woman who likes to live away from her family, away from her mother and father and loved ones. I visited other countries a lot, but it was just for touristic intentions. I never intended and wished to settle."

And Sevda noted:

> "I didn't speak to him (my spouse) for a week, and I cried for a week. I could never accept to go outside of Istanbul. I didn't accept it, but I also didn't want to wait for my spouse. Because I didn't want the people to tell me later that I couldn't have a better life due to my hesitation. And I also didn't want to leave my spouse alone. Because he was thinking that we would have a better future here after living abroad for a while. I faced a tough transition period. (...) Then I said, okay, let's head-on."

---

[4] Susan Donley DeSimone, Exploring the Effects of Guilt, Spousal Support and Role Conflict on the Psychological Well-Being of the Educated Full-Time Stay at Home Mother (San Diego, CA: University of San Diego Press, 2001).

Challenges as Experienced by the Participants

Nearly all the participants had hard times when they came to the UK for the first time. The majority had difficulty finding the support they required with their spouses working and with them staying at home with their children. They noted that perhaps one of the most challenging parts of living abroad is being distant from their comfort zones in Turkey and their families and the environment that may support them. For instance, Elif expressed the problems of both being with a small child and working abroad as follows:

> "When I look back, I'm thinking about how I did it. You're right. Of course, one is handling everything faced in that period. That was very hard for me. I was experiencing working abroad for the first time. For instance, people generally try to go abroad when they are young. I was 34. Okay, it was not too late, but I had difficulty. My spouse was already continuously travelling. And this time, he started to go to other countries. And we again became unable to see each other."

Reasons Behind Mother's Preference for Staying at Home

The participants said they were very interested in furthering their careers, but they were obliged to stay at home due to childcare. However, they are concerned about losing their skills due to the break in their professional lives. For instance, Fatma, who was an interior architect, explained that she wanted to work in the UK and keep up with her career, and added:

> "I don't know when I'll able to master this foreign language. I need a bit more time. Especially in my profession, it is required to be at a specific level. No matter how old I am. I stuck up on my dreams. That is to say, and I want to perform my profession in here too."

Hatice, a teacher with two children, said that she felt like having fallen into chaos due to a change of country. Faced with a lack of social life, she said the following with regards to working again:

> "In here, I tried to apply to a job once, but the hours are very different. I don't know who will take care of the children. Even if I leave one of them to someone who will take the other from school? That is to say; you have to think of everything. There are no close friends. Due to not having anyone to trust, we finally decided that I should take care of them."

Some of the participants had worked in various positions in the UK, but often they were over-qualified for these jobs. Nevertheless, they had been able to work in a foreign country. Some participants had to resign from these jobs as they did not want to neglect their family due to the inflexible working conditions. The women were especially desperate with regard to their children. Dependent for support on their spouses, they became their children's primary carers.

Conclusion

Some of these highly qualified women, immigrating to the UK by accompanying their spouses, became stuck in the lowest part of the labour market. A series of intertwined factors (inability to find a good job, lack of a foreign language, and some personal reasons) contribute to the challenges faced by these women who also have childcare responsibilities.

The high-priced childcare service in the UK when compared to Turkey has been a problem. The mothers have thus opted to stay at home to care for their children and this has had a negative impact on their careers.

The repeated moving with their spouses is also having a negative effect on these women. The study findings suggest that among married couples, priority is often given to the career expectations of the husband and the migration of family is associated with the husbands' career development. With the women unable to pursue successful careers, there is here a loss of human and social capital.

Another significant factor contributing to the challenges faced by the participants in this study is social gender roles. These roles seem to be the most influential factor in familial decisions among Turkish immigrant couples. Turkish social gender norms provide more power for the husband in a patriarchal family system. Contrary to the advocates of the power of marriage theory, these husbands are not required to bring in more valuable resources[5].

The findings of this study suggest that highly qualified Turkish women with children and a career who migrate to the UK along with their spouses seem to be unable to break the chains of traditional social gender roles. They are not only undertaking childcare responsibilities but are also assisting the careers of their spouses in order to maintain a harmonious family environment. As a result, they are facing a regression in their career and socio-economic status.

The UK government must better understand the problems faced by highly qualified immigrant women and develop policies to ensure their labour participation. Social cohesion is also as important as participation in the job market. For this reason, various activities should be organised by local administrations for such women to extend their social networks. More opportunities should be provided for immigrant women regarding language (including business English). Training and seminars can also be organised to enable them to refresh their business-related skills, and opportunities should be provided for them to meet with prospective employers.

References

Edward S. Shihadeh, 'The Prevalence of Husband-Centered Migration: Employment Consequences for Married Mothers', *Journal of Marriage and the Family*, Vol. 53, no.2 (1991), pp. 432–44.

Mike James, "Migration Statistics Quarterly Report," *Office for National Statistics*, 2020, August 27, https://www.ons.gov.uk/peoplepopulationandcommunity/populationandmigration/internationalmigration/bulletins/migrationstatisticsquarterlyreport/august2020.

Stephen Castles, Hein De Haas, and Mark J. Miller, *The Age of Migration: International Population Movements in the Modern World* (Palgrave Macmilllan: Basingstoke, 5th. Ed. 2014).

Susan Donley DeSimone, Exploring the Effects of Guilt, Spousal Support and Role Conflict on the Psychological Well-Being of the Educated Full-Time Stay at Home Mother (San Diego, CA: University of San Diego Press, 2001).

---

[5] Edward S. Shihadeh, 'The Prevalence of Husband-Centered Migration: Employment Consequences for Married Mothers', *Journal of Marriage and the Family*, Vol. 53, no.2 (1991), pp. 432–44.

WELSH ITALIAN LITERARY ACCOUNTS OF INTERNMENT IN WORLD WAR II: LES SERVINI'S A BOY FROM BARDI AND HECTOR EMANUELLI'S A SENSE OF BELONGING

Manuela D'Amore

Abstract

Unjustly neglected by academic criticism, Welsh Italian literary accounts of internment during World War Two are the product of non-professional writing which however supplement the meagre historical research on the Italian immigrant community in the Valleys. The purpose of this paper is to shed light on Les Servini's *A Boy from Bardi: My Life and Times* (1994) and Hector Emanuelli's *A Sense of Belonging: From the Rhondda to the Potteries. Memories of a Welsh Italian Englishman* (2010) while showing that the painful stories that they recount were written also to convey positive messages of strength and resilience. We believe it is now time for specialist and non-specialist readers to give them a complete social and cultural recognition.

Key-words: World War II – Internment – Welsh Italian literary narratives – Servini – Emanuelli

Introduction

Memory is a central component in British migration literature. Burrell and Panayi (2006) were the first scholars who explored the impact of contemporary history on transnational lives and writings; more recently, the concept of remembrance has more specifically been applied to war accounts and memoirs. Starting from Glynn's and Kleist's edited volume *History, Memory and Migration. Perceptions of the Past and the Politics of Incorporation* (2012), Writh (2015) and Damousi (2015) in particular have put an even stronger emphasis on WW2 in the shaping of immigrants' complex identities and integration processes.

Interestingly, despite the number of Italian victims in the tragic sinking of the Arandora Star (2nd July 1940), and the sheer violence that the whole community suffered in 1940-1945, there are virtually no academic contributions on British Italian war narratives. Published between the mid-1990s and 2010, Les Servini's *A Boy from Bardi: My Life and Times* (1994), Joe Pieri's *Isle of the Displaced: An Italian Scot's Memoirs of Internment During World War II* (1997), Hector Emanuelli's *A Sense of Belonging: From the Rhondda to the Potteries. Memories of a Welsh Italian Englishman* (2010), as well as Peter Ghiringhelli's *A British Boy in Fascist Italy* (2010), are all autobiographical and recount painful stories of persecution and internment in Britain, on the Isle of Man and in Canada.

Yet, even in such a small textual corpus, it is possible to find elements of peculiarity and uniqueness. They are related to the regional areas where these authors – first and second-generation Italian immigrants – came from, and also to the way they wanted to retell their war experiences. Although they never forgot what they had gone through, they all expressed their courage and resilience.

Building upon Marianne Hirsch's concept of post memory (Hirsch, 2012) and following a clear intertextual path, we shall thus try to enhance the meagre research on the Welsh Italian community, while focusing on Les Servini (1914-1999)[1] and Hector Emanuelli (1920-2018)[2]. They too can be considered members of the so-called "hinge generation" (Hirsch, 2012, p. 1) who helped to establish a closer link between the past and the present. As for their memoirs, they certainly affect "how the key events of the twentieth century can be remembered today" (Erll, 2011, p. 125).

Writing Retrospectively: From the Outbreak of the War to Captivity on the Isle of Man

In point of fact, both *A Boy from Bardi* and *A Sense of Belonging* were written "from factual experience" and express their authors' "personal views and thoughts": the reader may decide to "reject them all" (Servini, 1994, "Foreword", n.p.), yet it is undeniable that the Second World War was a key experience for them not only as individuals, but especially as immigrants.

It may be for this reason that two long chapters in each memoir are dedicated to those terrible years. They are rooted in a strong antifascist sentiment, which shows that, despite the national propaganda, Servini and Emanuelli were two innocent victims of the British persecution of the Italians. The following extract is clear on the link that they wanted to maintain between the past and contemporary times:

> Yes, the "Duce" was idolized, even by some Italians here, but there were well-hidden cracks in the glossy picture. I knew some stubborn folks who were "coaxed" into Fascism by beatings or liberal doses of caster oil! [...] Carlo Levi describes this so well in "Christ stopped at Eboli". Some who openly criticised were killed, the opponents were ruthlessly crushed as anarchists, Bolsheviks, trouble-makers.
>
> I have heard some say that Italy needs a Mussolini now. I can understand this, the graft and corruption, so rampant, calls for drastic remedies, but can we eradicate this only by a dictatorship? Is the loss of democracy the only cure? (p. 20)

There will be more rhetorical questions like these in the two authors' memoirs, which will also regard their new condition as "enemy aliens". This was the product of the severe measures that Prime Minister Winston Churchill adopted to prevent the formation of a "Fifth column" in Britain (Colpi, 1991; Hughes, 1991); as a result, MI5 started from the Case del Fascio in the country to compile the list of the most "dangerous" Italians, but finally imprisoned all Italian men aged 16-70 years. As neither Servini nor Emanuelli were British citizens, first they were taken to the local Police Station (Servini, 1994, p. 21; Emanuelli, 2010, p.71) and then they were interned on the Isle of Man.

A Boy from Bardi and *A Sense of Belonging* confirm that "the round up was swift" (Servini, 1994, p. 94), yet they also provide evidence of the shock, the rage and despair that the immigrant communities felt after 10th June 1940. Their members were "still Italian, and technically [...] enemies" (p. 21): they could not believe that after so many years Britain could consider them outlaws (p. 21).

They were thus moved from Maindy Barracks in Cardiff to the north of England. There is meagre research on enemy alien internment in Britain (Kochan, 1983; Sutherland and Sutherland, 2012; Chappell, 2017; Pistol, 2017), yet as Pistol maintains, "there were vacant lands where tents and barbed

---

[1] A first-generation Welsh Italian, Les Servini was originally from Bardi, a small town in the Ceno Valley in the province of Parma. He initially worked in the catering industry in south Wales; after the war, though, he completed his education and became a reputed language teacher. *A Boy from Bardi* is his only literary work.
[2] Hector Emanuelli too was from Bardi. As a boy he lived in the Rhondda Valley in Abercarn; then he moved to England with his family. After working in the catering industry, in the late 1960s he became a Home Sales Correspondent for Quickfit and Quartz. He published *Some Recollections of Adventures and Brief Encounters whilst Walking in Austria, Portugal and Italy* in 2013.

wire had been erected hastily" (Pistol, 2017, p. 33), yet the old factories and barracks near Liverpool were considered crucial in the project of expulsion of the Fascists and Nazis in the country.

Because of its convenient position, Warth Mills in Bury was one the most important ones. Servini associates the memories of his stay there with the tragic news of the sinking of the Arandora Star, but Emanuelli wanted to provide a short but realistic description of the "filthy condition" of Hanley Police Station:

> We were housed in D Wing, a part of the prison which had not been used since the days of the Suffragettes. It was in a filthy condition. Pigeon excrement seemed to be everywhere.
>
> I was there during the 'Christmas Blitz' of 1940. […] Being bombed is always scary, but it's really terrifying when you're locked up! Porridge was served to us in battered aluminium basins. To these days I have a dislike of it. (Emanuelli, 2010, p. 71)

Deprived of their freedom and mourning those in their families who had lost their lives on the Arandora Star, Servini and Emanuelli survived the first phases of their internment because they learned to make the most of their new friendships (Emanuelli, 2010, p. 73). It was so also when they arrived on the Isle of Man: Servini was sent to Palace Camp in Douglas, whereas Emanuelli resided on Peveril Camp in the small town of Peel. After such a hard experience, they would never be the same.

Interestingly, the chapters entitled "Isle of Man" and "Castaway" – which can be respectively found in *A Boy from Bardi* and *A Sense of Belonging* – express their authors' strength and resilience. After such a long period of detention, "conditions were [now] very favourable" (p. 78): Emanuelli, for instance, maintains that they "were able to choose with whom [they] shared a house" and that they "made [their] own rotas for cooking and household duties" (p. 78). As concerns Servini – who even provides precious details on his diet – he "actually put on weight!" (Servini, 1994, p. 28).

Writing extensively on his three-year internment on the Île St. Hélène in Canada, Scots Italian Joe Pieri depicts a far more complex picture of the dynamics on PoW camps. Human rights, for instance, were always at risk, but every time that he and his inmates managed to defend them, they felt a stronger sense of unity and achievement (Pieri, 1997, chapter 11, para. 16; D'Amore, 2020, p. 92). Chapters 11 and 13 of *Isle of the Displaced* clearly demonstrate how they learned to negotiate with the highest ranks of the military hierarchy.

Apart from a few references to the internal disputes and "disturbances" in the Douglas and Peel camps (Emanuelli, 2010, pp. 79-80), there is no trace of such important political issues in *A Boy from Bardi* and *A Sense of Belonging*. Yet, the authors' internment experience had a strong impact on their human and cultural growth: Servini, for instance, could never forget the names of his Italian inmates and wanted to add two large photos of them to his narration: the majority came from Bardi, his Italian hometown, while the rest came from Venice, Sorrento and even Sicily (Servini, 1994, p. 29). As for Emanuelli – who remained on the island until 1943 – he had even the chance to discover his artistic talent, which was essential when he left the catering industry in the late 1960s:

> I used my period of confinement to indulge my love of the theatre, designing posters and sets for revues that the detainees were allowed to put on at the Albert hall in Peel. […] I also had time to try my hand at painting, but having access only to watercolours I had no opportunity to make a renewed attempt at reproducing the miner's gloss I had loved as a child in the Rhondda. I did, however, manage to turn out some views of Peel. (Emanuelli, 2010, p. 79).

Conclusion

Today artistic materials like these are held at the archive of the War Museum in Douglas. They not only testify to the vitality of the internee community, but also to their hopes for the future. From this point of view, *A Boy from Bardi: My Life and Times* and *A Sense of Belonging. From the Rhondda to the Potteries: Memories of a Welsh-Italian Englishman* retain an even greater significance: blending precise historical details with vivid memories of a destructive past, they convey a message of courage and resilience, while putting a special emphasis on the success that their authors achieved in the post-war years.

In point of fact, Servini and Emanuelli are clear on the resentment and sense of frustration that they felt when they were released (Servini, 1994, p. 33; Emanuelli, 2010, p. 97). Looking back, though, they could both recognise that the Isle of Man had taught them a "valuable lesson in human relations" (Servini, 1994, p. 28), and that, compared to all those who had died, they had finally been able to make their professional dreams come true.

Two important representatives of a forgotten generation of British Italians, Servini and Emanuelli still show how they contributed to the social and cultural development of contemporary Britain, also – most importantly – that Welsh Italian writings now deserve a place within the canon of British migration literature.

References

Burrell, K. & Panayi P. (eds.). (2006). *Histories and Memories: Migrants and their History in Britain*. London: Bloomsbury.

Chappell, C. (2017). Island of Barbed Wire. The Remarkable Story of World War Two Internment on the Isle of Man. Ramsbury: The Crowood Press.

Colpi, T. (1991). *The Italian Factor. The Italian Community in Great Britain*. Edinburgh and London: Mainstream Publishing.

Damousi, J. (2015). Memory and Migration in the Shadow of War. Australia's Greek Immigrants after World War II and the Greek Civil War. Cambridge: Cambridge University Press.

D'Amore, M. (2020). Identità, straniamento e resilienza in Joe Pieri, *Isle of the Displaced: An Italian Scot's Memoirs of Internment in the Second World War*. In: Calì, V. (ed.). *Isolitudine, Confine, Identità*. Messina: Lippoli, 83-98.

Emanuelli, H. (2010). A Sense of Belonging: From the Rhondda to the Potteries. Memories of a Welsh Italian Englishman. Langenfeld: Six Town Books.

Erll, A. (2011). *Memory in Culture*. New York: Palgrave Macmillan.

Ghiringhelli, P. (2010). *A British Boy in Fascist Italy*. Stroud: The History Press.

Glynn I. & Kleist J.O. (eds.). (2012). History, Memory and Migration: Perceptions of the Past and the Politics of Incorporation. New York: Palgrave Macmillan.

Hirsh, M. (2012). The Generation of Postmemory. Writing and Visual Culture after the Holocaust. New York: Columbia University Press.

Hughes, C. (1991). Lime, Lemon and Salsaparilla. The Italian Community in South Wales 1881-1945. Bridgend: Seren.

Kochan, M. (1983). *Britain's Internees in the Second World War*. London and Basingstoke: The Macmillan Press.

Pieri, J. (1997). Isle of the Displaced: An Italian Scot's Memoirs of Internment in the Second World War. [Kindle Paperwhite version]. Retrieved from amazon.com.

Pistol, R. (2017). Internment during the Second World War. A Comparative Study of Great Britain and the USA. London: Bloomsbury.

Servini, L. (1994). *A Boy from Bardi. My Life and Times*. Cardiff: Hazeltree Press.

Sutherland, J. & Sutherland D. (2012). *Prisoner of War Camps in Britain During the Second World War*. Newhaven: Golden Guides Press.

Writh, C. (2015). Memories of Belonging. Descendants of Italian Migrants to the United States, 1884-Present. Leiden and Boston: Brill.

THE IMPACT OF COVID-19 ON ASYLUM SEEKERS AND MIGRANTS IN BELGIUM

Júlia Zomignani Barboza and Lisa Feirabend

Abstract

The COVID-19 pandemic has affected all sectors of the Belgian society, including its most vulnerable. In this contribution, we focus on the pandemic's effects on asylum seekers and migrants, who had their rights severely restricted by the sanitary measures enacted to contain the spread of the virus. More specifically, we will look into the limitations that were put in place to submit applications for international protection and the restrictions that apply to visits in detention centres, limiting independent oversight of such facilities. With the benefit of hindsight, we identify best practices and recommendations for the future.

Introduction

Asylum seekers and migrants in Belgium have seen important rights severely limited or even temporarily suspended by measures imposed to contain the spread of COVID-19. In this contribution, we focus on the measures that affected access to international protection, access to material assistance as well as those that impacted the conditions of detention in immigrations detention centres.

Requests for international protection: COVID-19 impact

Under normal circumstances, asylum seekers in Belgium can submit their request for international protection at the arrival centre of the Federal Agency for the Reception of Asylum Seekers (Fedasil), known as Le Petit Château, in Brussels. Following submission, the process of reception commences which screens the applicants and during this period, applicants are offered material assistance, including accommodation and financial and medical support, while awaiting their decision and any potential appeals.

However, during the onset of the COVID-19 pandemic in early 2020, the Immigration Office, following the issuance of several public health measures by the National Security Council, decided to close the arrival centre for asylum seekers between 17 March and 3 April 2020 [1]. The measure aimed to avoid the spread of the disease among those attending Le Petit Château to apply for international protection [1]. As a result, no one was allowed to request asylum in Belgium for almost three weeks, thereby effectively halting access to international protection and associated material assistance.

On 3 April, application for international protection became possible again, though the in-person system was replaced by a new online appointment one [2]. Everyone wishing to request international protection was required to fill in an online form, available only in French and Dutch, and wait to receive an email for an appointment.

This system presented many challenges. For example, the online form, only available in French and Dutch, presented a language barrier to those not proficient in those languages. Many applicants where therefore reliant upon third persons or non-profit organisations (NGO) to assist them in completing the application [3]. The system further required applicants to have access to the internet, through a computer with a Belgian IP address or a smartphone with a Belgian SIM-card, and an email address to receive their appointment invitation, practical requirements that many applicants did not have access to [3]. Moreover, applying online required some degree of digital literacy, which presented a further obstacle to applicants. Most importantly, the online system prevented asylum seekers from entering the reception network from the moment they expressed their desire to obtain protection (i.e. upon completion of the form). The appointments were sometimes scheduled for days or even weeks after the online application was completed. Only after the appointment would asylum seekers be housed in reception centres and start receiving material assistance. As such, asylum seekers were prevented from accessing often much needed material assistance immediately upon submitting their application for international protection.

A group of NGOs challenged this system in Court. On 5 October 2020, the francophone tribunal of first instance of Brussels ruled that the fact that asylum seekers could not obtain material assistance the moment they present their request online was *prima facie* illegal [4]. The Belgian State was requested to put an end to this practice and was given thirty days to ensure a registration system that guaranteed immediate access to material assistance upon submission of a request for international protection [3; 4]. Following the ruling, the in-person system was reinstated with the necessary sanitary restrictions by 30 October 2020 [5].

Requests for international protection: best practices and recommendations

The measures implemented to curb the spread of COVID-19 resulted in the temporary suspension and subsequent severe limitation of one of the most important avenues for asylum seekers to seek protection and obtain material assistance. The ability to submit a request is the only way to gain access to such international protection. It is an imperative step to become a recognised refugee and to gain access to associated material assistance during the application process.

While the COVID-19 pandemic was an unexpected and serious public health crisis that required adequate measures being implemented by authorities, public health concerns should have been weighed against the rights and protections put in place for asylum seekers and migrants. While reinstating the ability to register for international protection in April was a positive first step, the method and process employed by the government left much to be desired. As such, the Immigration Office's subsequent decision to restore in-person registration for international protection, thereby allowing for immediate access to associated material assistance, was a welcome development.

The restoration of access to international protection and related assistance should be considered essential and a best practice in ensuring the protection of asylum seekers and migrants in Belgium.

Immigration detention: COVID-19 impact

Sanitary measures also deeply affected migrants in closed detention centres. While multiple detainees were released as returns and expulsions were mostly halted due to travel restrictions, from March onwards those who remained in detention were not allowed to receive visitors, neither personal nor those from organisations providing oversight.1 Indeed, even a member of parliament was prevented from visiting the closed centre in Vottem [7]. Oversight of detention centres is of the upmost importance, especially as in early April media sources expressed concern over the situation in closed centres, reporting that expired food had been served and that sanitary measures were insufficient and

---

1 Under normal circumstances, NGO members of the so-called Transit Group conduct regular visits to closed detention centres in the country. See [6].

inadequate [8].

While both personal and NGO visits were restored in July, with the increase in COVID cases during the last quarter of 2020, new restrictions were put in place, once again limiting the extent of independent oversight of such facilities. Since fall 2020, NGO visits are limited to one visit a week of maximum two visitors and visitors are not allowed to enter the common areas. Instead, visits take place in a separate room with one detainee at a time. Visits by friends and family are limited to two adults (with minor children) per detainee, with multiple visits per week allowed [9]. For NGOs, these restrictions mean visitors have to wait for each detainee to be brought to the visiting area, which slows down the visiting process, resulting in less detainees being visited by them. Similarly, more first meetings are refused by the detainees, possibly because they are not aware of the reason why they are called to the visitors' parlour.2

Despite their limited oversight due to restrictions on visits, NGOs denounced that four detainees at the closed centre in Vottem who tested positive for COVID-19 were placed in solitary confinement to be isolated from other detainees. The NGOs criticised the use of solitary confinement as an isolation measure and the harsh conditions of such regime. The Immigration Office refuted these allegations, stating that these individuals were merely placed in isolation cells [9]. This shows, once again, the importance of independent actors having access to detention centres at all times, especially when extraordinary measures are in place.

Immigration detention: best practices and recommendations

The release of detainees at the early stages of the COVID-19 crisis was a positive development and can be considered a best practice as it not only facilitated the implementation of sanitary measures in centres but also released those who were not expected to be returned in the near future.

Another important step and a sign of lessons learned is that visits to centres were limited but not completely halted since their re-establishment in July 2020, despite the increase in cases that followed in the fall of 2020.

With the benefit of hindsight, however, the authors suggest that in the future more information should be provided to detainees about the work of NGOs in the centres and their oversight role so that detainees can make informed decisions on whether they wish to interact with such entities or not. Furthermore, even if the presence of visitors in the centre can be limited to protect the health of those detained, oversight visits to the common areas of detention facilities should continue to be organised, even if during such visits NGO or parliamentary representatives do not interact with detainees but merely observe the conditions and general atmosphere in the centres. This may also increase NGOs' visibility and encourage detainees to engage with them in the visitors' parlour, increasing the chances of independent oversight in times of emergency.

Lastly, it is of the upmost importance that those placed in detention centres who test positive for COVID-19 are isolated in medical areas of closed centres adapted to their health needs and not isolated in solitary confinement or isolation cells as the goal of such isolation is not to punish but to protect the health of those in the centre, including the infected detainees.

Conclusions

The rapid spread of COVID-19 around the world in early 2020 presented a great challenge to

---

2 This information was provided to the authors by members of the NGOs Nansen and JRS Belgium.

governments on how to handle the public health threat the new disease represented. This led to the enaction of restrictive measures that affected all sectors of society but were often especially harsh on the most vulnerable such as asylum seekers and migrants in closed detention centres.

With the evolution of the crisis in Belgium, measures adapted, and lessons learned were applied on how the government handled these populations. Despite positive developments, there is still room for improvement and in the continuance of the COVID-19 crisis as well as in future times of emergency, restrictive measures should more thoroughly take into account the fundamental rights of the most vulnerable to ensure the limitations imposed are not more restrictive than what is strictly necessary to protect public health.

References

Fedasil (17 March 2020), Le centre d'arrivée ferme ses portes. Available at: https://www.fedasil.be/fr/actualites/accueil-des-demandeurs-dasile/le-centre-darrivee-ferme-ses-portes.

Fedasil (3 April 2020), Reprise des demandes d'asile. Available at: https://www.fedasil.be/fr/actualites/accueil-des-demandeurs-dasile/reprise-des-demandes-dasile.

Vluchtelingenwerk Vlaanderen (31 December 2020), Country Report Belgium (Asylum Information Database), p. 29. Available at: https://asylumineurope.org/wp-content/uploads/2021/04/AIDA-BE_2020update.pdf.

Ordonnance 2020/105/C, 5 October 2020, Tribunal de première instance francophone de Bruxelles.

Fedasil (30 October 2020), Asil: adaption du système d'enregistrement. Available at: https://www.fedasil.be/fr/actualites/accueil-des-demandeurs-dasile/asile-adaptation-du-systeme-denregistrement.

CIRÉ (17 August 2011), Groupe Transit: le réseau des visiteurs ONG en centres fermés. Available at: https://www.cire.be/groupe-transit-le-reseau-des-visiteurs-ong-en-centres-fermes/.

Sarah Schlitz (26 March 2020), Coronavirus : l'office des étrangers refuse une visite parlementaire au centre fermé de Vottem. Available at: https://sarahschlitz.be/coronavirus-loffice-des-etrangers-refuse-une-visite-parlementaire-au-centre-ferme-de-vottem/?fbclid=IwAR3rtM7sXoRpdVxhdya74C-VVRsOQl2qEnjYUuZ0xuH0-Los-AlmxrPugZI.

RTBF (16 April 2020), Situation au centre fermé de Merksplas : Myria demande que des mesures soient prises. Available at: https://www.rtbf.be/info/societe/detail_situation-au-centre-ferme-de-merksplas-myria-demande-que-des-mesures-soient-prises?id=10483832.

European Union Agency for Fundamental Rights (2021), Migration: Key fundamental rights concerns - Quarterly Bulletin - 01.01.2021 -> 30.06.2021. Forthcoming at: https://fra.europa.eu/en/products/search.

RETOS PARA LA ADAPTACION ECONÓMIICA Y SOCIAL DE LA POBLACIÓN INMIGRANTE VENEZOLANA EN EL SUR DE ECUADOR

Jessica Ordóñez C.

acilities. With the benefit of hindsight, we identify best practices and recommendations for the future.

Introduction

Entre 2015 y 2021 han salido de Venezuela alrededor de 6,5 millones de personas migrantes y refugiadas hacia algunos países del mundo principalmente de América Latina donde se estima que residen alrededor de 4,6 millones, según (ACNUR, 2021) permanecen en Colombia, Perú, Chile, Ecuador y Brasil. Esta situación da un vuelco a la dirección de los flujos migratorios entre estos países, debido a que Venezuela pasa a ser un país de origen migratorio, lo opuesto sucede con Ecuador, Colombia y Perú que se convierten en países de destino migratorio.

Este colectivo es altamente vulnerable, debido al contexto de su éxodo migratorio, el cual surge de una situación de crisis en el país de origen: social, económica, y política, esto determina un éxodo apresurado e irregular. La inmigración irregular se da cuando una persona ingresa a otro país de forma indocumentada, por pasos ilegales o trochas. Según el Artículo 5 de la Convención internacional sobre la protección de los derechos de todos los trabajadores migratorios y de sus familiares, un migrante tiene la condición de irregular o no documentado si no,

> han sido autorizados a ingresar, a permanecer y a ejercer una actividad remunerada en el Estado de empleo de conformidad con las leyes de ese Estado y los acuerdos internacionales en que ese Estado sea parte (Convención Internacional Sobre La Protección de Los Derechos de Todos Los Trabajadores Migratorios y de Sus Familiares, 1990, artículo 5).

Esta denominación trata de eliminar el término de "migrante ilegal". Lo cual conlleva a estereotipos e incrementa la discriminación, limita las posibilidades de integración o inclusión.

Retomando el contexto de la migración irregular o no documentada, según Castles (2010), la "industria de la migración" o "las personas que viven de facilitar la migración" contribuyen a incrementar la migración irregular, cabe destacar que existen algunas formas y motivos de migración irregular pero aquí nos enfocamos en la que está estrechamente relacionada el tráfico de personas. Los traficantes de migrantes movidos por el dinero prometen a las personas migrantes el ingreso a otro país de forma ilegal, estos viajes se dan sin ningún cuidado, por rutas peligrosas y no oficiales, bajo el riesgo de que estas personas nunca lleguen a su destino, porque esta actividad ilícita está adicionalmente relacionada con el delito de trata de personas.

La trata de personas según el Ministerio de Gobierno de Ecuador (2021) implica la: captación, transporte, traslado, entrega, acogida o recepción de una o más personas dentro del país o fuera de él, cuyo principal fin es la explotación de la persona en cualquier forma. En este contexto, las personas son limitadas en el ejercicio de sus derechos humanos. Este es el reto más importante que tienen que enfrentar las personas migrantes, para superarlo se necesita del apoyo institucional de los gobiernos regionales y los organismos internacionales, en este punto recalco la existencia de numerosos tratados y convenios internacionales cuyo objetivo es justamente la migración ordenada y segura, de los cuales muchos países son signatarios, pero son pocos los resultados obtenidos.

La percepción negativa que tienen los residentes sobre las personas migrantes irregulares derivan en actitudes xenofóbicas, discriminatorias y de exclusion social. En este hecho tiene un protagonismo importante los medios de comunicación e influye en el sentido de las políticas migratorias que adoptan los países. Las malas percpeciones contribuyen con políticas restrictivas con la migración y viceversa.

Según Organización Internacional para las Migraciones (2015) en el informe How the World Views Migration, 2012-2014, ciertas características sociodemográficas están relacionadas con actitudes positivas respecto de la inmigración, de esta manera las actitudes positiva se observan en personas adultas con título universitario frente a los que tienen títulos más bajo, también en jóvenes y en los que perciben que la situación económica de su país es buena o está mejorando. Las actitudes negativas están relacionadas con las personas en desempleo frente a los empleados.

Según Esipova et al. (2020) a partir de la encuesta realizada por Gallup Migration Research Center en 2015, en Sudamérica existen actitudes positivas hacia mantener o incrementarse la inmigración, excepto en Ecuador y Bolivia, países donde un 62% y 51%, respectivamente, de las personas esperaría que se reduzca. Este mismo organismo calcula el Índice de percepción de migrantes, la cual tiene tres preguntas básicas: ¿tiene conocimiento de la existencia de inmigrantes en su país?, ¿qué haría si un migrante se convierte en su vecino? y si ¿se casa con un familiar suyo?, el indicador llega hasta un máximo posible es 9 puntos. Lo particular sobre esta información es que justamente estos países son receptores de inmigrantes venezolanos, Ecuador, Perú y Colombia este indicador se reduce de 2016 a 2019, periodo que coincide con el boom de la emigración internacional de los venezolanos. En Ecuador este indicador pasa de 6,13 a 3,51 de 2016 a 2019, en Colombia de 6,13 a 3,98 y en Perú de 6,33 a 3,61.

Según Organización Internacional para las Migraciones (2021), la xenofobia comprende las actitudes, prejuicios y otros comportamientos que implican rechazo o exclusión por el hecho de ser extranjero, en este caso. Y, la discriminación es el trato diferente o exclusión por diferentes motivos como la raza, el color, sexo, religión, nacionalidad, opinión política que tengan como resultado anular o menoscabar el reconocimiento, goce o ejercicio, en condiciones de igualdad, de los derechos humanos y libertades fundamentales de todas las personas.

El reto es sensibilizar a la población residente respecto de la situación en la que se encuentran las personas migrantes. De acuerdo con Rodríguez Chatruc & Rozo (2021), la efectividad de la provisión de información para cambiar actitudes y comportamientos resulta heterogéneo posiblemente porque el tipo de información proporcionada y la forma en que se entrega parecen ser importantes, por lo tanto, recomiendan proporcionar información sobre el tamaño real y las características de la población migrante puede mejorar las actitudes, pero no comportamientos o preferencias políticas con respecto a la migración indocumentada.

Adicionalmente, es importante mostrar a las personas información sobre los resultados de la investigación que muestra que ningún impacto adverso de la migración en el mercado laboral puede cambiar tanto actitudes y comportamientos hacia inmigrantes poco calificados de una manera más positiva. Además, de orientar esta información a jóvenes, debido a que en la edad de 18 a 15 años forman sus actitudes sociales.

Finalmente, el desarrollo de capacidades para la inserción laboral es determinante en el proceso de integración e inclusión. La integración tiene algunas tipologías según exponen Retortillo Osuna et al. (2006) entre las cuales están la: i) integración social, económica y cultural, la cual implica la inserción del migrante en el mercado laboral, la satisfacción de sus necesidades básicas y situación familiar; ii) integración cultural, implica la asimilación del inmigrante con las creencias, costumbres de la sociedad de acogida; iii) integración jurídica, es decir, la regularización del migrante. Por otro lado, la inclusión: tiene un carácter multidimensional, da cuenta del bienestar y reconocimiento social, a través del acceso a la vivienda digna, la salud, el empleo y la no discriminación.

Bibliografía.

ACNUR. (2021). *REFUGIADOS Y MIGRANTES VENEZOLANOS EN LA REGIÓN.* file:///C:/Users/jaordonezx/Downloads/2021.07.R4V_Stock_Esp.pdf

Castles, S. (2010). Migración irregular: causas, tipos y dimensiones regionales. *Migración y Desarrollo, 8*(n.15), 49–80.

Esipova, N., Ray, J., & Pugliese, A. (2020). *World Grows Less Accepting of Migrants.* GALLUP. https://news.gallup.com/poll/320678/world-grows-less-accepting-migrants.aspx%0A

Ministerio de Gobierno de Ecuador. (2021). *Trata de personas.* http://trataytrafico.ministeriodegobierno.gob.ec/conceptosTrata

Convención internacional sobre la protección de los derechos de todos los trabajadores migratorios y de sus familiares, (1990). https://www.ohchr.org/sp/professionalinterest/pages/cmw.aspx

Organización Internacional para las Migraciones. (2015). *How the World Views Migration.* https://publications.iom.int/books/how-world-views-migration%0A

Organización Internacional para las Migraciones. (2021). *Términos fundamentales sobre migración.* https://www.iom.int/es/terminos-fundamentales-sobre-migracion

Retortillo Osuna, A., Ovejero Bernal, A., Cruz Souza, F. R., Arias Martínez, B., & Lucas Mangas, S. (2006). Inmigración y modelos de integración: entre la asimilación y el multiculturalismo. *Revista Universitaria de Ciencias Del Trabajo, 7*, 123–139.

Rodríguez Chatruc, M., & Rozo, S. (2021). *Attitudes Towards Migrants during Crisis Times* (IZA DP No. 14319). https://ftp.iza.org/dp14319.pdf

www.ingramcontent.com/pod-product-compliance
Lightning Source LLC
Chambersburg PA
CBHW081356270326
41930CB00015B/3324